Science Of Light

An Introduction to Vedic Astrology

श्रीः

Science Of Light
ज्योतिर्विद्या
An Introduction to Vedic Astrology
वेदाङ्गज्योतिषप्रदीपिका

By
Freedom Tobias Cole

ISBN13: 978-0-9788447-8-3
ISBN10: 0-9788447-8-5

Cover Design: Freedom Tobias Cole
Cover Zodiac artwork by Leighton Kelly and Freedom Cole

Stipled Images by P. Stephen v. Rohr
Five Chakra images by Sarajit Podder
All other diagrams by Freedom Cole

Published by Freedom Cole, Nevada City, California

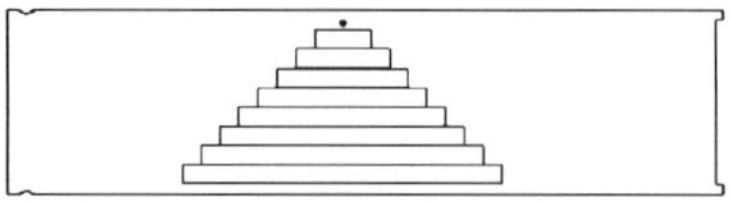

Each chapter cover contains an aspect of the Śrī-Chakra, starting with the bindu on the first chapter cover and gradually building to complete the entire yantra. The book from its side is therefore containing the three dimensional Śrī-Chakra. The building of the yantra outside is the building of the knowledge inside.

Introduction

Vedic Astrology is a beautiful, ancient science of self-discovery which teaches us how life works, how we fit into the bigger picture, our purpose for being here, and the goal of our lives. This study and practice enriches our own life and enables us to help other people enrich theirs, giving guidance in all matters of life, from career to love to health. As a teacher of yoga and āyurveda, I am amazed at the profound perspectives offered by understanding this often complex, yet always inspiring science.

I traveled all over the world to study with many Western and Indian teachers before meeting an Indian Guru who was able to answer any question I asked about this science. Sitting in classes with his advanced students literally made my head spin; sometimes I had to hold onto the seat of my chair. The way my brain processed information and viewed reality shifted - it was a change in my own consciousness from knowing that everything in the universe is connected, to understanding how it is all connected.

This book lays a firm foundation to expand the awareness toward the higher teachings of Vedic astrology. Many books aim to help a person read their chart and the charts of others; that important component is also taught in this book, but a deeper layer of astrological information is also presented here. It is by setting a proper foundation that the fully empowered flower of intuition will bloom. A technical understanding forms the roots, and it is the strength of the roots that show the might of the tree.

I have spent the last few years researching more advanced topics in Vedic Astrology, but have felt the lack of proper foundations limiting the audience of such research. This book attempts to create an honest, well-rounded understanding of Vedic astrological principles. I plan to follow this edition with two more books, completing the full set of tools a person will need to have a holistic approach and comprehension as a qualified Vedic Astrologer. This book is Vedic Astrology 101. Each chapter here could be a whole book in and of itself, but my goal is to make sure a person has the overall view of the field of this science.

I offer this book for students of Vedic Astrology to find the gems without wandering around for years looking for the mines. I have used the ancient text of Mahārṣi Parāśara, the grandfather of Indian astrology, as a basis for this book. His text is a gold mine filled with endless gems, and this book elucidates the secrets found therein. The systematic study of this text will open the doorway to the ancient science of light.

Dedication

This book is dedicated to my Parātparaguru, Śrī Jagannāth Rath.
He has made the secret science of Jyotiṣa accessible to people everywhere with the grace of Paramparāguru Śrī Achyutānanda Dāsa.

Vṛṣabhaṁ carṣaṇīnāṁ
Viśvarūpamadābhyam |
Bṛhaspatiṁ vareṇyam ||

Aum̐ Śrīṁ Dhlīṁ Jyotirbrahmāya Namaḥ

Acknowledements

The level of knowledge presented in this book would not be possible without the teachings of Pandit Sanjay Rath and the tradition of Śrī Achyutānanda Dāsa from Orissa, India. I need to thank all other SJC gurus and students, too many to list, for all they have done to help me on this path of Vedic Astrology.

The ability to complete this book would have been impossible without the support of my partner Amṛtā Kelley, as well as the support of my Mother and Grandmother.

ॐ

गणानां त्वा गणपतिं हवामहे कविं कवीनामुपमश्रवस्तमम्
ज्येष्ठराजं ब्रह्मणां ब्रह्मणस्पत आ नः शृण्वन्नूतिभिः सीदसादनम्

Gaṇānāṁ tvā gaṇapatiṁ havāmahe kaviṁ kavīnāmupamaśravastamam
Jyeṣṭharājaṁ brahmaṇāṁ brahmaṇaspata ā naḥ śṛṇvannūtibhiḥ sīda sādanam

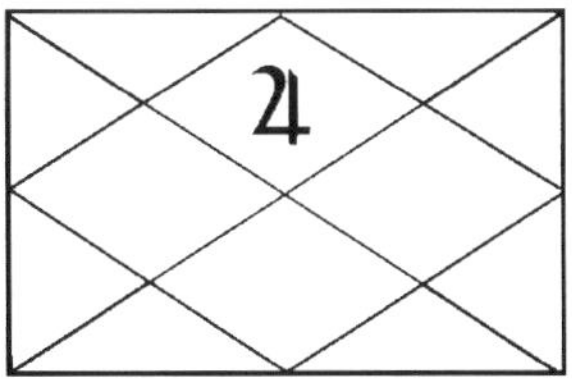

It is best to start any Jyotiṣa class or book when Jupiter (the Guru) is placed in the Ascendant.
When that is not possible, we need to put the Guru in the Ascendant.
The Ascendant (Lagna) represents our head.
When the Guru is on our head we are guided on the right path.
By the chanting of auṁ,
we are able to put the Guru on our head to insure
our intelligence is led in the right direction.

Present Edition

For many years I searched the waters of Vedic astrology trying to make sense of everything in this great ocean. Sometimes wishing I had just studied one subject or another a little bit earlier. This beginner's book is intended to introduce what I consider the foundation principles for a Vedic astrologer. The beginner doesn't know where to put importance on the multitude of techniques available in Vedic astrology, but with this guide the student knows what they need to understand and research more. There are various sources to deepen every topic found in this book; this is meant to be a guide to that learning process and to give direction in the vast ocean like a light house (*pradīpaka*).

This material is what I teach in my local classes and public lectures. Most of it was written during weekends and evenings in 2006 for Vyāsa SJC classes. Presently Eric Rosenbush has helped with content editing and Amṛta Kelley has helped with English grammatical editing. Vivek Nath Sinha has edited the Sanskrit in this finalized first edition. Any additional constructive suggestions on the text are appreciated.

I am grateful for all the lessons of life. Hard work has allowed me to understand my client's needs better and to develop humility. A story I'd like to share that brought realization to me came from a friend of mine who went to see the copper plate oracle at Kakatpur, Orissa. Normally we go early and sit in a long line at the temple waiting for the oracle reader to arrive. Though it was my friend's first time heading into the outback of Orissa and there was a miscommunication between him and the driver and the driver took him to the house of the oracle reader, Pandit Amaresvar Mishra. It was early morning before the Achyutānanda Center had opened, and the oracle reader was out plowing his field with two bulls. The situation reminded me of the message that Rāja-ṛṣi Janaka taught; even a great king should plow his own field. The duties of the king or a great oracle reader come after the basic necessities of one's own self-sufficiency. Hard work nourishes discipline and control of the senses. We are all busy, but we must make the time for this great study and still perform all tasks required of us in this world.

Comments can be sent to:

Freedom Cole
Vedic Astrology Introduction
119 Grove Street
Nevada City, CA 95959 USA
freedomfamily@gmail.com

Preface

Vedic Astrology is called Jyotiṣa in Sanskrit, the study of light *(jyoti)*. It is rooted in a tradition that goes back thousands of years. The Sage Parāśara lived in the time period of approximately 2 to 3,000 B.C. according to Indian historians. For the benefit of all, Parāśara left a scripture called the *Bṛhat Parāśara Horā Śāstra* (often abbreviated as BPHS), which has been a guide to astrologers for millenniums.

One day in correspondence, my Jyotiṣa guru, Pandit Sanjay Rath, told me, "Freedom, you have to work harder and get the text of BPHS *INSIDE* you completely." He had given me the assignment of teaching 12 students the ancient Sanskrit astrological text of Bṛhat Parāśara Horā Śāstra in two years. Many students were not even at a level to begin understanding those teachings, and needed to learn foundational principles first. I then began to teach beginner classes based primarily on the text of Bṛhat Parāśara Horā Śāstra, which led to the material in this book.

It is my vision to one day see Vedic Astrology taught in Western Universities. This text is written for the freshman university level mind. The aim is that a complete novice will be able to follow the text, but it is not baby food, nor watered down for the masses. It will require dedication and study to master this material. Utilizing a copy of Bṛhat Parāśara Horā Śāstra will greatly benefit the reader, though the first time through it may not be necessary.

The translations of BPHS and other Sanskrit in this text are mine unless otherwise noted. I have worked hard to make translations accurate, to provide the Sanskrit words that have manifold meanings for easy reference, and yet keep the reading enjoyable and flowing.

My study of this text has proven to me that BPHS is very systematic in its approach and order of chapters. There are some modern astrologers who believe BPHS is just a compendium of various ancient sources, but deep study and comparison will reveal otherwise. This present text aims to teach in a similar order as the material has been presented by the Ṛṣi Parāśara, and will reveal a traditional approach to Jyotiṣa that is found hinted at in other ancient texts on the subject. Once you study in this traditional format, the order of information presented in other ancient texts will be clarified. This reveals a style of teaching, or transmitting the knowledge, which I have tried to follow in this present text, while staying simple enough for the beginner to understand.

This text is designed to be an aid to prepare students to read and understand Bṛhat Parāśara Horā Śāstra. My Jyotiṣa Guru used to say that it is not about writing a new book, it is about understanding the ones we already have. This text will serve to guide one through BPHS in a systematic manner pointing out what to read, when and how. It is not possible for everything in BPHS to be covered in this introductory book, therefore further texts will go through the material at a higher level covering more aspects in greater detail. This text offers a foundation to understand classical Vedic Astrology. Upon completing this text one should have the ability to use BPHS as their primary Jyotiṣa text book, as has been the case for thousands of years in traditional study of Vedic Astrology. This text is not the end all; it is offered as the beginning of a journey into the tradition set out by the Sages of self mastery and universal understanding.

Tradition of Ṛṣi Parāśara

This text elucidates the fundamental teachings of Parāśara. The use of elements such as carakārakas, ārūḍhas, and argalā have been misunderstood in the West and labled as "Jaimini astrology". In the past, people have labeled anything they didn't understand in BPHS as Jaimini astrology. Ṛṣi Jaimini was a student of Parāśara, and his book is called *Upadeśa* (secondary notes heard from the teacher). This book gives a clear view of Parāśara's teachings from BPHS only. Jaimini's clarifications and additions will be studied in more advanced books. Only two notes of Jaimini are used in this text for clarification; Jaimini's order for analysis of strength and in the Argalā chapter where Parāśara says shadow planet (singular) and Jaimini clarifies that he is referring to Ketu, not Rāhu.

Chapter Overview for Teachers

The first chapter introduces the general idea of astrology and its basic principles. This is for the astrological beginner to become acquainted with fundamental terms and ideas. The astrological information is based on the first few verses of Parāśara's *Graha-Guṇasvarūpa-Adhyāya* (planet chapter) where Parāśara very briefly mentions the planets and stars. This text is supported with some basic astronomy (*Gola*), to get a person acquainted with the sky and the natural movement of the solar system before trying to interpret it. I notice people often get lost on the paper or computer screen and forget that astrology is not merely numbers written before them, but actual massive bodies of energy moving through the universe. The beginning section aims to allow that realization and understanding to become part of the psyche and hopefully broaden the perspective of the principles being studied.

The second chapter sets a proper Vedic foundation through understanding the framework of Vedic philosophy. One's awareness of the profound cosmology that Vedic Astrology exists within will deepen. Many of topics are often mentioned in the beginning of introductory Jyotiṣa works, but rarely are any deeper details given or is there any discussion on the important relationship the philosophical information has to the astrologer. This first section is an attempt to shed some light on this so the Vedas, their limbs, and the limbs of Jyotiṣa do not seem foreign, but feel like a part of oneself. I have avoided Euro-centric beliefs about the Vedas and have focused on acceptable philosophy of traditional Vedic scholars.

The third chapter goes into depth on the planets. The first section is based on Parāśara's *Graha-Guṇasvarūpa-Adhyāya* (planet chapter). I have focused on the teachings of Parāśara with a few noted additions from supplementary traditional sources to give a well-rounded understanding of the planets. The final section of this chapter introduces the three types of kārakas based on the *Kāraka-Adhyāya* (kāraka chapter). The next chapter, based on the *Avatārakathana-Adhyāya* (Avatār chapter) uses the descriptions of the Hindu Avatārs to deepen one's understanding of the planets. Parāśara does this first and then introduces the planets, I switched the two for a western audience that is unfamiliar with the avatārs. Then additional deities for the planets are introduced but depth will not be given till later volumes.

The chapters on rāśi (signs) and bhāva (houses) rely primarily on Parāśara's own chapters with only a few supplementary sources clearly noted in the text. The varga (divisions of the signs) are given while introducting the rāśis as this is how most classical texts mention the signs. I have followed the traditional order to reveal the sign as a collection or heap (rāśi) of many 'signs'. With the bhāvas chapter, I have first broken down the various house formats that are utilized through out India with explanations for each according to the Śri Achyutānanda tradition. The actual information on the houses is in a similar order as given by the Sage. The end of the chapter includes the houses of a praśna chart according to *HariHara's Praśna Mārga* to elucidate how the meanings of the houses change according to the situation. For the same reason, the varga houses of the D-9 and D-10 are analyzed only briefly and then covered in more depth in the divisional chart chapter. Appendix II contains a translation of the *Bhāveśa-Phala-Adhyāya* to compliment this chapter. It is archaic for some results but will deepen one's understanding of houses.

The chapter on strengths and states is a chronological collection and summary of various teachings on placement that Parāśara has mentioned throughout the text, from the *Graha-Guṇasvarūpa-Adhyāya* to the *Iṣṭa-Kaṣṭa-Adhyāya*. I have removed much of the mathematical calculation for this introductory lesson. The exact calculations of Viṁśopaka, Ṣaḍbala, etc. with their specific meanings will be covered in later lessons.

The chapter on bhāvapadas follows the chapter on strengths according to BPHS. It is a very abbreviated introduction with little attention paid to the *Upapada* (marriage point), but a benefical introduction for the beginner. This is followed by the Argalā chapter showing the interaction of houses from multiple lagnas to consider a more alive, free-moving approach to the chart. In this version I have not included a whole section on the kārakāṁśa as Parāśara has done, but instead include some beginner information on the kārakāṁśa in the divisional chart section.

The chapter on Yogas is a very brief introduction to the multiple chapters that follow in BPHS on a variety of Yogas. I have been more general here as it is a huge work in and of itself to explain all of these various chapters. Importance has been placed on understanding the conceptual framework of percieving planetary combinations and interaction.

The chapter on nakṣatras is supplementary to the general teaching of Parāśara. It is supported by the Sage's statement in the *Graha-Guṇasvarūpa-Adhyāya* (v.7) that says an "understanding of various nakṣatras should be learned from the general śāstra". For that purpose a chapter has been provided here. His brief mention implies that he assumes students have readily available access to this information as modern people have access to the 12 signs of the zodiac. Later, Parāśara speaks of various nakṣatra techniques where one will need to understand the informtion presented here in order to understand BPHS. I will devote a future text fully to the traditional use of the nakṣatras. A highlight of this chapter is the description of Vedic deities for each nakṣatra. These interpretations come from a combination of Vedic research, as noted, which was guided by Varāhamihira and Vaidyanātha Dīkṣita's interpretation of the nakṣatras and the professions advised in *Dhruva-Nāḍi* as translated by Sanjay Rath in *Crux of Vedic Astrology*.

The preceding chapters will correspond to what is presently the second volume of the English translations of Bṛhat Parāśara Horā Śāstra. The daśā chapter follows directly after the nakṣatras and only focuses on nakṣatra-based daśā techniques. Since it is a beginner's introduction, I have chosen to save other daśās for the next level. In this chapter, there are practice exercises where students are requested to follow-up on the techniques by reading specific sections in BPHS. This will serve a dual purpose of aquainting the student to the existence of other daśās given in the text and guide them to stay on track inside of the large amount of information offered in these chapters. Parāśara goes into great depth with aṣṭakavarga after speaking of daśās, but it is only briefly introduced here.

I have added a chapter on interpreting divisional charts after daśas. Parāśara does not speak directly about interpreting all these these vargas, he just ensures that planets are examined in all the divisions. The basic Parāśara principles of Argalā and yogas are used to understand most varga situations.

The final part of BPHS addresses curses, doṣas and their remedies. The remedy chapter in this book is primarily based on BPHS, with information from other traditional texts helping to understand the conceptual framework needed to use remedies. The Pañchāṅga chapter goes into the foundation principles of the five limbs of time as taught by the Śrī Achyutānanda Paramaparā. This is followed by a summary of Parāśara's teachings on flaws of time at birth and their remedies. This area has been extremely overlooked by modern Vedic astrology in the west as there are no western astrology correlations. Parāśara gives several chapters on this area including remedies showing the large emphasis that traditional astrologers place on these time conditions. The results indicated by the Pañchāṅga will show fruitful or barren results in chart interpretation. In āyurveda, herbs are prescribed along with a proper balancing diet. Without the foundation of a proper diet, the herb will have only a short-term effect. In the same way, the 'flaws of time' are the elemental foundation that needs to be balanced for other remedies to be effective.

In the final chapter on interpretation of the chart, I have tried to bring all previously mentioned techniques into perspective for proper application in reading a chart. Examples have been given in the oral classes, uploaded online at www.learnvedicastrology.org and www.vyasasjc.org, and it is advised to listen to them to see these techniques applied. It is important for a beginner to follow these principles step by step at first until it becomes second nature. Then one is advised to begin to develop their own approach to the chart, understanding the fundamental principles and utilizing intuition.

Freedom Tobias Cole
September 14, 2006
El Cerrito, California

Notes on Diacritical Marks:

Jyotiṣa is often translated as Vedic astrology. The word is sometimes written as 'Jyotish' which is the English spelling of the modern Hindi pronunciation of the word. Jyotiṣa is the correct transliteration from the ancient language of Sanskrit. Hindi relates to Saṁskṛta in the same way that English relates to Latin. A doctor learns Latin to speak about the human body, specifically referring to the bone in the upper leg as the femur, rather than the thigh bone. This text uses traditional Sanskrit transliteration throughout. A Sanskrit pronunciation guide accompanied by a small lesson is included in the appendix to aid in learning the diacritical marks used in this text and assist the reader to pronounce the Sanskrit words as best as possible without a live teacher. Diacritical marks are according to Omkarānanda Aśram's Itranslator and URW Palladio font which has become the standard for online Sanskrit and the protocol of all Śrī Jagannath Center material.

A few words have been left in non-transliteration to provide ease in understanding to those who are already familiar with the less 'correct' English translation as well as to assist students in recognizing these words in other modern texts; specifically, the transliterated word *Saṁskṛta* is written as *Sanskrit*, and *Svami* as the commonly used word Swami. A few words are written in both the correct transliteration and more common anglicized transliteration, particularly with the issue of *ca* and *cha*, were the anglicized word such as *Chandra* (Moon) would be *(छन्द्र)* and should be *candra (चन्द्र).* This issue is also there for *chara* (movable) which is properly transliterated as *cara*, or *Chatur* (four) which is properly *catur.* One should learn the words and say them correctly even in the mind, therefore correct Sanskrit pronunciation and awareness is promoted here.

Sanskrit has a method of combining words that are next to each other which changes the actual written form of the words. For grammatical purposes I have put a dash between words that should actually be written together but which are separate for the purpose of English comprehension. For example the chapter on significations is grammatically proper when written as *Kārakādhyāya* but is written as *Kāraka-Adhyāya* for ease of understanding.

There is no actual capitalization when transliterating. In general I have used English grammar rules in this regard. When studying Sanskrit verses I have tried to give the original Sanskrit, the transliteration and then the translation for students to study the actual verse itself as given by Parāśara. This is important as there are many controversial ideas and knowledge of the sage's original words is priceless. In some places where there are large sections of non-controversial material translated, I have only given reference to the original and left out the transliteration or the Sanskrit to save space.

Omkarānanda Aśram's Itranslator fonts

अ	अ	इ	ई	उ	ऊ	ऋ	ॠ
a	ā	i	ī	u	ū	ṛ	ṝ

ऌ	ॡ	ए	ऐ	ओ	औ	अं	अः
ḷ	ḹ	e	ai	o	au	aṁ	aḥ

क	ख	ग	घ	ङ
ka	kha	ga	gha	ṅa

च	छ	ज	झ	ञ
ca	cha	ja	jha	ña

ट	ठ	ड	ढ	ण
ṭa	ṭha	ḍa	ḍha	ṇa

त	थ	द	ध	न
ta	tha	da	dha	na

प	फ	ब	भ	म
pa	pha	ba	bha	ṁa

य	र	ल	व	श	ष	स	ह	क्ष
ya	ra	la	va	śa	ṣa	sa	ha	kṣa

Table of Contents

Introduction . . . v
Dedication . . . vii
Acknowledgements . . . viii
Present Edition . . . x
Preface . . . xi
Tradition of Parāśara . . . xii
Chapter Overview for Teachers . . . xii
Notes on Diacritical Marks . . . xv

Chapter One: The Overview

Planets . . . 4
Houses . . . 6
Signs . . . 6
Astronomy . . . 8
Time . . . 13

Chapter Two: Vedic Foundations

Backgound Understanding . . . 17
Four Veda Saṁhitās . . . 18
Four Parts of the Vedas . . . 26
Six Aṅgas . . . 28
Four Upāṅgas . . . 38
Jyotiṣa Foundations . . . 40
Karma . . . 42

Chapter Three: Grahas (Planets)

Planets . . . 47
Elements . . . 49
Guṇas . . . 50
Varṇa . . . 51
Naisargika-Kārakas . . . 51
Sūrya . . . 52
Candra . . . 54
Maṅgala . . . 57
Buddha . . . 59
Guru . . . 61
Śukra . . . 63
Śani . . . 65
Rāhu . . . 69
Ketu . . . 69
Upagrahas . . . 70
Natural Planetary Relationships . . . 70
Exaltation and Debilitation . . . 71
Retrogression . . . 72
Combustion . . . 72
Planet Maturity . . . 72
Natural Time Periods of Life . . . 73
Planetary Periods of Time . . . 73
Gocara . . . 74
Kārakas . . . 74

Chapter Four: Devatā (Deities)

Viṣṇu Avatārs of the Planets . . . 81
Paramaparā and Parāśara . . . 85
Additional Devatās . . . 96
Devī . . . 98

Chapter Five: Rāśi (Signs)

Basic Measurements of Time . . . 101
Ayanāṁśa . . . 103
Rāśi . . . 105
Guṇas . . . 108
Tattvas . . . 110
Directions and Distance . . . 111
Day and Night Rāśi . . . 112
Names of the Rāśi . . . 112
Rāśi Dṛṣṭi: Sign Aspects . . . 115
Rāśi Mantras . . . 117
Ādityas . . . 117
Jyotir-Liṅga . . . 119

Rāśi Divisions: Varga 121
Introduction to Divisional Deities 123
Parāśara Dreṣkaṇa. 125
Caturthāṁśa. 126
Saptāṁśa. 127
Navāṁśa. 128
Daśāṁśa 129
Viṁśāṁśa 130

Chapter Six: Bhāva (Houses)

Chart Types (Chakras) 135
Drawing the Chart by Hand 144
House Meanings 145
Bhāvat Bhāvam 146
Kendras. 147
Paṇaphara and Āpoklima 149
Dusthāna. 149
Upachaya 149
Parāśara: Bhāva-Viveka-Adhyāya 150
Bhāveśa: House Lords 152
Sixth and Eighth Lord. 154
Bhāva Kāraka. 156
Graha Dṛṣṭi: Aspects of Planets. 157
Houses in Praśna Charts 158
Houses in Varga Charts 159

Chapter Seven: Strength and Status

Natural and Temporal Friendships 163
Astaṁgata (Combustion) 165
Graha-yuddha (Planetary War) 165
Avasthā. 166
Maraṇa Kāraka Sthāna 169
Transition Points 170
Ṣaṣṭyamsa: The Sixtieth Division 171
Vaiśeṣikāṁśa: Division of Excellence. 175
Viṁśopaka: Divisional Strength 176
Prosperity and Destruction of a House 177
Ṣaḍbala 179
Ṣaḍbala of Houses. 183

Chapter Eight: Bhāvapadas (Perception)

Bhāvapada Calculation. 188
Dual Rulership of Aquarius and Scorpio 192
Meaning of each Ārūḍha Pada 192

Chapter Nine: Argalā (Interaction)

Principle of Argalā 197
Individual Houses 202
Argalā from Different Houses 204
Two Ways to Utilize Argalā 206
Śubha and Aśubha Argalā 208

Chapter Ten: Sambandha and Yogas

Sambandha and Yogas 213
Graha Sambandha 213
Bhāva Sambandha 214
Yogas in Jyotiṣa 215
Rāja-Yogas 218
Lunar Yogas 219
Solar Yogas 221
Introduction to Rāja-Yogas 222
Argalā 225
Additional Yogas 225
Pañca Mahāpuruṣa 229

Chapter Eleven: Nakṣatras (Stars)

Nakṣatras in the Sky 235
Division into 27 Nakṣatras 236
Nakṣatra Degrees 237
The 28th Nakṣatra 238
General Śāstra 238
Nakṣatra-Devatā 242
Other planets in Nakṣatras 271
Nakṣatra Symbols 272
Muhūrta 274
Divisions of the Nakṣatras: 108 275
Hoḍa-Cakra 276
Navatāra-Cakra 278
Special Tāras 280
Sarvatobhadra-Cakra 281
Nakṣatra-Dṛṣṭi 282
Ghātaka-Nākṣatra 282
Kālacakra 283

Chapter Twelve: Daśā (Timing)

Timing 289
Calculation of Viṁśottarī-Daśā 290
Conditional Daśās 298
Interpretation of Viṁśottarī-Daśā 300

Chapter Thirteen: Varga-Chakra (Divisionals)

Interpretation of Divisional Charts. 323
General Principles 327
Varga Arrangements. 329
Navāṁśa 330
Kārakāṁśa. 330
Deities 333
Trines: Skills and Abilities 333
Rectification 337
Spouse 338
Sexuality 339
Daśāṁśa 341
Saptāṁśa. 346
Horā Chart 348
Caturthāṁśa. 349
Pañcāṁśa and Ṣaṣṭāṁśa. 350
Dvādaṣāṁśa. 351
Ṣoḍāśāṁśa 352
Viṁśāṁśa 352
Caturviṁśāṁśa 354
Triṁśāṁśa 356
Khavedāṁśa / Akṣavedāṁśa 357
Ṣaṣṭyāṁśa 359
Higher Divisional Charts 362

Chapter Fourteen: Introduction to Remedies

Introduction to Remedies. 365
Cause of Affliction. 367
Planet Giving the Remedy 368
Form of the Remedy Planet or Rāśi 369
The Planet and Sign Placement. 372
House Placement, Trines and Aspects 375
Length or Amount of Remedy 375
Time to Perform the Remedy 378

Chapter Fifteen: Pañchāṅga

Five Limbs of Time 381
Vāra 382
Nakṣatra 386
Tithi 387
Kālachakra Remedies 392
Karaṇa. 394
Yoga. 396
Pañcāṅga-Doṣas: Flaws in Time 397

Chapter Sixteen: Interpretation

Interpretation 405
The Art of Interpretation 406
Proper Mantra 407
Lagna and Lagneśa 408
Planets in Houses 408
Planets Conjunct 408
Moon's Nakṣatra 409
Ātmakāraka and Ārūḍha Lagna 410
Curses and Blessings 411
Pañcāṅga Lords 411
Daśā Applicability 412
Navāṁśa Trines 412
Confirm the Chart 413
Assess the Issues of the Native 413
Talk about the Chart 414
Remedies 415

Appendix: Sanskrit Lessons 419
Appendix: House Lords 431
Bibliography 439
About the Author 445

Chapter 1

The Overview

•

Vedic Astrology/astronomy, known as Jyotiṣa, is one of the oldest sciences of mankind and in the ancient world reached heights beyond what is conceivable to modern man. As magical and implausible as a computer and its infinite capabilities would seem to someone 2,000 years ago, the science of Jyotiṣa remains just as mystical to modern man, though the foundations are based on logical principles derived from astronomy and the natural world. This is an introduction into the complex, yet logical ancient science of Jyotiṣa, which has survived thousands of years in India's Vedic tradition.

There are three important factors in Jyotiṣa from which everything else is derived; the *stars*, and *sky* and the *planets* moving through the two. The moving part of the sky (stars/constellations) is divided into **signs** and the stationary part of the sky is divided into **houses**. The houses show *areas of life*, common to all human beings, and the moving signs show the *situation* in that area of life. The planets will move within these two (houses and signs) to create the varied diversity of the living world.

Planets

There are nine planets used in Jyotiṣa. The better the planets are understood, the more this science of light will unfold as perfect intuitive understanding of the fully conscious universe we live in. Some of the information may seem very technical, but once understood it is a tool for perceiving this multi-dimensional interrelated life. In the same way that a painter goes to school and studies with a master for years before going and creatively making their own masterpieces based on the foundations of line and color, so too does one need to study basic foundations of Jyotiṣa before beginning to see the past, present and future of living beings and events. The archetypal energies represented by the planets are the building blocks of conscious reality. The more the planets are understood the better the universe and the fate of all beings will be understood.

Planet	Graha	Symbol	Rulership (Rāśi)	Weekday (Vāra)
Sun	Sūrya	☉	Leo	Sunday
Moon	Chandra	☽	Cancer	Monday
Mars	Maṅgala	♂	Aries/ Scorpio	Tuesday
Mercury	Buddha	☿	Gemini/ Virgo	Wednesday
Jupiter	Guru	♃	Sagittarius/ Pisces	Thursday
Venus	Śukra	♀	Taurus/ Libra	Friday
Saturn	Śani	♄	Capricorn/ Aquarius	Saturday
North Node	Rāhu	☊	Aquarius Co-ruler	None (Saturday Night)
South Node	Ketu	☋	Scorpio Co-ruler	None (Tuesday Night)

The seven major planets visible with the naked eye have been the focus of all cultures of the ancient world. The seven days of the week are based upon these seven planets. The two lunar nodes (Rāhu and Ketu) are mathematical points which when aligned with the ecliptic of the Sun cause eclipses of the Sun and Moon to occur. These unobservable points are called shadow planets *(chaya-grahas)* in Vedic astrology.

The planets are divided into *saumya* and *krūra*. Saumya means friendly, gentle, cheerful, cool, or auspicious. Krūra means cruel, fierce, ferocious, pitiless, or harsh; the same root of the English word cruel. Saumya (friendly) planets give good results to the areas of life they associate with. Krūra (cruel) planets harm or break the area of life they are associated with. For example, if in the area of marriage there is a benefic planet like Jupiter, the person will have tremendous growth and support in their relationship life. If a malefic like Mars is in the area *(house)* of relationship, there will be arguing and possibility of breaking the marriage. Jupiter rules good luck and expansion, while Mars rules fighting and breaking. In this way, the planets are considered either saumya or krūra.

Saumya	Krūra
Jupiter	Saturn
Venus	Rāhu/ Ketu
Mercury	Mars
Moon	Sun

The planets are given genders *(liṅga)* by Parāśara[1]. Moon and Venus are female *(yuvati)*. Sun, Mars and Jupiter are male *(nara)*, and Mercury and Saturn are neuter *(klība)*. Saturn represents the pre-pubescent boy who has not differentiated sexually. Mars is the teenage boy becoming a man. Jupiter is a married man, and the Sun is the individual becoming a father. When he becomes a widower he will become like Rāhu. A young girl before puberty is like Mercury, after puberty she is like Venus. When she is married with children she becomes the Moon and after her husband dies she is like Ketu. In this way, the planets represent each gender at all stages of life.

In chapter three, Ṛṣi Parāśara lists many significations of the planets:

Planet	Sanskrit Name	Attribute (verse 12-13)	Position (verse 14-15)	Color (verse 16-17)
Sun	Ravi	Soul of All *(sarvātmā)*	King	Dark red *(raktaśyāma)*
Moon	Chandra	Mind *(manas)*	Queen	Off white (gauragātra)
Mars	Maṅgala	Strength/power *(satva)*	Army chief *(neta)*	Red *(rakta)*
Mercury	Buddha	Speech giver *(vāṇi-pradāyaka)*	Prince *(rājakumāra)*	Dark Green Grass *(durvaśyāma)*
Jupiter	Guru	Knowledge and happiness giver *(jñānasukhdā)*	Counselor/ Minister	Whitish/Yellow/ Tawny *(gauragātra)*
Venus	Śukra	Vitality giver *(vīryapradāyaka)*	Counselor/ Minister	Dark Brown *(śyāva)*
Saturn	Śani	Giver of Grief *(dhuḥkhadā)*	Servant *(preṣya)*	Black *(kṛṣṇa)*
Rāhu	Rāhu	[delusion, *moha*]	Army [the masses]	
Ketu	Ketu	[spirituality, *mokṣa*]	Army	

Mercury is the speech giver. The position of Mercury will show the power of one's speech, in the same way that the position of the natal Moon will reveal the nature of a person's mind. Understanding what the planets mean, their strengths and weaknesses and how this relates to our lives, is the focus of a beginner's study of Vedic astrology.

[1]Bṛhat Parāśara Horā Śāstra, Chapter 3, v.19

Houses

Houses represent areas of our life; the area of our body and health, the type of food we eat, the situation of the home, etc. There are a total of twelve houses each representing a different area of life.

House	External Significations	People	Body
1	Body, health, strength	Self	Head
2	Wealth, food, sustenance	Close family	Throat
3	Effort, courage, willpower	Siblings	Arms, shoulders
4	Home, happiness, heart	Mother	Chest, breasts
5	Intelligence, decision ability	Children, students	Solar Plexus
6	Enemies, legal cases, sickness	Servants/Pets	Lower abdomen
7	Business, social interaction	Spouse	Pelvic region
8	Debt, loans, chronic disease	Lenders	Genitals
9	Guru, teacher, philosophy	Father	Thighs
10	Karma, career, occupation	Boss, biological father	Knees
11	Monetary income	Friends	Calves
12	Hospital, ashram, foreign lands, away time	Bill collectors, those who cause us loss	Feet

These twelve houses are the blueprint for life. Understanding them will not only allow one to read a Vedic astrology chart, but will also help elucidate how life works, by recognizing and appreciating the interconnectivity of the entire universe.

The eastern horizon where the Sun rises is the first house called the ascendant. In Sanskrit it is called the *lagna*, which means it is the tying down point of the chart. The place on the western horizon where the Sun sets is the seventh house. The houses exist in a static position in the sky above us; they are the divisions of the sky.

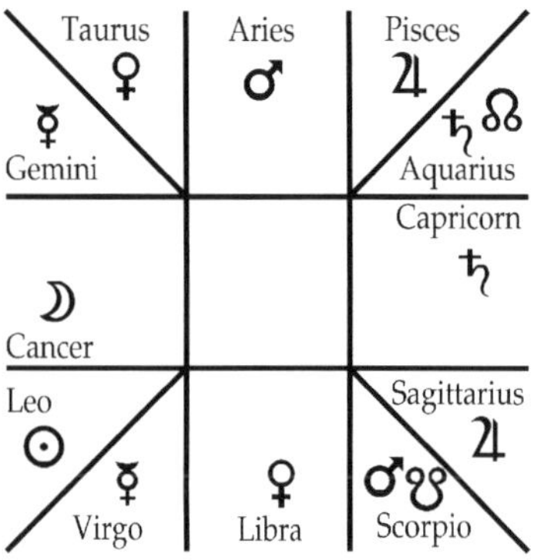

Signs

The signs/constellations, known as *rāśi* in Sanskrit, are moving through the sky. They move through the houses setting the situation for each area of life. Virgo rules gardens, and if it falls in the fourth house of home, the native will feel most comfortable in a home that has a well-cared for garden. Cancer rules watery places and Cancer ruling the fourth will make a person happiest in a home near water or with water in the yard. In this way, the houses are the area of life and the sign indicates the situation of that area of life.

The sign of the zodiac in the eastern horizon of the sky (first house) at the time of birth is the ascending sign, or lagna. It is the point that has tied down the position of all the signs in houses in the natal horoscope. The lagna changes on average every 2 hours throughout the day.

In Vedic Astrology this is considered one of the most important points in a chart as it dictates the house-planet relationship. In Western astrology most people are concerned about their Sun sign, but in Jyotiṣa people are more concerned about their ascendant. The Sun sign is important, as it is the place where the ātma (self) works through, but even this is understood by the proper house placement based on the lagna. The lagna shows our intelligence and how we apply it. It will also be the primary indication of the body, which is what ties one to this world.

#	Sign	Rāśi (verse 3)	Color (verse 6-24)	Places/Situations (Praśna Mārga XV.123-128)
1	Aries	Meṣa	Red *(rakta)*	*Forests*, gold/silver mines, diamond mines, canals, serpent's abode
2	Taurus	Vṛṣabha	White *(sveta)*	*Fields*, cultivated fields, farm houses, beautiful & lush places
3	Gemini	Mithuna	Green, emerald, or yellowish *(harit)*	*Cities*, parks, places of worship, places of precious stones, party & entertainment places
4	Cancer	Karka	Pink or rose *(paṭala)*	*Canals*, city water tanks, watery tracts, places where celestial nymphs frequent
5	Leo	Siṁha	Pale, yellow-white, or jaundiced *(pāṇḍu)*	*Hills*, places frequented by lions and other wild animals, elevated places, cowsheds, places visited by Brahmins and Devas
6	Virgo	Kanyā *(Kumārikā)*	Bright, various colored *(chitra)*	*Towns*, temples, horse and elephant stables, seacoast and ladies apartments
7	Libra	Tula	Black *(kṛṣṇa)*	*Market places*, streets, bazaars, forests
8	Scorpio	Vṛśchika	Red-yellow *(piśa)*	*Wells*, anthills, ponds
9	Sagittarius	Dhanu	Gold/Yellow *(piṅgala)*	*Forests*, rest houses, military barracks, battlefields, walls
10	Capricorn	Makara *(Nakra)*	Various colors, spotted *(karbura)*	*Rivers*, river deltas, forests, areas inhabited by wild tribes
11	Aquarius	Kumbha	Deep brown *(babhru)*	Lakes, same as Capricorn
12	Pisces	Mīna	Fish color *(mīna)*	*Oceans*, deep caves, watery places, temples

The lagna represents the body, and the sign placed there will have a large influence on the physical characteristics of an individual. As the fourth house rules home, the sign there will influence the conditions of the home. If a benefic (*saumya*) planet is placed in the fourth it supports all the good qualities of that sign by bringing good people into the home, while if a malefic (*krūra*) planet is placed in the fourth, it will bring out all the bad aspects of that sign by bringing negativities to the household. In this way, the various details are determined about the person's life. The sign represents the situation while the planets represent people or animate beings. The signs represent the inanimate surroundings.

There are multiple layers to a chart. It can be read as the native in relation to working in the world, or it can be read completely as the physical body. For example, the third house represents the arms and shoulders --if Mars, a breaking planet is placed there, then there is a large chance the arm may be hurt or damaged in some way. If Saturn is in the third house, there may be arthritis in the arm. The fourth house is the home, and if Saturn is placed there the home life will be more harsh or lonely. On the physical level, Saturn will also give irregularities in the heartbeat or a heart that needs more activity to warm up. In this way, the world is a maṇḍala that exists in the physical body, in the world outside of a person, and in every interaction in life. Everything is interconnected as seen through the Jyotiṣa chart.

The fixed *sky* above is divided into twelve houses that are 30 degrees each. The *stars* in the sky are divided into twelve constantly moving signs. While the houses remain stationary, the signs move. The houses represent areas of life, areas that everyone has, such as mother, father, physical body, etc. The signs move through these houses to indicate the situations in these areas of life. The *planets* show where the energy of life is more focused and whether it is positive or negative. Everybody has positive and negative planets and situations, everybody has a shadow and a light, it is just a matter of where and when.

Astronomy

Astronomy is the branch of Jyotiṣa called *Gola*. Before we get into the metaphysical meanings and mystical diagrams of Jyotiṣa, it is important to realize where all that information comes from. We are on a planet spinning around the Sun. We are part of a solar system interacting with an entire universe. Before reading this information, shut your eyes for a few moments and meditate on the fact that we are on a spherical planet that is *rotating* at hundreds of miles an hour. Feel that we are *revolving* around the Sun at the same time. Let your consciousness expand out and allow the realization of where you physically are in the universe to absorb into your awareness. Then visualize and become aware of the Moon circling the Earth as we are circling the Sun. Finally let your awareness expand out into the million other solar systems that appear as little stars in the sky above us. Just take a few moments to shut your eyes and be aware of where you are in relation to the universe.

Now if you visualized that fully, you probably feel a sense of expansion, a sense of the huge amount of energy contained in the movement of the universe. It is important to be aware that our solar system is basically flat. From a side view it would look flat like a plate. The solar system does not look like an atom with molecules moving about in different directions, but instead all the planets revolve within a seven degree latitudinal orbit around the Sun. This belt around the Sun where all the planets move within is called the ecliptic. In the diagram below, see how from a side view of our solar system, all the planets are moving in a single plane.

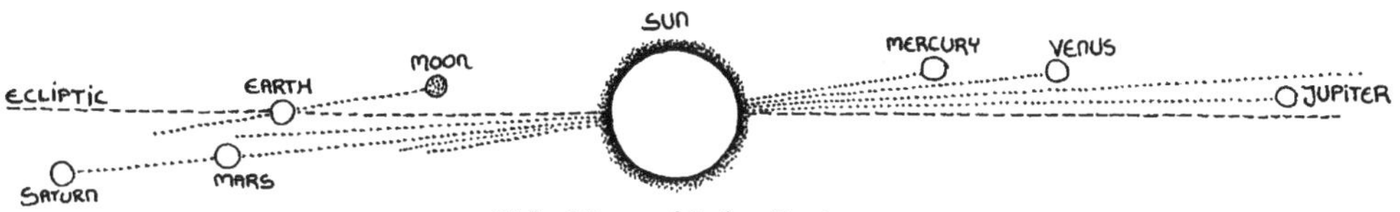

Side View of Solar System

Though the Earth is in the ecliptic of the Sun, from our view it looks as though the Sun is in the ecliptic with all the other planets. This change of perception is very important to keep in mind. While being aware of the heliocentric reality, Jyotiṣa uses a geocentric model to calculate how the stars and planets are affecting the energies on Earth. Our concern is what happens here on Earth; therefore we use a geocentric diagram to interpret the sky. In this way all the planets and the luminaries move through the ecliptic.

Side View of Earth-Moon System

Even the Moon is moving in approximately the same plane but with a five degree incline. This allows the Moon to be perceived as being in the same plane as the other planets.

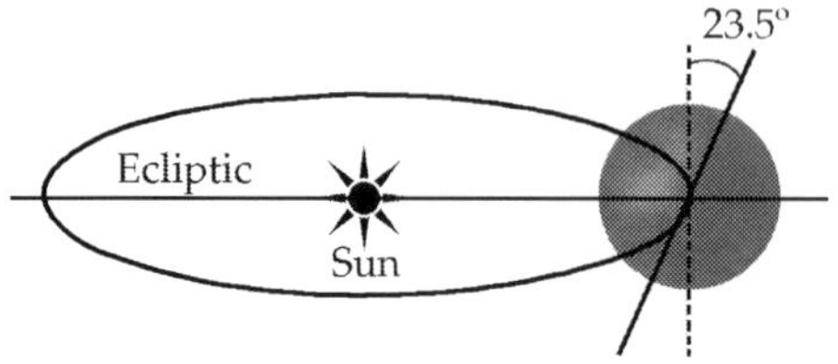

There are a few more variables to add in to get a holistic picture of astronomical relationships in our solar system. The Earth is not rotating in a perfect upright position – there is a slight tilt relative to the revolution around the Sun. The north/south pole is 23.5 degrees askew from the perpendicular angle to the ecliptic.

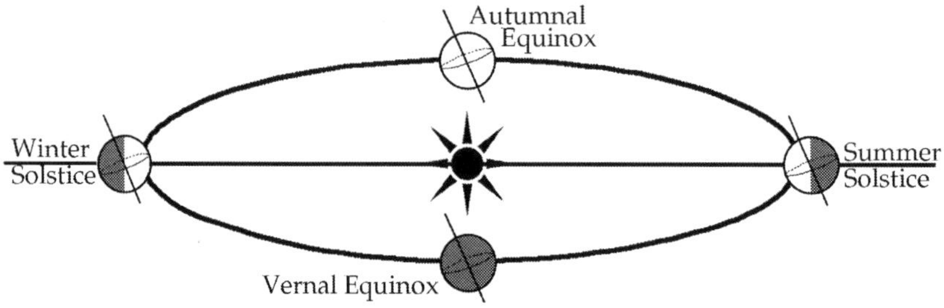

This difference in angle creates two important factors in Jyotiṣa. The first phenomenon it creates is the seasons as the Earth revolves around the Sun. This gives two equinoxes and two solstices.

The other important point of this 23.5 degree angle of the Earth from the ecliptic is the way the planets move through the sky. From our position on Earth, the ecliptic is seen as moving slightly across the side of the sky, not directly overhead. And it is in this ecliptic that all the planets will move within. The easiest way to understand this is to watch the path of the Sun throughout the day; this is why the ecliptic is called *Ravimārga* (Path-mārga of the Sun/Ravi) in Sanskrit. All the other planets will follow this path. Since the planets only move through specific stars along the ecliptic, those stars take on specific importance and are what make up the zodiac *(Bha-Chakra)*.

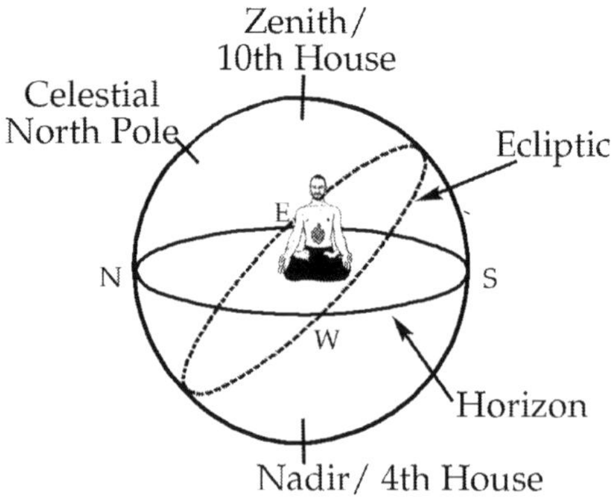

There is a slight variation in the apparent path of the Sun during the different seasons showing as a slight variation of height. In ancient observatories, huge buildings were made to calculate this. All over the world temples were constructed to align with this variation to allow light to pass into the temples during certain times of year. The diagram below shows the annual course of the Sun along the ecliptic.

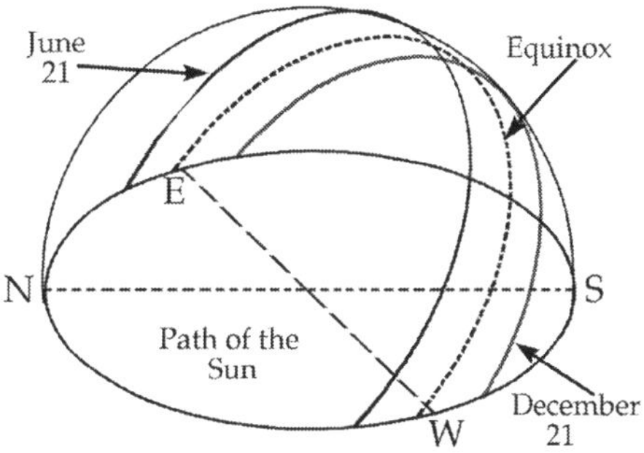

There may be billions of stars throughout the sky around us, but it is those that fall in the ecliptic that the planets are perceived as moving through. The Earth makes one complete rotation about its axis every 24 hours. Relative to the stars, it takes 23 hours, 56 minutes, and 4.09 seconds (about four minutes less than 24 hours). The Earth's rotation is creating the day and the night. The 12 hours that face the Sun are called day *(dina or ahar)* and the twelve hours that face away from the Sun are called night *(rātri)*. A day and night together is called an *ahorātra*.

By dropping the *'a'* in front and the *'tra'* at the end of a*horā*tra, the word for hour is called *horā* in Sanskrit. A Sun dial works by marking a circle with 15 degree increments to mark the hours or horās. Every hour the Earth rotates 15 degrees. There are twelve signs of the zodiac divided into 30 degrees. So each sign contains two horās of 15 degrees each. It takes the Earth 2 hours to rotate through a sign.The branch of Jyotiṣa dealing with horoscope interpretation is called *Horā Śāstra* (the science of hours- which is the movement of the Earth/sky).

From our perspective on Earth it looks like the signs are moving through the sky (even though we are the ones moving). From Earth, the stars are perceived as rising in the east and setting in the west.

The sign that is rising in the east is called the rising sign (*lagna*). It takes *approximately* 2 hours for it to rise. When someone or something is born the lagna sign is the most important point to consider. The *date of birth* gives the position of the planets while the *time and place* will show what stars are in the sky at the moment of birth and thereby show the lagna.

Just as the Earth's rotation makes it look like the stars are moving through the sky, the Earth's revolution around the Sun makes it look like the Sun is moving one degree a day. Therefore when we say that the Sun is in Libra, it is actually that the Earth is in Aries looking at the Sun with the background of Libra.

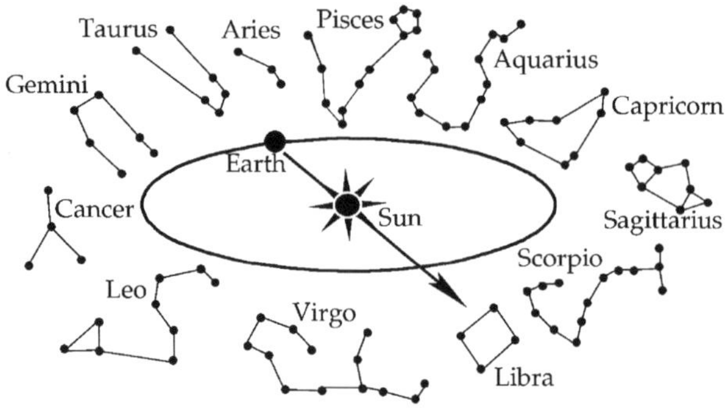

The zodiac moves in a clockwise motion through the sky. The perceived Sun, Moon & planets move forward through the zodiac, in a counterclockwise direction. As an example, if the Sun is in seven degrees of Aries, it will move clockwise through the sky as Aries moves clockwise through the sky in the seventh degree. As the Sun moves one degree every day, it will move counter clockwise to eight degrees of Aries the next day, and to nine degrees of Aries the following day. So while the zodiac is moving from East to West through the sky, the Sun is perceived to move from West to East through the zodiac.

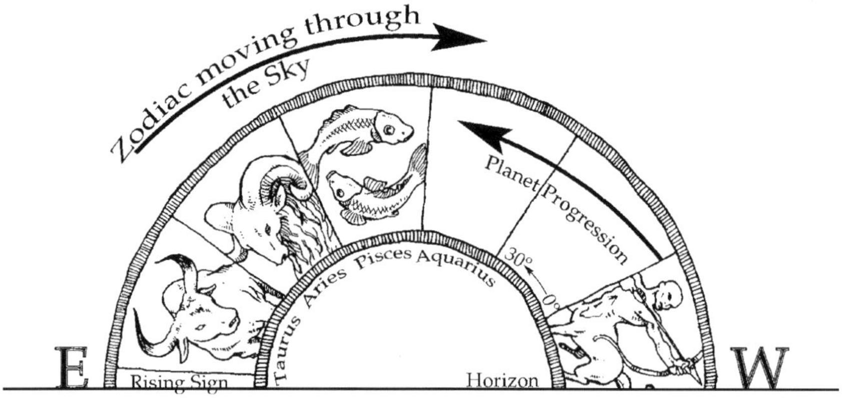

This leads to the next topic of Time (kāla). The zodiac is Viṣṇu's Kālarūpa[5] or manifestation through the zodiac as 'Time'. Our day is based on the rotation of the Earth, the week is based on the progression of the planets, the month on the cycles of the Moon, and the year on the revolution of the Earth around the Sun. Time by its very nature is based on the stars and planets. To have a working understanding of the basic features of time it is important to relate to the universe we live in. This understanding will also show the pertinence of the information presented in a Jyotiṣa chart and allow the mind to start computing the universe inside your head.

[5] Bṛhat Parāśara Horā Śāstra, Rāśi-Svarūpa-Adyāya, v. 2

Time

The first indication of time in Jyotiṣa is the Sun and Moon, representing the Father and the Mother. It is through time that all things happen. All things are born in, mature in, come to fruition in, and die in time. Therefore everything that will be seen or predicted must be done within the construct of time. In Jyotiṣa time is qualitative- it holds a particular energy. To understand the energy of time is to understand a dimension of being. The material being exists in the past, present, and future.

Time has five elements that make up the various energies felt in the quality of time. These are the five limbs of time in Vedic astrology. This lesson will introduce the Moon phases *(tithi)* to help give a sense of how the stars and planets are moving from a geocentric view. Their movement creates time and it is the birth time that determines the representative chart of the karma to be experienced in this life.

The planets move in a way that progresses through the zodiac, which is divided into twelve signs of thirty degrees each. The Sun progresses approximately one degree per day, so that it will circle the zodiac of 360 degrees in one year. The Moon moves approximately twelve degrees a day. Every month the Moon goes around the entire zodiac, while the Sun goes through one sign in a month of 30 days.

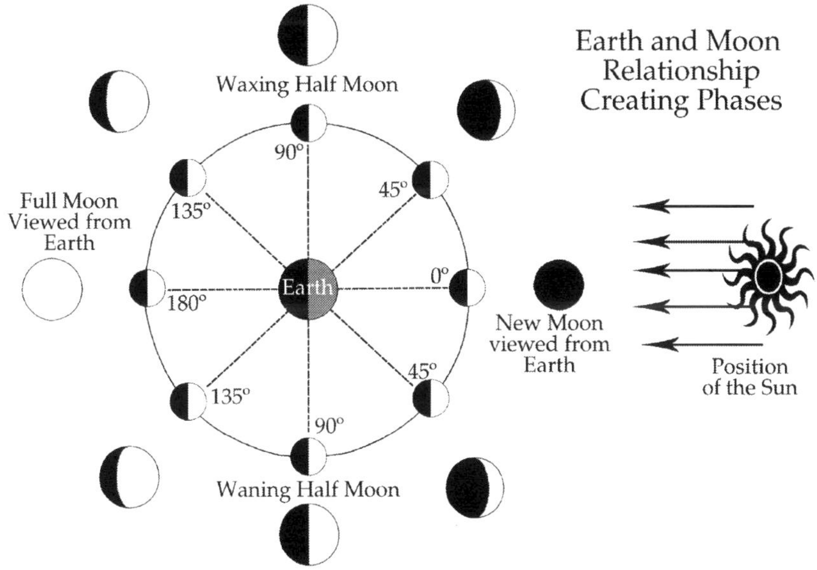

The above diagram shows the position of the Moon from the Earth in relation to the Sun. During each phase the Sun and Moon will have a certain angle of relationship to each other. In this way, the position of the Moon in the sky can be seen relative to the Sun.

During the Full Moon the Sun and Moon are 180 degrees apart (as shown in the above diagram) and when the Sun sets the Moon rises- meaning the Moon is in the sky the entire night and sets when the Sun rises. The table below summarizes the rising and setting times of the Moon. This was very important information to the ancients. Even within the Dead Sea Scrolls are tables explaining the time of the rising and setting of the Moon based on the phase. The Dead Sea Scrolls[3] say that when the Moon is full, it "rules all the night in the midst of the sky, and sets when the Sun rises, and thus begins the waning of the Moon".

The angle between the Sun and Moon will change and so will the rising time of the Moon also change. When the Moon is waning it will rise later and later in the night. At the waning half Moon it will rise at midnight. Until it reaches New where the Sun and Moon are perceived as being in the same place in the zodiac, and it will rise when the Sun rises and set with the Sun so it will not be visible in the sky. As it begins to grow more full it will begin rising almost an hour later each day; first an hour after sunrise, then after a day, two hours after sunrise, and after another day about three hours after sunrise. The waxing half Moon will rise at 12 noon, and be directly overhead when the Sun sets.'

Phase (*Tithi*)	**Time the Moon is ahead/behind the Sun**	**Moon Rises (eastern sky)**	**Moon in Mid-heaven**	**Moon Sets (western sky)**
New	within a few minutes	Sunrise	Noon	Sunset
Waxing ½	6 hrs behind	Noon	Sunset	Midnight
Full	12 hrs behind	Sunset	Midnight	Sunrise
Waning ½	6 hrs ahead	Midnight	Sunrise	Noon

With this technical information there should now be a better understanding of the Moon phases *(tithis)*. Take this information outside and start predicting when the Moon will rise. This is a beginner exercise to allow the study of astrology to be practically experienced outside in the sky above. In this way, you will be looking up into the heavens, and not down onto a piece of paper or computer screen,

You will become aware of the luminaries dancing in the sky, and slowly more aware of the natural cycles that living in a house with artificial light has obscured. This connection to the natural cycle of time will be the first Jyotiṣa practice *(sādhana)* for the beginner. The Sun, Moon, Planets and stars must come alive.

Practice Exercise:

Using a monthly calendar, note the phases of the Moon. Research and predict when the Moon will rise each day of the month. Check yourself by observation of the actual sky. Become aware of the heavenly bodies and their cycles similar to the ancient astrologers.

[3] Wise, Abegg, & Cook. Qumran texts, 4Q317

Chapter 2

Vedic Foundations

श्रीं

Background Understanding: The Foundation

Vedic Astrology is considered a limb of the Vedas. Without at least a small understanding of the Vedas, learning Jyotiṣa would be like teaching a person how to use a steering wheel without them knowing what a car is. If you went to a jungle tribe and told the tribal people that a car was a box on circles that took a person from one place to another very quickly, they may now have a definition for a car but they still wouldn't know what one is. So only a definition of the Vedas is not enough. Jyotiṣa is a limb of the Vedas, and understanding the Vedas and their goal will elucidate the purpose of Jyotiṣa. The Vedas are generally described as four texts which are a collection of prayers and teachings, but when an astrologer says "Vedas" they mean much more.

The Vedas have a literal meaning and manifold deeper meanings relative to worship, āyurveda, yoga, self-realization and other Vedic sciences. The Vedic texts have mantrik power behind each syllable and word. The different meters that verses are sung in also have their variety of meanings. The Vedas themselves are not meant to be read and studied in old books, they are meant to be alive and chanted. Therefore, for more complete study of the Vedas one must also learn to chant them properly. We will learn at least one verse from the Vedas and study its various aspects.

To fully understand the Vedas and all its limbs would take lifetimes, but a general knowledge is the first step. First we will understand the divisions of Vedic science (what are called abodes of knowledge). Then learn how each one works to support the whole (later small lessons will integrate all limbs of the Vedas into our study of Jyotiṣa). We will then be ready for learning the purpose of the Vedas. With this we will see the original purpose of Jyotiṣa thousands of years ago and how it still applies to human beings today.

The fourteen "abodes" of knowledge (caturdaśa-vidya) are:

I. The Four Veda Samhitas

1. Ṛgveda
2. Yajurveda
3. Sāmaveda
4. Atharvaveda

II. Six Añgas or limbs of the Vedas.

5. Śikṣā-Pronunciation, phonetics (nose/breath)
6. Vyākaraṇa- grammar and syntax (mouth)
7. Chandas- meter for Vedic recitation (feet/legs)
8. Nirukta- lexicon, etymology (ear)
9. Jyotiṣa- astronomy-astrology (eye)
10. Kalpa- manual of rituals (hands/arms)

III. Four Upangas

11. Mimāmsā
12. Nyāya
13. Purāṇas
14. Dharmaśāstra: Manusmṛti, etc.

IV. Four additional vidyasthānas (abodes of knowledge)

15. Āyurveda- medicine
16. Arthaśāstra- economics
17. Dhanurveda -warfare
18. Gandharvaveda- music

I. The Four Veda Samhitas

The four Vedas are composed of hymns that were 'seen' by sages (*ṛṣis*). They are said to have heard them, not to have written them or thought of them themselves, therefore they are not created by man (*Apauruṣeya*). The ṛṣis are called mantra-draṣṭās (those who saw the mantras). As Columbus did not create America by discovering it, the Vedas are believed to have always been present. They are the inherent nature of the universe that the ṛṣis saw in deep meditation. The words of the Vedas are multi-dimensional and have multiple levels of interpretation.

During the period just before the Mahābhārata war, Kṛṣṇa Dvaipāyana, who came to be known as Vedavyāsa (the compiler of the Vedas), took the 1,180 sakhas (sections) of Vedic mantras and divided them into four Vedas. Since then many sakhas have been lost. Yet, the Vedas are considered to be eternal, without a beginning or end. This eternal nature refers to the spiritual truths revealed within the Vedas themselves. Swami Śivānanda of the Divine Life Society says, "Vedas are eternal spiritual Truths. Vedas are an embodiment of divine knowldege. The books may be destroyed, but the knowledge cannot be destroyed. Knowledge is eternal. In that sense, the Vedas are eternal."

I.1 Ṛgveda

The Ṛgveda is the first Veda which contains prayers and praises to the devas (divinity). It is the foundation of the other Vedas and the root from which they evolve. Reference to the Ṛgveda and its verses gives substantiation to theories and practices in Vedic science. The Ṛgveda is written in verses called mantras (or Ṛks). It is composed of ten mandalas, 102 sūktas (hymns), and contains 10,552 mantras. The language is multi-dimensional and has many levels of interpretation.

The Vedas do not say that one path is right and another is wrong. They are worshiping the divine and invoking the highest truths that exist inside. They proclaim that with inquiry and wisdom we can go inside and find the Truth of the universe within ourselves. This is seen in the Hymn of Creation *(nāsadīya)* which is a famous stanza in the Ṛgveda for its poetic excellence and metaphysical depth:

1. There was neither non-existence nor existence then; there was neither the realm of space nor the sky which is beyond. What stirred? Where? In whose protection? Was there water, bottemlessly deep?

2. There was neither death nor immortality then. There was no distinguishing sign of day or night. That Oneness breathed without air by its own impulse. Other than that there was nothing beyond.
3. Darkness was hidden by darkness in the beginning; with no distinguishing sign, all this was water (potentiality of creation). The life force that was covered with emptiness, that One arose through the power of heat.
4. Desire came upon that One in the beginning; that was the first seed of mind. Poets seeking in their heart with wisdom found the bond of existence in non-existence.
5. Their ray of light (*raśmi*) was extended across. Was there below? Was there above? There were seed-placers; there were powers. There was impulse beneath; there was giving-forth above.
6. Who really knows? Who will here proclaim it? Whence was it produced? Whence is this creation? The gods came afterward, with the creation of the universe. Who then knows whence it has arisen?
7. Whence this creation has arisen- perhaps it is formed itself, or perhaps it did not- the one who looks down on it, in the highest heaven. Only he knows- or perhaps he does not know[4]."

The Ṛgveda has set the foundation of most concepts in Vedic Science including Indian Astrology. For example, individual beings are individual souls that have come from the One. As molecules of water leave a pot of boiling water so does the individual soul (*jīvātman*) leave the Supreme Soul (*Paramātman*) because of the heat of desire known as *rajas guṇa*. It is this creative energy (*rajas guṇa*) that causes the original creation and continues to cause the human being to create and make new things.

The Vedas support the pursuit of diverse paths fitting to the individual and do not claim a 'right way' nor a final word in everything; nor does it say that the final answer is even available, but 'poets seeking in their hearts with wisdom' have the ability to see the connection between what is here now and what was before this existence we are presently in. Inquiry and examination is the spirit that is ingrained in the Vedic texts[5]. Outer knowledge will never have an end or a final conclusion, while inner knowledge has an end in Universal truths of our true nature.

Below are some other important verses taken from the Ṛgveda:

अग्निमीळे पुरोहितं यज्ञस्य देवमृत्विजम् । होतारं रत्नधातमम् ॥

agnimīḷe purohitaṁ yajñasya devam ṛtvījam, hotāraṁ ratnadhātamam.

I glorify Agni, the high priest (*purohita*), the radiant light (*deva*), the one who invokes the devas (*ṛtvija*) to the sacrifice, who represents the oblation, and is the possessor of the greatest gems.

[4] Ṛg Veda X.129 translated by Burde, Jayante, *Rituals, Mantras, and Science*, p. 102
[5] Rao, S.K. Ramachandra, *Ṛgveda Darśana*, p.288

This is the first line of the Ṛgveda. The first line of each of the Vedas is important to understand the entire Veda. In this verse the fire is praised. The fire element (*agni tattva*) relates to spiritual insight and vision; it is the light of understanding, the light of realization. It is fire that offers up our prayers to the divine. The fire of the third eye opens the mind to higher consciousness, and the light within that awakens on the spiritual path. That light, Agni, is the high priest who has the power to invoke the devas and offer them our prayers. This invokes the awakening of the third eye to be able to tap into the higher realms of perception where the gems of wisdom await. Whole books are written on verses like this, so this is just a brief insight to gain some understanding and build a connection to these ancient texts. The following selected verses have various possible translations.

महो अर्णः सरस्वती प्र चेतयति केतुना । धियो विश्वा विराजति ॥
maho arṇaḥ sarasvatī pra cetayati ketunā , dhiyo viśvā virājati . (Ṛg Veda 1.30.12)

"Only education can help us to understand the knowledge of the universe, which is alike, an ocean. It enlightens everyone's minds."

"Sarasvati, like a great ocean, appears with her ray; she rules all inspirations."

"The great river (word), Sarasvati comes forward into perception illuminating all intelligence like that of a King."

"Sarasvati makes manifest by her acts a mighty river, and (in her own form) enlightens all understandings."

देवान् देवयते यज
devān devayate yaja (Ṛg Veda 1.15.12)

"A person who desires godliness should worship gods."

"One who practices the worship of the Gods is one who knows the Gods."

"One who worships the light-givers is one who has light."

इन्द्रं मित्रं वरुणमग्निमाहुरथो दिव्यः स सुपर्णो गरुत्मान्
एकं सद् विप्रा बहुधा वदन्त्यग्निं यमं मातरिश्वानमाहुः

indraṁ mitraṁ varuṇamagnimāhuratho divyaḥ sa suparṇo garutmān
ekaṁ sad viprā bahudhā vadantyagniṁ yamaṁ mātariśvānamāhuḥ (Ṛgveda 1.164.46)

They make offerings to the divine Indra,
Mitra, Varuṇa and Agni,
and then the great winged Garuḍa.
The seers speak in many ways of
That One Being.
They make offerings to Agni, Yama and Mātariśvān.

Translation of such ancient texts is very difficult. To convey the original meaning without adding too many extra words not in the original, or to choose which concept or aspect of the verse to bring out in translation and to keep some poetic flow is not easy.

This last verse starts with the worship of various devas, then says that the sages give various speech (*vadanti*) to 'the One', or you could say gives various names to the one, but it does not say the word *name*- it just says they call it or speak of it by different ways. The word *bahudhā* can mean different ways, or different forms, or different directions. So it could also be translated as they speak of it in different forms.

Ekaṁ sat means 'that one', or 'the real one', or 'the one existence' it is definitely intending a single form of divinity. With *bahudhā* translated as 'repeatedly' it could also mean that the 'one divinity' is invoked repeatedly even though there are many different names being used.

The verse ends again with the names of various deities. This is pure poetry, it would be like calling your wife by saying: honey, sweetheart, beloved, come my one wife, beloved, precious, beautiful. If the actual verse translation was over anglicized it could also sound like this: Oblations to the Divine King, divine Friend, great Punisher, Sacred Fire, and the celestial bird, the seers speak of the 'One Being' in many ways, Sacred Fire, Lord of Death, Fanner of the Flame, we offer to you.

'The One' is being invoked with many names, or many aspects of That One's presence. The verse says that these various deities are getting oblations- they are being worshipped (*āhu*), so in the midst of this worship of the various invocations the seer remembers that it is just 'That One' that is being offered to, not the many. This is the constant teaching of the Ṛgveda, that everything can be personified as divine, seen as god, and that there are not many but just one divine who manifests as this many. Everything is god and can be invoked but there is only 'One Being'.

From the ritualistic (*adhiyajña*) interpretation the deities are being worshipped outside of one's self. From the theological (*adhidaivata*) interpretation, the deities are being conceptually understood. From the internal (*adhyātma*) interpretation the deities all represent aspects of oneself. These different interpretations do not contradict each other but complement each other. The adhiyajña interpretation is used for ritual action (*karma*), the adhidaivata interpretation is used to understand the deity (*bhakti*), and the adhyātma interpretation is used to understand one's nature (*jñāna*).

On an adhyātma level, Indra is the inner controller. Mitra is the day- the friendly supporting voice in your head, while Varuṇa is the night- the pessimistic, punishing voice. Agni is consciousness as the cognition of reality and Garuḍa is the perceiving aspect of the self (the two wings being the two aspects relative to the two hemispheres of the brain). Garuḍa is the mode of perceiving, Agni is aware of that perception, Mitra and Varuṇa frame it, and Indra acts upon it. Yama is the guidance of our own mortality while Mārtariśvān is the desire to live. So the above verse could also be loosely translated as, "The inner ruler, the supportive and punishing self, consciousness and perception are all divine, the seers speak in many ways of the one self, they are aware of life and death".

I.2 Yajurveda

The Yajurveda is the second Veda which describes the rites and sacrifices supplementing the Ṛgveda mantras. It focuses on yajña (worship) and is used primarily by the priests. The Yajurveda is divided into two parts, white and black.

The Black Yajurveda is the older of the two. It is divided into seven kāṇḍas (books) of 44 praśnas (chapters) which each have 651 anuvākas (sections) and 2198 kaṇḍikās (pieces comprised of 50 words). The White Yajurveda consists of forty adhyāyas (chapters), 303 anuvākas (sections) and 1975 kaṇḍikās.

Below are some verses to help build a connection to the Yajurveda:

वसोः पवित्रमसि द्यौरसि पृथिव्यसि मातरिश्वनो धर्मोऽसि विश्वधा असि ।
परमेण धाम्ना दृहस्व मा ह्वार्मा ते यज्ञपतिर्ह्वार्षोत् ॥

vasoḥ pavitramasi dyaurasi pṛthivyasi mātariaśvano dharmo'si viśvadhā asi|
parameṇa dhāmnā dṛhasva mā hvāarmā te yajñapatirhvāarṣont||(Yajur Veda I.2)

"The Yajña (ritual) acts as a puifier, makes explicit, true and perfect knowledge, spread in space through rays, of Sun, purifies the air, is the mainstay of the universe, and also adds to our comfort through its exalted office. It behoves us, the learned ones and their followers, not to give up the performance of ritual[5]. "

अग्ने वेर्होत्रं वेर्दूत्यमवतान्त्वां द्यावापृथिवी अव त्वं द्यावापृथिवी
स्विष्टकृद्देवेभ्य इन्द्र आज्येन हविषा भूत्स्वाहा सं ज्योतिषा ज्योतिः ॥

agne verhotraṁ verdūtyamavatāntvāṁ dyāvāpṛthivī ava tvaṁ dyāvāpṛthivī
sviṣṭakṛddevebhya indra ājyena haviṣā bhūtsvāhā saṁ jyotiṣā jyotiḥ||(Yajur Veda II.9)

"Oh Fire, protect the Sun and Earth, who protect the ritual. Just as fire acquiring the fire ritual and acting as an envoy, protects the Sun and Earth, so protect us, Indra, the doer of the noble deeds for the learned. Just as the Sun combining light with light through the oblations put into fire, protects the heaven and the earth so God guard us with the light of spiritual knowledge. This is thus ordained the Veda[6]! ".

Chapter XV offers some beautiful sayings[7]:

Knowledge gives pleasure.
The practice of truth gives ease.
The cultivation of noble traits gives peace of mind.
Free movement like a river gives independence.
Life after death gives solace.
The Sun gives us knowledge.
The light of knowledge brings happiness.
The action which removes sin, gives light.
Concentration of mind gives strength.

[7] Yajur Veda Chapter XV.4-5, translated by Devi Chand

I.3 Sāmaveda

The Sāmaveda is sung as it is the musical interpretation of the Ṛg-mantras. The Ṛg and the Yajur are chanted in three notes while the Sāma is sung using the seven svaras (notes). Sāma-Gāna is thought to be the basis of the sapta- svara (seven notes) in Indian classical music. The Sāmaveda has 1875 mantras and only a few (less than a hundred) are its own mantras, the rest are the same as the Ṛgveda in different order.

In the Bhagavad Gitā, Kṛṣṇa identifies himself as the Sāmaveda. "Among the Vedas, I am the Sāmaveda" (10-22). He gives great importance to the Sāmaveda by identifying himself with it. The singing of the Sāmaveda can make the mind stable and lead one to peace.

Below are some verses taken from the Sāmaveda:

त्वमिमा ओषधीः सोम विश्वास्त्वमपो अजनयस्त्वं गाः ।
त्वमातनोरुर्वाश्न्तरिक्षं त्वं ज्योतिषा वि तमो ववर्थ ॥

tvamimā oṣadhīḥ soma viśvāstvamapo ajanayastvaṁ gāḥ।
tvamātanoruvāntarikṣaṁ tvaṁ jyotiṣā vi tamo vavartha।।

"Oh Soma (Moon), you have created herbs, the water, the cattle like kin,
You have expanded the vast atmosphere and cast aside darkness with Light[8]."

आ प्रागाद्भद्रा युवतिरह्नः केतुन्त्समीत्र्सरुत ।
अभुद्भद्रा निवेशनी विश्वस्य जगतो रात्री ॥

ā prāgādbhadrā yuvatirahnaḥ ketuntsamīrtsati।
abhudbhadrā niveśanī viśvasya jagato rātrī।।

"The Night, affording rest to the whole world, was a source of bliss.
Now has come this blissful young Dawn, that urges the lights of day[9]."

एष सुर्यमरोचयत् पवमानो अधि द्यवि । पवित्रे मत्सरो मदः ॥

eṣa suryamarocayat pavamāno adhi dyavi। pavitre matsaro madaḥ।।

"This all-pervading God, lends lustre to the Sun in heaven
and grants joy and happiness to the pure soul[10]."

"The sādhaka makes his life pure and divine by enkindling
the flame of knowledge in his mind[11]."

"Seeking the Shining Sun, being purified in the highest heavens,
the mind is cleared and passionately intoxicated."

---

[8] Authors variation on Devi Chand translation, Sāma Veda (604), Āraṇyaka Kāṇḍa, Chapter 3, Decade III.3

[9] Devi Chand translation, Sāma Veda (608), Āraṇyaka Kāṇḍa, Chapter 3, Decade III.7

[10] Devi Chand translation, Sāma Veda (1284), Book V, Chapter 2, Decade V.5

[11] Anonymous online translation

I.4 Atharvaveda

The Atharvaveda is the fourth Veda which contains spells for healing and harming. It has information on curing disease, human physiology, social structure, astrology, spirituality and yoga. There is a hymn that celebrates the wonder of creation called the *Pṛthvi-Sūkta*. There are mantras to ward off hardship and destroy enemies. There are mantras to correct the mispronunciations and wrong performances that may happen in the practices of the other three Vedas. It was not considered part of the orthodox three Vedas at the time f Ṛṣi Vāsiṣṭa, the father of Ṛṣi Parāśara. But at the time of Veda Vyāsa who was the son of Parāśara, the Atharvaveda was included as the fourth division. It was Parāśara's wish that his son learn all four Vedas. The gāyatri mantra has three steps (padas) and is said to relate to the first three Vedas. Therefore a separate initiation (Upanāyanam) is done for studying the Atharvaveda.

There was a ṛṣi by the name of Atharvan who was a great teacher of this Veda. Some say that the name means A (not) *tharva* (movement, fickleness) which would be 'devoid of movement' thereby meaning 'concentration'. The Atharvaveda is similar to the Ṛgveda, but puts more stress on practical worldly affairs. There are mantras to deities not mentioned in the other Vedas. The importance of the Artharvaveda is judged by the Upaniśads that are part of it: Praśna, Muṇḍaka, and Māndūkya Upaniṣads.

While the other three Vedas start with praises to the fire god, Agni, the Atharvaveda starts with praises to Vāchaspati, the lord of speech.

Below are some verses to make a connection with the Atharvaveda:

अक्ष्यौ नौ मधुसंकाशे अनीकं नौ समञ्जनम्।
अन्तः कृणुष्व मां हृदि मन इन्नौ सहासति ॥

akṣyau nau madhusaṅkāśe anīkaṁ nau samañjanam|
antaḥ kṛṇuṣva māṁ hadi mana innau sahāsati|| *(Atharvaveda, Kāṇḍa VII, hymn 36)*

"Sweet like honey be the lovely glances of the husband and
wife, may our faces look equally beautiful. Within thy bosom
harbor me; may one spirit dwell in both of us (1819)[12]."

यदि वासि तिरोजनं यदि वा नद्य स्तिरः।
इयं ह मह्यं त्वामोषधिर्बद्ध्वेव न्यानयत्॥

yadi vāsi tirojanaṁ yadi vā nadya stiraḥ|
iyaṁ ha mahyaṁ tvāmoṣadhirbaddhveva nyānayat||(Atharvaveda, Kāṇḍa VII, hymn 36)

"Oh husband, if you are far away beyond the rivers, far away from men, this
uptial vow will seem to bind thee fast and bring thee back to me (1825).

[12] Devi Chand translation, Atharvaveda (1819), Kāṇḍa VII, hymn 36

Mantra Against Sorcerers and Demons[13]

1. May this oblation carry hither the sorcerers, as a river (carries) foam! The man or the woman who has performed this (sorcery), that person shall here proclaim himself!
2. This vaunting (sorcerer) has come hither: receive him with alacrity! O Brihaspati, put him into subjection; O Agni and Soma, pierce him through!
3. Slay the offspring of the sorcerer, O soma-drinking *(Indra)*, and subject (him)! Make drop out the farther and the nearer eye of the braggart (demon)!
4. Wherever, O Agni Jātavedas, thou perceives the brood of these hidden devourers *(atrin)*, do thou, mightily strengthened by our charm, slay them, slay their (brood), O Agni, piercing them a hundredfold!

Mantra for Obtaining a Husband[14]

1. This Aryaman (wooer) with loosened crest of hair comes hither in front (of the procession), seeking a husband for this spinster, and a wife for this wifeless man.
2. This maid, O Aryaman, has wearied of going to the wedding-feasts of other women. Now shall, without fail, O Aryaman, other women go to her wedding-feast!
3. The creator *(Dhātar)* supports *(didhhra)* this earth, Dhātar supports the heavens, and the Sun. May Dhātar furnish this spinster with a husband after her own heart.

Mantra with licorice, to secure the love of a woman[14]

1. This plant is born of honey, with honey do we dig for thee. Of honey thou art begotten, do thou make us full of honey!
2. At the tip of my tongue may I have honey, at my tongue's root the sweetness of honey! In my power alone shalt thou then be, thou shalt come up to my wish!
3. Sweet as honey is my entrance, sweet as honey my departure. With my voice do I speak sweet as honey, may I become like honey!
4. I am sweeter than honey, fuller of sweetness than licorice. Mayest thou, without fail, long for me alone, (as a bee) for a branch full of honey!
5. I have surrounded thee with a clinging sugarcane, to remove aversion, so that thou shalt not be averse to me!

Mantra to allay jealousy[16]

1. From folk belonging to all kinds of people, from the Sindhu (Indus) thou hast been brought hither-from a distance, I ween, has been fetched the very remedy for jealousy.
2. As if a fire is burning him, as if the forest-fire burns in various directions, this jealousy of his do thou quench, as a fire (is quenched) with water!

---

[13] Maurice Bloomfield translation, IV.VI, 60
[14] Maurice Bloomfield translation, III. I. 8
[15] Maurice Bloomfield translation, IV.I, 34
[16] Maurice Bloomfield translation, IV.VII, 45

Four Parts of the Vedas

Each of the Vedas consist of four parts. The main book of the Vedas with its hyms are called the *mantra saṁhitas*. Second, are the *Brāhmaṇas* which are explanations of the mantras and rituals. Third, the *Āraṇyakas* are the philosophical interpretations of the rituals. The last part is the *Upaniṣads*, which are the knowledge portion of the Vedas. Each of the four parts relate to a loosely defined stage of life. The mantra saṁhitas of the Vedas, quoted above, are particularly meant to be studied during the student (*brahmachāra*) phase of life; the first 25 years of life. The relation of the four parts of the Vedas to the four stages of life does not mean that after 25 one stops studying the mantras of the Vedas, it is just a guide toward the primary place of focus on a topic that is bigger than a life time of study.

The **Brāhamaṇas** are similar to guide books which explain the Vedic practices. It is meant to be used by an individual during the householder (*gṛhastha*) phase of life (about 25 to 50 years of age); the time when the person marries and has children. Religious ritual is done in the home and for special occasions to ensure prosperity of knowledge, wealth and dharma. Rituals are done to purify one's karma and to purify oneself to be able to hold higher knowledge and understanding.

The **Āraṇyakas** explain why the various rituals are performed and the inner meaning in the prayers of the mantra samhitas. It explains the symbolic purpose of the rituals and teaches the symbolic/internal mode of worship. This part is meant for the third phase of life called *Vānaprashta*, from approximately 50 to 75 years of age, after one's own children become parents. Before this, ideally one is to support the proper functioning and health of society. Then, ideally one begins to slowly focus more on the non-material reality. The Āraṇyakas deepen the doorway to meditation and reveal the esoteric meaning of the Vedas. This section relates to the third eye chakra and the ability to perceive what is beyond. At the close of the Āraṇyakas comes the Upaniṣads. There is an analogy to nature that if the Vedic samhitas are the tree, the Brāhmaṇa are the flowers, the Āraṇyakas the unripe fruit and the Upaniṣads are the final fruit (*phala*)[17]. The preceding parts of the Vedas are meant to take one to the path of knowledge, while the Upaniṣads are the direct path of realization.

The **Upaniṣads** are the fruit of the Vedas, the concluding portion. 'Upa' means near or towards, 'ni' means into, śad means removal or destruction[18] . Therefore they can be considered teachings which take one toward the removal of ignorance, or teachings which take one towards the destruction of the individual self and its ignorance merging one into the Universal All-knowledge Self. The Upaniṣads teach the spiritual goal of the Vedas and are the foundation for modern Hinduism.

[17] Śrī Chandrasekharendra Sarasvati MahāSvāmiji, *HinduDharma: The Vedas*, The Upanishads

[18] "Upaniṣad is from dhātu sad meaning to destroy, to move, to loosen, with prefixes upa and ni and suffix kvip." Kaṭhopaniṣad Bhāṣhya by Śaṅkara

The Upaniṣads reveal the direct means of realizing the nature of the jīvātman (individual soul) and Paramātman (the Supreme soul). The Veda Samhitas and Brāhmaṇas are based on karma kāṇḍa[19]; the path of works and actions to purify the body and mind to be fit for realization. The Āraṇyakas deal with upāsana kāṇḍa which relates to worship and meditation which purify our heart. The Upaniṣads deal with jñāna kāṇḍa; the pure inner significance and the knowledge which leads to liberation.

The deepest revelations of Vedic understanding are clearly explained in the Upaniṣads. From the Upaniṣads comes the philosophy called Vedanta. *Anta* means, end, conclusion, final, the whole amount, inner part, inside, and nearness. In this way, Vedanta philosophy takes one near to the Vedas, giving the inside teaching of the Vedas. When understood, one attains complete knowledge of the Vedas, it is the final wisdom . . .

Each Veda Saṁhitā has Upaniṣads which are their spiritual essence. The essence of the Upaniṣads are condensed into 'great sayings' that are mantras to be meditated upon. These sayings are called the *Mahāvākyas* and reveal one's true nature. When an individual renounces the world for spiritual life (sanyas), they are initiated into the four principal Mahāvākyas that guide one to realize their unity with the Brahman (God beyond all perception).

Mahāvākyas

The Upaniṣads have been summed up in phrases or mantras which contain the core teachings. These key realizations extracted from the Upaniṣads are called the Mahāvākyas.

Mahāvākya	Upaniṣad
prajñānaṁ brahma (Supreme Knowledge is Brahman)	Aitareya of Ṛg Veda
ahaṁ brahmāsmi (I am Brahma/God)	Bṛhadāraṇyaka of Yajur Veda
aham-asmi /brahmāham-asmi	Taittirīya of Kṛṣṇa Yajur Veda
tat-tvam-asi (You are That)	Chāndogya of Sama Veda
ayam-ātmā-brahma (This indwelling Self is Brahman)	Māndūkya of Atharva Veda

The goal of the Vedas can be stated many ways. What I have tried to present here is the foundation so the essence of the goal can become visible. One can say that the goal is Self- knowledge or God-knowledge, but these are just words. Only learning, practicing, meditation and realization can enlighten one to the depths of the Vedas. As Jyotiṣa is a limb of the Vedas it is a way for the Veda to act and achieve its goal. This is why we must understand the goal of the Vedas if we are to understand the true goal of Jyotiṣa.

[19] Karma kāṇḍa is also known as purvamīmāmsā, and Jñāna kāṇḍa is also uttaramīmāmsā.

If the Vedas were personified as a person, the Upaniśads would be the crown of the head. This anthropomorphizing of the Vedas is called the *Veda Puruṣa,* which literally means the Vedas as a human being. When the Vedas are personified, the Veda Puruṣa has six limbs (aṅgas) through which to work in this world. The six Aṅgas are: Śikṣā (Phonetics), Vyākaraṇa (grammar), Nirukta (lexicon, etymology), Kalpa (manual of rituals), Chandas (prosody), Jyotiṣa (astronomy-astrology). Each branch/limb is interwoven with the other and knowledge of one helps in understanding all the others. Understanding of these limbs helps in understanding the Vedas and the path to the realization they contain.

II. Six Aṅgas or limbs of the Vedas

II. 1 Śikṣā-Pronunciation, phonetics (nose/breath of the Veda Puruṣa)

Śrota means ear and *śruti* means that which is heard. The Vedas are called śruti and have been handed down orally for thousands of years. Linguists have understood that human pronunciation changes every two hundred years, as one can see with old English relative to the English written in the U.S. Constitution, relative to modern spoken American English. The Vedic Ṛṣis were aware of this and developed the science of phonetics to a high degree to maintain the correct pronunciation of the Vedas through time. Śikṣā (pronunciation) is the life breath of Vedic mantras and keeps them alive and instilled with prana.

Wrong chanting is said to not give the intended results, as a different station on the radio will not give the correct musical program. The limb of śikṣā deals with all matters that work with proper pronunciation. Each letter-sound (phoneme) is to be pronounced correctly with the proper measure and proper tonal variations.

The phoneme is a sound syllable that needs to be pronounced clearly. This clarity is achieved by a thorough understanding of how sound is produced in the mouth. For example, in English the difference between a 'v' and a 'w' is that the 'v' is pronounced with the lower lip folded and the upper teeth come into contact with it to create the sound. The 'w' is pronounced with the lips turned round and no teeth contact to the lips. This clear, conscious understanding of how sound is created in the mouth and body is used to pronounce Sanskrit mantras correctly.

The measure of the phoneme is the length of time it is pronounced. There are short (*hṛsva*) and long (*dīrgha*) syllables. The short syllables are held for one beat (*mātrā*) and the long syllables are held for two beats. This affects the way the word/mantras are pronounced and chanted.

The tonal variation and accentuation (*svaras*) is a system meant to give tonal purity to the Vedic mantras. It is seen in the raised syllable (*udatta*), the lowered syllable (*anudātta*), and the falling syllable (*svarita*). These are to be learned from a teacher but can sometimes be seen marked in Sanskrit mantras above and below the letters.

Another element of śikṣā is the combining of letters called *sandhi.* When two letters are combined, they will change pronounciation. We can see this occur in English with the word cupboard which is composed of the words cup and board. When the 'p' and the 'b' are pronounced together it becomes as 'bb' (cubboard). The hard 'p' becomes a soft 'b' in pronunciation, but in English the written letters do not change. In Sanskrit they would change to fit the appropriate sound. The rules that govern the changing of the sound are part of śikṣā. An example in Sanskrit is seen with the word Jagat, which means universe. In Jagannātha, the 't' becomes an 'n' to mean lord (nātha) of the universe. In Jagadambā, the 't' becomes a soft 'd' for Mother (ambā) of the universe.

In this way the rules of pronunciation are very intricate as even small changes can affect the efficacy of a mantra. The branch of śikṣā forms the foundation of mantra yoga and śabda yoga. In Jyotiṣa it will be important for proper pronunciation of Vedic astrology terminology, correctly reciting mantras used for personal practice, and for giving successful remedies which may involve mantra.

Practice Exercises:

This is the Gāyatrī mantra, a key mantra from the Vedas which holds an important role for Jyotiṣis. First is the mantra, and second is the mantra's ghanapāṭha which is used to attain correct śikṣā of the mantra. It is similar to a tongue twister that makes you say it correctly instead of incorrectly. We will study this mantra through the various limbs of the Vedas.

तत्सवितुर्वरेण्यं भर्गो देवस्य धीमहि । धियो यो नः प्रचोदयात् ॥	tatsaviturvareṇayaṁ bhargo devasya dhīmahi dhiyo yo naḥ pracodayāt

॥गायत्रीमन्त्रः॥

||*gāyatrīmantraḥ*||

॥घनपाठः॥

||*ghanapāṭhaḥ*||

तथ्सवितु-स्सवितु-स्तत्तथ्सवितुर्वरेण्यं वरेण्यगं सवितु स्तत्तथ्सवितुर्वरेण्यम्।

tathsavitu-ssavitu-stattathsaviturvareṇyaṁ vareṇyagṁ savitu stattathsaviturvareṇyam|

सवितुर्वरेण्यं वरेण्यगं सवितु-स्सवितुर्वरेण्यं भर्गो भर्गो वरेण्यगं सवितु-स्सवितुर्वरेण्यं भर्गः।

saviturvareṇyaṁ vareṇyagṁ savitu-ssaviturvareṇyaṁ bhargo
bhargo vareṇyagṁ savitu-ssaviturvareṇyaṁ bhargaḥ|

वरेण्यं भर्गो भर्गो वरेण्यं वरेण्यं भर्गो देवस्य देवस्य भर्गो वरेण्यं वरेण्यं भर्गो देवस्य।

vareṇyaṁ bhargo bhargo vareṇyaṁ vareṇyaṁ bhargo devasya
devasya bhargo vareṇyaṁ vareṇyaṁ bhargo devasya|

भर्गो देवस्य देवस्य भर्गो भर्गो देवस्य धीमहि धीमहि देवस्य भर्गो भर्गो देवस्य धीमहि।

bhargo devasya devasya bhargo bhargo devasya dhīmahi
dhīmahi devasya bhargo bhargo devasya dhīmahi|

देवस्य धीमहि धीमहि देवस्य देवस्य धीमहि। धीमहीति धीमहि।

devasya dhīmahi dhīmahi devasya devasya dhīmahī| *dhīmahīti dhīmahi*|

धियो यो यो धीयो धियो यो नो नो यो धियो धियो योनः।

dhiyo yo yo dhīyo dhiyo yo no no yo dhiyo dhiyo yonaḥ|

यो नो नो यो योनः प्रचोदयात्प्रचोदयान्नो यो योनः प्रचोदयात्।

yo no no yo yonaḥ pracodayātpracodayānno yo yonaḥ pracodayāt|

नः प्रचोदयात् प्रचोदयान्नो नः प्रचोदयात्। प्रचोदयादिति-प्र-चोदयात्॥

naḥ pracodayāt pracodayānno naḥ pracodayāt| *pracodayāditi-pra-codayāt*||

II.2 Vyākaraṇa- grammar and syntax (mouth)

The word has life (the breath) with śikṣā, and through Vyākaraṇa (the mouth) it eats and sustains the Vedas. The Veda Puruṣa is sustained and nourished by grammar. Bhartṛhari said, "In this world no comprehension is possible except as accompanied by speech; all knowledge shines by means of speech. It is speech that binds knowledge of arts and crafts; everything, when it is produced, is differentiated through it[20]. " Without the knowledge of grammar, one cannot understand the Vedas. Vyākaraṇa brings understanding (*jñāna*) and therefore in India it is traditionally taught in Śiva temples. Grammar is the dance of words and it is believed that the dance of Śiva gave birth to the science of language. "Sound is the highest of the perceived forms of the Paramātman [the Supreme] and language is obviously connected with it. It is the concern of Śikṣā and Vyākaraṇa to refine and clarify it and make it a means for the well-being of our Self [Ātma/soul]." "If sounds are well discerned and employed in speech they will serve not only the purpose of communication but also of cleansing us inwardly[21]." Grammar is one of the most important branches of the Vedas.

Grammar makes complex and spiritual concepts possible to explain in writing. It also allows for embellishment making speech more beautiful. When Sanskrit was brought to China, the Chinese were amazed at the sophistication. Previous to this, Chinese written material was composed similar to lists and after the introduction of Sanskrit there was poetry. In this way, grammar is the dance of words, like Śiva dancing.

The three main texts of sanskrit grammar are written by Pāṇini, Vararuchi and Patañjali. In 700 B.C., Pāṇini was said to have composed his works on grammar after having done Śiva worship in the Himālayas. His *Aṣṭādhyāyī* contains comprehensive rules of grammar and insight into ancient Vedic language.. Pāṇini didn't just describe static grammar rules, he recorded a *generative* grammar. The rules were foundational so that new words could continually be made. Pandita Vāgīśa Śāstrī of Vārāṇasī took one root word and made 65,000 grammatically correct words from that root in order to show the generative power of Sanskrit grammar. Modern computer programming languages have many similarities to Sanskrit grammar because of their computing power.

Patañjali, famous for his *Yoga Sūtras*, also wrote on grammar because of its ability to purify the speech (*vaṇi*), the body (*śarīra*) and consciousness (*chitta*). He wrote the most authoritative commentary on Pāṇini which is called *Mahābhāṣya* (the great commentary).

Vararuchi, who wrote a commentary called Vartikā on Pāṇini's Sūtras, explains five objectives for grammar. The first objective is to protect (*Rakṣa*) the understanding of the Vedas. Second, grammar teaches how to derive words (*uha*). Third, it makes the words beautiful and flowing to the ear, and easy to understand (*laghu*). Fourth, grammar gives the foundation for understanding a word thereby removing ambiguity (*asandeha*) as often a word is understood by its context in a sentence. And finally it gives the ability to understand written texts (*āgama*) and record future works. In the beginning of Patañjali's

---

[20] Vākyapadīya, Ch.1, vv.123 and 125

[21] Śrī Chandrasekharendra Sarasvati MahāSvāmiji, *HinduDharma: Vyakarana*, Linguistic Studies and Religion

Mahābhāṣya he enumerates 13 purposes. These include the wealth of understanding through right meaning (*arthajñāna*), and the wealth of dharma (*dharma lābha*). Grammar is an important part of understanding the Vedas and related Sanskrit literature.

The primary Jyotiṣa scriptures are written in Sanskrit. To properly understand them one needs both knowledge of grammar and insight into Jyotiṣa given by the guru. In the present age, many people rely on faulty translations which lead to many misconceptions. One cannot rely on a paid translator instead of their own knowledge of grammar or a guru who cares for his students.

II.3 Chandas- meter for Vedic recitation (feet/legs)

Chandas is the various meters used for Vedic chanting. These meters are similar in structure to that of traditional poetry meters such as the sonnet. There are seven primary Vedic chandas called gāyatri, triṣṭubh, bṛhatī, paṅkti, uṣṇik, anuṣṭubh, and jagatī. Other meters developed later, but these seven are the original chandas in which the vedas are chanted. The Sun's chariot is described as having one wheel, representing the year, which is pulled by seven horses representing the seven colors emanating from the Sun. These seven horses and colors also relate to the seven meters *(sapta chandas)*, which pull the mantras of the Vedas to their goal. In the *Śatapatha-Brāhmaṇa*, the meters are each connected with a time of the year, a Ṛṣi, a direction, a vāyu, and other associations relating to the internal spiritual functioning. For example, Gāyatrī relates to Agni, the breath, the eastern direction, the spring time, Ṛṣi Vāsiṣṭa and the settling of the ten vāyus into one vāyu. Anuṣṭubh relates to heavenly lokas, the ear, the northern direction, the autumn time, Ṛṣi Viśvāmitra, and the settling of the desires of the ear into one sound.

Each verse of the Vedas is sung according to the proper chandas. Not only do the words and grammar have a meaning but the chandas adds yet another layer of meaning to the mantras. For example, the gāyatri chandas is 24 syllables in length and is composed of three lines (*padas*) of eight syllables (*akṣaras*). These are considered the three steps made by Viṣṇu in the Vāmana (Jupiter) incarnation. Therefore the Gāyatrī chandas is used for bhāgya (obtaining luck/blessings) in endeavors. The anuṣṭup chanda is four padas of eight akṣaras (32 syllables total). It is one pada (line/foot) more into bhakti (devotion). Anuṣṭubh is then a devotional meter. Triṣṭubh has 44 syllables with the four padas being made up of eleven syllables each. This meter relates to the destructive storm god Rudra and is used in verses that carry this destructive/removing energy. Each mantra has eight levels of interpretation and the chandas adds a deeper meaning and interpretation to the mantras of the Vedas. More details are found in Yakṣa's Nirukta and Śaunaka's Bṛhaddevatā.

Traditionally, information that is not written was easy to remember when it was in song or poetry. Since Vedic texts are meant to be committed to memory the meter helps to memorize large amounts of information otherwise impossible in prose form. Chandas also ensures that the mantra is preserved in its complete form, as any loss of information, even a syllable, will be noticed. The main reference text for meter is called the *Chanda Sūtra* by Piṅgala.

The Veda Puruṣa stands on chandas as the legs/feet. Chandas provides a foundation as well as locomotion. The correct chandas will ensure the mantra takes one to the mantra's goal/result as the meter moves one to the intended purpose. In this way the correct meter is important for remedial measures that involve mantras or stotras as remedies.

Practice Exercises:

After learning these chandas one can chant any verse from the ancient astrological texts. Compare the number of syllables in the Gāyatrī mantra above with the number of syllables in the mantra below. Which chandas is this mantra in? Look in the Bhagavad Gītā and other Jyotiṣa texts and count the syllables of the verses.

त्र्यम्बकं यजामहे सुगन्धिं पुष्टिवर्धनम्
उर्वारुकमिवबन्धनान् मृत्योर्मुक्षीय मामृतात्

tryambakaṁ yajāmahe sugandhiṁ puṣṭivardhanam
urvārukamivabandhanān mṛtyormukṣīya mā'mṛtāt

II.4 Nirukta - lexicon, etymology (ear)

Nirukta is the etymological interpretation of a word from its roots and its various variations. Sage Sāyaṇācārya describes nirukta as *"arthavabodhe nirpekṣatāya padjataṁ yatra tat niruktaṁ"* which means the collection of independent words to help in understanding their meaning. *Nairuktas* are etymologists who deal with the derivation of words.

Grammar is the correct use of the word but the deeper meaning of the words is understood through Nirukta. Remember that the Vedas hold the power of sound as that which created everything, which will reveal everything, and which can take you back to the source of everything. The sound vibration of the word is the essence of the nature of the object itself. The deeper aspects of Nirukta have found their greatest developments in the tantric texts, where huge amounts of literature has been written on the power of sound. At this level the sound is broken down into individual letters (*akṣaras*) and each has its own energetic meaning. The 'ra' sound is associated with heat, fire and burning, while the 'va' sound is associated with water. In this way all words have an energetic meaning behind them that can be understood without knowing the intellectual meaning of the word.

The more common use of Nirukta is the use of the roots of words to understand their meaning. Sanskrit is not a literal language like English has evolved to be. Sanskrit is a conceptual language. When one uses the Sanskrit language their conceptual mind will expand toward being able to think in more holistic and unified thought patterns. For example, the word car means something with four wheels that drives, it has a very specific definition. While the Sanskrit word is *vāhana*, which means bearing, carrying, conveying, or bringing. It is the word for car in that a car is something that carries you from one place to another, but a horse or motorcycle are also a vāhana. A spaceship is also a vāhana. In this way the Sanskrit language is conceptual, and allows the mind to think in a more fluid way. This root *vaha* became the Latin *veho*, which became the modern day word vehicle.

Nighaṇṭu is the Sanskrit term for a dictionary. The most famous nighaṇṭu was composed by Yāska (a predecessor of Pāṇini) in the eighth century B.C. It contains lists of words, synonyms and commentary. It is acknowledged in its antiquity and sheds light not only on language but also the social and scientific understanding in Vedic times. At the time of his nighaṇṭu, many words in the Vedas had already become archaic and not fully understood. Yāska gave derivations of words and the meanings known at his time. Yāska interpreted the Vedic words both from a ritualistic viewpoint (*adhiyajña*), a theological viewpoint (*adhidaivata*), and a symbolic viewpoint (*adhyātma*) setting the convention for three levels of interpretation. He lists the views of varying schools of thought in a very open minded approach that leaves the reader to meditate upon the word and come to their own conclusion. In this way, he exhibits the true nature of a spiritual person *(Brahmin)* being open to learning and always expanding the mind by understanding opposing views. One uses various views to understand the subject deeper, unattached to any particular view.

Yāska says that nirukta is a sort of 'tapas' which will enable us to appreciate the light that shines amidst the words used in a mantra. The process of nirukta involves understanding the root of a word, what that core root means. Then understanding the grammatical change that puts the root into its present form as a word. Then the comparison of various similar words that show the use of the word for a proper conceptual understanding. Sometimes a word can have two meanings, but from the level of nirukta it has one conceptual meaning. For example, the word Jīva means soul (the individual soul), and it is also a name for the planet Jupiter.

What is the soul? Why is Jupiter called by the same name while it is Sun that is supposed to represent the atma (soul) of a person? There are many different views relative to various religions and science on what the soul is. Our definition for these purposes must be *scientific* relative to Vedic *science.* The word Jīva comes from the root word *jiv* which according to Pāṇini means 'prāṇadhāraṇe'. This is translated as 'to support life, to keep alive, to nourish'. It literally means to hold (*dhāra*) life force energy (*prāṇa*). This same root *jiv* gives the Latin root *vivo* and *vita*[22] (life). In sanskrit we get the words jīvanti (life), jīvada (life-cutter, enemy), jīvadaśā (mortal existence), jīvadāna (life giving), jīvana (giving life energy, enlivening), jīvanavidambana (dissapointment in life, living in vain), Jīva has been defined by Monnier Williams as living, existing, alive, healthy, causing to live, vivifying, any living being, anything living, life, the principle of life, and the personal soul. So Jīva can be understood as "that which holds the lifeforce in the body". Whether you believe it to be a spiritual force or a chemical reaction in the brain, this definition can suffice for both views. Jupiter is the planet in Jyotiṣa that protects the life force. Malefic aspects and combinations for early death are removed by the aspect of Jupiter. In this way Jupiter is often called by the name Jīva.

Understanding a word at this level is nirukta. In Jyotiṣa, there are many terms which hide beautiful, deep, enlghtening concepts by the understanding of the words that name them.

[22] Hill & Harrison, *Dhātupāṭha*, p.344

Practice Exercises:

For this exercise we will just do a very simple level of nirukta, as an example is already given above of a single word. We will look at an entire Vedic mantra to be able to better understand it. Mantras should be understood, not said blindly. This is the power of the limb of nirukta which is the ear of the Vedas. The ear represents not just hearing, but the comprehension of what you hear. Nirukta is the ear to apprehend the word.

Tat - That, the self-evident, Parabrahma

Savituḥ - impeller, exciter, vivifier, awakener, the Sun as Āditya. Composed of the root *sa* which is creation (*sarga*) and the root *tṛ* which means doer- the one doing the creation or the producer. Savitṛ is the creative aspect of the Sun, also associated with Brahmā, the creator. It is also used in the Upaniṣads to refer to the Self (shining like the Sun) which creates our reality.

Vareṇyam - the root *vṛ* means 'to choose' and as an adjective literally means the choosable or that worthy of being chosen. The verb form *varaṇa* means the act of choosing, wishing, wooing, or honouring. Common translation is adorable, chosen by all, excellent, best among, desired, loveable, praiseworthy, invoking the heart.

'That' which is self evident is the highest awakener

Bargaḥ - light, power, radiance, brilliance, full of life, effulgent, consumer of all faults of avidyā, the self-effulgent source

Devasya - shining, divine, the illumiator or revealer of all, (literally: of the deva)

Dhīmahi - we meditate , the root is *dhyo* which also gives the word dhyāna

We mediate upon the self-effulgent source which is the illuminator of all

Dhiyo - wisdoms, plural of the word dhī which means intelligence, intuition, understanding, intention, disposition, opinion, the faculties of intelligence and intuition

Naḥ - our

Prachodayāt - should inspire, direct, impel us forward. The root *chod* means to inspire, instigate, or urge forward and the prefix *pra* means 'very much' which is emphasizing: much direction. It is the subjective mood (should) not an order but more of a request which requires the grace of the one being asked (*may he inspire* our wisdom).

Please direct/guide/enlarge all our intelligence and intuition.

II.5 Kalpa - Manual of Rituals (hands/arms)

Kalpa is the last Vedaṅga, but we will discuss it before Jyotiṣa so that we can understand Jyotiṣa within all the other limbs. Kalpa is the huge science of rituals in which one interacts with the personified universe. It utilizes the web of the universe as a matrix which can be effected by proper understanding of the elements that compose the universe and the balancing of those elements that compose our individual lives. By personifying and invoking various universal energies and balancing them with mantric sound vibrations and the proper elemental offerings, one can harmonize their life.

Kalpa is also the actual practice of the Vedic mantras and any ritual associated with them. For example, Agni Gāyatrī is done only facing east, in the early morning, with the hand over a container of water. The Savitṛ Gāyatrī is said after bathing and before eating while the Sun is rising. While Nirukta helps explain the meaning of the words in a mantra, Kalpa is the actual use of these words where the transcendental meaning is attained by the practitioner. Through actual practice the true inner meaning of the Vedic mantras is revealed.

There are many very elaborate rituals done for various problems in life. The main texts for Kalpa are the Śrauta Sūtras which explain the rituals and the Sulba which contain the calculation of the ritual space. It is said that the Dharma Sūtra (on ethics and customs) and the Gṛhya Sūtras (concerning domestic life) are also part of Kalpa as our everyday life is a ritual in and of itself. There are many different Kalpa Sūtras which relate to each of the four Vedas.

There is a large debate whether Tantra Śāstra originated from the Vedas or Buddhism or before both. The large body of Tantra is mainly Nirukta, Yoga and Kalpa Śāstra. Though not directly Vedic as Tantra uses non-Vedic deities, the underlying principles used by the Tantras are rooted in these Vedic Sciences as geometry is rooted in Algebra.

Practice Exercise:

Begin to chant the Savitṛ Gāyatrī, in the morning, after a bath and before eating. Use a mālā and do the mantra 108 times. Let the sound, light and understanding of the mantra awaken your highest potential. Try to do it every day or take a 40 day period where you do not miss a single day. The Ṛṣi is Viśvāmitra, chanda is Gāyatrī, and devatā is Savitā.

II.6 Jyotiṣa - Astronomy-astrology (eye)

Then we come to our main topic, Jyotiṣa as a limb of the Vedas *(Vedāṅga)*. Everything so far has fit together perfectly; the body of divine knowledge *(Veda)* and the method of transmitting it from one person to the next *(Vedaṅga)*. The rest of the text will be about Jyotiṣa so we won't go into the mechanics of it here, but just touch on how it is a Vedaṅga, and the Eye of the Vedas. The word for eye is netra, which means to lead and to guide. The eye is the guiding organ of the body. In the same way Jyotiṣa is the guiding light for the Vedic knowledge.

Jyoti is one of the words for light in Sanskrit. It represents light as the divine principle of life, the light of knowledge, the light of an enlightened one, the light of being alive. As the planets are the lights in the sky guiding us they are also called the Jyoti as well. It is this level of light that Jyotiṣa is studying.

The incredible web-like matrix through which everything is connected is perceived by Jyotiṣa. It is harmonized with rituals through the Kalpa Vedaṅga, but which ritual should be done and when is seen according to Jyotiṣa. Why it is done and how it works is also seen through the eye of Jyotiṣa. Kalpa is the offering of the dīpa (lamp) to the divine. Jyotiṣa is the eye that tells us when to offer the lamp and to which form of the divine in order to attain the results that will enlighten our life. Which of the thousands of mantras and rituals does each individual need to utilize is calculated by their individual karma seen in the birth chart. No person is the same and everyone needs their spiritual practices, life purpose, and path to fulfillment individualized according to their own karmic history. In the Upaveda (secondary Vedic branch) of Āyurveda it is said that no medicine is good for everybody and everything is good for somebody. This ability to understand the individual is core to Vedic Science. Jyotiṣa shows the way to attain the goals of life and the path to attain the goal of the Vedas. It is the eye to guide our lives to the highest fulfillment on every level of human existence.

The Savitur Gāyatrī is related to the rising Sun as Savitṛ, he who is the exciter, impeller, energizer and life giver. The Sun is connected to the first house of health as well as the tenth house of career/recognition. The main planet to destroy health is also Saturn (aging and disease). The main planet to destroy career and recognition is Saturn (poverty and bad name). When Saturn is in/aspects/transits the ascendant or the tenth house one needs to do the Gāyatrī mantra to protect themselves from the bad effects of Saturn. When Saturn afflicts the Sun one can do Gāyatrī mantra to uplift themselves from the suffering, bring health to the body and success in life. As the Sun is the representative of the self it also is a mantra to reveal the inner self knowledge hidden dark inside of us. In this way, Jyotiṣa perceives all mantras and rituals and uses them with understanding, as nirukta makes one understand the meaning of a mantra.

III. Four Upāṅgas

Upa means secondary and therefore these are the secondary branches of the Vedas.

Mīmāṁsā: Investigation and Inquiry

Mīmāṁsā consists of the rules for Interpretation of Vedic philosophy. One of the earliest and primary texts is the Mīmāṁsā Sūtra of Jaimini. The knowledge of the Vedas should not be taken blindly but should be understood deeply with reason through examination, investigation, inquiry, discussion and reflection. In this same way, the rules of Jyotiṣa are not meant to be blindly memorized and followed. The deeper reason behind all the principles is to be understood and applied properly.

Nyāya: Science of Logic

Nyāya is the ancient Indian system of logic similar to modern analytic philosophy. Traditional western logic is based on Aristotelian logical principles. Nyāya uses four means to attain knowledge (*pramāṇa*): Pratyakṣa (perception), Anumāna (inference), Upamāna (comparison) and Śabda (the teachings of authorities). These four methods separate false opinions from valid knowledge.

For proper research in the field of astrology, these components of Nyāya and Mīmāṁsā should be understood and applied. Many western astrologers try to practice Vedic astrology through intuition and modern channeled information, never learning the basics of Vedic logical analysis. This leads to the decadence of Jyotiṣa in the modern world. These methods of analysis are used in general among Vedic Sciences including Jyotiṣa.

Purāṇas: Histories and Mythologies

The Purāṇas are collection of traditional stories. Many of these stories are spiritual and astrological teachings hidden in ancient myths about sages and devas elaborated from the Vedas. Many take a story alluded to in the Vedas and give an explanation. For example, the Vedas called Viṣṇu as the one who conquers in three steps, but the full story of the three steps to conquer the world is found in the Purāṇas.

The Viṣṇu Purāṇa and Śrīmad Bhagavata are primary texts relative to Jyotiṣa, though all of them contain astrological teachings. Different religious schools hold specific Purāṇas in high regard. For example, goddess worshippers *(Śaktas)* use the Devi Mahātmyā which is a text that comes from the Markaṇḍeya Purāṇa. There are 18 primary texts *(Mahā-Purāṇas)* and hundreds in total. They play an important role in teaching Jyotiṣa students the mythology that goes along with all the various grahas and devas used in traditional Jyotiṣa.

Throughout this text, there will be references and retelling of Purāṇic stories, such as the churning of the ocean of milk. Purāṇic study or study of traditional stories/mythology composed of archetypal material is important for an astrologer. Much of this information has practical life lessons and spiritual growth understanding conveyed through stories that allow the mind to easily grasp a concept or to hold the story in memory until it eventually reveals its jewels of wisdom. Both the information in these stories and the ability to convey information through analogy is important for astrologers. One can begin studying the Purāṇas by focusing on a deity related to the present daśā (time period), for example during Jupiter daśā one can study the Vāmana Purāṇa.

Dharma Sāstra: Manusmṛti and Smṛti

Dharma Śāstra is the social, cultural, and national laws that govern people. The Dharma Śāstras are Smṛtis and have a seconday authority while Śruti takes precedent over anything stated chronologically later. Śruti is that which is **heard** (realized) by the Ṛṣis. Smṛti is what is **remembered** and composed by mortal humans. Both are authoritative sources. For example, the rules about the four stages of life (varnāśramas) are spelled out in these books. Brahmachārya is the first stage of life, which is approximately the first twenty-five years, where one is a student. Gṛhastaya is the householder working part of life which lasts from approximately age 25 to 50. Vanaprastiya is where one begins to step back from worldly life and focus on spirituality. Saṁyasin is the final stage of life where one focuses only on spirituality. The goal of the Dharma Śāstra is social regulation based upon the principles of Truth taught in the Vedas. Though laws change with the time and ancient laws do not look like modern laws. Sages like Yajñavalkya and Parāśara are known to have updated the laws to fit their times.

IV. Four additional vidyāsthānas (abodes of knowledge)

The fourteen authorities of dharma (*dharma-pramānas*) encompass all Vedic religious knowledge. The first fourteen are both abodes of dharma (*dharma-sthānas*) and abodes of knowledge (*vidyā-sthānas*). The last four (making 18 abodes of knowledge) are not dharmasthānas (abodes of dharma)[23] but they qualify to be vidyāsthānas (abodes of knowledge). These additional four subjects are commonly called Upa-Vedas or secondary Vedic texts. These subjects have complete Jyotiṣa teachings directly specific to there particular area.

- 15 Āyurveda- Science of life and medicine
- 16 Arthaśāstra- Science of politics and economics
- 17 Dhanurveda –Science of warfare and martial arts
- 18 Gandharvaveda- Science of music

[23] Śrī Chandrasekharendra Sarasvati MahāSvāmiji, *HinduDharma: The Vedas*, The Fourteen Abodes of Knowledge

Jyotiṣa Foundations:

Having caught a glimpse of the enormity of the Vedic Sciences one can understand that Jyotiṣa is subject with depth comparable to the ocean. Having broken down the main limbs of the Vedas which Jyotiṣa is among, now we break down the various branches of Jyotiṣa itself. There are three skandhas of Jyotiṣa. Skandha means section, part, or division; on a human it is the shoulder (region from the neck to the shoulder joint), on a tree it is the part of the trunk where branches begin to grow (or the places where branches come off the principle stem). Therefore, they are the principle departments within the science of Jyotiṣa of which other subjects exist within. They are sometimes called the three eyes.

Skandhas (parts of Jyotiṣa)

Gaṇita - the right eye (Sun)- the science of computation which includes algebra, spherical geometry, and other celestial mathematics for astronomy. It needs perfection of calculation because a small mistake can make a big difference. The main texts of this branch are called the Siddhāntas which are scientific treatises on mathematics, astronomy, and cosmology.

Horā - the left eye (Moon)- the science of astrology where the astronomical data is interpreted for interpersonal meaning. It is the study of the qualitative nature of time and its effect on life. The primary text for this is Bṛhat Parāśara Horā Śāstra. Bṛhat means large, vast, and abundant. Parāśara is one of the Ṛg Veda Ṛṣis and the father of Vedic Astrology. Horā Śāstra is the science of Horā. From the word horā we get the word horoscope and horoscopy. The word entered the Greek language and is the source of the word hour.

Saṁhitā - third eye (Jupiter/Agni)- saṁhitā means a compilation of verses, or text on a particular science. In Jyotiṣa, it is the various teachings on the understanding of natural phenomena, sometimes called natural astrology. All life is understood through Jyotiṣa and the various happenings in life are recorded and interpreted in these various texts. Earthquakes, comets, rainbows, palms of hands, marks and shapes of faces, dreams, omens, sounds, etc are aspects of saṁhitā. Horoscopes for states, countries or the masses also fall under saṁhitā. It is the ability to use the essence of all the Jyotiṣa knowledge for prognostication in all areas of life with all the elements of life.

Traditionally one learns Gaṇitā first with the various mathematical calculations needed to make a birth chart. Then one learns Horā for the interpretation of that data. Then after understanding the movements of the universe and how to interpret them one expands this understanding to every aspect of life in the branch of Saṁhitā. The time cycles affecting the movement of life, the relationship between internal personal elements and external phenomena, the significations of animals, colors, or people and what they reveal and mean for the past, present and future are the understanding given with these three branches. Life becomes a teacher. Life speaks to one who understands it and reveals that there are no secrets from an awake and aware universe. In this way Jyotiṣa is the eye of knowledge guiding the wise.

Ṣadaṅgas (six limbs) of Jyotiṣa

The six limbs which stem from these three branches are more defined areas of Jyotiṣa. They are areas which are necessary to understand to be a good Vedic astrologer.

1. **Gola** - is the science of astronomy. Gola literally means globe, and represents the aspect of being able to look at the sky and understand the motion of the planets and stars. It requires computation of planetary position and movement when a planet is on the visible side of the hemisphere, and when a planet is not visible relative to the season. Vedic astronomy is based on pratyakṣa which means visible, present before the eyes, perceptible, ocular evidence, direct perception, or apprehension by the senses, which is one of the modes of proof in Nyāya philosophy. Some say this is with the *unaided eye* only as if seeing through a telescope is not perception with ones 'own' eye. Traditionally this was a complex and deep science, but in modern practice has been largely replaced on the individual level by the existence of astronomical observatories and computer technology. This falls under the skandha of Gaṇita.

2. **Gaṇita** - is the individual branch composed of only mathematics. It is the more specific aṅga of the Gaṇita skandha focusing on computation of time periods and sphutas (degree points) with in a chart. With modern computers the importance of this is often overlooked, but proper knowledge of this branch will allow one to correct computer programs that do make mistakes. Calculation of charts and daśās (time periods) will allow one to understand the inner working of Jyotiṣa methods and better understand the results given by these methods. Computation of a chart also allows one to be better aware of the inner workings of the chart and allow it to become alive in one's consciousness.

3. **Jātaka** - is the science of interpreting individual horoscopes, sometimes called natal astrology. Jāta means born, to become present. Jātaka is the space/time of one who is born, it is the map of the sky one becomes manifest under which shows one's destiny. Jātaka is the main branch of Horā.

4. **Praśna** - is the interpretation of the sky for the moment a question arises. Praśna literally means a question, and in Jyotiṣa represents an inquiry into the past, present or future. When a question arises the same energy that invoked that curiosity holds the answer. That energy is seen by casting a chart of the position of the heavens at the time of answering a question and reading it accordingly. These praśna charts are used to answer question, to rectify birth time, determine intent of a person, determine immediate details of a situation or deepen a Jātaka understanding. The houses and planets will have different meaning relative to the question or reason for casting the praśna chart.

5. **Muhūrta** - is called electional astrology. Muhūrta means a moment, or an instant. It also refers to a space of time that is forty-eight minutes long. Electional astrology is used to choose a moment to begin a new endeavor. As a person's destiny can be seen from their birth chart, the birth of a business or marriage can show the future health and longevity of that union. Understanding this one takes into account planetary positions when starting important activities to ensure success and happiness.

6. **Nimitta** - is the science of omens or omenology. It is the ability to read life as a whole. Nimitta consists of understanding natural phenomena such as when the birds fly low it is going to rain. It takes into account a sound made by an animal, car, or object when a question is asked. It accounts for the state of the breath when you leave for a journey or receive a phone call to determine success and failure in your endeavors. Nimitta acknowledges whether a remedy will be beneficial or detrimental. It is a science of awareness and understanding that the world around you is alive and interacting with you constantly. This is the most important branch of Saṁhitā. Other branches of Saṁhitā like palmistry or face reading are good to know and give insight but are secondary to be able to interpret a basic natal chart or praśna chart.

These are the six branches of Jyotiṣa an astrologer must learn to become fully competent.

Karma: The Laws of Action and Reaction

The chart of the sky at the moment of birth is a map of one's karma. Ṛṣi Parāśara teaches that dharma is sustained by this law of cause and effect. Good actions receive good effects and negative actions receive negative effects. Viṣṇu, the energy associated with sustenance, takes the form of the nine Vedic planets (grahas) to maintain dharma through the law of karma. In this way, a Vedic Astrologer needs to understand the foundations of the laws of karma, and the effects produced by curses and blessings. There are four types of karma and three levels of intensity.

Four Types of Karmas:

Saṁchita Karmas: Saṁchita means piled together, accumulated, and dense. Saṁchita karma is the sum total of all actions one has performed in the past.

Prārabdha Karmas: Prārabdha means commenced, or undertaken. This is the portion of saṁchita karmas that one is destined to experience in the present life. The moment of birth is caused by the prārabdha karma which is revealed in the natal chart. This is the primary karma the astrologer is able to analyze based on the position of the planets in the natal charts.

Kriyamāṇa Karmas: Kriyamāṇa means being done. Karmas based on our choices in this present life are planting seeds for what we will receive in the future. Most astrologers believe in destiny for the previous two types of karma, as they are the results created by your own completed past actions. Kriyamāṇa karma brings up the debate about destiny and amount of freewill an individual possesses. The results of a person's present actions can be seen in Praśna.

Āgama Karma: Āgama means coming, or approaching. Āgama karmas are the ones being created by our desires. If one desires an object, action or position strongly, then the desires of the mind will cause these karmas to come about in either the future of the present life or future lives. Muhūrta charts are used to create the best results of the actions one plans to undertake.

Three Intensities of Karma:

Dṛḍha Karmas: Dṛḍha means fastened, tight, close, confirmed, certain, hard, strong, and solid. This is the fixed karma that is very difficult to change. The Buddha called it 'written in stone'.

Dṛḍha-Adṛḍha Karmas: Adṛḍha is the opposite of dṛḍha and means not firm. This is the intermediate level of intensity where change of karma can happen through determined effort and perseverance.

Adṛḍha Karmas: Can be changed easily through an individual's good actions or good choices and remedial measures, The Buddha called it 'written on sand'.

The three intensities of karma are based on the quantity of factors indicating a result in the particular chart. Indications are evaluated by four factors; the house, the house lord, the house kāraka, and the house arūḍha. Also fixed signs show the karma is more dṛḍha, dual signs are dṛḍha-adṛḍha, and moveable signs are adṛḍha.

Chapter 3

Grahas: *Planets*

Grahas: Planets

The Sanskrit word for planet is graha, which means seizing, laying hold of, holding, obtaining, perceiving, apprehending, or grasping. The English word 'grab' shares the same linguistic root. While the word 'planet' does not include the Sun and Moon, the term graha does. There are nine basic grahas in Jyotiṣa. They are called grahas as they are that which controlls the manifestation of elements in the material, pranic and mental plane. They are the instruments through which the law of karma is working. The Sage Parāśara explains,

अवताराण्यनेकानि ह्यजस्य परमात्मनः ।
जीवानां कर्मफलदो ग्रहरूपी जनार्दनः ॥ ३ ॥

avatārāṇyanekāni hyajasya paramātmanaḥ |
jīvānāṁ karmaphalado graharūpī janārdanaḥ || 3||

There are many incarnations of the unborn Supreme Spirit,
Janārdana[24] Viṣṇu takes the form of the nine grahas (planets) to give
living beings the results of their karma,

दैत्यानां बलनाशाय देवानां बलबृद्धये ।
धर्मसंस्तापनार्थाय ग्रहाज्जाताः शुभाः क्रमात् ॥ ४ ॥

daityānāṁ balanāśāya devānāṁ balabṛddhaye |
dharmasaṁstāpanārthāya grahājjātāḥ śubhāḥ kramāt || 4 ||[25]

To destroy the strength of the demons and increase the power of the devas
He took birth as the splendorous grahas to sustain dharma (to indicate dharma).

The Supreme Spirit (*paramātman*) takes many forms. He took the form of the grahas to give living beings (*jīva*) the results of their own actions. How does the law of karma work, through what mechanism does it work, when will the results of our actions return to us? The planets are setting the stage in which the script of our karma will be played out. When Parāśara says that Viṣṇu incarnated as the planets to destroy the strength of the demons, this means that it is to return the bad karma to those who perform bad actions. In this way the strength of our demon nature will be weakened. The law of karma gives blessings to the devas and thereby strengthens their power. The devas are our good thoughts, qualities and actions. By having good result from good, karma is strengthening these good qualities and we are encouraged to continue in the path of light (*deva*). It is by the law of karma executed through the grahas that Viṣṇu functions as the sustainer in this plane of existence; in this way, dharma is upheld. All good happenings have been earned and all calamity is learning from our mistakes with the hope of evolving towards a higher state of consciousness.

---

[24] *Jana* means generating, birth or those which are born (men and creatures). *Ardana* is to move, destroy or annihilate, therefore Viṣṇu can be the one who moves all creatures to manifest, all beings to be born, or He is the one who destroys the need to be reborn (the giver of mokṣa).

[25] Bṛhat Parāśara Horā Śāstra, Avatāra-Kathana-Adhyāya

This is the basic concept behind the functional purpose of the grahas in Vedic Astrology. They represent enactment of the various types of karma we have acquired. Karma is action and the grahas are kārakas through which action is done. All situations and occurances in life arise through the nine grahas. As the numbers begin to repeat themselves after reaching nine (...6, 7, 8, 9, 1+0, or 1+1, or 1+2), all numbers relate to the combination of one through nine. In the same way, if the universe was a computer program, all things would be made of the numbers one to nine and their variations. In this way, the planets and their combinations make up the actions of the entire manifest world.

Sun	Soul
Moon	Mind
Mars	Fire (agni)
Mercury	Earth (pṛthvi)
Jupiter	Space (ākāśa)
Venus	Water (jala)
Saturn	Air (vāyu)

The Sun is the soul (*ātma*) and the Moon is the mind (*manas*). Rāhu and Ketu are the mental and psychic disturbances of the mind and soul. The other five visible planets relate to the five elements. And it is through the ātma, mind, and five elements composing reality, that the grahas affect all things. The better one understands the five elements the better one will be able to understand the grahas from an intuitive level. Every manifestion in space and time is composed of and activated by the five elements.

Elements: The Essence of Reality (Tattva)

Earth *(pṛthvi)*	Form, creation of material reality, Creator, solid element defining form, manifests the solid aspects of the body like the bones and teeth, smell, apāna vāyu is related to earth creating downward flow of energy: excretion. Connected to sustenance and food/money/wealth and that through which we achieve this	
Water *(jala)*	*Sustainer*, love, flowing, connection, relationship, social, culture, creative, life-giving, immunity, healing, health, vitality, sexual attraction, reproduction, youth, young, malleable, beauty, voluptuous, growing, growth, rejuvenating, cleansing, cooling, taste, regulating temperature, circulation	
Fire *(agni)*	Digesting, transforming, heat, turns food to energy, nervous system activation, animation, movement, light, sight, eyes, understanding, discipline, celibacy, power, strength, anger, frustration, combustion, burning, irritatation, inflammation, boiling, cooking, alchemy	
Air *(vāyu)*	Separating, making difference, decreasing, waning, depleting, destruction, Destroyer, Rudra, movement, chitta- mindfield or movie screen of mind, Kālacakra, time and phalana (maturing), vāta in the body as what causes aging, decay, disease, suffering and death, relates to sense of touch through the skin	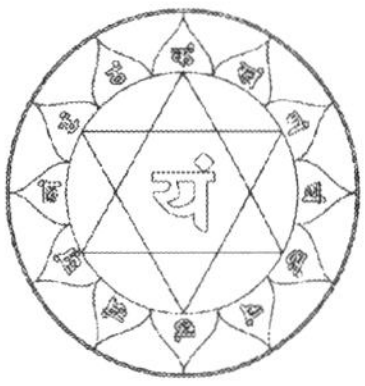
Space *(ākāśa)*	Abundant, everywhere, in everything, everything is in it, existence, soul, bringing things together harmoniously, lineage, Śrī Cakra, ear, hearing, the guru's teachings, true knowledge, fulfillment, true contentment (*santoṣa*), ākāśa awakens Guru in the body/ mind which gives intuition (*prātibhā*), inner guru, ākāśa allows space for life, good space (*sukha*), coordinates all other elements, ensures life continues, binding force, harmonizing glue	

Guṇas

The mind is influenced by the five elements and the three guṇas (attributes). The guṇas are qualitative states of nature. Tamas is heaviness densifying into the physical nature of things. Rajas is the fast moving creative energy of life and all activities. Sattva is balanced, sustaining energy. These three attributes are needed for the creation, sustenance, and transformation of all activities in life.

At a material level all elements of life can be classified into one of these three guṇas. Things that bring dullness, heaviness, inertia and lack of consciousness into the mind and body are tamas. Things that bring greed, anxiousness, turbulence, distraction into the mind/body are rajas. Things that bring harmony, knowledge, and understanding are sattva. Tamas is darkenss, rajas is too bright, and sattva is perfect illumination. Tamas is not moving when one need to move, rajas is moving when one needs to be still, sattva is moving when movement is needed and stillness when stability is needed.

Rajas	Sattva	Tamas
Creating, quick/rushed, greedy, desire filled, Brahma, Sarasvati, *Subhadra*	Sustaining, balanced, high consciousness, bringing truth and awareness, Viṣṇu, *Jagannātha*	Transforming, dull, slow, without thought or caring, unconscious, destruction, entropy, Śiva, *Balarāma*
Venus, Mercury	Sun, Moon, Jupiter	Mars, Saturn, *nodes*

The planets relate to the three guṇas. The sattva planets sustain life and bring harmonious benefit to one's life. The Sun provides resources, the Moon supports, and Jupiter shows the proper use of our intelligence. The rajas planets use energy to bring creativity into our life. Venus has creative energy through living beings, in love, sex, and sensory enjoyment. Mercury has creative energy through material things like business, business products, information, books, magazines, etc. The tamas planets transform life by removing the old and making room for the new. Mars breaks the material world and makes/engineers new objects. Saturn uses time, aging and disease to finish the life span and allow for rebirth.

In Jyotiṣa, the Sattva planets are called the tripod of life. As understanding deepens it becomes clear that they are the most important planets for a happy harmonious life. They represent the three eyes: the right eye (Sun), the left eye (Moon) and the third eye (Jupiter). Most remedies for a beneficial material and spiritual life involve these planets.

Varṇa: Caste of the Planets

Jupiter and Venus are Brāhmins. This means they indicate the paths of learning, knowledge, teaching, and guidance. A Brāhmin's job is to read the spiritual scriptures and guide the rest of society. Jupiter is a sattva planet as a Brahmin and represents spirituality for the larger sake of society (dharma) and for liberation (mokṣa). Venus is also a rajas planet as Brāhmin and represents spiritual learning for self gain (artha) and increasing life's enjoyments (kāma). In this way we begin to combine the various significations to deepen our understanding of the grahas. Sun and Mars are Kṣatriyas, which means they are the warrior and politician caste. Mars is the tamas kṣatriya who defends through physical means like the military and police. The sattva kṣatriya Sun defends by making laws and applying them through punishment.

Brahmins	Kṣatriyas	Vaiśyas	Śudras
Jupiter, Venus	Sun, Mars	Moon, Mercury	Saturn, nodes

Moon and Mercury are vaiśyas, the merchant caste. Mercury is a rajas merchant who is the classic businessman, selling products and increasing profit margins. Sattva Moon is more the social merchant who works with selling things beneficial to life as well as social services. Saturn and the nodes represent the working caste of śudras. Saturn is the normal craftsman or handy man laborer and Rāhu represents the foreign laborers (*mlecchas*).

Planets as Natural Significators (Naisargika Kārakas)

Each planet has many indications and therefore it is impossible to list them all. Everything written in an entire encyclopedia can be correlated to one of the nine planets. Yet, lists are given to help gain an understanding of a planet's energies and actions. Various authors will disagree on certain significations, so the important point is to not become attached to a particular object but to understand the principle, pattern, and archetype the planet represents. Significations can also be dividied further into infinite subgroups.

Forests are ruled by Leo, but the trees are ruled by Mercury. The wood to be used for carpentry is governed by Jupiter. The action of building is governed by Saturn. The architectural structure is ruled by Sun. The finished house is ruled by Ketu, while the land a home is built on is governed by Mars. The Feng Shui (vāstu) of the property is ruled by Saturn. The herbs in the garden are governed by the Moon, while the gems buried beneath the ground are ruled by Saturn.

In the forest there are many trees. Fruiting trees are ruled by Jupiter, while fruitless trees are ruled by Mercury. Thorny trees are ruled by Mars. Decorative trees are ruled by Venus. Barren trees are ruled by Saturn. Strong trees with thick trunks are ruled by the Sun. In the same way the natural significator of houses is Ketu, yet within that signification Moon and Venus togther give a luxurious house. Mars gives a house made of bricks, Jupiter gives a house made of wood, Sun gives a straw bale house, and Saturn gives a house made of stones. If you didn't know what type of house Jupiter gave you could surmise that since he rules wood, he would give a house with abundant wood work. In this way, the natural significations of the planets should be understood in a useable and applicable way.

The lists are endless, as everything in the created world can be classified accordingly. Therefore, first begin by understanding the energy of each of the planets. Then as you learn the various significations of each planet, try to understand why that particular object relates, such as why birds relate to the Sun and rams relate to Mars. Without a logical reasoning one is not able to remember long lists of significations, but after understanding, these significations become common sense.

Sūrya (Sun)

Parāśara describes the Sun as having "sweet brown colored eyes *(madhupiṅgala)* and a square figure, his constitution is pitta, he is intelligent *(dhīman)*, masculine, and tends towards baldness *(alpakacha)*"[26].

The Sun gives light energy for all things to prosper and grow. A seed needs the proper light to grow into a plant. Without enough light it will not grow well, with too much light it will burn. The Sun represents the resources we need to survive, for all of life to survive. All energy comes from the Sun, even coal and oil were created from ancient deposits originally brought to life by the Sun. Wind would not blow if not for the heat and cooling of the Sun. Solar power and even the food that grows to sustain all living beings would not exist if the Sun did not provide the energy for life.

The Sun represents the soul, the light inside that guides our lives and energizes our being. There are souls without bodies, but there are no bodies without souls. The soul is a key ingredient to life. If the soul is not happy the body grows sick and dies. The soul is the true guide.

The Sun represents position, respect, rulership and power. The Sun represents the king on a community level and the father on a personal level. The Sun shows dharma, the correct path to live. The king's job is to uphold the dharma of a country, to ensure society lives in a proper and harmonious fashion, in this way he is a sattva warrior (or what has become in modern times a politician). The father's job is to instill dharma, the proper way for an individual to live life. The father is responsible for instilling the sense of self (self esteem) in a child.

[26] Bṛhat Parāśara Horā Śāstra, Graha-Guṇa-Svarūpa-Adhyāya, v. 23

On a higher level the Sun represents the soul, but in the incarnated being this becomes the ahaṁkāra (the sense of self) when it identifies with the material creation. It is the planet Rāhu (north node) that obscures the mind with attachment to believe that the being is the material creation, instead of realizing that we are the soul behind the creation. Ignorance is not recognizing the true soul, but believing in this transitory world. The Sun is called the sarvātma (the soul of all), the level of 'soul' where there is no difference between you and me or anybody else. As the Moon and the other planets have no real light of their own but are just a reflection of the Sun, all the people in our lives are just reflections of the soul's karmic reality.

The Sun shows the reality where there is only One, sometimes called the Puruṣa (Cosmic Being). The reflection of this oneness as it becomes two is seen in the feminine Moon through which the material world is manifest. Through the masculine Sun, the souls of all beings come into existence. Together, the Sun and the Moon represent the god and the goddess who create reality. The Moon represents the dualistic world in which the mind works. The Sun represents the unity of one consciousness where the soul finds peace in that which is beyond the thought process.

The Sun represents spirituality, and will show one's relationship to spirituality in life. The Sun is light and knowledge and burns up untruth. When planets become too close to the Sun (combustion), their material nature is burned up, but their spiritual significations are purified and made clear. The highest knowledge of the Sun is beyond the material plane. The Sun is hot and pure and burns up the inertia of Tamas guṇa. As the rising Sun destroys the darkness of the night; the Sun burns up ignorance, darkness, sluggishness and untruth. The Sun removes the toxins from the body, and in this way is represented by majestic birds like an eagle who eats snakes. The mystical eagle, Garūḍa, is called upon when a person is suffering from toxins and poisons, to fight the dark energy that allows these elements to exist.

The Sun brings light which makes the truth visible. The Sun gives the ability to see clearly, the ability to have insight, the ability to perceive correctly. The famous Sun mantra called *Savitṛ Gāyatrī* is used to invoke the clarity of the Sun into the intellect, to enlighten the mind and the thinking process. Our true nature is clear, bright and brilliant. The Sun burns off the bad karma and darkness that obscures this true vision.

This Sun is the life giving energy of creation. All vitality comes from the Sun, therefore the Sun represents health while Saturn represents darkness and disease. Āyurveda stresses that regular routines are important for a healthy life. Saturn is irregular, while the Sun is the most regular planet. The Sun moves about one degree everyday. The 365 day year is rounded to 360 degrees of the zodiac. It is the movement of the Sun that has brought about the measure of a degree, and that has brought about the measure of a year, a month, and a day. The Sun is the most regular planet from whom all time consciousness rests upon, and creates the seasons of the year. The rhythms of the Sun create the bio-rhythms in plants and animals and relate to the heart and its pulsation. The Sun rules rhythm in nature as well as in sound, like the rhythm of music and musical instruments. The Sun is depicted in mythology with Seven horses driving his chariot. These seven horses relate to the seven ancient chandas (rhythms) of the Vedas. It is these rhythms/vibrations that manifest as the seven colors. Color comes from sound as everything manifests through sound first. The Sun is bright, colorful and musical. It is the soul of all life.

Medical Significations: Asthi dhātu. **Head**, *right eye*, eyesight, circulation, heart, general vitality, skeleton, spine.

Diseases: Pitta disorders, constitutional strengths and weaknesses, vitality, heart and circulation, bones, teeth, eye function, headaches, baldness, stomach, inflammations, fevers, head injuries, spinal problems, injuries from quadrupeds.

Candra (Moon)

Parāśara describes the Moon as being "very vāta-kapha constitution with a large/ wide body, she is wise *(prājñā)*, has good intuition *(dṛś)*, sweet speech, is changeable/ ficklminded, and is a hopeless romantic *(madanātura)*."

The Moon is a reflection of the Sun. Even though the Sun may physically be extremely larger than the Moon, from our vantage point they appear the same size. The Moon is the feminine yin energy and the Sun is the masculine *yang* energy. The movement of the Sun and the Moon is the dance of Śiva and Śakti (the god and goddess).

As the Sun relates to the father, the Moon relates to the mother. The Sun rules the day, and the Moon rules the night. The Sun is a provider of resources and the Moon is the utilizer of resources. In business astrology, the Sun shows supply and the Moon shows demand.

The Moon is the mother and shows nurturing and caring, providing the support to live and for all events to prosper. As a mother loves all her children the Moon is friendly towards all the planets. Planetary combinations with the Moon will show the quality of the mother in one's life, while the position of the Moon will show the presence of the mother in one's life. As the father instills dharma, the mother instills the psychological nature and emotional health in a child. The Moon represents the mother as well as the development in the womb and the early childhood development which affects the psychology of the human mind.

If the Moon is with Saturn the mother will be harsh and the child will have a pessimistic view of life. If the Moon is with Jupiter the mother will be gentle and concerned and the child will have an optimistic view of life. Ketu (the south node) with the Moon brings either psychic ability or schizophrenic tendencies, while Rāhu with the Moon (mind) brings confusion and addiction in one's mental tendencies. The Moon shows general mental health. The mind is very changeable and colored by its associations, while the Sun is one color, burning away untruth. The Moon is the mind mingling in material life with the illusions of name and form.

The Moon represents family; from the immediate family to the larger concepts of family such as a community of neighbors and social communities. The Moon represents society and social interaction, the interaction of many varied minds. The Moon determines one's level of social concern. When the Moon associates with Jupiter (expansion) the individual will have a high level of social concern, while if the Moon associates with Saturn (contraction) there will be disinterest, distancing, and the desire to be alone.

The Moon is fickle and changeable, like its many phases. The Moon is beneficial the closer to full, while it becomes malefic (darker, difficult) the closer it is to new. In Āyurveda, the Full Moon is Kapha (robust in body type) while the new Moon is Vāta (skinny in body type). The Moon is the fastest moving planet in the sky, just as the mind changes directions fast, thoughts and emotions moving quickly through the field of the mind.

The mind moves as the prāṇa flows in the body, and where the mind goes the prāṇa will follow. There is a direct relationship between the breath and the mind, when the mind is fearful, the breathing quickens. When the mind is calm the breathing slows. Yogis control the breath in order to control the mind. Through the breath yogis gain control of the mind and transcend the ephemeral world to attain the pure absolute.

The Sun shows the true reality, while the Moon represents the reflected illusion. The mind works through images which evoke emotions (emotions may reflect reality or may not). How the mind chooses to perceive reality is based upon an individual's natal Moon. The Moon will show the emotional balance of an individual. The lunar constellation (nakṣatra) of the Moon will show how the mind processes an individual's reality.

The mind works through the sense organs. In Mythology, the Moon is sometimes shown being drawn by five horses representing the five senses. It is the five senses which 'feed' the mind stimuli. In Āyurveda, the mind is treated through five sense therapies, and true rejuvenation of the mind happens when the mind is given rest from sensory stimuli, called pratyāhāra, the withdrawal of the senses by the mind. This is when the Moon firmly brings the five horses of the mind to a stop. Excess stimuli depletes the mind, creating anxiety, this is seen when Rāhu associates with the Moon.

The Moon is soft and vulnerable. It is easily hurt, disrupted and damaged. The Moon represents the home and the home is a place of security. The Moon is happiest when it is securely placed in a chart. The Moon suffers the most when it feels vulnerable. A weak Moon will show more difficulty processing emotions and feelings. Happiness and sadness are states of mind, illusionary states that fluctuate as all other emotions do. True happiness is found at the level of the Sun (soul), beyond the fluctuations and fickle nature of the Moon. But the Moon must be channeled in a direction that allows the prāṇas to be the healthiest and to create a fundamental state of happiness. This is achieved through bhakti yoga, the practice of devotion. When mental focus is one of devotion to a higher force, this brings the state of sukha (happiness) in the mind. The mind works through patterns of thought; negative patterns lead to mental unhappiness, positive patterns lead to well-being. Developing bhakti creates positive patterns that direct the mind to happiness. These patterns, and how to best correct them, are seen from the condition of an individual's natal Moon, indicating how to best direct the mind and through which archetypal forms. The Moon's mother was Anusūyā, the purest and most devoted woman in the world.

The Moon is watery and emotional, and relates to melody and singing. A person with the blessings of the Moon will be a good singer, with a melodious voice. When people wash themselves with water, the Moon is strengthened and creates a desire to sing, this is why people love to sing when they shower.

Rain nurtures and feeds all plant life on earth nourishing all forms of life. The Moon relates to the rain and to the growth of plants and herbs, being the primary significator for all food and herbs. Other planets relate to these secondarily. Chilies may be ruled by Mars, and black pepper by the Sun, but all herbs grow with the nurturance of the Moon, and all healing happens through the Mother's nurturance. It is the blessing of the Moon and Mercury that makes one a healer working with medicine. Mercury relates to the science and instruments of medicine, while the Moon relates to the energetic healing side of medicine. In the West these have been somewhat separated but the unison of both is needed for a complete healing system. It is said that the Moon is friendly to all planets, but Mercury has a dislike of the Moon. In this way, we see the natural circumstance of energetic healers to appreciate modern apparatus, while the modern science is less accepting of the lunar method of healing (calling it "alternative"). The Moon was the child of the Ṛṣi Atri, one of the main sages connected to Āyurveda.

The state of the mind directs the prāṇa, and a calm mind brings about the calming and balance of Vāta doṣa (the air humour). When the Vāta is balanced the Agni (digestion) is strong, and therefore the Ojas (immunity) is strong. True healing and health rests in the mind and finding balance and calmness in the mind. The best type of mental pacification (such as meditation) will be seen according to the state and placement of an individual's natal Moon.

Medical Significations: Rakta dhātu. **Face**, Blood, lymph, bodily fluids, stomach, lungs, *left eye*, breasts, uterus, ovaries, fertility, nutrition, mucous membranes.

Diseases: Vāta disorders (for a waning Moon) and kapha disorders (for a waxing Moon), mental and emotional disorders, epilepsy, dullness, laziness, moodiness, blood and lymphatic system, edema, menstrual and hormonal disorders, sleep disorders, TB, fear of watery animals.

Maṅgala (Mars)

Parāśara describes Mars as being "being cruel, inconsiderate, and tending to have blood-shot eyes, enjoys meat (pala) and his wife *(dāra)*, has pitta constitution, is easily angered *(khrodha)*, and has a thin waist".

Mars is hot like fire. He is fierce, aggressive, and forceful. The Sun is the king and Mars is the general executing the king's will. Mars has a soldier mentality and likes to fight. Mars has great leadership abilities but as a Tamas planet he does not think, he just follows orders. His job is to protect, and as a guardian relates to police as well as soldiers. The police do not make the laws, they just enforce them, a soldier does not choose the enemy, they just follow orders and fight.

Externally, Mars relates to fire, and cooks the food, thereby protecting the body from germs by killing them. Internally, Mars relates to the power of digestion, called Agni. When the Agni is strong it properly digests the food protecting the body from toxins *(āma)*.

The Sun is the vitality of the body, but it is the Sun's general as the Agni (digestion) that creates the health for vitality. According to Āyurveda, Agni regulates the strength of all body tissues *(dhātus)* through proper digestion and assimilation of energy. It regulates energy levels of the body and is the significator for strength.

The Ṛṣi Parāśara, teaches that Mars relates to the nerve tissue and the nervous system. The king (Sun) and queen (Moon) work through the general (Mars) who executes all their orders. In this way the soul and the mind, or the right and left sides of the brain command the body through the nervous system. The work is carried out by the servants (Saturn) who relates to the muscles. It is the muscles that carry out the hard work ordered by the nervous system. If the muscles stop working the nervous system has no one to order. If the nervous system malfunctions the muscles have no idea what to do. In this way the nerves and muscles have a tight inter-relationship when dealing with degenerative disease.

Mars is Pitta doṣa (fire humour) and relates to the body's bile. Excess bile, hyper-acidity, relates to Mars. When the Pitta doṣa increases so does irritability or frustration, often relating to an excess desire to control a situation. Mars people need to work at letting go and to try not to control everything. They need more faith and trust to balance out their warrior nature.

Mars is called Kuja or Bhauma, both mean 'born of the earth'. Mars is said to be born from a personification of the earth Mother herself. In this way Mars relates to earth, land and property. As a warrior Mars is one who protects the property/country or acquires other land through conquest. As a warrior Mars is the planet that significates celibacy. Worship of Martian deities like Hanumān or Kartikeya help one progress on the path of celibacy. Venus is water and love while Mars is fire and burning. Venus is a firefighter and has the power to put out Mars (end celibacy). When Mars and Venus are together, the ability to be celibate, or to be reserved with sex is extinguished leading the way for excess sexuality.

The deities associated with Mars are known for their strength. They are Rudras, great destroyers. Mars can create accidents, which are very harmful to the physical body. Mars is associated with harming, hurting, tearing, bleeding, killing and any sort of violence. When a planet is cursed and Mars is involved the planet experiences violence or anger. Mars burns therefore it is associated with the burnt smell. Irritated and inflamed skin or organs relate to Mars, as well as the smoking of cigarettes and the burning of herbs.

When Mars is giving its blessings, a person is skilled in martial arts, has talent for mechanical things and has a very good mind for technical subjects like engineering. Mars gives dynamism, high energy and radiance. Mars has the ability to look very deeply into a particular subject, giving it tremendous power to do research. Mars will often have a very deep understanding of a specific branch of knowledge, but not a well rounded knowledge like Mercury and Jupiter.

Mars has an attraction to occult knowledge. Mars particularly likes the darker side of the mystical reality and Parāśara says that Mars makes one skilled in dark mantras *(mantra-abhichāra-kuśalī)*. Not only does Mars have the power to control the mass of armies but he has the power to control the darker shadow energies. It is for this reason that māraṇa tantra is performed primarily on Tuesdays.

The son of the earth has the killing power and out of the seven realms (sapta loka) he is the lord of the earth plane (bhumi loka). That is why this realm is also called mṛtyu loka, the realm where everything dies. This is why beings of this plane are constantly engaged in the practice of war, as the mightiest will rule the mṛtyu loka. Mars rules breaking, and all things will break, even great mountains. Mars can be well behaved but it is not kind nor soft, and is very unhappy when a situation asks it to be.

Mars is a brother who is protective of his family. As we are all made of the mud of the Earth, we are all brothers when we relate to the Earth as Mother.

Medical Significations: Majjā dhātu. **Chest**, nerves, muscles, blood, stamina, strength, liver, spleen, gall-bladder, bone-marrow, hemoglobin, sex organs, endometrium, uterus, *eyebrows*.

Diseases: Pitta disorders, acne, ulcers, boils, accidents, injuries, cuts, bleeding, surgeries, burns, miscarriage, abortions, endometriosis, head injuries, liver, gallbladder, bile, blood disorders, sexual diseases, menstrual disorders, dysuria, weapons, hemorrhoids, hemorrhages, smoking and diseases caused by it.

Buddha (Mercury)

Parāśara describes Mercury as being "the handsome (having a beautiful form), distinguished *(śreṣṭha)*, uses words with double meanings, has a sense of humor/ makes jokes, is charming *(ruchira)*, and is tri-doshic (has a mix of all three constitutions)."

Mercury is the child born of the illicit relationship between the Moon and Jupiter's wife, Tārā. The Moon is the feeling, emotional nature of the mind, and Jupiter's wife is the Śakti (power) of intelligence. Together they create a child who represents the thinking, discriminating nature of the mind; that which makes decisions.

Mercury is a Rajas planet with lots of energy. Venus and Mercury are between the Earth and the Sun and move through the sky quickly by nature. They like to do lots with their time, more things than time allows, moving faster than the Earth itself. Mercury relates to business, trade, commerce and the business world.

Mercury has business skills, is good at organizing and management. The suits of business people relate to this aspect of Mercury. The fast moving markets relate to the work of Mercury.

Mercury relates to speech and articulation. Reading, writing and all forms of communication are ruled by Mercury. Mercury is studious and good at teaching or lecturing. Mercury loves learning and information, which is shared through speech or other methods of communication. Mercury is called *buddhipradāya*, the one who gives good thinking/ understanding/ intelligence. Mercury is skilled at organizing, and will create structures for knowledge and information. Mercury relates to the earth element, and it is this element which gives form to all things. Jupiter represents the wide vast ocean of knowledge, while Mercury is the departmentalization of colleges and universities that teach the information in a structured format. Mercury gives knowledge a definitive (earth) form as rows of vegetables in a garden, while Jupiter keeps the knowledge pulsing like the ocean which is intermingling beyond exact delineation. Jupiter relates to the information shared in a traditional guru-student relationship, while Mercury relates to the information shared in a class of large numbers of students. Jupiter relates to higher spiritual knowledge that feeds the soul, while Mercury relates to worldly knowledge that makes the world go around and has practical day-to-day application.

Mercury relates to the Prince and the Sun to the king. There is always an underlying tension of the prince waiting to become king; and therefore, in political astrology, Mercury relates to the one who is second in command or the one waiting to come to power. For a king to stay in power they will often do rituals to pacify Mercury as an energetic way of pacifying those who wish to overthrow the king's power and position. As Mercury relates to business and capitalism, it often has more power than the king in the way it influences the people and directs the focus of power. It is similar in the relationship of the boss (Sun) and the secretary who actually does the small work and understands some of the finer details of interaction, but does not have the power, position or control. Mercury relates to the position of administrating the information or processing the data.

Mercury rules memory retention, while Rāhu rules forgetfulness and loss of awareness. They are opposed to each other in this way, where if something is forgotten, it is not remembered, and what is remembered is not forgotten. Mercury is called *durbuddhināśa*, the one who removes or destroys bad comprehension/ bad discernment/ bad notions. Parāśara says that a strong Mercury lives a life of sattva *(sāttvika)*, and it is through sattva that Mercury overcomes Rāhu. Mercury rules greenery, and fresh foods from the garden; while Rāhu rules junk food and things that have been preserved or left over. Rāhu is unclear and messy, while Mercury is clear and concise. When Mercury becomes weak a person will use too many words to describe something that is simple. Rāhu creates conflict, while Mercury is interested in mediating between people, not arguing or fighting.

Mercury is known as *Saumyagraha*, the friendly planet. His disposition is friendly and helpful. Mercury relates to entertainment and rules the living room, or places of social interaction and entertainment. Mercury is into games and sports; games where there is a loser and winner and people are playing together not like Mars where there is the winner and the defeated where people are killed. Mercury rules pretending, and relates to actors. Mercury rules humor, as a child laughing, it is light and enjoys life (if un-afflicted). Mercury has wit and makes puns with words.

Mercury also relates to the in between, the *sandhi* time, between night and day. In Āyurveda, the taste (flavor) associated with Mercury is the the mixed taste. Mercury is known to be androgynous, not extremely masculine or feminine, but in between. The Greek hermaphrodite came from the union of Hermes (Mercury) and Aphrodite (Venus). Mercury is connected to the varieties of transgender people, as well as bi-sexuality. In the Purāṇas, Mercury even took as his wife a man who had been transformed into a woman by the curse of Śiva.

Mercury is often worshipped in the form of a young girl before puberty, as a child before the sexuality has developed. Mercury is seen as a child, and people strongly influenced by Mercury act young even as they age. The Sun acts proper, the Moon acts caring, Mars behaves like a bully, Saturn acts old, while Mercury acts young and is filled with fresh ideas. Mercury has agility and body awareness and makes a person skilled in Yoga *(yogavid)*. Mercury gives dexterity and skills with one's hands. Mercury is an independent thinker *(svatantra buddhi)*, unlike Mars who follows orders. The youth of Mercury leaves it to be highly influenced by other planets; it will act benefic if associated with good planets or behave malefic if associated with cruel planets. Mercury is very adaptable to whatever environment it is placed within, and therefore its company is very important.

Medical Significations: Rasa dhātu. **Hips**, skin, *forehead*, nervous system, throat, neck, mouth, tongue, forebrain, speech.

Diseases: Tridoshic imbalances, memory, discrimination, reason deficiencies, mental aberrations, skin problems, nervous system, nervous breakdowns, vertigo, speech disorders, tremors, ticks, ears, nose, throat and lung problems, hormonal weight disorders, impotence.

Guru (Jupiter)

Parāśara describes Jupiter as having "a large body, is heavy *(guru)*, has tawny hair and eyes, kapha constitution, intelligence *(dhīman)* and is skilled in all the scriptures."

Jupiter relates to the ākāśa (space/ether element), found everywhere in everything, all pervasive. From the Vedic perspective it is the glue that holds the universe together, creating harmony and health in all things. Jupiter is peaceful and represents peace and harmony on all levels. When Jupiter goes to battle, it looks like Gandhi fighting with ahiṁsā (non-violence) or a prayer to overcome obstacles. Jupiter does not try to win against the opposition, he tries to win over the opposition to his side.

Jupiter is strongest at sunrise when the day is beginning, and as such, the blessings of Jupiter are good to begin any new event. Jupiter is the planet with the most Sattva bringing happiness and contentment. Jupiter represents knowledge, wisdom and understanding. Jupiter represents the Vedas (or the pinnacle text of any religion), as the most high knowledge that is wide, holistic and all-encompassing. It is said that any mantra addressed to Jupiter is regarded as a eulogy of knowledge (*jñāna-stuti*).

Jupiter is the greatest benefic; he brings blessings, knowledge, grace, and wealth wherever he is placed. When he looks at another planet or house he gives energy and support helping to overcome any problem. Jupiter is generous and giving and relates to luck and wealth. Jupiter relates to the place money is kept, the bank safe or treasury. Jupiter shows the value of things, how much they are worth.

Jupiter shows personal values; what has meaning in life, what is thought to be important. If Jupiter is with Mercury, then writing is valued, if Jupiter is with the Moon then there are high social values, if Jupiter is with the Sun then spirituality and truth is highly valued. When Rāhu conjoins Jupiter it destroys the values. Jupiter is respect and Rāhu is disrespect, Jupiter is spiritual purity and Rāhu is material pollution. Jupiter is goodness and Rāhu is deceit. Jupiter removes the negative values of Rāhu, but Rāhu pollutes the beneficence of Jupiter. Rāhu is chaos and Jupiter is calmness, their actions and ideals are opposed each other.

Jupiter represents life, aliveness, the individual soul. The Sun is the soul of all, while Jupiter is the individual soul (jīvātmā). It is that which holds the lifeforce in the body. When death comes, it is Jupiter, or the individual soul, that has the power to stop death, otherwise nothing else can. Jupiter protects life and represents peace as opposed to Mars who represents war and killing. Their 'strengths' are opposed each other. But when they are together, Mars will follow Jupiter fully and the combination will give beneficial results.

In Āyurveda, Jupiter rules the sweet taste, and likes sweet foods (sweet but healthy-naturally sweet). Jupiter rules fruits and fruit trees. Venus rules flowers that look beautiful and smell good, while Mercury rules green plants that have no fruit or flower. Jupiter rules fruiting plants that have utilitarian use. Jupiter also relates to getting the end results *(phalana)*, the final fruit of one's hard work.

If the dharma was strong in previous lives the fruits it will bear in this life through Jupiter are a good partner and beautiful children. Children are not just the fruit of the womb but the fruit of one's past dharma (right living). A good spouse is one of the greatest blessings and the result of following the beneficial path of Jupiter in a previous life. Mars, the soldier, causes abortions and miscarriages, as it had given death previously. Jupiter gives life, contentment and the joy which arises through Sattva. In ancient times, Vedic sages served Jupiter in the form of god while their wives served Jupiter by taking care of the husband and children, both are service to Guru.

Jupiter is called Guru in sanskrit, which means teacher, guide, and advisor. The sounds of the name represent the light (Ru) shed on the darkness (Gu). Jupiter removes the darkness of ignorance. Jupiter is a ritualist and enjoys *pūjā* (ritual). Jupiter is called the *Devaguru*, the teacher of the gods, as he guides us to the higher realms and empowers the good tendencies of the mind. When Jupiter is in the mind (on your head) the mind will be guided in the right direction. When Saturn is on your head, there will be actions leading to hard work and suffering. Before performing Hindu ritual, a prayer will be said to Guru so the Guru sits on the head. The Guru is the guide to the Supreme, he is the priest of the king. In this way he relates to Jesus guiding us to the Father (Sun) of Truth.

The state and condition of Jupiter will indicate one's perception of the divine. Jupiter represents an individual's concept and experience of divinity. Jupiter is both god and the guru. It is said that God is the cause *(kāraṇa)* of a situation, while the Guru is the doer *(kārya)* of the actions in the sitaution. In this way, God is the cause of all things but it is done through and experienced through Guru. One's situation with the material guru is only reflective of one's own personal guru karma.

On a material plane, Guru may manifest as a spiritual teacher in one's life if there is enough *bhāgya* (accumulated good karma). The Guru may also manifest through multiple smaller forms of teachers in one's life, or as a transcendant form of Guru as indicated by the natal placement of Jupiter (showing Śiva, Viṣṇu, Dakṣiṇāmūrti, Dattatreya, Tripurasundari, or Jesus, etc). It is in this way that Guru is only a manifestation which is 'doing' the action 'caused' by the divine. Jupiter is the light of knowledge, truth and real understanding.

Medical Significations: Medas dhātu. Belly, fat, circulation, allergies, brain, liver, spleen, gallbladder, pancreas, ear, *nose*.

Diseases: Kapha disorders, obesity, liver, gall bladder, spleen, jaundice, diabetes, ear trouble, weight problems, laziness, chronic diseases, nutrition, tumors, swellings.

Śukra (Venus)

Parāśara describes Venus as "one who is happy, has a pleasing/desirable body, is of superior quality *(śreṣṭha)*, with beautiful eyes, is a poet, has a kapha-vāta constitution, and has curly hair."

Life on earth is only possible with the proper amount of water. A seed germinates into life with the addition of water. Venus represents this life giving power of water. Venus relates to the reproductive tissue in the body (semen and ovaries), and in this way is both the material of the creative process and the place of sustaining this creative process. Venus relates to the hormones of the body, specifically the ones that make reproduction possible. It is these hormones that direct the mind to be filled with thoughts of sexuality. This is the instinctual nature of a created being to procreate, and leads to the initial level of sexual attraction.

Sexuality relates to the water element, as do love and relationship. The ideals of love relate to the guṇa of the planet Venus in the natal chart. When Venus is placed in a sattva sign with sattva planets an individual will have ideals of true love and fidelity. When Venus is placed in a rajas sign or associated with rajas planets then love and sexuality become a desire to be fulfilled and the person's love life is driven by sexual desires. When tamas influences Venus then love becomes a means of sustenance and people marry for wealth, security, or other base acts. The guṇa of Venus will show how this instinctual sexual impulse arises in the individual, showing a person's ideals about love and what they are looking for in relationship.

When someone is in love they look on top of the world because love is energizing and enlivening. In Āyurveda there is a concept called Ojas, which relates to the healthy functioning of the immune system and seen in the glow of one's aura. Ojas is a subtle (higher vibration) form of the water element, showing the health and the protection/support of the health. Venus shows the state of Ojas and the ability to increase or deplete one's store of Ojas. It is in this way that Venus is the planet in charge of rejuvenation.

In Vedic Mythology, Venus is said to be empowered to bring the dead back to life. There are multiple levels from which to understand this. On the physical level, when a person is sick or near death, it is the power of Venus that can cure and bring a person back to health. One way Venus does this is with recitation of the famous Mahāmṛtyuñjaya mantra (Tryambakaṁ yajāmahe...) which exalts the power of Venus and can protect and instill life. On another level, Venus brings the dead back to life by ensuring one will be reborn through the procreative act. If no one was making babies, there would be no way for the soul to come back from the dead. In the same way, when a meditator puts carnal habits or thoughts out of their mind, it is the instinctual impulses of Venus that have the ability to restore them and bring them back into the thought process. One may work at removing the emotion of jealousy, but as soon as a situation arises, that emotion of jealousy will come alive again to attack the mind. Pure love is a deva emotion, while emotions like jealousy, greed or hatred are asura (demon) emotions.

Venus is called the guru (teacher) of the demons (asura-guru), he is the teacher of those who don't see the light, while Jupiter is the guru of the devas (gods). This represents Venus as the guiding force of all our desires. Venus teaches our lower nature, and works with our instinctual desires. Jupiter rules the right hand and Venus rules the left hand, and when a person takes the path of working with desire instead of disciplining desire then they are taking the left handed path of the asura-guru.

Mythically, Venus (Śukra) was born as a child of the great Ṛṣi Bṛghu. Though manifesting femininity at all levels, Vedic mythology perceives the planet Venus as male. Both the Moon and Venus represent women, but the Moon is a Sattva planet and shows the balanced nature of a mother, while Venus is a Rajas planet and shows the desire-filled dancing girl before motherhood. The Moon shows a caring and nurturing energy, while Venus shows the beauty and sexuality of a woman. Venus will invoke lust and a person with a strong Venus will invoke lust in uncontrolled minds.

The deity associated with Venus is Lakṣmī, the goddess of wealth and prosperity. Lakṣmī was born from the turning of the ocean of milk (the Milky Way) just as the Greek form of Venus (Aphrodite) was born from the ocean. As Lakṣmi represents abundance of prosperity in love and wealth, so too does Venus represent both abundance and wealth; money, love and health.

Medical Significations: Śukra dhātu. **Pelvis**, face, *cheeks*, kidneys, immune system, reproductive system, hormones, semen, ovaries, uterus, urinary system.

Diseases: Vāta and kapha disorders, sexual diseases, kidney and urinary tract problems, hormonal and endocrine disorders, diseases of face, eyes, tear duct, diabetes, autoimmune diseases.

Śani (Saturn)

Parāśara describes Saturn as "long and thin bodied, yellow/reddish brown eyes, vāta constitution, having large teeth, lazy/tired *(alasa)*, crippled in the legs *(paṅgu)*, is harsh *(khara)* and has bristly/course hair."

Water is the essence of life, and when water dries up there is the end of life. The air element dries up the water element and brings about the aging/dying process. When something has water and youth, it is malleable and fresh like a green tree sapling. When the air element increases things becomes hard and unbending like an old dry stick. Saturn as the air element is represented by an old gray bearded man.

As Saturn is the slowest moving of the seven Vedic planets, he is shown as walking slowly with a limp. Saturn is the planet connected to limping, being lame, or losing a limb/body part. Saturn is connected to the energy of separating. As the leaves of Autumn dry up and fall from the trees, Saturn rules this time of dying and turning inwards.

He relates to aloneness and meditation as well as the discipline of spiritual life, though to some, aloneness can be loneliness. Saturn is connected to the isolation of separation. Saturn controls death and dying and the loss of the people we love in life. Loss creates suffering in life because of our attachments, and through loss we learn to become unattached.

Everything must one day die and therefore age as the energy of Saturn increases inside. Aging bodies are prone to disease. Saturn brings disease in two ways: over time aging brings natural decay to the body, and secondly, as the body's natural processes stagnate, impurities and toxins build up inside creating disease. Saturn relates to dirt and impurity. On an inner energetic level the impurity of Saturn is removed with the mantra 'auṁ viṣṇave namaḥ'.

Saturn makes things come into maturity. He relates to aging which physically matures the body. He makes people suffer creating emotional maturity. He breaks attachments bringing spiritual maturity. In this way Saturn is connected to ripening, all things come in time.

While the Sun shows royalty and people in powerful positions, Saturn shows the common people that make a kingdom work. The Sun represents a king and his monarchy, while Saturn is democracy and the voice of the average person.

Jupiter shows expansion and growth, while Saturn shows contraction and a narrowing of focus. Jupiter shows good luck and ease in life. Saturn is a planet representing hard work and success through one's own sweat. If Saturn is strong in a natal chart, a person will work very hard in their life. Saturn relates to agriculture and the labor of creating the food from the earth. In many ancient civilizations he was personified as an agricultural deity that would punish through bad circumstances which would harm a harvest. Saturn rules traditional trades and skills and when Saturn rules one's blessings, the individual masters the skills of their forefathers.

Saturn is an old man and a great supporter of tradition, as tradition is about following "the old ways" or old established patterns and habits. When people become very traditional they wear the clothing of their ancestors and avoid change.

Saturn is personified as a punisher and one who invokes fear. As a karmic indicator, he represents the sins (bad karma) that one has done in the past. Any suffering 'caused' by Saturn is just the return of one's own negative actions that have been done in the past (this life or others). The best remedy for the suffering that Saturn brings is the purification of one's past karma through spiritual practice.

Medical Significations: Māṁsa dhātu. **Thighs**, muscles, nerves, *chin*, colon, rectum, knees, legs, joints.

Diseases: Vāta disturbances, chronic illnesses, arthritis, gout, rheumatism, paralysis, spasms, fear, phobia, melancholia, depression, cancer, exhaustion, aging, toxemia, constipation, diseases to legs, lameness, amputation, deafness, deformity, osteoporosis, tooth decay.

Rāhu and Ketu (North and South Nodes)

The story of Rāhu and Ketu comes from the famous story of churning of the ocean of milk (the Milky Way), and the arising of the *Amṛta* (nectar of immortality). The devas learned that by churning the milky ocean they could obtain Amṛta just like butter emerges from churning milk. But they could not do it alone and had to employ the demons *(asuras)* to help. They used a great mountain *(Mandara)* and a huge snake *(Ānanta)* as a churning

rod. The devas and asuras worked together to churn the ocean. When the Amṛta arose the asuras stole it for themselves. With the help of Viṣṇu, the devas were able to regain the nectar and Viṣṇu gave each of the devas a drop. He was avoiding giving any to the asuras. But one asura named Svarbhānu was smarter, disguised himself as a deva and got in line for the nectar. He hid between the Sun and the Moon. Viṣṇu poured a drop of nectar

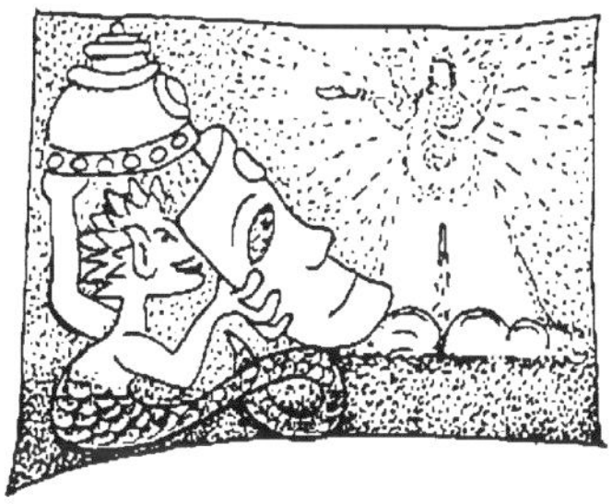

and as it fell the Sun and the Moon exclaimed that it was an asura. Viṣṇu took his chakra and severed Svarbhānu's head from the body at the same moment the nectar landed in his mouth. He thereby became immortal with his head separate from his body. He was put in the sky with the other immortals, but is continually chasing after the Sun and Moon for having caused his fate. The head is called Rāhu and the body is Ketu. It is said that Rāhu tries to swallow the Moon but as he has no body it comes right out after he swallows it. This is the lunar eclipse, while Ketu is related to the solar eclipse.

Rāhu and Ketu are bodiless entities, only having etheric form. They are called shadow planets (*chāya grahas*). They represent the forces that can not be seen. As Rāhu is the head he shows the delusion of the mind for the material world. As Ketu is a body with no head, he can either show the madness of having no mind (schizophrenia) or the spirituality of having the state of no-mind (sahaja, or Zen beginner's mind).

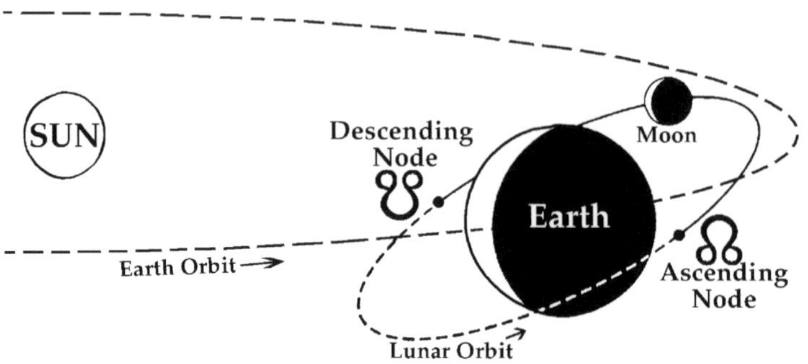

Astronomically, Rāhu and Ketu are created by the Sun, Moon, and Earth's alignment. There is a space of five degrees angular separation between the Earth's ecliptic plane around the Sun and the Moon's ecliptic plane around the Earth. The points where these two planes intersect are called the nodes of the Moon which is where eclipses can occur. These nodal points regress through the zodiac based on the wobble of the Moon.

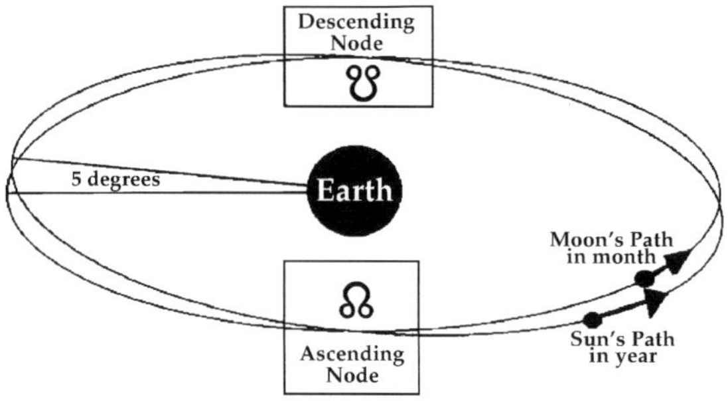

"True nodes" have a retrograde and direct motion because of a slight wobble, but Jyotiṣa *primarily* uses the "Mean nodes" which are always retrograde. The Mean nodes are calculated at an average motion without factoring in the wobble. In this way, the Sun and Moon are always direct and Rāhu and Ketu are always retrograde. It is the five planets related to the five elements that can go between retrograde and direct.

Rāhu

Parāśara describes Rāhu as "blue bodied, making smoke or obscuration (dhūmrākāra), living in the forests (tribal), invoking fear, intelligent (dhīman), and having a vāta constitution."

Rāhu is similar to Saturn in its airy nature of drying things. Saturn represents sorrow while Rāhu represents shock. Saturn is the natural dark side of life, while Rāhu is the demented dark side. He does not think clearly, the proper mind is obscured and deluded. Rāhu relates to addiction and foreign substances and rules all types of mind altering drugs.

Rāhu is impure and dirty and poisons whatever he associates with. Rāhu with Venus will create a dirty sense of sexuality, Rāhu with Mercury will make one use the mind in a deceitful way, Rāhu with Jupiter gives a disrespect to life. Rāhu is a disturbance and causes trauma.

On the beneficial side Rāhu gives the ability to work with chemicals, metals and heavy machinery. It will also give an attraction to things that are foreign, and may even give foreign travel. He is beneficial for business and politics where lying, cheating and stealing in the most deceptive way are things that get people ahead and make lots of money.

Medical Significations: Hands, nervous system, *mouth, lips, ears*, extrasensory functions.

Diseases: Vāta disorders, chronic illness, mental illness, phobias, hysteria, insanity, possession, addiction, obsessive/compulsive and bipolar disorders, poisoning, toxemia, parasites, cancer, psychic disturbances, leprosy, bad dreams, insomnia.

Ketu

Parāśara says that the serpents created from Svarbhānu are similar in appearance. Ketu is more like a nāga (higher vibration snake being) while Rāhu is sarpa (lower snake character). Ketu is like Mars in many ways, with heat and energy. Mars is the earth, and it was from the mud of the earth that the goddess Parvati created Gaṇeśa, the elephant headed deity related to Ketu. The earth of Mars was manipulated into form and became Ketu. In the same way, land and property is Mars but houses are ruled by Ketu, as a baked brick is the same as the earth but alive in form.

Gaṇeśa is the guardian at the doorway of the Mother. He resides in the root chakra and controls who has access to the kuṇḍalīni energy. Ketu rules doors and the locks on the doors. He gives the key or denies the key, he keeps obstacles in your way, or removes them. Ketu is beneficial for spiritual endeavors but not for material endeavors. Rāhu shows the path of *bhoga* (material enjoyment), while Ketu shows the path of spirituality and yoga.

Ketu and Rāhu both relate to disembodied entities and will show spirits and ghosts. Particularly, Ketu when with Saturn will show issues with ghosts. As they are disembodied, ethereal entities, there are ethereal remedies for these problems in Vedic astrology.

Rāhu destroys the Sun, the Moon and the sign it is placed in. Ketu destroys the planets (five elements) and the nakṣatra that it is placed in.

Medical Significations: Legs, *hair,* extrasensory functions

Diseases: Pitta disorders, mental confusion, schizophrenia, accidents, epidemics, eruptive fevers, viral and infectious diseases, catastrophes, parasites, viruses, TB, diagnostic confusion, wrong surgery, stuttering speech, psychic disturbance, possession by spirits.

Upagrahas

Important secondary planets in the traditional system are **Gulika** *(Gk)* and **Mandi** *(Md).* They are mathematical points based on the time of Saturn rising in the day. Gulika shows the poison one takes on to themselves while Mandi will show the poison (negativity) one gives to others. These are important planets relative to diseases like cancer.

Natural Planetary Relationships

The natural relationship between the seven main planets is listed by Parāśara in the graha chapter. Rāhu is said to act like Saturn and Ketu like Mars, so the friendships will be equivilant. These relationships are important to see how well planets work together when they interact. It will also show how the planet acts when it goes to another planet's house.

Graha *(Planet is)*	Mitra *(friendly to)*	Sama *(neutral to)*	Śatru *(enemy to)*
Sun	Moon, Mars, Jupiter	Mercury	Venus, Saturn
Moon	Sun, Mercury	Mars, Jupiter, Venus, Saturn	None
Mars	Sun, Moon, Jupiter	Venus, Saturn	Mercury
Merc	Sun, Venus	Mars, Jupiter, Saturn	Moon
Jupiter	Sun, Moon, Mars	Saturn	Mercury, Venus
Venus	Mercury, Saturn	Mars, Jupiter	Sun, Moon
Saturn	Mercury, Venus	Jupiter	Sun, Moon, Mars

Exaltation and Debilitation

Planets are strong or weak based on what sign and house they are placed in. Specific signs exalt *(uccha)* a planet and allow it to give its full results. Other signs debilitate *(nīca)* a planet and give the planet a hard time accomplishing its results. The Mūlatrikoṇa sign allows the planet to perform its duties (dharma) to its fullest potential. When a planet is in its own sign, it gives good results as it feels at home. Other signs will be positive or negative to the planet based on the planet ruling that sign (friend, neutral, enemy).

Graha *(Planet)*	**Uccha** *(exaltation)*	**Nīca** *(fallen)*	**Mūlatrikona** *(office)*	**Svakṣetra** *(own sign)*
Sun	Aries (10)	Libra (10)	Leo (0-20)	Leo (20-30)
Moon	Taurus (0-3)	Scorpio (3)	Taurus (3-30)	Cancer
Mars	Capricorn (28)	Cancer (28)	Aries (0-12)	Aries (12-30) & Scorpio
Merc	Virgo (0-15)	Pisces (15)	Virgo (15-20)	Virgo (20-30) & Gemini
Jupiter	Cancer (5)	Capricorn (5)	Sag (0-10)	Sag (10-30) & Pisces
Venus	Pisces (27)	Virgo (27)	Libra (0-15)	Libra (15-30) & Taurus
Saturn	Libra (20)	Aries (20)	Aquarius (0-20)	Aquarius(20-30) & Capricorn
Rāhu	Taurus/Gemini	Scorpio/Sag	Virgo[27]	Aquarius
Ketu	Scorpio/Sag	Taurus/Gem	Pisces	Scorpio

Rāhu and Ketu have two signs of exaltation on debilitation. Taurus and Scorpio are the āyus exaltations, which mean they are beneficial in health related matters. Gemini and Sagittarius are the bhoga exaltations and are beneficial in external matters.

Bṛhat Parāśara Horā Śāstra gives a summary of strengths with percentages. When a planet is exalted it is giving 100 percent of its effect. When debilitated it is giving close to zero percent of its results. The table below shows the ratios relative to planets' position in the signs.

Parāśara Strength Ratio *Graha Guṇasvarūpa Adhyāya, v.59-60*	
Exalted	100%
Mūlatrikoṇa	75%
Own sign	50%
Sign of a friend	25%
Sign of a neutral	12.5%
Debilitation or enemy	0%

[27] Bṛhat Parāśara Horā Śāstra, Daśāphalādhyaya, v.35. There are many opinions on the dignity of Rāhu and Ketu; some use Leo as the āyus exaltation of Ketu, some use Gemini and Sagittarius as the Mūla trikona signs, there are also other opinions.

Retrogression (Vakra)

The geometry of the different elliptical orbits of the planets and the Earth around the Sun can sometimes make a planet appear to be moving backwards in the zodiac. This motion is only in relation to our view from the earth. This apparent backwards motion shows that even what seems to be moving backwards is still evolving from a universal perspective.

Retrograde planets become three times stronger to give their effects. When a planet is direct it is acting like the Sun and the Moon. When a planet goes retrograde it is acting like Rāhu and Ketu. It shows past desires that need to be fulfilled relative to the natural indications of that planet. Jupiter retrograde will give strong desires for children, wealth, or learning. Venus retrograde will give a strong desire for love and relationship, etc.

When a debilitated (nīca) planet becomes retrograde it acts exalted (uccha). This is called nīca bhanga, the reversal of debilitation. When an uccha planet is retrograde it acts debilitated- uccha banga.

Combust (Aṣṭaṅgata)

Planets too close to the Sun get their natural significations burnt. This hurts the external significations but is sometimes beneficial to internal or spiritual significations. Generally seen as 8° to 12° from the Sun, but some use more specific degrees. When a planet leaves combustion it is called the*Udaya* or the *heliacal rising*.

Planet Maturity:

The grahas mature at different times in life. There are different maturity times, the graph shows the primary time period. When the person turns sixteen their sense of dharma and spirituality develops. When they turn 21 their sense of identity will mature into who they believe they are. At age 24 the mind matures and the emotional life is fully developed. The understanding of love and relationship matures at age 25. The right use of passion develops at age 28. Business skills reach maturity around age 32. And the understanding of how time moves in life matures at age 35. These maturities show that there is a natural progression to understanding and maturing in life. An elder is wiser in a way that they have experienced more of life and have reached maturity of these planets.

Planet	Age
Jupiter	16
Sun	21
Moon	24
Venus	25
Mars	28
Mercury	32
Saturn	35
Rāhu	42
Ketu	48

Each of these planets is placed in everyone's chart differently. Venus may show the maturity of sexuality, but for one person that may mean they decide to settle and get married while for another it may mean they decide to become gay or not marry. The particular situation indicated by the planet will show what situation reaches fruition. The placement will also indicate some material phalana (fruition) in life, as Mars in the house of investment may show the investment in land at 28, while Sun in the house of vehicles may show a new car at the age of 21.

Natural Time Periods of Life

The natural life span is ruled by a particular planet, showing the focus of human development during those years. The first year of life is ruled by the Moon which shows the development is focused on being nurtured and adjusting sensory awareness. The next period of Mars indicates the development of independent living. Mercury period shows the individual will begin their education to learn how to live in the world. Venus indicates sexual maturity and the development of affection. Jupiter shows the step up for higher purposes in one's life. The Sun shows the pinnacle of reaching the top of ones material life and the beginning of the spiritual journey of the ātmā (soul). Saturn shows that the development has turned to the aging process. These periods are based on natural human development. Each phase is broken down again into smaller phases (Antardaśā) which show more particular development within that particular phase of life.

Planet	Age
Moon	0-1
Mars	1-6
Mercury	6-12
Venus	12-32
Jupiter	32-50
Sun	50-75
Saturn	75+

Planetary Periods of Time

Each planet represents a special amount of time. These are not the transit times. They are used for praśna[27] to indicate when an event will happen. When the Moon indicates the start of an event it will happen very soon. When Mars indicates when a person will get a new job it will be a matter of weeks. When Jupiter indicates when you will get married it will be a matter of months. When Sun determines the time before reincarnation it will be a matter of ayanas before the person will be reborn. In this way, the period indicated by the planets is used to time events.

Planet	BPHS v.33	Time period
Sun	Āyana	Six months
Moon	Muhūrta	48 minutes
Mars	Vāra	Day of 24 hours
Mercury	Ṛtu	Season: two months
Jupiter	Māsa	Month
Venus	Pakṣa	15 days (fortnight)
Saturn	Samā	Year

The Sun Rules an Ayana which is six months. This relates to the Sun's movement from one solstice to the next. The Moon rules a Muhūrta, which indicates that the results will be quick, as the Moon is the quickest moving planet.

Mars rules a day as it is associated with the fire element, and the energy that only lasts a day before needing rejuvenation. Mercury rules the seasons as it relates to the variations of the year and its effect on the plant world.

Jupiter rules the month (ie. full Moon to full Moon) as it relates to the fruition of the Full Moon completing a period of time. Venus rules a fortnight as it is half of the

[27] See Chapter 2: Vedic Foundations, page 41

lunar cycle containing fifteen tithis (tithis are ruled by Venus). Venus has both a dark and light half which is differentiated, while Jupiter does not separate things into good or bad but sees the utility and proper place of all things. Jupiter is the deva-guru and Venus is the asura-guru (teacher of those without the light). When the ocean of milk was being churned, a great snake was used. The asuras had the choice of which end of the snake to use and they chose the head thinking it was the best. But it was a thousand headed snake with fangs spitting poison. So the devas took the tail which was a singularity of vision and they had oneness, while the asuras took the head with many views that were filled with all sorts of poisons and differentiations.

Saturn represents a year, the longest period, which shows he is the slow motion of things coming to fruition. Saturn represents the patient time of things coming to maturity.

Gochāra: The movement of the planets (transits)

The planets are constantly moving and a good astrologer has a general understanding of how fast each planet is moving. This chart is the 'average' longitudinal motion. One should be formiliar with these motions for later usage.

Graha	Daily *(Bhukti)*	Through a Sign *(Bhabhoga)*	Degrees Annually	Complete 360° *(Bhagaṇa)*
Moon	13° 20′	2.5 days	-------	1 month
Mercury	1° 40′	About one month	About 360°	88 days
Venus	1° 36′	About one month	About 360°	224.7 days
Sun	1°	One month	360°	1 year (365.25 days)
Mars	0° 31′	Two months	191°	687 days (1.9 years)
Jupiter	0° 5′	One year	30°	361.04 days (11.9 years)
Rāhu	0° 3′	1.5 years	20°	18.6 yrs (6793.4 days)
Saturn	0° 2′	2.5 years	12°	29.5 years

Kāraka: Significators

Kāraka means making, doing, acting, who or what produces or creates, and instrumental in bringing about an action. The kāraka is the instrument to bring about a certain effect. For example, if you are sick what planet will indicate this, if your mother is sick what planet will show this result. The importance of kāraka is to determine the correct planet to evaluate for specific results. In Parāśara's chapter on kāraka (*Kāraka-Adhyāya*), he mentions different types of kārakas. We will divide them into three main groups, Brahma, Śiva and Viṣṇu.

Deity	Guṇa	Kāraka	#	Use
Brahma	Rajas	Naisargika- Natural	9	Natural instrument of action
Viṣṇu	Sattva	Cara- changing	8	Inner soul nature
Śiva	Tamas	Sthira- static	7	Health and longevity

Naisargika Kārakas

Brahma is the creative energy of the universe known as Rajas. It is through this energy that all things are created. Things that are percieved with the eye and things that are beyond perception were created by rajas. The nine planets as discussed earlier each have significations related to them. These are the natural (*naisargika*) indications. They are the way the universe naturally works through an object. The Sun works through black pepper, the Moon works through salt. This is the natural way the creative energy made the world.

Carakārakas

Viṣṇu is the sustaining energy of the universe known as sattva. Living beings are sustained through the individual soul (*jīvātmā*) within them. Non-living things have a *jaḍātmā* which sustains them. *Jīva* means living, and *jaḍa* means inanimate. When a chair is broken its purpose is no longer for sitting, it has become just bits of wood, its jaḍātmā has left. When a person dies, they become rotting flesh and bones, it is their jīva that has left. Both after breaking/dying will then return to the elements from which they came. The force that keeps them alive and maintains their purposeful existence is Viṣṇu (sustaining energy). The inner soul of people and things will change according to various situations. To understand *this level of being* we use the carākārakas.

The highest degree planet represents the Ātmakāraka (soul-significator). It is the planet that represents your soul. To calculate this Ketu is not used, as it is the planet showing mokṣa (liberation) and souls that have attained Ketu Ātmakāraka are not here on earth anymore. Rāhu always moves backwards through the signs and therefore his degree is calculated backwards. Take the degree of Rāhu and substract it from 30 degrees, this will give you the distance Rāhu has moved in a sign. Then see which planet has the highest degree to see the soul of the individual.

Parāśara says[28] that the Ātmakāraka (AK) is the principle kāraka, a king among all others. As a king has governance over a country, and the country affairs will be controlled by the king, in the same way the AK controls one's life. If the king of a country is good then all his ministers do good acts. If the king of a country is evil, his cabinet will be filled with scandels and negative acts. The planet which becomes AK will show the internal nature of the person, it is the seed of the ahaṁkāra (the sense of self).

The Sun is the natural (*naisargika*) kāraka representing the soul, it is the same for every person. When referring to the concept of the soul in general we utilize the Sun as the natural kāraka. The Ātmakāraka planet shows the personalized nature of the individual's soul. It shows the soul color or soul flavour of that particular person. It is the planet that we have the most karma to work with in this life. When we speak about the nature of a person's soul we utilize the Ātmakāraka planet.

Planets as Ātmakāraka[29]:

Sun	When the Sun becomes AK it indicates the individual will hold a deep value for power, position, and respect. This indicates the person has to learn humility to overcome their karma associated with ego.
Moon	Indicates that the individual should be very caring and compassionate, and family and social life are important. The person needs to overcome small family attachment and realize the whole world is one's family.
Mars	Indicates that the individual may be competitive or aggressive. They need to learn to have playful competition and refrain from all forms of violence following the path of non-violence (*ahiṁsā*).
Mercury	Indicates the individual is very interested in communication (such as mail) and information (such as books). The person needs to control their speech, debate less, and be truthful at all times.
Jupiter	Indicates that the individual has an affinity for expansiveness and wisdom. The person needs to be open to others' opinions, and should always respect the Guru, husband and care for children.
Venus	Indicates that the individual is concerned about aesthetics, music and creativity. The person needs to control their sexual energy, and refrain from lust and illegitimate sex.
Saturn	Indicates that the person will see sorrow in their life and understand the suffering of others. They need to practice not giving others sorrow but instead share the sorrow of others.
Rāhu	Indicates that the individual maybe cheated often or not conscious of situations that they become entangled within. They need to practice good discernment and refraining from deception.

[28] Bṛhat Parāśara Horā Śāstra, Kāraka-Adhyāya, v. 6-12
[29] Information based on lesson: *Ātmakāraka I* by Sanjay Rath

The Ātmakāraka planet is the planet that we have the most karma to work with in this life. Therefore the natural significations of that planet play an important role in our life. If there are problems with this planet in the chart then they will be issues that affect one at a soul level. If the Ātmakāraka planet is afflicted in the horoscope the individual will have soul-level suffering regarding that planet's natural significations. There are also other combinations with the Ātmakāraka planet that can make a person powerful and famous.

The placement of the AK relative to the other carakārakas will show the interaction with other souls in the person's life. The Ātmakāraka planet will show the flavor of the individual's soul. The second highest degree planet will show the nature of those who advise an individual. As the AK is king, the Amātya-kāraka (Amk) is the minister or that which guides your accomplishments in life. All the planets except Ketu represent a soul level relation or soul level quality which one interacts with in life. The lowest degree planet will show the nature of the spouse's soul. It also represents wealth (*Śrī*) and so will show the soul level relationship with money.

Degree	Carakāraka[30]	
Highest	Ātmakāraka	Individual soul, the inner nature, like the Sun, karma for the soul to work with and overcome,
Second	Amātya-kāraka	Minister, advisor, guide, leadership, like the Moon, karma yoga, what to do for the world
Third	Bhrātṛ-kāraka	Siblings, who stands by in time of need, knowledge, sharing of knowledge, Guru
Fourth	Mātṛ-kāraka	Mother, guides to understanding, heart, healing, devotion (*bhakti*)
Fifth	Pitṛ-kāraka	Father (biological implanting of the soul), sense of duty/dharma, ability to give protection to others
Sixth	Putra-kāraka	Children, that which carries your future, Power and that which you have power over
Seventh	Jñāti-kāraka	Relatives, those intimately aquainted, kinship, group, gang, those who share a common objective
Lowest	Dara-kāraka	Spouse, witness to your life, wealth

Parāśara teaches[31] that there are two types of carakāraka schemes, one which uses 8 planets and one that uses 7 planets. The Achyutānanda tradition teaches that the 8 planet scheme is for living beings and the 7 is for non-living beings. The cause of creation is desire, which is represented by Rāhu. If we are free of desire and attachment we would not have incarnated. It is our own desires that again stimulate us to procreate and bring another living being into this plane of existence. So from a soul level we are incarnated from our own desire

[30] Bṛhat Parāśara Horā Śāstra, Kāraka-Adhyāya, v. 13-16

[31] Bṛhat Parāśara Horā Śāstra, Kāraka-Adhyāya, v. 1-2

and on a physical level we are incarnated because of our parents desire. In this way, for living beings Rāhu shows the desire and the Putra kāraka shows our offspring. For non-living things like a car, there was no desire of its own to be born, nor does it have desire to reproduce itself, therefore there is no need of Rāhu or the Putra kāraka. In this way, for the charts of living beings we use 8 carakārakas, and for the charts of non-living things we use the 7 carakārakas without Rāhu.

Parāśara teaches carakāraka replacement[32], which is when two planets obtain the same degree (irrelavant of sign) and the one planet replaces another's role in the carakāraka placement. For example if the Ātmakāraka is Venus (23-29) and the Amātya-kāraka is Sun (23-22), then there will be a replacement at the planet's natural age. The lower degree planet will become the AK, in this case the Sun, and the soul will then reflect more solar qualities. This will show major transformations at a soul level in one's life.

Sthira Kārakas

Śiva is the destructive/transforming energy of the universe known as tamas. It is because of tamas that the five elements took their physical form and gave us a physical body. And it is because we were born into a physical body that we will have to grow old and die one day. The Sthira-kārakas are used when looking at health and longevity in the chart. Rāhu and Ketu are not incuded in here because they do not have physical bodies and therefore will not show physical longevity.

Stronger of Sun and Venus	Father
Stronger of Moon and Mars	Mother
Mars	Younger sister/brother, brother-in-law
Mercury	Maternal relatives, uncles, aunts, cousins
Jupiter	Paternal grandparents, *husband*
Venus	*Wife*, maternal grandparents, father/mother-in-law
Saturn	Children, *elder brother/sister*

These significations will not be used much by the beginner, but they are important to understand that phalita-jyotiṣa (predicting the future results) and Āyurjyotiṣa (predicting and curing health) have certain different foundations.

When looking at the nature of the Mother one will observe the situation of the Moon. When understanding the Mother's inner nature one will look at the Mātṛ-kāraka. When predicting the health of the Mother one would use the stronger of the Moon or Mars as the significator of her health and longevity.

[32] Bṛhat Parāśara Horā Śāstra, Kāraka-Adhyāya, v. 17

Chapter 4

Devata: *Deities*

Devatās

Sage Yajñavalkya is asked "who are the thirty-three thousand deities?" and he replies, "33,000 are their powers, but indeed there are thirty-three gods[33]. " The gods or deities, called devatās, ***are all manifestations of the root astrological forces*** seen as the 33 devas. Therefore it is important to understand how these root astrological forces manifest through various different planets, strengths, guṇas and other combinations. The various forms can enlarge our understanding of the planets as the planets can enlarge our understanding of the devatās. We can perceive the planets from many different angles, as each planet can be a form of Śiva, a form of Gaṇeśa, a form of the divine Mother, but the first forms we will study are the forms of Viṣṇu.

Myth has the power to input images into the unconscious mind which opens a thousand doorways to understanding. Whether you believe in the Hindu deities or not-the myths will awaken a deeper understanding both conscious and unconscious of the planetary energies.

Viṣṇu Avatāra of the Planets

The first forms of devatās that Parāśara describes are the Viṣṇu incarnations (avatāras). An avatāra is a deity who descends to take birth in a physical body to interact on earth. The following are short introductions to the Viṣṇu Avatāras in order to more fully develop the planets through them. The Viṣṇu forms of the planets show the highest sattvic qualities of each planet.

Planet Viṣṇu Incarnations[34]	
Sun	Rāma
Moon	Kṛṣṇa
Mars	Nṛsiṁha
Mercury	Buddha
Jupiter	Vāmana
Venus	Paraśurāma
Saturn	Kūrma
Rāhu	Sūkara (Varāha)
Ketu	Mīna (Matsya)

Parāśara teaches that Viṣṇu incarnates as the planets to uphold dharma. The planets are that which sustain dharma through the law of karma. If you do bad action you have a bad placement *(doṣa)* and you suffer in life. The planets make sure we get our bad and our good karma. This is how the planets are upholding dharma and why the planets are incarnations of Viṣṇu; they are sustaining the world through the law of karma. Parāśara gives us a list of all the avatāras relative to the planets, and each of these ten avatārs relate to the nine planets and the ascendant; but Parāśara gives us the nine planets and the nine avataras relative to that, he doesn't give us all ten. The next section is a transcription of a lecture given on the Avatāras.

[33] XI Kaṇḍa, 6 Adhyāya, Third Brāhmaṇa, v. 4-5
[34] Bṛhat Parāśara Horā Śāstra, Avatārakathanādhyāya, v.5-7

Varāha: The Boar

Rāhu shows desire and it was the *seed of desire* that started the whole universe, as well as our individual incarnations on this planet. The avatāra of Rāhu is the boar incarnation. The story of the Varāha avatāra begins with the Earth being under water. Viṣṇu incarnates as a boar to go down into the water and lift the Earth out. After this the Earth was ready for living beings to populate. In many cultures there is a similar creation myth of the earth coming through the waters. The Sumerians killed *Tiamat* and spread her body all over the waters and created the earth. It is also written in the Bible, "In the beginning God created the heaven and the earth. And the earth was without form, and void; and darkness was upon the face of the deep. And the Spirit of God moved upon the face of the waters. And God said, Let there be light: and there was light."[35] There was the face of the deep water, not nothing. This concept exists in many traditions. The manifestation of the earth from the cosmic waters; the waters give birth to the earth. The Bible says that we're created in God's image. The Vedic view is that we are the microcosm reflecting the universe which is the macrocosm. In the same way the universe is created, so are we created. Just as the earth came from the waters; so also, we live inside the womb in the amniotic fluid and when the water breaks we are born.

Varāha avatāra relates to the cause of our birth as the Viṣṇu incarnation of Rāhu representing that sustaining desire. It is desire that caused us to come into this body and have these karmas that created the need to be *re-born*. Rāhu pulls us into a body through his desires, (Ketu represents the period of time when we are leaving the body). Viṣṇu incarnated as a boar bringing us the Earth, showing the desire for the *material* creation. Rāhu represents desire, and more specifically the desire for material creation; material desire. If our desire is for God we don't reincarnate on the earth plane. It is our desire for the material world that brings us to the physical plane.

Rāhu represents the ahaṁkāra, the I-sense or ego, and when Rahu is negative in a chart then the sense of 'I' is incorrect. The mind thinks about what the 'I' can get out of each situation. Varāha takes the sense of 'I' to a larger scale; you are sharing this planet and made up of a larger network of interacting people. The Ahirbudhnya Saṁhita says that Varāha avatāra rescues those who have drowned (in the material world) and detroys ignorance in the heart. Worship of the Varāha avatāra removes unhealthy selfish motivations and gives proper focus.

Remedies:

The practical application of the Varāha avatāra is used as a remedy for Rāhu. Viṣṇu avatāras show the exalted aspect of planets, how the planets function when they are operating at the highest level of sattva. Varāha saved the Earth, so Rāhu in his highest state is material desire that is beneficial to the world. Examples of this are people with the

[35] Genesis 1:1-1:3

desire to create a school or a hospital; to create the places or situations where others can go and enjoy the kāma (enjoyment) they need to experience in life, or the extreme is a person who chains themselves to a bulldozer to save a forest from being cut down. So the highest form of Rāhu is saving the material world and making the world a more beneficial place for all. This takes a non-selfish desire for the world, at the highest level of desire, wanting to save the world and make it a better place.

When we worship Rāhu in the Viṣṇu form as Varāha avatāra, we invoke this energy.

When we are balancing bad karma we have to create good karma relative to the negative karma we've created. For remedies to work, the positive karma we create in the future by donating to humanitarian efforts balances out the negative things we've done in the past. There's a concept called *Deśakālapātra*; the country *(deśa)* the time *(kāla)*, and the person *(pātra)*. As astrologers we take the person, the time period and the place all into account at the same time to make our analysis. At this time on earth, ancient remedies such as giving a Brahmin a cow or offering a snake gold eggs are not very practical, they are minute compared to what is happening in the world today. We need to give donations to places that are working to save the planet, helping life on earth because we're becoming a global community. In the same way, our karma, when we do something negative, is affecting the global community. When we're doing a remedy based on the Varāha avatāra, we should do something to try and improve the global community.

Making donations to places like Greenpeace, or the Sierra Club and other organizations working to protect nature and the earth would be a practical way to propitiate Rāhu as this energy.

Matsya: Fish Incarnation

Ketu takes the form of *Mīna*, which means fish, or better known as the Matsya avatāra. The story of Matsya is similar to the story of the Judeo-Christian flood myth. All these various myths, archetypal in nature, are found throughout world cultures, in the bible, the Vedas, and African cultures, etc. And so it is with the story of the flood.

The Ṛṣis (sages) had known that Viṣṇu had taken birth as a fish. The king had found this fish in his washing water. The small fish said that "fish devours fish" and while he was small it was dangerous for him. He asked the king to keep him till he was large and then to release him. The king did so and when he eventually released the fish he was told to make a boat for the coming flood[36].

When the flood eventually came the sages tied a boat to the fish and the king got into the boat with the Vedas and let the fish lead him during the time of the flood. There were no oars, and no where to go as everything was flooded. The symbolic meaning of the boat having no oars shows that when we can't control what's happening, we need to surrender to the divine (Viṣṇu- the all-pervasive). With the Vedas (spiritual knowledge) in hand, we can hold tight and trust that Viṣṇu will carry through these periods of unknowing change.

[36] Śatapatha Brāhmaṇa, Manu-Matsya Kathā, 1.8.1.1-11

Time periods of a negatively placed Ketu can sometimes be phases of confusion where the logical aspect of the mind becomes dysfunctional, or in the worst case people experience psychological breakdowns or 'lose their mind' for a period of time. In these times one needs to look for the higher guiding forces in life. A beneficially placed Ketu will often give times of great spiritual insight and alignment with aspects of life that are beyond the visible realm.

The deeper spiritual teaching is that when we leave the body, if we try to control where our soul is going, we may get lost. All we have to do is call on the divine (in the form most comfortable to one's religion). Trusting in divinity and keeping our minds steadfastly on God, we are guided through the afterlife. Carrying only Veda, the spiritual knowledge we have acquired in this life, we surrender to the divine. The actual material nature of what we have learned doesn't traverse through various lives with us. Only that Veda, the root knowledge of the soul, comes with us and is carried through to the other side. If we keep our mind on Viṣṇu (the all-pervasive divine), we will be guided through to a new birth or wherever it is we are supposed to go after we die, according to our karma. Matsya avatāra relates to spirituality, as Ketu is the spiritual indicator (mokṣa kāraka), and shows the nature of offering up our soul to the omnipotence of God. If your ahaṁkāra (I-sense) thinks its in control, you deny the Omnipotence. It does not work to say "okay God I offer myself to you an hour here but the rest is all in my hands." Ketu teaches that we have to fully offer ourselves, not just physically, but mentally and at the level of our soul. We have to offer our full selves to the divine *(ātma-nikśepa)* so the divine can fully guide us. The *Ahirbudhnya Saṁhitā* compares the path of surrender *(śaraṇāgati)* to a boat where the pilgrim climbs in and sits allowing the boatman to row. In this way, Matsya allows us to let go of the oars and be guided.

Remedies:

Matsya avatāra shows us the exaltation of Ketu, bringing out the highest, most sattva nature of Ketu. Ketu shows our spiritual perception as well as our general nature of perceiving; it is this internal perception, as Ketu doesn't have a head. When Ketu is weak or not well placed in the chart he will give fundamentalism and close-mindedness, the person isn't open to new understanding or new ways of perceiving. When Ketu is well placed the person has an open-minded, expansive view of things and is easily able to see and understand new ideas, perceiving the unity of all creation. So Matsya avatāra is needed when we need to take Ketu up to an open-minded/tolerant level of understanding.

When Ketu is the planet sustaining a marriage (2nd from UL), if Ketu isn't strong that marriage won't last because there will be a certain fundamentalist, close-minded nature present. If Ketu is strong, the marriage will be sustained and nourished through an understanding and expansive perception. When we are able take Ketu to the level of Matsya avatāra the person or marriage will have an accepting, open-minded quality and that nature will sustain the marriage or relationship.

We use the forms of Viṣṇu to *sustain* marriage. If Rāhu was sustaining a marriage then the person could be too materialistic and it would destroy the marriage. By raising Rāhu to that high level of Viṣṇu where it's working for the sustenance of the world and for dharma, this in turn sustains the relationship. In this way we are using the Viṣṇu forms to pull the planets up to their highest level of sattva. More than merely worshiping the graha forms, we invoke Viṣṇu as he incarnated as the planets for sustaining.

Traditional ways to propitiate Ketu were feeding fish, or keeping fish in an aquarium/ pond and feeding them. Examples of practical ways to propitiate Ketu would be by supporting efforts to protect the ocean and marine life, helping save wild stream salmon, supporting the Sierra Club's Marine Fish Conservation Act, clean water initiatives, and other organizations of this nature. Varāha has the focus of uplifting the material world and remedies directly relate to this. Matsya is about the spirit and the improvement of one's spiritual karma- practicing surrender is a key element when propitiating Ketu.

Paramparā and Parāśara

A student asks: Where does this information come from and how does it relate to the teachings of Parāśara?

Reply: Parāśara expects you to know this information. This is the tradition, the guru teaches this according to the Purāṇas. Parāśara indicates clearly that the Sun incarnates as Rāma, what do you do with that information? You can't do anything unless the teacher teaches you, and that is the tradition. Parāśara gives us tons of information and only with the proper knowledge can we apply it. Our tradition comes from Parāśara. Vyāsa, the son of Parāśara, traveled around India teaching and the knowledge came teacher to student, teacher to student until arriving to us right now, that's the tradition called paramparā. When you have a real guru of a Vedic paramparā, it's coming from this lineage.

That's why after studying with my guru I began to understand the Vedas, because everything he is saying is coming from this Vedic knowledge. That is what paramparā is about. The knowledge is passed down. It is alive, it is living. If you could just read Parāśara and know everything then everyone would be a perfect astrologer. Every single verse needs multiple levels of teachings to fully understand. Parāśara just says Rāhu is the boar incarnation. He doesn't tell you the story of Varāha, he expects you to go read your Vedic history. He is giving you the main points. No one can argue that the Rāhu incarnated as Kṛṣṇa or the Rāhu incarnated as Sai Baba. Rāhu incarnated as Varāha, the Moon incarnated as Kṛṣṇa. This is what Parāśara is doing, he's making that reality clear. And then the deeper part we go into; the teacher and the tradition.

Kūrma: Turtle Incarnation

Saturn incarnated as *Kūrma,* which means turtle, during the myth of the churning of the ocean of milk. All of these stories of the Viṣṇu avatāras should be studied in depth. The Purāṇas are the storybooks from which all of these myths are found. During certain periods when working with a planet, one can study the avatāra stories further as a way to uplift and get the most from that time period.

The churning of the ocean of milk begins with 54 gods *(devas)* and 54 demons *(asuras),* the 54 good qualities and 54 bad qualities of man. The devas decide to churn the ocean of milk. On a macro-cosmic level the ocean of milk is the Milky Way in the sky, and the 54 devas and asuras are the 108 divisions of the sky seen in the *navāṁśa.*

The Sun rules half a year, called an āyana[36], where Saturn rules one whole year called a Samā. It takes the Sun one year, or 108 navāṁśas, to go all the way around the 360° zodiac. It takes the Sun 54 navāṁśas to go through an āyana (solstice to solstice). Half of this time is spent in the southern course in the time of the asuras and half in the northern course in the time of the devas. This turning of time is connected to Saturn.

Astronomically, this becomes the churning of the cosmic ocean, the churning of the Milky Way. On an internal level, this is represented by our good and bad qualities and our consciousness. The Milky Way is the consciousness. As explained earlier, in order to churn the ocean of milk the devas and asuras put a mountain in the middle to be like a churning rod and used a snake to churn the milk of the Milky Way with the goal of extracting out the nectar of immortality *(amṛta).*

On the macro-cosmic level, the mountain is the pole star with the zodiac turning through the sky, and the Sun going back and forth to the devas and asuras churning our lives. On a micro-cosmic level the snake represents the kuṇḍalīni and the mountain represents the *suṣumna,* the central axis that runs through the body representing balance. The devas represent the right and left channels, hot and cold. When we churn the consciousness with the central mountain *(suṣumna)* we seek that which is beyond death *(amṛta).*

---

[36] See planetary periods of time in the Graha Chapter, page 73

When the mountain was first put into the ocean, it would not turn. Therefore Viṣṇu took the form of Kūrma (a turtle) underneath the mountain so it would be able to churn on top of something. That churning is the churning of our karma. On a macro level this will happen as the Sun moves through the sky and time will naturally insure that all karma gets fulfilled. On the internal level our spiritual practice can churn our karma more quickly. Saturn represents all the negative accumulated karma that needs to be experienced or burned through. It is the suffering of Saturn that turns people to spirituality or to begin work burning their suffering and negative karmas that attach us to this world. When we begin spiritual practice and we start working with the kuṇḍalīni energy we start churning our consciousness and working through our negative karma. Saturn in this way is the foundation and support of spiritual practice.

Saturn sets the stage so we can begin the churning. Saturn is connected to the *apāna vāyu*, the grounding energy. He grounds the root chakra so energy can begin to turn and from there spiritual growth starts to happen. The Kūrma avatāra represents the proper burning up of our bad karma. We either suffer our bad karma or we start doing tapasya and remedies and practising spirituality, burning up this karma and purifying our consciousness. This is the proper way to face our bad karma, through spirituality and spiritual practice, or we just suffer through life. This is the beginning of the spiritual path. Spiritual progress comes when we start facing all the negative karma we have done which is stored as negativities in our consciousness and revealed as the negative qualities in our actions.

Remedies:

Kūrma represents the activation and purification of our karmas, taking Saturn to the highest level.The Kūrma avatāra is about dealing with our past negative karma in the most productive way, a very important element of spiritual progress. Saturn as the Kūrma avatāra allows us to start dealing with the negativity in our life in a way that we can properly digest and churn it making it into something better.

Saturn can make a person harsh from bad experiences in life (past and present). Bad experiences are best when they humble us and make us better people- not when they make one hard-hearted and harsh. Kūrma brings the moving force to break up blocked and stagnant energy.

In the case that Saturn is sustaining a relationship, there may be a lot of obstacles (from past karma) that come up which can break harmony between partners. A relationship centered on dealing with the partner's problems is unsustainable. Ways to sustain a Saturnian relationship involve growing and achieving, learning from past lessons, taking on new spiritual learning together and progressing in this way, doing sādhana, and burning up inner negativities. This builds a solid foundation that a relationship can be based on. The arising problems are the basis for this spiritual growth. This is the difference between Saturn being weak and Saturn taken to the level of Viṣṇu.

Narasiṁha: Man-Lion

The avatāra of Mars is called Narasiṁha, *nara* means man and *siṁha* means lion. It is the last animal and is half-lion and half-man. If you notice, all the malefics are animal avatāras: Ketu, Rāhu, Saturn and Mars. This is the last animal avatāra, having evolved to that of a lion.

The story of the Narasiṁha avatāra starts with a demon who had become emperor of the world. He had magical powers protecting him that he had aquired through tantric practice. He couldn't be killed by a human, he couldn't be killed by an animal. He couldn't be killed at day; he couldn't be killed at night. He couldn't be killed inside and he couldn't be killed outside. He couldn't be killed on the ground, and he couldn't be killed in the sky. He believed that he was worth worshiping not some unseen power. The demon was worse than atheist; he was anti-God.

When the demon got his wife pregnant the other devas (light beings) found their way to intercede. The Divine Ṛṣi, Nārada Muni, would visit and tell spiritual stories to the pregnant wife and thereby the baby would hear these stories and became very spiritual in the womb. This is an important lesson in raising children and shows the importance of the time while the baby is in the womb. Everything the mother hears or does influences and conditions the *mind* of the child, even the mother's mental state is very important as it directly conditions the mind while still in the womb. So Nārada told all kinds of stories of Viṣṇu and spiritual teachings so the child was born incredibly spiritual, a great devotee of God. The demon father was not pleased. His son, named Prahlāda, was spreading spiritual teachings about the love for god and converting people away from mass consumerism/ materialism into simple spiritual lives.

The demon father created all kinds of strategies to "accidentally" have his son die, like stampedes of elephants. Nothing would work as Viṣṇu would always protect Prahlāda because he was filled with such supreme devotion. Finally the demon father became frustrated with trying to covertly destroy the son. He faced Prahlāda directly and said, "What is this God trash you keep talking about," ready to put an end to it. And they got in to a whole argument about God, where is the omni-present, what is the All-knowing, and the demon father said, "There's no God. And if so, where is he?"

Prahlāda replied, "He's everywhere, *Sarvavyāpakeśvara*, everywhere in everything." Viṣṇu is all-pervasive, in everything, the space element (ākāśa tattva).

The demon couldn't be killed during day or during the night, yet the argument just happened to be at sunset; in the inbetween. In the argument, the angry demon mockingly says, "If God is everywhere, are you telling me God is in this stone pillar here?"

They were standing on the doorway to one of their palaces, not inside, not outside. Prahlāda said, "Yes" and then his angry father punched and shattered this stone pillar. And out of that shattered pillar, inside, was this Lion-headed form of Viṣṇu, ferocious and angry having just been hit. Narasiṁha picked the father up and put him on his lap, so he wasn't on the ground, he wasn't in the sky, it wasn't day time, it wasn't night time, he wasn't inside the house, he wasn't outside the house, he was in the doorway. Narasiṁha killed the father. Then Prahlāda became a very spiritual king.

Remedies:

Narasiṁha represents the protection of those devoted to the divine. When we surrender to divinity, let down our hands and don't fight, that's when God comes and protects us. Narasiṁha teaches us to acknowledge the need to be protected. The path of *goptṛ* is when we take god as our sole protector and we open ourselves to divine protection. With this comes *viśvāsa* - confidence and trust in a supreme benefactor to make our endeavors successful.

The exalted aspect of Mars is protecting those who are devoted. At a deeper level the demon was killed because he did not allow himself to see god everywhere, and used that ignorance *(avidyā)* to promote his own personal gains. The lower nature of Mars was destroyed by being the pure child and having devotion. Mars is generally shown as a young child, as in his Śiva form (Kartikeya). It's very important to approach Mars as a young child because if we try to be too controlling, Mars energy can be very dangerous and destructive. When we approach Mars in an innocent, unselfish way, the childlike devotion removes all obstacles and the ego is destroyed.

Mars in the lower nature will give us a lot of fighting, quarreling and control type issues (related to the fire element). When we invoke the Viṣṇu form of Narasiṁha we are removing the negative controlling ego and awakening the devotional child that exists within. This removes the fighting energy, as the highest level of Mars is that of the internal warrior, fighting the spiritual battle. Narasiṁha removes the over aggressive attitude that is projected to make up for one's own weakness. By worshipping Narasiṁha we invoke the exalted energy of Mars that gives inner strength through a firm faith in divine protection and guidance.

Vāmana: Brahmin Boy with an Umbrella

The Jupiter incarnation of Viṣṇu is as a small Brahmin boy. He carried an umbrella to protect himself from the Sun. The umbrella is symbolic of a position of power, as well as gentle protection and comfort from the harshness of life.

After Narasiṁha killed the demon, his son, Prahlāda, became king. His son was Virochana, and his son was Bali. When Bali became king, he conquered the earth and began doing all kinds of magic rituals to get the power to overtake the three worlds. Having conquered the earth and sky the demon, Bali, had one more ritual to do in order to conquer heaven. As he was about to begin his final ritual, all the gods pleaded for Viṣṇu to intervene in the situation. Vāmana shows the aspect of Jupiter that comes in to redirect us on the right path when negativity has taken over our lives.

The demon king, Bali, had one final pūjā to perform. All Brahmins, priests, and spiritual people were able to come to him and ask for what they needed as part of the ritual. Viṣṇu incarnated as Vāmana, a little Brahmin boy, and went before King Bali.

The Demon saw Vāmana and said, "I see you are so holy, ask anything of me, what can I give you?" And Vāmana said, "I have no need of wealth. I just want the land that I can take in three steps. Give me three steps worth of land." Symbolically, this represents the three steps needed to be buried. Back then, traditionally, Indians were cremated. And they would collect the bones and put them in a pot and bury them. The three steps were just that piece of ground needed to bury one's urn.

So Vāmana asked for three steps. And the King said, "Come on, I can give you anything, even an entire kingdom, you can have anything you want, because I will give it to you." And Vāmana said, "just three steps, promise me three steps."

The Guru of the demon King said, "No, no, don't give him this, he is not a normal Brahmin." And the King said, "what this little guy, come on, I own everything. I'll give him whatever he wants." The king did the ritual to guarantee Vāmana three steps.

After the ritual, the little Brahmin boy grew bigger and bigger. And with his first step, he stepped across the whole earth. He grew even bigger and with the second step he crossed the whole of heaven. And with nowhere else to step, Bali bowed down and said, "Step on my head." He surrendered, he offered himself, and so Vāmana put the third step on Bali's head, destroying the demonic quality in the king and restoring dharma to the world. This is the power of Jupiter, to bring things back into their natural state. Vāmana in his huge form is known as *Trivikrama*, the one who conquers with three steps. With three steps Vāmana conquered everything.

The Martian Viṣṇu incarnation, Narasiṁha, was fierce and violent. He surprised the demon King and tore apart the demon with the claws of his hands. The Jupitarian Viṣṇu incarnation was peaceful and gentle and respectfully approached the demon king. Through modesty he conquered and restored order to the world. Both incarnations found the loop holes to overcome the demons (representing obstacles), and in the same way, their worship helps one find steps or a way to overcome the planet's respective obstacles.

Remedies:

As the most benefic planet, Jupiter gives abundance but sometimes even this is not enough. When Jupiter is retrograde or weak, there is discontentment. When Jupiter is raised to exaltation, there is inner contentment. When Jupiter is sustaining a relationship, it will need abundance and dharma. And that highest level of Jupiter is showing that the whole of the three worlds, everything, belongs to God, it's all God.

There is not as much negativity with Vāmana avatāra as with the other incarnations. Even Bali wasn't that bad of a demon, relative to demons; he was a pretty nice guy. Some say he was even a better organizer than the gods themselves. But he developed a monopoly on power and disturbed the natural order. Through Vāmana we bring the highest exalted state of Jupiter where everything realigns with its purpose and dharma is fulfilled. Great bounds and great achievements can be made at this natural state.

The full power of the inherent dharma, when awakened, will achieve everything. Jupiter achieves victory with peaceful methods, not war. Gandhi's peace movement was called Satyagraha (which means 'holding truth'), Jupiter is the kāraka for truth and significates non-violent action. Bali gave three steps to the modest brahmin and then seeing the might of Vāmana he surrendered. In this way, Jupiter achieves victory by upholding dharma.

Paraśurāma: Warrior turned to Meditator

Venus is the water element that removes excess fire, like a firefighter. The Venus Viṣṇu avatāra is a powerful warrior, highly skilled, who incarnated to remove the excess bloodthirsty politicians from the earth. The Viṣṇu avatāra Paraśurāma incarnated during a time where political powers were becoming very corrupt and there were wars, fighting, and unneeded bloodshed. Paraśurāma was known for his battle-axe, where as Rāma carries a bow, and Kṛṣṇa carries a flute. These weapons speak to an aspect of each of their power, the battle-axe having two sides to it, showing a dual nature. The axe is said to cut out the roots of the trees of karma.

During the time of Paraśurāma, the Ṛṣis' ashrāms were being burned down and people were not safe. Due to the heavy bloodshed and brutality, Viṣṇu incarnated as Paraśurāma and vowed to kill the kṣātriya/political-warrior class that was creating all this destruction. At that time, even Parāśara's ashrām was destroyed by the Haihayas. Paraśurāma incarnated to restore dharma by killing all these kṣaitriyas. This is representation of Venus' nature towards vengeance. When the heart gets hurt in love, a vengeful energy can follow and become very dangerous and painful on an emotional level. An afflicted Venus can bring about this type of suffering.

Paraśurāma was known as a skilled and masterful warrior. Venus relates to grace, the dancer. When Paraśurāma was on the battlefield, his skill was unmatched. He was a great guru of many lineages of arts similar to kung fu and tai chi. He created all kinds of weapons with his creative ability; he was a great master of warfare. Later, at the Mahābhārata war, people would brag, "oh, I studied with someone who was a disciple of Paraśurāma."

Paraśurāma was a partial avatāra and after meeting Rāma he went to Ṛṣikeśa and did sādhana (spiritual practice). In this time he purified himself of all the killing he had committed so that incarnation could leave cleansed of these actions. In the same way that the Sun purifies Venus, the meeting of Rāma brought the purification of Paraśurāma. Vaiṣṇavas worship him as *Hṛṣīkeśa*. *Hṛṣ* means to rejoice, to excite, or to arouse and *hṛṣīka* are the sense organs which do this to the mind. Hṛṣīkeśa is the lord of the senses who has won the battle over excitement, etc. This symbolizes the Venus avatāra as the warrior who has finished the battle and has now gone to work on purifying the inner evil, not as the bloodthirsty vengeful Paraśurāma.

Remedies:

Venus can be jealous, vengeful, and have a competitive type of nature. When Venus is sustaining or upholding a relationship there will be issues related to jealousy. By invoking the Hṛṣīkeśa avatāra, we are appealing to this energy of Viṣṇu representing the completion of the battle, where there is no longer need for competition. We can let go of battling and go to work on culturing inner beauty. Looking at a chart, Venus has the most difficulty in the sixth house, the house of competition. A healthy Venus shows where we are working on creatively beautifying our inner selves rather than competing with others. Art is somet hing that we work on culturing from within. So the worship of the Hṛṣīkeśa avatāra helps raise Venus up to the point where Venus is working on the self-culture art and beauty not external competition.

Rāma: The Ideal King

The energy of the Sun incarnated as the famous King Rāma. To really understand Rāma requires reading and developing an understanding of the great classic called the Rāmāyaṇa. The two primary Viṣṇu avatāras are Rāma and Kṛṣṇa. By looking into these two most important deities we are deepening our understanding of the Sun and the Moon. Where the other planets are the five tattvas, or five elements, the primary forces of Sun and Moon are that of the soul and the mind respectively; and as such, they are above that of physical creation.

The Mahābhārata contains the stories central to Kṛṣṇa and the Rāmāyana relates to Rāma. These are epic stories that go into incredible detail and intricacies that help us understand the various energies and aspects of these avatāras. The Mahābhārata and Rāmāyaṇa fall under the classification of Purāṇas, and are often referred to as 'The Great Epics'.

In the Rāmāyaṇa, Prince Rāma is heir to the throne, but when his father dies he loses the throne to his younger brother and is sent into the jungle for fourteen years, during which time he was in his Saturn mūla daśā[37]. Rāma was supposed to be king but he fell from power and was exiled to the jungle, and grew dreadlocks. While spending time in the jungle, his wife was stolen from him. And thus begins the quest where Rāma gathers an army (of monkeys and bears) with Hanumān as a general to conquer the demon, Rāvaṇa who has stolen his beloved wife Sītā.

The Sun is the King, and is supposed to be in charge, to be on the throne making the country run. When the Sun has problems, there's a fall from power. Saturn is what causes a fall from power. Saturn and the Sun have an inimical relationship, Saturn brings down the King. Here, the Sun, instead of being King is sent to the woods during a Saturn period, showing the fall of the Sun due to the curse of Saturn. Rāma with the help of Hanumān, who was an incarnation of Rudra (Śiva), conquered Lanka, the city of Rāvaṇa, and rescued Sītā. On an internal level, the demon king had ten heads representing the five senses and their five actions. The arrow of Rāma which kills Rāvaṇa is right discrimination and through worship of Rāma one becomes tranquil[38]. Through inner tranquility one becomes king of themselves, just as Rāma is restored to his kingdom.

Considering the inimical relationship between the Sun and Saturn, whenever we have Saturn problems, we try to strengthen the Sun. The Sun is life force, vitality, the only true light in the sky. Saturn is death, aging decay, the opposite. Protection from Saturn is achieved by strengthening the Sun to its highest level of sattva, done through worshipping Rāma. Rāma allows us to be the king in our life that we're supposed to be. Whatever status we are supposed to achieve in our life, we will become with the power of Rāma. Gandhi threw out the British from India with only one mantra; the mantra of Rāma. He stood up and repetitively said, "Rāma Rāma Rāma." This is the only mantra he said, this name, and with that, he won India. That's the power of the exalted Sun and the Rāma avatāra. With this name, he allowed India to rise up and be in charge of itself.

[37] The mūla daśā is a timing technique that shows our curses and our blessings.
[38] Sātvata Saṁhitā 12, 151-152

Remedies:

When there are health problems and we are being afflicted by Saturn, when we're feeling down-trodden and need to rise up in life, we need the power of Rāma. The Sun represents government and problems with government officials and policies. The worship of Rāma will raise one to a proper position.

When the Sun is sustaining a relationship, there should be health power and vitality in the relationship. If the Sun is weak (or Saturn is causing it affliction), there may not being enough energy, power or vitality to uphold the relationship, or even chance of disease destroying the relationship. The worship of Rāma lifts this distress, bringing power, light, health, and proper living. It elevates the person and brings an empowering relationship instead of a downtrodden, controlling relationship like Saturn.

Kṛṣṇa: The Flute Player

In the Bhagavad Gītā, Kṛṣṇa repeats what his distant grand-uncle, Parāśara, said earlier about the avatars,

यदा यदा हि धर्मस्य ग्लानिर् भवति भारत।
अभ्युत्थानम् अधर्मस्य तदाऽत्मानं सृजाम्यहम्॥७॥

yadā yadā hi dharmasya glānir bhavati bhārata।
abhyutthānam adharmasya tadā'tmānaṁ sṛjāmyaham।।IV.7।।

Whenever a decrease in righteousness (dharma) comes into being,
And the wrong path (adharma) becomes prominent, I incarnate myself.

परित्राणाय साधूनां विनाशाय च दुष्कृताम्।
धर्मासंस्थापनार्थाय संभवामि युगे युगे॥८॥

paritrāṇāya sādhūnāṁ vināśāya ca duṣkṛtām।
dharmāsaṁsthāpanārthāya sambhavāmi yuge yuge।।IV.8।।

For the protection of the righteous, and destruction of the evil-doers,
In order to establish the correct path (dharma), I manifest from yuga to yuga

The teachings of the Mahābhārata and Bhagavad Gītā are what we use to understand Kṛṣṇa. Many associate Kṛṣṇa with the image of a blue cartoon god running around doing super miracles. Reading some of the traditional stories, we learn that Kṛṣṇa was a real person. Looking at the living saint Mātā Amṛtānandamayī as an example, we see a real woman; a human being we can see and touch, with a body.

And in the same way Kṛṣṇa was born, he was a human being. Looking at Kṛṣṇa from the outside you would see a normal human, yet he did supernatural things which allow us to know that he was a higher being incarnate in a physical body. He was a political leader with a small kingdom in India, some believed he was divine, others didn't. He went to parliament and argued his politics. In a family war, he gave the teachings in the Bhagavad Gītā, some of the highest teachings on yoga; including jñāna yoga, karma yoga and bhakti yoga.

Kṛṣṇa is the Viṣṇu icarnation of the Moon. The Moon shows the mind. Patañjali's definition of yoga is *yogas-chitta-vritti-nirodaha*: yoga is the cessation or control of the mind-waves. The thought waves exist in the mind; a bundle of thought waves. Kṛṣṇa teaches how to balance those waves and come into peace with the mind. Kṛṣṇa carries the flute. Some of the stories about Kṛṣṇa, tell of him playing the flute and how all the Gopis (cow-girls) come running to dance with him and how he divides himself up into multiple realties spending time with, dancing and making love to all of them. That flute is the nāda talked about in yoga. It represents the internal vibration of Auṁ that exists within. When we meditate and listen to that internal sound, all the senses turn inward creating *pratyāhāra*, and merge and dance with the Lord who is found in the many but emanates as the One.

Kṛṣṇa is all about the mind; the pratyāhāra of the mind, the control and working of the mind, as well as all the playful aspects of the mind. So there exists all these fun stories of Kṛṣṇa doing many playful things. Many of the other avatārs conquer one demon, and with Kṛṣṇa there're so many demons he's conquered in the stories from the Purāṇas, specifically the Bhagavat Purāṇa. This is due to the constant besiegement of negative thoughts and feelings and the things we need to overcome. Kṛṣṇa represents the exalted state of the mind, which is seen in the mind that knows how to control itself.

Remedies:

When the Moon is sustaining something it can be quickly changing with many ups and downs. Using Kṛṣṇa to take the Moon to its highest state, uplifting the Moon to create that stability of mind also creates the knowledge of how to understand and balance the mind. Nothing balances the mind more than devotion and that is why devotion is so much associated with Kṛṣṇa. When we think of Kṛṣṇa, the first thing that comes to mind is devotion and this is because of the ability of bhakti to control the mind, creating the proper balance of mind to allow things to be properly sustained and fructified. All aspects of yoga as taught in the Bhagavad Gītā will be beneficial to the mind and empowerment of the Moon.

Buddha: The Awakened One

Buddha, besides being a name of Mercury, literally means wise, learned, intelligent, as well as awake or aware. It comes from the root *Buddh* which means comprehension, apprehension, understanding, and discernment. The Buddha is one who has achieved these qualitites. To the Buddhist religion it has a deeper meaning of the aware state of consciousness that comes through proper discernment, also known as enlightened awareness or enlightenment. Sometimes over-orthodox Hindus will say that Buddha can't be an avatāra of Viṣṇu and that this part of Parāśara is corrupted. This is what the verse says, so to say it's wrong is not our job; our job is to understand why Parāśara has made the statement.

Bṛhat Parāśara Horā Ṣāstra is older than the time of the Buddha Avatār. So does some author add in Buddha's name or does Parāśara speak of the Buddha avatāra and when Gautama comes along he says, I am the Buddha? The name of Mercury in Sanskrit is Buddha, and that is all Parāśara was saying for his time. Parāśara teaches that Mercury follows his own dharma, his own way, is very independent *(sva-tantra)*. In this way, the Buddha avatāra became independent of the Vedas which leads fundamentalist Hindus to discredit the Buddha as an incarnation of Viṣṇu. But the whole of Hinduism sees not only Buddha but also Jesus as an incarnation of Viṣṇu.

During the time of the Buddha, some of the Brahmins were doing really crazy things, similar to the time when Jesus came into the temples and threw over the tables and wanted reformation. In the same way, the Buddha wanted to bring about purity. Most of his teachings primarily give the essence of the Vedas, but without the Vedic rituals that were becoming more of a money-making scam than a sharing of spiritual teachings.

Remedies:

When the Mercurial form of Viṣṇu incarnated, the Buddhist teachings were about the discernment of mind. Using the intellect to understand what is real and what is not real, digging into reality to properly use the intellect.

To see the practical application of the Buddha avatāra we use the discriminating mind and intelligence, the *buddhi*, and properly apply this knowledge. When Mercury becomes negative, there is an over-discriminating, prejudice without reason and hypercritical nature present. The Buddha avatāra takes that critical, discriminating mind and makes it work in the right direction: discerning the real from the unreal, the truth from the untruth, differentiating that which is transitory from that which is eternal and uncovering our eternal nature. If Mercury is sustaining a relationship there can be an over-criticalness that can destroy the relationship. The worship of Buddha avatāra will allow an individual to use their intellect in a more harmonious and productive way; to go inside and evolve themselves rather than focusing outside and trying to pick something apart.

Planet	Bhagavata Dvādakṣari Mantras
Sun	auṁ namo bhagavate rāmachandrāya
Moon	auṁ namo bhagavate vasudevāya
Mars	auṁ kṣauṁ namo bhagavate nṛsiṁhāya
Mercury	auṁ namo bhagavate budhadevāya (or balabhadrāya)
Jupiter	auṁ namo bhagavate śrīvāmanāya (or trivikramāya)
Venus	auṁ namo bhagavate hṛṣīkeśāya
Saturn	auṁ namo bhagavate kūrmadevāya
Rāhu	auṁ bhūr namo bhagavate varāhāya
Ketu	auṁ namo bhagavate matsyadevāya

Additional Devatās

Parāśara mentions more variations of deities further into Bṛhat Parāśara Horā Śāstra which are used for other purposes. The planets rarely appear as just planets in our life or spirituality. They will take manifestation through various deity forms. As a Vedic astrologer (*Jyotiṣī*), one needs to learn which form the planet is appearing as in the person's life. Then the person can interact with the planet energy in the most direct way possible. Below is a list given by Parāśara as way to approach the planet to ask for assistance (*krama*). Then a list is given by Jaimini who was a student of Parāśara which is used for propitiation of the planets.

Planet	BPHS Parāśara v.18	Jaimini 1.2.72-81
Sun	Agni (Vahni)	Śiva
Moon	Water (Ambu)	Gaurī
Mars	Skanda (Śikhija)	Skanda
Mercury	Viṣṇu	Viṣṇu
Jupiter	Indra (Viḍojas)	Sāmba Śiva
Venus	Indrāṇi (Śachī)	Lakṣmī
Saturn	Brahma (Khagānā)	Viṣṇu/lower gods
Rāhu		Tāmasī, Durgā
Ketu		Gaṇeśa, Skanda

This list can become even more specified for the individual chart. This is a complex science of understanding the devas, understanding the light bearers in your life. HariHara is a classic author of a Kerala Jyotiṣa text called Praśna Mārga. He says, "Whether one's past karma is favorable or unfavorable and in what manner it expresses itself, should be carefully divined by the astrologer[39]." Below is a more detailed list given by him:

	Harihara Praśna Mārga Ch.XV	
Sun	All Signs	Śiva, [Jyotir-Liṅga]
	1st drekkana of dual sign	Subramanyam
	2nd drekkana of dual sign	Ganeśa
Moon	Strong Moon	Durgā
	Weak Moon	Kālī
	Weak and in Martian signs	Cāmuṇḍā
Mars	Odd signs	Skanda, Bhairava, etc
	Even signs	Cāmuṇḍā, Bhadrakālī, etc
Mercury	Moveable and dual signs	Viṣṇu āvātara
	1st and 2nd drekkana of fixed	Śrī Kṛṣṇa
	3rd drekkana of fixed sign	Viṣṇu avatara [or Śakti]
Jupiter	Represents divinity in all signs	Mahāviṣṇu, signs and conjunctions will specify form
Venus	Sattva signs	Annapūrṇā
	Rajas signs	Lakṣmī
	Tamas signs	Yakṣā [Rādhā]
Saturn	Śāstādika	Traditional Teachers, Viṣṇu
Rāhu	Sarvagaṇa	Every kind of deity [serpants]

"Jupiter represents that one supreme divinity. If he is favorable, all deities will favor the native. If he is not favorable, all the deities will be unfavorable."

In general the Sun will represent the Śiva-liṅgam in all signs. The Moon will show various forms of the divine mother. Mars will show itself as a male deity in odd/male signs and a female deity in even/female signs. Mercury will show Viṣṇu avātaras as it is a rajasic planet and differentiates these forms. Jupiter will represent the greater form of Viṣṇu or the god figure in the person's specific religion.

Venus will show itself in three different aspects of the three guṇas. Anna-pūrṇa means filled with food, complete nourishment, or perfect sustenance. This sattva goddess is prayed to when we are content with what we have, or for just the basic needs of life. Lakṣmī is Rajas in that she represents wealth and prosperity as well as the comforts of the

[39] Raman, B.V. trans *Praśna Mārga*, chapter XV, v.1, p.496

water element. She is prayed to when we want more than our basic needs met. The Tamas signs will show worship of Yakṣas which are nature spirits. Our tradition recommends the use of Rādhā for this position as she has the power to remove the Tamas from Venus and raise the ideals of the individual.

For Saturn the devatā is Śāstā. Ādi Śaṅkara gave this definition, "Śāstā is he who instructs all by means of śruti, smṛti, etc[40]." The tradition will often use Nārāyaṇa as Jaimini mentions Viṣṇu for Saturn. The name Śāstā directly refers to Viṣṇu in Utpala's *Spandapradīpikā* (which quotes the *Pāñcarātra Upaniṣad*) as well as the *Lakṣmī Tantra.*

Rāhu is mentioned as all types of deities or gaṇas which are lower types of deities. The tradition teaches that Durgā is best for Rāhu as she is who removes all durgati (misfortune and distress). Not mentioned here, Ketu represents Gaṇeśa, the elephant headed devatā. Rāhu represents obstruction and Ketu is always opposite Rāhu showing the doorway out of this blockage. In this way Ketu removes all obstacles when invoked in its particular form of Gaṇeśa relative to the birth chart.

Devī

When a planet is in its exaltation it will act like Viṣṇu. When a planet is weak (*nīca*), it will need to take the form of the Mother (*Śakti*). The Mother is she who nurtures, comforts, protects and allows us to become strong (*Śakti*). The Mother forms of the planets are important to understand. When something is weak it lacks understanding, it lacks knowledge (*vidyā*). These Mahāvidyā (great knowledge) forms are the knowledge (*vidyā*) aspect of the creation (*prakṛti*). Through their worship the understanding of a planet's energies are gained and the planet becomes purified of its ignorance.

The Mahāvidyā forms are to be used with a qualified guru only. There are other forms of the Mother like Durgā, Sarasvatī, and Lakṣmī who are always beneficial to a person and generally good to worship. The Mahāvidyā are *Nīla Śakti*, which is how they purify a planet. They are the pinnacle of Tantra and should be used wisely. There use is for more advanced astrologers who are fully aware of what they are doing with remedial measures.

The Mother is Vidyā (Knowledge). If She is not with you then you are in avidyā (ignorance). This is why the worship of the Devī is crucial for a Jyotiṣī or any other person seeking knowledge or mastery of a Vedic science, from the lowest level of aparavidyā to the highest level of ātmavidyā and god-knowledge.

[40] Harisson, Hill, *Dhātu-Pāṭha*, Bhāṣya on Viṣṇu Sahasranāma 35 by Śaṅkara

Chapter 5

Rāśi: *Signs*

Rāśi

There are twelve rāśi (signs) in both Western and Indian astrology. The word Rāśi means a heap, pile, group, compilation, or a measure of quantity. In Jyotiṣa a rāśi represents a quantity of degrees. It takes 365 days for the Sun to go around the earth and through the zodiac. This was converted to 360 for purposes of division. Thereby, the Sun moves through approximately one degree everyday. This too explains why a circle is measured in 360 degrees and not using a decimal system of 100 or 1,000 degrees.

There are about 12.3 lunar months in every revolution of the Earth around the Sun. This 360 degree path is broken up into 12 months, each composed of 30 degrees (or 30 days). The mathematical calculations of the months are created by This is the root of the months in a calendar of which once correlated to the Sun's exact movement. The Rāśi is the grouping of these 30 degrees each with its own qualities.

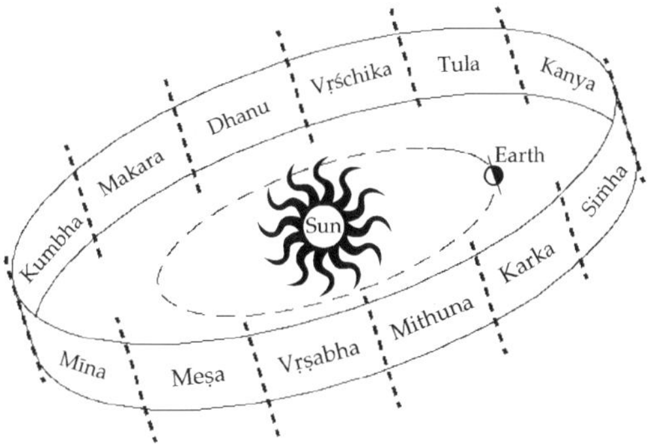

In Western astrology there exists controversy regarding a 13th sign. This is fine as the western zodiac is symbolic, 'sign' literally means symbol. But the Indian Zodiac cannot have a 13th sign, as it is based on a calculation of time. This time is then overlaid in space to make the 12 'signs' of the Sun.

Basic Measurements of Time

Lunar Month

Sidereal month: period of time wherein the Moon passes through all twelve constellations (27.3217 days)

Synodic month: period of time from one full Moon to the next (29.5306 days)

Intercalary Lunar Month

12 synodic months average 354.3672 days (10.9 less than a solar year)

36 synodic months/3 solar years average 29 days or 1 synodic lunar month

As the year is 12.3 lunar months, an intercalary lunar month is added every $2\frac{2}{3}$ years to synchronize the cycles of the Sun and the Moon. An intercalary time period is an important part of many traditional cultures. The Vedic system uses a full lunar month, making it a holy time, to align the Sun and the Moon, or a holy time to align the Mind and the Soul.

Solar Day: period of time between one sunrise and the next. Varāhamihira uses the first ray of the Sun as the start of the day. Others take the center of the Sun disk.

Solar Year

Tropical year: period of time from one vernal equinox to the next (365.2422 days) Sidereal year: period of time wherein the Sun passes through all twelve Rāśi (365.2564 days)

Days	Hours	Minutes	Seconds
365	5	48	45.2
365	6	9	9.8

(1 minute of arc is equal to 2 minutes of time)

The difference between the tropical and sidereal year is 20 minutes. These twenty minutes create the ayanāṁśa. Each year this distance increases, creating a greater variation between the sidereal and tropical zodiac.

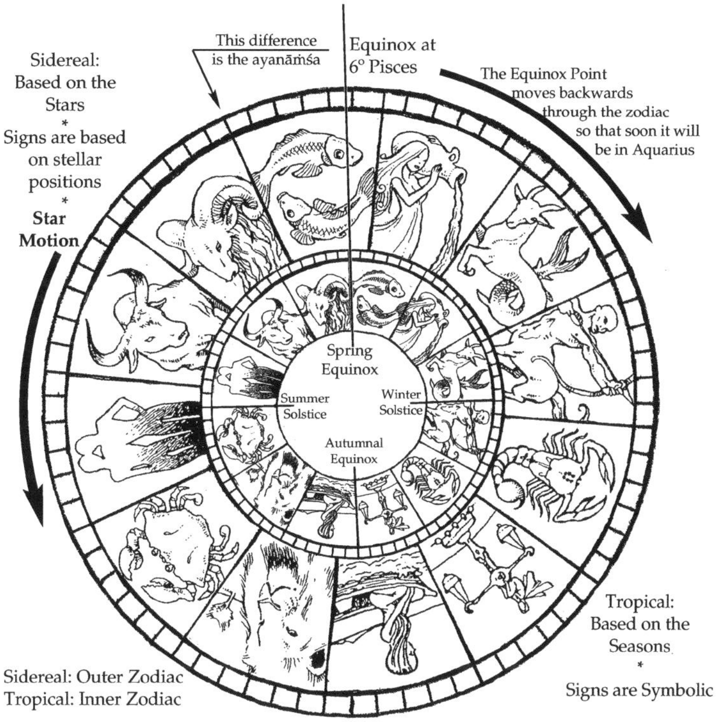

Ayanāṁśa

There are slight disagreements on the exact degree of the ayanāṁśa based on variations of astronomical calculation. The charts below will show the variation based on the point of calculation where the zodiac signs actually begin. These points show what seems a small difference but when doing very refined astronomical calculations the difference can change time periods in the chart by months. The commonly accepted ayanāṁśa, made official by the government of India, is called Lahiri ayanāṁśa.

Name of Ayanāṁśa	Reference Point
Lahiri (Chitra Pakṣa)	Spica (Chitra) at 0 Libra
Fagan-Bradley	Spica (Chitra) at 29:06:05 Virgo
De Luce	Zeta Piscium (Revati)
Raman	Calculation of B.V. Raman
Krishnamurti	Calculation of Krishnamurti

At one point in time the two zodiacs corresponded. But there is a slow precession that creates a steadily increasing difference between the two zodiacs. The Sanskrit word *Sāyana* is the calculation of the planets from the vernal equinoctial point, which begins the tropical zodiac. The *nirayana* position of planets begins the sidereal zodiac. Common Western astrology is tropical (sāyana), and Vedic astrology is sidereal (nirayana).

The chart below gives the time when the primary ayanāṁśas correlated to the tropical zodiac. The difference is due to the difference in reference points in the sky. Before that time period the sidereal zodiac was ahead of the sign Aries, now it is after the signs Aries. The procession moves backward through the zodiac.

Ayanāṁśa	1900	1950	2000	2050	Correlation
Lahiri	22:28:02	23:09:34	23:51:17	24:33:41	290 AD
Raman	21:00:28	21:42:00	22:23:43	23:06:07	395 AD
Fagan-Bradley	23:20:56	24:02:28	24:44:11	25:26:35	221 AD
De Luce	18:45:00	19:26:32	20:08:15	20:50:39	560 AD

The difference between the tropical and sidereal year creates twenty minutes of difference that increases each year. The equinox point moves approximately 1 degree every 72 years, and about 1.4 degrees every 100 years. This means it moves about 14 degrees (one nakṣatra of 13°-20′) every 1,000 years. The various ages of mankind can be marked by the movement of the procession of the zodiac through the nakṣatras.

The Ṛg-Veda depicts the spring equinox in Rohini Nakṣatra (Taurus). Then later it is marked in Krittikā Nakṣatra (the Pleiades). Presently the equinox is in Uttarābhādra nakṣatra and will move into Pūrvābhādra nakṣatra before moving into the sign of Aquarius.

Rāśi

In the chart below we will study the signs (rāśi) in what is called the Bṛhaspati chakra, also known as the South Indian Chart. The signs remain fixed within this style chart. Each sign is ruled by a planet called the lord of the sign. Understanding this lord will help in understanding the quality of the sign as they are representative of the planetary energies. Each sign corresponds to a number starting with one at Aries and ending with twelve at Pisces. The odd numbers show masculine, outgoing energy. The even, female numbers reflect a soft, inward energy. Referring to the chart below, each planet has both an odd and even number related to it. The Sun and Moon rule one sign each. The Sun, a masculine planet, rules the odd sign Leo (number five). The feminine, inward energy of the Moon rules the even sign of Cancer (number four).

Pisces	Aries	Taurus	Gemini
Aquarius			Cancer
Capricorn			Leo
Sagittarius	Scorpio	Libra	Virgo

On each side of Cancer and Leo (the signs of the king and queen) are the signs of Mercury the prince. These are Gemini (number three), the outward direct energy of Mercury showing skill in communication and love of games, and Virgo (number six) as the feminine, inward energy of Mercury which shows the qualities of refinement, purity, and perfectionism. Venus rules two signs on each side of Mercury. Libra is the odd sign showing the outward energy of Venus performing and in the market place. Taurus is the even, inward energy of Venus that shows the desire for comforts, good foods, and beautiful possessions. On each side of this is the sign Aries lorded by Mars. Aries as the odd sign shows the male, outward, aggressive force of Mars while Scorpio being the even sign shows the inward, more feminine energy and the spiritual warrior related to Mars. Jupiter's lordship is to either side of Mars in the signs of Sagittarius and Pisces. Sagittarius shows the masculine control of justice through law, the judicial system, and battle related to dharma. Pisces shows the feminine expression of

1	Aries	♈	Odd/male	Mars
2	Taurus	♉	Even/female	Venus
3	Gemini	♊	Odd/male	Mercury
4	Cancer	♋	Even/female	Moon
5	Leo	♌	Odd/male	Sun
6	Virgo	♍	Even/female	Mercury
7	Libra	♎	Odd/male	Venus
8	Scorpio	♏	Even/female	Mars (Ketu)
9	Sagittarius	♐	Odd/male	Jupiter
10	Capricorn	♑	Even/female	Saturn
11	Aquarius	♒	Odd/male	Saturn (Rāhu)
12	Pisces	♓	Even/female	Jupiter

Jupitarian spirituality in an ocean of oneness. Opposite Leo and Cancer are the signs of Saturn. Capricorn is the even, feminine sign showing the dedicated work of Saturn and Aquarius is the odd, masculine sign showing the creative work Saturn makes as a craftsman.

Each sign has a certain physical appearance and complexion. The appearance of the sign will affect the physical features of a person as the house shows the area of life and the sign shows what that area looks like. In the same way, the ascendant will show one's body and the sign ruling the ascendant will indicate what the person's body is shaped like. Thereby, the ascendant can be obtained based on certain characteristics of a person. Planets in signs will dominate over the features of the sign, so it is important to take into account the natural state of the sign compared to the sign modified by a planet's features. If the sign is weak then the related significations will be weak.

#	Rāśi	BPHS, Rāśi Svarūpādhyāya v.6-24	Doṣa
1	Aries	Large body *(bṛhad-gātra)*	Pitta
2	Taurus	Tall/long *(dīrgha)*	Kapha
3	Gemini	Vāta, well proportioned body *(sama- gātra)*	Vāta
4	Cancer	Thick body *(sthaula tanū)*	Kapha-vāta
5	Leo	Large body *(bṛhad gātra)*	Pitta
6	Virgo	Medium body *(mādhya)*	Vāta-kapha
7	Libra	Medium body *(mādhya tanū)*	Vāta-kapha
8	Scorpio	Short/slender *(svalpa)*, hairy	Kapha-pitta
9	Sagittarius	Well proportioned body *(sama gātra)*, Strong brilliance *(tejas)*	Pitta-kapha
10	Capricorn	Large body *(bṛhad gātra)*	Vāta-kapha
11	Aquarius	Medium body *(mādhya tanū)*	Vāta
12	Pisces	Medium body *(mādhya deha)*, healthy *(svastha)*	Kapha

Parāśara teaches that the signs are Time personified *(kālarūpa)*. Each sign relates to a region of the body as well as has its own Ayurvedic constitution. This is important relative to health, disease, accidents, and constitution determination.

#	Rāśi	BPHS Verse 4	Common Associations
1	Aries	Head	**Head**, brain, nerves
2	Taurus	Face	**Neck**, face, nose, eyes, mouth (teeth, tongue, oral cavity), throat, tonsils
3	Gemini	Arms	**Upper chest,** neck, shoulders, clavicles, arms/hands, esophagus, trachea
4	Cancer	Heart, breast, chest *(hṛd)*	**Chest cavity**, breasts, heart, lungs, diaphragm, esophagus
5	Leo	Stomach, abdomen *(kroḍa)*	**Solar Plexus**, (above navel), stomach, liver, gallbladder, spleen, duodenum, small intestines, heart
6	Virgo	Hip/loins/ Buttocks *(kaṭi)*	**Lower abdominal region**, lower abdomen, large intestines
7	Libra	Lower abdomen *(basti)*	**Pelvic region**, urinary tract, kidney, uterus, ovaries, testes, prostate, bladder, urethra, groin, semen, ovum
8	Scorpio	Privates/anus *(guhya)*	**External genitalia**, scrotum, testicles, colon, rectum, the sweaty/dirty genitalia area
9	Sag	Thighs	**Hips** and thighs, lumbar region, sciatic nerve, walking ability
10	Cap	Knees *(jānu)*	**Knees**, patella, popliteal fossa,
11	Aqua	Calf *(jaṅgha)*	**Calves**, ankles, shins
12	Pisces	Feet	**Feet**

The classic work *Sārāvalī* says that a malefic planet acting adversely in a sign will show lack of development or some type of deformity relative to the corresponding organ of the KālaPuruṣa. Therefore if Saturn is in Pisces with malefic aspects the person could have foot problems.

The Guṇas[41]

There are two aspects of guṇas to consider when understanding the rāśis, the intrinsic nature and the outer objective. For the intrinsic nature of the sign one looks to the planet which lords that sign. For example, the sattva planets, Jupiter, Sun and Moon have sattva rāśis. This shows the intrinsic, or **natural state** of the sign. Then there is the outer objective of the guṇa related to each of the moveable (cara), dual *(dvisvabhāva)*, and fixed *(sthira)* signs. The chara signs have lots of energy and are of rajas guṇa, the sthira signs are more steady and are of tamas guṇa, while the dvisvabhāva signs are a mix of these two energies and are sattva in their **objective**.

#	Rāśi	Lord	Nature		Rāśi Quality	Objective		Result
1	Meṣa	Mars	Tamas		Cara	Rajas		Sattva
2	Vṛṣabha	Venus	Rajas		Sthira	Tamas		Sattva
3	Mithuna	Mercury	Rajas		Dvisvabhāva	Sattva		Tamas
4	Karka	Moon	Sattva		Cara	Rajas		Tamas
5	Siṁha	Sun	Sattva		Sthira	Tamas		Rajas
6	Kanya	Mercury	Rajas		Dvisvabhāva	Sattva		Tamas
7	Tula	Venus	Rajas		Cara	Rajas		Rajas
8	Vṛśchika	Mars	Tamas		Sthira	Tamas		Tamas
9	Dhanu	Jupiter	Sattva		Dvisvabhāva	Sattva		Sattva
10	Makara	Saturn	Tamas		Cara	Rajas		Sattva
11	Kumbha	Saturn	Tamas		Sthira	Tamas		Tamas
12	Mīna	Jupiter	Sattva		Dvisvabhāva	Sattva		Sattva

The guṇa of the sign lord shows the intrinsic nature of the sign or the sign's natural quality. The order of creation, sthira, cara, dvisvabhāva, shows the guṇa of the sign's objective. The combination of these two will show the end result a sign actually accomplishes (shown in the last column).

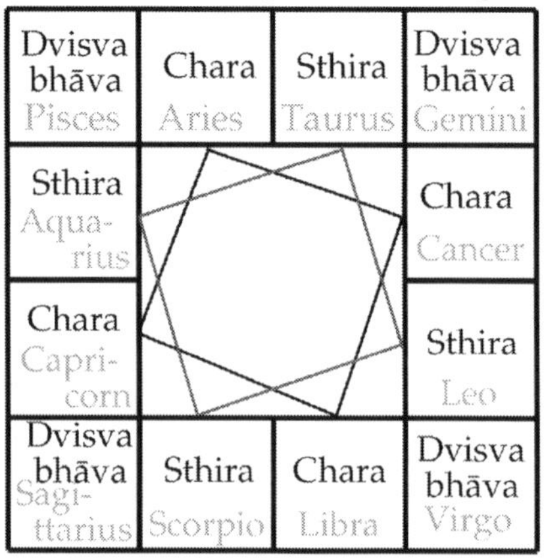

Aries is lorded by the tamasic planet Mars so its intrinsic nature is tamas, slow, heavy, sleeping all the time, and lazy. The sign is cara (moveable), so the objectives are too many, an excess of energy. Being of a lazy nature the Aries native only accomplishes the very important tasks set out to accomplish and the end result is sattva. In this way, the guṇa not already given becomes the result. Scorpio is also ruled by the tamas planet Mars. The sign is sthira

[41] Rath, Sanjay, Introduction lecture for Vyāsa SJC, 2005

(fixed) so it has little objective. With little energy and little objective, not much is attained, so the accumulated energy (result) is tamas. Scorpio is the best sign for tamas activity.

Taurus is ruled by the rajas planet Venus and therefore naturally has lots of energy to do many things. Being a sthira (fixed) sign, this tamas gives little objective, or want to share energy. With lots of energy and little objective the end result is sattva, all tasks are completed, or completed with careful expenditure of energy. Libra is also ruled by the rajas planet Venus and therefore has lots of intrinsic energy to create. Libra is a chara (moveable) sign and so has many desires and objectives. Having lots of objectives and lots of energy it becomes very successful in rajas activities. When the intrinsic nature and outer objective align there is success along that quality of activity.

Gemini is ruled by the rajas planet Mercury giving it lots of creative energy. It is a dvisvabhāva (dual) sign so it has a sattva objective, very high intentions. But sattva can only be attained with sattva so the end objective is tamas as the objective is not achieved. Virgo is the same as Gemini, ruled by a rajas planet and dvisvabhāva sign, leading to a tamas result. These signs need to calm down, and learn to take on a more sattva nature.

Cancer is ruled by the sattva Moon so it has a balanced caring intrinsic nature. It is a cara sign giving it the desire to attain a lot of results. Rajas will often use all types of methods to attain results. The end result is tamas as it is not able to accomplish sattva through rajas. Because of Cancer's ambition it burns itself out and falls into tamas. By setting realistic goals the Moon will allow itself to achieve without losing. Leo is ruled by the sattva Sun who wishes to uphold dharma. The sign is sthira which shows a tamas objective, as the King's job is to punish the wrongdoer. The accumulated energy (result) is rajas, the growing of the *ahaṁkāra* (egotism), and the belief in power.

Sagittarius has the sattva lord Jupiter and is dvisvabhāva giving it a sattva objective. The sattva objective signs are those ruled by Jupiter and Mercury, which show learning, teaching, studying and the pursuit of knowledge. The end result of Sagittarius is sattva. Pisces again is sattva both in its nature and objective making these signs strong for successful sattva activity.

Capricorn is ruled by the tamas graha Saturn giving it a naturally heavy, lazy, and dark nature. It is a cara rāśi, which gives it many objectives. The final result is sattva. This is the goal of the Aghori practitioners who hope to attain sattva knowledge and a balanced mind through their tamas nature and rajas activity. Aquarius is also ruled by the tamas planet Saturn and being a sthira sign makes its final outcome successful in tamas activities.

Tattvas

The signs are each ruled by one of the four gross elements. Ākāśa (space) doesn't rule any signs as it permeates everything -is in all signs. The elements of the signs are used in conjunction with the quality (chara, dvisvabhāva, and sthira) of the signs. For example, Meṣa (Aries) is chara fire, it is movable fire so it changes quickly, and is easy to anger but also quick to settle down. Siṁha (Leo) is sthira fire, fixed fire, so it burns steady and continues down its path with force not giving up or changing its mind easily. Dhanu (Sagittarius) is dvisvabhāva fire, it works for justice, changes views sometimes but not without reason. It works with long-term governing and short term-war. In this way, the combination of these two aspects must be brought together in order to understand the complete motivation of each of the signs.

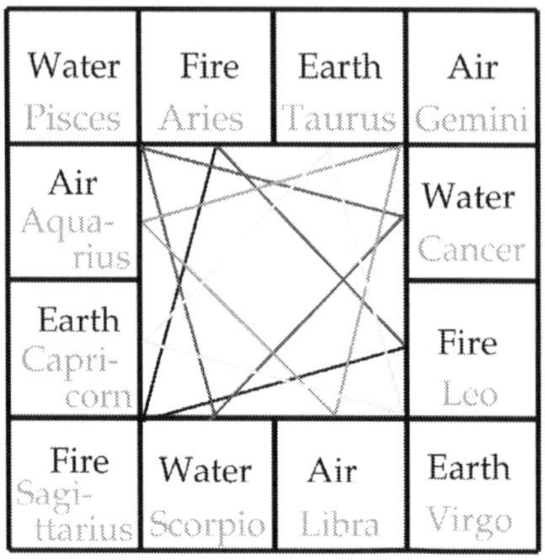

The tattvas are in a trinal (trikoṇa) or 120° relationship to each other. The guṇas are in a quadrant (kendra) or 90° relationship to each other. When planets are in kendra to each other they have the same guṇa, and guṇa works on the level of mind. They therefore think the same way and help each other out. When planets are in trikoṇa to each other they share the same element. Elements work on the physical plane and show the planets will support each other's actions, as they are getting things done in the same way and with the same support. Therefore the trines from the Sun and the quadrants from the Moon become important.

3	Guṇas	Quadrants *(kendra)*	90°	Support the Mind/perception
4	Tattvas	Trines *(trikoṇa)*	120°	Support Resources/materials

There are four tattvas corresponding to the four yugas[42]. The yugas are often thought of as the cycles of time the universe passes through on the grand scale of evolution. They are huge phases in time, but there are also smaller phases of the yuga reflected within our own lives. It is best to learn about the large scale phases that happen throughout time and then later it will be easy to see how we pass through these periods in our life on a smaller scale.

Satya	Fire	Dharma- life purpose
Tretā	Earth	Artha- wealth
Dvāpara	Air	Kāma- pleasure
Kali	Water	Mokṣa- spirituality

Satya yuga relates to the Fire signs (Aries, Leo and Sagittarius) as fire (agni) is the most spiritual and dharmic element. Fire and water do not get along so in Satya Yuga there is strong dharma but little chance of *mokṣa* (liberation). *Tretā yuga*

[42] Raman, B.V. *Praśna Mārga of Harihara*. XVI.122

relates to the earth signs. As earth and air do not get along in Tretā yuga there is plenty of *artha* but little happiness in relationship. The story of the Rāma avatāra was during the time of Tretā yuga and the story revolves around the loss of his wife and the battle to get her back.

Dvāpara Yuga relates to the air signs. Again, air and earth do not get along so in the Dvāpara yuga there is plenty of relationship enjoyment but little wealth. In the story of the Kṛṣṇa avatāra, Kṛṣṇa has multiple wives and lovers (kāma), but there is a battle over a kingdom (wealth).

Kali yuga relates to the water signs. Water and fire do not get along, so in Kali yuga there is a chance to attain liberation but there is no dharma. Dharma is present when things are done according to the natural law, or one's innate purpose in life. Kings are good people and crooks are put in jail. In Kali yuga, crooks become kings and good people are put in jail -the dharma of nature is not followed, yet mokṣa is easy to attain. Of course when the good guys are too busy as kings it's hard to focus on spirituality, but while you are stuck suffering it is easy to remember and call out to one's concept of god.

Directions and Distance

The elements will each show one of the cardinal directions. The cara and sthira signs show the distance in that direction. Each direction has a far distance (cara), short distance (sthira) and a medium distance (dvisvabhāva).

The directions of the elements relate to the natural directions or cara rāśis. In this way, East is the fire signs from Meṣa, South is the Earth signs from Makara, West is the Air signs from Tula, and North is the water signs from Karka.

Tattva	Diś
Fire	East
Earth	South
Air	West
Water	North

The cara signs have lots of energy/rajas and indicate a far distance, like out of state or overseas type of distance. The sthira signs indicate a relatively small distance, where one works in their own hometown, meets their wife in their own hometown, etc. The dvisvabhāva rāśi show a medium distance, which will range from outside one's own hometown to outside one's home state depending on the strength of the indications. Combining these two significations, Aries is a long distance to the East. Leo is a very short distance to the East and Sagittarius is a medium distance to the Eastern direction. The same method of combining distance and direction is applied for all the other signs.

Cara (moveable)	far
Sthira (fixed)	close
Dvisvabhāva (dual)	medium

Day and Night Rāśi

The below chart gives the day and night rāśis with the back rising *(pṛṣṭodaya)* and front rising *(śirṣodaya)* together. Varāhamihira makes a statement that makes remembering the direction of rising easy. "Vṛṣabha, Mithuna, Dhanu, Meṣa, and Makara possess strength in the night. These excepting Mithuna rise with their rear portion[43]." So all the night strong signs rise with the back while the day strong signs rise with their front, except for Mithuna (Gemini). Mīna rises with both its front and back as it is two fish together and therefore one is always facing forward and one is always facing backwards. This information is used for particular timing and strength calculations. It is noted here for reference.

Both *Mīna*	Back *Meṣa*	Back *Vṛṣa*	Head *Mithuna*
Back *Kumbha*			Back *Karka*
Back *Makara*			Head *Siṁha*
Back *Dhanu*	Head *Vṛśchika*	Head *Tula*	Head *Kanya*

Names of the Rāśi

There are many names for each sign which reveal the various meanings of the sign itself. A small introduction to these names will help shed light on the signs. It is also said in *Jātakapārijāta* that the signs inhabit the region appropriate to its symbol. For example, Aries is represented by a ram and these animals live in hilly regions, so Aries correlates to hilly areas.

Venus	Sun	Moon	Rahu
	Exaltation Uccha		Jupiter
Mars			
Ketu		Saturn	Mercury

Aries is known as Meśa which translates to a ram, sheep or anything woolen. The Latin word Aries also means ram. Aries relates to hilly areas and places where there is mining for minerals and gemstones. Aries is also called *Aja* which means a he-goat or ram but also means an instigator or mover and the leader of a flock. This leadership energy of Meṣa gives the Sun its exaltation here, while its harshness puts too much burden on the working class debilitating Saturn here.

Taurus is the word for bull in Latin. In Sanskrit, *vṛṣa* means a bull, the male of any animal or a strong and potent male. Taurus relates to farm land, pastures, forests, small villages. The Moon ruling dairy products, plants, and herbs is exalted in Vṛṣabha, which represents the places these things come from. It also gives the Moon, a lusty graha, the vitality to express itself in this sign.

[43] Vaidyanātha, *Jātakapārijāta*, I.14

Gemini comes from the Latin *geminus* which means twin, and refers to Castor and Pollux in Greek mythology. In the Western tradition they are seen as two twin males. In the Vedic tradition Gemini is seen as a couple in loving embrace. Parāśara describes Mithuna as a couple holding a mace and a lute. Mithuna literally means a couple (male/ female), or copulation. It also refers to the other part of something, or the compliment or companion of something. Gemini relates to places of pleasure like parks, entertainment places, and gambling areas. Rāhu the planet of underhanded business gets its bhoga exaltation in Gemini for its links to gambling and prostitution.

Cancer means crab in Latin. In Sanskrit, *karka* means a female crab. It relates to lakes, ponds, sandbanks, rivers and other watery places. It shows the clean and purifying aspect of the Moon, and because of this Jupiter is exalted here. Mars is rough and dirty and too tamasic for Cancer and is therefore debilitated there. Emotions are watery and soft; Jupiter brings contentment and fulfillment while Mars will show trauma or violence.

Leo means lion in Latin. *Siṁha* also means lion in Sanskrit, as well as a hero or eminent person. Siṁha relates to deep mountain caves and forests. It is the rāśi signficating jungles and wilderness. It is also the sign of authority, power and control and relates to the government.

Virgo means a virgin in Latin. *Kanyā* means a girl, a virgin or a daughter. It has the sense of being chaste and undefiled. *Jātaka Pārijāta* describes the rāśi Kanyā as a woman in a boat holding grains and fire in her hands. Kanyā represents cultivated land and gardens. Mercury is exalted in this cultivated, manicured type of environment, which constantly needs care and attention to stay beautiful. Venus is debilitated here because of the control and limitation the purity rules put upon the element of love.

Libra means a balance scale in Latin and *tulā* means the same thing in Sanskrit. The word tulā represents weighing, comparing, finding an equal measure or equal quantity, it represents equality in general. *Jātaka Pārijāta* says that Libra is symbolized by a person holding a balance scale. The scale represents both the marketplace and place of business. Libra also shows the delicately balanced weight needed on both sides of a scale to fulfill its job. Tula relates to the market place or bazaar of a city with valuable items, entertainment, and social activities. The Sun is debilitated here, as it likes to have power and control over all things. Saturn is exalted here as it represents the common working person and the power of democracy.

Mercury	Saturn		Ketu
			Mars
Jupiter	Neecha		
Rahu	Moon	Sun	Venus

Scorpio means scorpion in Latin and *vṛśchika* means the same in Sanskrit. It relates to deserts, places having holes, and is also associated with places of murky, stale or dirty water. The poison of the scorpion shows the dangerous powers that scorpio hides. It is ruled by both Mars and Ketu, and shows both the occult side of Mars and the inner quest of Ketu.

Sagittarius means archer, as *sagitta* is arrow in Latin. Dhanu means a bow in Sanskrit, which an archer would hold. *Jātaka Pārijāta* describes Dhanu as a man armed with a bow and arrow and the lower part of his body being that of a horse. Parāśara says it is two-legged for the first 15 degrees and four-legged for the second 15 degrees, and holds a bow *(dhanudhāra).* Sagittarius is connected to places containing horses, chariots and elephants. And it is the upper class, politicians, warriors, etc., that would normally have stables for these animals so it also represents the upper class.

Capricorn comes from the Latin *caper* meaning goat and corn meaning horn. Makara means a kind of sea monster in Sanskrit, which has the body of a crocodile and the head of a deer or goat. Its also called *nakra* which means crocodile and is associated with river regions. In India the dead are traditionally burned near a river and remains are thrown in and eaten by makara type creatures. These burning grounds are also associated with left-handed tantrics who reveal the darker side of *Ma-kāra* (performing the five M's). Mars is exalted here as it has the ability to work with the occult power of Makara while Jupiter the priest is debilitated here as it needs to be pure to achieve success with the devas.

Aquarius is Latin for water bearer as *aqua* means water. Parāśara says that Kumbha is represented by a man holding a pot. Kumbha shows the water pot/storage or holding places of water. Dams and water containment places are connected to Aquarius.

Pisces is plural for the Latin word *piscis* which means fish. Parāśara says that Mīna is represented by two fish tied together with the heads and tails in reverse position. Mīna relates to the ocean and large expanses of water. That expansiveness gives Mercury its debilitation by being unable to structure the vastness lost in words. Venus reaches exaltation here as boundless, limitless love. The Viṣṇu avatāra of Venus practiced deep meditation at the end of his incarnation in Ṛśikeśa, the city of ṛṣis. Pisces is the sign of the ṛṣis where Venus attains its higher vision.

Rāśi Dṛṣṭi: Sign Aspects

Each sign has an aspect on certain other signs. Dṛṣṭi means sight, to view, to behold, to regard, to consider. The word *aspect* itself can mean 'appearance to the eye from a certain vantage point', or 'a way in which something can be viewed by the mind'. The word aspect comes from the Latin *ad* (at) and *specere* (to look). In this way, dṛṣṭi and aspect have the same root meaning. Sign aspect (*rāśi dṛṣṭi*) is the act of one sign looking at and influencing another sign. All chara signs aspect the sthira signs except the one next to it. All sthira signs aspect chara signs except the one next to it. Dual signs aspect each other. If one of these signs contain a planet that planet will also aspect those signs.

The Mahā-Dṛṣṭi Chakra shows the aspects through a diagram described by Parāśara. Follow the line from Gemini (3) to Sagittarius (9) and from there across to Virgo (6), and from there to Pisces (12) and then to Gemini (3). All dual signs aspect each other. The sign Aries (1) aspects Leo (5), Scorpio (8), and Aquarius (11). As a chara rāśi it aspects all sthira rāśi except the one next to it (Taurus). Rāśi-dṛṣṭi will show the material resources influencing a sign and its house.

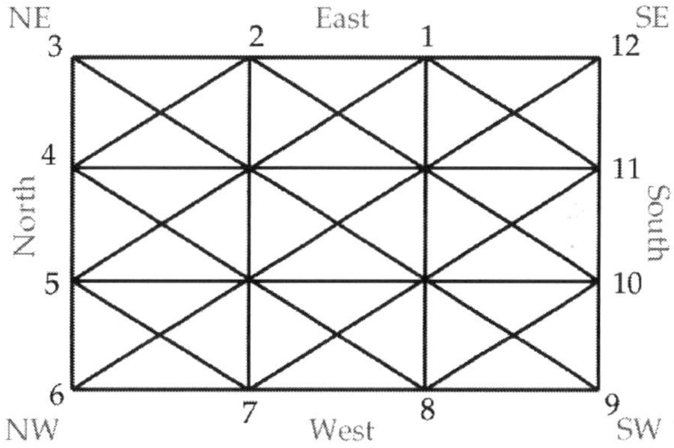

The Dvisvabhāva signs are sattva guṇa and thereby interact with themselves. It is the teachers (Jupiter) and students/scholars (Mercury) interacting. The chara signs are rajas and have excess energy they need to get rid of. The sthira signs are tamas and have deficient amounts of energy. Therefore these signs are constantly interacting back and forth. It is a natural tendency of nature for sattva to maintain sattva with itself. It is a natural tendency of rajas and tamas to interact back and forth. For example, when one drinks coffee (rajas) one gets hyper with extra energy, but the after effect is less energy (tamas) and tiredness. This is the case with rajas and tamas interacting.

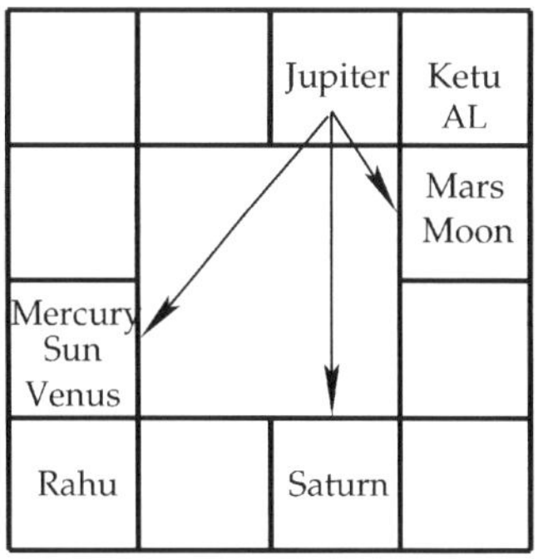

In the chart of Oprah Winfrey, Jupiter is in Taurus. Taurus aspects all chara signs except the one next to it; Cancer, Libra and Capricorn. Taurus does not aspect Aries. If a planet is in a sign it is also aspecting the same places as the sign. Jupiter is in Taurus and has rāśi dṛṣṭi on Cancer (containing Mars and Moon), Libra (containing Saturn), and Capricorn (containing Mercury, Sun, and Venus). The aspect of Jupiter shows the abundance of resources available to the signs (situation and places) and planets (people she interacts with) that Jupiter aspects. In Oprah's chart, all planets except the nodes have the support of Jupiter. This is considered a great blessing and empowers the signs and planets that receive Jupiter's aspect. At the same time, Saturn is in Libra aspecting all the sthira signs, except the one next to it. That means it does not aspect Scorpio. It does aspect Aquarius, Taurus and Leo.

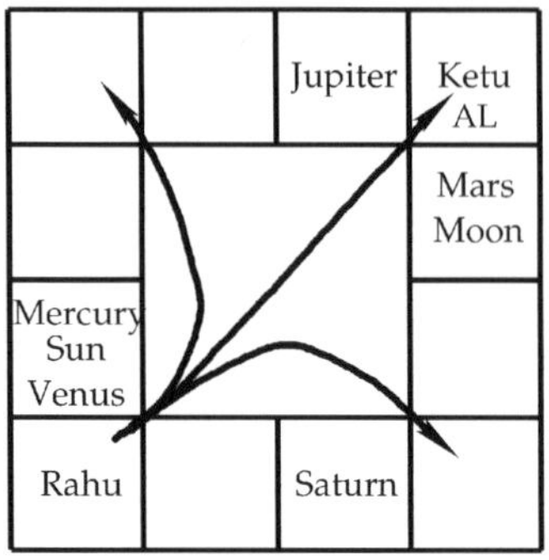

For a dvisvabhāva (dual) sign the other dvisvabhāva signs are aspected. Therefore Sagittarius aspects Pisces, Gemini and Virgo. Rāhu, who shows shock, causes trauma, and creates blockages is placed in Sagittarius in Oprah's chart. It is aspecting Pisces with no planets, Gemini which contains Ketu and Virgo which contains no planets. Rāhu is hurting very few planets in Oprah's chart.

Benefic aspects strengthen a planet and sign, malefic aspects damage a planet or sign. The aspect of a planet to its own sign is strong protection for the house, even if it is a malefic. A malefic will never hurt its own sign. The best aspect is Jupiter as it shows there is plenty of support and resources for the house. Mercury is the second best aspect as it shows the house has the skills to prosper. The houses own lord is the next best aspect to strengthen and protect a house. Saturn will bring hard work to a house. Ketu will bring spiritual help or spiritual objects. In this way, each of the planets will help according to their natural significations.

Rāśi Mantras[44]

Rāśi Mantras are used to strengthen a sign and make it friendly. These mantras relate to the various aspects of Viṣṇu, invoking the sustaining, sattva energy of the signs.

Aries	ॐ विष्णवे नमः	Aum̐ viṣṇave namaḥ Aum̐
Taurus	ॐ वासुदेवाय नमः	Aum̐ vāsudevāya namaḥ
Gemini	ॐ केशवाय नमः	Aum̐ keśavāya namaḥ
Cancer	ॐ राधाकृष्णाय नमः	Aum̐ rādhākṛṣṇāya namaḥ
Leo	ॐ हरिहराय बालमुकुन्दाय नमः	Aum̐ hariharāya bālamukundāya namaḥ
Virgo	ॐ ह्रीं पिताम्बराय परमात्मने नमः	Aum̐ hrīm̐ pitāmbarāya paramātmane namaḥ
Libra	ॐ श्रीरामदाशरथये नमः	Aum̐ śrīrāma-dāśarathaye namaḥ
Scorpio ♂	ॐ नराय नमः	Aum̐ narāya namaḥ
Scorpio ☋	ॐ नारायणाय नमः	Aum̐ nārāyaṇāya namaḥ
Sagittarius	ॐ ह्रीं श्रीं क्रीं धरणीधराय नमः	Aum̐ hrīm̐ śrīm̐ krīm̐ dharaṇī-dharāya namaḥ
Capricorn	ॐ श्रीं वत्सलाय नमः	Aum̐ śrīm̐ vatsalāya namaḥ
Aquarius ♄	ॐ क्लीं गोविन्दगोपालाय नमः	Aum̐ klīm̐ govinda-gopālāya namaḥ
Aquarius ☊	ॐ श्रीं उपेन्द्राय अच्युताय नमः	Aum̐ śrīm upendrāya acyutāya namaḥ
Pisces	ॐ क्रीं रथाङ्गचक्राय नमः	Aum̐ krīm̐ rathāṅga-cakrāya namaḥ

Ādityas

The twelve signs are seen as the twelve children of Mother Aditi, hence they are called Ādityas. *Diti* means cutting, splitting, dividing, and *Aditi* is that which is not divided or limited. The Mother Aditi is the universal mother that is unlimited, boundless and everywhere. Diti is the sister of Aditi, who represents the separateness and differentiating aspect of the mind. Diti gave birth to all the asuras (beings without light) called demons. Aditi represents the unity consciousness, and the ability to see the oneness of all life and living beings, from her were born all the devas, the light bearers.

The twelve Ādityas are the twelve Sun signs of the zodiac *(bhachakra)*. They represent the aspect of creation which gives rise to the fruits of life. The Sun makes everything on Earth work. The day comes with the Sun, life energy comes from the Sun, all things grow with the Sun which fuels the body, all fuels come from the Sun, either directly or from oil/coal that was vegetation thousands of years ago made by the Sun. Without the Sun the Earth would die and no longer produce the things needed for life. The Ādityas represent this life giving nature of the Sun, and its various aspects of giving throughout the year.

[44] These mantras are from the Śrī Achyutānanda Paramparā, given here according to VRA p.181

The availability of resources to survive and achieve all things in life are given through the Sun signs. The Sun signs represent not just the situation in a particular area of life but also the resources in that area. The Sun grows all resources, in the same way, the rāśi give all the resources in one's life, relative to the sign's placement. The Rāśi show the fruit (phala) we will receive. When the Ādityas are strong there is prosperity and abundance, and when they are weak there is poverty and scarcity of particular resources.

Āditya mantras are made by saying *Auṁ* which is an invocation starting the mantra, then the request *ghṛṇiḥ*, which means 'please shine'. Then the name of the Āditya is said with the word *Āditya* after it[45]. These are the general Āditya mantras asking the rāśi to shine brilliantly.

Rāśi Mantras are used to pacify a sign and make it friendly, and sattva. It will strengthen the sign in a friendly holistic way. Āditya mantras energize a sign and activate its resources. They relate to the creative energy of the sign. Jyotir-liṅga mantras purify and exalt a sign, allowing its higher nature to manifest. They relate to Śiva's aspect of purifying and removing the tamas guṇa.

Rāśi	Āditya	Āditya Mantras	
Aries	Dhata	ॐ घृणिः धातादित्य	Auṁ ghṛṇiḥ dhātāditya
Taurus	Aryamā	ॐ घृणिः अर्यमादित्य	Auṁ ghṛṇiḥ aryamāditya
Gemini	Mitra	ॐ घृणिः मित्रादित्य	Auṁ ghṛṇiḥ mitrāditya
Cancer	Varuṇa	ॐ घृणिः वरुणादित्य	Auṁ ghṛṇiḥ varuṇāditya
Leo	Indra	ॐ घृणिः इन्द्रादित्यषप	Auṁ ghṛṇiḥ indrāditya
Virgo	Vivasvān	ॐ घृणिः विवस्वानादित्य	Auṁ ghṛṇiḥ vivasvānāditya
Libra	Pūṣān	ॐ घृणिः पुषादित्य	Auṁ ghṛṇiḥ puṣāditya
Scorpio	Parjanya	ॐ घृणिः पर्जन्यादित्य	Auṁ ghṛṇiḥ parjanyāditya
Sag	Aṁśumān	ॐ घृणिः अंशुमानादित्य	Auṁ ghṛṇiḥ aṁśumānāditya
Cap	Bhaga	ॐ घृणिः भगादित्य	Auṁ ghṛṇiḥ bhagāditya
Aqua	Tvaṣṭa	ॐ घृणिः त्वष्टादित्य	Auṁ ghṛṇiḥ tvaṣṭāditya
Pisces	Viṣṇu	ॐ घृणिः विष्णवादित्य	Auṁ ghṛṇiḥ viṣṇavāditya

[45] Mantra (and grammar) based on the aṣṭākṣari mantra of the *Sūrya Upaniṣad*

Jyotir-Liṅga

The Jyotir-liṅgas relate to the signs, as the Sun relates to the ātmā. The Siva-liṅga is the ātmā in creation, both the Puruṣa in the Prakṛti, as well as the ātmā in the body. The ātmā is Sun, the Sun is Śiva, and Śiva is the guru. The ātmā is the highest guru. Before god-realization comes self *(ātmā)* – realization *(vidyā)*. The Sun manifests as twelve different Adityas which are the twelve solar energies known as the Sun signs. The rāśi are created by the relationship of the Sun and Moon, the Puruṣa and Prakṛti, or the soul and the mind. Rāśis are the stellar Śiva-liṅgas. The Jyotir-liṅgas are the core essence of the rāśi, their innermost light. Worship of the Jyotir-liṅga takes one into that core light knowledge.

Rāśis show the place and situation while grahas show the animate beings. Rāśis show the Puruṣa merged into Prakṛti to create substantiated reality that the planets/ātmās exist within. It is the lights and shadows creating reality. The Jyotir-liṅgas enlighten the mind to this higher essence awakening the soul-light-consciousness in various areas of our life. The Jyotir-liṅgas burn up tamas so knowledge/sattva can exist. Viṣṇu forms support the planet and take it to sattva by uplifting the planet. Śiva *(Jyotir-liṅga)* takes one to sattva by burning up the negativity present.

Jyotir-liṅgas[46]			
Aries	Rāmeśvara	Libra	Mahākāla
Taurus	Somanātha	Scorpio	Guśmeśvara
Gemini	Nāgeśvara	Sagittarius	Viśvanātha
Cancer	Omkāreśvara	Capricorn	Bhimaśaṅkara
Leo	Vaidyanātha	Aquarius	Kedārnātha
Virgo	Mallikārjuna	Pisces	Tryambakeśvara

Various remedies will be prescribed based on these Śiva-liṅgas as one learns more Jyotiṣa. The first teaching/remedy will be about purifying one's own ātmā. The re-telling of the stories of the avatāras of Viṣṇu will give the inner teaching. Rāma, the incarnation of the Sun, was going to battle the demon king Rāvaṇa. Before setting out for battle he installed the Rāmeśvara Jyotir-liṅga relating to the sign Aries, the exaltation of the Sun. Śri Kṛṣṇa, avatāra of the Moon, installed the Somanātha Jyotir-liṅga relating to the sign Taurus, the exaltation of the Moon. In this way they both worshiped the Śiva Liṅga which naturally exalted who they were. Therefore we take the Ātmakāraka and worship the Jyotir-liṅga that exalts who we are, to purify our ātma. This allows the ātmakāraka to be a good King and therefore help all the other grahas to act according to their higher nature.

To practice this, one either does Śiva-liṅga worship with the Jyotir-liṅga mantra or meditates on the ātmā while repeating this mantra.

[46] Śiva-Mahāpurāṇam, Śatarudra Saṁhitā, Chapter 24 and Koṭi Samhitā, Chapters 14-32. See also Ādi Śaṅkara's Dvādaśa Jyotirliṅga Stotra.

To create the Jyotir-liṅga mantra we use a little Sanskrit grammar; first we say *Auṁ*, which is an invocation starting the mantra, then the mantra *Namaḥ Śivāya*, which means "praises to that which removes tamas." Then we add the word *namo*, which means again praises, reverence, or adoration. Then we change the name of the Jyotir-liṅga into the dative form (so that we are offering to the Jyotir-liṅga). In Sanskrit the preposition goes on the end of the word as a postposition. So the translation of "to Śiva" is *Śivāya*. The ending 'āya' is the preposition 'to'. Below is an example of the first mantra for Rāmeśvara Jyotir-liṅga. The other mantras can be made accordingly using the same formula.

Auṁ Namaḥ Śivāya Namo Rāmeśvarāya

Practice Exercises:

1. Read the chapter in Bṛhat Parāśara Horā Śāstra on the signs.
2. One should have already studied and meditated upon the qualities of the grahas. Now take each of the signs relative to the day of the planet. Meditate upon how the signs reflect their particular lord, masculine or feminine energy, the element, and the quality of cara, sthira, and dvisvabhāva.

Rāśi Divisions: Varga

The Rāśis show the broad overview of life, but there are many more details that need to be looked into. For example, you may have good karma with children, but if you have five of them you will need a way to differentiate each one. The division of the signs into smaller sections allows the creation of other placements for the planets. This section is an introduction to the division of the signs, the interpretation will be expanded on later. The divisions of the signs are used to assess the planets strength, as the planets will be placed in various signs in different divisions *(vargas)*. The classics introduce the varga charts in the same section as the Rāśi explanations; this is because the vargas are divisions of the Rāśi chakra.

Varga means a division, a separate class, or everything included under a category. When the signs are divided into another chart it is called a varga (a division). The Rāśi is called the D-1 (or first divisional chart). When each sign is divided in half it is called a D-2, or the *Horā* chart. When the Rāśi is divided into three portions it is called a D-3 or a *dreṣkāṇa* chart. There are 16 primary divisions. Below is an example of the sign Aries broken down from the first to its tenth varga. Notice that the Sun at two degrees of Aries is exalted in six of these divisions making it very strong while the Sun at 27 degrees is exalted in only one division and debilitated in another.

<table>
<tr><th>D-1</th><th>D-2</th><th>D-3</th><th>D-4</th><th>D-7</th><th>D-9</th><th>D-10</th></tr>
<tr><td rowspan="10">Aries
0-30°</td><td rowspan="5">Leo
0°-15°</td><td rowspan="3">Aries
0-10°</td><td rowspan="2">Aries
7° 30′</td><td>Aries 4°17′8.57″</td><td>Aries 3°20′</td><td>Aries 3°</td></tr>
<tr><td>Taurus 8°34′17″</td><td>Taurus 6°40′</td><td>Taurus 6°</td></tr>
<tr><td rowspan="3">Cancer
15°</td><td rowspan="2">Gemini 12°51′25″</td><td>Gemini 10°</td><td>Gemini 9°</td></tr>
<tr><td rowspan="4">Leo
10-20</td><td>Cancer 13°20′</td><td>Cancer 12°</td></tr>
<tr><td rowspan="2">Cancer 17°8′34″</td><td>Leo 16°40′</td><td>Leo 15°</td></tr>
<tr><td rowspan="5">Cancer
15-30°</td><td rowspan="3">Libra
22°30′</td><td>Virgo 20°</td><td>Virgo 18°</td></tr>
<tr><td rowspan="2">Leo 21°25′43″</td><td>Libra 23°20′</td><td>Libra 21°</td></tr>
<tr><td rowspan="3">Sag
20-30</td><td>Scorpio 26°20′</td><td>Scorpio 24°</td></tr>
<tr><td rowspan="2">Cap
30°</td><td>Virgo 25°42′52″</td><td rowspan="2">Sag 30°</td><td>Sag 27°</td></tr>
<tr><td>Libra 30°</td><td>Cap 30°</td></tr>
</table>

Each small portion of a division is called an aṁśa (a part or portion). So the D-10 has 10 (*daśa*) portions (*aṁśa*), and is called the *daśāṁśa* in Sanskrit. Parāśara lists 16 primary vargas in Bṛhat Parāśara Horā Śāstra, and each one has a different use relative to a specific area of life. Maitreya, the student of Parāśara asks, "Muni, I have heard from you about the qualities of the planets and the qualities of the signs, please tell me about the divisions of the signs."

Parāśara replies, "Maitreya, there are 16 vargas that have been described by the great grandfather of the world, Brahma, I will explain them."

Aṁśa	Size°	Name v.3-4[47]	Purpose (consideration, viveka) v.1-7[48]
1	30°	Rāśi	*Deha*, the body and its appearance, [general all aspects of life]
2	15°	Horā	Wealth
3	10°	Dreṣkāṇa	Coborn *(bhrātṛ)*, health, welfare *(saukhya)*
4	7°30′	Turyaṁśa	Blessings, good luck, *(bhāgya)*, [property]
7	4°17`8.5″	Saptāṁśa	Children and grandchildren *(putrāpautra)*
9	3°20′	Navāṁśa	Spouse, consort *(kalatra)*, [skills]
10	3°	Daśāṁśa	Abundant fruits, success, career, *(Mahatphala)*
12	2°30′	Sūryāṁśa	Father, mother, parents, *(pitṛ)*
16	1°52′30″	Ṣoḍāśāṁśa	Comfort and prosperity *(sukha)* or lack of it (asukha), vehicles *(vāhana)*
20	1°30′	Viṁśāṁśa	Worship *(upāsana)*
24	1°15′	Vedabāhvāṁśa	Knowledge, learning, school, science *(vidyā)*
27	1°6′40″	Bhāṁśa	Strengths (bala) and weaknesses *(abala)*
30	1°00′	Triṁśāṁśa	Results of misfortune, bad-luck *(ariṣṭaphala)*
40	0°45′	Khavedāṁśa	Good *(śubha)* and bad *(aśubha)*, [also used for maternal lineage]
45	0°40′	Akṣavedāṁśa	All indications, [paternal lineage]
60	0°30′	Ṣaṣṭyāṁśa	All indications, [karma from previous life]

Parāśara then gives to examples. He says that a planet placed in a malefic *ṣaṣṭyāṁśa* will hurt its house significations, and a planet placed in a benefic *ṣoḍāśāṁśa* will ensure prosperity. In this way, the vargas will show the strength of a planet in different areas of life.

One should always see the planet's sign in both Rāśi and Navāṁśa to make an accurate assessment of the planet. The Navāṁśa will show what resources and blessings a person has in their life. The Rāśi will show what a person does with those resources. For a simplified example, if the planet Mercury (which rules speech) is exalted in the Rāśi, it can make the person a good speaker, but if it is debilitated in the Navāṁśa the person may have nothing to speak about, or little opportunity to speak. If the planet is debilitated in Rāśi the person will not be a good speaker, but if it is exalted in the Navāṁśa the person will have lots to speak about and many opportunities to lecture. These blessings in the Navāṁśa will not be utilized unless the Rāśi has strength to utilize them. And the utility of the Rāśi will not be able to achieve its heights unless it is supported by the Navāṁśa. Therefore the various strengths and weaknesses of the placements in the vargas need to be analyzed together. When a planet is in the same sign in Rāśī and Navāṁśa it is called *vargottama*, and this makes it very strong for its indications. The first portion of chara signs, the middle portion of sthira signs, and the last portion of dual signs is vargottama.

[47] Bṛhat Parāśara Horā Śāstra, Ṣoḍaśavargadyāya
[48] Bṛhat Parāśara Horā Śāstra, Vargavivekādayāya

Introduction to Divisional Deities

Besides the grahas being in different signs, the vargas are each ruled by various devattas. These deities are used to better understand the planet in that area of life and for use as remedies.

D2	Horā Lord (0-15°)	Horā Lord (15-30°)
Aries	Sun (Devas)	Moon (Pitṛs)
Taurus	Moon (Pitṛs)	Sun (Devas)
Gemini	Sun (Devas)	Moon (Pitṛs)
Cancer	Moon (Pitṛs)	Sun (Devas)
Leo	Sun (Devas)	Moon (Pitṛs)
Virgo	Moon (Pitṛs)	Sun (Devas)
Libra	Sun (Devas)	Moon (Pitṛs)
Scorpio	Moon (Pitṛs)	Sun (Devas)
Sagittarius	Sun (Devas)	Moon (Pitṛs)
Capricorn	Moon (Pitṛs)	Sun (Devas)
Aquarius	Sun (Devas)	Moon (Pitṛs)
Pisces	Moon (Pitṛs)	Sun (Devas)

The first division of signs is the Horā. It takes a sign approximately two hours to rise. It takes one hour (*horā*) for 15 degrees of a sign to rise. The horā chart (D-2) is the division of the sign into these 15 degree portions. There are only two lords of the D-2, the Sun and the Moon. The first horā of an odd sign is ruled by the Sun and the second horā is ruled by the Moon. The first horā of an even sign is ruled by the Moon and the second portion by the Sun. The Sun relates to the Devas and the Moon relates to the Pitṛs (the Ancestors). The Devas or Ancestors therefore become the deity of a planet relative to wealth and sustenance. Masculine planets are stronger in solar horās, and feminine planets are stronger in lunar horās. The Horā chart relates to wealth and sustenance, similar to the indication of the second house. Those who practice business astrology will focus on this divisional chart in great depth.

D3	1st (0-10°)	2nd (10-20°)	3rd (20-30°)
Aries	Aries Movable Rajas Manuśya Śrī Durvāsa	Leo Fixed Tamas Rākṣasa Śrī Agastya	Sagittarius Dual Sattva Devata Śrī Nārada
Tau	Taurus Fixed Tamas Rākṣasa Śrī Agastya	Virgo Dual Sattva Devata Śrī Nārada	Capricorn Movable Rajas Manuśya Śrī Durvāsa
Gem	Gemini Dual Sattva Devata Śrī Nārada	Libra Movable Rajas Manuśya Śrī Durvāsa	Aquarius Fixed Tamas Rākṣasa Śrī Agastya
Can	Cancer Movable Manuśya Śrī Durvāsa	Scorpio Fixed Rākṣasa Śrī Agastya	Pisces Dual Devata Śrī Nārada
Leo	Leo Fixed Rākṣasa Śrī Agastya	Sagittarius Dual Devata Śrī Nārada	Aries Movable Manuśya Śrī Durvāsa
Virgo	Virgo Dual Devata Śrī Nārada	Capricorn Movable Manuśya Śrī Durvāsa	Taurus Fixed Rākṣasa Śrī Agastya
Libra	Libra Movable Manuśya Śrī Durvāsa	Aquarius Fixed Rākṣasa Śrī Agastya	Gemini Dual Devata Śrī Nārada
Sco	Scorpio Fixed Rākṣasa Śrī Agastya	Pisces Dual Devata Śrī Nārada	Cancer Movable Manuśya Śrī Durvāsa
Sag	Sagittarius Dual Devata Śrī Nārada	Aries Movable Manuśya Śrī Durvāsa	Leo Fixed Rākṣasa Śrī Agastya

D3	1st (0-10°)	2nd (10-20°)	3rd (20-30°)
Cap	Capricorn Movable Manuśya Śrī Durvāsa	Taurus Fixed Rākṣasa Śrī Agastya	Virgo Dual Devata Śrī Nārada
Aqu	Aquarius Fixed Rākṣasa Śrī Agastya	Gemini Dual Devata Śrī Nārada	Libra Movable Manuśya Śrī Durvāsa
Pisces	Pisces Dual Devata Śrī Nārada	Cancer Movable Manuśya Śrī Durvāsa	Scorpio Fixed Rākṣasa Śrī Agastya

Parāśara Dreṣkaṇa

The division of the chart into three portions (aṁśas) of ten degrees each is called the dreṣkaṇa (which has many variations). Each sign is divided into three parts. The first portion is the sign itself, the second is the sign that is fifth from it, and the third portion is the sign that is ninth from the original sign. Therefore the dreṣkaṇa divides each sign into the three qualities (guṇas) it is in trines to.

For example, in the fire sign Aries the first ten degrees is *chara* fire (Aries), the second ten degrees is *sthira* fire (Leo), the third ten degrees is *dvisvabhāva* fire (Sagittarius). In the same way, the earth sign Taurus is divided into sthira, dvisvabhāva and chara earth signs. Gemini is divided into dvisvabhāva, chara, sthira air signs. Each sign is divided into the guṇas of its element.

Each portion in the D-3 is ruled by a Ṛṣi; if the aṁśa is chara (moveable) it is ruled by the Ṛṣi Durvāsa, who is known for his power and his anger. If it is a sthira (fixed) sign it is ruled by Ṛṣi Agastya, one of the seven great Ṛṣis of the big dipper and associated with Jyotiṣa. The dvisvabhāva (dual) signs are ruled by the deva Ṛṣi Nārada, related to the all-pervasive nature of Viṣṇu.

In the previous section of this chapter, the 12 signs of the zodiac were first understood as ***one***, they each had an individual ruler. Then the signs were labeled into ***two*** categories, odd and even (yin and yang). Then the signs were categorized into the ***three***, the three qualities of chara, sthira, and dvisvabhāva, or rajas, tamas and sattva. Then the signs were categorized into ***four***, earth, water fire and air. These significations all need to be added together to understand the root principles of the signs. Aries is ruled by Mars, it is a male/odd sign, it is chara (moveable), and it is of the fire element. From this information all the basic knowledge of the sign's nature arises.

In this section on rāśi divisions, the signs are individually divided into parts within themselves. The 12 signs of the zodiac were first categorized into odd and even (yin/yang). In the vargas they are divided individually into yin and yang with the D-2. Then the signs of the zodiac were categorized into the three qualities, and in the D-3 the individual sign is divided into the three qualities. Then the 12 signs are categorized into the four elements, and in the D-4 the individual signs are divided into the four elements. In the same way, humans have a particular nature, as a sign ruled by a planet. Humans are either male or female on the outside. But on the inside, each person has male and female aspects in their being. A person may be the nature of rajas like Aries, but inside themselves they still have all three guṇas. In the same way, each sign is divided into one of the four elements but inside it will still contain some aspect of all four elements.

Chaturthāṁśa

The fourth divisional chart, relates to the blessings one attains in life. It also relates to property, land ownership and a person's situation at home. The first quarter of the sign is ruled by the sign itself, the next quarter is ruled by the next sign in a kendra to it (the 4th sign from the original). The third quarter is the second kendra from the original sign (the 7th sign from original), and the fourth quarter is the last kendra to the original sign (10th sign from original). In this way each guṇa is divided into all four elements. For example, Aries is chara and is composed of chara fire (Aries), chara water (Cancer), chara air (Libra) and chara earth.

D4	Deity	Aries	Tau	Gem	Can	Leo	Virgo	Libra	Sco	Sag	Cap	Aqu	Pisc
(0* - 7*30′)	***Sanaka***	Aries	Tau	Gem	Can	Leo	Virgo	Libra	Sco	Sag	Cap	Aqu	Pisc
(7*31′ - 14*59″)	***Sānanda***	Can	Leo	Virgo	Libra	Sco	Sag	Cap	Aqu	Pisces	Aries	Tau	Gem
(15* - 22*29′)	***Kumāra***	Libra	Sco	Sag	Cap	Aqu	Pisces	Aries	Tau	Gem	Can	Leo	Virgo
(22*30′ - 7*30′)	***Sanātana***	Cap	Aqu	Pisces	Aries	Tau	Gem	Can	Leo	Virgo	Libra	Sco	Sag

Saptāṁśa

The D-7 relates to creative endeavors and children. The D-7 starts what are called the cyclic ordered divisions. Each division is ruled in the natural order of the Rāśi chakra. Every odd sign lines up to start its division with its own sign. The lords of the varga are the various *rasas* (tastes/juices/ emotions). In the odd signs the first rasa is kṣāra.

In this varga, the odd/masculine signs start with kṣāra (acidic juice), while the even/ feminine signs end with kṣāra. The even signs start with cooling jala (plain water), while the odd signs end with jāla. The odd even variation is a regular feature in varga charts. There are 84 saptāṁśas in the zodiac, 42 in odd signs and 42 in even signs.

	Odd	1	3	5	7	9	11
Division/Degrees	**Rasa**	**Aries**	**Gemini**	**Leo**	**Libra**	**Sag**	**Aqu**
1st (0 - 4* 17′)	Kṣāra *(acidic juice)*	Aries	Gemini	Leo	Libra	Sag	Aqu
2nd (4*-18′ - 8*-33′)	Kṣīra *(Milk)*	Taurus	Cancer	Virgo	Scorpio	Cap	Pisces
3rd (8*-34′ - 12*-50′)	Dadhi *(Curd)*	Gemini	Leo	Libra	Sag	Aqu	Aries
4th (12*-51′ - 17*-07′)	Ghṛta *(Ghee)*	Cancer	Virgo	Scorpio	Cap	Pisces	Taurus
5th (17*-08 - 21*-24′)	Ikṣu *(Sugarcane)*	Leo	Libra	Sag	Aqu	Aries	Gemini
6th (21*25′ - 25*-41′)	Madhu *(Honey)*	Virgo	Scorpio	Cap	Pisces	Taurus	Cancer
7th (25*-42′-30*)	Jala *(Pure Water)*	Libra	Sag	Aqu	Aries	Gemini	Leo
	Even	**2**	**4**	**6**	**8**	**10**	**12**
Division/Degrees	**Rasa**	**Taurus**	**Cancer**	**Virgo**	**Scorpio**	**Cap**	**Pisces**
1st (0 - 4* 17′)	Jala *(Pure Water)*	Scorpio	Cap	Pisces	Taurus	Cancer	Virgo
2nd (4*-18′ - 8*-33′)	Madhu *(Honey)*	Sag	Aqu	Aries	Gemini	Leo	Libra
3rd (8*-34′ - 12*-50′)	Ikṣu *(Sugarcane)*	Cap	Pisces	Taurus	Cancer	Virgo	Scorpio
4th (12*-51′ - 17*-07′)	Ghṛta *(Ghee)*	Aqu	Aries	Gemini	Leo	Libra	Sag
5th (17*-08 - 21*-24′)	Dadhi *(Curd)*	Pisces	Taurus	Cancer	Virgo	Scorpio	Cap
6th (21*25′ - 25*-41′)	Kṣīra *(Milk)*	Aries	Gemini	Leo	Libra	Sag	Aqu
7th (25*-42′-30*)	Kṣāra *(acidic juice)*	Taurus	Cancer	Virgo	Scorpio	Cap	Pisces

Navāṁśa

The D-9 chart is one of the most used divisional charts. It is always referred to before giving any statements or predictions. Twelve signs divided by nine divisions is 108 aṁśas. The signs are cyclic and the chara (moveable) signs start with their own sign. It shows the support and resources of a planet indicated by its strength. It shows the skills that one has carried over from previous lives. It also shows the nature of the spouse in one's life. The signs are either of deva, rākṣasa (demon), or manuśya (mankind) temperment. The deva signs relate to sattva and the search for knowledge. Manuśya signs relate to mankind and the search for wealth. Rākṣasa signs relate to the search for power and dominion.

D9	Aries	Taurus	Gemini	Cancer	Leo	Virgo	Libra	Scorpio	Sag	Cap	Aqu	Pisces
0* - 3*20′	Aries Movable Rajas Manuśya Brahma	Cap Movable Rajas Manuśya Brahma	Libra Movable Rajas Manuśya Brahma	Cancer Movable Rajas Manuśya Brahma	Aries Movable Rajas Manuśya Brahma	Cap Movable Rajas Manuśya Brahma	Libra Movable Rajas Manuśya Brahma	Cancer Movable Rajas Manuśya Brahma	Aries Movable Rajas Manuśya Brahma	Cap Movable Rajas Manuśya Brahma	Libra Movable Rajas Manuśya Brahma	Cancer Movable Rajas Manuśya Brahma
3*21 - 6*39	Taurus Fixed Tamas Rākṣasa Shiva	Aqu Fixed Tamas Rākṣasa Shiva	Scorpio Fixed Tamas Rākṣasa Shiva	Leo Fixed Tamas Rākṣasa Shiva	Taurus Fixed Tamas Rākṣasa Shiva	Aqu Fixed Tamas Rākṣasa Shiva	Scorpio Fixed Tamas Rākṣasa Shiva	Leo Fixed Tamas Rākṣasa Shiva	Taurus Fixed Tamas Rākṣasa Shiva	Aqu Fixed Tamas Rākṣasa Shiva	Scorpio Fixed Tamas Rākṣasa Shiva	Leo Fixed Tamas Rākṣasa Shiva
6*40′- 9*59′	Gemini Dual Sattva Devata Viṣṇu	Pisces Dual Sattva Devata Viṣṇu	Sag Dual Sattva Devata Viṣṇu	Virgo Dual Sattva Devata Viṣṇu	Gemini Dual Sattva Devata Viṣṇu	Pisces Dual Sattva Devata Viṣṇu	Sag Dual Sattva Devata Viṣṇu	Virgo Dual Sattva Devata Viṣṇu	Gemini Dual Sattva Devata Viṣṇu	Pisces Dual Sattva Devata Viṣṇu	Sag Dual Sattva Devata Viṣṇu	Virgo Dual Sattva Devata Viṣṇu
10* - 13*19′	Cancer Movable Manuśya	Aries Movable Manuśya	Cap Movable Manuśya	Libra Movable Manuśya	Cancer Movable Manuśya	Aries Movable Manuśya	Cap Movable Manuśya	Libra Movable Manuśya	Cancer Movable Manuśya	Aries Movable Manuśya	Cap Movable Manuśya	Libra Movable Manuśya
13*20′ - 16*39′	Leo Fixed Rākṣasa	Taurus Fixed Rākṣasa	Aqu Fixed Rākṣasa	Scorpio Fixed Rākṣasa	Leo Fixed Rākṣasa	Taurus Fixed Rākṣasa	Aqu Fixed Rākṣasa	Scorpio Fixed Rākṣasa	Leo Fixed Rākṣasa	Taurus Fixed Rākṣasa	Aqu Fixed Rākṣasa	Scorpio Fixed Rākṣasa
16*40′ - 19*59′	Virgo Dual Devata	Gemini Dual Devata	Pisces Dual Devata	Sag Dual Devata	Virgo Dual Devata	Gemini Dual Devata	Pisces Dual Devata	Sag Dual Devata	Virgo Dual Devata	Gemini Dual Devata	Pisces Dual Devata	Sag Dual Devata
20* - 23*19′	Libra Movable Manuśya	Cancer Movable Manuśya	Aries Movable Manuśya	Cap Movable Manuśya	Libra Movable Manuśya	Cancer Movable Manuśya	Aries Movable Manuśya	Cap Movable Manuśya	Libra Movable Manuśya	Cancer Movable Manuśya	Aries Movable Manuśya	Cap Movable Manuśya
23*20 - 26*39′	Scorpio Fixed Rākṣa	Leo Fixed Rākṣa	Taurus Fixed Rākṣa	Aqu Fixed Rākṣa	Scorpio Fixed Rākṣa	Leo Fixed Rākṣa	Taurus Fixed Rākṣa	Aqu Fixed Rākṣa	Scorpio Fixed Rākṣa	Leo Fixed Rākṣa	Taurus Fixed Rākṣa	Aqu Fixed Rākṣa
26*40′ - 29*59′	Sag Dual Devata	Virgo Dual Devata	Gemini Dual Devata	Pisces Dual Devata	Sag Dual Devata	Virgo Dual Devata	Gemini Dual Devata	Pisces Dual Devata	Sag Dual Devata	Virgo Dual Devata	Gemini Dual Devata	Pisces Dual Devata

There are a few simple fundamentals to remember to make mental calculation of the navāṁśa easy. Each of the moveable signs begins with the sign itself; the first navāṁśa of Aries is Aries, the first navāṁśa of Cancer is Cancer, the first navāṁśa of Libra is Libra, and the first navāṁśa of Capricorn is Capricorn. Each sign begins with the navāṁśa of its moveable sign in trines; the first navāṁśa of Taurus is Capricorn which is the moveable sign of its trine, the first navāṁśa of Gemini is Libra which is the moveable sign of its trine.

In this way if a planet is in the third navāṁśa of Scorpio, and Scorpio begins with Cancer (its moveable trine) then the third navāṁśa is Virgo.

Daśāṁśa

The D-10 relates to the work life. In this chart debilitated planets are good for money as they show that any means is taken to acquire wealth. The deities relate to the lords of the eight directions, upwards and downwards- relating to ten types of work. Odd/male signs start with their own sign showing a self focus, while even/female signs start with the ninth sign from them showing focus on dharma.

D10	Deity	Aries	Taurus	Gemini	Cancer	Leo	Virgo	Libra	Scorp	Sag	Cap	Aqu	Pisces
0* - 3*	***Indra***	Aries	Cap	Gemini	Pisces	Leo	Taurus	Libra	Cancer	Sag	Virgo	Aqu	Scorpio
3* - 5*59′	***Agni***	Taurus	Aqu	Cancer	Aries	Virgo	Gemini	Scorpio	Leo	Cap	Libra	Pisces	Sag
6* -8*59′*	***Yama***	Gemini	Pisces	Leo	Taurus	Libra	Cancer	Sag	Virgo	Aqu	Scorpio	Aries	Cap
9* -11*59′	***Rākṣasa***	Cancer	Aries	Virgo	Gemini	Scorpio	Leo	Cap	Libra	Pisces	Sag	Taurus	Aqu
12* - 14*59′	***Varuṇa***	Leo	Taurus	Libra	Cancer	Sag	Virgo	Aqu	Scorp	Aries	Cap	Gemini	Pisces
15* -17*59′	***Vāyu***	Virgo	Gemini	Scorpio	Leo	Cap	Libra	Pisces	Sag	Taurus	Aqu	Cancer	Aries
18* -20*59′	***Kubera***	Libra	Cancer	Sag	Virgo	Aqu	Scorpio	Aries	Cap	Gemini	Pisces	Leo	Taurus
21* -23*59′	***Īśana***	Scorpio	Leo	Cap	Libra	Pisces	Sag	Taurus	Aqu	Cancer	Aries	Virgo	Gemini
24* -26*59′	***Brahma***	Sag	Virgo	Aqu	Scorpio	Aries	Cap	Gemini	Pisces	Leo	Taurus	Libra	Cancer
27* - 30*	***Ānanta***	Cap	Libra	Pisces	Sag	Taurus	Aqu	Cancer	Aries	Virgo	Gemini	Scorpio	Leo

Viṁśāṁśa

The D-20 relates to spiritual practice and worship. Each sign relates to a form of the divine Mother. This shows the forms of the Mother that give the mind direction in spiritual life.

The calculation is reversed for odd and even signs. This first graph shows the odds signs and the second graph shows the deities for even signs.

D20		Odd Signs					
	Devi	Aries	Gem	Leo	Libra	Sag	Aqu
0* - 1*30′	*Kāli*	Aries	Leo	Sag	Sag	Leo	Aries
1*31′ - 2*59′	*Gauri*	Tau	Virgo	Cap	Taur	Virgo	Cap
3* - 4*29′	*Jayā*	Gem	Libra	Aqu	Gem	Libra	Aqu
4*30′ - 5*59′	*Lakṣmi*	Can	Sco	Pisces	Can	Sco	Pisces
6*- 7*29′	*Vijayā*	Leo	Sag	Aries	Leo	Sag	Aries
7*30′ - 8*59′	*Vimalā*	Virgo	Cap	Tau	Virgo	Cap	Tau
9* - 10*29′	*Sātī*	Libra	Aqu	Gem	Libra	Aqu	Gem
10*30′ - 11*59′	*Tārā*	Sco	Pisces	Can	Sco	Pisces	Can
12* - 13*29′	*Jvālāmukhi*	Sag	Aries	Leo	Sag	Aries	Leo
13*30′ - 14*59′	*Śvetā*	Cap	Tau	Virgo	Cap	Tau	Virgo
15* - 16*29′	*Lalitā*	Aqu	Gem	Libra	Aqu	Gem	Libra
16*30′ - 17*59′	*Bagalāmukhī*	Pisces	Can	Sco	Pisces	Can	Sco
18* - 19*29′	*Pratyangra*	Aries	Leo	Sag	Aries	Leo	Sag
19*30′ - 20*59′	*Śachī*	Tau	Virgo	Cap	Tau	Virgo	Cap
21*- 22*29′	*Raudri*	Gem	Libra	Aqu	Gem	Libra	Aqu
22*30 - 23*59′	*Bhavāni*	Can	Sco	Pisces	Can	Sco	Pisces
24* - 25*29′	*Vardā*	Leo	Sag	Aries	Leo	Sag	Aries
25*30′ - 26*59′	*Jayā*	Virgo	Cap	Tau	Virgo	Cap	Tau
27* - 28*29′	*Tripurā*	Libra	Aqu	Gem	Libra	Aqu	Gem
28*30′ - 30*	*Sumukhī*	Sco	Pisces	Can	Sco	Pisces	Can

D20	Even						
	Devi	Tau	Can	Virgo	Sco	Cap	Pisces
0* - 1*30′	***Dayā***	Sag	Aries	Leo	Aries	Sag	Leo
1*31′ - 2*59′	***Medhā***	Cap	Tau	Virgo	Cap	Tau	Virgo
3* - 4*29′	***Chinnamastā***	Aqu	Gem	Libra	Aqu	Gem	Libra
4*30′ - 5*59′	***Piśāchini***	Pisces	Can	Sco	Pisces	Can	Sco
6*- 7*29′	***Dhūmavati***	Aries	Leo	Sag	Arie	Leo	Sag
7*30′ - 8*59′	***Mataṅgi***	Taur	Virgo	Cap	Tau	Virgo	Cap
9* - 10*29′	***Baglāmukhī***	Gem	Libra	Aqu	Gem	Libra	Aqu
10*30′ - 11*59′	***Bhadrā***	Can	Sco	Pisces	Can	Sco	Pisces
12* - 13*29′	***Arunā***	Leo	Sag	Aries	Leo	Sag	Aries
13*30′ - 14*59′	***Analā/Śītalā***	Virgo	Cap	Tau	Virgo	Cap	Tau
15* - 16*29′	***Piṅgalā***	Libra	Aqu	Gem	Libra	Aqu	Gem
16*30′ - 17*59′	***Chuchchukā***	Sco	Pisces	Can	Sco	Pisces	Can
18* - 19*29′	***Ghorā***	Sag	Aries	Leo	Sag	Aries	Leo
19*30′ - 20*59′	***Varāhī***	Cap	Tau	Virgo	Cap	Tau	Virgo
21*- 22*29′	***Vaiṣṇavi***	Aqu	Gem	Libra	Aqu	Gem	Libra
22*30 - 23*59′	***Sītā***	Pisces	Can	Sco	Pisces	Can	Sco
24* - 25*29′	***Bhuvaneśvarī***	Aries	Leo	Sag	Aries	Leo	Sag
25*30′ - 26*59′	***Bhairavi***	Tau	Virgo	Cap	Tau	Virgo	Cap
27* - 28*29′	***Maṅgala***	Gem	Libra	Aqu	Gem	Libra	Aqu
28*30′ - 30*	***Aparajitā***	Can	Sco	Pisces	Can	Sco	Pisces

Practice Exercises:

Take your own birth chart and using the degrees of the planets, find the division of each planet and its deity in the various varga charts. You will need to use BPHS, or another source to complete this entire chart. An example is done in gray, which can be written over.

	Lagna	Sun	Moon	Mars	Merc	Jupiter	Venus	Saturn	Rāhu	Ketu
D-1	12° Aries	18° Aqu								
	Mars	Saturn								
D-2	Sun/Leo	Moon/Can								
	Devas	Pitṛs								
D-3	Leo	Gemini								
	Agastya	Nārada								
D-4	Cancer									
	Sānanda									
D-7	Gemini									
	Dadhi									
D-9	Cancer									
	Brahma									
D-10	Leo									
	Varuṇa									
D-12										
D-16										
D-20										
D-24										
D-27										
D-30										
D-40										
D-45										
D-60										

Chapter 6

Bhāva: *Houses*

Bhāvas: Houses

There are twelve houses called *bhāvas* in Sanskrit. Bhāva literally means being, existence, occurring, appearance, state of mind, manner of acting, conduct, the state or condition of something, state of being, truth, reality, that which is or exists, all earthly objects. All things that exist and every aspect of our lives can be divided into these 12 areas of existence known as bhāvas.

All over India and throughout the world people use different formats for viewing the houses. These diagrams are called *yantras*; vehicles that display the twelve areas of existence. In the West a circle chakra is used, while in India there are three main chakras.

Chart Types (Chakras)

All three chakras display the same information but each in a unique format, placing emphasis in a different area. It is advised to begin with the North Indian chakra, then to learn the South Indian and finally learning to use the East Indian. Developing familiarity with all three chakras allows one to interpret a chart with a multi-dimensional viewpoint, being able to use any house, planet or sign as the ascendant. This allows for greater flexibility and a more versatile approach as a jyotiṣī.

North Indian	Bhṛgu-chakra	Venus	Counter-clockwise	House based, signs move
South Indian	Guru-chakra	Jupiter	Clockwise	Sign based, houses move
East Indian	Surya-chakra	Sun	Counter-clockwise	Sign based, houses move

North Indian (Bhṛgu Chakra)

The North Indian Chart is made of diamonds and is different from the other two charts in that the houses always remain the same. The lagna is always the first house and is shown in the top-most center diamond. The signs move through the houses in a counter-clockwise motion. This is how the sky looks from earth, the houses remain the same but the stars are moving through the sky. The first house is always sunrise (East) and the 7th house is always sunset (West). The sign rising on the eastern horizon takes residence in the first house and is referred to as the lagna or ascendant. The signs of the zodiac (Rāśi) are then placed in each house in a counter-clockwise direction according to their number following the ascendant.

North Indian Style Chart: Houses

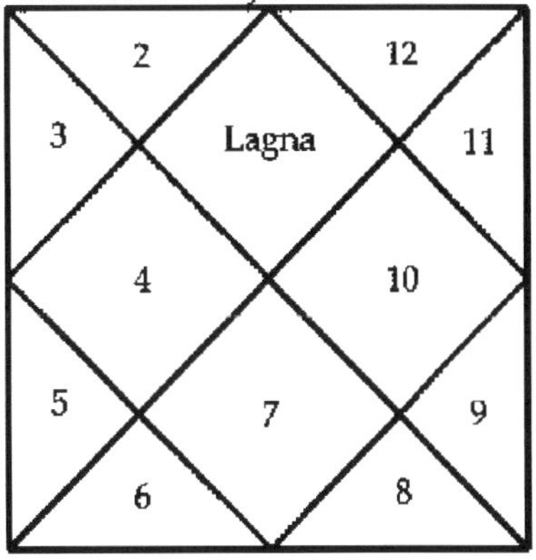

1	Aries	7	Libra
2	Taurus	8	Scorpio
3	Gemini	9	Sagittarius
4	Cancer	10	Capricorn
5	Leo	11	Aquarius
6	Virgo	12	Pisces

Gemini (3rd sign) Ascendant

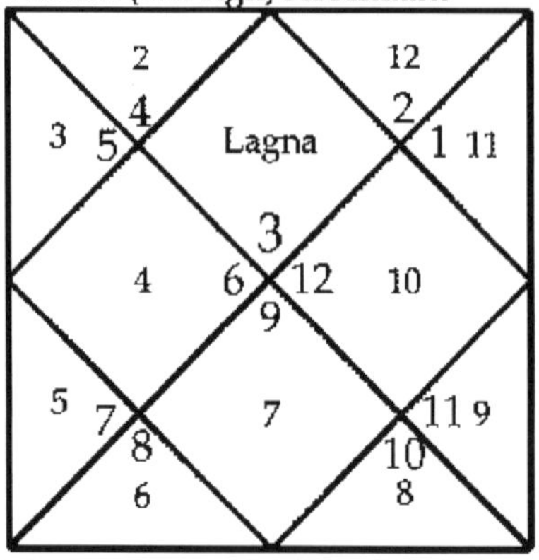

The example chart has Gemini as the Lagna, so the number 3 representing Gemini is placed in the 1st house. The 2nd house then becomes Cancer with the number 4 placed there to represent the sign. The houses will always remain the same, while the signs of the zodiac will circulate accordingly through the houses.

Practice Exercise:

1. Take your own chart and write it by hand. Put the number of the sign in the lagna and write in the numbers of the corresponding signs in each house. This will help to learn to separate the houses from the signs within them.

Bringing Life to the North Indian Chart

The Bhṛgu-chakra is turned on its side from the horizon. The horizon line cuts the first house in half, so half the lagna is under the horizon and the other half is above the horizon. The chart on the left is turned on its side to show the horizon.

The Sun rises in the first house and sets in the seventh house. From the first house to the seventh is the night: reflective of the inward spaces.

The seventh house to the first is the day: showing the visible/outward expression of life. The fourth house is midnight while the tenth house is high noon.

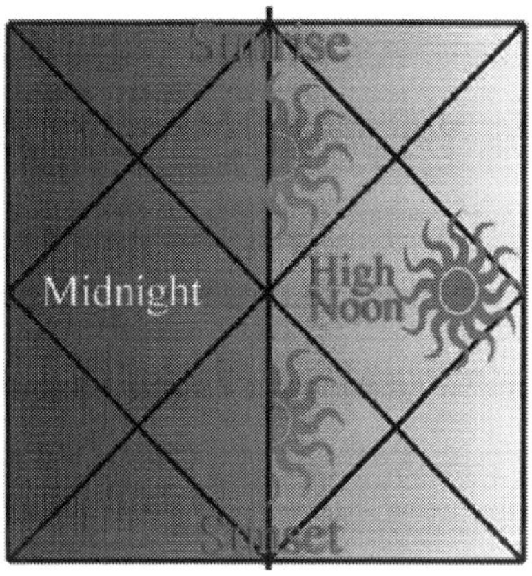

Then examine the Bhṛgu-chakra right side up. When the Sun rises it is seen as a half globe and is right at the ascendant line. It is important to visualize this outside in the environment.

When the chakra is turned on its side, it can be laid over the visible sky to see the position of the planets. All the planets take the same course as the Sun, moving along the ecliptic. When it is turned right side up, it shows the left (night) and right (day) side of oneself.

Using the Sun as the first example as it is the keeper of time, we begin to see its movement within the chart and how that relates to sky above as well as to the houses.

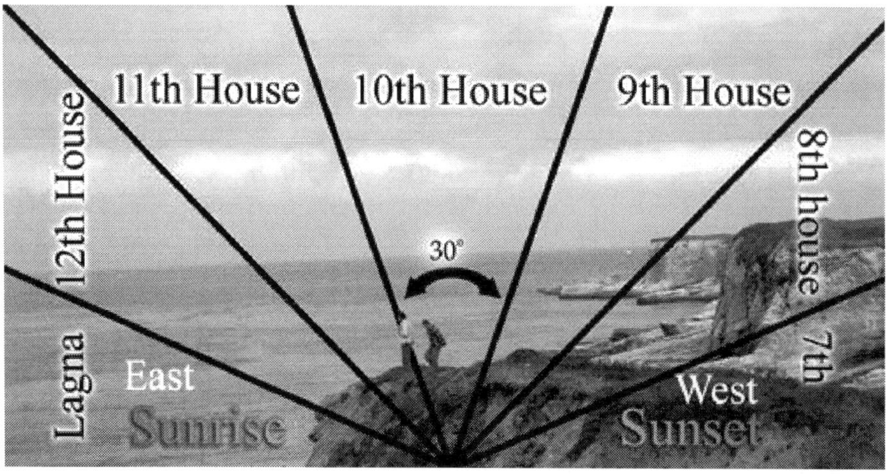

We will generalize for learning sake, and take sunrise at 6:00AM and sunset at 6:00PM. The Sun rises in the center of the lagna at 6AM. It will be in the first house/lagna till 7AM. At that point it will enter the twelfth house and be there from 7 to 9AM, after which time it will enter the 11th house and remain there until 11AM. The Sun will be in the 10th house from 11AM to 1PM. This center most point (near 12PM) where the Sun is the highest and hottest is called the mid-heaven.

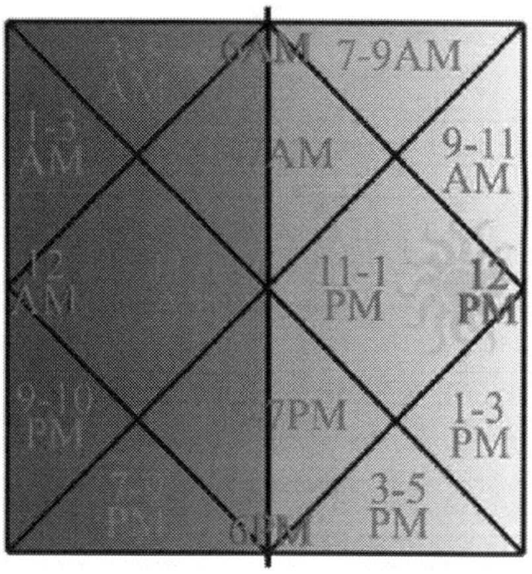

Practice Exercises:

2. Look at the position of the Sun in your chart and see how it correlates to the time of your birth. Take into account some variation at different times of the year depending on the sunrise.
3. Watch the Sun throughout the day and cast a few charts to see how it moves through the houses.

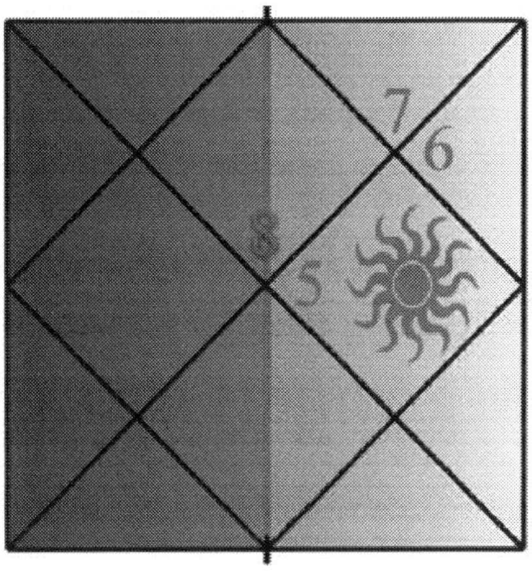

One must become accustomed to reading the chart and perceiving it properly before beginning metaphysical interpretation. The first example chart shows a native born at 12:00PM during the time of the year when the Sun was in Leo. This places the Sun in the 10th house as well as makes the tenth house ruled by Leo. If the Sun is in the 10th house ruled by Leo then the ascendant must be Scorpio as the houses are always the same and Scorpio is four signs from Leo.

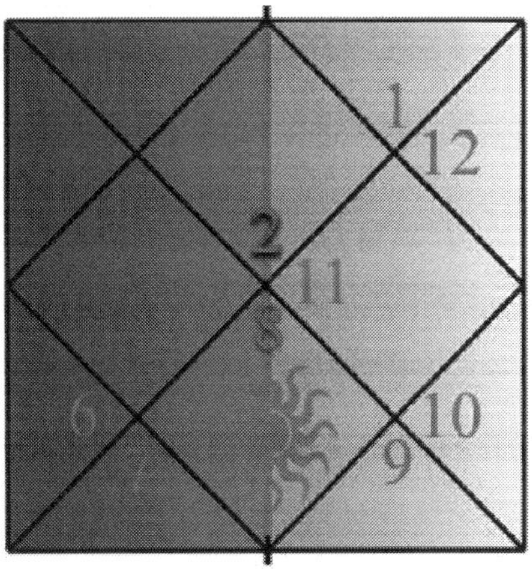

In the second example chart, the native was born at Sunset while the Sun was in Scorpio. This will make the lagna Taurus, so as the Sun set the constellation of Taurus was rising on the eastern horizon.

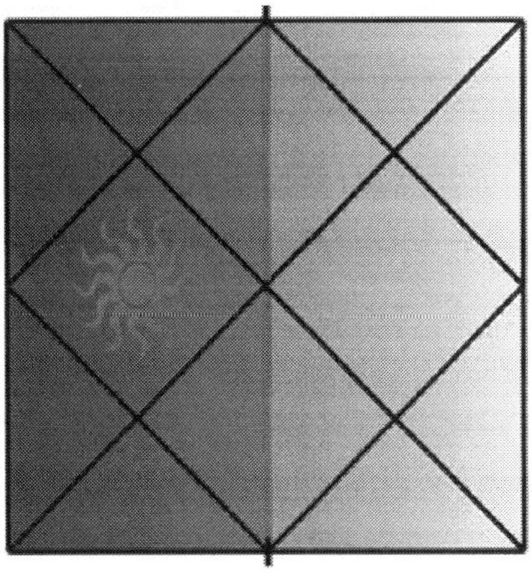

Practice Exercise:

4. The next chart belongs to a native who was born at midnight while the Sun was in Sagittarius. What was the lagna (stars rising on the eastern horizon) when the native was born?

5. In the next example, what house is the Sun in? About what time was the native born? If they were born on November 20th, what would be the lagna? If they were born on April 1st, what would be the lagna?

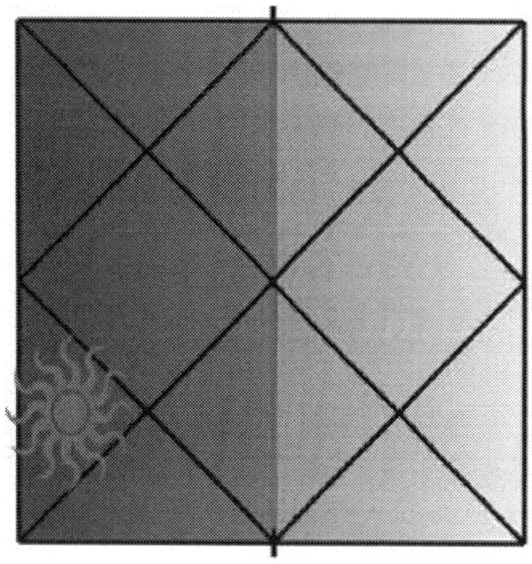

6. In the next example, what house is the Sun in? About what time was the native born? If they were born on November 1st, what would be the lagna? If they were born on April 21st, what would be the lagna?

Now that the houses have a physical reality to you in the sky, you can use the Bhṛgu chakra consciously.

7. Look at your chart to see what was in the sky when you were born and where the planets were above you by bringing the chart into the sky. Where in the sky or below the Earth was your Sun when you were born? What other planets were located in the daylight part of the sky?

8. Take some time to cast the chart just after sunset for your location. Go outside and locate the planets, and the Moon. Predict where they will be before going out by looking at the sky. Predict when Venus will set, or when it will rise and take time to watch this. What times of year is Jupiter visible in the sky? Calculate and observe this.

South Indian Chart(Guru-chakra/Bṛhaspati-chakra)

The South Indian chart is made of squares and places the signs in a clockwise manner. This was used to teach the signs because they never change; instead, the houses are what move in the chart. The ascendant is placed in a sign and the houses proceed clockwise from that sign. The Lagna is marked by a line crossing the house or by either writing Lag (Lagna) or Asc (Ascendant). The clockwise motion of the signs is as it is perceived from the Sun's viewpoint.

In this example, a line is crossed through Gemini, the 3rd sign. Gemini is then the first house (lagna). The Sun is placed in Virgo in the 4th house (it is four signs away from the lagna). The house count is always inclusive of the house the counting starts from. In this way the signs remain the same and the houses will change depending on the lagna.

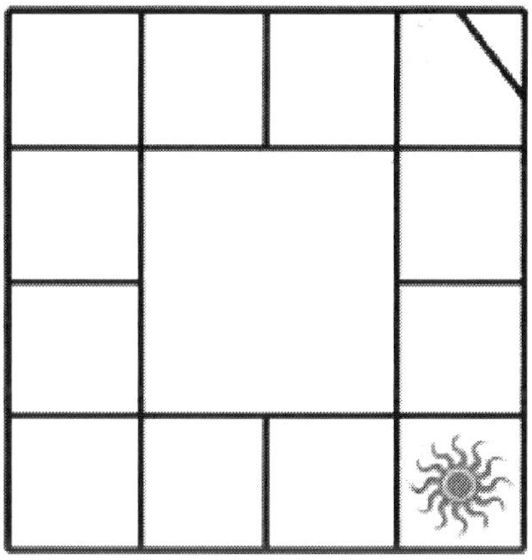

9. In the next South Indian chart, which sign (rāśi) is the lagna? What rāśi and house (bhāva) contains the Sun?

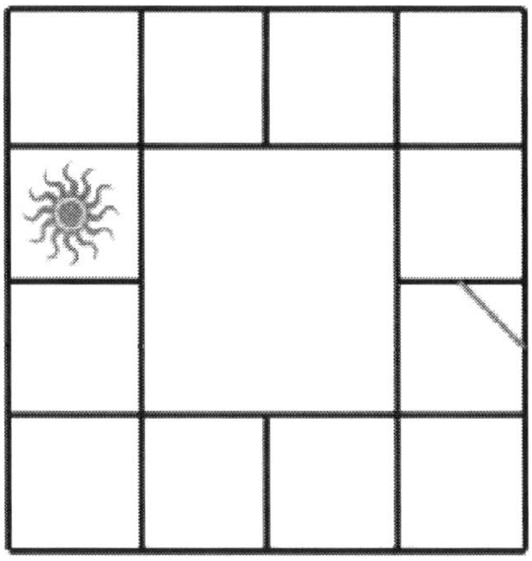

Where the North Indian chart represents the view of the houses from the vantage point of Earth, the South Indian chart represents the movement of the Earth while the signs remain still in the universe. The signs and the Sun remain still and the revolving Earth changes houses as if a higher power outside the earth is watching. This chart is considered to be ruled by Jupiter (called Guru or Bṛhaspati in Sanskrit). It is said to bring prosperity to those who use it, as Jupiter is the kāraka of wealth. This style chart is called the Guru Chakra.

10. First draw your own chart in the South Indian style, placing all the planets in the appropriate signs.

11. Which planets are *uccha* and which planets are *nīca*?

The Guru Chakra is always used when doing *Vāstu* (Indian Feng Shui). The rāśi of Aries is lined up to the Eastern most direction. According to the rules of Vāstu, the center of the room should remain empty. The center is called the *Brahmasthānam* (the place of god). It is the all-encompassing emptiness (śūnya) in the center of everything. For this reason, the Center is best left open and uncluttered.

In the example diagram, Aries has been lined up to the East of a person's bedroom. The doorway falls in Aries. The altar is in Pisces and Aquarius. The circular table is in Gemini. The desk is in Sagittarius and Capricorn while the desk chair is in Scorpio. The bed is falling in Leo and Virgo. If a person was to enter the room and take a seat, we could see what sign they were sitting in. Will they sit by the door in Taurus, or will they sit near the bed in Libra, or will they sit on the desk chair in Scorpio. When looking at the signs upon the Earth one will always use the Guru Chakra.

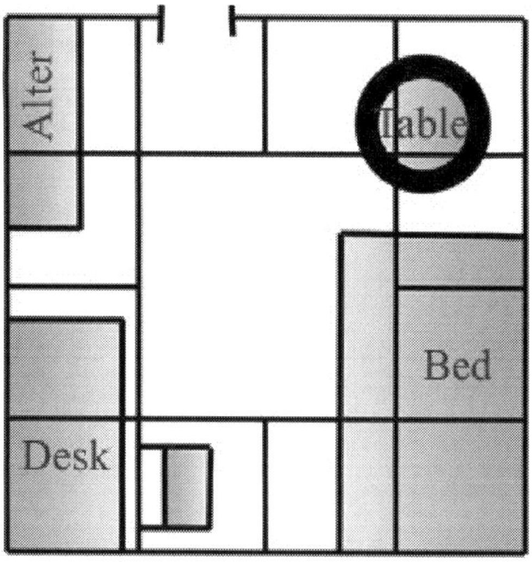

12. Draw a map of the floor plan of your house. Then overlay the Guru Chakra over the house with Aries in the Eastern-most direction. Which room contains your Lagna, which room contains your Lagna lord? [In Vāstu, house design is based upon the *aṣṭakavarga* (strength calculation) of the signs.]

13. Draw a map of your bedroom. Then overlay the Guru Chakra. Where is Venus in your bedroom? If possible, try to arrange your bed to be in the place of Venus, as Venus is the karaka of beds. [The room layout is based on the position of the karaka for the purpose of the room.] If you have a standing light, try to place it in the position of the Sun. Noticing these factors, how suitable is this room for your individual purposes?

East Indian Chart (Sūrya-chakra)

The north Indian chart is made of all diamonds/diagonals; the south Indian is made of all squares/ straight lines. The East Indian chart is made of both diamonds and squares. It is meant to look like the Sun with rays coming from it.

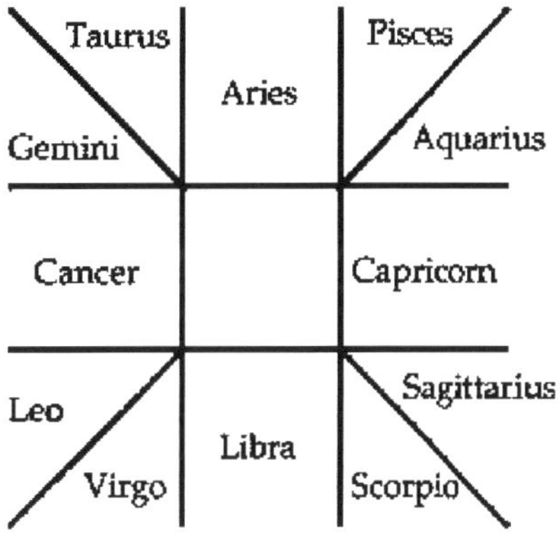

The signs remain in the same position and the houses move. The Ascendant is placed in a sign and the houses are reckoned from it. From there, the signs are placed counter-clockwise in the chart, as they are perceived from Earth looking at the sky.

In the example chart, the ascendant is Gemini and the Sun is in the fourth house in Virgo. The Moon is in the 11th house in Aries.

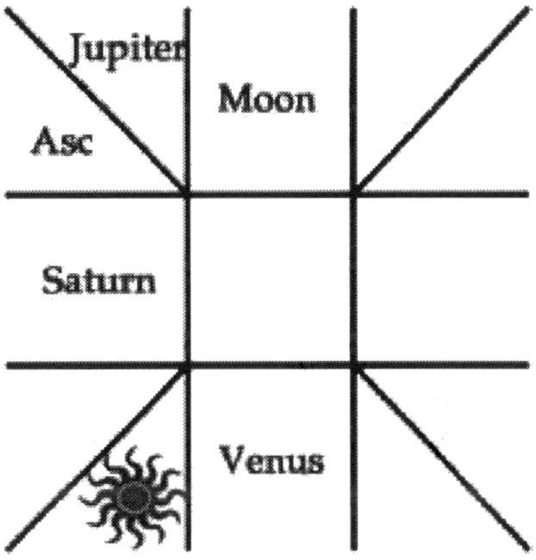

The cara rāśis are all square and in the center. The sthira rāśis are all the triangles that point clockwise against the zodiac. The dvisvabhāva rāśis are triangles that point counter-clockwise with the zodiac.

Sūrya is the planet which rules vision, to see, to perceive. Sūrya must be strong to be able to read an astrological chart. The Sūrya-chakra is considered the best for predictive purposes.

Drawing the chart by Hand

It is important to be able to draw the chart by hand, especially as a beginner. The chart is a yantra of the human incarnation; it contains all potentialities of an individual. It is a sacred diagram and should be studied by hand before moving to computer generated charts. Before drawing any type of chart, first a small mantra to Gaṇeśa is recited. Then one says a small mantra to Sūrya, the Sun god.

The chart itself should be drawn in black pen [when using the North Indian the signs are also written in black]. The planets are placed in the chart with red pen. When the planets are written in red it is said they become alive and will reveal much more to the astrologer.

To be a good astrologer one should be able to read any of the three chakras, but that will come in time. To not get too attached to a single style, and remain flexible it is important to use different chakras.

14. Now that you have a better grasp, draw your chart in each style. Draw the North Indian chart 3 times:
    a. one with Lagna in the first house (physical body)
    b. the second with Moon as the first house (subtle body) which is called Chandra Lagna
    c. the third with Sun as the first house (causal body) which is called Sūrya Lagna.

15. Draw a South Indian chart in the proper procedure with proper colors.

16. Draw an East Indian chart in the same way. Use these hand drawn charts for the practice exercises given in this book.

House Meanings

There are many levels of meaning for each of the 12 houses, reflecting every aspect of life. The chart below shows multiple significations of each house; the primary external and internal significations, the people the house represents and the region of the body ruled by the house.

House	External Significations	People	Body	Internal
1	Body	Self	Head	Strength
2	Wealth, Sustenance	Close family	Throat	Speech
3	Effort	Siblings	Arms, shoulders	Courage
4	Home	Mother	Chest, breasts	Emotional heart, feelings
5	Intelligence, decision ability	Children, students	Solar Plexus	Pratibha-intuition
6	Enemies	Servants/pets	Lower abdomen	Bad habits
7	Business	Spouse	Pelvic region	Desires
8	Debt	Lenders	Genitals	Vulnerability
9	Guru, Teacher	Father	Thighs	Dharma
10	Karma, career, occupation	Boss, biological father	Knees	Respect
11	Gains	Friends	Calves	Achievement
12	Away time, hospital, ashram, foreign lands	Bill collectors, those who cause you loss	Feet	Sleep, rest, meditation

Bhāvat Bhāvam

Bhāvat Bhāvam is an important principle in Jyotiṣa which helps us to understand the various indications of the houses. The principle is that the signs from a house will have the same significations for that particular area of life, as the lagna has for oneself. For example, the fourth house relates to the Mother. The fifth house is the second from the fourth making it the signification of the mother's immediate family. The sixth house is the third house from the fourth making it a signification of the mother's siblings, representing the native's maternal uncles and aunts. The seventh house is the fourth from the fourth representing the native's maternal grandmother. This method of counting from one house to the next is applied to all the houses giving multiple layers of meaning. The Rāśi chart is primarily used for one generation prior, while the D-12, D-40, and D-45 are used for going further back in the family history.

[49] Bṛhat Parāśara Horā Śāstra, Vargavivekādhyāya, v. 33-36

Parāśara defines the houses by various groups: Kendras (angles), Paṇapharas (succedent), Āpoklimas (cadent), Koṇa (trine), Duḥsthānas (suffering houses), Chaturāśrayas (protection), and Upachaya (increasing) . These groupings are important to understand for interpretation as well as in calculating the timing of events.

Kendras

The *Kendras* (angles) are the four center houses: first, fourth, seventh, and tenth. These four houses show the four pillars or goals of life, (ayana) that a human life aims toward to achieve success and find fulfillment. The four goals are dharma, artha, kāma, and mokṣa.

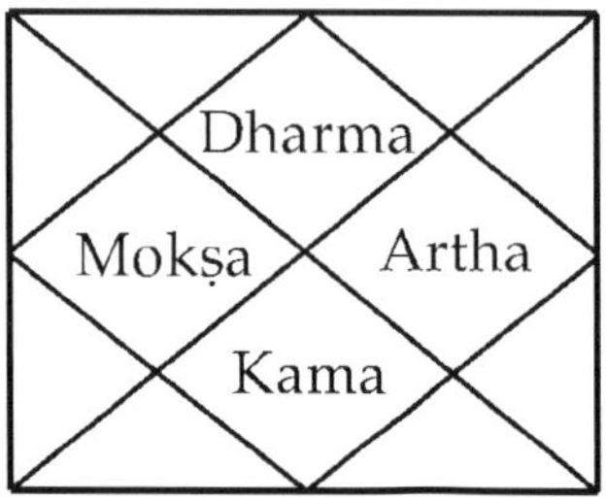

Dharma is defined as the purpose for which an individual has taken birth. A cow has no religion but it has a dharma- to make milk, so dharma is not religion. It is what the person needs to do for themselves and society to better the world. It is an innate aspect of one's contribution to the world. The dharma of a carpenter is to build houses, the dharma of a writer is to write, the dharma of a chair is for providing a place to sit, etc. The natural path and purpose of an object or person is seen from the dharma kendra and its trines (1, 5, 9). The first house shows the innate self, the fifth shows intelligence and learning, and the ninth shows respect for elders and the blessings of guru and knowledge.

Artha is that which sustains; in Western culture represented by money, wealth or acquisition of valuable objects. In ancient times this could have included bartering items as well. Artha is the human goal to attain a material livelihood and financial security done primarily through work and money. One's artha and dharma may be different. For example, a carpenter who does carpentry during the day may be pursuing artha and in the evening teaches yoga practicing his dharma. It is a blessing when one's dharma and artha are the same, and one can actually earn a livelihood through one's dharma. Our work and earning is seen from the artha-kendra and its trines (10, 2, 6). The tenth shows career work, the second shows money saved from that to support oneself, and the sixth shows the hard work and service done.

Kāma is basic desire and the human need for love, enjoyment, emotional and sensory happiness. Kāma relates to sexuality, marriage, partnership, children, and the acquisition of the things we desire in life for our own enjoyment. The fulfillment of kāma is seen from the kāma-kendra and its trines (7, 3, 11). The seventh shows the spouse or partner, the eleventh house shows the money one acquires and the things purchased with it, the third house shows games, hobbies, socialization and all that comes from that.

Mokṣa is freedom or liberation, and refers to our spirituality and spiritual growth. It includes whatever liberates our inner spirit and sense of Being. The mokṣa houses are 4, 8 and 12. The fourth house relates to the heart and its focus or direction (gati) in life. The eighth house trine is the internal work that one needs to do to grow spiritually, it relates to the kuṇḍalinī. The twelfth house is the time one spends alone or in spiritual practice away from the world.

The North Indian chart makes the trines very easy to see and work with. The middle four houses stand out showing the four ayana. The trines to each of these in turn stands out very distinctly. The four inner diamonds (Kendras-1,4,7,10) are called *Viṣṇu-sthānas,* places of Viṣṇu, the energy of sustenance. The trines (Koṇa-1,5,9) are called *Lakṣmi-sthānas,* places of Lakṣmi (the power of sustenance). The trines from each kendra are important to it, and will support the ayana or weaken it.

Paṇaphara and Āpoklima

The fifth house trine from each kendra is called a paṇaphara house. When looking cyclically the house next to every kendra is a paṇaphara. The house following that is an āpoklima, which is also the ninth house from every kendra. The paṇaphara houses relate to the past and the resources one has to achieve the goal and the effort needed to realize that goal . The āpoklimas show the future, what the other two houses are aspiring towards. There is a relation to the natural signs of the zodiac, the natural sthira (fixed) signs relate to the resources of the paṇaphara houses. The dvisvabhāva (dual) signs relate to the end goal of the āpoklima houses. The chara (moveable) signs relate to the natural rajas which instigates the goal in the first place.

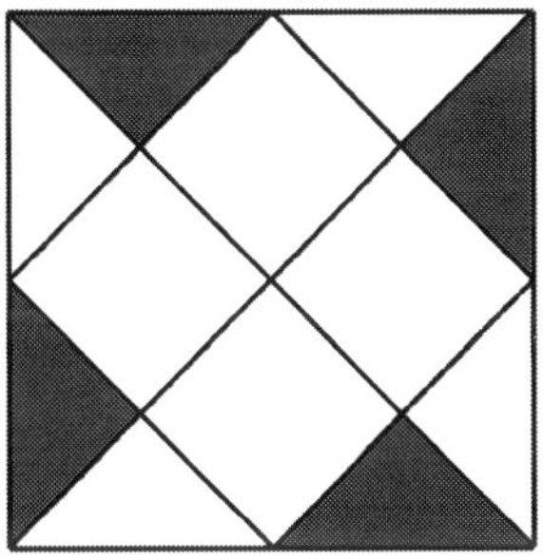

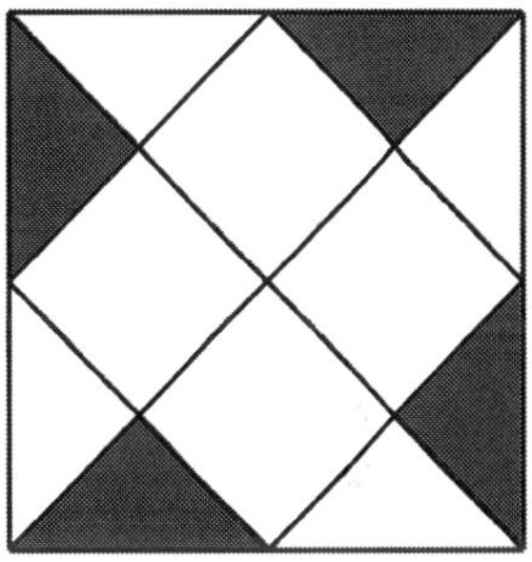

In the dharma trines (1/5/9), the Lagna is the kendra which shows the essence and nature of the person. If Mars is there the person may be a fighter and intend to be a soldier. The fifth house shows the person's intelligence that supports the type of soldier they will be and to what level they will rise. The fifth house is the person's dharma showing their sense of duty to serve and protect. The artha trines (2/6/10) have the tenth house in a kendra, showing the nature of the person's career, what line of work they may be interested in. The second house is the paṇaphara which shows past resources, the person's wealth, their investment potential, as well as the family they come from and the traits picked up from their immediate family. The sixth house is the āpoklima which shows the future, what work or service the person intends to do or how many employees they tend to hire and work with. In this way the houses are analyzed relative to the goals of life.

The overall personality of a person will be shown by the strongest planets in a kendra. The area of life associated with that kendra will show what shapes their personality. The tenth is the strongest kendra (work), next to the seventh (spouse), next to the fourth (home life) and finally the innate personality seen from the lagna.

Practice Exercises:

17. In the translation of the significations of houses (on page 150), notice the use of the Bāvat Bhāvam principle in the significations given for the sixth, ninth and eleventh houses. These small examples point to the multiple ways this principle can be applied. The ninth house shows the wife's brother because it is the third house (siblings) from the seventh house (spouse). Explain the other examples of Bāvat Bhāvam given here.
18. Using the ninth house for father, which house will indicate the father's brothers, and which will show the father's children?
19. Calculate which planets are in which ayana of life. Which ayana has the most planets?
20. Which ayana is the planet ruling the lagna placed in? The Moon? The Sun? Which planets dominate the kendra and shape your personality, and how was it shaped (what ayana experience)?

Dusthāna

There are three dusthāna, often called the trik houses ("the three houses"). *Duḥkha* means pain, suffering, and sorrow, and *sthāna* means place. So the dusthāna are the three houses that cause natural suffering to the individual. These are the sixth house of enemies and disease, the eighth house of debt, suffering, and death, and the twelfth house of loss. Planets in these placements indicate some type of suffering. Malefics in the sixth will make one a good fighter but will give them lots of enemies to fight. Benefics in the sixth will make the native prone to not fight and will make the enemies very smart. Both types of planets become more susceptible to disease when placed in a dusthāna. Planets in the eighth will feel vulnerable and weak. Mercury in the eighth shows high level research and Saturn in the eighth shows knowledge of longevity, but even with benefics there is still suffering. The twelfth house shows loss, secret enemies, and expenses and only two planets handle the 12th house well. Venus in the 12th shows benefits from foreign trade and the bādhakeśa (the obstacle causing planet) does well in the 12th as it is loss of obstacles.

Upachaya

Upachaya means growth, accumulation, elevation. The upachaya houses are those that grow and improve over time. They are the third, sixth, tenth and eleventh houses from the lagna. Kriyamāṇa karma, the karma being created in this life, comes primarily from these houses. Some say they are the houses of free will. Indications of these houses will grow as the person ages. The third house shows how we start a communication, or get what we want. The sixth shows how we handle things when we don't get what we want. The third house is the first response and the sixth house is the second response. Benefics in the third and sixth make a person soft and gentle, while malefics make a person more aggressive and able to defend their viewpoint. The tenth and eleventh show the work we do and what we get for it. The work you choose to do can either better your self and the world or not. What you choose to gain from that work, how you spend the money earned, and the energy put forth into acquiring material gain for pleasure will change your future for better or worse.

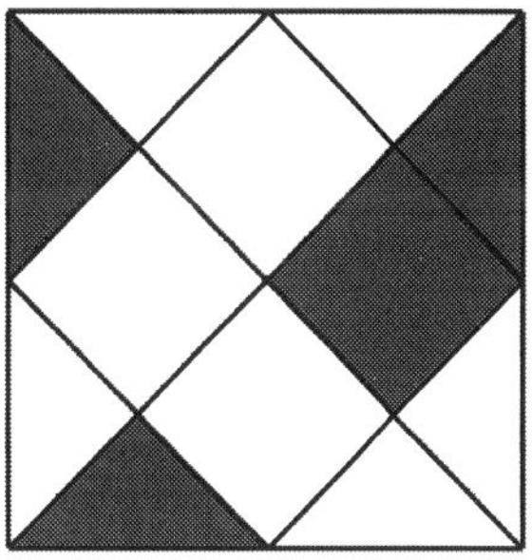

Parāśara: Bhāva-Viveka-Adhyāya

The Ṛṣi Parāśara gives a list of the indications of each house. Adhyāya means chapter and viveka means to discern or distinguish, so the chapter is on the distinguishing factors of each house as given by the Muni (sage).

First House (Lagna-Bhāva): body *(deha)*, appearance/form *(rūpa)*, intellect *(jñāna)*, complexion *(varṇa)*, strength and weaknesses *(bala-abala)*, happiness *(sukha)* and sorrow *(duḥkha)*, innate nature *(svabhāva)*.

Second House (dhana-sthāna/place of wealth): wealth/riches *(dhana)*, gains/food *(dhānya)*, family *(kuṭumba)*, death/longevity *(mṛtyu)*, friends *(mitrika)*, metals *(dhātu)*, precious stones *(ratna)*, and all things of monetary value, etc. *(sarva)*.

Third House (duścikya-house of bad/foolish thoughts): courage, strength, power, heroism, intensity *(vikrama)*, servants/attendants/support *(bhṛtya)*, siblings *(bhrātrādi)*, teaching of the guru or knowledge coming from hearing the guru *(upadeśa)*, short journeys/march/walk *(prayāṇaka)*, parent's death *(pitrorvai maraṇa)*.

Fourth House: vehicles *(vāhana)*, relatives, kindred, friends *(bandhu)*, mother *(matṛ)*, happiness, welfare, comfort *(saukhya)*, purity *(kanya)*, treasures/place for storage of treasures *(nidhi)*, lands/property *(kṣetra)*, and house/home *(gṛha)*.

Fifth house: amulets/sacred diagrams *(yantra)*, sacred spells/prayers *(mantra)*, learning/knowledge *(vidyā)*, intellect *(buddhi)*, management ability *(prabandhaka)*, children *(putra)*, corruption/falling from high position *(rājya-apabhraṁśa)*, mental distress *(dīna)*.

Sixth house: maternal uncle *(mātula)*, causing death *(antaka)*, enemies *(śatru)*, wound, boil, scar, sore, cancer, *(vraṇa)*, step mother *(sapalīmātṛ)*, bearing bow/weapons *(chāpī)*.

Seventh House (jāyā-bhāva): wife/spouse *(jāyā)*, medium distance journey *(madhya-prayāṇa)*, commerce/trade (vāṇijya), misplaced items, momentary loss *(naṣṭa-kṣaṇa)*, death *(maraṇa)*.

Eighth House: longevity *(āyus)*, battle, war, enjoyment of fighting *(raṇa)*, enemies, deceit *(ripu)*, bearing weapons *(chāpī)*, forts *(durga)*, inheritance *(mṛtadhana)*, knowledge of the past and future *(gatyanukādika)*, and all things like this, etc (*sarva*).

Ninth House (dharma-sthāna): Fortunes *(bhāgya)*, wife's brother *(syāla)*, justice *(dharma)*, brother's wife *(bhrātṛpatnyā)*, journeys to holy places/shrines, pilgrimages *(tīrtha-yātrā)*.

Tenth House (vyoma-sthāna/the place of sky): power, rule, authority, royalty *(rājya)*, changeable work, livelihood, present profession (*ākāsha-vṛtti*), respect, honor, arrogance, pride *(māna)*, father *(pitṛ)*, foreign business assignments, living away from home *(pravāsya)*, obligation/debt/duty *(ṛṇa)*.

Eleventh House (bhava sthāna-aquistion/prosperity place): receipt of various valuable items *(nānā-vastubhavasyāpi)*, son's wife *(putra-jāyā)*, income, revenue, gain, profit *(āya)*, growth, increase, prosperity *(vṛddhi)*, farm animals which were used like money in ancient days *(paśu)*.

Twelfth House: expenses, loss, waste, spending *(vyaya)*, knowledge about the enemy/ the working or opportunity of one's secret enemies *(vairivṛttānta)*, one's own losses are to be known *(vyayācchaiva hī jñātavyamītī)*.

These are general aspects of each of the houses. One should not expect one text at one time to explain something as vast as a chakra that represents all aspects of existence. As one's study of Jyotiṣa deepens, there will be various layers that will unfold taking one deeper into the essence of each house. For example, the ninth house represents the guru, yet Parāśara has not mentioned this in his significations of houses. Though, later he teaches that benefics in the ninth make one respectful to elders and teachers while malefics in the ninth house will make a person doubt and disrespect the guru and elders[49]. In this way, the various layers of the houses reveal themselves through other teachings.

Always try to utilize logic and understand why a house relates to a certain area. In some cases there will be disagreement between astrologers, such as whether the ninth or tenth house should be used for showing the father. Logically this is solved in that the tenth house is the seventh from the fourth house, which shows the lover of the mother and therefore the biological father. The ninth is the house which guides you (dharma) and which protects you. The Vedic sages define the father as the one who raises an individual teaching the ways of life and providing protection and shelter, which shows the acting father is the ninth house.

Jyotiṣa is never just logic though, one must balance logic (solar/masculine) with feeling (lunar/feminine) to fully open the third eye and get the complete intuitive understanding. For example, logic memorizes that the fourth bhāva relates to house, home, mother, happiness, and the physical and emotional heart. The sensitive mind can connect how this bhāva shows the home as a reflection of how a person feels, and mother's impact on the emotional reality of the native, and the difference of the person's heart based on the planets placed in the fourth bhāva. Then together one can predict the nature of a person's childhood, happiness and events that influences the individual's life with empathic clarity.

[49]Bṛhat Parāśara Horā Śāstra, Kārakāṁśa-Adhyāya, v.50-53

Bhāveśa: House Lords

Each house contains a sign. The planet ruling this sign becomes the house *(bhāva)* lord *(īśa)*, called the *bhāveśa*. The lord of the lagna is called the lagneśa. This planet's status and placement becomes very important for the house. Parāśara lists indications for each lord in each house in the Bhāveśa-Phala-Adhyāya[50], the chapter on the results/effects of the house lords. Here is a small section related to the Lagneśa in the twelve houses.

Lagna Lord in:

First house: happy and blessed body *(dehasukhabhāg)*, strong arms, good strength *(bhuja-vikramī)*, intelligent, clever *(manasvī)*, unsteady, fickleminded *(cañcala)*, having two wives *(dvibhārya)*.

Second House: strength *(bāla)*, one endowed with earnings or gains *(lābhavān)*, teacher, scholar *(paṇḍita)*, happy *(sukhī)*, well mannered/cultured *(suśīla)*, law abiding *(dharmavi)*, respectable *(mānī)*, having many wives *(bahu-dāra)*, good qualities *(guṇairyuta)*.

Third House: brave as a lion *(siṁha-tulya-parākramī)*, able to accomplish, meeting with success *(sarva-sampadyuta)*, respected *(mānī)*, having two wives *(dvibhārya)*, good intelligence *(matimān)*, happy *(sukhī)*.

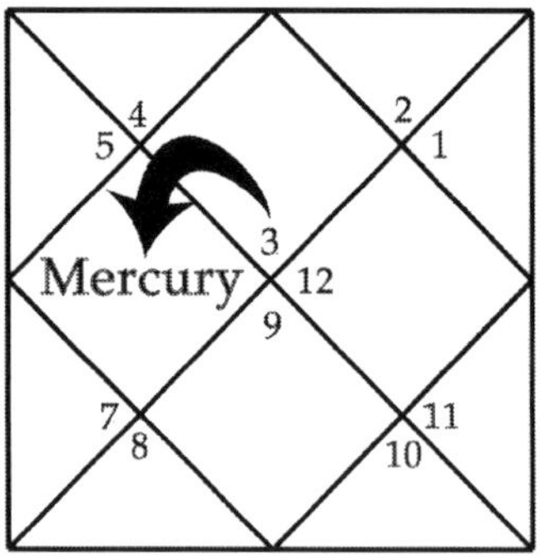

Fourth House: strong *(bāla)*, gives the mother and father happiness *(pita-mātṛ-sukhānvita)*, has many siblings *(bahu-bhrātṛ-yuta)*, having love, affection, passion *(kāmī)*, having good qualities and form *(guṇa-rūpa-samanvita)*.

Fifth House: happiness from children *(suta-saukhya)*, moderate, reasonable *(madhyama)*, loss of first child *(prathama-apatya-nāśa)*, respectable *(mānī)*, easily angered *(krodhī)*, liked by authorities *(nṛpa-priya)*.

Sixth House: troubled by health complaints, lacking happiness through the body *(deha-saukhya-vivarjita)*, problems with enemies if aspected by malefics *(pāpādhye-śatrutaḥ)*, misfortune, affliction, pain if not aspected by benefics *(pīḍā saumyadṛṣṭivivarjite)*.

Seventh House: if the 7th lord is a malefic it hurts the longevity of the partner or the relationship *(bhāryā tasya na jīvati)*, a benefic planet can make the person a wanderer *(śubhe'ṭano)* and poor *(daridra)*, indifferent *(virakta)*, or associated with authority *(nṛpa)*.

[50] See Appendix II

Eighth House: skilled in the knowledge of supernatural powers/occult knowledge *(siddha-vidyā-viśārada)*, diseased *(rogī)*, a thief, dishonest *(caura)*, gets very angry very easily *(mahākrodhī)*, one who gambles or fights *(dyūtī)*, adulterous *(paradāraga)*.

Ninth House: fortunate *(bhāgya)*, well liked by people *(vāñjana-vallabha)*, worshipper of sattva devatās *(viṣṇubhakta)*, clever and eloquent in speech *(paṭurvāgmī)*, happiness from spouse and children and wealth *(dāra-putra- dhanairyuta)*.

Tenth House: having happiness and comforts from father *(pita-saukhya-samanvita)*, leadership, respect, royal honor (nṛpa-mānya), well known among the public, popular *(jane khyātaḥ)*, self acquired wealth, self-made *(svārjita)*.

Eleventh House: always gaining/acquiring *(sadā lābhasamanvita)*, well mannered/ cultured *(suśīla)*, popularity *(khyāta)*, fame *(kīrti)*, many wives *(bahudāra)*, good qualities *(guṇairyuta)*.

Twelfth House: troubled by health complaints, lacking comfort in the body *(deha-saukhya-vivarjita)*, if the graha is not aspected by or conjunct benefics *(śubha-dṛgyoga-varjita)*, the person wastes money on useless/unprofitable items *(vyartha-vyayī)*, and is easily angered *(mahā-krodhī)*.

The lagna lord shows our intelligence and how it is applied. The kāraka for the lagna lord is Jupiter (intelligence). The significations of the house will show how and to what end a person directs the use of their intelligence. The type of house it is will also reveal the nature of the significations of the house. For example, the lagneśa in the second house will show a person who has a lot of wealth as they will apply their intelligence to achieve this end. The second being a positive house allows the significations of the house to do well. The first house shows the health and the body. If the lagneśa is in the second health is ok, but if it goes to the sixth or eighth house the health and body suffer. In this way the significations of the house are affected by the placement of the lord. The placement of the lord of the house *from lagna* shows the experience of that aspect of life. The placement of the lord of a house *from that house itself* shows how that house applies its intelligence.

The second house shows stored wealth, if the house lord is placed in the ninth the person has luck with wealth, if it is in the sixth the person will have loss of wealth through enemies (litigation). In this way, all the houses should be seen and the interpretation becomes an art.

The quality of the sign lord also has an effect on the house it occupies. Beneficial houses have beneficial lords. For example, the ninth lord brings luck into whatever area it is placed. While the twelfth lord brings expenses to whatever house it occupies. The fourth lord brings happiness to whatever house it occupies. The sixth and eighth lords bring trouble along with disease in the houses they are positioned.

Sixth and Eighth Lords

Disease is caused by malefic planets as well as the sixth and eighth lords. The *house placement* of the sixth lord and the *rāśi placement* of the eighth lord become important in determining health problems.

The signs are created by the universe itself and show the innate nature of the native. In this way the eighth lord will show the flaws we have inherited from our family, society and that we have been created with *(nija-doṣa)*. These are internal flaws/weaknesses that we need to work with to purify. If the eighth lord is in Cancer it can show problems with the chest and lungs, independent of the house it is placed in.

The houses are determined by the period in time when the soul took birth and show the karma we create for ourselves. Therefore the sixth lord's house placement takes importance, as it is the negative actions performed against oneself *(ṣaḍripu)*. The sixth lord needs discipline to live in a right way in order to avoid disease caused by it. The sixth lord placed in the fourth house will cause problems with the chest, heart, lungs, independent of what sign it is placed in.

Bādhakasthāna and Bādhakeśa

Bādhaka means hindering or oppressing from an obstacle. Gaṇeśa is asked to remove these obstacles. A particular house becomes a bādhaka house (*bādhaksthāna*) and its lord becomes the obstacle causing graha (*bādhakeśa*). This is a more advanced topic that will be only briefly mentioned here, as the bādhakeśa works on the subtle level and is only remedied with subtle methods.

The bādhakeśa changes depending on the quality of the lagna. For a movable (*cara*) lagna the bādhakasthāna is the eleventh house making the eleventh lord the bādhakeśa. For a fixed (*sthira*) lagna the bādhakasthāna is the ninth house making the ninth lord the bādhakeśa. For a dual (*dvisvabhāva*) lagna the bādhakasthāna is the seventh house making the seventh lord the bādhakeśa.

The kāraka for the bādhakeśa is Rahu, which means that the planet which becomes badhākeśa will some times act like Rahu causing obstacles to the house it is placed in. It becomes an important planet in medical astrology (*āyur-jyotiṣa*) as it will confound diseases and make them hard to cure. In other areas it will create blockages, delays, confusions and other obstacles.

Cara	Sthira	Dvisvabhāva
Aries, Cancer, Libra, Capricorn	Taurus, Leo, Scorpio, Aquarius	Gemini, Virgo, Sagittarius, Pisces
11th House	9th House	7th House
11th Lord	9th Lord	7th Lord

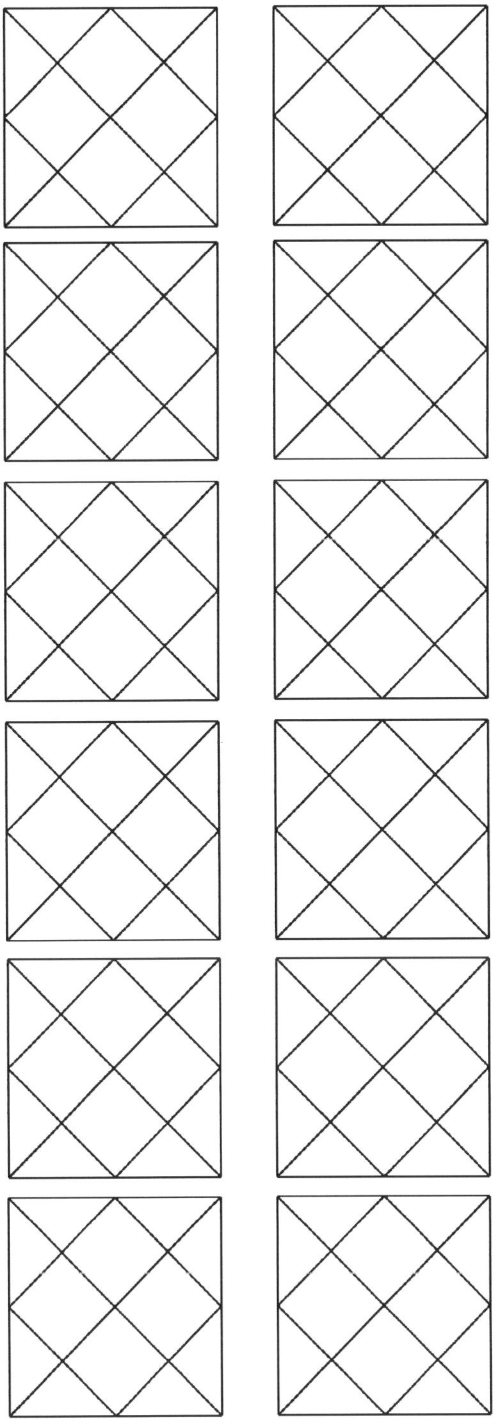

Practice Exercises:

21. Calculate all the house lords and their placements in your chart, for example, First lord Jupiter in First house (own sign), Second lord Mars in seventh house (neutral sign), Third lord Venus in fifth house (neutral sign).

22. Draw out each Lagna, accounting for all twelve. Analyze the planets lording beneficial houses and the planets lording malefic houses for each ascendant. Notice the relationship between these beneficial and malefic lords for each lagna. Get familiar with the house lord situation for each Lagna.

23. Calculate the bādhakasthāna and bādhakeśa for each lagna.

24. Look through the *Bhāveśa-Phala-Adhyāya* (chapter on Effect of Bhāva Lords) in Bṛhat Parāśara Horā Śāstra translated in appendix II. Then choose one house lord and make your own indications for its placement in each of the twelve houses. This will allow you to utilize the significations in a practical way.

Bhāva Kāraka

Each house has a *primary kāraka* that shows the natural significations of the house, and some have a few *secondary kārakas*. This is where the significations of the planets and houses begin to mix for proper analysis. When the bhāva kāraka is well placed in angles or trines it strengthens the qualities of that house.

For example, the fifth house is intelligence and indicates the person's mental abilities. Jupiter is the planet that significates intelligence, if Jupiter is weak, the fifth house cannot be completely strong on its own. If Jupiter is strong, the fifth house cannot be completely weak. If the fifth house has malefics in it, this could show the person makes wrong decisions. If Jupiter is also weak, the intelligence *(dhi)* is less in the person and they will have a tendency to make wrong decisions (or use bad judgment). If Jupiter is strong, they will be more aware of the wrong choices they make and work harder to avoid the house inclination. In this same way, benefics in the fifth show a person making good decisions. If Jupiter is weak, the person can have a good idea of what to do but lack the intelligence to know the exact path, or lack the full knowledge of the correct choice, or lack the intelligence to follow their own good advice. In this way, the house and its kāraka are taken into account to give the final results of the house.

Kāraka-Adhyāya v.34	
Lagna	Sun
2nd	Jupiter
3rd	Mars
4th	Moon
5th	Jupiter
6th	Mars
7th	Venus
8th	Saturn
9th	Jupiter
10th	Mercury
11th	Jupiter
12th	Saturn

Some houses have multiple kārakas. For example the fourth house can show Mother, property, houses, and vehicles. The kāraka for mother is the Moon, for property is Mars, for houses is Ketu, for vehicles is Venus. So if the fourth house is weak, but the Moon is strong the mother does not suffer much. If the fourth house is weak and Venus is weak, then the person will have trouble with vehicles. If the fourth house is strong and Ketu is weak, the person will not have the best of luck with houses, but if Mars is strong they may do well with properties. Therefore when looking at the strength of a signification of the house, one must look at the house and the kāraka of the house. The tenth house has four kārakas: Mercury for skills, Saturn for hard work, Jupiter for the intelligence in the work and its fruits, and Sun for the respect of one's position. The seventh house has Jupiter for husband and marriage, and Venus for wife and love.

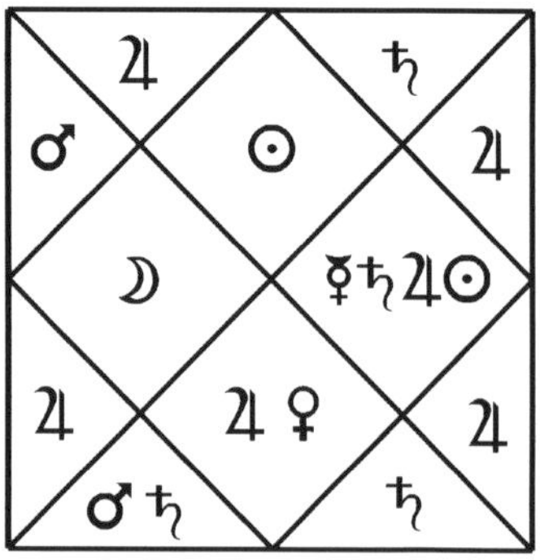

Graha-Dṛṣṭi: Aspects of Planets

Full Graha-Dṛṣṭi	
Saturn	3rd & 10th
Mars	4th & 8th
Jupiter	5th & 9th
Rahu	5th, 9th, (2nd)
All	7th

The planets each aspect particular houses from themselves. Rāśi aspect shows that which is *supporting* or afflicting the sign and house receiving the aspect. Graha aspect shows what the planet *desires*. It shows what the planet is *looking* at because it wants to affect, intervene and influence that area of life (signified by the house) or affect the particular planet it is looking at. It is the natural innate desire *(svabhāva)* of the planet to look *(dṛṣṭi)* in this way.

All planets cast a full aspect *(pūrṇa dṛṣṭi)* on the seventh house from itself. Mars gives a full aspect on the 4th and 8th house from its position. Jupiter gives full aspect on the 5th and 9th house from its position, and Saturn casts a full aspect on the 3rd and 10th from its position. Full aspects are the most important as all other aspects are partial- as can be seen in the chart below. Full aspects should be memorized and one should be able to see them quickly when analyzing a chart. In general, planets are taken to aspect the entire house. Though specific strength of an aspect on a planet can also be mathematically calculated with its degrees and is called *sphuṭa-dṛṣṭi*.

	3rd & 10th	5th & 9th	4th & 8th	7th
Saturn	**Full**	One foot (¼)	Two feet (½)	Full, Three feet (¾)
Jupiter	Three feet (¾)	**Full**	One foot (¼)	Full, Two feet (½)
Mars	Two feet (½)	Three feet (¾)	**Full**	Full, One foot (¼)
All	One foot (¼)	Two feet (½)	Three feet (¾)	**Full**

In other classics, Rāhu is given full aspects of the 5th, 9th and 12th from its placement. But Rāhu aspects in reverse, so the 12th house aspect falls on the 2nd house from Rāhu, the 5th house aspect falls on the ninth house from Rāhu, and the 9th house aspect falls on the 5th house. Ketu is headless, and therefore has no eyes to see. Without eyes to see it has no sight (*dṛṣṭi*), and no *desires* for this world and therefore no *graha aspects*.

Benefic aspects strengthen a planet and sign, malefic aspects damage a planet and sign. Benefics aspecting a bad combination provide the individual with ways to improve the situation. Malefics aspecting a bad combination make a negative situation more severe or more likely to happen as it increases the intensity of the karma. Two or more malefics aspecting a house (by graha dṛṣṭi) shows a *curse* (dṛḍha karma for suffering) to the house or grahas placed in the house. Two or more benefics similarly aspecting a house show a *blessing* or area of good results to the house and its contents.

The aspect of a planet to its own sign is very good protection for the house, even if it is a malefic. A malefic will never hurt its own bhāva, as a gangster takes care of his own home. Though the malefic aspect will not be good for the planets inside the house, and will still cause suffering to them. If you have a mean landlord it is better that they don't look over your shoulder.

Houses in Praśna Charts

In praśna charts, the houses have different meanings. Praśna are the charts cast for specific questions where the sky holds the answer at the moment the question is asked. The houses relate to the question being asked. Here are two examples of how to look at a chart for specific types of praśna.

The first diagram shows a bhojana (feeding/eating) question. If someone asked a bhojana question before going out, 'what am I going to have for lunch?' You would cast a chart for the moment they asked the question and interpret accordingly. If Mars is in the second house the plate they eat on is cracked, if Mars is in the fourth house their food is burnt, if Mars is in the eighth house they added chilies on their food. If Mars was in the sixth house they were in an agitated mood while they ate. If Mars was in the ninth house they ate with some policemen, or soldiers. If Mars is in the eleventh house they argued while they ate. In the same way if Moon is in the eleventh house they talked about their feelings while they ate. If Jupiter is in the eleventh, they will have spiritual discussion while eating.

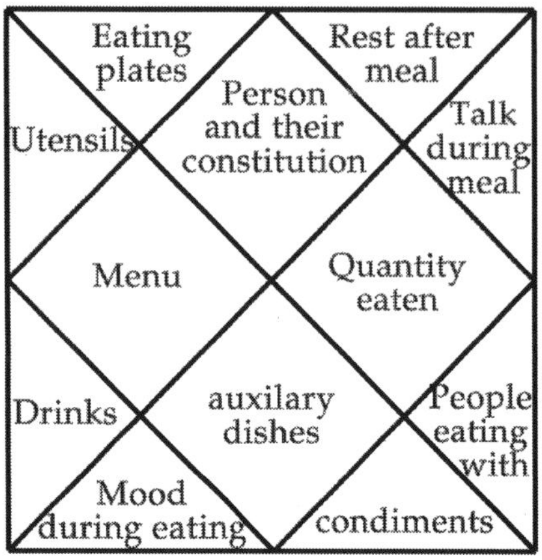

For political forecasts one can also do a praśna. Kings and businessmen always need to know the future as many important decisions are at stake. In these cases the lagna represents the king, or president, or prime minister. The second house will represent the country's treasury. The third house which normally represents what a person may hold in their hand, pen, hammer, gun, will show the army of the nation. The fifth house will show the country's diplomacy. If Rāhu or a malefic is placed in the fifth the person will challenge a nation much bigger than himself to war. If Jupiter is in the fifth the politics will insure prosperity for everyone. This shows how the use of houses will change depending on the intention and question.

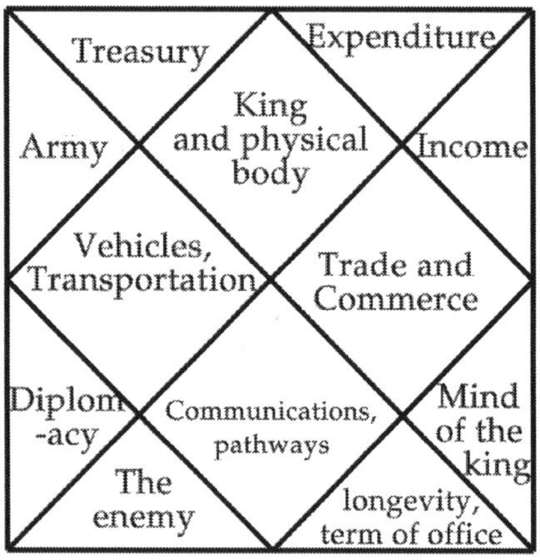

Houses in Varga Charts

The same chakras (house charts) are used for the divisional charts. The sign the lagna is placed in that particular varga becomes the first house and all the other planets go into the sign division they are positioned in that varga. A new and more specific chart is created for that area of life. The houses in these charts have different significations as they are a more detailed look into a specific area of life.

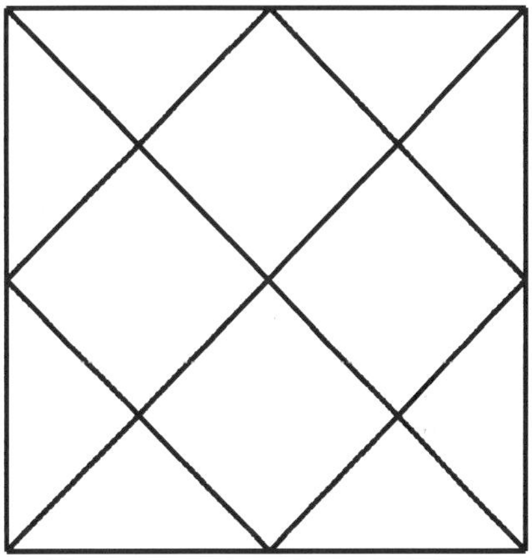

First let's construct a varga chart. Calculate the navāṁśa of the lagna (on page 128 if you haven't already filled it out on page 132). Put that navāṁśa lagna sign in the first house of the practice chart. Then find the navāṁśa sign of the Sun based on its degrees in the rāśi chart, and place it in the sign according to the navāṁśa lagna. Complete this for all the grahas to see the house placements in the navāṁśa.

Planets in the navāṁśa first house show the abilities you were naturally born with. Planets in the fifth house show the skills and abilities you easily learn in this life. Planets in the ninth house show skills you are blessed to acquire through a teacher in this life. The signification of planets in the sixth, eighth and twelfth are a struggle to achieve. The fourth house of mother and nurturing relates to cure in the navāṁśa. Benefics in this fourth house protect health, malefics can bring health problems or lack of cure. The tenth house relates to career, and is a money (*artha*) trine showing the fortune (*bhāgya*) with money in career. Malefics in the navāṁśa tenth house make income hard to attain and benefics placed there make it come easily. In this way there is a conceptual similarity to the houses in the rāśi chart but the navāṁśa houses have slightly different significations relative to the nature of the varga.

The carakārakas become very important in the navāṁśa in a different more spiritual way. The trines from the ātmakāraka will show the desires of the soul. If the ātmakāraka is in the navāṁśa lagna the person has great rise in life because their soul desires and their skills and abilities align. The relationship between the ātmakāraka and the bhrātṛkāraka will show how close one is to their guru in this life. The amātyakāraka will show what divine energies are supporting/ sustaining you in life. In this way, the spiritual support of a soul is seen from the carakārakas in the navāṁśa.

The daśāṁśā (D-10) is another good example of how the houses are different in the varga charts. The daśāṁśā chart shows the career, a finer tuning of the tenth house. Take the data from the previous lesson and make your daśāṁśa chart. The rāśi chart (D-1) changes every two hours, the horā chart (D-2) every hour. The navāṁśa chart (D-9) changes about every 15 minutes, and the daśāṁśa chart (D-10) changes about every 12 minutes. As the divisions increase the accuracy needed also increases.

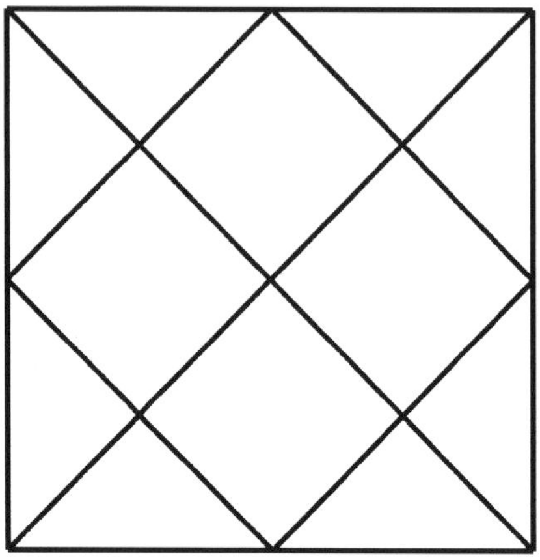

The first house is you; the first house of every divisional chart (*varga*) shows you in relation to that area of life. So the first house shows how you are in the work place. The fourth house shows your office (the work home). Planets there and the lord of the house will show what your office(s) looks like. The tenth house is the work you are doing, the type of work and quality of it. The seventh house is used for those who are self-employed or who have their own business, and it shows business partners instead of love partners. The sixth house is used for those who work for other people. The eighth house shows big business loans. The fifth house (eighth from the tenth) shows changes of jobs. It shows one's job education and skill. If there are benefics in the daśāṁśā fifth house then the person changes their jobs for better ones (promotions) because of their intelligence at their work. If there are malefics in the fifth house the person will often lose jobs without good standing. The third house which indicates short journeys in the rāśi chart will show time off or vacations (the twelfth from the office).

This brief introduction to these charts has been for the purpose of showing that houses in these charts must be seen according to the relevant area of life as represented by the divisional chart. The chakra of twelve houses has many layers of meanings according to the frequency of the view.

Practice Exercises:

24. Take a few charts and calculate the graha dṛṣṭi. With a light colored pen write this into the houses of the charts. Write in the rāśi dṛṣṭi of planets with a different colored pen so that you can visually see the aspects affecting the houses. Which houses are the most supported and how has this manifested in the person's life.
25. Using logic and explaining your reasoning- what do you think the ninth house of the daśāṁśa represents? (The answer to this will be found in chapter 13.)

Chapter 7

Strengths and Status

Strength, States and Results

Planets and houses both signify good and bad results to different degrees. To know what results they will give one needs to calculate two factors: how strong a planet or house is acting and whether giving good or bad results. Specifically, is the planet giving bad results in small amounts or large amounts, or is the planet giving good results in small or large amounts.

There are multiple factors to take into account. I have gone in the order of the information as presented in Bṛhat Parāśara Horā Śāstra. At first the material may seem somewhat overwhelming, and take a long time to calculate, but eventually it becomes more fluid and easy to read, just like learning a new language and knowing the grammar.

Natural and Temporal Friendships: Naisargika and Tatkālika Sambandha

The planets have natural (naisargika) friends and enemies. This was discussed in the section on grahas. Parāśara also mentions temporary (tatkālika) relationships which are based on how a planet is placed from the lord of its sign.

Temporary relationships:	
Friend	2, 3, 4, 10, 11, 12
Enemy	1, 5, 6, 7, 8, 9

The placements of planets in these houses become temporal friends or enemies. This temporal status is added with the natural status to find out the end result of the planet's status. If a planet is not exalted, mūlatrikoṇa, in its own sign or debilitated, then it needs to be more finely calculated as a great friend, friend, neutral, enemy or great enemy. First one must see the natural relationship the planet has with its lord. Then one sees the temporal relationship it has with its lord. These factors are added together for the final result. If Mercury and Jupiter are in the first house in Sagittarius, Jupiter is in his own sign. Mercury is a natural friend of Jupiter but it is in the same house as its lord so it is a temporal enemy. A friend plus an enemy equals a neutral. If Jupiter was placed in the second house, then it would be a temporal friend of Mercury and a friend plus a friend is a great friend. But if Jupiter is in the second from a Sagittarius lagna it is in debilitation in Capricorn.

Friend + Friend	Great Friend
Friend + Neutral	Friend
Enemy + Neutral	Enemy
Enemy + Enemy	Great Enemy

Natural Relationships Between the Planets							
	Sun	**Moon**	**Mars**	**Merc**	**Jupiter**	**Venus**	**Saturn**
Sun	-	F	F	N	F	E	E
Moon	F	-	N	F	N	N	N
Mars	F	F	-	E	F	N	N
Mercury	F	E	N	-	N	F	N
Jupiter	F	F	F	E	-	E	N
Venus	E	E	N	F	N	-	F
Saturn	E	E	E	F	N	F	-
Rāhu	F	E	N	N	N	F	N
Ketu	E	N	F	N	N	N	N

The example chart is given in a South Indian chart format. The ascendant is Gemini with Sun, Moon and Mars. The Sun is in Gemini ruled by Mercury. The Sun is neutral towards Mercury in natural relationship. Mercury is second from the Sun making it temporal friends. A natural neutral combined with a temporal friend creates a friend, so the Sun holds the status of *'friend'*. Moon is in Gemini and is natural friends towards its house lord Mercury, while Mercury is in the second house from Moon making it again a temporal friend. A natural friend combined with a temporal friend gives the Moon the status of *'great friend'*.

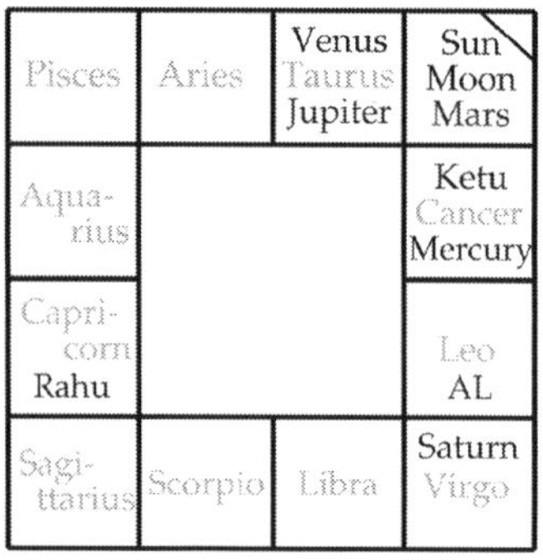

Mars is in Gemini and is an enemy towards house lord Mercury, yet Mercury is placed in the second house from it making it a temporal friend, these added together give Mars the status of *'neutral'*. Mercury is placed in Cancer and a natural enemy to the Moon while the house lord Moon is twelfth from Mercury making it a temporal friend. These combined factors therefore give Mercury the status of *'neutral'*.

Jupiter is in Taurus ruled by Venus and is a natural enemy towards Venus. Venus is in the same house (1) which makes it a temporal enemy which when combined gives Jupiter the status of *'great enemy'*. Venus in Taurus has the beneficial status of *'own'* sign. Saturn is in Virgo and is natural friends towards Mercury, while the house lord Mercury is eleventh from Saturn making it a temporal friend, thus in this chart Saturn has the status of *'great friend'*.

Practice Exercise:

1. Calculate the great friends, friends, neutrals, enemies and great enemies in your chart and in one other chart.

Astaṁgata (Combustion)

Combustion is when the planet is too close to the Sun. This ruins a planets ability to give external results. It may give very good internal and spiritual results. For example, if Venus is combust, the external significations of lover or dancing may be hurt, but the internal signification of love and a refined eye may be purified by the Sun. Planets getting combust show that they are undergoing the cleansing of bad karmas in this life. Various authors have given different degrees for what is considered combust. The graph here is the opinion of the ancient Indian astronomer and master of spherical geometry named Āryabhaṭa.

Planet	Direct°
Mars	17°
Saturn	15°
Mercury	13°
Jupiter	11°
Venus	9°

Graha-yuddha (Planetary War)

When two planets are within a degree of each other within the same sign they fight over that space and it is called a war (yuddha). For example, if Mercury is 3°15′ of Aries and Venus is 3°54′ of Aries they are in a war. Also if Mercury is 3°15′ of Aries and Venus is 4°05′ of Aries they are still within one degree of each other. One degree is sixty minutes of arc. It is important to remember that after 59 minutes and 59 seconds it becomes one degree, not 60 minutes.

$$\begin{array}{rccl} & 4^\circ\ 05' & & 3^\circ\ 65' \\ - & \underline{3^\circ\ 15'} & \text{is} & \underline{3^\circ\ 15'} \\ & & & 0^\circ\ 50' \text{ the remainder is under 60 minutes} \end{array}$$

If the planets are under 60 seconds which is one degree then they are engaged in a war. Generally, the planet with the highest degree will win. When this higher degree planet wins it will take the strength of the losing planet. If the losing planet is a benefic it will become a weak benefic unable to help much in the chart. If the losing planet is a malefic it will became angry and though weak will give negative results.

Avasthā

Avasthā means to abide in a state or condition. It shows the state of the planet, how it is feeling. There are different types of avasthā calculations, as you can be young, sleepy and lonely, or old, awake and happy. We will study four types of avastha; *bālādi, jāgrādi, dīptādi and lajjitādi.* They are named after the first state of being in each of there groups, *ādi* is like the English abbreviation *etc.*

I. Bālādi Avasthā

The signs are divided into six sections. They are related to the stages of life from infancy to old age. The avasthā shows how the planet is feeling, and will therefore act relative to that state of being (*avasthā*) it is situated in. When we feel young we will do more adventurous things, when we are feeling old we move slower. In this way one can stereotype the actions of certain stages of life.

Odd signs		Avasthā		Even
0°-6°	0°-2°	Bāla	Infant	24°-30°
6°-12°	3°-9°	Kumāra	Youth	18°-24°
12°-18°	10°-22°	Yuva	Adolescent	12°-18°
18°-24°	23°-28°	Vṛddha	Adult	6°-12°
24°-30°	29°-30°	Mṛta	Old	0°-6°

The odd signs begin with infancy and end with old age, while the even signs begin with old age and end with infancy. In the diagram, the main numbers are those recommended by Parāśara, while the column in italics is that considered by some other authors. **Bāla**[51] means young, infantile, not fully grown, early, newly arisen, simple, foolish, pure, and childlike. It does not give all of its energy as it is not fully developed and matured yet. **Kumāra** refers to a pre-pubescent child, it also means one who does not contain the traces of death and aging. The planet here will like a youth be open to possibilities but still needing guidance and protection. **Yuva** means young, a young adult, strong, and healthy. It is the strongest of the bālādi avasthās as it is in the prime of its strength and energy, ready to accomplish anything. **Vṛddha** means full grown, adult, advanced in years, aged, experienced, and eminent. It shows a planet that is matured in its qualities though it is older and more preoccupied with its own duties. **Mṛta** means finished, deceased, useless, and will show a planet that has not much energy to give. In the scheme that uses only one degree for mṛta, this is a degree where the planet is too old to do very much. There are variations of age within the avasthā as well, as 24° will be the start of old age, and 29° 59′ will be the time just before leaving the body. Just as below one degree a planet is too young to really be able to stand on its own, but grows older as it moves through the signs.

[51] *Bāla* with a long *ā* means child, and *bala* with a short *a* means strong.

II. Jāgrādi Avasthā

A planet that is exalted (*uccha*) or in own sign (*sva*) is in the avasthā of **Jāgrat**. This means it is awake, watchful, attentive, and caring. A planet that is in a friend (*mitra*) or neutral (*sama*) sign is **Svapna**. This means it is dreaming, sleepy, or tired. A planet in an enemy (*śatru*) or debilitated (*nīca*) sign is in the state of **Suṣupta**. This means it is fast asleep/deep sleep, and lacking in awareness. This avasthā shows the awareness of a planet, and the results are according to the name.

Jāgrat	awake	Uccha, svakṣetra
Svapna	dreaming	Mitra, Sama
Suṣupta	sleeping	Śatru, nīca

III. Dīptādi Avasthā

There are nine states of the planets known as *dīptādi* based on the first one of this type called dīpta-avasthā. An uccha graha is **Dīpta**, shining, bright, brilliant, blazing, and excited. A planet in its own sign (*sva-kṣetra*) is in a svastha state, which means it is content, confident, comfortable, self-sufficient, and taking care of itself. A planet in its great friend's sign is **Pramuditā**. This means it is delighted, pleased, and filled with the fun energy of one visiting a friend's house. A planet in a friend's sign is **Śānta**, which means it is peaceful, tranquil, content, and calm. When a planet is in a neutral sign it is Dīna, which means timid, depressed, or sad. It is a general boring feeling. A planet in an enemy's sign is **Duḥkhita**, which comes from the word duḥkha (suffering). The planet is unhappy, distressed, or pained to be in this situation. A planet conjunct (*saṁyukt*) a malefic has the avasthā of **Vikala**, meaning it feels confused, sorrowful, mutilated, maimed, crippled, or impaired.

A planet in its enemy sign has the avasthā of **Khala**. Khala is the ground where grain is threshed. When grain is threshed it is beaten against the floor, so this is a feeling of doing base work, and being beaten down and used. When a planet is conjunct the Sun it is burnt up and the avasthā is **Kopa**. Kopa means it feels irritated, angry, enraged.

Dīpta	Excited	Uccha
Svastha	Comfortable	Own sign
Pramuditā	Delighted	Extreme friend
Śānta	Content	Friend's sign
Dīna	Sad	Neutral sign
Duḥkhita	Unhappy	Enemies sign
Vikala	Sorrowful	Conj. malefic
Khala	Burdened	debilitated
Kopa	Angry	Combust

IV. Lajjitādi Avastha

This is one more fine tuned avasthā to consider. **Lajjita** means to be ashamed or to have done something to cause shame. **Garvita** means proud, haughty, or conceited and shows the planet thinks highly of itself. **Kṣudhita** avasthā means the planet feels hungry for something more, or something else, it is lacking what it needs and is becoming agitated by its state. **Tṛṣita** avastha is when the planet is thirsty for something more, more rasa, more emotion or experience. It is a desirous thirst that cannot really be quenched. **Muditā** avasthā is when the planet feels delighted and joyful to be rejoicing in the company of someone who takes care of it, and showers beneficence. **Kṣobhita** avasthā is when the planet has become disturbed, is trembling, shaking, and in an agitated situation which it does not enjoy the pressure of.

Lajjita	Ashamed	Conjunct Sun, Saturn, Mars or Nodes
Garvita	Proud	Uccha or Mūlatrikoṇa sign
Kṣudhita	Hungry	Conjunct an enemy in enemy sign
Tṛṣita	Thirsty	Enemy aspect, no benefic aspect, watery sign
Muditā	Delighful	Conjunct a benefic
Kṣobhita	Disturbed	Combust with enemy/malefic aspect

Maraṇa-Kāraka-Sthāna

Each planet has a position *(sthāna)* where its significations *(kāraka)* feel like it is dying (maraṇa). Parāśara does not mention these placements but they are found in *Garga Horā* and *Jātaka Pārijāta* (VII.34-36). When a planet is in these placements it is suffering in such a way that it feels like it is dying.

Saturn	Lagna
Ketu	2nd house
Jupiter	3rd house
Mercury	4th house
Venus	6th house
Mars	7th house
Moon	8th house
Rāhu	9th house
Sun	12th house

Saturn the lord of disease is maraṇa in the first house of health, he feels like he is dying when you try to make him take care of your health. Ketu the lord of renunciation is maraṇa in the second house of wealth. The holy man feels like he is dying when you make him do the accounting. Jupiter, the priest, is maraṇa in the third house of partying and gambling. Mercury the planet of duality has two different places of maraṇa. For Gemini Mercury, the child, is māraṇa in the seventh house of sexuality. For Virgo Mercury, the sports player, is maraṇa sitting in the fourth house of being in a classroom all day.

Maraṇa kāraka sthāna (MKS) is cancelled when a planet is in its exaltation sign. For a Gemini lagna the fourth house is Virgo, the exaltation of Mercury, therefore Mercury cannot be the maraṇa placed there. For other ascendants, particular planets cannot become MKS. For example, for Taurus lagna the third house is Cancer and Jupiter cannot become MKS, as well as the Sun being exalted in the twelfth cannot be MKS. For Libra lagna Saturn is exalted in the first house and cannot be MKS, nor can Venus who is exalted in the sixth house of Pisces.

Venus, the planet of love and sensuality, is maraṇa in the sixth house of celibacy. Mars, the celibate warrior, is maraṇa in the loving seventh house of sensuality and sex. Moon, the planet of life, breath and sustenance is maraṇa in the vulnerable eighth house of debt. Rahu, the planet of deceit, is maraṇa in the ninth house of upholding the dharma. For Rāhu (Taurus) and Ketu (Leo) the āyus exaltation is utilized for cancellation of maraṇa.

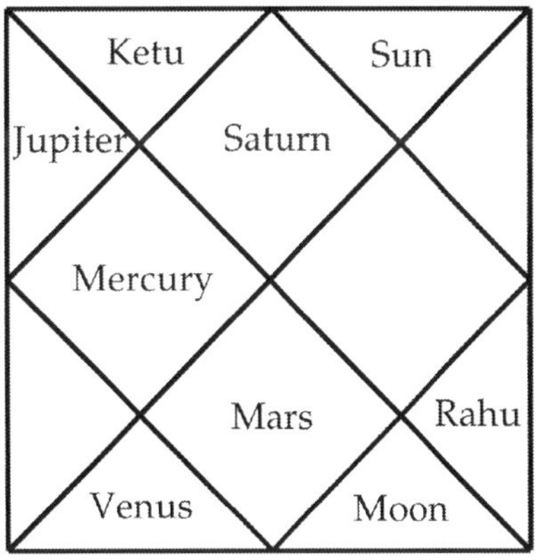

The Sun, king who supports all, is maraṇa in the twelfth house of loss. These are the maraṇa kāraka positions of the planets based on the houses. They will be used similar to avasthas as well as in medical astrology.

Transition Points

Sandhi

Sandhi means to contain a conjunction or transition from one point to another. This is when a planet is in a position where it is changing from one sign to another. It also refers to changing nakṣatras and navāṁśas. When a planet is under 1° or over 29° it is at the transition from one sign to the next and it is called *Rāśi Sandhi*. This placement will weaken a planet. I will be in either extreme infancy or extreme old age and not have the ability to do much. It can also be compared to when one is moving houses and everything is packed up in boxes and therefore it is not easy to maneuver oneself.

Gaṇḍānta

There are three sandhi that are more detrimental than the others. This is when the rāśi, navāṁśa, and the nakṣtra sandhi all line up at their sandhi points. This happens between Cancer and Leo, Scorpio and Sagittarius, and Pisces and Aries. It relates to the split of the torso by the diaphragm (Cancer-Leo), the split between the legs and torso (Scorpio-Sagittarius), and the split between the feet and the head. Planets here will struggle more than the other sandhis with the Scorpio-Sagittarius transition being the most difficult.

Practice Exercises:

2. Calculate the avasthās of the planets in your chart and one other.
3. Look for planets placed in maraṇa-kāraka-sthāna and see which significations are making a person suffer.
4. Look for any sandhi or gaṇḍānta planets in those charts. If a planet is placed there, see what significations are hurt and which houses are weakened.

Ṣaṣṭyāṁśa: The Sixtieth Division

The ṣaṣṭyāṁśa is the D-60 chart and relates to past life karma. The lords of the D-60 will show what type of past life karma the particular planet is carrying and thereby influence the results the planet will give. Some of these aṁśās are benefic and others are malefic. Parāśara says,

शुभषष्ट्यंशसंयुक्ता ग्रहाः शुभफलप्रदाः ।
क्रूरषष्ट्यंशसंयुक्ता नाशयन्ति खेचारिणः१ ॥

śubhṣaṣṭayaṁśasaṁyuktā grahāḥ śubhaphalapradāḥ|
krūraṣaṣṭayaṁśasaṁyuktā nāśayanti khecāriṇaḥ||41||

Planets in good a ṣaṣṭyāṁśa give good results,
Planets in cruel ṣaṣṭyāṁśa can destroy the beneficial nature of a planet.

The practical application of this information is to refine the type of results a planet will give. For example, if malefics are placed in the ninth house, the person will tend to be disrespectful towards elders, gurus or tradition. The ṣaṣṭyāṁśa of the ninth lord will confirm whether the person is slightly not honoring tradition, or very disrespectful to teachers. If the ninth lord was in the *ghora-ṣaṣṭiamsa* (awful-division) the person will definitely be disrespectful at some time, and commit some type of awful show of disrespect. If the ninth house has malefics but the ninth lord is in *amṛta-ṣaṣṭiamsa* (nectar-division), the person may argue with the teacher/tradition but still serve and work with them fully, as they have much nectar (life giving energy) to give to the tradition.

Previously, one should have calculated all the deities of the vargas, as we will begin to use them as we progress. Here we are learning to use the deities of the ṣaṣṭiamsa, which reveal the type of karma the planet is carrying with it.

Practice Exercise:

5. Calculate the D-60 lord of all your planets and one other chart.

Odd Signs				Even Signs	
1	0° – 30′	**Ghora**	Awful, frightful, violent, pained by disease	30°00′	**60**
2	1°00′	**Rākṣasa**	Protective, aggressive, demonical	29°30′	**59**
3	1°30′	**Deva**	Happy joyful expression, light bringer	29°00′	**58**
4	2°00′	**Kubera**	Lord of wealth, benefactor, acts like a rich person, in past life was probably a rich person, may not mean that they are or will be rich in this life.	28°30′	**57**
5	2°30′	**Yakṣa**	Spiritual creatures, elves, tree spirits, fertility goddesses, nature spirits, In past dharma had to do with working with nature spirits.	28°00′	**56**
6	3°00′	**Kinnara**	Half bird-half man holding lutes in their hands. Representing knowledge (viydā) of the birds/Sun, Sun=jyotiṣa, spirituality. Knowledge of Spirituality.	27°30′	**55**
7	3°30′	**Bhraṣṭa**	Corrupted principles, fallen, a sign that its all gone wrong. They didn't follow certain principles in past life, in this life, there is a corrupting influence.	27°00′	**54**
8	4°00′	**Kulaghna**	One who destroys the family, home wrecker, stops the lineage which is also a kula (family).	26°30′	**53**
9	4°30′	**Garala**	The venom of the snake. Someone hurts someone in a past life or they were very hurt too. Resentful.	26°00′	**52**
10	5°00′	**Agni**	Agni, energy, motivation hard work, bright, spiritual, understanding, transformation, offering	25°30′	**51**
11	5°30′	**Māyā**	Don't see things clearly, given confusion, deception, being deceived, materiality.	25°00′	**50**
12	6°00′	**Purīṣa**	Dirty, the person defiled something. I.e. polluting the environment, or living in a polluted place.	24°30′	**49**
13	6°30′	**Appati**	Lord of the waters.Varuṇa- Lord of the milky way-ocean of milk, Universal cosmic waters, lord of secrets, mystical understanding. Incarnated as Janaka Ṛṣi-wisest king who acted in perfect dharma.	24°00′	**48**
14	7°00′	**Marutvān**	Wind , strength, power, considered more benefic	23°30′	**47**
15	7°30′	**Kāla**	Dying, death, decay, disease, a name of Saturn. Someone associated with death in last life, (malefic)	23°00′	**46**
16	8°00′	**Ahi**	Sarpa/snake, deceiving, deceit, changeability, changes, shifting, traveler, (when Ketu is causing a bondage-trapped by snakes= Ahi-bandhana)	22°30′	**45**
17	8°30′	**Amṛta**	Nectar, nourishing, taking care of others in last life, in this life being given to. Rejuvenating, uplifting.	22°00′	**44**
18	9°00′	**Indu**	Chandra/Moon, feminine	21°30′	**43**
19	9°30′	**Mṛdu**	Easy to deal with, moderate, soft	21°00′	**42**
20	10°00′	**Komala**	Tender, gentle	20°30′	**41**
21	10°30′	**Heramba**	Very bright form of Gaṇeśa, a boastful hero, related to Buddhist Heruka	20°00′	**40**

Odd Signs				Even Signs	
22	11°00′	**Brahma**	Creative, making things happen, starter, the creation of it, the beginning of it, universal father.	19°30′	39
23	11°30′	**Viṣṇu**	Sustaining, someone who holds things together, person who keeps peace in the family.	19°00′	38
24	12°00′	**Maheśvara**	The person worked for knowledge and learning. Śiva- someone good at removing tamasic energies.	18°30′	37
25	12°30′	**Deva**	Divine, light bringer, light bearer, deity, spiritual.	18°00′	36
26	13°00′	**Ārdra**	Wet, damp, fresh, not dry, succulent, green as a plant, new, full of feeling, (Beneficial)	17°30′	35
27	13°30′	**Kalināśa**	Destruction, removal, the pains of time. Either someone who caused a lot of pain and has to remove the pain, and also a healer who has helped others to remove the pains of life.	17°00′	34
28	14°00′	**Kṣitīśa**	The ruler of the earth, connected to Mars- bhūmi kāraka, protective energy, protection of the land, more beneficial aspect of Mars, royal quality.	16°30′	33
29	14°30′	**Kamalākara**	The one who makes the lotuses bloom: the Sun.	16°00′	32
30	15°00′	**Gulika**	The child of Saturn, Gulika represents the poison you drink, the suffering you take on. Sometimes many spiritual people have this as they take on other people's suffering. (note: The upagraha Mandi represents the poison you give.)	15°30′	31
31	15°30′	**Mṛtyu**	Death personified, son of Mars.	15°00′	30
32	16°00′	**Kāla**	Dying, death, decay, disease, a name of Saturn.	14°30′	29
33	16°30′	**Dāvāgni**	Someone associated with death in last life, (malefic)	14°00′	28
34	17°00′	**Ghora**	Forest fire. Loss of control, fast transformation.	13°30′	27
35	17°30′	**Yama**	Awful, frightful, violent, pained by disease	13°00′	26
36	18°00′	**Kaṇṭaka**	The Lord of Death. Transformation, people who make change happen, righteousness, judging. Thorn, slows you. (ex: Kaṇṭaka-śani - 10th from lagna or moon or AL.)	12°30′	25
37	18°30′	**Sudhā**	Ease, comfort, juice, flower nectar, nourishing, light of the moon, beauty, happiness.	12°00′	24
38	19°00′	**Amṛta**	Nectar, nourishing, taking care of others in last life, in this life being given to. Rejuvenating, uplifting.	11°30′	23
39	19°30′	**Pūrṇa- chandra**	Full Moon, completeness, finishing things.	11°00′	22
40	20°00′	**Viṣa-dagdha**	Destroyed by venom, person burning with resentment or grief	10°30′	21
41	20°30′	**Kulanāśa**	Destroy traditional family, someone who destroys the larger sense of family or tradition.	10°00′	20

Odd Signs				Even Signs	
42	21°00′	**Vaṁśa Kṣaya**	Not growing, wasting away, stale, not wanting to change.	9°30′	**19**
43	21°30′	**Utpāta**	Bad omen, portentous or unusual phenomenon. Bad things foreboding calamity.	9°00′	**18**
44	22°00′	**Kāla**	Dying, death, decay, disease, a name of Saturn. Someone associated with death in last life.	8°30′	**17**
45	22°30′	**Saumya**	Friendly, happy, joyful, having qualities of Moon	8°00′	**16**
46	23°00′	**Komala**	Tender, gentle	7°30′	**15**
47	23°30′	**Śītala**	Cold, goddess connected to Saturn-Rāhu. Measles, colds, disease caused by cold, not very emotional.	7°00′	**14**
48	24°00′	**Karāla-daṁṣṭra**	Frightful teethed, "vampire", fangs, someone who aquires desires harshly.	6°30′	**13**
49	24°30′	**Chandra-mukhi**	Woman with a face like a moon, charming, enchanting, attractive energy.	6°00′	**12**
50	25°00′	**Pravīṇa**	Clever, expertise, dexterity with hands, the person perfected a skill from a past life, perfectionist.	5°30′	**11**
51	25°30′	**Kāla-pāvaka**	Fire that burns, removing/desroying the old, removing tamas, (a malefic division).	5°00′	**10**
52	26°00′	**Daṇḍā-yuddha**	Staff, fighting, yudh-means war, from lagna-unfinished fight in past life that came into this life. If ninth ninth lord is here it means struggling between dharmas.	4°30′	**9**
53	26°30′	**Nirmala**	No dirtiness, sinless, non-toxic, pure, truthful, free of bad qualities. Nir="free from" and mala= wastes.	4°00′	**8**
54	27°00′	**Saumya**	Friendly, happy, joyful, nice, social like the Moon, handsome, auspicious.	3°30′	**7**
55	27°30′	**Krūra**	Cruel, harsh, person had harsh things done to them.	3°00′	**6**
56	28°00′	**Ati-śītala**	Very cold or extra cold, lacking emotions, harsh.	2°30′	**5**
57	28°30′	**Amṛta**	Nectar, nourishing, well taken care of in last life, in this life being given to. Rejuvenating, uplifting.	2°00′	**4**
58	29°00′	**Payodhi**	Ocean, bountiful, abundant, resourceful, lots of ideas, having plenty.	1°30′	**3**
59	29°30′	**Bhramaṇa**	Wandering, doesn't have a goal, no real direction, can even be confusion. In past life may have stopped others from achieving their goals.	1°00′	**2**
60	29°30′ – 30°00′	**Chandra-rekha**	Crescent Moon- growing just out of new, 'green'- someone who just started something, just learning, open to all possibilities.	0° – 30′	**1**

Vaiśeṣikāṁśa: Division of Excellence

Vaiśeṣika means special, distinguished, excellent, and pre-eminent. When a planet is in its exaltation (uccha), mūlatrikoṇa, or own sign (sva) in multiple divisions it enters a vaiśeṣika (special) aṁśa (division). Therefore the planets need to be analyzed in multiple divisions that it exists within. This shows the strength of the planet to uphold planetary combinations for wealth and power (as spoken of in the *Rāja Yoga* and *Dhana Yoga* chapters). . Therefore, when looking at combinations that make one famous or rich one should consider this source of strength.

There are different ways to use the divisional charts (discussed soon). When looking at the chart of an average person ten vargas are used (D1, D2, D3, D7, D9, D10, D12, D16, D30, D60). When looking at the chart of royalty (nṛpa= kings, princes, leaders, protectors) one uses all sixteen varga charts. When a planet attains uccha, mūlatrikoṇa, or sva in more than one varga it takes on special properties to give better results. For example, if a planet was in its own sign for twelve vargas it would become Sūryakānti, shining like the Sun. The results of these special divisions are canceled if the planet is combust, loses a planetary war, or is in a negative avasthā.

BPHS, Ṣoḍaśavarga-Adhyāya v.42-53				
#	Daśavarga	(for average people)	Ṣoḍaśavarga	(for royalty)
2	Parijāta	Red flowered tree	Bhedaka	piercing
3	Uttama	Best	Kusuma	a flower
4	Gaupura	Sweet place	Naga-puṣpa	serpant flower
5	Siṁhāsana	Throne	Kanduka	a serving vessel
6	Pārāvata	A Dove	Kerala	
7	Devaloka	Realm of gods/light	Kalpavṛkṣa	Wish-fulfilling Tree
8	Brahmaloka	Pious Realms	Chandanavana	Grove of Sandalwood
9	Śakra-vāhana	Strong vehicle	Pūrṇachandra	the Full Moon
10	Śrīdhama	Containing Glory	Uccaiḥśrava	the King of Horses
11	-		Dhanvantari	the God of Medicine
12	-		Sūryakānti	Sunlight
13	-		Vidruma	Coral
14	-		Śakra-siṁhāsana	Strong Throne
15	-		Gauloka	Sweet Existence/ heavenly
16	-		Śrīvallabha	The Highest Beloved

Viṁśopaka: Divisional Strength

Viṁśopaka-bala is a mathematical strength calculation based on a planet's position in the divisional charts.

स्थूलं फलं च संस्थाप्य तत्सूक्ष्मं च ततस्ततः ॥१९॥

sthūlaṁ phalaṁ ca saṁsthāpya tatsūkṣmaṁ ca tatastataḥ||19||

It [viṁṣopak] shows the results given by a planet on a general (*sthūla*) level, the precise (*sūkṣma*) results are to be seen by the exact position of the planet.

The viṁśopaka-bala shows up as a little graph on modern computer programs. It is a generalized idea of planet strength in the varga charts. More than the actual resultant number the calculation gives us certain clues to the importance of certain charts. The final number of points for all the vargas add up to twenty (*viṁśa*).

For example, with the ten vargas, the rāśi chart (D-1) is given 3 points, the ṣaṣṭyāṁśa (D-60) is given 5 points and all other charts are given 1.5 points each. From this we can tell the rāśi chakra and the D-60 are given primary importance in affecting the life.

In the sixteen vargas, the rāśi chart is given 3.5 points, the navāṁśa is given 3 points, the kalāṁśa is given 2 points, and the ṣaṣṭyāṁśa is given 4 points. Again the weight given to the D-60 shows the power of our past tendencies (*saṁskāras*) to influence our life.

	Daśa Varga	Ṣoḍaśa Varga
D1	3.0	3.5
D2	1.5	1
D3	1.5	1
D4	1.5	1
D7	1.5	0.5
D9	1.5	3.0
D10	1.5	0.5
D12	1.5	0.5
D16	1.5	2.0
D20	-	0.5
D24	-	0.5
D27	-	0.5
D30	1.5	1.0
D40	-	0.5
D45	-	0.5
D60	5.0	4.0
Total: 20 points each		

When a planet is exalted, mūlatrikoṇa, or sva it receives the full 20 points. When it is in a great friends sign it receives 18 points, decreasing to 15 points in a friends sign, 10 points in a neutral sign, 7 in an enemy's sign, 5 in a great enemies sign, and nothing in debilitated signs. This is averaged together for the final result.

A planet with 0-5 points will give no effects. With 5-10 the planet will give minute (*svalpa*) results. With 10-15 points the planet will give medium results. With 15-20 points the planet will give its full results.

During the time period (*daśā*) of the planet one should analyze the placement of the planet and the viṁśopaka strength for the prediction of accurate results.

Prosperity and Destruction of a House

First Parāśara listed strengths of the planets, then he listed how they become strong through the signs. Next, he begins to speak of how they influence houses to make those particular areas of life prosper or fail. It is first mentioned at the end of the Judgement of Houses chapter (*Bhāva-Viveka-Adhyāya*, v 14-16).

A house will prosper (saukhya) when it is:
- occupied by or aspected by benefics
- or aspected by its own lord
- or the lord of the house is in the tenth house
- or when the lord of the house is in a good avastha

A house will be unsuccessful (naṣṭa) when its:
- lord is destroyed or conjunct malefics
- or not aspected by its own lord or benefics
- or is in combination with dustana lords
- or losing a planetary war
- or in a bad avasthā

I. The first thing to notice is that benefics in or aspecting a house make it prosper just as malefics will damage the area of life the house signifies. The sign's own lord will protect the house and make it prosper, even if it is a malefic. The own lord is powerful support for a house. Later, Parāśara mentions the importance of *Jupiter* and *Mercury* aspecting a house. Mercury shows the house has the skills to accomplish its needs and Jupiter shows a house has the 'money' to get its needs fulfilled.

For example, the fourth house is the house of happiness; if Mercury aspects one has the *skills* to work on themselves to attain a happy state of feeling, while Jupiter's aspect gives the person the resources to attain happiness, yet if Saturn is aspecting the person is *lacking* something and will experience some *suffering*. The own lord of the fourth house is the lord of the house of happiness, and when the lord of the house of happiness is in or aspecting the house of happiness then happiness is more likely. The tenth house is the house of work and career. If it is aspected by Mercury then one has the skills to get a good job, if Jupiter is aspecting then the person has the *resources/connections* to get a good job. If benefic Venus is aspecting then the person will have the charm to get a good job with *luxuries.* If Rāhu is in or aspecting the tenth, then there can be confusion with career goals and in the work place. Therefore, planets will give their significations to the houses they are in and aspecting. If the tenth lord is not aspecting its own house, then the lord of career is not able to watch over its own place of work and there will be less protection in the workplace and less awareness of what is happening there as a result.

II. The next thing to notice is that Parāśara says houses are good if their lord is in the tenth, and destroyed if combined with duḥsthāna lords. This shows that planets need to be seen not only according to their natural significations, but also according to their house lordships as well as their placements.

First, see where the lord of a house has gone. If the lord has gone to a positive house (like the tenth or ninth) then it makes the house strong. If the house lord has gone to a negative house like the (sixth or eighth) then it damages the house. There are two differentiations to make here- the placement from lagna and the placement from the sign itself.

The placement of one's individual lagneśa will show how they apply their intelligence in life. From lagna all other placements will show how the individual experiences the house and its significations. From the house itself, the placement will show how that person, etc is applying their intelligence. For example, if the fourth lord is in the eighth house, it is showing a negative experience with the mother from the individual's perspective, but being in the fifth house from the fourth, the Mother experiences it as her learning and quest for understanding. Or, if the fourth lord was in the eleventh house from the lagna, it would show the individual makes great gains with the mother and happiness. But being the eighth house from the fourth, the mother will have trying times and many hardships.

Second, see which house that lord is benefiting or harming. For example, the sixth lord is hurting the house it is placed in, giving some enmity and fighting there. The fourth lord benefits a house by bringing some way of finding happiness there. The ninth lord brings luck to a house, while the eighth lord brings bad luck. The twelfth lord brings losses to a house while the second lord brings gains to a house.

III. The third factor Parāśara teaches is to be aware of the avasthā of the lord. The state the house lord is in will show how we feel when that house gets activated. If the fourth lord is exalted we will feel dīpta (excited) when we are home. If the tenth lord is combust the Sun, we will feel kopa (angry) when we are at work. If the lord of the Upapada (marriage point) is in an enemies sign, the person will feel dirtied when they get married. In this way, the avasthās are factored into making a house strong and weak.

Parāśara also mentions a planet losing a planetary war destroys the house it lords. This is also understood as any negative combination like gaṇḍānta, sandhi, etc that damages a planet will also damage the houses it lords.

If you thought that was a lot, that is just the beginning of evaluating strength in the chart. It is the important foundation, but then there are many other techniques to fine tune strength, as well as many short cuts to find the strength of a house very fast. The fine tuning techniques will differentiate between specific areas of life. For example, to differentiate the strength of your health, we can see the constitution, digestion, tissue formation, and pranic flow, etc. The general rules are when we are looking at a chart and we need to know which house is stronger quickly, then we use the shortcuts.

Below are two more sections. One is on Ṣaḍbala, which is a fine tuning of planetary strength. The second section has the strengths rules used by Ṛṣi Jaimini, who was a student of Parāśara. Jaimini made some rules which are used as a shortcut to determine house strength very quickly.

Ṣaḍbala

Parāśara gives a chapter on Ṣaḍbala which is a calculation for seeing the strength of the planet. Then a chapter on Iṣṭa and kaṣṭa-balas which are a calculation to see how the good or bad the results will be during a time period of the planet (śubhāśubha-daśa-phalam).

Graha-bala is the power, strength, might that is expected from a planet. It is calculated based on the combination of *position* and *time* and a few other factors *(sthān kālādi)*. Ṣaḍ means six, so the ṣaḍbala are six strength calculations used on planets. These calculations are put into a number form and then graphed.

Numerical calculation averages together strong and weak areas that will not fully give the planets variety of strengths as one would see by looking at it manually. Here we will break down the various aspects of the Six Strengths. The important part for you as a beginner is to understand what is being given more strength. Later you will learn specific calculations, but for now it is important to understand that kendras are stronger than paṇapharas, or that malefics are stronger when the Moon is waning and benefics are stronger when the Moon is waxing. The foundations of the calculations, what is given importance, is important to be aware of.

I. Sthāna-Bala: Positional Strength

The planets will show what status and position one rises to in life. They will show how powerful or weak we are. There are five aspects of sthāna-bala.

A. Uccha-Bala: Exaltation Strength

The position of a planets in exaltation (uccha) mūlatrikoṇa, friendly/neutral, enemy signs, and debilitation are observed. There is a mathmatical calculation which gives a planet in its exaltation 60pts, and zero points in debility. Every 3° away from exaltation it loses a point until debilitation and then every 3° towards its exaltation it gains a point.

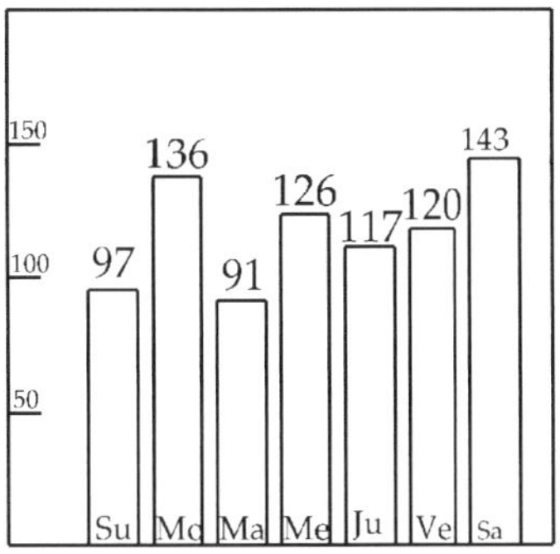

B. Saptavargaja-Bala: Strength born from the Seven Vargas

The position in the seven vargas, Horā, Drekkana, Saptāṁśa, Navāṁśa, Sūryāṁśa, and Triṁśāṁśa, will give a certain strength value. If a planet is in its own sign it gets 30 points, in the sign of a great friend 22.5 pts, in the signs of a friend 15 pts, in the signs of a neutral 7.5 pts,in the signs of an enemy 3.75 pts and in the sign of a great enemy it will get only 1.875 points.

C. Sugam-Yugma Bhāṁśa: Even and Odd Sign Strength

When female planets are in female signs in the rāśi and navāṁśa they get 15 points. Male and neuter planets get points in male signs. Male and female are based on odd and even signs.

D. Kendrādi-Bala: Angular Strength

Planets are stronger in angular houses. In general, benefics are better in angles as they give prosperity to the native. Malefics planets are better to be weak in kendras and strong in dusthānas. While benefics are better strong in kendras and weak in dusthānas.

In kendras (angular houses) planets get 60 points of strength. In paṇaphara (succedant) houses planets get 30 points, and in āpoklima (cadent houses) planets get 15points only.

E. Drekkana-Bala: D-3 Strength

Male planets get 15 points in the first drekkana of a sign (00° to 09°60′). Female planets get 15 points in the second drekkana of a sign (10° to 19°60′). Neuter planets get 15 points in the third drekkana.

These five aspects of are calculated together to get the sthāna bala.

II. Dig Bala: Directional Strength

Digbala shows the direction where planets are strong for career and self development. Planets in these positions bring the qualities of these planets heavily into the life. Jupiter and Mercury are strongest Rising in the first house. Moon and Venus are strongest in the midnight of the fourth house. Sun and Mars are strongest in the high noon position of the tenth house, the throne, where they have power and command. And Saturn is strongest in the seventh house of the setting Sun.

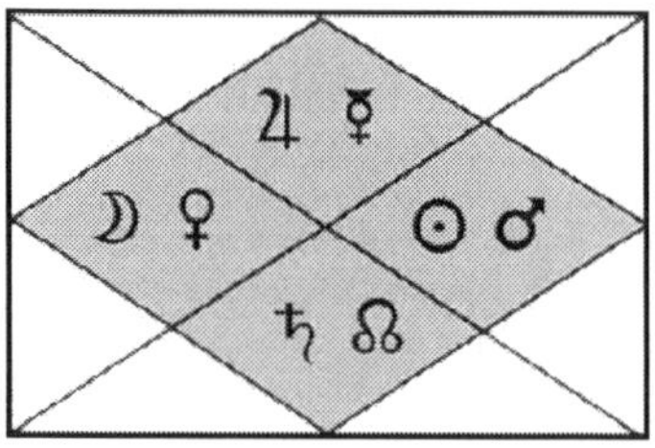

III. Kāla-Bala: Strength Accorded by Time

Kāla-bala is sometimes called temporal strength or time strength. It shows which time the different planets are strong. What parts of the year, month, day, etc., support the actions of the graha.

A. Natonnata: Day-Night Strength

Moon, Mars and Saturn are stronger at night or closer to the zenith (nata), while Sun, Jupiter and Venus are stronger during the day or closer to the mid-heaven (unnata). When a day planet is closer to the day or a night planet is deeper into the night it gets 60 points. Every 24 minutes (ghaṭikā) away it will lose a point. Mercury is strong both during the day and night and gets full day/night strength. The Greek astrologers (and a few Indian texts) varied slightly in teaching that the Moon, Mars and Venus had nocturnal strength and the Sun, Jupiter and Saturn had diurnal strength.

B. Pakṣa-Bala: Waxing-Waning Strength

Benefics are strong when the Moon is waxing and get 60 points of strength the closer the Moon gets to being full. Malefics are stronger during the waning half of the Moon. And the closer the Moon gets to being New the stronger a malefic becomes. Therefore when there is a good yoga in the chart it becomes stronger closer to the time of the full Moon. When there is a malefic causing a bad effect it will be stronger (worse) near the new Moon

4 hours	Day	Night
First Third	Mercury	Moon
Middle	Sun	Venus
Last Third	Saturn	Mars
Jupiter has strength at all times		

C. Tribhāga: Three Parts Strength

If the twelve hour day or twelve hour night is divided into four hour sections it is then three sections called the tribhāga. Each planet gets strength in a particular third while Jupiter always has the full tribhāga strength of 60 points. Only one planet and Jupiter get tribhāga strength at any given third of the day.

D. Varṣādi-Bala: Year-month-day Lord Strength

Just as the day is ruled by a planet, Sunday by the Sun, Monday by the Moon, etc., the hour, month, and year have a planet that rule over them. The planet that becomes the lord of the year, Abdapati, gets 15 points of strength. The lord of the month, Māsapati, gets 30 points of strength. The lord of the day, Vārapati, gets 45 points of strength. The lord of the hour, Horāpati, will get 60 points of strength. This shows the lord of the hour is a very strong planet.

E. Ayana-Bala: Declinational Strength

The declination (krānti) of a planet is based on how high (north) or low (south) it is from the celestial equator. The Sun, Mars, Jupiter, and Venus are stronger north of the celestial equator. The Moon and Saturn are stronger south of the celestial equator.

F. Yuddha-Bala: Planetary War Strength

If two planets are in a war, find the difference between their ṣaḍbala. Add the difference to the winning planet and subtract it from the losing planet.

IV. Naisargika-Bala: Natural Strength

The natural strengths of the planets are a constant in all charts. It shows which planets will be able to more naturally give their results. If two planets have the same ṣaḍbala, then this will be the determining factor. The Sun is the strongest with 60 points. The Moon has 51 points, Venus has 43 points, Jupiter has 34 points, Mercury has 26 points, Mars has 17 points, and Saturn gets only 9 points.

V. Dṛg-Bala: Aspectual Strength

Dṛg is the look or aspect that shows the support of the planet. Benefic aspects add points and malefics aspects subtract points. Mercury and Jupiter are given extra weight.

VI. Cheṣṭa-Bala: Motional Strength

The motion (cheṣṭa) strength shows the power of the desire of a planet. It shows how much strength it has for its wants. This shows which planets desires will lead us more.

The cheṣṭa-bala of the Sun is the same as its ayana-bala, it is stronger in the northern course (spring to fall) and weaker in the southern course (fall to spring). The cheṣṭa-bala of the Moon is the same as its pakṣa-bala, it is stronger in the waxing phase andweaker in the waning phase.

60	Vakra	Retrograde
30	Anuvakra	Retrograding into previous sign
15	Vikala	Stationary (stambhi)
30	Manda	Slower than normal
15	Mandatara	Slower than slower
7.5	Sama	Even speed, not fast or slow, (madya-gati)
45	Chara	Faster than average
30	Atichara	Entering next sign in accelerated motion

The other planets are in one of eight motions a planet is capable of. The most important aspect to see is that retrograde planet become very strong relative to desire. A retrograde planet will have a very strong desire for the aspects of life it significates naturally.

Ṣaḍbala of Houses

Parāśara mentions that mathematical strengths can also be calculated for the houses. This can then be graphed as well. Malefics subtract points from a house and benefics add points. Jupiter and Mercury add full points to a house showing their beneficence in aspect. Saturn, Mars and the Sun subtract full points. Mathematical calculation is done to see if the house is left positive or negative.

Houses containing front rising *(śirṣodaya)* signs are stronger when the individual is born during the day. Houses containing back rising *(pṛṣṭodaya)* signs are stronger when the person is born during the night. Signs with both rising *(ubhayodaya)* are strong during the sunrise and sunset times (*sandhya*). In this way mathematical strengths are also calculated for the houses.

Practice Exercises:

6. Evaluate house strengths of each house in your chart and one other chart using the three factors given by Parāśara.
7. What planets are retrograde in your chart? Factor in the natural signification of that planet in that house, and explain the strong desires it gives you.
8. Find the Ṣaḍbala calculations for planets and houses in your computer program. See the other mathematical strength calculations available.
9. Look at the Ṣaḍbala of your planets. Research the strongest planet and the weakest planet and see what strengths they have and which they are missing.

Jaimini Strength Rules

There are specific strength rules given by Jaimini in his *Upadeśa Sūtras*[55] verses 2.3.5 to 2.3.17. They are meant to simplify calculations when many are needed for things like calculation of time periods. They are based on the principle of exclusion. There is a long list of strengths, but as soon as one sign wins in strength, the process if finished. There is no need to continue down the list looking at all the other strengths. The only finer detail is that among the four sources of strength, different sources are used for different purposes.

The First Source of Strength

- Presence of the Ātmakāraka
- Conjunction of larger number of planets
- Status of planets (uccha/nīca)
- Natural order of strength (dvisvabhāva, sthira, chara)
- Lord is Ātmakāraka
- Lord more advanced in degrees
- Lord of odd sign in even sign, or lord of even sign in odd sign is stronger

The first source is the presence of the Ātmakāraka, but this is only used when referring to spiritual events or timing. Therefore, the first source of strength is the conjunction of more planets in a house. If one is comparing the strength of the lagna to the seventh house, the one with more planets is stronger. If by chance, they have the same number of planets, then the next rule applies. The status of those planets is examined, and the sign with uccha planets is stronger than a planet in a lesser status. The higher status will win. But if the same number of planets happen to be the same status, like Moon in Aries and Mars in Libra. Then the natural order of sign strength is used. Since Moon is in a chara sign and Mars is in a chara sign it would still be the same, so the next source is used. If the lord of the sign happens to be the Ātmakāraka then it is stronger. If neither are AK, then the degrees of the lords are seen. In the example, the lord of Aries (Mars) and the lord of Libra (Venus) would be seen to who has the higher degrees. If Venus has higher degrees then Libra is stronger. There is no need to go to the next strength rule, one is finished. But if they just happened to be the same then the next rule would be used.

The Second Source of Strength

- The aspect or conjunction of own lord, AK, Jupiter or Mercury

The second source is pretty simple. It is the aspect of the sign's own lord as discussed by Parāśara. Then the aspect of the Ātmakāraka, followed by the benefics Jupiter and Mercury. In some cases, only this source of strength is used, like when timing events (calculating Nārāyaṇa daśā). In this case the second source is used first and then if there

[55] Standard Translation in Indian Universities is by Sanjay Rath, Sagar Publications.

is no stronger sign, then the first source of strength is used. Where when looking at the ārūḍha of houses, the first source of strength will show the stronger situation, and only after that will the second be used if needed.

The Third Source of Strength

- The placement of the lord from the Ātmakāraka (kendra, paṇaphara, āpoklima).

A sign lord placed in the kendra from the AK is stronger than the lord placed in paṇaphara, etc. This source of strength is used for seeing spiritual events in the life.

The Fourth Source of Strength

- The conjunction or aspect of malefics (or lorded by malefics)

The fourth source of strength is used for longevity and health calculations where the stronger sign to cause disease or death is calculated. It is also used in legal situations to see the stronger of enemies when this is needed to be seen. This source of strength is to see which sign is stronger to do harm, or damage. It is used only in these situations.

These are shortcuts compared to the lengthy mathematical calculations of ṣaḍbala. It is important to have an understanding of them as they will be used frequently.

Chapter 8

Bhāvapadas: *Perception*

Bhāvapadas: House Ārūḍhas

Each house has a manifestation that arises from it in the world. The *bhāvapada* is the image that arises from a house. *Ārūḍha* is another word for bhāvapada which means arisen.

The lagna represents the body and personality, from that arises ones fame and reputation in society. The fifth house is one's intelligence and from that arises one's degrees and awards for achievement. The sixth house shows enmity and fighting and that which arises from there are enemies. The science of bhāvapadas gives the ability to fine tune our understanding of how a house manifests in the world.

Bhāvapada Calculation

The methodology to calculate these images arising from a house are given by Parāśara in the chapter on bhāvapadas or house ārūḍhas (*Padādhyāya*) in Bṛhat Parāśara Horā Śāstra[56].

लग्नाद् यावतिथे राशौ तिष्ठेल्लग्नेश्वरः क्रमात्।
ततस्तावतिथे राशौ लग्नस्य पदमुच्यते ॥ २ ॥

lagnād yāvatithe rāśau tiṣṭhellagneśvaraḥ kramāt |
tatastāvatithe rāśau lagnasya padamucyate || 2||

If as many signs from the ascendant lord as he is away from the ascendant house are counted, the sign that is arrived at is called the Pada of the ascendant.

The ārūḍha is the reflection of a sign through its lord. So the houses are counted (inclusively) from the lagna to its lord and then that many houses (inclusively) from the lord. The sign arrived at will be the ārūḍha (reflection) of the house it was counted from.

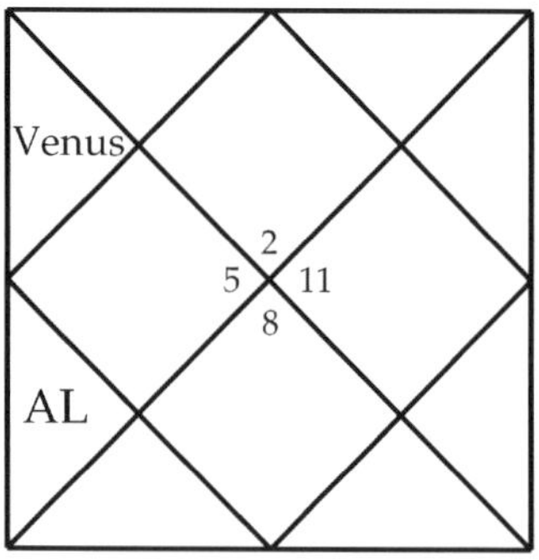

In the example chart, the lagna is Taurus which is lorded by Venus. Venus is three signs away (third house). Counting inclusively three houses from Venus the ārūḍha lagna (AL) falls in the fifth house in Virgo. If Venus was placed in the fifth house, then the ārūḍha lagna (AL) would be placed in the ninth house. In this way the ārūḍha is a reflection of the house from which it is counted.

[56] Bṛhat Parāśara Horā Śāstra, Chapter 29/31

सर्वेषामापभावानां ज्ञेयमेवं पदं द्विज ।
तनुभावपदं तत्र बुधा मुख्यपदं विदुः ॥ ३ ॥

sarveṣāmāpabhāvānāṁ jñeyamevaṁ padaṁ dvija |
tanubhāvapadaṁ tatra budhā mukhyapadaṁ viduḥ

The padas of all the other houses should be known in the same way. The learned know that the pada of the ascendant (*tanu-bhāva-pada*) is the principle pada (*mukhya-padaṁ*). || 3 ||

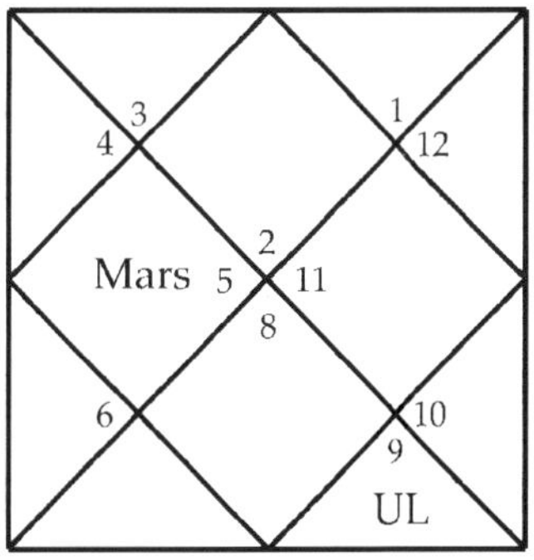

The ārūḍha lagna (AL) is the primary ārūḍhapada to be calculated, it shows what people think about you. The next most important ārūḍha is the upapada lagna, which is the ārūḍha of the twelfth house. The upapada lagna is the marriage point of the chart and shows all about one's marriage partner, the one next to you, and the marriage itself. The upapada lagna (ārūḍha of the 12th) can be written as 'A12' or more commonly as 'UL'. The same rule of reflection is applied; counting from the twelfth house to its lord and the same number of signs from that lord. Using the same chart, with Taurus lagna, the twelfth house is Aries ruled by Mars. Counting (inclusively) from the twelfth house to Mars in the fourth house gives five signs. Counting inclusively again from Mars in Leo for five signs goes to Sagittarius in the eighth house. The UL (ārūḍha of the 12th) falls in the eighth house.

In the same way the ārūḍhas of all the houses are calculated as A2, A3, A4, A5, A6, A7, A8, A9, A10 and A11. They are called ārūḍhapadas but they also have multiple names according to their use. For example, the A4 will be called the mātṛpada when examining the mother, or the sukhapada when looking at happiness, or the vāhanapada when looking at the manifestation of vehicles. The names are often poetic, sometimes they are changed to reveal deeper meaning and other times they are changed to fit the meter of the verses. English nomenclature has become shorthand and people speak in abbreviations; such as A4 when talking of the ārūḍha of the fourth house. Below are some commonly used names collected from various texts.

Ārūḍha	Common Names
AL	Ārūḍha lagna, pada-lagna, 'pada'
A2	Dhanapada, kośapada
A3	Bhrātṛpada, vikramāruḍha, sodarārūḍha
A4	Matṛpada, sukhapada, vāhanapada, vidyāpada
A5	Mantrapada, putrapada, tanayapada
A6	Śatrūpada, rogapada, matulārūḍha, ṣaṣṭhāruda
A7	Dārapada, kalatrapada, bhāryapada, jāyāpada
A8	Mṛtyupada, randhrapada
A9	Bhāgyapada, pitṛpada, gurūpada
A10	Karmapada, rājyapada
A11	Lābhapada
A12	Upapada lagna, vyayapada

Important Exceptions

There are certain exceptions to the calculation that must be taken into account. The ārūḍha is the image, the māyā of a house and cannot be in the axis of truth: the 1st or 7th house from the house it is calculated from, or else the truth would be clearly visible as it already is, with no room for projection. For the ārūḍha lagna, it cannot be in the 1st house or the 7th house. The UL cannot be in the 12th house or the 6th house. Any ārūḍha cannot be in the 1st or 7th house from its place of origin. Parāśara says,

स्वस्थानं सप्तमं नैवं पदं भवितुमर्हति ।
तस्मिन् पदत्वे विज्ञेयं मध्यं तुर्यं क्रमात् पदम् ॥ ४ ॥

svasthānaṁ saptamaṁ naivaṁ padaṁ bhavitumarhati |
tasmin padatve vijñeyaṁ madhyaṁ turyaṁ kramāt padam || 4||

The same house or the seventh house from it cannot become the house's pada. Therefore when the pada is in its own house, the tenth house there from should be percieved (*vijñeya*) as the pada.

When an ārūḍha is calculated into the 1st or 7th, one then proceeds to take the 10th house from that bhāva. An ārūḍha calculated into the 1st will end up in the 10th house from that bhāva, while the ārūḍha calculated into the 7th will go to the 10th from it which is the 4th house from the concerned bhāva.

In the example chart, the lagna is Gemini which is lorded by Mercury, and Mercury is in the fourth. So the ārūḍha is first calculated as being in the 7th house. Then it is put into the 10th house from the 7th which ends up being in the fourth with the lagneśa itself.

This rule will be the same for any ārūḍha from any house. For example, the A4 cannot be in the 4th or the 10th house, so it will follow the same rules of moving to the tenth house from it if it lands in the 4th or 10th house which is its 1st and 7th house. In this chart, the 4th lord Mercury is in the fourth house of Virgo. You can count 1 house to the lord of the 4th and then count one inclusive house from that which will keep you in the same house. The A4 (ārūḍha of the fourth house) cannot be in the fourth house or its 7th, so it will go to the 10th house from it which is the rāśi lagna.

The aruḍha shows your interaction with the world. If you are not interacting with the world then aruḍha is not as important. One's primary interaction with the world is through their work and career, in this way the tenth house becomes the aruḍha as it is what the person projects in order to fulfill their karma. The tenth from the lagna is where the Sun attains digbala, where it is the most seen. The aruḍha also goes to the tenth, as it is the most visible house.

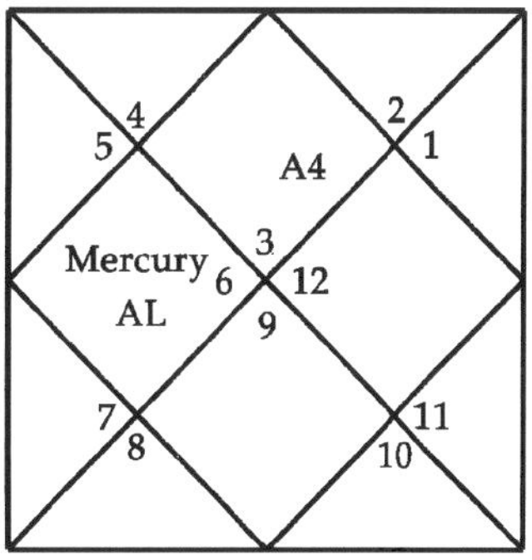

Parāśara gives a more direct way to calculate the ārūḍha when it falls in the first or seventh house:

यथा तुर्यस्थिते नाथे तुर्यमेव पदं भवेत्।
सप्तमे च स्थिते नाथे विज्ञेयं दशमं पदम्॥ ५॥

yathā turyasthite nāthe turyameva padaṁ bhavet |
saptame ca sthite nāthe vijñeyaṁ daśamaṁ padam || 5||

If the lord of the house is in the fourth from it,
then that fourth house becomes the pada.
When the lord is in the seventh house the pada is tenth from the original.

There are four situations when the exception can arise. One can calculate the tenth house from the first bhāvapada or just remember:

- If the lord of the lagna is in the lagna itself, then the ārūḍha becomes the 10th house
- If the lord of the lagna is in the 7th house, the ārūḍha becomes the 10th house
- If the lord of the lagna is in the 4th house, the ārūḍha becomes the 4th house itself
- If the lord of the lagna is in the 10th house, the ārūḍha becomes the 4th house

Dual Rulership of Aquarius and Scorpio

One must also take into account the dual rulership of Rāhu and Ketu in the signs of Aquarius and Scorpio as mentioned by Parāśara in multiple places. Since Aquarius is lorded by Saturn and co-ruled by Rāhu there are two possible ārūḍhas produced. The same happens for Scorpio which is ruled by Mars and co-ruled by Ketu. In cases when Mars is alone in Scorpio then Ketu is used to determine the primary ārūḍha or if Ketu is in Scorpio then Mars is used primarily. This is the same for Aquarius' dual lordship of Rāhu and Saturn. Otherwise two ārūḍhas are created and the strongest one is used.

Meaning of each Aruḍha Pada

The aruḍha represents the visible, tangible significations of a house. The other internal significations are seen according to the house and lord strength. So for each house one must understand the visible significations related to that house to understand the meaning of the ārūḍha. For example, the second house aruḍha shows money, stored wealth, and the immediate family. The third house ārūḍha shows brothers. The aruḍha is not used to see courage or valor, because these are internal significations, but the ārūḍha will show the daring acts a person does (which is based on the internal attribute). The fourth house shows ones happiness and education. The fourth house ārūḍha will show things that make one happy like cars, houses, and other luxuries. It will also show educational degrees that are the manifestation (image) of our education that hang on the walls of a professional's practice. In this way one can interpret all the bhāvapadas.

The bhāvapadas are used for interpretation. A house (area of life) is judged by four main factors:

- The house- the actual environment of that area of life
- The house lord- the direction that energy is working
- The house kāraka- the relationship to the natural significations
- The house ārūḍha- the manifestations arising from that area of life

Example Chart: Dalai Lama

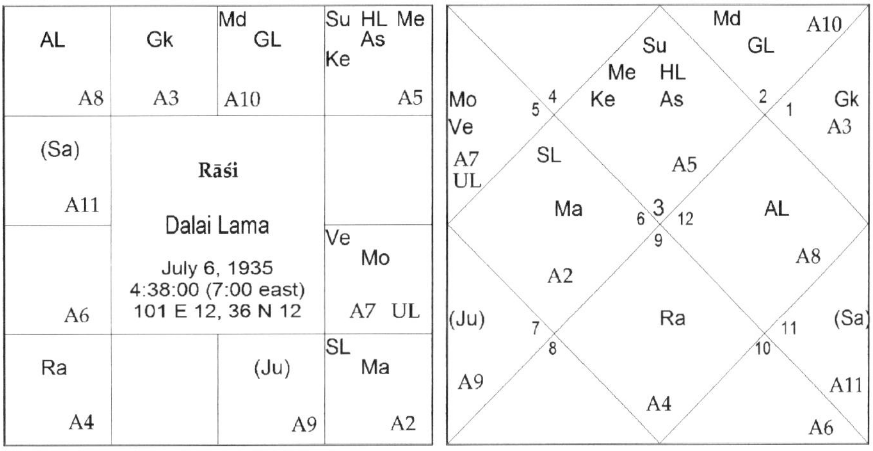

As:	13 Ge 29	Su:	19 Ge 58 (BK)	Mo:	16 Le 40 (PiK)	Ma:	25 Vi 19 (AK)
Me:	2 Ge 33 (GK)	Ju (R):	20 Li 31 (AmK)	Ve:	5 Le 17 (PK)	Sa (R):	17 Aq 06 (MK)
Ra:	29 Sg 27 (DK)	Ke:	29 Ge 27	HL:	4 Ge 22	GL:	12 Ta 23

Let's apply what we've learned so far to the chart of the Dalai Lama, looking first at his fourth house of home.

I. The fourth house:

A malefic Mars is placed in this house showing there is some fighting related to the home. The fourth house also contains the A2 so there was much wealth and traditional learning where he lived. The fourth house is ruled by Virgo which shows refinement and order in his home.

It is a dual sign aspected by other dual signs, therefore it has the rāśi aspect of Rāhu, Ketu, Mercury and Sun. The Sun is the third lord, showing colleges, giving spiritual advice about the home. Mercury is the fourth lord, therefore it works to protect the home through writing, speaking and other skills the native has. The aspect of Mercury is beneficial as well as the aspect of the own lord. But this must be combined with the negative aspect of Rāhu and Ketu as well as the situation of Mars in the house. Rāhu represents outsiders or deceit disrupting the fourth house, and Ketu adds to this.

There are no full graha aspects to the house.

II. The house lord:

Mercury the lord of the fourth is strong in his own sign in the first house. From the lagna this means he will have a strong focus on his home/homeland. From the fourth house, Mercury has gone to its tenth which shows there is much work being done related to the home. The placement of the lord is good and will strengthen the focus of the house, but it is conjunct malefics which will bring much difficulty.

III. The house kāraka

For home the natural kāraka representing home is the Moon. The Moon is in the third house which is not a strong house for the Moon. Malefics are good in the third, sixth and eighth, while benefics are not. Benefics in these houses make a person very passive and gentle, it is a good combination for a monk.

The Moon is in a fixed sign so it is aspected by the chara signs. Therefore the Moon has the rāśi aspect of Jupiter strengthening its resources. It has the graha aspects of Rāhu and Saturn. When more than two malefics cast a graha aspect on a planet then the aspected planet is considered cursed to suffer some of its past karma. The Moon is aspected by Rāhu (shock) and Saturn (suffering). The conjunction with Venus is a blessing showing comfort and beneficial nature of home, but the malefics aspects show negative experiences that must be experienced.

IV. The house ārūḍha

The fourth lord Mercury has gone ten houses from the fourth house (counting from 4, to 5, 6, 7, 8, 9, 10, 11, 12, 1). Inclusively counting ten more houses (1, 2, 3, 4, 5, 6, 7, 8, 9, 10), the bhāvapada falls in the tenth house. It is in the seventh from the fourth and since the ārūḍha cannot be in the first or seventh from the fourth house, ten more houses are counted. The A4 then takes residence in the seventh house with Rāhu. The A4 is disturbed by malefics like Rāhu and can show either disruption in the home, or living in a place foreign to the homeland. Rāhu is not well placed in Sagittarius and so causes more problems than normal.

The factors of these results are seen together in the summary chart below. The house does not do well, and the native left his home being exiled from his own homeland.

Prosperity	Loss
Mercury/own lord aspect	Malefic Mars in the house
Lord has gone to good house- lagna	Rāhu aspect
House kāraka conjunct Venus	Ketu aspect
	Sun aspect
	Lord of house conjunct malefics
	House kāraka aspected by Rāhu
	House kāraka aspected by Saturn
	Bhāvapada conjunct Rāhu

Practice Exercises:

1. Calculate all the bhāvapadas for your chart and one other.
2. Analyze three houses in each chart in the same way as above.

Chapter 9

Argalā: *Interaction*

Principle of Argalā

Maharshi Parāśara devotes a chapter, *Argalā-Adhyāya*, to the results of argalā. It is found between the bhāvapada chapter and the kārakāṁśa[57] chapter which relates to the importance of using the principle of argalā with the ārūḍha lagna, and the kārakāṁśa (as well as all other points in the chart). Sage Parāśara directly indicates to use argalā from all points of reference with special importance given to the lagna and ārūḍha lagna. Argalā is a foundational principle to be applied by all astrologers. Monnier Williams defines argalā as "a wooden bolt or pin for fastening a door or the cover of a vessel." In Jyotiṣa, it is meant to be that which is influencing (locking in) the results of a house, lagna, special lagna, ārūḍha, or the lord of a time period.

In the chapter on argalā, the student, Maitreya, says to Parāśara,

भगवान् याऽर्गला प्रोक्ता शुभदा भवताऽधुना ।
तामहं श्रोतुमिच्छामि सलक्षणफलं मुने ॥ १ ॥

bhagavān yā'rgalā proktā śubhadā bhavatā'dhunā |
tāmahaṁ śrotumicchāmi salakṣaṇaphalaṁ mune || 1||

Oh one giving blessings, you have spoken of the goodness that will be given
by Argalā, I am anxious to hear the particulars of these results, oh Sage.

The Guru, Parāśara, responds to the properly asked question. He decides to give his student some more specific details.

मैत्रेय सार्गला नाम यया भावफलं दृढम् ।
स्थिरं खेटफलं च स्यात् साऽधुना कथ्यते मया ॥ २ ॥

maitreya sārgalā nāma yayā bhāvaphalaṁ dṛḍham |
sthiraṁ kheṭaphalaṁ ca syāt sā'dhunā kathyate mayā || 2||

Maitreya, that which is called argalā gives the definite *(dṛḍha)* results of a house
and the fixed *(sthira)* results of the planets. It will be expounded greatly by me.

[57] Kārakāṁśa is the ātmakāraka in the navāṁśa

Argalā can show definite results for every house and planet. Argalā shows the *objectives* of the native, while graha aspects show the *desires* of the native, and rāśi aspects show the *physical influences* on situations of the native. Aspects of a sign/planet show its specific effect on certain houses/planets, while the argalā shows the interaction of every house/graha with every other house and graha. Every house is affecting every other house, as the chart is a complete whole. The results indicated by a planet in a house to all the other houses show the planets influence on every area of life. Parāśara says,

चतुर्थे च धने लाभे ग्रहे ज्ञेया तदर्गला।
तद्बाधकाः क्रमात् खेटा व्योमरिष्फतृतीयगाः ॥ ३॥

caturthe ca dhane lābhe grahe jñeyā tadargalā |
tadbādhakāḥ kramāt kheṭā vyomariṣphatṛtīyagāḥ || 3||

Know that a planet in the fourth, second, and eleventh gives argalā, respectively;
a planet taking position in the tenth, twelfth, and third becomes an obstacle.

Primary Argalā (Direct Intervention)	2	11	4
Virodha (Obstruction)	12	3	10

Argalā links houses into pairs. One house gives intervention while its pair obstructs the intervention. The twelfth, third, and tenth gives virodha (blockage, hindrance, prevention, impediment, opposition). The virodha will show who or what will come to obstruct your objectives and the objectives of the houses. Therefore, the second house gives while the twelfth house blocks that result. The eleventh house is giving while the third house is blocking that house's result, and the fourth house gives while the tenth house blocks that result.

निर्बला न्यूनसंख्या वा बाधका नैव सम्मताः।

nirbalā nyūnasaṅkhyā vā bādhakā naiva sammatāḥ |

When the obstruction is there without strength,
or of lesser number it will be destroyed.

The obstruction is removed if the sign of the obstruction is weaker than the argalā or if there are more planets giving argalā than planets in obstruction. The main strength calculation is best done according to Jaimini's second source of strength which is the larger number of planets means the sign is stronger (2.3.8). The third source of strength is the status of the planets (2.3.9). The sign receiving more rāśi aspects will give results according to the signs indications (the situation becomes an argalā or obstruction).

For example, the ability to have the money *(dhāna)* of the second house is obstructed by the expenditure *(vyaya)* of the twelfth. If you are spending more than you are saving, your savings are obstructed. But if you are saving more than you are spending then you will have a good second house argalā. If there is a planet in the twelfth and nothing in the second then there is obstruction to gains. If the second house has two planets and the twelfth house has one planet then the obstruction is overpowered. The planets giving the argalā will show the methods of removing the obstruction. For example, if Moon is in the second and Mars and Ketu are in the twelfth, then Mars and Ketu are blocking the results of the argalā the Moon is giving. On the other hand, if the Moon and Venus are in the second and Mars is in the twelfth then the blockage is overcome. It will be overcome by the significations of Venus and Moon.

In the same way, the third house causes blockage to the eleventh house. The personal desires for entertainment, pleasure or sports can block the ability of the eleventh house of making money/gains. There is one exception though called *viparītā argalā*. Parāśara says,

तृतीये व्याधिकाः पापा यत्र मैत्रेय बाधकाः ॥ ४ ॥

tṛtīye vyādhikāḥ pāpā yatra maitreya bādhakāḥ || 4||

Malefics in the third change the obstruction, Maitreya.

तत्रापि चार्गला ज्ञेया विपरीता द्विजोत्तम ।
तथापि खेटभावानां फलमर्गलितं विदुः ॥ ५ ॥

tatrāpi cārgalā jñeyā viparītā dvijottama |
tathāpi kheṭabhāvānāṁ phalamargalitaṁ viduḥ || 5||

Best of Brahmins, that is known as viparītā argalā, and thus should be known the planet and house results from the division of the chart.

The third house gives obstruction *(virodha)* to the argalā if there are benefics placed there. This shows the person does not take the force needed to achieve the house's goals. From lagna the person's actions are not strong enough to achieve, while from ārūḍha lagna the person is too nice and is considered a "push-over". The virodha caused by benefics blocks the ability to take aggressive action when needed to accomplish a job. Modern assertiveness therapy can be the remedy for these people. Malefics in the third cause viparītā argalā *(reversal of argalā)*, the reversal of the virodha to become an argalā. Malefics in the third make one assertive and even aggressive to attain the results of the house. These people will use *parākrama* (courage, exertion, boldness) to attain results. If the results of the house are denied the person will work even harder until they are achieved. These people can sometimes be considered aggressive and 'non-violent communication' programs can be used to teach them to use this energy constructively and still relate well with others.

When benefics are third from the lagna and malefics are third from the ārūḍha lagna or the other way around there is confusion created. Sometimes they are nice people who are perceived as aggressive, or the opposite situation where they are aggressive and have a sugar ārūḍha coating that makes them be perceived as sweet and nice. The viparītā argalā from lagna shows how the person is applying their intelligence. The viparītā argalā from the AL shows how the person is being perceived as they interact with others.

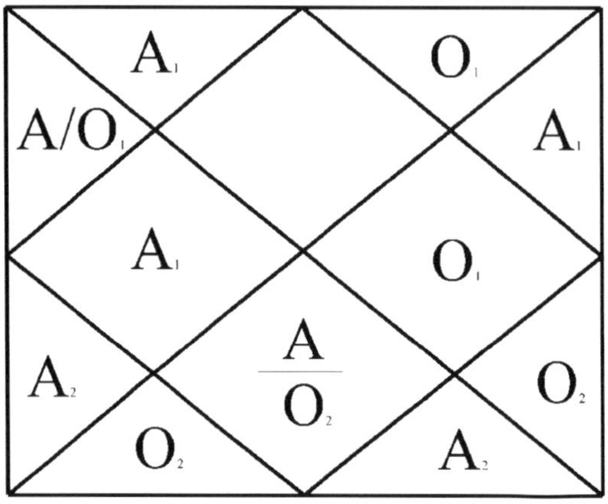

पञ्चमं चार्गलास्थानं नवमं तद्विरोधकृत् ।

pañcamaṁ cārgalāsthānaṁ navamaṁ tadvirodhakṛt ।

The fifth house is a place of argalā, and the ninth house gives it virodha.

The argalās previously given in the other verses are called primary argalā. The argalā and virodha from these houses will have a more direct interaction with the concerns of the house/graha. This verse lists the first secondary argalā which will have a more subtle intervention on the concerned position.

The paṇaphara (2, 5, 8, 11) represent the future. The āpoklima (3, 6, 9, 12) represent the past. The kendras show the present. In this way the past blocks the future. Old conditioning of the past obstructs new possibilities of the future. What has been done in the past controls what will be done in the future.

The eighth house also has secondary argalā while the sixth house has obstruction to that. The seventh house will have tertiary argalā or virodha on the lagna depending on the relationship between the planet's natural significations and the house's significations.

All houses are interacting with every other house. The diagram shows primary and secondary argalā and obstruction for all houses on the lagna or other point of reference. Planets give pronounced results, and the more planets creating an Argalā or obstruction the more powerful the results. Planets represent people interacting with an individual and the actions being done to get results.

When there are no planets placed within the house, the rāśi (signs) in these houses will cause argalā or obstruction (based on their strength). The signs represent the place or situation intervening. For example, if there are no planets in the second or twelfth house, then the signs become important. For example, if the lagna is Gemini then Cancer is giving argalā from the second and Taurus is giving obstruction from the twelfth. Cancer gives sustenance through caring, nurturing, water creatures, etc and is obstructed by Taurus which shows expense on luxuries, excess possessions or material pleasures. The stronger of the two signs will be the dominating influence in the chart.

Argalā is calculated both from houses and from planets. Parāśara mentions an exception -that the dark planets are calculated in reverse,

तमोग्रहभवा सा च व्यत्ययाज् ज्ञायते द्विज ॥ ६ ॥

tamograhabhavā sā ca vyatyayāj jñāyate dvija || 6||

The houses are understood in reverse from the dark planet.

Jaimini in his *Upadeśa Sūtra* clarifies that this reverse reckoning is done from Ketu only,

विपरीतं केतो

Viparītaṁ Keto ||1.1.9||

Reverse reckoning is from Ketu.

Therefore, argalā from Ketu is reckoned in reverse. The twelfth, third, tenth, ninth, and sixth give argalā to Ketu. Argalā from a kāraka shows the planet's *objectives*. All the planets are focused on manifesting things in this world, except mokṣa-kāraka Ketu whose objective is to liberate us from this world. Accordingly, look at argalā from Jupiter to see things related to money, children, Jyotiṣa, etc. Look at argalā from the Sun to see health, spirituality, etc. Look at argalā from the Moon to see influences on the mind, mental health, etc. For all planets, the significations can be seen from them in the natural order of argalā. But for Ketu see the argalā for spiritual liberation in reverse order. While for Rāhu see argalā in direct order (as his objectives are for the world) yet his dṛṣṭi (aspects) are in reverse (12th house is in the 2nd, 5th is in the 9th and 9th is in the 5th) because his *desires* are causing rebirth.

Argalā of Individual Houses

Parāśara gives a brief explanation of what each house represents using the concept of argalā. This can be applied from multiple reference points using all the rules taught earlier. The second house argalā can be seen from the lagna (sustenance of body), second from ārūḍha lagna (sustenance of image), and second from the kāraka Jupiter (sustenance of luck and wisdom). In this way, the chart becomes an even more multi-demensional chakra to perceive life and its levels of interaction.

सार्गले च धने विप्र धनधान्यसमन्वितः ।
तृतीये सोदरादीनां सुखमुक्तं मनीषिभिः ॥ १३ ॥

sārgale ca dhane vipra dhanadhānyasamanvitaḥ |
tṛtīye sodarādīnāṁ sukhamuktaṁ manīṣibhiḥ || 13||

The second house Argalā makes one wealthy and fortunate,
The third gives co-born, happiness, indulgent (*mukta*), and intelligence

चतुर्थे सार्गले गेहपशुबन्धुकुलैर्युतः ।
पञ्चमे पुत्रपौत्रादिसंयुतो बुद्धिमान्नरः ॥ १४ ॥

caturthe sārgale gehapaśubandhukulairyutaḥ |
pañcame putrapautrādisaṁyuto buddhimānnaraḥ || 14||

The fourth house Argalā gives houses, livestock, and family, the fifth gives children, grandchildren, etc., and a person endowed with understanding.

षष्ठे रिपुभयं कामे धनदारसुखं बहु ।
अष्टमे जायते कष्टं धर्मे भाग्योदयो भवेत् ॥ १५ ॥

ṣaṣṭhe ripubhayaṁ kāme dhanadārasukhaṁ bahu |
aṣṭame jāyate kaṣṭaṁ dharme bhāgyodayo bhavet || 15||

The sixth gives fear from enemies,
the seventh gives much wealth and happiness from spouse,
the eighth gives misery and trouble (*kaṣṭaṁ*), while the ninth gives bhāgya.

दशमे राजसम्मानं लाभे लाभसमन्वितः ।
सार्गले च व्यये विप्र व्ययाधिक्यं प्रजायते ॥ १६ ॥

daśame rājasammānaṁ lābhe lābhasamanvitaḥ |
sārgale ca vyaye vipra vyayādhikyaṁ prajāyate || 16||

The tenth gives kingly respect, the eleventh gives profits/gains,
And the intervention of the twelfth gives abundant expenses.

1	***Focal point.*** Planets in lagna will obstruct marriage as focus is more on self than other. Planet in lagna will shape personality and physical appearance. Planet with AL will color image.	7	***Virodha/Argalā:*** Wealth and happiness from spouse, more planets in the 7th house means more spouses or more focus on spouse. More planets in lagna means a disinterested or unavailable attitude to spouses. It is the doorway to get signified objective- benefics or exalted planets help achieve the objective, malefics block the doorway to objective.
2	***Dhānārgalā:*** That which sustains the bhāva: wealth, food, etc. Jupiter 2nd from lagna shows wealth and good food, while Rāhu shows a combination for imprisonment. Dhānārgalā from AL is that which sustains one's image/ fame- Jupiter there allows the image to rise, Rahu 2nd from AL shows image falling due to ill fame.	12	***Virodha:*** Abundant expenses, what takes away from the task at hand, where energy is expended, energy depletes focus on the task of the house.
3	The parākrama (force/courage) needed to get house's goals met, makes one mukta ('freed up', wanton, indulgent). Intelligence relative to application of skills. ***Benefics (virodha):*** siblings and supporters, will talk sweetly, too nice, good for sannyāsa. ***Malefics (viparītā-argalā):*** able to get what one wants through whatever means. Attainment of goals with less work.	11	***Labhārgalā:*** Profits, the work one makes money or gains from, hopes, fulfillment of dreams. Benefics: person gains from good work. Malefics: the person may gain from illicit or harsh activities. Planets here allow the individual or house to makes gains and growth.
4	***Sukhārgalā:*** To Lagna shows gains from properties and vehicles. Who is doing work for you, shows the ability to deligate work. A person or bhāva's definition of happiness/ comfort, mental balance needed to attain goal- Jupiter shows spirituality makes the person happy, while Rāhu shows the attainment of materiality makes the person happy. Sukhārgalā to the 2nd house: investments/ plans for money that bring comfort. Sukhārgalā to the 3rd house: the condition of the enemy. Sukhārgalā to the 4th: condition of the partner determines the happiness to the home life.	10	***Virodha:*** The respect of a king, The work you will perform to get results, if stronger than fourth then less deligation of power and more work carried by the person. Work takes one away from the home. The tenth house argalā from the fifth is the second house in which all planets obstruct children for the pursuit of the planet's significations. Tenth house virodha from the 11th house is the 8th house of loans –earning is blocked due to paying debts (its either in the bank-2nd house or to the debt collector-8th house).
5	***Argalā:*** The intelligence and planning needed, the future, children/students support. Plans to make objectives. Benefics: good plans that will fructify, a blessing. Malefics: bad plans to get power and authority, damage the future therefore need śānti mantras. 5th house argalā from the 6th house shows the job planning for the work to be done, a benefic will show good work plans. A malefic in the tenth will show problems with one's work-related planning.	9	***Virodha:*** Protection, past karma, past experience, advice of elders. Benefics: good advice that will override plans, Sun=father, Venus=wife/sister, Mercury=business partners/uncles will block bad plans. Good fortune, waits for objectives to be fulfilled. Malefics: Bad advice= avoid the advice of person significated by the planet. Malefics the 9th house from AK destroy ones bhāgya. From the 2nd house the ninth house argalā is the 10th house showing the actual work of making the money or not. Malefics show bad employer (father of one's money).

6	*Virodha:* Enemies, obstacles, bad habits (*shadripu*) that shorten longevity, stress laws/ code that hinders new beginnings of business or marriages or other social/legalistics, planets here will make the already delicate transformations of the eighth more difficult.	8	*Argalā:* Misery and suffering. The new beginning after a transformation, longevity, inheritance (things coming without work), disease that comes without work for it in this life, best if there are no planets in the sixth or eighth house (but signs will still show the argalā and obstructions.

Argalā from Different Houses

The results listed by Parāśara are for the first house and need to be adjusted according to each house argalā is seen from. One must understand each house in relation to every other house, and each house relative to every planet. For example, look at the argalā from the fourth house relative to education. The dhanārgalā for the fourth house is the fifth house which represents intelligence. Often people argue the fifth is the house of education because there is lots of schooling with benefics there and less with malefics. But according to argalā, the fifth will show how much of the persons intelligence is getting applied to education. The fifth house is intelligence and the wealth of education is the intelligence -the moreintelligencetherichertheeducationwillbe.

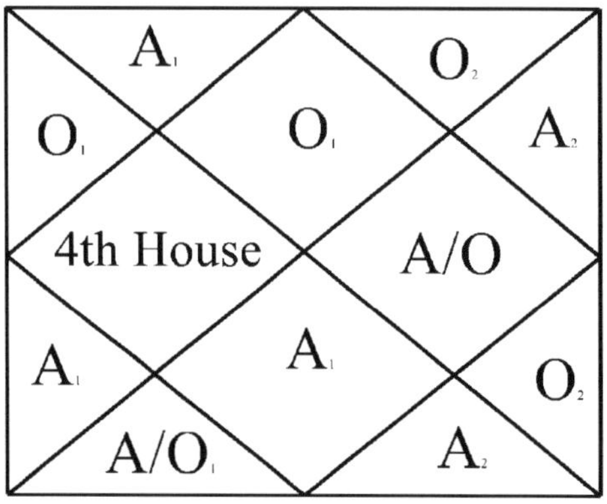

The third house from lagna has twelfth house obstruction on the fourth as it is the house of personal hobbies, musical/artistic performance, as well as the house of skilled trade using the hands; it is vocational studies instead of formal studies. The second house from lagna has labhārgalā showing that the support of family as well as monetary means are important to sustain the rise of good education. The sixth house is an obstruction if benefics are there. This shows too many enemies/bad habits during school, while malefics will give argalā by making the person work hard to achieve. The seventh house will have argalā by the person having a social network to achieve their studies, while the lagna obstructs based on too much focus on personal needs and fulfillment. The eighth house from lagna gives the fifth house secondary argalā which allows the person to do the study and research needed to be a successful student. The twelfth house has secondary obstruction by making too much time and energy spent on things other than study. The eleventh house from lagna has secondary eighth house argalā showing the friends one associates with will have a subtle influence on one's studies. The more professional and hard working one's friends are the better the longevity of education will be. Relative to the fourth house signification of land the eleventh house from lagna will show inheritance of property and in the same way it is knowledge that is gained through works outside of school. The ninth house obstructs this as it takes away focus from material plane oriented work. The tenth house obstructs the fourth if the work/job a person is performing is inimical to the fourth house or planets in it. If it is friendly to the fourth house it will support the education by allowing the person to earn through a similar vein which supports the education. In this way, all planets and houses are giving results for education. The chart is a holistic diagram that shows the unity and interwovenness of all life.

Argalā Compared to Bhāvat Bhāvam

There is sometimes confusion between the concept of Bhāvat Bhāvam (a house from a house) and argalā. Using the tenth and fourth house from a house as an example, should clarify the difference.

The fourth house is home and mother, while the tenth house is work and career. Bhāvat Bhāvam is used to see the various meanings of the houses; the fourth house from the fourth is the mother's mother, or the home of the mother. The tenth house from the tenth is the mother's career.

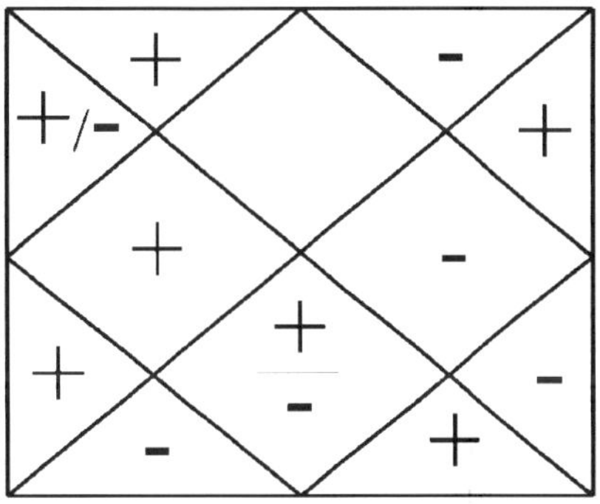

Argalā is used to see where the energy of the person is going. The argalā houses are similar to positive charges, while the obstruction houses are similar to negative charges. If Jupiter is in the fourth house and Saturn in the tenth, then Saturn is taking energy from you and away from the home, while Jupiter is giving energy to you and to the home. This would be someone who has a beautiful home and enjoys it, but is taken away from it by a lonely job. If Saturn was in the fourth and Jupiter was in the tenth, then the home would be a lonely place and Jupiter would take one away from that loneliness, showing that the person may enjoy being at work more than at home and will spend more time there. The stronger of the two planets will bring the person more to one place than the other. The stronger planet will show whether the positive or negative charge is stronger.

Fourth house argalā and tenth house virodha from the fourth house (relative to formal education) shows whether the person is putting more energy into themselves and self progress (tenth house from fourth) or more energy into developing social networks at the place of learning (fourth from the fourth).

Two Ways to Utilize Argalā

One area of life affects every other area of life, and this is seen through argalā. The rāśi shows the inanimate situation in the area of life, the bhāva shows the internal signification or area of life relative to the concerned house, and the planet shows the animate beings in your life represented by the graha.

राशितो ग्रहतश्चापि विज्ञेया द्विविधाऽर्गला ।
निर्बाधका सुफलदा विफला च सबाधका ॥ ८ ॥

rāśito grahataścāpi vijñeyā dvividhā'rgalā |
nirbādhakā suphaladā viphalā ca sabādhakā || 8||

Argalā is to be known in two ways; from the rāśi and from the grahas.
With no obstruction there is good results, with obstruction it bears no fruit.

There are two ways that argalā shows the interaction of the bhāva, rāśi, and graha in a chart: how a bhāva/rāśi affects your life and how your life affects the bhāva/rāśi. As an example we will use the tenth house.

- Argalā given by planets ***in*** the 10th house to other houses show how career influences the life
- Argalā given by planets in other houses ***to*** the 10th house show how life influences career

Notice the subtlety of grammar that sets these two dictums apart. This is why grammar itself is a limb of the Vedas -it is absolutely crucial for a person to comprehend interactive material correctly.

Now, the argalā of planets in the tenth house show how career influences the rest of the chart (the life of the individual). For example, Jupiter placed in the tenth gives a *dhānārgalā* to the 9th house, making the gains of dharma very fruitful. It gives *sukhārgalā* to the seventh house, making the spouse very happy. It gives *labhārgalā* to the twelfth house allowing for very good sleep. In this way a beneficial planet in the tenth will give beneficial results in these other areas of life, while tenth house malefics which cause problems in career will bring problems in these areas accordingly.

The argalā given by planets to the tenth house show how life (the rest of the chart) influences the career. For example, if Moon and Venus were in the eleventh house, giving large earnings, they would be giving *dhānārgalā* to the tenth house showing the career has good gains. Planets in the lagna show what the happiness of the career will be as it is giving *sukhārgalā* on the tenth. This *sukhārgalā* is blocked by the seventh house, which shows the spouse can override the happiness we have or don't have. Planets in the eighth house will be giving *labhārgalā* on the tenth and will increase gains in career. Planets in the second show the plans and decisions one will make regarding career. If they are strongly beneficial planets, they will show good decisions made about career and therefore being the second from lagna will show a large bank account. In this way, planets in all houses have an effect in some way on the tenth house of career. There is no house nor planet that is not affecting career. When you read a chart in this way, you will begin to understand the holistic nature of the universe we live in and how anything and everything we do will ripple throughout all facets of life.

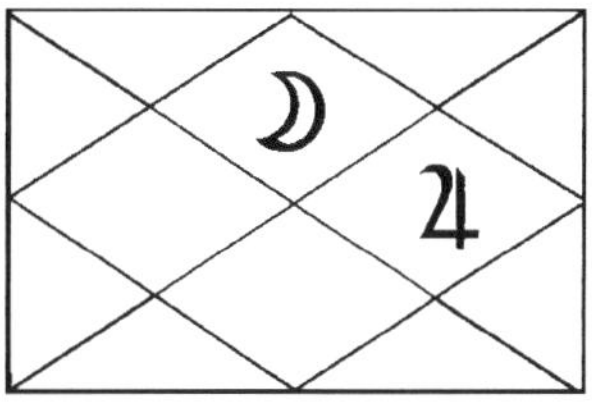

This is a tough principle to understand, but very important for a holistic view of the chart. This next part clarifies the above principles using Jupiter in the tenth as an example. There are two ways that argalā shows interaction but multiple ways to express this.

Dictum: Planets in X house give argalā/virodha to Y house/planet.

1. Jupiter **in** the 10th house gives 2nd house argalā to the 9th house

2a. Moon **in** the 1st house gives 4th house argalā to the 10th house/Jupiter

2b. Moon gives 4th house argalā **to** the 10th house/Jupiter

2c. Jupiter gets 4th house argalā **from** the Moon

Therefore analyzing Jupiter's position:

1. Jupiter in the tenth giving second house argalā to the 9th shows *how career effects the life*. A beneficial career gives support to dharma (9th house), or makes the person more dharmic.
2. Jupiter getting fourth house argalā from Moon shows how *life affects career*. The person's social popularity (Moon in lagna) gives them happiness (sukhārgala) in career, or allows them to attain happiness in career.

Also Jupiter as kāraka of children with the Moon giving subhārgala shows that there will be a lot of happiness through children or other significations of Jupiter.

Śubha and Aśubha Argalā

Benefics and malefics will give a different type of argalā. Parāśara explains,

शुभग्रहार्गलायां तु सौख्यं बहुविधं भवेत्।
मध्यं पापार्गलायां च मिश्रायामपि चोत्तमम्॥ १७॥

śubhagrahārgalāyāṁ tu saukhyaṁ bahuvidhaṁ bhavet |
madhyaṁ pāpārgalāyāṁ ca miśrāyāmapi cottamam || 17||

Benefics giving argalā will give many types of happiness,
Pāpārgalā (argalā caused by a malefic) gives partial happiness,
and mixed planets gives mixed results.

Benefics giving argalā, called *śubhārgalā*, give their results through well- intentioned, positive activities. After the results are achieved everyone involved is happy. When malefics give argalā, called *pāpārgala*, they achieve their ends through whatever means necessary. In this case there is often negative repurcussions from other people or the conscience. For example, when malefics give labhārgalā, the person may attain money through illegal means. This can lead to paranoia, or other things resulting from negative karmic acts (*duṣṭa-karma*). Therefore the person has happiness from attaining their goal but not full happiness as a śubhārgalā will give.

Malefics giving argalā can also give the results but of a less desirable quality. For example, Saturn having labhārgalā on lagna can give crooked friends; Saturn having labhāragalā on the ārūḍha lagna will show gains of money through illicit means. Pāpārgalā on the fourth house can give a house in a dangerous place or a house that needs a lot of remedial work. Malefics giving dhānārgalā to the lagna can make the person eat rajas or tamas foods.

Planets obstructing (*virodha*) Pāpārgalā can be beneficial as they will stop the native from performing harsh actions. Saturn in the second can make a person eat tamas foods. Jupiter in the twelfth can obstruct the native from eating these foods. Take the fifth and ninth house as an example. The fifth house shows one's speculation and planning for the future. This is why it relates to children who show the future of the family, or students who show the future of the lineage. The ninth house argalā shows the past karma and the bhāgya earned; it is that which is recieved because of past good karma, and that is why it shows dharma (of the ancients) and the father. The past is an obstruction for the future. Benefics in the fifth house will show good planning, while malefics will show wrong planning. Malefics in the ninth will obstruct one's plans whether they are good or bad. Benefics in the ninth will obstruct one's plans because of better plans. If a malefic has argalā on the fifth house and a benefic is removing it, this will be a person who makes bad plans but has the guidance of that planet in the ninth giving good advice. The Sun in the ninth shows the father gives good advice, Jupiter shows the guru gives good advice,

Moon shows the mother gives good advice, etc. A benefic in the fifth shows good planning and a malefic in the ninth shows it will be interrupted by the problem significated by the ninth house malefic. No one likes their plans to change, but if they do it is most beneficial to have them change for better purposes.

The kāraka's relationship to the house has to be taken into consideration. For example, using the fourth house of the chart, the fifth house gives dhanārgalā. A benefic there will support all aspects of the fourth house. Mars (*bhūmi-kāraka*) will support the person owning land but not other fourth house significations. Ketu will support buildings on one's land, Saturn is inimical to the Moon (fourth house kāraka) and will not give the most benefical help to the fourth house, it may show accumulation of trash, waste, or damage to the home. If Saturn is weak it may be a large junk pile collection on the land, if Saturn is strong it will be the collection of great antiques in the home. The ninth house is dharma and the dhanārgalā is given by the tenth house. If given by a benefic, there will be very good work that will support one's dharma. Jupiter is the kāraka of the ninth house and Rāhu is its most inimical planet. If Rāhu is giving unobstructed argalā on the tenth house it will show work that is not supporting one's dharma, thereby damaging the ninth house. In this case a benefic in the eighth house can be beneficial for one's dharma by obstructing Rāhu.

Planets which are kārakas for a house will not obstruct results of that house; instead they will force the effects onto that house. It is important for timing of events: when Moon has obstruction on the 4th house, in Moon daśā the person will be forced to go home.

For special ascendants, the relationship of planets to the kāraka of the special ascendant is important. Friends to Moon support the ārūḍha lagna. In the same way, the planets' support needs to be seen relative to the individual kārakas of the bhāvapadas. For example, the kāraka of the A6 is Saturn, while the kāraka of the A5 is Jupiter. The kārakas of the bhāvapadas generally relate to the kāraka of the house they originate from. Therefore, when looking at children, one can see the argalā houses from the fifth house, the argalā houses from putrakāraka Jupiter, and the argalā houses from the A5.

When one can recognize the argalā that is giving good results, then that planet or sign can be strengthened to improve the good results. For a planet, the remedies for weak grahas can be used; mantra, gems, etc. When there is a sign giving a beneficial argalā (or blocking a malefic argalā), it can be strengthened with rāśi mantras to assure the attainment of the results. The rāśi mantras are all Kṛṣṇa mantras which stabilize the mind with reference to that bhāva -they pacify, purify and strengthen the sign. Āditya mantras activate a sign but they activate all the good and bad associated with the house as well.

This is one of the hardest chapters for any beginner. But the principle of argalā underlies many of Vedic astrology's most important techniques: from interpretation of time periods to understanding divisional charts and many principles in between. When you understand the foundation, all the rules make sense. Therefore, take time with this chapter and allow yourself to fully digest it to unbolt the secret of argalā.

Chapter 10

Sambandha and Yogas:
Association and Combination

Sambandha and Yogas

Sambandha means binding, joining together, connection, or relation. Sam means with, along with, or together with. *Bandha* means binding, *sambandha* is the way things are bound or connected together, or the way planets associate with each other. There are various combinations that can connect two planets. Some of these sambandhas are called yogas. Yoga means to join for an application or type of employment, as a cow is yoked to help it drive the plow. A yoga is a sambandha with a purpose or intention behind it, and thereby it can be given a name.

There are two-planet yogas, such as Jupiter and Saturn conjunct makes *Brahma Yoga* (the person is curious about creation and existence). Saturn and Moon conjunct is *Kālika Yoga*, Sun and Rāhu is *Dakṣiṇamūrti Yoga*, etc. There are three and four-planet yogas. There are yogas formed when the planet lording one house joins the planet lording another house, like when the ninth lord and the lagneśa conjoin it is called *Lakṣmi Yoga*, which offers prosperity to the individual. When the the ninth lord of dharma conjoins the tenth lord of karma it creates *Dharma-karmādipati Yoga* where one's work and dharma align. In this way there are many planetary combinations that create yogas through various sambandhas.

Graha Sambandha

Grahas have specific ways they create sambandha. There are stronger connections and weaker connections. Just as a brother is closer than a second cousin, yet you are still related to both. When planets are in the same house, they create a Yuti (union); this ties them together very tightly. *Parivartana yoga* is when planets trade houses, and this ties them together even more tightly. For example, if Mars was in Taurus and Venus was in Aries they would be in each other's houses. These two types of sambandhas are the strongest and work throughout life.

Strength	Sambandha
100%	Parivartana
80%	Conjunction
60%	Mutual Aspect
50%	Graha Aspect

Mutual aspect is when the planets aspect each other, so they are both concerned and influencing the affairs of each other[58]. It becomes less strong of a sambandha when one aspects the other and is not aspected back. This creates concern and desire from one but not the other. The association through aspect, *dṛṣṭi sambandha*, is based upon *icchā-śakti*, the power of the planets desire and will. This desire will change depending on the daśa. Therefore the sambandha will give effect sometimes and not other times.

If a planet is being aspected by another planet while it is in that planet's sign, this is stronger than a simple aspect. For example, if the Moon was in Aquarius and aspected by Saturn from Taurus this would be a stronger sambandha than Moon in Cancer aspected

[58] Dṛṣṭi-sambandha is caused by graha aspect as rāśi aspect will always be mutual.

by Saturn, as it only has one association not two. A planet also is connected to a planet who is its lord by placement in that planets house, but this will be very less if it is not aspected by the planet. In this way, there are many ways to create sambandha, and some are stronger than others. Just as you are related to your uncle's wife's cousin, so also does a planet conjunct the lord of its house gain some distant sambandhas. It is important to see how planets are connected to each other and how strong the connection is.

Bhāva Sambandha

There are seven relationships that a planet can have through the bhāvas. They can be in the same sign, called yoga (joined). One planet can be in the second from the other planet which places the second planet in the twelfth from the first, this is a 2-12 relationship. If the first planet is in the third from the second, then the second is in the eleventh. This is a 3-11 relationship, as whenever the planet is third the other planet is eleventh. These relationships take on certain predictable energies.

Yoga is when planets are conjunct in the same sign. They share similar views and intentions. In graha sambandha the planets create Yoga for a certain purpose with various combinations, while in regards to bhāva sambandha the planets are situated in the same house showing that they will work well together. How well will depend on how naturally friendly the planets are to each other.

5-9 (trikoṇa) is the best relationship because the planets are working well together. They are in the same element and therefore share the same goals in life, and will work for the same purposes. Planets in this position have a healthy mutual relationship.

4-10 (kendras) show the significatons will work or live together in a harmonious way. The intention rests around using the other planet to attain career goals or home/happiness goals. The planets are in the same guṇa and work well with the other.

3-11 The third house is the house of desires, and shows the desires of that planet, while the 11th shows the gains of the other planet. The relationship revolves around the planets using each other to attain their ends. It can show friendship relative to the eleventh house but will be one based on getting something desired.

1-7 is called opposition and the planets are sitting opposite each other. They are the complimentary nature of opposites and can open the doorway for each other. They are always in a mutual dṛṣṭi sambandha and thereby strongly influencing each other.

2-12 is when one planet is in the house of giving while the second planet is in the house of losing (12th). One planet is enjoying the other but it is not an equal exchange. When relationships are like this one person will feel ignored or unreciprocated towards.

6-8 is the *worst* relationship between planets. There is friction and the relationship between the planets or bhāvapadas will not end on good terms. The sixth house is fighting and the eighth house has troubles. In this relationship the planets or bhāvapadas will be fighting and feeling hurt making both unhappy. [Occasionally there is a planet that harmoniously links the two planets and this will indicate the remedy for the situation.]

The bhāva sambandha interaction of planets/bhāvapadas is a key component of horoscope interpretation. Parāśara teaches in the bhāvapada chapter to look at the relationship between the AL and other bhāvapadas to understand how these people are interacting with the individual. Parāśara says,

[34] If the ārūḍha lagna (AL) and the dārapada (A7) are in mutual kendra (4-10) or trikoṇa (5-9) the couple stay together. If they are in trik houses (2-12 or 6-8) there will be false friendliness and hostility.

[35] The gain of friendship or enmity between people is seen from the respective house ārūḍha, as child and parent relationship is seen from the lagnapada (AL) relative to the tanayapada (A5).

If the AL and A7 are in the same house (yoga) then there are similarities between the desires of the partners and a beneficial relationship. If the AL and A7 are 4-10 or 5-9 there is a positive connection that holds the relationship together. If the AL and A7 are 6-8 then there can be quarrelling between lovers, if they are 2-12 there is false friendliness and hidden agendas. In this way the relationship between many points of importance are seen in the chart.

Yogas in Jyotiṣa

There are thousands of special combinations listed in various texts with names and a multitude of indications. This section will focus on a few primary yogas given by Parāśara that give definite results. The first yogas mentioned in Bṛhat Parāśara Horā Śāstra by Parāśara are the Nābhasa Yogas which lay out the tone of the indications in the chart[59]. These combinations though mentioned first give a more subtle result that is not easily utilized by the beginner student of Jyotiṣa.

Parāśara next has a chapter on various combinations (*vividha yogas*), followed by chapters on yogas for specific results. The next section looks at some of the various yogas mentioned by Parāśara, but keep in mind there are hundreds of special combinations and one will constantly be learning and exploring more. Below is a foundation for understanding how to look at and use the yogas taught by Parāśara and others which are found in the various Jyotiṣa texts.

[59] These have been explained by Sarajit Podder in Jyotish Digest 3-1

Śubha and Aśubha Yogas

The first yogas mentioned in the Various Combinations Chapter are the Śubha (good) and *Aśubha* (not good) Yogas. *Śubha Yoga* is when benefics only are in the ascendant. *Aśubha Yoga* is when malefics only are in the ascendant. When there is a benefic in the second and twelfth house a Śubha Yoga called *Śubha-Kartari Yoga* is formed. *Kartari* means scissors and shows that it is supported from both sides of itself. The second house of sustenance is full and supporting, while the house of loss is losing to beneficial areas. Malefics in these areas show the house of support is weakened and money is spent on malefic *(pāpa)* things. The condition of the planets must be factored into interpretation.

Śubha Yoga	Well spoken (*vāgmin*), possessed of beauty (*rūpaśālin*), endowed with virtues (*guṇānvita*)
Aśubha Yoga	Lustful (kāmi), will do negative acts (*pāpa-karman*), dependant on others wealth (*parārthayuk*)
Śubha-Kartari	Well supported and spends money for good purposes
Pāpa-Katari	Lacking support and spending money on the wrong objects

Parāśara teaches this Yoga from the ascendant, but every house is an ascendant for some aspect of life. If the fourth house has a Pāpa-Kartari Yoga then the mother suffers the indications. If the seventh house has a Śubha-Kartari Yoga then the spouse has these blessings. In this way, the ārūḍha lagna and other bhāvapadas can also benefit or suffer from these Yogas.

These combinations can be understood by good Jyotiṣa logic without remembering the yoga. But the memorization of these yogas aid one in being able to quickly see important combinations and quickly interpret them. There are also many hidden rules that the sages reveal by the various interpretations of these combinations.

Gajakesarī Yoga

Gaja means elephant and Kesarī means lion (literally, the one with the mane). These animals are symbols of respect and status which this Yoga can give. *Gajakesarī Yoga* is formed when Jupiter and Moon are in kendra (angles) from each other. The Moon must have benefic sambandhas and both planets need to not be debilitated or in an enemy sign or duṣṭāna. Therefore a strong Jupiter and beneficial Moon in a kendra creates Gajakesarī Yoga which makes one wealthy *(dhanavān)*, well-educated *(medhāvin)*, endowed with good qualities *(guṇasampanna)*, and favored by the government/rich and powerful *(rājapriyaka)*.

At a general level, just remember that Jupiter in kendra to the Moon is an auspicious combination that brings learning and wealth as well as greater support from society. This basic understanding will help with client readings. Then one can look deeper into the yoga and begin to understand more about Jyotiṣa. For example, the kendras are very important to the Moon. Where the Moon and its seventh house are on the Earth, the ocean is in high tide while the 4th and 10th houses from the Moon are in low tide. Planets in these kendras are highly influential to the Moon's nature. Good planets here bless the Moon and malefic planets cause suffering to the Moon. This rule about importance of kendras applies to the ārūḍha lagna (AL) as well as its kāraka is the Moon. The strongest planets in the kendras from AL will show what the person becomes known for. In this way, many deeper principles of Jyotiṣa are hidden within the yogas mentioned by the sages.

Amala Yoga

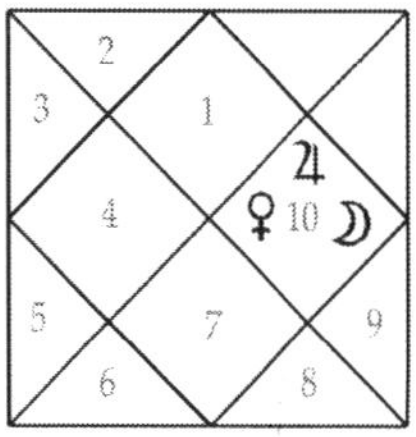

Amala means spotless, pure, shining and is created by only benefic planets placed in the tenth from lagna or tenth from Moon. Parāśara says it makes the native have long lasting fame, be honored by the government *(rājapujya)*, have great enjoyment of worldly comforts *(mahābhogī)*, be charitable *(dātā)*, fond of family and colleagues *(bandhu-jana-priya)*, helpful to others *(paropakārī)*, and one who follows dharma.

When only benefics are in the tenth house from the lagna the person's actions (*karma*) are beneficial and for the upliftment of all. The tenth from the Moon shows similar good karma, though relative to how a person procures their wealth. By doing good karma one makes themselves amala (pure and shining).

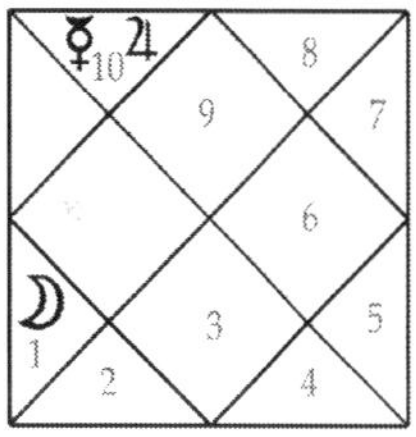

The first example chart shows benefic planets in the tenth house from the lagna, while the second example chart shows the Moon placed in the fifth house from lagna with benefics tenth from it. Amala Yoga from the Moon is more beneficial when it involves beneficial houses. Moon in the fourth with benefics tenth from it in the lagna is very nice. Moon in the third with benefics in the twelfth is not as beneficial. In this way, general factors are utilized to give the final analysis.

Practice Exercises

1. Similar and more complicated yogas are in the chapter on Miscellaneous Yogas (*Vividha-Yoga-Adhyāya*) in Bṛhat Parāśara Horā Śāstra. Read this chapter and check for these yogas in your own chart and one other chart.
2. Most modern software calculate these yogas, find where they are displayed in your software.

Rāja Yogas

Rāja Yoga is a combination in the horoscope that can show a rise to prominence, power, wealth and position. *Rāja* literally means king, royalty or chief. In the present time, the use of the word rāja can be interpreted as leader, boss, or government/ political position. Parāśara says that Rāja Yoga makes one honored like a king *(rājapūjya)*. An owner of a large business with many employees has the same power as a traditional king who ruled over a small city in pre-modern times. And people like Bill Gates or Andrew Carnegie who had huge businesses which influenced the lives of many people are similar in power to ancient kings. Mayors, governors, and presidents are those that hold power and position politically. To rise into a position of power in any of these situations, shows Rāja Yoga in the individual's life. Parāśara lists many of these combinations and says that they were long ago taught by Śiva to Parvati[60].

There are many aspects to understanding and interpreting Rāja Yogas. First they can be calculated from both the lagna and the kārakāṁśa. Second, upon identifying a Rāja Yoga, one must judge how strong the planets causing the yoga are and to what degree they can allow one to rise. The lagneśa, fifth lord, tenth lord, ātmakāraka, and putrakāraka all play important parts in Rāja Yoga. The effects due to their association will be full, or partial relative to the strength of the planets involved.

The yoga should have some connection to the lagna or the ascendant lord for the person to get the entire fruit of the combination. A Rāja Yoga without lagna association and instead association with the sixth lord can show that one's uncle is a powerful person. Rāja Yoga connected to the fourth lord and not the lagna lord will make the mother a powerful person, etc.

The third aspect is about the energy and resources needed to start the Rāja Yoga - does the combination have the power to raise an individual to a high position? The Sun represents confidence, initiative and resources. It will show the ability of the Rāja Yoga to be ignited. Then, can the Rāja Yoga be sustained once it makes a person rise? Some people rise to power and then fall from power. How long the yoga has the ability to last will be based upon the strength of the Moon as the Moon shows sustenance and support.

Varāhamihira says that the Sun shows the inner core strength and the Moon shows the mental strength and physical luster[61]. If the Sun is weak then the Rāja Yoga will have trouble starting, if the Moon is weak then there will be problems sustaining the rise to power and maintaining an elevated position. The lord of the Sun's sign should be strong and the lord of the Moon's nakṣatra should be strong. Parāśara has given some specific yogas to show the support of the Sun and Moon. These are to be analyzed before looking at Rāja Yogas in a chart.

[60] Bṛhat Parāśara Horā Śāstra, Rāja-Yoga-Adhyāya, v.2
[61] Varāhamihira, Bṛhat Saṁhitā, chapter LXIX

Lunar Yogas

Parāśara says the the lunar yogas have the power to destroy other yogas or to grant their own fruit[62]. To make correct predictions about beneficial combinations in a chart one needs to understand the strength of the Moon relative to this section[63].

The first two combinations mentioned below show the strength of the Moon relative to the Sun and the strength of the Moon relative to the Navāṁśa. Then the houses from the Moon are taken into account.

House Placement: The house placement of the Moon from the Sun is analyzed. The Moon is strongest in Āpoklima from the Sun, middle strength in Paṇaphara from the Sun and least strength in Kendra from the Sun to give wealth *(dhana)* intelligence *(dhi)* and skill *(naipuṇya).*

Jupiter-Venus Apect: If the Moon is in its own Navāṁśa or in a friendly Navāṁśa, it will do well if aspected by Jupiter for a day birth or aspected by Venus for a night birth. This supports one having wealth and happiness; while the opposite, Venus in the day and Jupiter in the night, is not supportive.

Below are the standard Lunar Yogas taking the situation of the houses from the Moon into account. The Sun does not count for a planet in these combinations as it causes the waxing and waning of the Moon. Rahu and Ketu also do not factor in as planets here because of their relationship to the Moon- only the physical planets are utilized for these yogas.

Candra-Adhi Yoga: occurs when benefics are simultaneously occupying the sixth, seventh, and the eighth houses from the Moon. Then planets are causing Śubha and Śubha- Kartari Yoga by aspect in this case. Parāśara says the person will be either a king *(rāja)*, minister *(mantrī)*, or general *(sena)* depending on the strength of the planets. This shows that benefics 6th, 7th, and 8th from the Moon prove beneficial and protective -they open the doorway by giving social support.

Candra-Upachaya Dhāna Yoga: occurs when all the benefics are in upachaya houses from the Moon (houses 3, 6, 10 and 11). The individual is wealthy *(mahādhani).* If only two benefics are in upachaya from the Moon there will be medium effects and only one benefic so placed will give even less results.

[62] Bṛhat Parāśara Horā Śāstra, Candra-Yoga-Adhyāya, v. 13
[63] Bṛhat Parāśara Horā Śāstra, Candra-Yoga-Adhyāya, v. 1-12

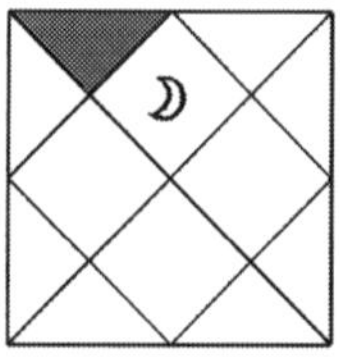

Sunaphā Yoga: occurs when a favorable planet (other than Sun) is located in the 2nd house from the Moon. This gives rise in life *(rāja vā rājatulya)*, endowed with intelligence *(dhi)*, wealth *(dhana)*, fame *(khyāti)*, and is self made. The second from the Moon shows that which is supporting the mind, emotions and providing sustenance.

Anaphā Yoga: occurs when a favorable planet (other than Sun) occupies the 12th house from the Moon. The twelfth from the Moon shows what the mind dwells on and what the mind wants to put money and energy into. Parāśara says it makes one have a position of power *(bhūpa)*, free from disease *(agada)*, gives good character *(śīlavān)*, and happiness *(sukha)*.

Duradhurā Yoga: occurs when favorable planets (except Sun) occupy the 2nd and 12th houses from the Moon. This gives the enjoyment of the best happiness *(utpanna sukhabhuj)*, makes one charitable *(dātā)*, wealthy with nice cars *(dhana-vāhana)* and good attendants *(subhṛtya)*.

Kemadruma Yoga: no planets (except the Sun) in the 2nd, 12th or conjoining the Moon and no planets in a kendra from the ascendant. This makes the native suffer disgrace, deprived of learning and intellect *(buddhi-vidyā- vihīna)*, poor *(daridra)* and have menial work *(patti)*. The aspect of Jupiter is said to cancel this combination.

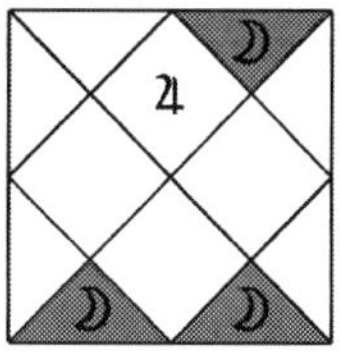

Sakaṭa Yoga: is formed when the Moon is sixth, eighth, or twelfth from Jupiter. It will often show a lack of motivation as the native will work only as much as they need to in order to get by (this yoga is located in the *Vividha-Yoga-Adhyāya*, verse 14, but placed here because of its focus on the Moon).

Solar Yogas

Solar yogas are similar to lunar yogas except they relate to the Sun which shows the strength of resources and the ability to ignite Rāja Yoga. Parāśara says the good results are according to benefics (*śubha-grahas*) while opposite results are caused by malefics (*pāpa-grahas*). The Moon isn't included in solar yogas, just as the Sun doesn't count in lunar yogas. For example, if there is only one benefic in the second house from Sun and it's the Moon it won't count to make a yoga.

Veśi Yoga- any planet (excluding the Moon) in the 2nd house from the Sun.

Subhaveśi- benefics in the second from Sun gives one balanced vision (*sām-dṛk*), makes them truthful (*satyavāt*) and gives long life (*martya-dīrgha*). Planets here are generally supportive of the Sun's significations.

Papaveśi- malefics in the second from the Sun make one lazy (*ālasa*), and happy with trifling earnings (*sukha-bhāga-alpa*).

Vośi Yoga- any planet (excluding the Moon) in the twelfth house from the Sun.

Subhavāśi- benefics in the twelfth make one skillful *(nipuṇa)*, charitable *(dātā)*, possessing fame *(yaśovat)*, learning *(vidya)* and strength *(bala)*. The person will put their resources into beneficial areas.

Papavāśi- malefics in the twelfth from the Sun will show loss of resources and energy on unimportant or worthless activities and objects.

Ubhayachari Yoga- planets second and twelfth from the Sun.

Benefics in the second and twelfth from the Sun will give the happiness *(sukha)* of a king or equal to this *(bhūpo vā tatsama)*. Bhūpa means king or sovereign, but literally means 'protector of the earth' or land owner. This shows better support through the resources the person has available.

It is important to analyze these yogas from the Sun and Moon to see what is uplifting or hurting them. If Saturn is causing Veśi Yoga (which makes one happy with small earnings) then the Rāja Yoga will have trouble starting because of this reason and will need to be remedied. If Jupiter is causing Veśi Yoga, then it is the person's balanced mind and truthfulness that will help draw the resources they need to ignite the Rāja Yoga. Bhāvapadas with the Sun will also show support for igniting the yogas. For example, if the Sun is with the upapada (UL), then the spouse will be the one who helps acquire the resources to rise up to Rāja Yoga.

Introduction to Rāja Yogas

There is a whole chapter given by Parāśara on combinations that make one a king and combinations that give royal association. Many of these combinations will be fully covered in more advanced lessons. This section will introduce a few Rāja Yogas from the *Rāja-Yoga-Adhyāya* in order to become familiar with the nature of these yogas given by the sages. Studying these yogas and understanding how they work reveals many of the fundamentals of Jyotiṣa. More important than the actual yogas is to be able to understand why the combinations are causing the person to rise to power and position in life.

Parāśara states that Rāja Yoga needs to be seen from both the lagna and the Kārakāṁśa. The Kārakāṁśa is the sign that the Ātmakāraka is placed in the navāṁśa. This becomes the lagna showing what the soul desires in this life. Many important combinations should be seen relative to the soul's desire as well as the placement in the rāśī chakra.

लग्नेशात् कारकाच्चापि धने तुर्ये च पञ्चमे ।
शुभखेटयुते भावे जातो राजा भवेद् ध्रुवम् ॥ ९ ॥

lagneśāt kārakāccāpi dhane turye ca pañcame |
śubhakheṭayute bhāve jāto rājā bhaved dhruvam || 9||

तृतीये षष्ठभे ताभ्यां पापग्रहयुतेक्षिते ।
जातो राजा भवेदेवं मिश्रे मिश्रफलं वदेत् ॥ १० ॥

tṛtīye ṣaṣṭhabhe tābhyāṁ pāpagrahayutekṣite |
jāto rājā bhavedevaṁ miśre miśraphalaṁ vadet || 10||

When there are benefics in the second, fourth, and fifth houses from the lagna/kārakāṁśa or malefics in the third and sixth houses, the native becomes like a king. If there is a mixed combination then the results are mixed.

Benefics in the second bring good money; in the fourth house they bring happiness, land and conveyances; and in the fifth house they give good intelligence and decision making. If they are strong, they are all supportive of a rise in life. Malefics in the third and sixth give one the force to go out and achieve what is desired. The person does not take no for an answer and fights their way to success. Remember this causes Rāja Yoga but the Moon and Sun must be supportive of the rise in life. The planet causing the Rāja Yoga must also be strong. One can only rise as high as the strength of these planets.

पदे शुभ सचंद्रे च धने देवगुरौ तथा।
स्वोच्चस्थखेटसन्दृष्टे राजयोगो न संशयः॥ १६॥

pade śubha sacandre ca dhane devagurau tathā |
svoccasthakheṭasandṛṣṭe rājayogo na saṁśayaḥ || 16||

There will undoubtedly be Rāja Yoga when the Moon is conjunct benefics in the ārūḍha lagna, Jupiter is second from the ārūḍha lagna, and it is aspected by exalted planets.

This Rāja Yoga teaches some important information. The Moon with the ārūḍha lagna makes one well liked, if it is strong with a benefic conjunction the person becomes well known. Benefics second from anything sustain that signification. If Benefics are second from the AL then it will be well supported to make one famous if the AL indicates that. Strong beneficial aspect to the AL will show what makes a person famous in life. Exalted Sun can show a high government opportunity, exalted Mercury will show high publishing/communication opportunities. If the planets aren't exalted they will show that the people and opportunities helping one become known are not as high of stature.

स्वोच्चस्थो हरिणांको वा जीवो वा शुक्र एव वा।
बुधो वा धनभावस्थः श्रियं दिशति देहिनः॥ १८॥

svoccastho hariṇāṅko vā jīvo vā śukra eva vā |
budho vā dhanabhāvasthaḥ śriyaṁ diśati dehinaḥ || 18||

Moon, or Venus, or Jupiter, or Mercury being exalted in the second house will make one wealthy.

This principle is simple to understand. An exalted benefic will give the significations of a house in abundance. The second house is the house of support and sustenance. But one must remember that the Moon and the Sun need to be supportive of any Rāja Yoga to give the full effect. This combination in the second house from the lagna gives monetary wealth while the same from AL gives the wealth of good name.

Lakṣmī-Nārāyaṇa Yoga

Rāja Yogas can also be formed when a lord of a angle (*kendra*) is in the sambandha with a lord of a trine (*trikoṇa*)[64]. The kendra houses (1,4,7,10) are called the *Viṣṇu-sthānas*, or places of Viṣṇu-Nārāyaṇa. The trikoṇa (1, 5, 9) are called *Lakṣmī-sthānas*, places of wealth and fortune. When these lords combine they create a *Lakṣmī-Nārāyaṇa Yoga* which gives power and success to a person, and allows a person to rise to prominence.

The most powerful of these combinations is the combination of the tenth lord of *karma* (*kendra*) and the ninth lord of dharma (*trikoṇa*). This is called *Dharma-karmādipati Yoga*, and is a combination for ones work and dharma being the same. Doing one's dharma is merged with one's career, and will involve the house in which the yoga is placed. In this way, kendra and koṇa lords create Rāja Yoga together.

Argalā

The principle of argalā plays an important role giving or blocking a Rāja Yoga. In the Rāja Yoga chapter, Parāśara says,

शुभे लग्ने शुभे त्वर्थे तृतीये पापखेचरे ।
चतुर्थे च शुभे प्राप्ते राजा वा तत्समोऽपि वा ॥ १७ ॥

śubhe lagne śubhe tvarthe tṛtīye pāpakhecare |
caturthe ca śubhe prāpte rājā vā tatsamo'pi vā || 17||

If the lagna, second house and fourth house have benefic planets,
and the third house has malefic planets, the native will be a king or equal to a king.

The lagna having benefics gives a good personality and attitude. The second and fourth house have a *primary argalā* on the lagna and the benefic placed there. A malefic in the third house gives *viparītā-argalā* which gives the ability to be aggressive to achieve one's goals. When a person has multiple śubhārgalās there are great blessings to achieve one's objectives. The benefic placements give the individual the means, while the malefic planets giving the power to achieve one's desires. This allows a person to achieve a high position in life.

When a time period activates a śubhārgalā in a chart, the individual achieves through benefical means. If it is a single argalā then it is a small achievement, while multiple argalās give a larger achievement. When a time period activates a viparītā-argalā the individual achieves through whatever means is necessary. When all these placements are present without obstruction then great objectives are accomplished.

[64] Bṛhat Parāśara Horā Śāstra, Viśeṣa-Dhana-Yoga-Adhyāya, v. 28

One can calculate the level of Rāja Yoga based on the argalā principle. Argalā is a crucial concept that will deepen the understanding of the entire chart. Since every house and planet is influencing each and every other house and planet, they will be affecting the level a Rāja Yoga can rise to. Sometimes helping to rise and other times blocking a rise. Parāśara says in the argalā chapter,

एकग्रहा कनिष्ठा सा द्विग्रहा मध्यमा स्मृता ।
अर्गला द्व्यधिकोत्पन्ना मुनिभिः कथितोत्तमा ॥ ७ ॥

ekagrahā kaniṣṭhā sā dvigrahā madhyamā smṛtā |
Argalā dvyadhikotpannā munibhiḥ kathitottamā || 7||

It is taught that argalā by one planet is smallest (*kaniṣṭhā*),
by two planets medium (*madhyamā*),
and argalā produced by more planets is called the best (*uttamā*).

One planet causing argalā gives minor upliftment. Kaniṣṭhā (smallest) is also the name of the smallest finger, and represents that the indication is held but not tightly. Two planets are called madhyamā (middle), which is also a name of the middle finger. This shows a stronger hold on the indications. Argalā caused by three or more planets is uttamā (excellent), as one having something firmly held in the hand. This strength of argalā can be seen from various points (lagna, AL, kāraka, etc) having three planets giving unobstructed argalā in any of the argalā houses. These placements will allow the person to achieve their objectives in the time period *(daśā)* activating these argalās. This will also affect Rāja Yogas in a chart.

When you see a Rāja Yoga see if it has any obstruction that will limit or stop the activation of that yoga. Then see how many other argalā planets are supporting the Rāja Yoga to fructify. This will fine tune how effective or blocked a Rāja Yoga is in the person's life. Using the principle of argalā, one can also understand the blockages *(virodha)* and see what the person can do to remove them. First, see how the obsruction will come -if the Sun is present it may be the father or government, or the ego that causes the obstruction. Understand the blockage using the natural significations as well as the house placement from the lagna. Then help the individual to see the blockage and the ways to overcome it.

Additional Yogas

After this Parāśara teaches wealth giving combinations (*Dhana Yogas*), followed by combinations for bondage and jail. He also teaches an entire chapter on yogas that make one renounce the world (ascetic yogas). These will be covered in depth in advanced classes. Here we will briefly cover wealth and poverty yogas and then focus on the yogas that make one a great personality with the ability to impact the world.

Dhana Yoga

Dhana means wealth and Dhana Yogas are combinations that make one wealthy. These occur by combinations between the houses that rule wealth.

2nd house	Money in the bank, savings, liquid assets
4th house	Land, conveyances, fixed assets
5th house	Investments, stocks, speculative gains
9th house	Luck with wealth and prosperity
11th house	Income, gains, profits, money earned

When these lords have a sambandha it is a combination for wealth. For example, if the 9th house lord is in the second house it gives luck with savings. If the 2nd house lord is in the 11th house it shows the persons savings are earning them more money. If the eleventh lord is well placed in the 5th, the person can make good gains from the stock market and other forms of speculation. These are combinations that show wealth *(dhana)*. Parāśara teaches that the lagna, fifth and eleventh houses are the most important houses to analyze for Dhana Yoga. Parāśara teaches that the fifth and ninth lords are the most important of the house lords for bestowing wealth.

धनदौ धर्मधीनाथौ ये वा ताभ्यां युता ग्रहाः ।
तेऽपि स्वस्वदशाकाले धनदा नाऽत्र संशयः ॥ १६ ॥

dhanadau dharmadhīnāthau ye vā tābhyāṁ yutā grahāḥ |
te'pi svasvadaśākāle dhanadā nā'tra saṁśayaḥ || 16||

The fifth and ninth lords or planets conjoined them
each give wealth during their, time period.

These fifth and ninth lord will help bring prosperous times as long as they are strong and well placed to be able to do so. In this regard, Parāśara utilizes the strength of the Vaiśeṣikāṁśa[65] along with normal strength rules. If these planets are strong, even planets joined them will give prosperity.

[65] Vaiśeṣikāṁśa is introduced in the strength chapter on page 175 and more in depth information is found in BPHS in the chapter on Yogas for Wealth (*Viśeṣa-Dhana-Yoga-Adhyāya*).

Daridra Yoga

Daridra Yoga is the opposite of combinations to make one rich. They instead make one poor or give problems with not enough money. They occur when houses of wealth or lords of houses of wealth associate with dusthāna lords or dusthāna houses. The sixth can show loss or debts related to litigation or theft. The eighth house and lord show loss related to loans, interest on debts, bad decision and bad luck with money. The twelfth house and lord show loss which may be due to taxes, wrong decisions, slow reaction time, delays, or other events related to the planet in the house or lord of the house.

षष्ठाष्टमव्ययगते लग्नपे पापसंयुते।
धनेशे रिपुभे नीचे राजवंश्योऽपि निर्धनः॥ ५॥

ṣaṣṭhāṣṭamavyayagate lagnape pāpasaṁyute |
dhaneśe ripubhe nīce rājavaṁśyo'pi nirdhanaḥ || 5||

If the lagneśa is in the sixth, eighth or twelfth conjunct a malefic
and the second lord is in its enemies or debilitation sign
then even a king will become poor.

This yoga shows the importance of the lagneśa relative to prosperity. When the lagna lord is in a dusthāna and conjunct a malefic the intelligence does not work properly and the individual wastes monetary opportunities. This combined with a weak second house lord does not give the ability to keep money. The native cannot manage money properly. Remedy is given by the aspect of a benefic on the situation, especially if it is the fifth or ninth lord.

कोणेशदृष्टिहीना ये त्रिकेशैः संयुता ग्रहाः।
ते सर्वे स्वदशाकाले धनहानिकराः स्मृताः॥ १३॥

koṇeśadṛṣṭihīnā ye trikeśaiḥ saṁyutā grahāḥ |
te sarve svadaśākāle dhanahānikarāḥ smṛtāḥ || 13||

A planet conjunct the sixth, eighth, or twelfth lords and devoid of the
aspect of a trinal lord will be detrimental to all finances in its time period.

Just as the time periods of the fifth and ninth lord bring prosperity, the time period of the dusthāna lords and planets conjunct them are not good for finances- especially when placed in a postion to hurt wealth. Parāśara mentions here that the trikoṇa lords remove the poverty issues. They will do so through their indications, so one can prescribe work related to the indications of that planet, to seek the help and advise of the people indicated by that planet and to perform remedies to strengthen the planet relieving the poverty yoga.

स्वांशाल्लग्नात् पदाद्वाऽपि द्वितीयाष्टमभावयोः ॥ ९४ ॥
केमद्रुमः पापसाम्ये चन्द्रदृष्टौ विशेषतः ।

svāṁśāllagnāt padādvā'pi dvitīyāṣṭamabhāvayoḥ || *94b*||
kemadrumaḥ pāpasāmye candradṛṣṭau viśeṣataḥ |*95a*|

If the second and eighth house from lagna, ārūḍa lagna or svāṁśa each have malefics then there is kemadruma, and it is worse if the Moon aspects.

Kemadruma Yoga

Kemadruma Yoga is a combination where the individual *suffers* poverty. The primary indication is malefics in both the second and eighth houses from lagna. If this is also from AL then the poverty will be worse, and self choosen if the combination is from the Kārakāṁśa[66]. If there are malefic planets in both the second and eighth houses from lagna, there will be monetary issues throughout life and it will be worse in the time periods of the malefics giving the poverty combination.

The Kemdruma Yoga can be broken if there is a benefic conjunct one of these malefic planets. If that benefic also has association with the second and eighth houses from the AL then it defintely has the potential to break the poverty yoga. If there are no benefics conjunct the poverty causing planets, then utilize a benefic or beneficial house lord that has aspect to the combination. If this is not available then use the lord of the second house if it is a benefic.

The main factors in the wealth and poverty combinations have been explained here but one should study the intricacies of the Dhana and Daridra Yogas in more depth in their relative chapters in Bṛhat Parāśara Horā Śāstra and other traditional texts.

[66] Bṛhat Parāśara Horā Śāstra, Kārakāṁśa-Phala-Adhyāya, v. 94-95

Pañca Mahāpuruṣa

Pañca means five, *mahā* is great, and *puruṣa* means person. The five planets correlating to the five elements can each produce a great person by the element becoming strong and predominant in the life. Planets in kendra will have a heavy influence on who the person becomes. When these planets become very strong, they will make a person powerful. That person will have the ability to make a big difference in the world. When Jupiter *(ākāśa)*, Saturn *(vāyu)*, Mars *(agni)*, Venus *(Jala)*, or Mercury *(pṛthvī)* are in their own sign or exaltation in a kendra it will form a Mahāpuruṣa combination. These combinations happen in kendra from the lagna and therefore relate to the intelligence of the person.

Mars- Ruchaka Mahāpuruṣa

Ruchaka means very large, an object bringing luck, as well as the citrus flavor. It can also mean a gold ornament. In general the person will have the best strengths of the planet Mars and the fire element. They will be able to work hard, overcome obstacles, and excel in areas ruled by Mars.

According to Parāśara, a person who is Ruchaka Mahāpuruṣa has a long face *(dīrghānana)*, high energy and enthusiasm *(mahotsāha)*, is healthy *(svaccha)*, has great strength *(mahābala)*, an attractive brow *(cārubhrū)*, dark hair *(nīla keśara)* and slender thighs. Their complexion is dark reddish *(raktaśyāma)*, radiant (*suruci*) and they enjoy war (*raṇapriya*)[67].

The person is a chief of gangsters *(chora-nāyaka)* and they are good at killing and destroying enemies (*arihan*). They can be cruel and abusive *(krūrabhartā)*, but are respectful to Brahmins *(dvijapūjaka)*. They are skilled in dark mantras *(mantra-abichāra-kuśalī)*, will die by fire *(vahni)* or enemies *(śatreṇa)* and attain the realm of the gods *(surālaya)*.

Mercury- Bhadra Mahāpuruṣa

Bhadra means blessed, auspicious, fortunate, and friendly. The person will have the good qualities of Mercury. They will be known for their large circle of friends, be skilled, good at communication and knowledgable.

Parāśara says they will have the wisdom and appearance of the lion *(śārdūla- pratibhā)*, have a muscular chest *(pīna-vakṣa)*, walk like an elephant *(gaja-gati)*, have muscular limbs and joints *(pīna-jānu-bhuja)*, with well formed feet *(śobha-aṅghri)*. There have moderate weight *(bhārapramita)*, dark and curly hair *(kṛṣṇākuñcita-keśa)*, a handsome nose *(sunāsā)*, and good quality beard *(śobha-śmaśru)*.

They have a well rounded understanding *(prājñaścaturasra)*, are skilled in Yoga *(yogavid)*, and live a life of sattva *(sattvika)*. They enjoy comforts and desire *(kāmī)*, have knowledge of weapons *(astravid)*, are clever, wise, skillful *(dhīra)*, independent, self willed,

[67] Varāhamihira adds that they have thin calves and knees *(kṛśa janu jaṅga)*

and possessed of freedom *(svatantra)*. They are good at all business *(sarvakāryeṣu)*, able to entertain their social circle *(svajana-prīṇana-kṣama)*, and possessed of wife and children (*strī-suta-anvita*). Varāhamihira says they have the smell of the earth after it has rained (*navāmbu-sikta-avani*). He also mentions that their penis becomes smaller than normal when flaccid and grows larger when aroused, just like a horse or elephant's penis disappears when it is not aroused. He also says that Bhadra Mahāpuruṣa people are independent thinkers *(svatantra-buddhi)*.

Jupiter- Haṁsa Mahāpuruṣa

Haṁsa means swan and spirit. The swan is a pure white bird gracefully floating on top of the water of māyā which is the world yet it stays unsullied by the water and graceful like the ātmā (soul) inside of each person. A realized being becomes a paramahaṁsa (a great soul) because of their realization of this ātmā. One of Jupiter's names is Jīva, or the individual soul, and its name as 'so ham' or 'haṁsa' comes from the sound of the breath emanating from the jīvātmā. The Haṁsa Mahāpuruṣa has the best qualities of Jupiter, they are knowledgable and are benefactors of the spiritual sciences.

Parāśara says they have the voice of the 'swan' *(haṁsa-svaro)*, are fair complexioned *(gaura)*, have a good face *(sumukha)*, a noble/prominent nose *(uttana-nāsika)*, honey or light brown eyes *(madhupiṅgakṣa)*, and a reddish tint to their finger and toe nails *(rakta-varṇa-nakha)*. They suffer excess kapha/phlegm *(śleṣmala)*, have fleshy well mounded cheeks *(pīna-gaṇḍa-sthala)*, a round head *(vṛtta śira)*, and well formed feet *(sucharaṇa)*.

They have good intelligence *(sudhī)*, are land owners, or sovereigns *(nṛpa)*, owning land between rivers. They enjoy water sports *(jala-krīḍa-rati)*, and cannot satisfy their love and passion enough[68] *(kāmārtha-naiti-tuṣṭatām)*. They die after having enjoyed all happiness on earth (*bhuktvā sarvasukhaṁ bhuvi*).

Venus- Mālavya Mahāpuruṣa

Mālavya means one who wears a garland or worthy of being garlanded. Artists, musicians, and politicians are all often adorned with garlands to show respect and appreciation. These people have the best aspects of Venus. They have the creative energy of the water element, and shiny eyes. Venus finds digbala in the fourth house, where it gives all the comforts of life. In the same way, Mālavya Yoga brings comforts and enjoyments.

Parāśara says they have well shaped lips *(samauṣṭa)*, nice teeth *(samasavaccharada)*, the face is slightly longer than it is wide, and they possess the loveliness of the Moon *(Chandra-kānti-ruchi)*. They are not too red in their complexion *(nāti raktāṅga)*, and has a good smell *(sugandha)*. Their waist is thin *(kṛśa madhya)*, and they are not too short *(na-hrasva)*, and not too tall *(nāti dīrgha)*, but have long arms *(ājanu-bāhu-dhṛk)*. Their voice is deep and loud

[68] Varāhamihira adds that their semen is thick and copious *(śukra sāratā dviguṇa)*

like an elephant *(hasti-nāda)*. They enjoy themselves *(bhuktva)*, live happily *(sukha)*, and go to the heavenly realms *(surālayam)* after death. Varāhamihira adds that they leave their body in a sacred place through yoga and penance.

Saturn- Śaśa Mahāpuruṣa

Saturn gives the strength of the vāyu (air) element. These people are strong and powerful *(śūra)* and make things happen. They have a soft face and small teeth *(tanudvijamukha)*, and the teeth may be projecting some *(dantura)*. They are not short *(nāti hrasva)*, but have a slender abdomen *(kṛśira-udara)*, and the middle of the body is very thin *(Madhya-kṣāma)*, while the calves are strong *(sujaṅgha)*.

They are intelligent *(matimān)*, and have very good knowledge and understanding of people's weaknesses *(pararandhravid)*. They are competent *(śakta)*, and may be a leader of an army or group *(senānī)*, but may be inconsistent or inconsiderate *(cañcala)*. They live in or own places that are hard to access like mountains and forests *(vana-adri-durgeṣu)*. These people have knowledge of minerals and metals *(dhātu-vādī)*. They are happy *(sukhi)*, very capable with women *(strīśakta)*, and seek after other people's wealth *(anya-dhāna-anvita)*. They own land *(bhūpo'yaṁ)*, and are lords of producing things from the earth *(vasudhā)*. Varāhamihira adds that they may suffer from abdominal/colon/gas problems as well anal fistula. When they die they will go to the abode of Yama, the lord of death.

The five planets represent the five elements (tattvas) which are the essence of everything created. These five tattvas in their perfected states exist in the five faces of Śiva, as told in the Purāṇas and Tantras. Śiva is the primal Mahāpuruṣa, the original Great Person. The five mantras used in Śiva pūjā are known to activate these Yogas in a chart.

Ākāśa	Jupiter	Haṁsa	auṁ īśānāya namaḥ
Vāyu	Saturn	Śaśa	auṁ tatpuruṣāya namaḥ
Agni	Mars	Ruchaka	auṁ aghorāya namaḥ
Jala	Venus	Mālavya	auṁ vāmadevāya namaḥ
Pṛthvi	Mercury	Bhadra	auṁ sadyojātāya namaḥ

When there is more than one Mahāpuruṣa Yoga in the chart, the strongest one is predominant. This will be based upon the one conjunct the most planets. If they have the same number of planets then the strength is based on sign (uccha, mūlatrikoṇa, and then own sign). If these are the same then the tenth house is strongest followed by the seventh, the fourth and lastly the lagna.

Practice Exercises:

4. Aquire the charts of people you know who are wealthy and see which combinations are causing this. Aquire the charts of people that have financial problems and find the factors that are causing this.
5. Read through the characteristics of Pañca Mahāpuruṣa chapter (*Pañca-Mahāpuruṣa-Lakṣaṇa-Adhyāya*) in Bṛhat Parāśara Horā Śāstra, chapter 75/77. Note the physical and personality characteristics of each of the planets. Note the symbols that are found on the palm for each planet.
6. Work on putting the general combinations listed in this chapter into memory, so they can be quickly found in a chart. There are many yogas, these listed here are the first to begin with.

Chapter 11

Nakṣatras: *Stars*

Nakṣatras

Parāśara gives very little information on the nakṣatras except for moments of actual application as it relates to interpreting a birth chart. He says in the very beginning of Bṛhat Parāśara Horā Śāstra,

संज्ञा नक्षत्रवृन्दानां ज्ञेयाः सामान्यशास्त्रतः ।
एतच्छास्त्रानुसारेण राशिकेटफलं ब्रुवे ॥ ७ ॥

sañjñā nakṣatravṛndānāṁ jñeyāḥ sāmānyaśāstrataḥ |
etacchāstrānusāreṇa rāśikeṭaphalaṁ bruve || 7||

Complete and total knowledge of the nakṣatras
is to be known from the general śāstras.
From these śāstras one will also learn about the results of the rāśi and planets.

Parāśara is telling us here that complete knowledge of the nakṣatras should be learnt from the general scriptures (*śāstras*). He is expecting one to already have this knowledge as it was as common in his time as the classroom history lesson is in our time. It is therefore important to learn about the general mythology and attributes of the nakṣatras from various sources.

As an aid to understand Parāśara's teachings on the nakṣatras, the first section will briefly look at the relevant astronomy *(gaṇita)*. The middle section and bulk of this chapter presents some of the mythological stories relating to the presiding deities of each of the 27 nakṣatras. The last section will touch on a few of the various applications of nakṣatra in the chakras found throughout the Jyotiṣa classics, Purāṇas and Tantras.

Nakṣatras in the Sky

We live in a spiral galaxy called the Milky Way. Our Sun is one of 200 billion stars that constitute our Galaxy. All objects in the Milky Way orbit their common center of mass called the Galactic Center. Our solar system is located toward the outer part of the Milky Way. In the diagram to the left, notice the Galactic Center relative to the location of our solar system's Sun. We are about 28,000 light years from the Galactic Center. Because of the disk-like spiral shape of our galaxy it is perceived as a milky trail through the night sky. From our perspective, the center is in Sagittarius, specifically in a section of the sky called Mūla, which means "the root".

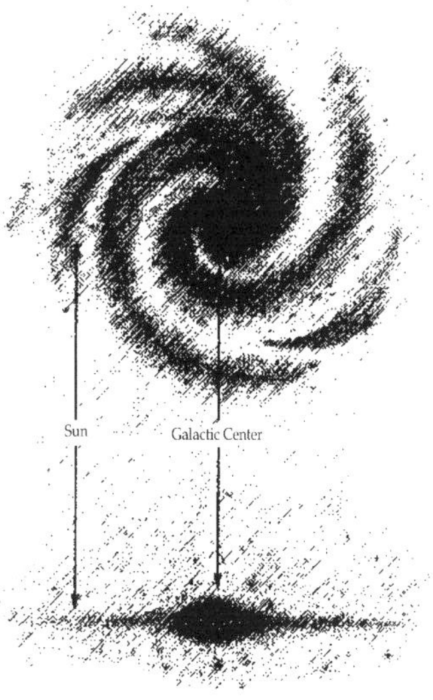

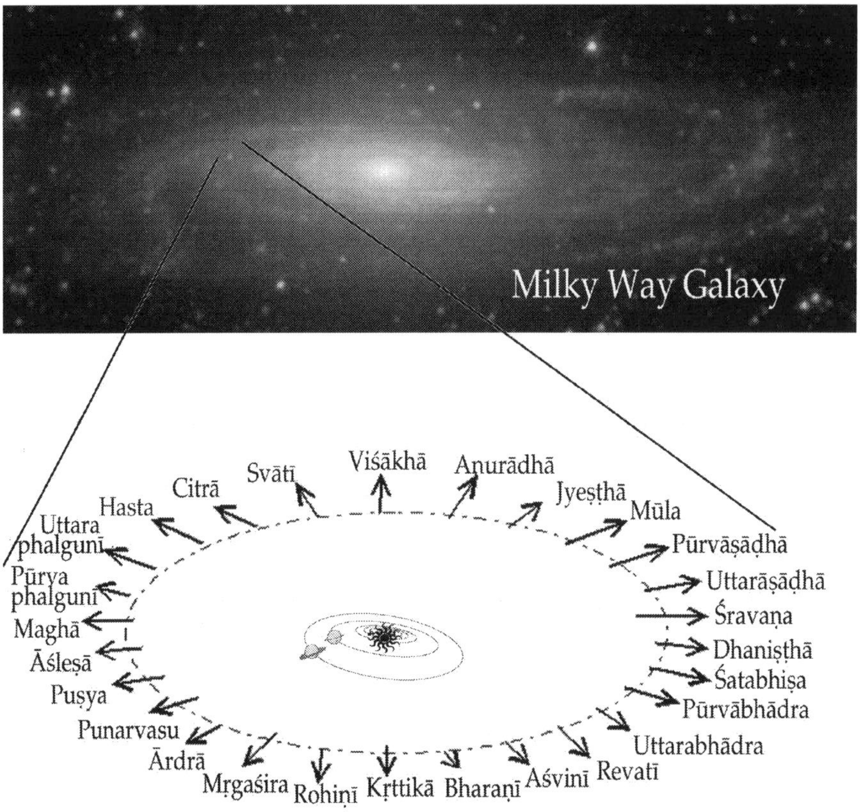

Division into 27 Nakṣatras

The Moon takes 27.3217 days to make one revolution around the zodiac, this is called a *sidereal* month. The sky is therefore divided into this sidereal interval of 27 constellations called the Nakṣatras. Each nakṣatra is 13° and 20′ of the sky and overlaps the Sun signs.

The tithis are based on the *synodic* month, the period from one full Moon to the next. The synodic month covers 29.5306 days, rounded to 30 tithis. This relates to the Sun's movement of 30 degrees per month creating the Sun signs that are common to most modern day cultures. In this way, the lunar *synodic* months create the Sun signs, and the lunar *sidereal* months creates the nakṣatra. The Sun signs show the quantitative and qualitative material resources while the lunar signs show the quantitative and qualitative *mental* and *emotional* resources.

The Moon takes 27 days to go around the zodiac, and will continue to move forward another two and a half days until it becomes full. This progressively puts each full Moon in the next Sun sign. The Moon is therefore referenced by its nakṣatra (lunar constellation) and tithi (lunar phase).

Nakṣatra Degrees

To the left is a chart with the degrees of the nakṣatras showing how the Moon's constellations (shown in the nakṣatra column) overlap the Sun's signs (shown in the degrees column). There are three sets of nine nakṣatras, as shading indicates.

The nakṣatras and the rāśi line up in three places which divide these nakṣatras into three sets. These are the Gaṇḍānta points mentioned in the previous strength chapter. Gaṇḍānta happens in the Rāśi between Cancer (Āśleṣā) and Leo (Maghā), Scorpio (Jyeṣṭhā) and Sagittarius (Mūla), and Pisces (Revatī) and Aries (Aśvinī). These are points of major transition and when the lagna or important planets are placed at the end of these signs, close to these transition (*sandhi*) points, they are weakened. Parāśara lists very specific Pūjās to remedy the Moon, lagna or a planet placed in Gaṇḍānta. There are additional specific pūjās for placements in Jyeṣṭhā and Mūla as these are more severe transition points. In this way Parāśara teaches about the nakṣatras in a utilitarian, practical format.

	Nakṣatra	Degrees
1	Aśvinī	00°00′- 13°20′ Aries
2	Bharaṇī	13°20′- 26°40′ Aries
3	Kṛttikā	26°40′Ari - 10°00′ Tau
4	Rohiṇī	10°00′- 23°20′ Taurus
5	Mṛgaśiras	23°20′ Tau- 6°40′ Gem
6	Ārdrā	06°40′- 20°00′ Gemini
7	Punarvasu	20°00′ Gem- 3°20′ Can
8	Puṣya	03°20′- 16°40′ Cancer
9	Āśleṣa	16°40′- 30°00′ Cancer
10	Maghā	00°00′- 13°20′ Leo
11	Pūrvaphalgunī	13°20′- 26°40′ Leo
12	Uttaraphalgunī	26°40′ Leo - 10°00′ Virg
13	Hasta	10°00′- 23°20′ Virgo
14	Citrā	23°20′ Virg - 6°40′ Lib
15	Svātī	6°40′- 20°00′ Libra
16	Viśākhā	20°00′ Lib - 3°20′ Sco
17	Anurādhā	3°20′- 16°40′ Scorpio
18	Jyeṣṭhā	16°40′- 30°00′ Scorpio
19	Mūla	00°00′- 13°20′ Sagittarius
20	Pūrvāṣāḍhā	13°20′- 26°40′ Sagittarius
21	Uttarāṣāḍhā	26°40′ Sag - 10°00′ Cap
22	Śravaṇa	10°00′- 23°20′ Capricorn
23	Dhaniṣṭhā	23°20′ Cap - 6°40′ Aqu
24	Śatabhiṣa	6°40′ - 20°00′ Aquarius
25	Pūrvābhādra	20°00′ Aqu - 3°20′ Pisc
26	Uttarabhādra	3°20′- 16°40′ Pisces
27	Revatī	16°40′- 30°00′ Pisces

Practice Exercise:

1. Study the relationship of the nakṣatra degrees to the signs of the zodiac. See where they line up and where they do not. Study the degrees enough to be familiar with the general patterns.
2. Look in the end chapters of the second volume of Bṛhat Parāśara Horā Śāstra and find the pūjās mentioned for births in Gaṇḍānta. Check to see if you have planets placed in these positions.

The 28th Nakṣatra

There are two systems of nakṣatras, one with 27 portions and one with 28. The sidereal month takes 27.3217 days to transit the 360 degree zodiac. The 27 nakṣatra system averages this to 27 signs each making up 13 degrees and 20 minutes of arc. The 28 Nakṣatra system calculates the remaining 7 hours and 38 minutes into a portion called *Abhijit* spanning 4 degrees 14 minutes and 13 seconds of arc. Abhijit is calculated from 6° 40′ to 10° 53′ 20″ Capricorn (or 276° 40′ to 280° 54′ 13″). The 27 nakṣatra system is for all mundane purposes. The 28 nakṣatra system is for spiritual purposes as its lord is Hari. It is important when using nakṣatra techniques to be aware of whether it is a 27 or 28 nakṣatra system and to know when it is appropriate to use one or the other.

General Śāstra

There are a variety of verses throughout the Jyotiṣa literature on the nakṣatras. Sometimes the scriptures can be very extreme in how beneficent or malevolent a nakṣatra will be. This is not to be taken literally. The nakṣatra will show how the mind filters information and sensory stimuli, showing the psychology of the native and how they are percieving and interacting with their environment. Meditation and inner work can change the general indications as one gains the ability to control their mind.

The positive or negative indications will be modified due to the lagna and lagna lord (how the person uses their intelligence), the fourth house (the clarity of their heart and feelings), conjunctions and aspects to the Moon, general strengths and the condition of the ātmakāraka. A good astrologer can look at a chart and see how these indications modify the native's current condition. A beginner can look into the eyes of the native and look for light and clarity. This light and clarity will show how much the native has overcome the obstacles of their own mind and personality. The less light and clarity, the more the negative features of the mind will be indicated. This is utilizing *Saṁhitā* and *Horā* together.

One should study the nakṣatra as delineated in official texts. Provided below is a comparison of Varāhamihira's Nakṣatra-Jātaka-Adhyāya (birth Nakṣatra chapter) as found in *Bṛhat Saṁhitā*. It is compared side by side with another official text, Vaidyanātha Dikṣita's Nakṣatra Phalam (results of nakṣatra) section in *Jātaka Pārijāta*. The Sanskrit word has many English meanings; the reader is advised to meditate on the general nature of the indications presented, being aware of translation difficulties.

Varāhamihira's Bṛhat Saṁhitā

	Varāhamihira's Bṛhat Saṁhitā Nakṣatra-Jātaka-Adhyāya [100]	Vaidyanātha Dikṣita's Jātaka Pārijāta Nakṣatra Phalam
Aśvinī	Fond of decorating themselves *(priya bhūṣaṇa)*, handsome, well-formed *(su-rūpa)*, fortunate *(su-bhaga)*, talented, dextrous *(dakṣa)*, intelligent *(matimat)*	Great intelligence *(mati buddhi)*, famous, well known *(vitta)*, good conduct *(vinaya)*, wise *(prajña)*, happy *(sukhī)*
Bharaṇī	Determined, resolved, certain *(kṛtaniścaya)*, sincere, honest *(satya)*, free from disease *(aruja)*, talented, dextrous, industrious *(dakṣa)*, happy *(sukhī)*	Agitated, exhausted, as a woman menstruating *(vikala)*, delighting in anothers wife *(anya dāra nirata)*, cruel, harsh *(krūra)*, ungrateful *(kṛtaghna)*, possesing riches *(dhanī)*
Kṛttikā	Eats a lot *(bahubhuk)*, enjoys themselves with other's spouses *(paradāra-rata)*, energetic, brilliant, respectable *(tejasvī)*, known *(vikhyāta)*	energetic, bright, dignified *(tejasvī)*, very productive *(bahulodbhava)*, lord-like in status *(prabhusam-murkha)*, wealth is in learning *(vidyādhanī)*
Rohiṇī	Honest, *(satya)*, clean, virtuous *(śuci)*, agreeable speech *(priyaṁ vada)*, stubborn, persevering *(sthira)*, good form, handsome *(surūpa)*	Knowledge of people's weaknesses *(parrandhravid)*, thin body *(kṛśa-tanu)*, illuminated *(bodhī)*, enjoys/desires other people's spouses *(parastrī-rata)*
Mṛga	Inconsiderate, fickle, unsteady *(capala)*, skillful *(catura)*, timid *(bhīra)*, crafty, cunning, clever speaker *(paṭu-ruta)*, powerful *(sāhī)*, wealthy *(dhanī)*, enjoys comforts of life *(bhogī)*	Friendly disposition *(saumya-manas)* traveler *(aṭana)*, crooked, dishonest *(kuṭila)*, love-sick *(kāmātura)*, sickly *(rogavān)*
Ārdrā	False, deceitful *(śaṭha)*, conceited, proud *(garvita)*, feirce, passionate, violent *(caṇḍa)*, ungrateful *(kṛtaghna)*, cruel, hurtful *(hiṁsra)*, having many vices, sinful *(pāpa)*	Fickle *(cala)*, abundant strength *(adhika bala)*, performing base/vulgar actions *(kṣudra-kriyā)*, ill-behaved *(aśīlavān)*
Punar-vasu	Patient, self-controlled *(dānta)*, happy *(sukhī)*, good natured *(suśīla)*, dull-witted *(durmedha)*, sickly *(rogabhāj)*, thirsty *(pipāsu)*, easily pleased *(alpena ca santuṣṭa)*	Simple *(mūḍhātmā)*, strong wealth *(dhana bala)*, well-known *(khyāta)*, poet *(kavi)*, a lover, lustful, *(kāmuka)*
Puṣya	Tranquil minded *(śāntātmā)*, fortunate, liked, favored *(su-bhaga)*, scholarly *(paṇḍita)*, wealthy *(dhanī)*, fixed in dharma *(dharma-saṁśrita)*	Fond of gods and spiritual people *(vipra-sura-priya)*, wealthy with all that goes with wealth *(sadhanadhī)*, enjoys benefits from government *(rājapriya)*, surrounded by their relations *(bandhumān)*
Āśleṣa	False, deceitful *(śaṭha)*, one who eats anything *(sarva bhakśya)*, sinful *(pāpa)*, ungrateful *(kṛtaghna)*, cunning, cheating, decieving *(dhūrta)*	Simple *(mūḍhātmā)*, disrespectful, ungrateful speech *(kṛtaghna-vacana)*, ill-tempered *(kopī)*, bad luck, hard to cure *(durācāravān)*

	Varāhamihira's Bṛhat Saṁhitā Nakṣatra-Jātaka-Adhyāya [100]	**Vaidyanātha Dikṣita's Jātaka Pārijāta** Nakṣatra Phalam
Maghā	Has many servants *(bahu bhṛtya)*, wealthy *(dhanī)*, enjoys life *(bhogī)*, devotion to the gods and ancestors *(sura-pitṛ-bhakta)*, industrious, exerting great efforts, busy *(mahodyama)*	Proud, arrogant *(garvī)*, religious, holy *(puṇya)*, enjoys sex*(rata)*, having an obedient spouse *(kalatravaśaga)*, honoured, esteemed *(mānī)*, wealthy *(dhanī)*
Pūrva-phalgunī	Kind and sweet speech *(priya-vāg)*, generous *(dātā)*, bright, dignified *(dyutimān)*, traveler *(aṭana)*, employed by important people or government *(nṛpasevaka)*	Inconsiderate, fickle, restless *(capala)*, performs negative acts *(ku-karma-carita)*, liberal, giving *(tyāgī)*, persevering *(dṛḍha)*, filled with desires, lustful *(kāmuka)*
Uttara-phalgunī	Fortunate, liked, favored *(su-bhaga)*, earns through their learning *(vidyā-āpta-dhana)*, enjoys life *(bhogī)*, happy *(sukha)*	Enjoys life *(bhogī)*, venerated, loved *(bhajanita)*, high-minded, revered *(mānī)*, correct in conduct, grateful *(kṛtajña)*, religious, intelligent *(sudhī)*
Hasta	Powerful, energetic, active *(utsāhī)*, bold, courageous, daring *(dhṛṣṭa)*, addicted to alcohol *(pānapa)*, incompasionate, cruel *(aghṛṇī)*, a thief *(taskara)*	Sometimes *(yadi)* sensual *(kāma)*, virtuous *(dhamani)*, enjoying sex *(rata)*, does favors for the wise *(prājña-upararta)*, wealthy *(dhanī)*
Citrā	Wears nice clothing and necklaces *(ambara-mālya-dhara)*, has beautiful eyes *(sulocana)*, and well shaped limbs *(āṅga)*	Secretive *(gupta)*, in constant study *(śīlani)*, enjoys sex *(rata)*, honorable *(mānī)*, enjoys other's spouses *(parastrī-rata)*
Svātī	Patient, self-controlled *(dānta)*, merchant, trader *(vaṇik)*, compassionate *(kṛpālu)*, sweet speech, kind words *(priya-vāg)*, follows virtue and justice *(dharma-āśrita)*	One who pleases the gods and brahmins *(deva-mahīsura-priyakara)*, enjoys life *(bhogī)*, wealthy *(dhanī)*, simple, slow understanding *(manda-dhī)*
Viśākhā	Jealous, envious *(irṣyu)*, covetous, greedy *(lubdha)*, bright, dignified *(dyutimān)*, eloquent, skillful in speech *(vacana-paṭu)*, argumentative *(kalahakṛd)*	Proud, arrogant *(garvī)*, under the power of the spouse, uxorious, devoted *(dāra-vaśa)*, conquered and subdued by enemies *(jita-ari-radhika)*, ill-tempered *(krodhī)*
Anu-rādhā	Abundant wealth *(āḍhya)*, foreign residence, *(videśa-vāsī)*, continually hungry *(kṣudhālu)*, traveler *(aṭana)*	Very pleasant speech *(supriya-vāg)*, wealthy *(dhanī)*, happy *(sukha)*, enjoys sex *(rata)*, honorable*(pūjyo)*, beautiful, famous *(yaśasvī)*, strong and powerful *(vibhū)*
Jyeṣṭhā	Not many friends *(na bahu mitra)*, contented *(santuṣṭa)*, performing dharma, virtuous *(dharmakṛt)*, angry, very irritable *(pracura-kopa)*	Angry thoughts, mentally irritated *(mati-kopavān)*, fond of other women *(paravadhū-sakta)*, strong sense of dharma *(vibhudhārmika)*
Mūla	Honourable *(mānī)*, wealthy *(dhanavān)*, happy *(sukhī)*, not malicious or hurtful *(na hiṁsra)*, firm, steady-minded *(sthira)*, enjoys life *(bhogī)*	Eloquent, Skillful speech *(paṭu-vāg)*, agitated, disheveled *(vidhūtakuśala)*, deceptive *(dhūrta)*, ungrateful *(kṛtaghna)*, wealthy *(dhanī)*

	Varāhamihira's Bṛhat Saṁhitā Nakṣatra-Jātaka-Adhyāya [100]	**Vaidyanātha Dikṣita's Jātaka Pārijāta** Nakṣatra Phalam
Pūrva-aṣāḍhā	Desirable spouse who gives happiness, *(iṣṭ-ānanda-kalatra)*, bold, courageous *(vīra)*, a steady friend *(dṛḍha-sauhṛda)*	Inconstant, undergoing change for the worse, constantly falling in love *(vikāracarita)*, honorable *(mānī)*, happy *(sukhī)*, tranquil, gentle nature *(śāntadhī)*
Uttara-aṣāḍhā	Well behaved, humble, polite *(vinīta)*, righteous, virtuous *(dhārmika)*, many friends *(bahu-mitra)*, grateful, mindful of help *(kṛtajña)*, fortunate, liked, favored *(su-bhaga)*	Respectable *(mānya)*, tranquil nature *(śāntaguṇa)*, happy *(sukhī)*, wealthy *(dhanavān)*, scholarly *(paṇḍita)*
Śravaṇa	Illustrious, eminent, possessed of fortune *(śrīmān)*, learned, one having heard the teachings *(śrutavān)*, very upright, noble spouse *(udāra-dāra)*, aquires wealth *(dhana-anvita)*, well known *(khyāta)*	Reverence to the gods and brahmins *(dvija-deva-bhakti-nirata)*, in government, or a leader *(rājā)*, wealthy *(dhanī)*, virtuous *(dharmavān)*
Dha-niṣṭhā	Generous *(Dāta)*, wealthy *(āḍhya)*, brave *(śūra)*, fond of music *(gīti-priya)*, greedy for money *(dhana-lubdha)*	Wealthy, having treasures *(vasumān)*, large thighs/neck *(pīnorukaṇṭha)*, happy *(sukhī)*
Śata-bhiṣa	Clear and specific speech *(sphuṭa-vāg)*, having addictions *(vyasanī)*, destroys their enemies *(ripuhā)*, reckless, overworking oneself *(sāhasika)*, obstinate *(durgrāhya)*	An astrologer *(kālajña)*, peaceful *(śānta)*, sparing diet *(alpa-bhuk)*, reckless, overworking oneself *(sāhasī)*
Pūrvā-bhādra	Suffer from grief and sorrow *(udvigṇa)*, controlled by the opposite sex *(strī-jita)*, skilled with making money *(dhanapaṭu)*, miserly *(adātā)*	Confident in speaking *(pragalbha-vacana)*, deceitful *(dhūrta)*, fearful, cowardly *(bhayārta)*, gentle, weak *(mṛdu)*
Uttara-bhādra	Speaking ability *(vaktā)*, happy *(sukhī)*, many children, fruitful *(prajāvān)*, conquering enemies *(jita-śatru)*, virtuous *(dhārmika)*	Gentle-natured *(mṛduguṇa)*, liberal, open minded *(tyāgī)*, wealthy *(dhanī)*, scholarly *(paṇḍita)*
Revatī	Well-developed and proportioned limbs *(sampūrṇa-aṅga)*, fortunate, favored *(su-bhaga)*, brave *(śūra)*, clean, pure, honest *(śuci)*, wealthy, full of self-worth *(arthavān)*	Large marking/ sign on the body *(uru-lāñchana upagatanu)*, love-sick *(kāmātura)* beautiful *(sundara)*, counselor *(mantrī)*, accompanied by children, spouse, friends *(putra-kalatra-mitra-sahita)*, will produce steady prosperity *(jāta-sthira-śrīrata)*

Nakṣatra Devatā

Of the many attributes related to the nakṣatras the two most important to understand are the devatā and the symbol. The qualities of the devatās give us the primary meaning of each nakṣatra and form the foundation for the interpretation of the lunar constellation. The most important nakṣatra is the one containing the natal Moon, called the *janma nakṣatra*.

The lunar constellations represent the mind, conditioned by the devatā ruling the nakṣatra of the Moon. By understanding the nature of the deity we will understand the qualitative nature of the individual's thinking. To completely understand the deity one needs to read the various stories of Vedic literature and become familiar with these devatās. The more one understands these gods, the more one will be able to appreciate the motivation and the nature of the mind.

Twenty-seven devatās may seem like a lot of gods to remember, and a bit pantheistic. What is important is to understand these gods in a symbolic or philosophical (*adhyātma*) perspective. Yāska, the nirukta scholar, teaches that there is just one divinity who becomes distinguished according to the function in a particular realm[69]. Śaunaka in his *Bṛhad-devatā* distinguishes the temperaments, moods, and inclinations of the various devatāś[70] which are found within the various mythologies. Therefore it is the function and nature of the devatā that must be understood.

Some scholars have judged the importance of Vedic deities found in the Vedas by how many verses they had addressed to them. From our perspective, they are all equally important as they each rule an equal portion of the sky. Therefore we should try to understand them and how to approach each one equally. Rudra is approached for protection. Nirṛti is asked to stay away. Bhaga is approached for conjugal happiness, lovingly and with charm; Āpas through emotion and feelings. Indra is approached as one would a king, while Bṛhaspati is approached as one would a spiritual teacher.

Sometimes, in the texts, the nakṣatra will be called by the deity who owns it. For example, Anurādhā can be called *maitrā*, that which belongs to Mitra. Pūrvāṣāḍhā is called *jaladeva*, that which belongs to the water god. In this way, the lunar signs are the domains of the devatā. It is their energy that rules over that particular portion of the sky. Understanding their mythology reveals the deeper workings of the nakṣatra, and opens the doorway for intuitive understanding of the native's psychology. Below is a brief introduction to the deities for the beginner.

[69] Rao, S.K. Ramachandra, Rigveda Darsana, p.110, 169, 170
[70] Rao, S.K. Ramachandra, Rigveda Darsana, p.83

#	Constellation	Deity	
1	Aśvinī	Aśvini-kumāra	Healing, rejuvinating,
2	Bharaṇī	Yama	Dying, death, transformation
3	Kṛttikā	Agni	Burning, purifying, clarity,
4	Rohiṇī	Brahmā	Creating, culture
5	Mṛga	Chandra	Growth, ojas, procreative power
6	Ārdrā	Rudra	Anger, power of destruction
7	Punarvasu	Aditi	Learning, understanding, Expanding
8	Puṣya	Bṛhaspati	Knowing, awareness
9	Āśleṣa	Sarpa	Deception, illusion, over confidence
10	Maghā	Pitṛ	Authority, karma
11	Pūrvaphalgunī	Bhaga	Relationship and sexuality
12	Uttaraphalgunī	Aryaman	Love, marriage, and family
13	Hasta	Savitṛ	Waking up, realizing
14	Citrā	Viśvakarma	Building, planning
15	Svātī	Vāyu	Movement, strength to build
16	Viśākhā	Indrāgni	Alliance, support systems
17	Anurādhā	Mitra	Friendship, fine detail
18	Jyeṣṭhā	Indra	Sensory control, controlling urges
19	Mūla	Nirṛti	Breaking
20	Pūrvaaṣāḍhā	Āpas	Feeling, searching
21	Uttaraaṣāḍhā	Viśvadeva	Noblity, good character
22	Śravaṇa	Viṣṇu	All-pervasive, expanding
23	Dhaniṣṭhā	Vasudeva	Fame, shining, being seen
24	Śatabhiṣa	Varuṇa	Punishment, repentance
25	Pūrvābhādra	Ajaikapada	Tapasya, penance
26	Uttarabhādra	Ahirbudhnya	Unseen, hidden
27	Revatī	Pūṣān	Nourisher, safe and fruitful journeys

There are various levels by which to perceive the deities. They can be seen as natural forces, mental tendencies, or cosmic archetypes that are sometimes personified for ease of human grasping. Each of these levels simultaneously includes the other and it is the responsibility of the astrologer to not only perceive the multi-dimensionality of these energies, but to also comprehend how they influence every aspect of an individual's life. Understanding the deity will help one get a 'feeling' for the devatā so as to understand the nakṣatra from an energetic standpoint, instead of as a list.

Aśvinī: Aśvini Kumāra

| | auṁ aśvinīkumārābhyāṁ namaḥ | |

The Aśvin twins, Dasra and Satya, are two handsome men known as the doctors of the gods. *Aśva* means horse; their father was the Sun god (*Sūrya*), who conceived them while in the form of a horse. Kumāra means young boy; they are said to be always young, handsome and healthy as masters of Āyurveda.

The Aśvin twins possess magical healing powers and as such this nakṣatra is associated with the ability to heal. The old, blind Sage Chyavanna was rejuvinated and made young and healthy again by the Aśvins, showing the power of this nakṣatra to heal, prevent aging and to rejuvinate, a branch of Ayurveda known as *Rasāyana*. The healing was done for the benefit of Chyavanna's young wife, so it also relates to *Vājikaraṇa* (sexual health/potency/ fertility). The horse *(aśva)* is a symbol of strength, stamina and vitality, and good health is feeling alive in this way. Horses are also known for the power of making anti-venom for snake bites, and this shows Aśvinī's power to fight poison. This nakṣatra will not tolerate dark, deceitful or harmful behavior in a person's personality. It also relates to fighting toxins in the body and purifying the body's natural processes from extraneous poisons.

The Aśvins were always testing people, as they tested the wife of Chyavanna before healing him. As handsome male gods they asked Chyavanna's wife to marry one of them, instead of being with the old blind sage. They only restored youth to her husband after she proved faithful to him. In this way, people with Aśvini nakṣatra will often be critical of situations, testing them before believing, helping or engaging themselves. They need to find proof, and will test the situation sometimes openly, sometime covertly.

The Aśvins are highly intelligent and skilled in many arts. They are good at not only medicine but music and other skilled arts. Natives with this nakṣatra will be refined, intelligent, and skillful. This star's association with horses will show a love of horses and working with them. In ancient days, horses were an elevated method of transportation. This star will also relate to transportation in all its modes in the modern world.

Bharaṇī: Yama

||auṁ yamāya namaḥ||

Yama is the lord of death and so called Dharmarāja (king of Dharma), as all who die see him after death to have their karma weighed indicating the direction they will go in the afterlife. Yama literally means self-control, restraint, or any great moral rule, and can also refer to a driver or charioteer. Yama is the restraint we have to not do the negative things in life, and it is our own yama that weighs the direction we go upon death.

Yama carries a noose *(pāśin)* and a punishing stick *(daṇḍa)*. Natives of this nakṣatra will both, follow the rules, and often times even be an enforcer of them, being in roles dealing with law and judgment as Yama executes the law. They will often act cruel or harshly without compassion. Death is not someone you can barter with, though in the story of Mārkaṇḍeya, found in various Purāṇas, it was predicted by the best astrologers that he was to die at the age of sixteen. He did intense sādhana to Viṣṇu, the sustainer, and overcame death. In this way, the native of Bharaṇī may not be easily overcome directly, but can be won over by the actions one does to others (service, etc).

In the *Uttara-Rāmāyaṇa*, Yama, who was sent by Brahmā, came disguised as a Maharṣi to Rāma to bring him back to Vaikuṇṭha. Similarly, Bharaṇī natives are reminding one of where they belong and giving advice. In the *Mahābhārata*, Yama was born as Vidura, who was a famous advisor giving wise and intelligent counsel. He was known to give the 'bitter' truth in his advice.

Bharaṇī also relates to killing and butchers, as well as animal sacrifice. Many of the cannibalistic tribes of ancient India worshipped the Buffalo god, as this is the vehicle of Yama. Bharaṇī is the birthstar of Rahu and can show the impurity of Rahu's acts. Planets placed in this star can show harsh acts or crimes done against the planet's kāraka. Worship of the goddess Durgā is the remedy to purify this nakṣatra.

The Ṛṣi Vālmīki had Bharaṇī janma-nakṣatra. He was originally a thief and bandit, who could cut off the fingers of his victims. Vālmīki realized the absurdity of being a thief, left his wife and children and became a celibate Ṛṣi, but first he had to go through the transformation. Bharaṇī nakṣatra relates to transformation and change in a person's life. It also relates to the transition from this life into the next, as death just is a journey from one body into another. Natives of this star are good at working with death, dying and transformative experiences. Healing therapies that involve harsh/quick transformation are good for them.

Kṛttikā: Agni

||auṁ agnaye namaḥ||

Agni is the Sacred fire god, he is fire itself. On the physical plane he is the fire which offerings are made to, transporting those offerings to the gods and thereby serving as an intermediary between mankind and the gods. He rules over the digestion of food, the digestion of sensory input, the digestion of knowledge and is the giver of insight. He is connected to the third eye and higher knowledge. In this way he is also an intermediary between mankind-consciousness and higher god-consciousness.

The Ṛgveda begins with a prayer to Agni as he is the connection to the higher realms through sacred fire so the essence of the offerings reach the gods. When the Ājñā chakra is open and activated the prayers are heard by the higher realms of mind. Natives with this star make the best priests as they are truly interested in helping people connect to the higher realms of god, or good spiritual teachers as they are trying to teach others how to attain higher realms of mind and burn up their past karmas.

Agni as the fire god shows strong Tejas in an individual. Strong Tejas shows inner radiance in a person. As fire cooks and purifies food, tejas cooks the individual to evolve one's consciousness.

Kṛttikā nakṣatra will make one bright and physically and mentally energetic. Its radiance gives good intelligence and thinking ability. Natives of this star are educated and ingenuitive, which makes them good inventors and engineers, or a good astrologer as the perception is clear, sharp and precise. It may also give an attraction to fire and working with fire through metallurgy or chemistry.

The mythology of Agni is the understanding of fire. His mothers are two kindling sticks and he devours them as soon as he is born. He is produced every morning and is therefore young. He is praised as the lord of the house *(gṛha-pati)*, but also called the guest *(atithi)*. Wood is his food, and ghee his beverage. He is the mouth through which the offerings are fed to the gods. And by that offering, the gods are brought nearer in order to be receptive.

Agni is decribed as black/smokey, red and golden, with a golden brown moustache, eyes, and hair, though he takes on a fierce form when he becomes *Kravyāda* to devour the body in the funeral pyre. In this form, Agni is known for dispelling ghosts, spirits and black magic.

Fire is sharp and cutting. These natives are often very precise and exact. They generally don't engage in excessive talk and can be very direct.

Rohiṇī: Brahmā/Prajāpati

||auṁ brahmaṇe namaḥ ||

Brahmā is the creator god relating to the rajas guṇa in the trinity of gods. He is the creator god who has created the universe and through the power of his energy creation continues. Prajāpati (Pati of prajās = lord of progeny) is also known as Brahmā. Prajāpati means the divinity presiding over creation and is more general as it refers to various deities or even the first men who progenate a race.

From the center (navel) of All-pervasiveness comes Brahmā to create the entire universe. It is a creative and artistic star, but because of the prevalence of rajas guna it can become materialistic. Brahmā's wife is Saraswati, the goddess of art, music and learning, whom he himself created so often she is called his daughter as well. This makes natives of this star very cultured and interested in music, performing arts and other esthetic expressions. At the same time, as the creator had as his wife his own creation, sexual appropriateness is a concern for these natives. Instinctual creative energy brings excess of passion and sexuality in these natives, yet makes them skilled in the many arts of love. It is a good star for activities involving fertility rites and acts.

Kṛṣṇa, known as Mohana, the object of desire (*moha*), being attractive, charming and playful has his birthstar in Rohiṇī which aids to his alluring nature. Rohiṇī also relates to cows in a cowshed, and the cows represent kāmadeva, the god of desire. Rohiṇī relates to fulfilling desires and represents foods that are good for both the body and the mind. It also has the ability to bring resources together or to organize, as Brahmā classified all created things by giving them names.

There are so many stories found throughout classic Vedic literature of Brahmā creating, getting cursed, and giving boons. One important story is when Brahmā and Viṣṇu tried to find the end of Śiva's Jyotir-liṅga. The pillar of light was endless but Brahmā lied and said he found the top and Śiva caught him in his lie and pinched off one of Brahmā's five heads. This left Brahma with only four heads to see in the four directions (but not above). This is a lesson in the egotistical nature of rajas guna not acknowledging a higher power, and losing the full vision because of it. Natives of this star need to remember the source of all their creativity to stay beyond the traps of the material world.

Brahmā is rarely worshipped in his form as Brahmā, some say to do so is similar to worshipping the body or material nature which would increase materialistic tendencies. Instead it is said that to get married and have children is in itself the worship of Brahmā. Others will worship him as Sūrya (*Sūrya-Prajāpati*) during Brahma-muhūrta (early morning) as propitiation to Brahmā.

Mṛgaśiras: Soma/Candra

| | auṁ candramase namaḥ | |

Soma is the ancient Vedic name of the Moon. The Moon is the lord of all the nakṣatra as the Sun is lord of all the Rāśi. The ninth Maṇḍala of the Ṛg Veda is devoted to Soma.

The qualities of this nakṣatra relate to the Moon god as male. These natives will still express the caring nature of the Moon, but the mental nature is understood by the disposition of Soma, the Moon god. They will be fickle changing their likes and dislikes often as the Moon moves quickly and changes phases, sleeping in a different nakṣatra every night. The nakṣatra are said to be Soma's 27 wives; this gives him the quality of constantly moving as that of a traveler. The Moon's favorite wife is Rohiṇī because of her creativity, cultured behavior and skills at pleasing Soma. Natives of this star care about manners and expect a good host when they visit. They may be shy because of the timid nature of the Moon, but they will be sly in their speech to make up for any missed opportunities.

The Moon is known for his high sexual libido and power of procreation. He is lusty and often falling in love, attracted to external beauty. He even ran off with his Guru's wife, Tārā, and got her pregnant, illustrating his lustful nature.

The Moon is a friendly planet; he enjoys being an entertainer and making his guests happy. The Moon relates to clothing and comforts, and natives of this star enjoy nice clothing or working with textiles, delighting in the comforts of life and striving to be wealthy. There is love of tradition and ancestral practices as the Moon relates to the place of transition of the ancestors. In this way the significations of the Moon should be understood.

Soma is the lord of plants and represents their potency, as he is the one who gives plants their nourishing energy (*ojas*). In ancient times, when the division between men and devas was less, there was an herb called soma. In the divine medicine *(divyauṣadhi)* section of the *Charaka Saṁhitā*[69] the herb Soma is called the "King of medicines *(Oṣadhi-Rājā)*." It is described as having 15 leaves which increases *(vardha)* and decreases (*hīya*) like the Moon waxes and wanes. This correlates to the 15 tithis (phases) of the Moon; there are no leaves on the new Moon increasing to 15 leaves on the full Moon. On the material plane this relates to the potency in a plant being pulled into the leaves on the waxing Moon and being pulled into the roots on the waning Moon determining the best time to harvest. In the same way, these natives are more social during certain periods.

[69] Charaka Saṁhitā, Cikitsāsthānam, Chapter I.4 Rasāyanādhyāya v.7

Ārdrā: Rudra

| | auṁ rudrāya namaḥ | |

Rudra was born from a moment of the creator's anger. He is a destructive god who makes one cry. He is associated with storms and natural disasters as well as sickness and disease.

When Brahmā was creating the world, his four "mind-born" sons, called the *Sanāta Kumāra*, refused to procreate. They were mind-born, meaning they existed only in the mental realm of existence. Brahmā grew angry and the emotion of destruction came upon him. This manifested as heat in his third eye and from this was born the form of Rudra. Therefore Rudra is partially the manifestation of anger and is representative of destruction and storms. Natives of this star are easily angered or may be malicious in their anger.

The *Viṣṇu Purāṇa* says that as a freshly born child Rudra was wailing, he would not stop crying until the creator named him properly. Brahmā named him Rudra (he who cries) because he was crying *(rodana).* It wasn't until another seven names that he stopped crying showing the need of Ārdrā natives to have big titles or names to be happy.

The wailing of Rudra was the movement of energy relating to prāṇa. It is a densification from the mind-born reality to the manifestation at the prāṇic level. It is the prāṇas that give life, and the removal of life that makes a human wail. The Chāndogyopaniṣhad says, "The Prāṇas are indeed the Rudras for they cause all creation to weep."[70] Rudra is the father of the Maruts (winds), which can be understood externally as storm gods or internally as the five types of Prāṇa in the body. It is the proper flow of prāṇa that ensures health and freedom from disease. Rudra is always seen carrying medicine and called the chief physician among all physicians, the healer of healers.[71] Rudra is prayed to for protection and propitiated to not bring sickness, strife, or injury. In this way natives of this star will often find health through prāṇayam or other methods of prāṇa control.

Rudra is considered the strongest of the strong[72] and armed with a bow and arrow. His arrows are quick and sharp. In this way natives of this star are often known for their strength and fierceness. In the *Rāmāyaṇa,* Rudra incarnates as Hanumān, and in the *Mahābhārata,* he incarnates as Bhīma; both famous for their strength and power. Both were known for their inability to be gentle, always being a little rougher than would be beneficial.

[70] Chāndogyopaniṣhad 3.16.3 (prāṇa vāva rudra aite hīdṁ sarva rodayanti)
[71] Ṛg Veda 2.33.4 (bheṣajenhirbhiṣakta)
[72] Ṛg Veda 2.33.3 (tavastamsa tavasāṁ)

Punarvasu: Aditi

| | auṁ adityai namaḥ | |

Aditi in the Vedas is the formless absolute Mother of all goodness. She sets us free when we need help, filled with the abundance a mother showers on her children. She is limitless, un-bound, un-differentiated abundance.

Taking form, Aditi was the daughter of Dakṣaprajāpati, and was married to Kaśyapa along with her 12 sisters. It is said that through them all living things were given birth. Aditi gave birth to the 33 devas: the 12 Ādityas, 11 Rudras, the 8 Vasus, Indra and Prajapati. She is the expansive foundation of the universe, the mother being everywhere and in everything,and as such the mother of the devas (gods). On an internal level she represents the unitive consciousness. Her sister is Diti (difference) and she was mother to all the demons, the dualistic/ divided thoughts which create ignorance. Aditi is non-difference, or equinamity of mind *(sama)* which is spoken of in the Bhagavad Gītā as the foundational attitude for liberation.

Śrī Aurobindo has written extensively on Aditi. She is called the consort of Truth *(ṛtasya patnī)*[73]. Aditi gave birth to Viṣṇu in the celestial worlds and when he incarnates, so does she to give birth to him. In the *Mahābhārata*, she incarnated as Devakī[74] where she gave birth to Viṣṇu, as Kṛṣṇa. She is propitiated to remove hinderances, as she provides the resources to prosper. Natives of this star are helpful, with good qualities, and blessed with the resources to provide for others. The abundance of Aditi also manifests as wealth and fame on the material plane. The *Matsya Purāṇa* tells a story of how Indra gave her a beautiful pair of earrings found at the churning of the ocean. These were stolen from her and rescued by Kṛṣṇa while she was in the form of Devakī.

As a mother and protectress, she is easily pleased by what her children offer her, in this way, natives of her star are easy-going and easily satisfied. She is not intellectual, and natives of this star may not be intellectually smart, but they are also unpretentious. Her wisdom is simple and quiet like Rāmaṇa Maharṣi who had this nakṣatra as his birth star. These natives are patient and have good composure. Śrī Aurobindo translates,

> *"May we call to Aditi for protection, who is, verily, the great builder of those who are engaged in happy works, who is the* ***Consort of Truth****, whose strength is manifold; who embraces the vast, who is a happy shelter, who is perfect in her leading."*

[73] Yajurveda21.5 and Atharvaveda VII.6.2

[74] Devībhāgavata, Skandha 4

Puṣya: Bṛhaspati

||auṁ bṛhaspataye namaḥ ||

Bṛhaspati is the priest of the gods, the devaguru Jupiter. He had vast knowledge and his advice was sought in all major decisions of the gods (*deva*).

Bṛhaspati was the son of sage *Aṅgirasa* and *Vasudā*. Aṅgirasa was the son of Brahmā. Sometimes Bṛhaspati is called the son of Agni, but this is because the tapas of Aṅgirasa was so intense that Agni said his brilliance surpassed his own so he should be called the fire god as well. The father is the ninth house and in the case of Jupiter it is shining like fire itself. A benefic ninth house shows respect for elders and tradition as well as love of the gods and temples. As the guru, Bṛhaspati empowers sacred knowledge and supports the growth of his followers. Natives of this star are knowledgeable and promote dharma. Through dharma they acquire wealth, luck and fortune. They have an internal 'knowing' and are often ministers, advisors or caregivers.

Bṛhaspati once forcefully slept with his elder brother's wife, Mamatā[75]. They produced a child, the sage Bharadvāja, and hid the fact of his birth. Because of this, Bṛhaspati's wife, Tārā, ran away with (or was kidnapped by) the Moon, returning home pregnant with a child. Bṛhaspati at first denied the child, Mercury, but later claimed him after seeing how brilliant he was. In this way, there is a social appropriateness or religiousness that these natives need to overcome to be more truthful. Jupiter is also called *Vachaspati*, lord of the word, showing those with this star need to keep their word in order to manifest all the support, abundance, spirituality and splendour of this nakṣatra.

Bṛhaspati represents the planet Jupiter, and is the wisest of the planets; the priest and the ritualist, he is always helping the devas (good thoughts) to win over the asuras (negative thoughts), and therefore natives of this star often have calm minds. Once when Venus was off doing tapasya for a thousand years, Bṛhaspati disguised himself as the asura-guru and took the place of Venus. In ten years[76] time, Bṛhaspati had converted all the bad qualities in the demons and when Venus returned the asuras didn't believe he was their guru. In this way, the intention is generally good, though these natives often *assume* they know what's best. Those with this birthstar can make good clergymen or personal growth counselors.

[75] Bhāgavata, Skandha 9

[76] Viṁśotarri daśā of the Moon

Āśleṣā: Sarpa

||auṁ sarpebhyo namaḥ ||

Sarpa means snake or small serpant. It can also mean creeping or crawling, which is how most snakes and serpants move along. Ṛṣi Kasyapa had two wives and granted them each a boon before he entered into retreat. The first wife, Kadru, asked for a thousand splendorous snake sons. The second wife, Vinatā, asked for two glorious bird sons[77]. The snakes were born first and enslaved Vinatā until her son, Garuḍa, was born. Garuḍa freed his mother and became an eater of snakes. Therefore Guruḍa is invoked to remove the poison of snakes and troubles that they cause *(kṣipa auṁ svāhā).*

Not all snakes are negative. Śeṣa (*Ananta*), Kadru's first born, did intense penance to purify himself and was granted a boon by Brahmā to have a heart delighting in virtue and penance. Brahmā asked him to live deep underground and give steadiness to the Earth. Vāsuki, the second born, was the snake used to churn the ocean of milk. Other snakes became vile and used their poison to kill and harm. Snakes have powerful energy and can do great harm.

The lunar nodes represent serpants. Rāhu represents *sarpas,* those snakes that used their powers negatively. Ketu represents *nāgas,* those snakes who use their powers beneficially. Though sometimes a sarpa may do something nice and a nāga my use a little black magic they generally go to extremes. Natives of Āśleṣā will often be in extreme negative or positive situations.

Sarpas are sinful, cheating and have a power of deceiving with their speech, their split tongues. Natives of this star can be dangerous with the poison of these sarpas, they may engage in illicit sale of drugs or sex. They have excess sexual energy which can lead to deviances if not channeled properly. They are also known as con artists, and will even cheat their own family as they enslaved Vinatā and their brother, Garuḍa.

Nāgas are known to have gems growing out of their third eyes because of the intense study and research they perform, they become keepers of wisdom, and percieve subtle energy. Natives of this star may be interested in occult studies and mystic knowledge. They can become healers, particularly the branch of āyurveda known as *agadatantra* (toxicology), which can include working with cancer or diseases related to external pollutants, and even modern day pharmacology. The mesmerizing serpant energy also relates to hypnotherapy and other trance state therapies, or entrancing music.

[77] Mahābhārata, Book 1 Adi Parva, Astikā Parva

Maghā: Pitṛ

||auṁ pitṛbhyo namaḥ ||

Pitṛ generally means ancestors but, also has many other levels of meaning. It can directly relate to the father, *pitṛ* shares the same linguistic root as the latin word *pater* meaning father which gives us the word paternal. It can also refer to both parents, or to the close ancestory that has passed on (father, grandfather, great-great-grandfather). Pitṛ can also refer to the ancestors who started a lineage or the progeninators of mankind as well as the great Vedic Ṛṣis. By worshipping the ancestors one gives respect to that which has come before them. This reminds one to stay humble and remember the past. Maghā is a bright star of authority and respect. Natives of this star can become proud or arrogant, so need to remember the past that helped them achieve where they have presently risen to.

Our karma is affected by our ancestors of seven generations. Not only will a king's karma affect the entire country, but his family's karma seven generations ago to present will influence the country as well. By propitiating the ancestors we remove karmic debts and blockages. This allows for prosperity, happy married life, proper sex life, high position or status, and success in career. The full enjoyments of life are blessings of the ancestor's desires and are enjoyed by natives of this star.

Hindu tradition has specific ceremonies, like *śrāddha*, for the immediate ancestors to be propitiated, or for rememberance of the ancient Ṛṣis from which we trace our heritage back to. In Judaism, they constantly invoke the founding fathers Abraham, Issac and Jacob and remember the past. In Islam, there is full attention paid to the final prophet, Mohammed. In some Asian culture there is even more direct focus on ancestors, where a differentiation between one's personal and ancestoral karma is not made. Just as a family unit shares prosperity and loss, one shares the karmic gains and debts of the ancestors. One shares the sins a grandfather made by stealing during difficult times, or shares the blessings he received by visiting a true saint during more prosperous times. With the blessings of the ancestors one has a firm karmic foundation to rise high in life. All blocks to accomplish get removed and one achieves the honor offered by the ancestors.

Natives of this star often take jobs in government or positions related to the general role of a father. There is a masculine energy present in these individuals which can make a person chauvinistic. They may also be in positions concerned with the past like preservationists, historians, curators or archaeologists.

Pūrvaphalgunī: Bhaga

||*Auṁ Bhagāya Namaḥ* ||

Bhaga is one of the twelve Ādityas born of Aditi and Kaśyapa. The Ādityas, in general, rule over the resources we have in life. They are forms of the Sun god and like the rāśis they show potentialities we can achieve. Bhaga Āditya is connected to the sign Sagittarius. He is the 'dispenser' and considered a lord of wealth and happiness. The ninth house is called the bhāgya bhāva, the house of luck and fortune, and the blessings of the actions from the past life. The navāṁśa shows ones bhāgya as well. Bhāgya means relating to Bhaga or lucky, fortunate, and also one's fate, destiny or welfare. Individuals with this birth star are often generous, dignified and kind in their speech. Bhaga's wife is Perfection *(Siddhi)* and he had three sons named Greatness *(Mahimān)*, Power *(Vibhu)*, Sovereignty *(Prabhu)*, and a daughter named Hope *(Āśi)*[78].

Bhaga presides over love and marriage as a blissful form of the Sun god. Associated with love, affection, amorous pleasure and sexual passion, natives of this star will be lovers of life, charming and attractive. They will often be involved in professions such as dance, art, music, or other creative expressions. The may work in relationship counseling or anything involving love and affection.

As Bhaga is usually invoked with Aryaman the two should be understood together. Both relate to marriage and have a bed as their symbol, though Bhaga resides in the part of the bed that shows the pleasure one enjoys from relationship and marriage. While Aryaman resides in the portion of the bed that shows the long term reasons for marriage.

"May Aryaman and Bhaga lead us, and may the union of wife and husband be easily accomplished, oh gods "[79].

[78] Bhāgavata Purāṇa, Canto 6, Chapter 18, verse 2. translation based on Danielou, Alain
[79] Wilson, H.H. Ṛg Veda Saṁhitā, Maṇḍala 10, Sūkta 86, 23

Uttaraphalgunī: Aryaman

||auṁ aryamaṇe namaḥ||

Aryaman is also one of the twelve Ādityas. He relates to sustenance and gives health and strength of the body. Aryaman is a deity of arranging marriage, companionship, and the one who brings children. He is the 'friendly companion' aspect of the Sun. These natives are interested in seeing others enjoy marital happiness and good at arranging marriages and match-making. Aryaman shows prosperity through marriage, accumulation of wealth and family. Natives of this star are generally good with finances, trade, and business.

He is the chief of the ancestors and the milky way is his path[80]. From the Vedic perspective, marriage and children is a way to repay the ancestors. In this way, the ārūḍha (external manifestation) for marriage is calculated from the twelfth house. The twelfth house ārūḍha (UL) shows how we will repay our anscestors, and it is the bhāvapada for marriage.

The symbol for the phalgunī stars is a bed. Uttara means northern, or higher in vibration. Uttaraphalgunī is the higher vibration of the bed and shows the upper part of the body, and the higher aspects of the bed pleasures which are marriage and children. The previous star, Pūrvaphalgunī, relates to the more base vibrations of the bed, and shows the lower sexual parts of the body. The stars of phalguni relate to love, sexuality and relationship. Uttara also relates to the future, or what will come to be, and is more concerned about the long term situation.

A Vedic prayer to the newly married wife says,

"May Prajāpati grant us progeny, may Aryaman unite us together until old age;
free from all evil omens enter your husband's abode,
be the bringer of prosperity for our people and animals[81]."

In the word phalgunī, *phala* means the fruits or results, guṇi comes from guṇa and means qualities. It shows the attributes that bring fruit or progeny. *Phalgunibhava* is a name of Jupiter, he who gives the fruits, or decides the fruits you'll get.

The month of Phalguni is in the spring, during a time of fertility, flowers and colors. The Indian festival of Holi is celebrated at this time with many colors. It is the best nakṣatra for marriage, irrespective of doṣas (except Tuesday). Even the gods get married in the time of the phalgunī nakṣatras[82], with the palanquin of Maghā nakṣatra leading them to the ceremonial place. It is a good nakṣatra for making contracts that will lead to a fruitful outcome. Therefore marriage contracts are made at this time as well as other types of beneficial contracts or agreements.

---

[80] Monier Williams Sanskrit Dictionary
[81] Wilson, H.H. Ṛg Veda Saṁhitā, Maṇḍala 10, Sūkta 86, 43
[82] Wilson, H.H. Ṛg Veda Saṁhitā, Maṇḍala 10, Sūkta 86, 13

Hasta: Savitṛ/Arka

||auṁ savitre namaḥ ||

The diety ruling this star is Savitṛ, the form of the Sun just before the Sun rises signaling dawn. All Brahmins worship him, he determines all births and is the cause of the lagna. The lagna represent one's intelligence and ideals, the awareness of an individual. Savitṛ is the awakener, the light-giver who impells life. Natives of this star are motivated in life and are often interested in techniques and studies related to expansion of consciousness.

Savitṛ has the light of knowledge and gives good insight. Natives of this star are often interested in techniques that reveal deeper levels of understanding. This includes astrology and all its branches, such as omenology and samudrika śastra. Palmistry specifically relates to these individuals given the symbol of this nakṣatra is the hand, representing the ability to look at one holographic aspect of reality, such as reading the palm, or face, and understand the nature of the person's entire life. Planets in this nakṣatra give some magical power to the hand of the native. To activate this quality, one can wear something associated with the planet in Hasta on the hands. For example, if Mars is placed in Hasta one can wear a copper ring, if Jupiter or Mercury one can wear a gold ring, etc. If the Moon is there, one can wear silver on the hand as well as recite the Savitṛ Gāyatrī mantra (often called '*the* Gāyatrī'), and this will invoke magic for this nakṣatra.

The insight of Savitṛ can also be applied to speculation-based professions, like the stock market, real estate, or even certain aspects of business and trade that require good foresight. *Savitra* means to generate, or an instrument of production. These natives are skilled and able to make things happen by creating the situation or tool that is required. They are intelligent and give themselves in service to things related to wisdom and its flourishing.

Negative tendencies can develop when these natives use their inherent insight for the wrong purposes. They can be cruel with their intelligence. They may also use their insight illicitly, or the skill of their hand for thievery like a good pick-pocket. To avoid these negative tendencies one should avoid that which hurts the Sun, such as elements ruled by Saturn and Rāhu.

Chitrā: Viśvakarmā/ Tvaṣṭa

||auṁ viśvakarmaṇe namaḥ ||

Tvaṣṭa is the divine architect later known as Viśvakarmā[83]. "He is the author of a thousand arts, the carpenter and mechanic of the gods, the fabricator of ornaments, the chief of artists, the constructor of the self-moving chariots for the deities, and by whose skill men obtain subsistance[84]." His name literally means the all *(viśva)* worker *(karmin)*, so he relates to work and production, which he has tremendous energy to accomplish. He is an Āditya who has the power to bring resources into our lives. He is sometimes considered an incarnation of Brahmā, as the manifest form of the world creator who makes all things.

These natives are known to be honorable (*mānī*), especially when they use their energy for community service or to perform karma yoga. In this way, these natives can become great karma yogis. Propitiation of Viśvakarmā gives the blessings of children, similar to Brahmā and the Pitṛs.

Chitrā means 'to be painted' and represents the ornamentation the native either wears or creates. It may also indicate that visual mediums and imagery play an important role in their lives. Natives of this star are known to wear nice clothing and jewelry, either made by themselves, or with an eye paid to the detail in the craftmanship of the item. Chitrā also refers to the future projections we make for our life, and is linked to the dhyana yoga aspect of meditation. Viśvakarmā is all about planning, figuring out what and how to build. The entire zodiac is actually built from Chitrā, and this is why the *ayanāṁśa* comes from this star.

When the Sun was too bright for his wife, Viśvakarmā trimmed one-eighth of his rays. From this he made the discus of Viṣṇu, the trident of Śiva, the spear of Kārttikeya and all the weapons of the other gods. These natives can be skilled artisans working with metals and stones, marble, gems and jewelery. They find success in careers related to this type of work or weaving, sewing, fashion design, interior decoration, architecture, engineering, mathematics, machines, creating new things, or making old things better.

The body of these natives is generally well formed with good features as they have received the blessing of the divine architect himself. They can also be very secretive as the craftsman keeps his private life separate from his work. Natives of this star enjoy learning to constantly expand themselves.

---

[83] Viṣṇu Purāṇa, Part I, Chapter 15, says he incarnated through Bṛhaspati's sister, Yogasiddhā, and the eighth Vasu, Prabhāsa, to become the patriarch Viśvakarmā.

[84] Viṣṇu Purāṇa, Part I, Chapter 15

Svātī: Vāyu

||*auṁ vāyave namaḥ*||

Vāyu means wind or air, from the linguistic root vā which means to blow. He is the cosmic life born from the breath of the cosmic man *(puruṣa)* as the Moon *(candra)* was born of the cosmic mind, and the Sun (*sūrya*), born of the eyes[85]. Vāyu relates to the prāṇa inside the body and the five vāyus that cause all things to properly function inside the body. When the internal vāyus are balanced one is physically and mentally healthy, when imbalanced there is disease. Vāyu is worshipped as the breath of the gods, the impeller of life, and the essence of speech (*vāc*).

Vāyu is one of the eight Vasudevas, as a source of illumination among the 33 devas, natives of this star tend to be religious, patient and follow the path of dharma.

Anila is another name of the wind god, and *anilaya* means to have no resting place. 'Ani' is a negation and 'la' is the earth seed sound, therefore it means no earth, or no grounding. As the wind has no home, these natives can be fond of traveling or of making changes. They do not like things to stay static. They feel that situations should come into their life, serve their purpose and then move on. These natives like airplanes or vehicles for traveling. They make good merchants, who travel and need to be both harsh and gentle.

Vāyu personified is white with all white attributes. He rides a deer and carries a bow and arrow. There is a link between Rudra and Vāyu in that they both carry a bow and arrow; one is the lord of wind (as he is the air itself), while the other is the calamity of the storm, including the fierce winds and rain. Both Bhīma and Hanumān were the sons of Vāyu, famous for their strength and power. The strength of the Rudras comes from Vāyu. The difference is that Vāyu can be the harsh wind scattering and destroying things or it can be the cool refreshing breeze on a hot day. Vāyu is a powerful force that when on your side can fill the sails of a boat and carry you across the world.

As wind tends to cool things off, these natives may be unattached to their feelings or not very expressive of their emotions. They will often put on a cold face that does not reveal their emotions. This lack of sharing the emotions (water) is often the cause of many of the prāṇic blockages in these natives. To befriend them it is important to give them the proper space since they are slow to warm up socially.

[84] Ṛg Veda, Maṇḍala 10, Sūkta 90, v. 13

Viśākhā: Indrāgni

||auṁ indrāgnibhyaṁ namaḥ||

Indra and Agni are the king and the high priest, the political power and the spiritual power; together they rule over the star Viśākhā. As Vāyu was born of the cosmic breath, Indra and Agni were born of the mouth *(mukha)* of the Cosmic Being *(puruṣa)*[86]. The cosmic mouth is the portal to make offerings, the place the gods can 'eat' the offerings. All offerings pass through these two deities *(behind these two deities are (all) the other gods)*. If a sick person offers, or if a person offers for abundance, these deities will sustain the offerer[87]."

Indra and Agni are two separate deities in the Vedas, but sometimes two deities combine to create something together, such as when Mitra-varuṇa gave birth to the sage Viśvamitra. Śaunaka says in the *Bṛhad-devatā* that when a Vedic mantra speaks of two distinct devatās in the same context, then they are regarded as constituting single devatā.

Traditionally there is a relationship between the king (Indra) and the priest (Agni), in that the priest perfoms the sacrafices to make the king rise to and stay in power. And the king takes care of the priest's livelihood. The king may hold the political power, but will lose it without his priest, and the priest has no political power but is indispensible for his sacraficial power.

Natives of this star will be aimed at accomplishment and will work to cultivate alliances that prove beneficial to them. They are competitive and understand the roles that people play to help them achieve their aims, as a king and priest interact. They make good businessmen and leaders. Their aggressive desire to achieve can tend toward an argumentative nature. They believe in repayment of personal favors. They can also be greedy or jealous of other people's accomplishments.

There is one story where Indra and Agni took the form of birds to test the charity of an emperor named Śibi[88]. Indra took form as a hawk and Agni that of a dove. The dove flew onto the lap of the emporer while engaged in ritual worship. The hawk flew in demanding the emporer not withhold his food but the emperor protected the bird as it had come to him for protection. He offered the hawk other foods and even his kingdom but the hawk would not settle for anything except the same weight of the dove in the emporer's own flesh. The dove was put on a scale and the emperor cut away the flesh from his own thigh, but no matter how much he cut out, the dove was still heavier. Finally as he was about to put himself on the scale the birds revealed their true form, blessed him and took him to the heavenly realms. The path to true success with these natives is learning about self-less service.

---

[86] Ṛg Veda, Maṇḍala 10, Sūkta 90, v. 13

[87] Śatapatha Bhrāhmaṇa, XI Kāṇḍa, 8 Adhyāya, 3 Brāhmaṇa, v.3 (p.128)

[88] Mahābhārata, Vanaparva, Chapter 131

Anurādhā: Mitra

||auṁ mitrāya namaḥ||

Mitra is an Āditya, a form of the Sun who relates to friendship. The word *mitra* literally means friend, companion, ally. He is a very supportive and sustaining form of the Sun that helps when help is needed just as a friend would.

Mitra relates to the day, while Varuṇa relates to the night. They are often invoked together in prayer to gain the blessings of the entire 24 hour day, or the yin-yang aspects of the Sun. Mitra is your friend and protector, while Varuṇa is looking over your shoulder making sure you behave. Natives of this star are dependable, honorable, and often well-known. They form tight alliances and are faithful to them. When too extreme, their faithfulness to one area will lead them to be stuck in a clique and not extend themselves to others, or other available resources. They are known for their appetite and may use eating as a way to deal with frustration, discomfort, or insecurity.

These natives are generally happy, friendly and give compliments readily. They achieve wealth based on being well connected and knowing the right people. If natives of this star are struggling in career (or any area), they just need to get to know the right people for doorways to open. Mitra gives the blessings of wealth and power through friends. These natives are good at customer service, social services, connecting people, or overseeing meetings. Jobs that involve customer interaction or signing of contracts are beneficial for this star, as well as jobs needing detail, like a fine carpenter. Mitra, representing the day, is always changing and renewing. These natives like to travel and change residence on a regular basis.

In the *Śatapatha Brāhmaṇa* there is the story of Prajāpati creating the goddess Śrī (beauty, prosperity, Lakṣmī), a story helpful in elucidating many of the Vedic deities. "Prajāpati was becoming heated while creating living beings. From him, worn out and heated, Śrī came forth. She stood there resplendent, shining, and trembling. The gods, beholding her thus resplendant, shining, and trembling, set their minds upon her[89]."

Ten devas came to her and took ten different aspects of her. First Agni came and took food, Soma took royal power, Varuṇa took universal soveriegnty, Mitra took noble rank, Indra took power, Bṛhaspati took holy lustre, Savitṛ took dominion, Pūśan took wealth, Sarasvati took prosperity, and Tvaṣṭā (Viśvakarmā) took her beautiful form. She then asked it back from them all in sacrifice and received ten sacrificial dishes offered to her.

[89] Śatapatha Brāhmaṇa, XI Kāṇḍa, 4 Adhyāya, 3 Brāhmaṇa, v. 1

Jyeṣṭhā: Indra

||auṁ indrāya namaḥ||

Indra is king of the devas (gods). He uses a thunderbolt (*vajra*) as his weapon. He is the god of rain and releases open the gates of the clouds. When dependency on the rain god decreased, Indra's position became less prominent[90].

Indra, as the king of the pantheon of gods, engages in dharmic works, so natives of this star have a strong sense of dharma. They do well in leadership roles and enjoy government jobs. Indra's position was not secure and consequently he was always defending, losing and regaining heaven. Natives of this star will be competitive, seeking power and position with the ability to rise and fall equally. They enjoy being the boss or in charge of a situation, but must watch for excess pride.

The Upaniṣads call Indra the life-force (*prāṇa*) in the body which becomes the conscious self (*prajñātmā*)- and to worship prāṇa is to worship Indra[91]. Śaunaka, author of *Bṛhad-devatā*, says that Indra, the aspect of the One divinity, is the prāṇa of all creatures and therefore the inner-ruler (*antaryāmin*). *Indriya* means belonging to Indra, it is also the word denoting the sense organs, or power of the senses. In this way, Indra is the lord of the internal sensory faculty. He is king in the way that the senses are king over the human body and mind. In this way, natives of this star are easily affected by their senses, and can often become easily irritated due to this sensitivity. It also allows for a refinement of the senses to be developed which can lead to extra sensory perceptions or other occult powers and interest. In this regard these natives also tend to seek power through magical practices. Heaven is inside, and being ruled by the senses is like being tossed into battles for peace of mind. This is the meaning behind the symbolism of the demons (negative thoughts) taking over heaven and the battle of the gods to restore heaven (good thoughts and control over the senses).

Indra is a god known for his sexual exploits. One well known situation was when he disguised himself to seduce Ṛṣi Gautama's wife, Ahalyā. When the Ṛṣi discovered the situation, to make known Indra's lust, he cursed Indra to be covered with a thousand vaginas all over his body[92]. Through severe penance Indra was able to turn the vaginas into a thousand eyes, symbolizing this nakṣatra's need to transform sexual energy into spiritual energy so it does not manifest in physically grotesque acts, but can be used as fuel for higher perception.

Indra defeated the serpent demon, Vṛtra, who had hoarded all the earth's water. His son Arjuna, was the hero of the war in the *Mahābhārata*. These natives can be known for their heroism, and desire to make things right, therefore they can be good generals, police officers, and soldiers.

[90] This is seen in the story of when the natives of Uttar Pradesh stopped worshipping Indra and he sent a storm. Kṛṣṇa protected the people with Mount Govardhana representing the change from the times of being dependant on rain.

[91] Kauśītaki-brāmaṇa-upaniṣad (3,1), Aitareya-āraṇyaka (2,2,3), Rao, *Rigveda Darsana*, p.219, 220

[92] Padma Purāṇa 1:56:15-53, and Vālmīki Rāmāyaṇa

Mūla: Nirṛti

||*auṁ nirṛtaye namaḥ*||

Nirṛti *(pronounced near-rrrri-tea)* is the wife of Adharma (not dharma, sin)[92]. She has three sons named *Bhaya* (fear), *Mahābhaya* (great danger), and *Antaka* (causing death). *Ṛta* means the natural law, or the natural order of the universe. The prefix *nir* means away from, without, or lacking. Nirṛti is that which does not follow divine law, or the natural order, going against the natural way, as her husband, Adharma, is that which is not dharmic, nor socially acceptable, but sinful. Parāśara also calls her 'Rākṣasa', or sometimes known as Rākṣasī; she is said to be the mother of all the beings Rākṣasas (demons or merciless people).

The dark goddess is mentioned in Vedic hymns to dispel her or ask her to stay away. In the Atharvaveda, prayers are made for sick people to be rescued from her lap and restored to health.

"Let the Prāṇa and Apāna restore thy life that has vanished through misdeeds. Agni has snatched it from the lap of Nirṛti, and restores it into you[93]."

Prayers for protection are recited to keep the demons, ghosts, strife and the destructive energy of Nirṛti away. She is strong, vigorous, and disheveled. Her tendency is to tear things apart, or pull them out of place. Natives of this star have the ability to remove things they don't like, this is very beneficial when working with medicine to remove disease. It is also good for work that requires destruction, like demolition, remodeling, or even garden maintanence where one is pulling out the excess vegetation.

These natives can have attributes like that of Nirṛti or possess the power to keep her away. When Nirṛti is present there is poverty and suffering, where she is absent there is wealth, honor and familial happiness. Before a big yajña, priests propitiate Nirṛiti by offering black rice to a woman unable to have children (meaning she is possessed by Nirṛti) and ask for the blessing that Nirṛiti not come near[94]. It is important for these natives to regularly clear energy, and dispell negative vibrations.

Nirṛti rules over the south-western direction considered by Vāstu as a place to put the office, or a seat of power. She has power and force, and when unattended to can create distrubances. When the prāṇa gets scattered in this direction, it is spent partying and imbibing intoxicants which lead to disease. The physician prays,

"If life has faded, with a hopeless case, and brought one close to death, I snatch them from the lap of Nirṛti, and grant them the strength to live for a hundred years[95]."

[92] Mahābhārata, Sambhava-Parva LXVI
[93] Long life Prayer, Atharvaveda, Kāṇḍa VII, Hymn 53, v. 3 (1860)
[94] Śatapatha Brāhmaṇa, Kāṇḍa V, Adhyāya 3, Brāhmaṇa 2, v. 2
[95] Atharvaveda, Kāṇḍa III, Hymn XI, v. 2 (463)

Pūrvāṣāḍhā: Āpas

| | auṁ jaladevāya namaḥ | |

Āpas is the goddess of water *(jala)* or the energy of water personified as a deity. Water represents emotions, purification, and rejuvenation.

Āpas relates to flowing water[96]; when water is moving it stays fresh and clear, renewing itself. Therefore, water gives clarity and freshness, as a bath purifies the body. Water is used for cleansing as well as clearing in rituals. Dhruva Nāḍi says that these natives will be successful in professions related to water in any way, sailing, fishing, building dams or canals, etc. They enjoy an honest profession. As water continues to flow and passes against all it encounters along the way, these natives push forward to achieve their aims.

Water relates to love and emotion. Natives of this star value love and relationship highly. They are often falling in love and will often look for happiness through relationship. In the Ṛgveda, Āpas is invoked to bind the hearts during marriage,

"May the Universal-gods (Viśvadeva) and the Waters (Āpas) unite both our hearts[97]."

Natives of this star have sensitive feelings. They are gentle and caring, and faithful to their friends. They are community oriented and are concerned about family.

Emotional positivism and balance are very important for health. The negative flow of emotions can disturb the mind and body. In this way, love is an important medicine for health and longevity. The subtle essence of air/vāta is *Prāṇa*, the subtle essence of fire/ pitta is *Tejas*, and the subtle essence of water/ kapha is *Ojas*. It is Ojas that gives a glow and luster to the body and aura. Without Ojas a person looks worn-out and tired. Therefore, the water deity has the power to enliven and make a person glow with health and well being, as the Sun of vitality rises from the ocean of water renewed and brilliant[98] each day. This star is good for preparing medicines, especially those that relate to rejuvenation or increasing Ojas in general.

In the creation of the elements, first there is space, then air, then fire, and from fire comes water. The Upaniṣads[99] say that Āpas came forth from fire *(tejas)*, and because of that when people get hot they perspire. In this way water comes forth from heat and from water comes food and grains (earth). In this way, natives of this star may work with food production or cultivation.

---

[96] Ṛg Veda, Maṇḍala 10, Sūkta 76, entire Sūkta with specific reference to v. 7

[97] Ṛg Veda, Maṇḍala 10, Sūkta 85, v. 47

[98] Ṛg Veda, Maṇḍala 1, Sūkta 95, v. 4-8

[99] Chāndogya Upaniṣad, 6.2.3-4 [463]. Danielou, p.244

Uttarāṣāḍhā: Viśvadeva

||auṁ viśvadevebhyo namaḥ||

The Viśvadevas are sometimes called the all-gods, or the universal principles. *Viśva* means all, whole, everywhere, universal. Dharma-deva with his wife Viśva gave birth to the Viśvadevas.[100] The names of these all-gods are Goodness *(Vasu)*, Truth *(Satya)*, Determination *(Kratu)*, Talent *(Dakṣa)*, Time *(Kāla)*, Enjoyment *(Kāma)*, Firmness *(Dhṛti)*, Ancestors *(Kuru)*, Abundance *(Purūravas)*, Joy *(Mādrava)*, as well as Pleasantness *(Rochana)*, Sight *(Lochana)*, Fame *(Dhvani)*, and Leadership *(Dhuri)*, all strong qualities of one's character. The watery sensitivity of feeling in previous *(purva)* aṣāḍhā is developed into a character made up of all the greatest attributes in the later (*uttara*) aṣāḍhā. It is the awareness of other people's feelings that leads to the natural development of positive character traits. These natives tend to be polite, ethical, mindful of others, and respectable. They utilize these good qualities to climb their way to success in life.

These natives are talented and fortunate, often being able to work in physically strenuous conditions or in scholarly studies. All the various attributes shown by the Viśvadevas lead to success. *Dhruva Nāḍī* recommends physically demanding work such as wrestling, rodeo feats like catching and riding elephants, working at recreation resorts, or being an astrologer for natives of this star. The Viśvadevas give one the ability to overcome challenges and obstacles, allowing a person to keep sight of their objective. Natives of this star will look for a secure job or position of power, not the variability of Indra's throne.

It is through adharmic activity that one falls from position and power. Only Saturn can pull one down from position through one's own self-generated sin. Through the honorable (*dharmic*) living of Uttarāṣāḍhā one removes the obstacles that would cause one to fall from heights they have risen to. While Indra rises to power by whatever means and thereby loses friends due to it, the Viśvadevas gain friends because of their ethical practices. Therefore these natives often have many friends and associates as they ascend to the heights they are capable of.

The *Bhāgavata Purāṇa* says that people worship the Viśvadevas when they want to attain a kingdom, or royal success.[101] Natives of this star follow the saying that some people have dreams and others stay awake to make them happen.

[100] Sometimes Viśvadeva can refer to a particular group of deities, other times Viśvadeva refers to"all the gods" (as in Ādityas, Rudra and everyone else).
[101] Bhāgavata Purāṇa Canto II, Chapter 3, v. 4

Śravaṇa: Viṣṇu

||*auṁ viṣṇave namaḥ*||

The name Viṣṇu means the 'all-pervader', like the ākāśa (space) element he exists everywhere. In the same way the ākāśa creates harmony, Viṣṇu creates harmony and solidity, and especially firmness in dharma. Ākāśa is the element through which comes hearing and the transmission of dharma.

In the Ṛg Veda, Viṣṇu is mentioned in the Vāmana form where he took three steps to traverse the three realms of earth, sky (solar system) and heaven (universe). Two steps are visible, but the third is beyond the vision of men and birds. Viṣṇu is described as the friend of Indra, both being able to immediately grant desires[102]. Natives of this star are often wealthy or have good fortune with money (Śrīmān= one who has Śrī). They generally have an honorable spouse and are well-known.

Viṣṇu, who takes three steps, is the protector *(gopa)* who upholds dharma *(dharmāṇi dhārayan)*. His abode is called the Paraṁ-padam[103]. This literally means the supreme *(para)* footing or abode *(pada)*, or the 'supreme station' of Viṣṇu. It can be seen as the foot of the supreme, or the base/foundation of the transcendent. Natives of this star tend to be religious, and they are fond of learning about ancient teachings. Śravaṇa literally means to hear, study or learn, and this represents hearing the teachings. Spiritual teachings and oral tradition promote dharma, and therefore this nakṣatra relates to knowledge that has been passed down. Natives of this star are often involved in religious or spiritual professions, as well as teaching language, literature, and other related sciences.

In the Vedas, Viṣṇu is shown as an ally in the battles of king Indra.[104] As Kṛṣṇa, Viṣṇu was a politician, showing the native's propensity toward politics or positions of power, positions in which they intend to uphold dharma. Viṣṇu is often changing forms and using sly tricks to win. In this way, these natives can also be good at deception and cheating in order to win a battle or situation. They will often use intellectual intelligence to outsmart their opposition or competition.

Viṣṇu, who expands his body beyond all measure[105], conquers the worlds in three steps and is praised for his expansiveness. He gives a broad, open-minded perspective.

[102] Ṛg Veda, Maṇḍala 1, Sūkta 154-6, and Maṇḍala 8, Sūkta 25, v. 12
[103] Ṛg Veda, Maṇḍala 1, Sūkta 22, v. 16-21
[104] Ṛg Veda, , Maṇḍala 7, Sūkta 99, v. 4-7
[105] Ṛg Veda, , Maṇḍala 7, Sūkta 99, v. 1

Dhaniṣṭhā: Vasu

||auṁ namo bhagavate vāsudevāya||

The linguistic root *vas* means to shine, to grow bright or to bestow by shining upon. Vasu means excellent and wealthy, to dwell in their shining. The Vasus bring wealth and fame into ones life.

As part of the 33 devas, the eight Vasu-deva are the sources of illumination and prosperity. It is said that "the world dwells in them and they dwell in the world." The eight Vasu-devas can be seen collectively as the aspect of the planets and stars that are manifesting the material plane *(ādhibautika)*, as: the Moon *(Soma)*, the Sun *(Pratyuṣa)*, Water *(Āpas)*, Earth *(Dhara)*, Air *(Anila)*, Fire *(Anala)*, Space *(Dhruva)*, and the Spledourous Light of the stars *(Prabhāsa)*.

Parāśara says in the Viṣṇu Purāṇa that they originated from the light (jyoti)[106], or that they are the origins of Jyotiṣa. They are born as the children of Dharma and his wife Vasu, and have children of their own. For example, Prabhāsa, became the father of Viśvakarmā. The Vasus are siblings to the Viśvadevas who are born of Dharma and Viśva (another one of Dharma's ten wives).

It is said that "those who desire wealth (vasu) worship the Vasudevas.[107]" This is a star of wealth and prosperity, and can also be a place of greed, or excess drive to make money. Natives of this star tend to be generous and sharing, though they have a detached attitude toward their work, and often perform impersonal jobs.

The Vasudevas represent the key indications of manifestation on the material plane, and therefore there is a lot of creativity in this star. There is also a strong desire to share this creative spirit, especially that which is considered novel or misunderstood. The Vasudevas are the indicators, shedding light on a situation. Natives of this star like to make things known, making announcements, and sharing information. They enjoy attention and focus as they like to shine.

Individuals of this star enjoy music, and the messages being expressed through the music are very important to them. They often have refined senses.

[106] Viṣṇu Purāṇa, Book I, Chapter 15, v. 110, (ye tvanekavasuprāṇā devā jyotiḥ purogamāḥ)
[107] Bhāgavata Purāṇa, Canto II, Chapter 3, v. 3

Śatabhiṣa: Varuṇa

||auṁ varuṇāya namaḥ||

Varuṇa is the guardian of Ṛta, the universal law. He is said to have a thousand eyes[108] to see everything. He sends his spies (Rāhu) throughout the worlds as police men looking to punish the wrongs people have done. There is no escape from Varuṇa, the Saturnine Āditya. *Va* is the seed syllable of water, and Varuṇa is the lord of the waters of the Milky Way. As Mitra relates to the rules over man-made laws, Varuṇa, who is mysterious like the night, rules over the laws made by the gods and the suffering or blessings of fate.

Varuṇa rules over unseen (invisible) obstacles (*adṛṣṭa-bādhaka*). When disease starts in Śatabhiṣa know that it is serious, the noose of Varuṇa is put on by Rāhu and tightened by Saturn. Disease started when the Moon is in Śatabhiṣa is said to be incurable by even Dhanvantari, the god of medicine. The Aśvins and Dhanvantari heal disease that is caused by something visible. Varuṇa rules over diseases and suffering from previous sin, in this and previous lives. That is why this star can make a good astrologer, as they can show you the way to balance out karma.

When Varuṇa is against you nothing in the three worlds can remove his noose from tightening around your neck. Natives of this star are very harsh against their competition and work hard to defeat their enemies. They are known to be reckless, forceful and sometimes even brutal. They may lack grace in their manners and make enemies of people who wish to help them. Varuṇa is worshipped with salt water or in the ocean, and when Varuṇa is pleased one gets the blessings of his children, Lakṣmi[109] and Soma, who give prosperity and cures.

Varuṇa is often refered to as 'King' or even the king of kings *(rājā rāṣṭra)*. Sage Vasiṣṭha calls Varuṇa 'Samrāj,' the universal ruler or overlord. Sage Vasiṣṭha also calls Indra 'Svarāj', the self-ruler or independent lord[110]. While Indira is the king of heaven- his job is to rule the self (to rule over the senses). Varuṇa is the king ruling with the universal law *(Ṛta)*, and his duty is to keep all things in their natural order.

Natives of this star are successful at professions like hunting or situations where traps or 'catching' is required. They can work in jails or prisons or places of punishment and rehabilitation. There is an association of this star with addictions and alcohol. These natives are also comfortable working with chronic and mental disease. They are often known for overworking themselves.

Varuṇa is known for his immense knowledge, like an ocean, this quality is found in Śatabhiṣa. In the *Rāmāyaṇa*, Varuṇa incarnated as Rāja Ṛṣi Janaka, known for his great wisdom, even while he lived a simplistic life.

---

[108] Ṛg Veda, Maṇḍala 7, Sūkta 34, v. 10

[109] Ṛśi Bṛghu is also the son of Varuṇa, Śatapatha Brāhmaṇa, Kaṇḍa XI, Adhyāya 6, Brāhmaṇa 1

[110] Muller, Max, and Eggeling, Julius, *The Śatapatha- Brāhmaṇa*, p.xxii

Pūrvābhādra: Ajaikapada

| | auṁ ajaikapadāya namaḥ | |

This nakṣatra is ruled by Aja-ekapada. *Aja* can mean goat which is one of the Veda murtis (forms of the Vedas) that brings knowledge. Generally Ajaikapada refers to a form of Śiva standing on one leg doing penance, like the Sun moving through the sky in a one-wheeled chariot, making this a nakṣatra of penance and tapasya.

Aja is considered one of the Rudras, and later developed into a Bhairava form of Śiva, as well as a form of the Sun[111]. Aja translates as 'he-goat' or a leader of a flock, driver, instigator. Ādi Śaṅkara comments that the lord is Aja "because he impels, or moves everywhere, casting off evil[112]."

These natives are either driven to practice darker forms of tantra (black magic) or driven to practice tapasya (austerity) or rituals of purification. Lorded by one of the Rudras, this nakṣatra will present many problems eventually leading the native to live a more austere life. These natives can often perform menial or cruel work, or may be disinterested in work. They do not have two feet in this world; one is here and the other is in another realm.

Ajaikapada was one of the sons of Viśvakarmā[113], in charge of preserving all the gold in the world[114]. These natives are known to be skilled with making money and to not be generous as they are trying to save for some other purpose. As one foot needs balance, these natives will often lean on their spouses for support or be under the control of the spouse.

Aja can also mean 'not born' (*a-ja*) or the 'first created' who is not born. Ekapada means having only "one foot" or a "single word." This can be translated as a 'one footed goat', or on a more spiritual level as the 'unborn single word'. He is sometimes also called aja-devatā[115]. The one foot shows a single pointedness, a balance and centeredness that has the power of Rudra.

Pūrva means backside, *bhādra* means auspicious, and *pada* means foot. When standing or walking, it represents the back foot. This nakṣatra shows someone who can balance the impossible, making for good doctors, giving the ability to heal impossible conditions.

This symbol is the burning of the funeral cot, opposite the phalgunīs in the sky. The phalgunīs are represented by a bed used for creating, a function of the Ādityas. The bhādrapadas are ruled by forms of Rudra, represented by a funeral cot which carries the dead body to be burned. They show the purification and death that is needed to understand that which is beyond the material plane.

---

[111] Varāha Purāṇa 26.5, as translated by Danielou, Alain, p. 97
[112] Śaṅkara's Bhāṣhya on Viṣnu Sahasranāma Bh.35, (*ajati gacchati kṣipatīti vā ajaḥ*)
[113] Viṣṇu Purāṇa, Part I, Chapter 15
[114] Mani, Vettam, Purāṇic Encyclopedia p. 20
[115] Monier Williams Sanskrit Dictionary

Uttarabhādra: Ahirbudhnya

||auṁ ahirbudhnyāya namaḥ||

Ahirbudhnya is one of the sons of Viśvakarmā and his wife Surabhī. *Ahi* is often interpreted as serpant and *Budhnya* as 'below' or 'bottom'. He is called the serpant of the deep or serpant of the nether regions. He lives in the abyss which is the region of mist[116]. The serpant symbolizes untapped energies that lie hidden within our subconscious mind, as the kuṇḍalini is the serpant in the depths or base of our body. Natives of this star have an affinity for secret knowledge, or subjects that deal with the hidden or unseen.

"Divine Heaven, Earth, and Ahirbudhnya,
I praise you with water, as those searching for treasure desire passage
over the ocean into which all the rumbling rivers disappear[117]."

These natives are scholarly, and will often study Vedic sciences or other traditional literature. Ahirbudhnya is associated with the protection (*gopāya*) of the mantras of the Vedas in their particular divisions; the mantras to be chanted (Ṛgveda), the mantras to be sung (Sāmaveda), and the mantras for ritual (Yajurveda). In this way, these individuals will often seek to classify knowledge and keep the purity of its background.

They are similar to the previous star in the performing of austerities, but are much more ritualistic in their approach. This star is therefore associated with magic and tantra. These natives do not like to lose and work very hard to win in events of competition, often overcoming their opposition.

Ahirbudhnya is a Rudra who removes calamity and misfortune and has the power to grant refreshment, delight, and enjoyment *(mayas)* as a cow takes care of her calf[118]. These natives are often happy and are known to be fruitful in their endeavors, having many children or many projects that they are involved in. Ahirbudhnya is sometimes associated with mist or fog, as he is associated with the upward movement of water which leads to rain.

There is a connection to Śeṣa nāga as he is deep underground giving steadiness to the earth. In the same way, natives of this star seek to find steadiness in their life which is often filled with moving and changing. They are often known as either ascetics or kings.

[116] Monier Williams Sanskrit Dictionary
[117] Ṛg Veda, Maṇḍala 4, Sūkta 55, v. 6
[118] Ṛg Veda, Maṇḍala 1, Sūkta 187, v. 5

Revatī: Pūṣan

||auṁ pūṣṇe namaḥ||

Pūṣan means the nourisher, coming from the linguistic root *puṣ* which means to flourish, prosper, increase, and nourish. He is one of the twelve Ādityas who is like a shepherd tending his flock. His cattle are never lost, for he is the protector of all beings (*anaṣṭapaśu*[119]). These natives prosper in caretaking jobs, or jobs where they are looking after people or animals. They are often surrounded with friends and relatives as they hold family and the family unit as very important.

Pūṣan is called "*Āghṛṇi*" which means he is very bright and shining. He is known for finding the animal that has wandered from the herd and his light is invoked to help find lost articles. Āghṛṇi also means very warm, friendly, and compassionate. Natives of this star are generally honest, clean and fortunate.

"Pūṣan, convey us over the road, and remove obstacles."[120]

Pūṣan is the protector of all paths (*pathas pathaḥ paripatiṁ*[121]), and is invoked for protection on journeys. He is asked to remove thieves and those who delight in evil from one's path. These natives are good in business and find success sailing or traveling, or working in places where people travel to. Pūṣan shows the easiest way, helps the journey be comfortable, and knows the location of hidden treasures.

The blessing of Pūṣan leads one to good pastures (*suyavasa*). This refers to leading the cattle to a place of abundant eating, and leading humans to a place of abundant wealth (food and money). He is a guardian for journeys in the material world, in the astral world and after one has left the body.

These natives are often handsome, with well-proportioned limbs. Pūṣan is considered handsome with braided hair, golden-hued, and carrying a golden spear. He has a chariot drawn by goats, and is called the friend/brother of Indra as he fights battles with him. In battle he is invoked to be close like a friend and help defeat the enemy. Natives of this star are brave, they are not just caring, but are also very protective of those around them.

Pūṣan is also associated with fruits, flowers and watery plants, like the lotus. According to the Brāhmanas, Pūṣan is propitiated with porridge or oatmeal *(karamba).* He likes food that does not need to be masticated (can be eaten without chewing). Pūṣan is associated with milk, a symbol for nourishment; the type of nourishment a cow gives to her calf.

[119] Ṛg Veda, Maṇḍala 10, Sūkta 17, v. 3
[120] Ṛg Veda, Maṇḍala 1, Sūkta 42
[121] Ṛg Veda, Maṇḍala 6, Sūkta 49, v. 8

These deities are perceived through natural phenomenon; in that, Puṣan is nourishment (cow nursing a calf), and Āpas is water. It is not the actual water that is being worshipped, but the deity as these elements and qualities. Water is a powerful, miraculous medicine and life-giving element. It is the power of water that is respected through the Vedic deity Āpas. Yama can be seen as the lord of death, the energy that enters a house when someone is dying or has died. He can be seen as the death process, the time of something dying and transitioning; or, the process of the soul preparing its exit from the body and finally departing. The Aśvins are the divine doctors, they represent healing energy, or the healing potential in all things. In this way, one does not need to take an image and worship it, but instead to watch and be aware of the natural phenomena of the world, learning how things work and the lessons that the natural world presents. How do people act when they don't get enough water, how do they feel when they go swimming, is swimming ever a somber experience? In this way, the deities are archetypal phenomena that exists both outside in nature, in the working of the physical body, and in the dynamics of the psychology.

Practice Exercise:

3. Learn more about your janma nakṣatra devatā. Write on a calendar when the Moon enters this nakṣatra each month and utilize this day for research or do pūjā to this devatā.

Other planets placed in the Nakṣatras

The nakṣatra deity of the planets in the rāśi chakra relate to the *external* significations of the planets. For example, if the Sun is in Citra, the father will be very creative and enjoy craftsmanship. The psychology of the *internal* significations of the planet relate to the nakṣatra deity of the planet's D-27 position. For example, if the Sun was in the D-27 of Śravaṇa, then there will be a large amount of vitality around learning. The lagna and lagna lord in the D-27 relate to the psychology of how a person intellectually thinks, while the D-27 lord of the Moon relates to a person's behavior. The D-27 of Jupiter relates to a person's thinking or mental processing related to religion and god. This is a more advanced area which becomes very important in the branch of Āyurveda called *Mānasa Roga*, the treatment of mental disorders (psychology). It is important to notice that in the D-27 the nakṣatras no longer line up with the signs, and therefore one should avoid using the signs of the zodiac or their lords to interpret the nakṣatra meanings.

Nakṣatra Symbols

The symbols of the nakṣatra are archetypal images used to trigger the natural understanding of the activities, skills, and strengths of each nakṣatra.

#	Constellation	Translation	Symbol	Body Part
1	Aśvinī	Horseman	**Horse's head**	Upper feet
2	Bharaṇī	The bearers	**Yoni (vagina)**	Lower feet
3	Kṛttikā	The razor	**Axe, scalpel, flame**	Head
4	Rohiṇī	Female deer	**Ox cart**	Fore-head
5	Mṛga	Antelope's head	**Deer head with antlers**	Eye-brows
6	Ārdrā	The moist	**Teardrop, perspiration**	Eyes
7	Punarvasu	Return of light	**Quiver of arrows**	Nose
8	Puṣya	The nourisher	**Milk giving cow udder**	Face
9	Āśleṣa	The serpant	**Coiled serpent**	Ears
10	Maghā	The beneficient	**Throne room, palaquin**	Lips & chin
11	Pūrvaphalgunī	Earlier fig tree	**Back legs of a bed**	Right hand
12	Uttaraphalgunī	Later fig tree	**Front legs of a bed**	Left hand
13	Hasta	The hand	**Hand or fist**	Fingers
14	Citrā	The brilliant	**Shining Jewel**	Neck
15	Svātī	The sword	**Sprout, sword, coral**	Chest
16	Viśākhā	The two branches	**Decorated gateway**	Breast
17	Anurādhā	Near success	**Decorated gateway**	Stomach
18	Jyeṣṭhā	The eldest	**Talisman, an earring**	Right side
19	Mūla	The root	**Bundle of Roots, or lion's tail**	Left side
20	Pūrvaaṣāḍhā	The earlier victory	**Tusk of an elephant, winnowing basket, fan**	Back
21	Uttaraaṣāḍhā	The later victory	**Planks of a bed, Tusk of an elephant**	Waist
22	Śravaṇa	The famous	**3 footprints, trident, ear**	Genitals
23	Dhaniṣṭhā	The most famous or most wealthy	**Drum (tabor)**	Anus
24	Śatabhiṣa	Has a hundred medicines	**Empty circle or a charm**	Right thigh
25	Pūrvābhādra	The earlier auspicious one	**Front of funeral cot, a 2 faced man**	Left thigh
26	Uttarabhādra	The later auspicious one	**Back legs of funeral cot**	Shins
27	Revatī	The rich splendorous	**Drum for keeping time**	Ankles

The horse's head of Aśvinī will show all the attributes of horses, with their strength, power, transport abilities, etc. The yoni (triangle representative of a vagina) of Bharaṇī shows the creative potential and śakti power of transformation. It reveals that the lord of death is not just taking you out of one body but he is putting you into another, transformation. He is the Dharmarāja and insures you come into this world through the correct yoni, and into a family that you have karmicly earned to be a part of.

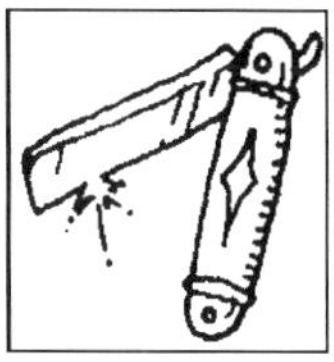

The scalpel of Kṛttikā shows the sharp cutting nature to perceive things clearly, as well as their precise nature. The cart of Rohiṇī shows the ability to move resources. As a trader would take his goods to the market or a farmer to carry his harvest, the cart shows the gathering and transport of resources. Stellar astrology looks even closer and differentiates whether the Moon is behind, in or in front of the stars creating the cart to give more specific details.

The symbol for Mṛgaśira is the head of a deer with antlers. These antlers start as little nubs and grow branching out in many directions. They are ornamentation and a protective system. This shows both the growth of this nakṣatra and its skills to branch out in many directions. In Āyurveda, the powder of deer antlers *(mṛga-śṛiñga-bhasma)* is used as a nutritive medicine to improve immunity *(ojas)* and often included as an ingredient in chyavanprash (a rejuvinative medicine). The Chinese often mix deer antlers with ginseng as a tonic, especially for women who use it as a calcium supplement that strengthens the bones and hair. It is also used in aphrodisiac medicines. Each year the antlers of the deer fall off and then grow anew, like the Moon waxing and waning. The antlers on the head also relate to the nature of the internal Soma of the yoga tradition being seated in the crown of the head.

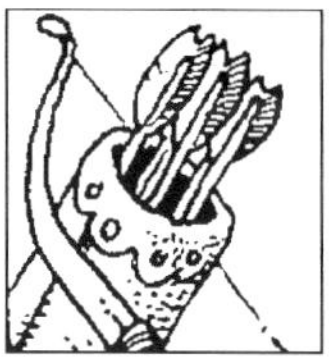

Punarvasu (return of the light) is represented by arrows and their quiver. It relates to constant practice or revisiting something again and again. As an archer shoots arrows, picks them up and shoots them again- patiently practicing for perfection. Or an astrologer who will read a text again and again to perfect their art. The arrows revisiting the quiver represent this constant returning to the basic foundations to reach a complete understanding, or expansion of consciousness. This nakṣatra shows the repetition and practice that becomes understanding. That knowledge becomes the *knowing* found in Puṣya, where the complete giving and nourishment of the universe provides as the udders of a cow provide milk.

In this way, the symbols are to be meditated upon and understood. For this introductory text, the devatās will be the main focus. So take time with each one and understand them. Volume two will focus on the symbols.

Muhūrta

There are seven qualitative divisions among the nakṣatras. They are used with the Moon's transit to determine the quality of actions on a particular day. For example, putting out rat traps is better on an ugra nakṣatra to ensure the removal of rats. Introducing yourself to someone you want as a friend is better on a mṛdu nakṣatra if you want them to like you. Below is a list according to Varāhamihira's *Bṛhat Saṁhitā*.

Quality	Nakṣatra	Nakṣatra-Karma-Guṇa-Adhyāyaḥ [97]
Dhruva (fixed): indicates that it is good for stable, permanent and persevering results	Rohiṇī U.Phalgunī Uttarāṣāḍhā Uttarabhādra	Commencement of coronations *(abhiṣeka)*, remedial measures *(śānti)*, planting trees *(taru)*, benefits for the town *(nagara)*, dharmic works *(dharma)*, sowing seeds *(bīja)*, etc.
Tikṣṇa (Sharp and dreadful): A cutting nature, ability to make decisions, and executive ability	Ārdrā Āśleṣā Jyeṣṭhā Mūla	Success in: attacks, retaliation, arguments *(abhighāta)*, spells *(mantra)*, working with ghosts *(vetāla)*, imprisonment *(bhandha)*, hurting or killing *(vadha)*, murders, breaking unions/relations *(bheda-sambhanda)*, etc.
Ugra: (fierce and severe): when action must be aggressive or harsh	Bharaṇī Maghā P.Phalgunī Pūrvāṣāḍhā	Success in: destroying, ruining, interrupting *(utsāda)*, destruction/removal *(nāśa)*, deceit/ dishonesty *(śāṭhya)*, imprisoning *(bandha)*, working with poison *(viṣada)*, slaughtering *(hana)*, work with weapons *(astra)*, injuring *(ghāta)*, etc.
Laghu (light): not heavy, quick, active, prompt, graceful, easy	Pūrvābhādra Aśvinī Puṣya Hasta (Abhijit)	Business/ trade *(paṇya)*, sexual enjoyment *(rati)*, pursuit of knowledge *(jñāna)*, jewelry, decorative clothing, adornment *(bhūṣaṇa)*, practical skills/arts *(kalā)*, artisan/ skilled labor/handicraft *(śilpa)*, use of herbs/medicines *(auṣadha)*, travels and journeys *(yāna)*, etc.
Mṛdu (soft/ mild/ tender): indicates easy going nature and bhoga (indulging in pleasure/ enjoyments)	Mṛgaśira Citrā Anurādhā Revatī	Gaining friends *(mitra-artha)*, delightful activities, sex *(surata)*, rules, ordinances *(vidhi)*, clothing, new outfits *(vastra)*, jewelry, adornment *(bhūṣaṇa)*, anything auspicious or ceremonial *(maṅgala)*, singing *(gīta)*, etc.
Mṛdutīkṣṇa (Mixed- Soft and hard): Combination of results Also called *sādhāraṇa*: general or common	Kṛttikā Viśākhā	These nakṣatra will give mixed *(vimiśra)* results *(phala)*, mingled, miscellaneous results.
Chara (moveable/ ephemeral): easily changing nature	Punarvasu Svātī Śravaṇa Dhaniṣṭhā Śatabhiṣa	Good for benefitng one's own or other people's welfare *(cara karmaṇi hitāni)*.

Divisions of the Nakṣatras: 108 Padas

Each 13° 20′ nakṣatra is divided into four *padas* (parts) of 3° 20′ each. Each of the four parts relate to the four *ayana* (goals): dharma, artha, kāma, and mokṣa. The first pada is dharma, the second pada is artha, the third pada relates to kāma and the final pada of each nakśatra is mokṣa.

Varāhamihira defines a rāśi as nine nakṣatra padas[122]. The rāśi chart divided by nine is called the navāṁśa, one of the most important divisions of a sign. Use the above chart to see the rāśi, nakṣatra, and the navāṁśa divisions, these are either four per nakṣatra or nine per rāśi, both are 3°20′.

A rāśi divided into nine *aṁśas* (divisions) gives us the navāṁśa, a division which shows many aspects including the inherent qualities of the soul, a native's dharma, bhāgya, and one's spouse. Each navāṁśa is 3° 20′, and nine aṁśas multiplied by twelve rāśis equals 108. So the navāṁśa is the 108-sign chart.

[122] This is stated in Jātaka Pārijāta, Bṛhat Jātaka and Bṛhat Saṁhitā.

The Sun is kāraka for the first and ninth house, while the Moon is kāraka for the fourth house. There are four padas in a nakṣatra each equating to 3° 20′. Twenty-seven nakṣatras multiplied by four padas equals 108. Each pada relates to a tone, and when used properly, the tone can activate a planet. The Moon has 108 padas and 108 tones.

The 3° 20′ division is the most crucial division. The Moon's nakṣatra padas and the Sun sign's navāṁśas line up with the number 108. One hundred and eight is the number where the Moon (*manas/mind*) and Sun *(ātman/soul)* line up. It is where the Moon's çycle can be aligned with the Sun's cycle. 108 is a number that aligns the mind and the soul.

The 3° 20′ division aligns the Sun and Moon, creating alignment of *Śiva* and *Parvati* or the *Puruṣa* (consciousness) and *Prakṛtti* (creation). The 108 division reflects the creation of the world; it is a powerful force that can do anything. Tantra (both positive and negative) taps into this force. We have 108 beads in a mālā which allows us to tap into this vibration of the supreme creative force of the god and goddess, Puruṣa and Prakṛtti.

Hoḍa Cakra

H*oḍa* means raft or boat. The Hoḍa Cakra is composed of 108 sounds, each nakṣatra pada has one sound. The sounds start at Kṛttikā which contains the primary vowel sounds *(pañca-svara)*; a, i, u, e, o. Long and short vowels are interchangeable here. These vowels repeat in this order with the addition of various consonants. Each of the dual rāśis has an extra three letters (*akṣaras*) included.

There are two main varieties of this cakra, one with 27 nakṣatras and one with 28 nakṣatras. This is the 27 nakṣatra/108 sound chakra. For those wishing to use the 28 scheme the additional akṣaras have been added in the center based on Pandit Sanjay Rath's teachings in his book *Vedic Remedies in Astrology*.

There are various sources (best being *Phaladīpikā*) that have a slight variation of the exact syllables. I have tried to stay along the lines of BV Raman. One's best judgment is advised, as akṣaras vary depending on source. The most questionable akṣaras are put in italics for known variability, these are mostly the additional akṣaras added in the dual signs.

These sounds are used primarily for naming where the sounds give the first letter. A name can be given according to the Moon's pada or the most beneficial planet. In this way, whenever someone says the name, they are activating the Moon or the most beneficial aspect of the individual. Naming can be a very complex science with deeper understanding of the pañcha-svara and the placement of sounds in trines from Moon and ārūḍha lagna. This chakra is a foundational understanding that can be used in general for people and businesses.

Hoda Chakra

26 40 - 30 00	chi
23 20 - 26 40	cha
20 00 - 23 20	do
16 40 - 20 00	de
13 20 - 16 40	tha
10 00 - 13 20	jha
03 20 - 06 40	*śa*
06 40 - 10 00	du
00 00 - 03 20	di

26 40 - 30 00	da
23 20 - 26 40	so
20 00 - 23 20	se
16 40 - 20 00	su
13 20 - 16 40	si
10 00 - 13 20	sa
03 20 - 06 40	go
06 40 - 10 00	ge
00 00 - 03 20	gu

26 40 - 30 00	gi
23 20 - 26 40	ga
20 00 - 23 20	*gha*
16 40 - 20 00	jo
13 20 - 16 40	je
10 00 - 13 20	ju
03 20 - 06 40	ji
06 40 - 10 00	ja
00 00 - 03 20	bo

chu	0 00 - 03 20
che	03 20 - 06 40
cho	06 40 - 10 00
la	10 00 - 13 20
li	13 20 - 16 40
lu	16 40 - 20 00
le	20 00 - 23 20
lo	23 20 - 26 40
a	26 40 - 30 00

i	0 00 - 03 20
u	03 20 - 06 40
e	06 40 - 10 00
o	10 00 - 13 20
va	13 20 - 16 40
vi	16 40 - 20 00
vu	20 00 - 23 20
ve	23 20 - 26 40
vo	26 40 - 30 00

ka	0 00 - 03 20
ki	03 20 - 06 40
ku	06 40 - 10 00
gha	10 00 - 13 20
ṅa	13 20 - 16 40
Cha	16 40 - 20 00
ke	20 00 - 23 20
ko	23 20 - 26 40
ha	26 40 - 30 00

hi	0 00 - 03 20
hu	03 20 - 06 40
he	06 40 - 10 00
ho	10 00 - 13 20
ḍa	13 20 - 16 40
ḍi	16 40 - 20 00
ḍu	20 00 - 23 20
ḍe	23 20 - 26 40
ḍo	26 40 - 30 00

ma	0 00 - 03 20
mi	03 20 - 06 40
mu	06 40 - 10 00
me	10 00 - 13 20
mo	13 20 - 16 40
ṭa	16 40 - 20 00
ṭi	20 00 - 23 20
ṭu	23 20 - 26 40
ṭe	26 40 - 30 00

ṭo	0 00 - 03 20
pa	03 20 - 06 40
pi	06 40 - 10 00
pu	10 00 - 13 20
ṣa	13 20 - 16 40
ṇa	16 40 - 20 00
ṭha	20 00 - 23 20
pe	23 20 - 26 40
po	26 40 - 30 00

be	26 40 - 30 00
ḍha	23 20 - 26 40
bha	20 00 - 23 20
dha	16 40 - 20 00
bu	13 20 - 16 40
bi	10 00 - 13 20
ba	06 40 - 10 00
yo	03 20 - 06 40
ye	0 00 - 03 20

yu	26 40 - 30 00
yi	23 20 - 26 40
ya	20 00 - 23 20
no	16 40 - 20 00
ne	13 20 - 16 40
nu	10 00 - 13 20
ni	06 40 - 10 00
na	03 20 - 06 40
to	0 00 - 03 20

te	26 40 - 30 00
tu	23 20 - 26 40
ti	20 00 - 23 20
ta	16 40 - 20 00
ro	13 20 - 16 40
re	10 00 - 13 20
ru	06 40 - 10 00
ri	03 20 - 06 40
ra	0 00 - 03 20

Abhijit
ju je jo khi

Śravaṇa
ju je jo gha

Practice Exercise:

4. Calculate the ayana (dharma, karma, etc) of each of your planets in the nakṣatra padas. Note the relationship the ayana has with the navāṁśa sign.
5. Find Kṛttikā in the Hoḍa Cakra. Starting with the primary vowels, see how other letters are added to these same vowels repeatedly- understand the pattern. Find the sound connected to each of the planets in your chart.

Navatāra Cakra

The Moon is the lord of the nakṣatra, the lord of the mind. The ātmā is entangled to the mind, wherever the body goes the ātmā must go. Therefore the nakṣatras are all very important. *Tāra* means star and *nava* means nine, so the Navatāra Cakra is the 27 nakṣatras divided into three groups of nine. Place your natal Moon nakṣatra in the first box (1/1) and list the consecutive nakṣatras accordingly. Having covered the first nine nakṣatras, the subsequent nakṣatras again begin from the beginning in nakṣatra group 2, and the same process is repeated in the third group.

Navatāra Cakra					
	Nakṣatra		Nakṣatra group 1	Nakṣatra group 2	Nakṣatra group 3
1	Janma				
2	Sampat				
3	Vipat				
4	Kṣema				
5	Pratyak				
6	Sādhana				
7	Naidhana				
8	Mitra				
9	Parama-mitra				

This cakra is used for fine-tuning the timing of results (especially in viṁśottari daśā) as well as for making muhūrta (starting times) specific to an individual chart. This is a list of the meaning of each of the nine nakṣatras:

1. **Janma-** birthstar, one's own nature, most influential nakṣatra.
2. **Sampat-** wealth, prosperity, it shows the kind of wealth you should possess, how your mind works in receiving and utilizing the resources available.
3. **Vipat-** separated, struck down, to fall apart, shows dangers to life and business.
4. **Kṣema-** giving rest, well-being, ease, cure, time to get healed, if there is a disease and it is not healed here then problems can be caused in next nakṣatra.
5. **Pratyak-** obstacles, bādhaka, can cause death or death-like suffering, if an activity is started on this nakṣatra there will be many obstacles.
6. **Sādhana-** achievement, good for starting activities as they will succeed.
7. **Naidhana-** death, the worst of the negative stars (3, 5, 7).
8. **Mitra-** friend, friends who are close.
9. **Parama-mitra-** best friend, supporters, community, friends will meet you, good for things dealing with crowds.

A person will progress through each of the first nine nakṣatras throughout their life (discussed next chapter). The time periods of the beneficial nakṣatras will bring more comfort to an individual's life. The periods of the negative nakṣatras will be more difficult. Parāśara utilizes the Navatārā chakra when he teaches about timing death in the *Māraka-Bheda-Adhyāya*[123] (literally the chapter on 'being pierced by the planets with the power to kill'). In this section he mentions that certain nakṣatra periods can be a time when a person will be weaker in health or even die. Parāśara says,

[15] Now I will speak some about a person *(nṛṇāṁ)* who has signs of death *(māraka-lakṣaṇa)*. A person with short life combinations *(alpa-āyur-yoga)* will die in the daśā of the *vipat nakṣatra*. [16] A person with medium life combinations *(madhya-āyur-yoga)* will die in pratyak star daśā. A person with long life yogas *(dīrgha-āyur-yoga)* will die in the daśā of the *naidhana nakṣatra*.

[17] After that, the lord of the 22nd drekkāṇa *(dvāviṁśa-tryaṁśa)* is a death inflicting lord along with the lord of the *vipat*, *pratyak* and *naidhana tārā*. **[19]** In the daśā of the sixth, eighth and twelfth lord death is possible, and will happen in the antardaśā of the sixth, eighth, or twelfth lord. **[20]** The planet must be endowed with strength to become a māraka, and in that planet's antardaśā there is disease *(roga)* or suffering *(kaṣṭa-adi)*.

	Short life *(alpa-āyus)*	**Medium life** *(madhya-āyus)*	**Long life** *(dīrgha-āyus)*
Māraka Chapter v.10-11	0-32	32-64	64-100
Aṣṭottari (108)	0 - 36	36 - 72	72 - 108
Viṁśottari (120)	0 - 40	40 - 80	80 - 120

This chapter focuses on timing death which becomes very important in medical astrology. There are combinations which show which third of life a person will die, and then calculations are determined within that third of life. The above table relates to the three divisions of life and depending on which of these a person will die the 3rd, 5th or 7th nakṣatra period becomes dangerous. We won't focus on timing death here, but instead use the example to see how Parāśara is utilizing the Navatāra Cakra.

During the time period related to the negative stars there is a chance of ill-health or death (activating indications already present in the chart). The other nakṣatras will give results similar to their indications at the proper time and according to the general strength of factors in the chart as a whole.

[123] Bṛhat Parāśara Horā Śāstra, Māraka-Bheda-Adhyāya, Chapter 44/46

Special Tāras

There are also special tāras (stars), or nakṣatras that take on more specific attributes according to one's natal Moon placement. The number in the first column relates to the nakṣatra's placement from the Moon.

#	Special Tāras	Meaning	Nakṣatra
1			
10			
18			
16			
4/26[124]			
7			
12/27			
28			
19			
23			
11/25			

1. **Janma-** You, the crucial reference point
2. **Karma-** Profession, 10th from the janma-nakṣatra, needs to be well placed to work properly, transits here affect one's work.
3. **Samudāyika-** Crowd, 18th in cycle, samudāya means totaling or sum total, all the people coming together.
4. **Saṅghāṭika-** Group, 16th in cycle, inner (core) group
5. **Jāti-** Community, caste, one's social group, 4th in the cycle, it is the same as the kṣema star which is community, so a strong community represents good well-being (bad community will deny the proper advice that leads to well-being).
6. **Naidhana-** Death, 7th nakṣatra, as the janma-nakṣatra is both a navatāra and a special tāra it shows that these are very important points in birth and death.
7. **Deśa-** Country, nation, culture (California versus the United States), 12th star
8. **Abhiṣeka-** Coronation, 28th star
9. **Ādhāna-** Conception, 19th star, this is 9 stars before the Janma nakṣatra which shows circumstances around the conception. Malefics will confirm troubles with pregnancy
10. **Vaināśika-** Destruction *(vināśa)*, 22nd nakṣatra
11. **Mānasa-** Mind, the 11th nakṣatra, that which controls the mind

[124] There is a difference of opinion depending on source. The first one is the one used in JHora Software. Also see Jātakapārijāta, Janma Tāra Adhāya.

Sarvatobhadra Cakra[125]

This is just a tiny introduction to the vast area of working with the nakṣatras. The *Sarva* (all) *bhadra* (auspicious) cakra is used for various purposes like observing the transit of planets through nakṣatras. Planets will have vedha (affect) on the nakṣatra diagonal to it, and directly across from it. In this way, planets can affect special tāras by being located within them or having vedha on them.

North

West

ई ī	Dhaniṣṭhā	Śatabhiṣa	P.bhādra	U.bhādra	Revatī	Aśvinī	Bharaṇī	अ a
Śravaṇa	ॠ ṝ	ग g	स s	द d	च ch	ल l	उ u	Kṛttikā
Abhijit	ख kh	ऐ ai	Aq	Pi	Ar	ऌ lṛ	अ a	Rohiṇī
U.āṣāḍhā	ज j	Cp	अः aḥ	Rikta Friday	ओ o	Ta	व v	Mṛga
P.āṣāḍhā	भ bh	Sg	Jaya Thursday	Purna Saturday	Nanda Sunday Tuesday	Ge	क k	Ārdrā
Mūla	य y	Sc	अं ṁ	Bhadra Monday Wednesday	औ au	Cn	ह h	Punarvasu
Jyeṣṭhā	न n	ए e	Li	Vi	Le	ॡ lṝ	ड ḍ	Puṣya
Anurādhā	ऋ ṛ	त t	र r	प p	ट ṭ	म m	ऊ ū	Āśleṣā
इ i	Viśākhā	Svātī	Chitrā	Hastā	U.phal	P.phal	Maghā	आ ā

East

South

[125] For those interested in further research on the Sarvatobhadra Cakra see *Phala Dīpikā* 26.26-29 and *Collected Papers in Vedic Astrology*, Chapter 5 by Sanjay Rath, Sagittarius Publications.

Nakṣatra Dṛṣṭi

The planets also have nakṣatra aspects which show likes and dislikes. They will show what the planet has a taste for and enjoys. These can be calculated very easily with the Sarvatobhadra Cakra.

Sun[126]	14th, 15th
Moon	14th, 15th
Mars	1st, 3rd, 7th, 8th, 15th
Mercury	1st, 15th
Jupiter	10th, 15th, 19th
Venus	1st, 15th
Saturn	3rd, 5th, 15th, 19th

Practice Exercise:

6. Fill out the navatāra chakra with your own chart.
7. Fill out the Special Tāras in the graph with your nakṣatras. Then make notation of them in the Sarvatobhadra Cakra with your natal planets.
8. Calculate nakṣatra aspects and see if any planets are relating.

Ghātaka Nakṣatra

Ghātaka means one who hurts, afflicts pain, maims, destroys, or kills. Each Moon rāśi has a ghātaka nakṣatra, which causes problems to the native. The ghātaka nākṣatra is an inauspicious time, whether the Moon is transiting that star, or the Muhūrta with that star in lagna, etc., it will indicate negative results that are dangerous to the individual's health or physical well-being. The nakṣatra are connected to vāyu (air/ Saturn) according to the Pañcāṅga which relates to the prāṇas, longevity, and life. Mars is the kāraka for ghātaka, as it injures, hurts, kills.

The ghātaka nakṣatra is a serious matter because it can cause death. The day the Moon transits the ghātaka from one's own Moon, the person should not start any important things, begin journeys or have any possibly dangerous adventures. Athletes will be more likely to injure themselves on this nakṣatra. If a person gets married at this time they may die from the marriage. If one is starting a business on the ghātaka, then the business will fail as its prāṇas will suffer.

	Rāśi		Nakṣatra[127]
1	Aries	10	Maghā
2	Taurus	13	Hasta
3	Gemini	15	Swāti
4	Cancer	17	Anurādhā
5	Leo	19	Mūla
6	Virgo	22	Srāvaṇa
7	Libra	24	Śatabhiṣā
8	Scorpio	27	Revatī
9	Sagittarius	2	Bharaṇī
10	Capricorn	4	Rohiṇī
11	Aquarius	6	Ārdrā
12	Pisces	9	Āśleṣā

[126] Rath, Sanjay, Crux Of Vedic Astrology, p.11
[127] Daivagya Acharya Shri Ram's Muhurta Chintamani, 11.32

Prāṇa

The nakṣatra are ruled by vāyu tattva (air) according to the Pañcāṅga. Vāyu (air) becomes prāṇa (life force) when it enlivens the body/mind mechanism according to the Moon nakṣatra. The Moon nakṣatra shows the direction of the mind, and where the mind goes the prāṇa follows. Therefore the nākṣatra shows the strength of our prāṇas and any afflictions to them.

The nakṣatra will guide us by guiding the mind and prāṇa in the directions the deity indicates. For general health improvement the nakṣatra deity is worshiped with puja and preferably on the day of its nakṣatra. One can use the mantras given in the deity section to worship the deity of the nakṣatra to improve the direction of the mind, focus of the prāṇa, and over all health.

Kālachakra

The Kālacakra will show the health of the native and especially times of sickness. It shows how a person uses their prāṇas (energy) and the directions in life this will lead them. The natal chart is mapped onto the Kālacakra to be read.

The first nakṣatra starts at the center of the top horizontal line, in the diagram there is the number one. The Kālacakra has multiple ways to be set up, but for primary purposes use the janma nakṣatra called the birth star, the natal Moon's nakṣatra. The Kālacakra is a 28 nakṣatra system so add 1 to any nakṣatra over 21 in the 27 cakra system.

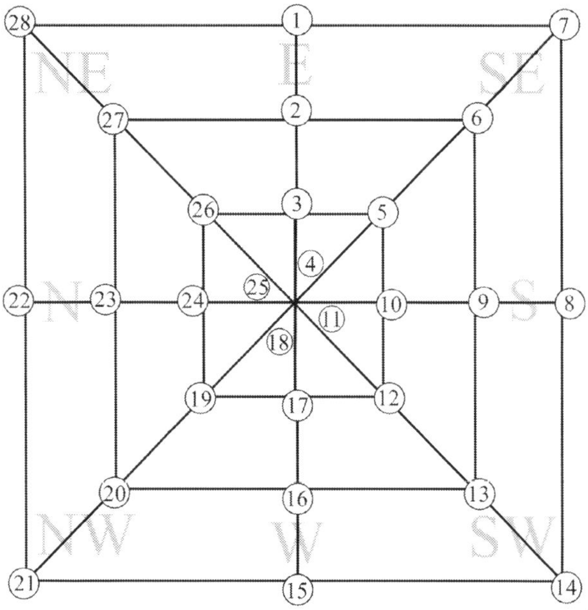

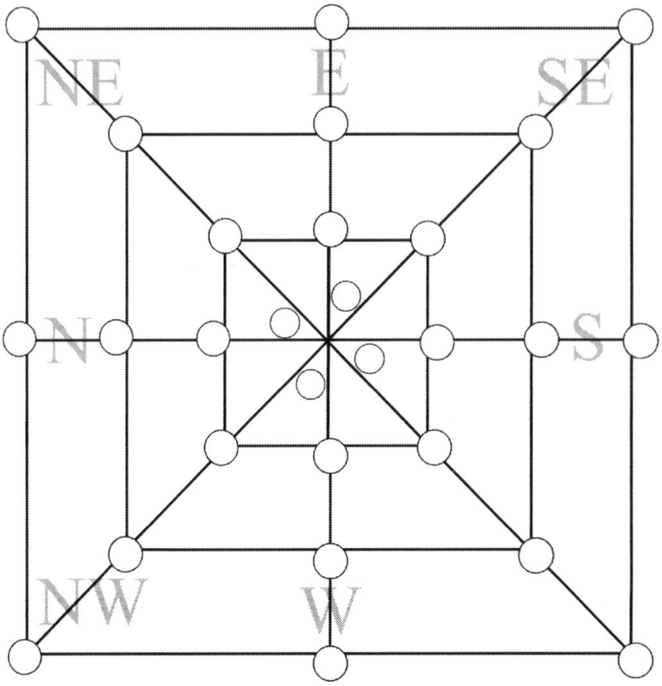

Human beings are made of three external things: Body, Prāṇa and Mind. This can be seen in the Kālacakra as the external layer, the middle level and the internal level. The outer body layer is often referred to as the Exalted Body Maṇḍala. The middle prāṇic level is called the Exalted Speech Maṇḍala. The inner Manas level is called Exalted Mind Maṇḍala.

What is visible is what is outside, on the outer level. The Moon is always visible, like the conscious mind is always seen. So the birth star of the Moon starts the Kālacakra. The Moon is placed where you see the number one in the above diagram. Other planets are placed in their respective nakṣatras.

There are techniques other than the one I will be demonstrating that use different configurations. The Moon in the East is aligned with the natural Sun and therefore shows the prāṇas in the body. The moon in the North East shows the manas (as the mind is always under the influence of Rāhu). Sometimes the Sun nakṣatra is also used starting the sequence from the North East direction; this is used to see evils in the chart. There is also another system used for receiving knowledge from and about the devas. In this Kālacakra the nakṣatras will go in a counter clockwise order.

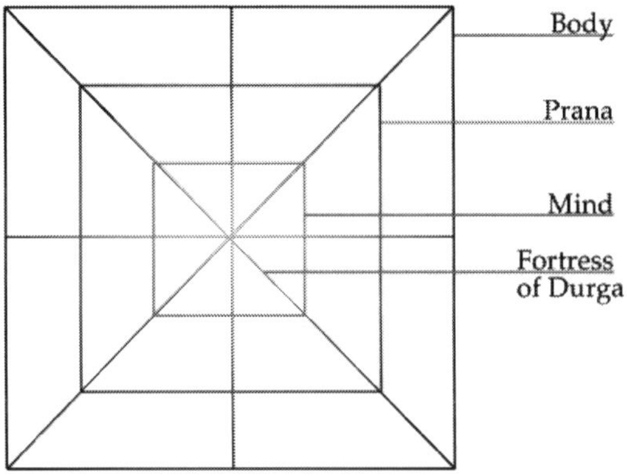

The following is an example using the chart of the Dalai Lama.

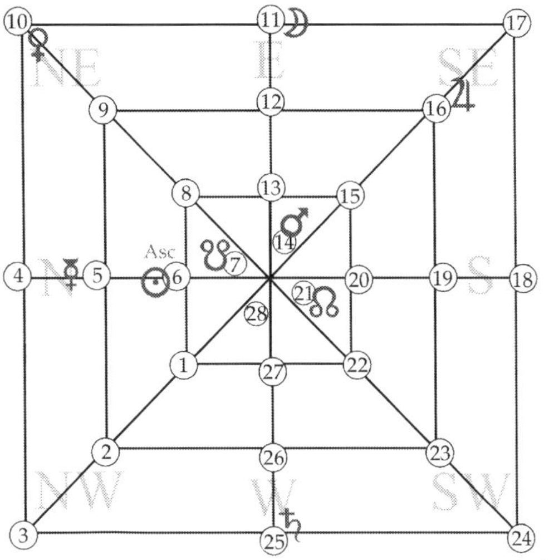

Dalai Lama
Date: July 6, 1935
Time: 4:38:00 am
Time Zone: 7:00:00 (East of GMT)
Place: 101 E 12′ 00″, 36 N 12′ 00″

Body	Longitude	Nakṣatra	Pada	Rāśi	Nava
Lagna	13 Ge 28′ 53.22″	Ārdrā	3	Ge	Aq
Sun	19 Ge 57′ 38.48″	Ārdrā	4	Ge	Pi
Moon	16 Le 39′ 55.11″	P. Phal	1	Le	Le
Mars	25 Vi 18′ 31.49″	Chitrā	1	Vi	Le
Mercury	2 Ge 33′ 25.32″	Mṛga	3	Ge	Li
Jupiter (R)	20 Li 30′ 39.83″	Viśākhā	1	Li	Ar
Venus	5 Le 16′ 36.18″	Maghā	2	Le	Ta
Saturn (R)	17 Aq 05′ 37.27″	Śatabhiṣa	4	Aq	Pi
Rahu	29 Sg 26′ 48.52″	U. Ṣāḍhā	1	Sg	Sg
Ketu	29 Ge 26′ 48.52″	Punarvasu	3	Ge	Ge
Maandi	5 Ta 33′ 26.60″	Kṛttikā	3	Ta	Aq
Gulika	24 Ar 23′ 09.29″	Bharaṇī	4	Ar	Sc

The Moon is in Pūrvaphalgunī which is the 11th nakṣatra. Therefore the Kālacakra starts with 11 and goes from there forward. The Moon is on the top middle horizontal line in Pūrvaphalgunī. The Sun is in Ārdrā nakṣatra, which is the 6th star and therefore you see the Sun placed next to number six which represents Ārdrā. Mars is in Citrā which is the 14th star and so Mars is placed within the Fortress of Durgā by the number 14 representing Citrā nakṣatra. Other planets and points (*sphuṭa*) are placed accordingly.

Direction

The prāṇa moves in the same way the nakṣatras have been placed in the Kālacakra. Energy comes in the Kendras (straight lines) and energy goes out the Koṇas (diagonal lines). Planets placed in a Koṇa axis are taking energy out, they need to be guarded/ stopped/regulated. Benefics placed in Kendras are beneficial to bring energy into the person's life.

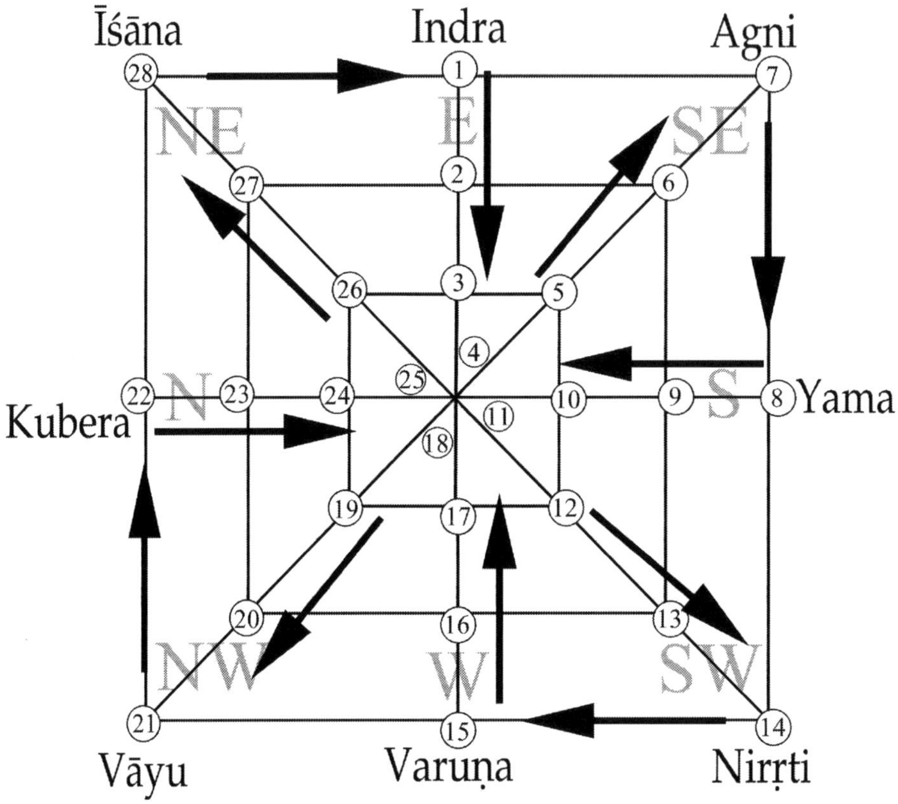

This is just a small introduction to some uses of nakṣatras in Vedic Astrology. There are many other cakras found in the local Jyotiṣa texts as well as Purāṇas and Tantras. For example, the Kurma (turtle) Cakra is used to observe the nakṣatra transit of Saturn, and his relation to property. The Phaṇīśvara (serpant lord) Cakra is used to see the success and failure of a journey. In this way the use of chakras involve an understanding of the psychological qualities of the nakṣatra, their timing for the success of events and they add more specific utility.

Chapter 12

Daśā: *Timing*

Timing

Timing when an event will happen is very important, both in understanding the past, correctly perceiving the present and making decisions and predictions about the future. In general, when beginning to look at a chart an astrologer will first time key past events to check the accuracy of the birth time. Next they consider the present life conditions, and finally after insuring the chart is correct will give predictions about the future. This methodology is traditional even in the advanced Nāḍī texts and palm leaf readings. There are as many ways to time events in our lives as there are aspects of life. The mind may be strong but the native may be money-less. Spiritual growth may be very good, but the health may be bad. All the different areas of life will have various ways to time themselves. Time is qualitative and like a map of a country, time can also be mapped out. The mountains and the valleys of emotions, health, spirituality, suffering, etc can all be seen using Jyotiṣa.

A Vedic Astrologer has many tools for timing. The key is to know which tools to use when, and also how to combine them for the most complete results. There are natural (naisargika) progressions of time that are the same for everyone, like natural planet maturities, or house maturities- when the planet or house naturally reaches an age where it will give the results that it indicates in the chart. Then there are graha daśās that show which planet has predominant energy in a particular area of life. And rāśi daśās that show the areas of life that get activated in our lives. Within those time periods one also analyzes the present movement of the planets called Gochāra (transit). Then there are lots of other small techniques for fine tune timing. Eventually, it is possible to learn all these methods. First it is important to learn one tool and be able to use it correctly. Then one can slowly fine tune an understanding of karmic unfoldment with other techniques of timing.

The most used system of timing is the Viṁśottarī daśā calculated from the Moon. The 120-year cycle relates to the three zodiacal divisions into 120 degrees making up the signs/nakṣatras from Aries to Cancer, Leo to Scorpio, and Sagittarius to Pisces. Each third of the zodiac contains nine nakṣatras which are given a Viṁśottarī daśā lord and this cycle repeats three times through the zodiac. Each of the nine planets repeated three times relates to the 27 nakṣatras in the navatāra chakra.

Calculation of Viṁśottarī Daśā

It is very important to have the ability to calculate Viṁśottarī daśā. In modern times people are lazy and let the computer do it for them; but understanding the cycle and the various daśā lengths are key for fast and good predictions. Learning to calculate Viṁśottarī daśā will also teach a beginner about calculating degrees, minutes and seconds as well as days, months and years.

How to calculate Viṁśottarī daśā:

1) Find exact location of native's Moon at birth:
Traditionally one should (A) see how much Moon moved during the day, (B) look this up with GMT in Diurnal Planetary Table and (C) add to 0hr. in the ephemeris for the day of the person's birth. These tables have not been included here, but one is advised to learn how to calculate the position with the help of their teacher and the proper books. For the moment, take the degrees for the position of the Moon in your chart.

Example: The Moon is in 13° 48′ Aries for Native born 9th October, 1976.

2) Take exact location to Table I and see which sign and X° X′ it is within:

Example: Moon in 13° 48′ Aries which is Bharaṇī nakṣatra and the Viṁśottarī lord is Venus. This means the native was born in Venus Mahādaśā and therefore Venus was a very influential factor in the native's early development. Venus Daśā lasts for twenty years.

3) Subtract the Moon location from the end of the period of time to see how much of that dasa is left in Degrees° and Minutes′. There are 30 degrees of arc (30°) in a sign, 60 minutes of arc (60′) in one degree (1°), and 60 seconds of arc (60″) in one minute (1′).

Example: Bharaṇī is 13° 20′ to 26° 40′ and the Moon is 13° 48′ so

26° 40′	which is also	25° (60′ +40′)	or	25° 100′	
- 13° 48′		- 13° 48′		- 13° 48′	
				12° 52′	remaining in Bharaṇī

4) The remaining degrees are how much of that daśā is left to be experienced. Take this number to Table II and III to find out the exact amount of time in years, months and days (using 30 Days in 1 Month, 12 Months in 1 Year).

Example: 12° 52′ are left in Bharaṇī, ruled by Venus.

In the Venus column of ***Table II***, see 12° which is 18 years, 00 months, and 00 days. Find the minutes of arc in the Venus column of ***Table III***, where 52′ is 1 year, 3 months, and 18 days. Add these two results together to get the final result. The amount of time left of the daśā is 19 years, 3 months and 18 days.

Time Periods	Years	Months	Days
Time from Table II (Degrees)	18	00	00
Time from Table III (Minutes)	1	3	18
Total:	19	3	18

5) Add the *daśā time* remaining to the birth date to find time of next daśā.

Example: native born 9th October, 1976 or

Year	Month	Day	
1976	10	9	
+19	3	18	
1995	13	27	(Subtract 12 months and add 1 to the years)
1996	1	27	(this will be the end of Venus daśā and beginning of the next daśā which is ruled by the Sun)

6) Go back to Table I to find length of each daśā and add onto each date continuously to find the Mahādaśās.

Example:

Year	Month	Day	
1976	10	9	Venus Mahādaśā
+19	3	18	
1996	01	27	Sun Mahādaśā (six years)
+6	00	00	
2002	01	27	Moon Mahādaśā (ten years)
+10	00	00	
2012	01	27	Mars Mahādaśā (7 years)
+7	00	00	
2019	01	27	Rāhu Mahādaśā (18 years)
+18	00	00	
2037	01	27	Jupiter Mahādaśā (16 years)
+16	00	00	

7) The Mahādaśās break down into smaller sub-daśās (antar daśā). Start with the daśā the person is running and go to Table IV to find the break down of individual daśās. The Viṁśottarī sub-periods begin with the same planet as the Mahādaśā.

Example: The native is presently in Moon Mahādaśā.

Year	Month	Day	
1976	10	9	Venus
+ 19	3	18	
1996	01	27	Sun
+ 6	00	00	
2002	01	27	Moon
+10	00	00	
2012	01	27	Mars
+7	00	00	
2019	01	27	Rahu
+18	00	00	
2037	01	27	Jupiter

2002	01	27	Moon Moon
+00	10	00	
2002	11	27	Moon Mars
+00	07	00	
(2002	*18*	*27)*	
2003	06	27	Moon Rahu
+01	06	00	
2004	12	27	Moon Jupiter
+01	04	00	
(2005	*16*	*27)*	
2006	04	27	Moon Saturn
+01	07	00	
2007	11	27	Moon Mercury
+01	05	00	
2009	04	27	Moon Ketu
+00	07	00	
2009	11	27	Moon Venus
+01	08	00	
2011	07	27	Moon Sun
+00	06	00	
2012	01	27	Mars Mahādaśa

8) Each of the Mahādaśās has a certain length, then within the Mahādaśā it is broken down into the same proportional parts within the time of that planet. For example, Venus is 20 years out of a 120 year cycle-- 20/120 (1/6) of the sequence, and it will be that same percentage of the antar-daśā. Then the antar-daśā is broken down into similar proportions.

Practice Exercise:

1. Calculate the Viṁśottarī daśā of your own and three other charts. Make sure you understand the pattern of calculating the daśās.
2. Read *Bṛhat Parāśara Horā Śāstra,* where Parāśara mentions calculation: Mahādaśās (BPHS chapter 46/48 v.12-16), and Antaradaśās (BPHS chapter 51/53).
3. Continue calculating Sub-sub daśā (*pratyantar-daśā*) in this same way. Calculated charts are available in *Bṛhat Parāśara Horā Śāstra.*

Table I: Nakṣatra and Daśā Period

Sign (Rāśi)	Degrees ° ′	Nakṣatra	Degrees ° ′	Lord	
Aries (Meṣa) Taurus (Vṛṣabha)	0° to 30°	Aśvinī Bharaṇī Kṛttikā	0 00 to 13 20 13 20 to 26 40 26 40 to 40 00	Ketu Venus Sun	7 20 6
Taurus(Vṛṣabha) Gemini(Mithuna)	10° to 30° 0° to 6°40′	Rohiṇī Mṛgaśira	10 00 to 23 20 23 20 to 36 40	Moon Mars	10 7
Gemini (Mithuna) Cancer(Karka)	6°40′ to 30° 0° to 3° 20′	Ārdrā Punarvasu	6 40 to 20 00 20 00 to 33 20	Rāhu Jupiter	18 16
Cancer (Karka)	3°20′ to 30°	Puṣya Āśleṣā	3 20 to 16 40 16 40 to 30 00	Saturn Mercury	19 17
Leo (Siṁha) Virgo (Kanyā)	0° to 30° 0° to 10°	Maghā P.phalgunī U.phalgunī	0 00 to 13 20 13 20 to 26 40 26 40 to 40 00	Ketu Venus Sun	7 20 6
Virgo (Kanyā) Libra (Tula)	10° to 30° 0° to 6°40′	Hasta Citrā	10 00 to 23 20 23 20 to 36 40	Moon Mars	10 7
Libra (Tula) Scorpio(Vṛśchika)	6°40′ to30° 0° to 3°20′	Svātī Viśākhā	6 40 to 20 00 20 00 to 33 20	Rāhu Jupiter	18 16
Scorpio (Vṛśchika)	3°20′ to 30°	Anurādhā Jyeṣṭhā	3 20 to 16 40 16 40 to 30 00	Saturn Mercury	19 17
Sagittarius(Dhanu) Capricorn (Makara)	0° to 30° 0° to 10°	Mūla Pūrvāṣāḍhā Uttarāṣāḍhā	0 00 to 13 20 13 20 to 26 40 26 40 to 40 00	Ketu Venus Sun	7 20 6
Capricorn (Makara) Aquarius (Kumbha)	10° to 30° 0° to 6°40′	Śravaṇa Dhaniṣṭhā	10 00 to 23 20 23 20 to 36 40	Moon Mars	10 7
Aquarius (Kumbha) Pisces (Mīna)	6°40′ to 30° 0° to 3°20′	Śatabhiṣa P.bhādra	6 40 to 20 00 20 00 to 33 20	Rāhu Jupiter	18 16
Pisces (Mīna)	3°20′ to 30°	U.bhādra Revatī	3 20 to 16 40 16 40 to 30 00	Saturn Mercury	19 17

Table II: Daśā Balance by Degrees of Arc

	Ketu			Venus			Sun			Moon			Mars			
°	y	m	d	y	m	d	y	m	d	y	m	d	y	m	d	°
1	0	6	9	1	6	0	0	5	12	0	9	0	0	6	9	1
2	1	0	18	3	0	0	0	10	24	1	6	0	1	0	18	2
3	1	6	27	4	6	0	1	4	6	2	3	0	1	6	27	3
4	2	1	6	6	0	0	1	9	18	3	0	0	2	1	6	4
5	2	7	15	7	6	0	2	3	0	3	9	0	2	7	15	5
6	3	1	24	9	0	0	2	8	12	4	6	0	3	1	24	6
7	3	8	3	10	6	0	3	1	24	5	3	0	3	8	3	7
8	4	2	12	12	0	0	3	7	6	6	0	0	4	2	12	8
9	4	8	21	13	5	0	4	0	18	6	9	0	4	8	21	9
10	5	3	0	15	0	0	4	6	0	7	6	0	5	3	0	10
11	5	9	9	16	6	0	4	11	12	8	3	0	5	9	9	11
12	6	3	13	18	0	0	5	4	24	9	0	0	6	3	18	12
13	6	9	27	19	6	0	5	10	6	9	9	0	6	9	27	13

	Rāhu			Jupiter			Saturn			Mercury			
°	y	m	d	y	m	d	y	m	d	y	m	d	°
1	1	4	6	1	2	12	1	5	3	1	3	9	1
2	2	8	12	2	4	24	2	10	6	2	6	18	2
3	4	0	18	3	7	6	4	3	9	3	9	27	3
4	5	4	24	4	9	18	5	8	12	5	1	6	4
5	6	9	0	6	0	0	7	1	15	6	4	15	5
6	8	1	6	7	2	12	8	6	18	7	7	24	6
7	9	5	12	8	4	24	9	11	21	8	11	3	7
8	10	9	18	9	7	6	11	4	24	10	2	12	8
9	12	1	24	10	9	18	12	9	27	11	5	21	9
10	13	6	0	12	0	0	14	3	0	12	9	0	10
11	14	10	6	13	2	12	15	8	3	14	0	9	11
12	16	2	12	14	4	24	17	1	6	15	3	18	12
13	17	6	18	15	7	6	18	6	9	16	6	27	13

Table III.A: Daśā Balance by Minutes of Arc (1′-30′)

	Ketu		Venus		Sun		Moon		Mars		Rāhu		Jupiter		Saturn		Mercury		
′	m	d	m	d	m	d	m	d	m	d	m	d	m	d	m	d	m	d	′
1	0	3	0	9	0	3	0	5	0	3	0	8	0	7	0	9	0	8	1
2	0	6	0	18	0	5	0	9	0	4	0	16	0	14	0	17	0	15	2
3	0	9	0	27	0	8	0	14	0	7	0	24	0	22	0	26	0	23	3
4	0	13	1	6	0	11	0	18	0	13	1	2	0	29	1	4	1	1	4
5	0	16	1	15	0	13	0	23	0	16	1	11	1	6	1	13	1	8	5
6	0	19	1	24	0	16	0	27	0	19	1	19	1	13	1	21	1	16	6
7	0	22	2	3	0	19	1	2	0	22	1	27	1	20	2	0	1	24	7
8	0	25	2	12	0	22	1	6	0	25	2	5	1	28	2	8	2	1	8
9	0	23	2	21	0	24	1	11	0	28	2	13	2	5	2	17	2	9	9
10	1	1	3	0	0	27	1	15	1	1	2	21	2	12	2	26	2	17	10
11	1	5	3	6	1	0	1	20	1	5	2	29	2	19	3	4	2	24	11
12	1	8	3	8	1	2	1	24	1	8	3	7	2	26	3	13	3	2	12
13	1	11	3	27	1	5	1	29	1	11	3	15	3	4	3	21	3	9	13
14	1	14	4	6	1	8	2	3	1	14	3	23	3	11	4	0	3	17	14
15	1	17	4	15	1	10	2	8	1	17	4	2	3	18	4	8	3	25	15
16	1	20	4	24	1	13	2	12	1	20	4	10	3	25	4	17	4	2	16
17	1	24	5	3	1	16	2	17	1	24	4	18	4	2	4	25	4	10	17
18	1	27	5	12	1	19	2	21	1	27	4	26	4	10	5	4	4	18	18
19	2	0	5	21	1	21	2	26	2	0	5	4	4	17	5	12	4	25	19
20	2	3	6	0	1	24	3	0	2	3	5	12	4	24	5	21	5	3	20
21	2	6	6	9	1	27	3	5	2	6	5	20	5	1	6	0	5	11	21
22	2	9	6	18	1	29	3	9	2	9	5	28	5	8	6	8	5	18	22
23	2	12	6	27	2	2	3	14	2	12	6	6	5	16	6	17	5	26	23
24	2	16	7	5	2	5	3	18	2	16	6	14	5	23	6	25	6	4	24
25	2	19	7	15	2	8	3	23	2	19	6	23	6	0	7	4	6	11	25
26	2	22	7	24	2	10	3	27	2	22	7	1	6	7	7	12	6	19	26
27	2	15	8	3	2	13	4	2	2	25	7	9	6	14	7	21	6	27	27
28	2	18	8	12	2	16	4	6	2	28	7	17	6	22	7	29	7	4	28
29	3	1	8	21	2	18	4	11	3	1	7	25	6	29	8	8	7	12	29
30	3	4	9	0	2	21	4	15	3	4	8	3	7	6	8	17	7	20	30

Table III.B: Daśā Balance by Minutes of Arc (31′-60′)

	Ketu		Venus			Sun		Moon		Mars		Rāhu			Jupiter			Saturn			Mercury			
′	m	d	y	m	d	m	d	m	d	m	d	y	m	d	y	m	d	y	m	d	y	m	d	′
31	3	8		9	9	2	24	4	20	3	8		8	11		7	13		8	25		7	27	31
32	3	11		9	18	2	26	4	24	3	11		8	19		7	20		9	4		8	5	32
33	3	14		9	27	2	29	4	29	3	14		8	27		7	28		9	12		8	12	33
34	3	17		10	6	3	2	5	3	3	17		9	5		8	5		9	21		8	20	34
35	3	20		10	15	3	5	5	8	3	20		9	14		8	12		9	29		8	28	35
36	3	23		10	24	3	7	5	13	3	23		9	22		8	19		10	8		9	5	36
37	3	27		11	3	3	10	5	17	3	27		10	0		8	26		10	16		9	13	37
38	4	0		11	12	3	13	5	21	4	0		10	8		9	4		10	25		9	21	38
39	4	3		11	21	3	15	5	26	4	3		10	16		9	11		11	3		9	28	39
40	4	6	1	0	0	3	18	6	0	4	6		10	24		9	18		11	12		10	6	40
41	4	9	1	0	9	3	21	6	5	4	9		11	2		9	25		11	21		10	14	41
42	4	12	1	0	18	3	24	6	9	4	12		11	10		10	2		11	29		10	21	42
43	4	16	1	0	27	3	26	6	14	4	16		11	18		10	10	1	0	8		10	29	43
44	4	19	1	1	6	3	29	6	18	4	19		11	26		10	17	1	0	16		11	7	44
45	4	22	1	1	15	4	2	6	23	4	22	1	0	5		10	24	1	0	25		11	14	45
46	4	25	1	1	24	4	7	6	27	4	25	1	0	13		11	1	1	1	3		11	22	46
47	4	28	1	2	3	4	7	7	2	4	28	1	0	21		11	8	1	1	12		0	0	47
48	5	1	1	2	12	4	10	7	6	5	1	1	0	29		11	16	1	1	20	1	0	7	48
49	5	4	1	2	21	4	12	7	11	5	4	1	1	7		11	23	1	1	29	1	0	14	49
50	5	7	1	3	0	4	15	7	15	5	7	1	1	15	1	0	0	1	2	8	1	0	22	50
51	5	11	1	3	9	4	18	7	20	5	11	1	1	28	1	0	7	1	2	16	1	1	0	51
52	5	14	1	3	18	4	20	7	24	5	14	1	2	1	1	0	14	1	2	25	1	1	7	52
53	5	17	1	3	27	4	23	8	29	5	17	1	2	9	1	0	22	1	3	3	1	1	15	53
54	5	20	1	4	6	4	26	8	3	5	20	1	2	17	1	0	29	1	3	12	1	1	23	54
55	5	23	1	4	15	4	29	8	8	5	23	1	2	26	1	6	6	1	3	20	1	2	1	55
56	5	26	1	4	24	5	1	8	12	5	26	1	3	1	1	13	13	1	3	29	1	2	8	56
57	6	0	1	5	3	5	1	8	17	6	0	1	3	12	1	20	20	1	4	7	1	2	16	57
58	6	3	1	5	12	5	7	8	21	6	3	1	3	20	1	28	28	1	4	16	1	2	24	58
59	6	6	1	5	21	5	9	8	26	6	6	1	3	23	1	6	6	1	4	21	1	3	1	59
60	6	9	1	6	0	5	12	9	0	6	9	1	4	6	1	12	12	1	5	8	1	3	0	60

Table IV: Daśā and Sub-periods (bhukti)

Nakṣatra	Aśvinī			1	Bharaṇī			2	Kṛttikā			3	Rohiṇī			4
	Maghā			10	P-phalgunī			11	U-phalgunī			12	Hasta			13
	Mūla			19	Pūrvāṣāḍhā			20	Uttarāṣāḍhā			21	Śravaṇa			22
Mahādaśā	KETU 7 0 0				Venus 20 0 0				Sun 6 0 0				Moon 10 0 0			
Sub-Periods * Antar Daśā		Y	M	D		Y	M	D		Y	M	D		Y	M	D
	Ke	0	4	27	Ve	3	4	0	Su	0	3	18	Mo	0	10	0
	Ve	1	2	0	Su	1	0	0	Mo	0	6	0	Ma	0	7	0
	Su	0	4	6	Mo	1	8	0	Ma	0	4	6	Ra	1	6	0
	Mo	0	7	0	Ma	1	2	0	Ra	0	10	24	Ju	1	4	0
	Ma	0	4	27	Ra	3	0	0	Ju	0	9	18	Sa	1	7	0
	Ra	1	0	18	Ju	2	8	0	Sa	0	11	12	Me	1	5	0
	Ju	0	11	6	Sa	3	2	0	Me	0	10	6	Ke	0	7	0
	Sa	1	1	9	Me	2	10	0	Ke	0	4	6	Ve	1	8	0
	Me	0	11	27	Ke	1	2	0	Ve	1	0	0	Su	0	6	0

Mṛgaśira			5	Ārdrā			6	Punarvasu			7	Puṣya			8	Āśleṣā			9
Citrā			14	Svātī			15	Viśākhā			16	Anurādhā			17	Jyeṣṭhā			18
Dhaniṣṭhā			23	Śatabhiṣa			42	Pūrvābhādra			26	Uttarabhādra			26	Revatī			27
MARS 7 0 0				RĀHU 0 0 18				JUPITER 16 0 0				SATURN 19 0 0				MERCURY 17 0 0			
	Y	M	D		Y	M	D		Y	M	D		Y	M	D		Y	M	D
Ma	0	4	12	Ra	2	8	12	Ju	2	1	18	Sa	3	0	3	Me	2	4	27
Ra	1	0	24	Ju	2	4	24	Sa	2	6	12	Me	2	8	9	Ke	0	11	27
ju	0	11	6	Sa	2	10	6	Me	2	3	6	Ke	1	1	9	Ve	2	10	0
Sa	1	1	18	Me	2	6	18	Ke	0	11	6	Ve	3	2	0	Su	0	10	6
Me	0	11	18	Ke	1	0	18	Ve	2	8	0	Su	0	11	12	Mo	1	5	0
Ke	0	4	0	Ve	3	0	0	Su	0	9	18	Mo	1	7	0	Ma	0	11	27
Ve	1	2	24	Su	0	10	24	Mo	1	4	0	Ma	1	1	9	Ra	2	6	18
Su	0	4	0	Mo	1	6	0	Ma	0	11	6	Ra	2	10	6	Ju	2	3	6
Mo	0	7	18	Ma	1	0	18	Ra	2	4	24	Ju	2	6	12	Sa	2	8	9

Conditional Nakṣatra Daśās

In the Viṁśottarī daśā the lifespan is calculated to be 120 years, and the planet's daśās all add up to 120 thus establishing the name of the daśā system. Aṣṭottarī daśā is a 108-year daśā system with each nakṣatra given an Aṣṭottarī daśā planetary lord and length which when all are totaled up equals 108 years. Both of these are a type of daśā (timing period) based on the Moon and are known as *Uḍu-daśās*. The main Uḍu-daśā is Viṁśottarī which is considered to have universal application while the other Uḍu-daśās are conditional[128], meaning their use will depend on the chart and will only relate to specific areas of life, while Viṁśottarī relates to all areas.

Daśā	# of years	Governor	Conditions for applicability[129]
Viṁśottarī	120	Moon	Universal applicability
Aṣṭottarī	108	Ketu	1) Rāhu should be quadrant or trine to the lagna lord without being in the lagna itself, and 2) Birth in Śukla Pakṣa in the night or Kṛṣṇa Pakṣa in the day
Ṣodaśottarī	116	Rāhu	Birth in Kṛṣṇa Pakṣa with the lagna in Moon Horā or in Śukla Pakṣa with the lagna in Sun Horā
Dvādaśottarī	112	Venus	Rāśi lagna in sign which contains Venus in Navāṁśa (lagna in Śukrāṁśa)
Pañchottarī	105	Ascendant	Cancer Lagna in the short range 0-2°30′
Śātābdikā	100	Ascendant	Vargottama lagna i.e. lagna occupying the same sign in Rāśi and Navāṁśa
Ṣaṭ triṁśata Samā	36X3=108	Mercury	Birth in day time with lagna in Sun Horā or in night time with lagna in Moon Horā
Chaturaśitī Samā	12X7=84	10th Lord	10th lord in 10th House
Dvisaptatī Samā	9X8=72	Hora/Moon	Lagna lord in 7th house or 7th lord in lagna
Ṣaṣṭi-hāyanī	60	Sun	Sun in lagna

[128] More information on conditional Uḍu-daśas in *Viṁśottari and Uḍu Daśās* by Sanjay Rath, Sagar Publications

[129] Bṛhat Parāśara Horā Śāstra, Daśā-Adhyāya, v. 1-43

Viṁśottarī is governed by the Moon and specifically shows what experiences the person will have. It uses 9 planets and 27 nakṣatras. Aṣṭottarī daśā uses 8 planets and 28 nakṣatras like the Kālachakra. Its governor is Ketu and it will give fine tuning on importing and exporting, as well as foreign residence and travel. Dvādaśottarī daśa is ruled by Venus and will show details about artistic ventures. Ṣaṣṭi-hāyanī daśā is ruled by Sun and will give details about people of high status, or people who start or carry a spiritual lineage. In this way, Viṁśottarī is giving a general overview of experience and other daśās will fine-tune the details of that experience.

		120	108	116	112	105	100	36	84	72	60
1	Aśvinī	Ketu	Rāhu	Ketu	Ketu	Venus	Moon	Venus	Saturn	Moon	Jup
2	Bharaṇī	Venus	Rāhu	Moon	Jupiter	Moon	Venus	Rāhu	Sun	Mars	Jup
3	Kṛttikā	Sun	Venus	Merc	Sun	Jupiter	Merc	Moon	Moon	Merc	Jup
4	Rohiṇī	Moon	Venus	Venus	Moon	Sun	Jupiter	Sun	Mars	Jup	Sun
5	Mṛga	Mars	Venus	Sun	Saturn	Merc	Mars	Jupiter	Merc	Venus	Sun
6	Ārdrā	Rāhu	Sun	Mars	Mars	Saturn	Saturn	Mars	Jupiter	Saturn	Sun
7	Punarvasu	Jupiter	Sun	Jupiter	Merc	Mars	Sun	Merc	Venus	Rāhu	Sun
8	Puṣya	Saturn	Sun	Sun	Rāhu	Venus	Moon	Saturn	Saturn	Sun	Mars
9	Āśleṣa	Merc	Sun	Mars	Ketu	Moon	Venus	Venus	Sun	Moon	Mars
10	Maghā	Ketu	Moon	Jupiter	Jupiter	Jupiter	Merc	Rāhu	Moon	Mars	Mars
11	Pūrvaphalgunī	Venus	Moon	Saturn	Sun	Sun	Jupiter	Moon	Mars	Merc	Moon
12	Uttaraphalgunī	Sun	Moon	Ketu	Moon	Merc	Mars	Sun	Merc	Jup	Moon
13	Hasta	Moon	Mars	Moon	Saturn	Saturn	Saturn	Jupiter	Jupiter	Venus	Moon
14	Citrā	Mars	Mars	Merc	Mars	Mars	Sun	Mars	Venus	Saturn	Moon
15	Svātī	Rāhu	Mars	Venus	Rāhu	Venus	Moon	Merc	Sun	Rāhu	Merc
16	Viśākhā	Jupiter	Mars	Sun	Merc	Moon	Venus	Saturn	Moon	Sun	Merc
17	Anurādhā	Saturn	Merc	Mars	Ketu	Sun	Merc	Venus	Mars	Moon	Merc
18	Jyeṣṭhā	Merc	Merc	Jupiter	Jupiter	Merc	Jupiter	Rāhu	Merc	Mars	Venus
19	Mūla	Ketu	Merc	Saturn	Sun	Saturn	Mars	Moon	Jupiter	Sun	Venus
20	Pūrvaaṣāḍhā	Venus	Saturn	Ketu	Moon	Mars	Saturn	Sun	Venus	Moon	Venus
21	Uttaraaṣāḍhā	Sun	Saturn	Moon	Saturn	Venus	Sun	Jupiter	Saturn	Mars	Venus
22	Śravaṇa	Moon	Saturn	Merc	Mars	Moon	Moon	Moon	Sun	Merc	Saturn
23	Dhaniṣṭhā	Mars	Jupiter	Venus	Rāhu	Jupiter	Venus	Sun	Moon	Jup	Saturn
24	Śatabhiṣa	Rāhu	Jupiter	Sun	Merc	Sun	Merc	Jupiter	Mars	Venus	Rāhu
25	Pūrvābhādra	Jupiter	Jupiter	Mars	Ketu	Merc	Jupiter	Mars	Merc	Saturn	Rāhu
26	Uttarabhādra	Saturn	Rāhu	Jupiter	Jupiter	Saturn	Mars	Merc	Jupiter	Rāhu	Rāhu
27	Revatī	Merc	Rāhu	Saturn	Sun	Mars	Sun	Saturn	Venus	Sun	Rāhu

Interpretation of Viṁśottarī Daśā

There are many types of daśā and one should be clear what is to be seen in each in order to use them all correctly. Viṁśottarī Daśā (the 120 period) is calculated from the Moon Nakṣatra and will show the guṇa coming into and leading the mind. It will show what the mind wants; whether this desire is rajas, tamas or sattva and whether moving in that direction will lead to similar actions and results. Whether the guṇa is beneficial or not will depend on the nature of the person, which can be determined by evaluating the guṇa of the native's lagna, (revisit the Rāśi chapter for greater detail). The interaction of guṇas is the first level and basic energetic to understand when interpreting the Viṁśottarī Daśā.

The following section lists the many factors to be considered when interpreting a daśā in a systematic order. All the factors need to be taken into account and a final consensus made, as the final outcome will be a mix of all factors. As a beginner, start with the first few teachings, understand and utilize them, as they will give general results. The additional techniques are tools to continue to fine-tune these general results, which are to be mastered after the first ones. Specific techniques are worthless without the proper understanding of the general results. Parāśara is very systematic in his own approach.

Maitreya is enlightened to have learned about all the various daśā systems and requests Parāśara to teach him how to get results *(phala)* using daśā. Parāśara begins,[130]

साधारणं विशिष्टञ्च दशानां द्विविधं फलम् ।

sādhāraṇaṁ viśiṣṭañca daśānāṁ dvividhaṁ phalam |2a|

The daśā gives two particular types of results;

ग्रहाणं च स्वभावेन स्थानस्थितिवशेन च ॥२॥

grahāṇaṁ ca svabhāvena sthānasthitivaśena ca ||2b||

That based on the planet's intrinsic nature (*svabhāva*),
and that based on the place of residence (*sthāna sthiti*).

ग्रहवीर्यनुसारेण फलं ज्ञेयं दशासु च ।

grahavīryanusāreṇa phalaṁ jñeyaṁ daśāsu ca |3a|

Know the results of the daśā to manifest according
to the nature of the planet's strength.

[130] Bṛhat Parāśara Horā Śāstra, Daśā-Phala-Adhyāya (47/49), v.2

1) Intrinsic Nature of the Planet (Svabhāva)

The natural (*naisargika*) nature of the planet will show itself during its daśā time; this is its own (*sva*) state of being (*bhāva*). In a Venus period, a person will be more artistic, in a Sun period a person will become higher status, succeed in profit making, etc. The natural characteristics of the planet will be more prevalent than in other daśās. Jupiter is said to bring religious work, assets in elephants, the blessings of the king, conception with the blessings of the devoted deity, etc. Saturn is said to bring success in business, agricultural land, as well as trouble from enemies and atrocities from various persons[131].

2) Modified Nature of Planet by Placement (Sthāna Sthiti)

The place (*sthāna*) the planet is situated (*sthiti*) will modify its results. The Moon in the first will give social fame, the Moon in the second house will give monetary pursuit, the Moon in the third house will give a soft nature and desire for theatrical performance, the Moon in the fourth will give a compassionate heart and the possession of a nice home or property as well as an educational focus. The Moon in the sixth will give arguments, or desire to learn about health, the Moon in the seventh will give relationship or new business partners. In this way, the effect of the natural planetary significations will be modified by their house placement. The daśā will activate the physical significations and experiences that are possible through that house.

The classic text, *Jātaka Pārijāta* (18.17), says that "a planet produces its effect upon the bhāva it occupies during its daśā, this effect will be good or bad according to the nature of the planet," meaning that benefics give good results and malefics give malefic results to that house.

Each planet will have its own results in a specific house relative to the significations of that house. Moon in the ninth house will give religious motivation during its daśā, while Rahu in the ninth house will make the person renounce religion in its daśā. Both will bring the ninth house significations into the focus of the individual's life but in a different way.

First, analyze the daśā by understanding what the natural significations are of that planet, and second, how that planet will act in the position it is placed in, analyzing the significations of that planet channeling through that particular house. Third, analyze the strength of the planet as we will discuss next.

[131] Bṛhat Parāśara Horā Śāstra, Daśā-Phala-Adyāya

3) Modified Nature of Planet by Strength (Graha Vīrya)

The planet's strength *(graha vīrya)* will determine the favorable or unfavorable nature of the results. The modified nature of planets is caused by the position/ placement, strength, aspects, avasthā, and all indications spoken of in the strengths section. In the chapter of the results of daśā (*Daśā-Phala-Adhyāya*), the sage Parāśara says,

दशारम्भे दशादीशे लग्नगे शुभदृग्युते ।
स्वोच्चे स्वभे स्वमैत्रे वा शुभं तस्य दशाफलम् ॥ ५ ॥

daśārambhe daśādīśe lagnage śubhadṛgyute |
svocce svabhe svamaitre vā śubhaṁ tasya daśāphalam || 5||

If the lord of the daśā is in the ascendant, or having benefic aspects, or conjunct with the benefic planets, or exalted, or in its own sign or in a friendly sign, favorable (*śubha*) results will be felt from the beginning of the daśā.

षष्ठाऽष्टमव्ययस्थे च नीचास्तारिपुभस्थिते ।
अशुभं तत्फलं चाऽथ ब्रुवे सर्वदशाफलम् ॥ ६ ॥

ṣaṣṭhā'ṣṭamavyayasthe ca nīcāstaripubhasthite |
aśubhaṁ tatphalaṁ cā'tha bruve sarvadaśāphalam || 6||

If the planet is placed in the 6th, 8th, or 12th house, or debilitated, or in an enemy's sign or combust, results will be the unfavorable *(aśubha)* qualities of the planet.

The Sun can make one a king or give great business success. The Sun can also give low self esteem, punishment from the government and even exile to a foreign land. Which result it will give will be determined according to the planet's strength. Mars in the fourth can give new properties if it is friendly and can give litigation over properties if it is weak. In this way the favorable and unfavorable nature of the planet is to be understood.

The various rules of strength will show how the planet gives good or bad results. As mentioned in the strength chapter, the aspect of Jupiter brings monetary resources and the aspect of Mercury brings the appropriate skills for success. An exalted planet will create a high status situation for itself and the houses it lords. A debilitated planet will bring dysfunction in the same way. A planet in rāśi sandhi will cause grief *(śoka)* and disease *(roga)* in its daśā[132]. The avasthā of the planet will also be felt at this time. The natural level of all the techniques learned must be applied. An astrologer who says it will be a good daśā because it is an exalted planet is still not fully interpreting the chart. Understand what uccha does, it makes a rise in life, situation and status. So the daśā will be "good" because of these things. In this way, utilize the full understanding of all techniques to speak about life and its natural unfolding.

[132] Jātaka Pārijāta 18.27

Good results in the daśā will come from the aspects of strength, and bad results will exist according to the results of the various factors of weakness. Jātaka Pārijāta (18.13) says that "during an auspicious daśā of a planet, the inner soul (antarātma) assumes a benefic character and leads one to attain happiness and wealth". If the planet is well placed but is lacking strength then the results will be only in the person's day dreams *(svapnachintā)*. In this way the various aspects of strength and placement should be understood and used in interpretation of the results of daśā.

The first three principles of intrinsic nature, placement and strength are demonstrated by Parāśara in the *Daśā-Phala-Adhyāya*. This is a small excerpt from the results of the Sun:

मूलत्रिकोणे स्वक्षेत्रे स्वोच्चे वा परमोच्चगे ।
केन्द्रत्रिकोणलाभस्थे भाग्यकर्माधिपैर्युते ॥ ७ ॥
सूर्ये बलसमायुक्ते निजवर्गबलैर्युते ।
तस्मिन्दाये महत् सौख्यं धनलाभादिकं शुभम् ॥ ८ ॥
अत्यन्तं राजसन्मानमश्वांदोल्यादिकं शुभम् ।

The Sun, if positioned in its mūlatrikoṇa, own or exalted sign or its highest point of exaltation *(parama-uccage)* and occupies angles *(kendra)*, trines *(trikoṇa)* or the eleventh house *(lābhasthāna)* and is conjunct with the lords of ninth or tenth house or other beneficial lord and has strength and placed in his own or well placed vargas during the daśā of the Sun the individual acquires great comforts and happiness, there is good wealth and earning and everything that accompanies this, and great *(atyanta)* respect is given by the king and he moves to a good place. ||7-9a||

सुताधिपसमायुक्ते पुत्रलाभं च विन्दति ॥ ९ ॥
धनेशस्य च सम्बन्धे गजान्तैश्वर्यमादिशेत् ।
वाहनाधिपसम्बन्धे वाहनात्रयलाभकृत् ॥ १० ॥

The Sun conjunct the lord of the fifth house gives gain of a son and other earnings,
With the eleventh lord it gives elephants *(gajāntaiśvaryamādiśet)*,
With the fourth lord the individual aquires three vehicles *(vāhanā)* ||9b-10||

नृपलतुष्टिर्वित्ताढ्यः सेनाधीशः सुखी नरः ।
वस्त्रवाहनलाभश्च दशायां बलिनो रवेः ॥ ११ ॥

In the daśā of a strong Sun, the individual causes the satisfaction of the king *(nṛpa)*, becomes a leader/boss *(senādhīśa)*, with gains of happiness, clothing and vehicles ||11||

नीचे षडष्टके रिःफे दुर्बले पापसंयुते ।
राहुकेतुसमायुक्ते दुहृस्थानाधिपसंयुते ॥ १२ ॥
तस्मिन्दाये महापीडा धनधान्यविनाशकृत ।
राजकोपः प्रवासश्च राजदण्डो धनक्षयः ॥ १३ ॥

If the Sun is nīca, without strength, in the sixth, eighth, or twelfth house
or conjunct a malefic, Rahu or Ketu or with the lords of dusthānas,
during the daśā there is great pain *(mahāpīḍā)*, destruction of wealth and grain,
anger of the king, foreign residence or exile *(pravāsa)*,
punishment by the government, dimunition of savings *(dhanakṣaya)*, ||12-13||

ज्वरपीडा यशोहानिर्बन्धुमित्रविरोधकृत ।
पितृक्षयभयं चैव गृहे त्वशुभमेव च ॥ १४ ॥
पितृवर्गे मनस्तापं जन्द्वेषं च विन्दति ।

suffering of fevers *(jvarapīḍā)*, loss of honor *(yaśohāni)*, hostility with relatives
and friends, fear of father's death, and other negative results to domestic life.
Mental anguish of the father's affairs, hatred from the public ||14-15a||

शुभदृष्टियुते सूर्ये मध्ये तस्मिन् क्वचित्सुखम् ।
पापग्रहेण सन्दृष्टे वदेत्पापफलं बुधः ॥ १५ ॥

If the Sun has benefic aspects or conjunctions it will at times give good results,
With malefic planets and aspects it will give negative results *(pāpaphala)* ||15||

Practice Exercise:

3. Analyze these verses to see how Parāśara is determining strength and weakness. On a separate sheet of paper, list and graph these strengths and weaknesses into two columns. Correlate these criteria to those listed in the above three sections.
4. Notice what is bringing favorable experiences in a bad daśā. Apply these three techniques in a few charts before moving on in this chapter.
5. Read the chapter on the Results of the Daśās *(Daśā-Phala-Adhyāya)* in BPHS.

4) Association: Yogas

The planets will give results related to planets they are associated with. As seen in the previous verses, Parāśara mentions that planets conjunct the 6th, 8th, or 12th lord or conjunct malefics will give some unfavorable (aśubha) daśā results while those conjunct beneficial house lords will give more favorable (śubha) daśā results. In this way, the planets conjunct another planet will get activated with good and bad indications of that planet. If Jupiter and Rāhu are conjunct, Jupiter daśā will be less fruitful as it will be darkened by Rāhu, but Rāhu daśā will not be as bad since it is conjunct Jupiter. The malefic planets pull down the benefic planet results, while the benefics uplift the malefic planets. In Rāhu daśā, Jupiter will be activated and there will be learning and some sattva guna present. But in Jupiter daśā, when Rāhu gets activated, the balance and peace of Jupiter is lessened by the troubles and trials of Rāhu.

Yogas are formed in a chart by combinations (*sambandha*) of planets. These yogas are activated in the various daśās. There are various yogas based on planets, houses, and other points that can be activated by daśā.

If the Sun is with Rāhu, during Sun daśā Rāhu will also get activated. During Rāhu daśā Sun will also get activated. When there are multiple planets in a house, there will be certain planets that interact more with each other, and thereby activate each other more than others. The dictum of the tradition is that the most malefic planets will interact with the most benefic planets.

If there are only two planets they interact with each other. If there are three planets the most malefic will interact with the most benefic and the middle will remain less affected.

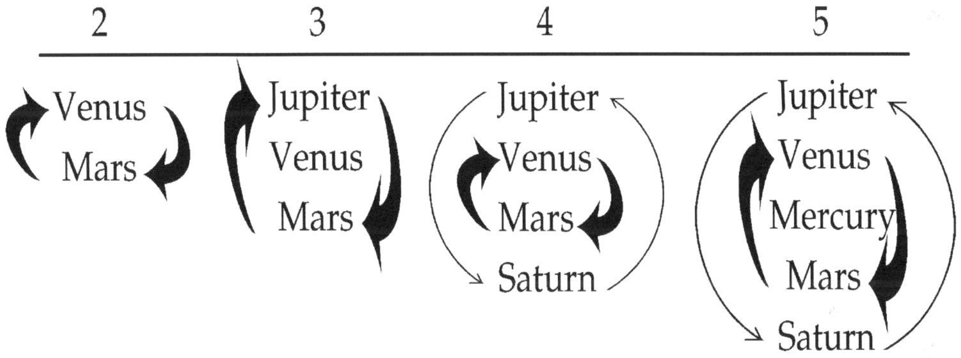

If there are four planets then the most malefic will interact with the most benefic and the second most malefic will interact with the second most benefic. In the case of five planets, the same thing as four planets takes place with a fifth planet being neutral to itself in the center.

In the example, when Venus and Mars are conjunct they interact with each other. When a third planet is added, the most benefic (Jupiter) interacts with the most malefic (Mars). Therefore during Mars daśā Jupiter will also get activated and during Jupiter daśā Mars will also be activated. Yet Venus daśā will be able to give its own results. When Saturn, a fourth planet is added, the most benefic (Jupiter) will interact with the most malefic (Saturn), while the second most benefic (Venus) will interact with the second most malefic (Mars). In this way the activation and shared results of planets is seen in the daśās.

5) House Lordship of Planet

There are two aspects of house lordship. The planet will give particular favorable or unfavorable results according to the house it lords. The daśā of the sixth lord brings disease and enemies, while the daśā of the ninth lord brings wealth, and good luck. In this way the houses lorded by the daśā planet are very important and all aspects of that house will become predominant in the lords daśā. Parāśara simplifies the house lord daśā results, but one must remember to use all aspects of the house according to the strength of the planet, the time of life, and overall indications of the chart.

During the daśā of lord of the...	Chapter on the Results of Nakṣatra Daśā (*Viśeṣa-Nakṣatra-Daśā-Phala-Adhyāya v.1-8*)
Ascendant	Enjoys sounds health, high fame
2nd house	Conflicts, fear of death
3rd house	Unfavorable results be anticipated
4th house	Luxury of house and land (property)
5th house	Progress in education and pleasure of children
6th house	Physical sufferings and danger from the enemies
7th house	Danger to wife, fear of death
8th house	Loss of wealth, danger to life
9th house	Fabulous gain of wealth and fame
10th house	Recognition from state or authorities
11th house	Gains, obstacles and fear of sickness
12th house	Faces extensive distress

Most planets own two houses (except the Sun and the Moon). They will give general results of both houses. When conjunct, there is a technique to determine whether a planet is more than one of the other lord. The planet will support the sign of opposite sex. For example, Saturn has two signs: Capricorn (10-even-female), and Aquarius (11-odd-male). If Saturn is in an odd sign it supports Capricorn more. If Saturn is in an even sign it supports Aquarius more. A planet placed in an even sign will support its odd sign and a planet placed in an odd sign will support its even sign more.

The placement of the daśā lord from the sign it owns will also be taken into account. If the ninth lord of luck goes to the second house of wealth there will be luck with money and savings felt during its daśā. If the ninth lord goes to the eighth house then loss of luck and wealth will be felt during its daśā. Parāśara lists a few indications; he does not list all possible indications. One is supposed to study the indications he has listed, understand why he has said what he has said and then apply the principles his statements are based upon.

This will teach one how to think and use their rational mind properly. In Jyotiṣa, you can say things not in the texts but they need to be based on principles enunciated there. The first step is understanding these principles, then elaborating on them by using them in different situations. This is the proper use of the rational and creative mind. Only logic or only creativity will not give good Jyotiṣa. Proper logic with creativity balances both sides of the mind and opens the 3rd eye.

Bṛhat Parāśara Horā Śāstra, Viśeṣa-Nakṣatra-Daśā-Phala-Adhyāya v.9-20	
Favorable/Auspicious Results	**Unfavorable/Inauspicious results**
Daśā of the 10th lord occupying the ascendant or ascendant occupying the 10th house (will certainly bring gains from the king)	The daśā of the auspicious planets posited in the 3rd, 6th or 11th house or their lords or the planets connected with their lords
Daśā of planets posited with the 5th lord	Daśā of a planet placed in the 8th house
Daśā of 10th lord if conjunct with 5th or 9th lord	The daśā of a planet combining with lords of the 2ndor 7th houses or posited therein
Daśā of Planets conjunct 9th lord	
Daśā of 9th lord when conjoined 4th lord	
Daśā of 10th lord if posited in the 5th house	
Daśā of trine lords occupying angles (extremely auspicious)	
Daśā of kendra lords in trine houses (extremely auspicious)	
Daśā of 6th, 8th, 12th lord if they have conjunction of the lord of trines	
Daśā of planets having the conjunction of the trine lords posited in angles	
Daśā of planets having the conjunction of the angle lords posited in trines	
Daśā of ascendant lord that occupies the 9th	
Daśā of 9th lord that occupies the ascendant	

In the daśā of a planet, the houses it lords are activated. Planets and ārūḍhas in these houses will also become activated. Therefore if a planet is dispositor (the lord of) a benefic then there will be some beneficial results from that. If the planet is dispositor of a malefic then there will be effects of the malefic's position felt. In this way the lordship of the planet will also show results in a daśā. *Jātaka Pārijāta* (18.5) specifically says that the planet can give negative results when it lords the upagraha Mandi, or is placed in the bhāva with Mandi. In this way, upagrahas, ārūḍhas, and other special points can be activated with dasa.

Jātaka Pārijāta (18.28) reiterates the factors considered so far in this chapter in the following verse: "A planet in debilitation in the natal chart cannot give good results, nor a planet associated with it. If the nīca planet is conjunct Rāhu it can do harm to the native in its daśā, this is also true of the planet lording that rāśi and the planet in rāśis owned by that planet".

Practice Exercise:

6. Take the last verse from *Jātaka Pārijāta* and break down the various parts of the verse and how it applies to the various rules learned. Reverse all the indications for the situation with an exalted planet and a benefic planet conjunction.
7. Read Chapter on Results of Special Nakṣatra Daśās *(Viśeṣa-Nakṣatra-Daśā-Phala-Adhyāya)*, which teaches about house lord daśās. Analyze the lords of your present and previous daśās.
8. If possible, find a copy of *Jātaka Pārijāta* and read chapter eighteen.

6) Mahādaśā Lord and Antardaśā Lord

The lord *(nātha)* of the daśā is called the *daśānātha*. The main (mahā) daśā is broken down into smaller daśās inside of the *mahādaśā*. Antara means internal, inside, or within. The daśā inside the mahādaśā is called the *antardaśā*.

The Mahādaśā lord *(mahādaśānātha)* and Antardaśā lord *(antardaśānātha)* are treated as if a conjunction between the two planets. Jupiter and Moon conjunction is Gajakeśarī Yoga and this daśā will give similar results as the yoga of these two planets. Rāhu and Mars together is called Agni Stambhana yoga (the blocked fire combination) and the daśā will have similar results.

The interaction of these two planets will flavor the results of the daśā for positive or negative. They will work to attain the significations of the attributes related to their conjunction. Moon-Jupiter daśā will be more auspicious while Moon-Rahu will have the nature of confusion which Rahu gives the Moon in conjunction.

[133] Bhāva sambandha combinations are listed in the chapter on Yogas, page 214

7) Bhāva Sambandha of Daśānātha

The bhāva sambandha[134] between the mahādaśā lord and antardaśā lord will indicate how that yoga is acting in the daśā. It can give favorable or unfavorable results. If the mahādaśā lord and antardaśā lord are in a 5-9 relationship then those two planets will give their respective better results together. If the planets are in a 6-8 relationship, they will create friction between each other. *Jātaka Pārijāta* (18.30) says when the daśā and antardaśā lord are in a 6-8 relationship to each other there may be danger, exile or some malefic event, especially if the planets are inimical to each other, but less if they are friendly to each other.

For example, the Moon and Jupiter in a Yoga, 1-7 or 4-10 relationship are forming Gajakeśarī Yoga and will make the native famous and fortunate. During this daśā the blessings of this yoga will be activated. If Moon and Jupiter are in a 6-8 relationship it forms a Sakata Yoga and the native is lazy and lacks motivation to achieve higher social goals for themselves. During this daśā they will need to face their issues with this and the daśā will not be as fruitful as a better bhāva sambandha could be. In general the mahādaśā lord shows the situation and the antardaśa lord shows our mind's desires. When the situation and the mind don't work well together there may be suffering. When the situation and mind work together, then there will be a better chance of success.

Parāśara lists the results of all the antardaśās in Bṛhat Parāśara Horā Śāstra. This is an excerpt from Moon-Jupiter daśā and Moon-Saturn daśā:

[22] In Moon mahādaśā- Jupiter antardaśā, if Jupiter is situated in an angle, trine, or eleventh from lagna or in its own signs or exaltation then there is gain of a kingdom *(rājyalābha)*, great enterprise *(mahā-utsava)*, **[23]** clothing, position, ornaments, gain of favor from the king/boss/governement, pleasure of the guiding deity *(iṣṭadeva-prasādena)*, conception *(garbhā-dhānādikaṁ)*, **[24]** auspicious works *(śobhana-kāryāṇi)*, home, the affection of goddess Lakśmī *(lakṣmī kaṭākṣakṛt)*, respectable position *(rājāśraya)*, wealth, land, elephants/vehicles, **[25a]** kindness of the ruling governement *(mahārāja)*, accomplishment of things important to oneself *(sveṣṭasiddhi)*, activities that make one happy *(sukhāvahā)*.

[25b] Jupiter placed in the sixth, eighth, or twelfth house, in debilitation, combust, **[26]** or conjunct malefics gives unethical actions *(aśubha karma)*, afflictions to the teacher, children, and other significations of Jupiter *(guru-putra-adi-nāśa)*, fall from one's position/rank *(sthāna-bhraṁśa)*, mental affliction due to deciet or quarrel *(manoduḥkha-makasmātkalaha)*, **[27a]** affliction to one's home or property *(gṛha-kṣetra-adi-nāśa)*, as well as problems with vehicles and apparel *(vāhana-ambara-nāśa)*.

[134] Bṛhat Paraśara Horā Śāstra, (54-62 Sharma, 52-60 Santhanam)

[27b] Jupiter placed in an angle, trine, third, or eleventh from the mahādaśā lord **[28]** gives gains of food, apparel, higher learning *(paravādi)*, comforts, happiness with brother and friends, patience *(dhairya)*, vigour *(vīrya)*, strong willpower *(parākrama)*, **[29]** ritual *(yajña)*, penance *(vrata)*, marriage *(vivāhādi)*, and acquisition of dowry *(śrī-dhana-sampada)*.

Jupiter placed in the sixth, eighth, twelfth houses from the mahādaśā lord or without strength results in **[30]** inferior quality food (*kutsinānna*), and travelling abroad (*videśagamana*). It is said that the beginning of the antardaśā will be beneficial (*śobhana*), but it will end in difficulties (*kleśakara*).

[31] If Jupiter is the lord of the second or seventh house, it indicates illness or pre-mature death *(apamṛtyu)*. It is said that doṣa can be avoided *(parihāra)* by chanting the thousand names of Śiva *(śiva-sāhasranāma)*, and donating gold to keep away *(nivāraka)* all troubles *(sarva-kaṣṭa)*.

[32] In Moon mahādaśā- Saturn antardaśā, if Saturn is situated in an angle, trine or eleventh house from lagna or in own sign in rāśi, or own sign in navāṁśa or exalted *(tuṅga-aṁśa-saṁyuta)*, **[33]** or aspected / conjunct benefics, or with strength *(balasaṁyuta)* then there is acquisition of children *(putra)*, friends *(mitra)*, earnings *(artha)*, coming together with capable workers *(śūdra-prabhu-samāgama)*, **[34]** claiming lost wages *(vyayasāyāt-phalādhikya)*, increase of land *(kṣetra-adi-vṛddhi)*, gains from son *(putralābha)* good reputation *(kalyāṇa)*, and high position *(vaibhava)* received from the king *(rāja-anugraha)*.

[35] If Saturn is placed in the sixth, eighth, or twelfth house, or debilitated or in the second house, that antardaśā will give visiting *(darśana)* and ablution *(snāna)* at sacred pilgrimage places (puṇyatīrtha), **[36]** trouble with many people *(anekajanatrāsa)*, and pain from enemies *(śastrapīḍā)*.

Saturn placed in angle or trine or strong from the mahādaśā lord **[37]** will have comforts *(saukhya)* and aquisition of wealth *(dhanāpti)* cause quarrel with the spouse and children *(dāra-putra-virodha-kṛt)*. Saturn in the second, seventh, or eighth will give bodily affliction *(deha-bādha)*. **[38]** It is said that doṣa can be avoided *(parihāra)* and one be free of disease *(ārogya)* by chanting the mṛtyuñjaya-mantra and donation of a black cow or buffalo.

Practice Exercise:

9. Study and note how Parāśara is giving results of the daśā from both the lagna and the lord of the daśā (*daśānātha*).
10. Locate your specific daśā within these chapters of Bṛhat Parāśara Horā Śāstra and see how this and previous daśās relate to your experiences at these times; note the remedies.

8) Stage of Life: Āśrama

There are four stages of life according to traditional Vedic philosophy. These are the brahmachāra (student) phase, Gṛhastha (householder) phase, Vānaprashta (partially retired) phase, and sanyasin (complete spiritual focus) stage of life. These stages of life will determine how a planet expresses itself. An event in the fourth house could cause one to go to University in the student phase, may make someone buy a house in the householder phase, will make one begin spiritual study in the semi-retired phase of life and will bring internal awakening in the last phase of life. All results and predictions should take the age of the individual into account.

In this same way, the *naisargika daśā* should be integrated into the interpretation of the *nakṣatra daśā*. The naisargika daśā is the natural evolution of a human being, and is the same for all people based upon their age. The Moon rules the first year of life, as the baby needs its mother and nurturing to survive. Mars rules the next three years as the child learns sensory-motor control of the body. Then Mercury daśā comes and the child learns the social and intellectual skills needed to live in the world. During Venus naisargika daśā the person will go through puberty, engage with the opposite sex, and eventually marry. During the Jupiter daśā the native will raise their children and accumulate wealth in the householder stage of life. In the Sun daśā the person will take semi-retirement and begin to open to their spiritual life. In the final Saturn daśā the individual will begin to become unattached to the material world, focusing on the knowledge of the Upaniṣads. This prepares them for a healthy transition into the next life.

Age	Natural Daśā
0-1	Moon
1-3	Mars
3-12	Mercury
12-32	Venus
32-50	Jupiter
50-75	Sun
75-108	Saturn

The naisargika daśā is the natural tendency of human life, which is the same for everyone. The Viṁśottarī daśā will show how this varies due to the guṇa of the mind, and the places our desires lead us. If one of these planets is afflicted, then the native will suffer those significations naturally at that time. If Mercury is afflicted the person may have learning difficulties during Mercury daśā. If Venus is afflicted the person may not marry during Venus naisargika daśā. If Jupiter has some kind of sambandha with Venus then the person will still be interested in marriage during Jupiter daśā. In the same way, if the Sun has sambandha with Venus the native will still be interested in marriage during Sun naisargika daśā. People who remarry in their eighties after their first partner dies must have Saturn in association with Venus. In this way the natural interaction of the planets is seen in naisargika daśā. The specific direction of the mind seen in Viṁśottarī daśā will be influenced by these variations in the age of the person.

9) Levels of Daśā

The Viṁśottarī daśā can be divided into six levels. The finer the level the more accurate the birth time must be. There is a story that Śrī Jagannath Rath watched someone get on a train for a particular journey. He looked at his watch and with that time rectified the daśā down to the sixth level. The six levels are Mahā, Antar, Pratyantar, Sūkṣma, Prāṇa, and Deha.

As a beginner, one should be able to at least utilize the first three levels of daśās. There is a simple way to remember the area of each level. The *tripod of life* are the three sattva planets; the Sun, the Moon and Jupiter. These three sattva (sustaining) planets support and guide all life. The mahādaśā relates to the Sun, the antardaśā relates to the Moon, and the pratyantardaśā relates to Jupiter.

The **Sun** *(Āditya)* shows our energy and resources; how we get them, what they are, when they come and where they are from. Therefore the **mahādaśā** will show what resources are available, what situations we are in and how prosperous those situations are going to be. The **Moon** shows sustenance, the mind, thoughts and emotions. Therefore the **antardaśā** will show where the mind is directed, how we are applying ourselves, what emotions are being experienced, etc. **Jupiter** relates to our intelligence and power of understanding *(dhi-śakti)*. The **pratyantardaśā** will show how we are applying our intelligence, where are we putting the mental understanding, and how the intelligence is serving us.

For more advanced information on the daśā, the mahādaśā lord should also be examined from the Sun to see the full attainment of the situation and position offered by the planet. The antardaśā lord should be observed from the Moon for mental state and attitude during the daśā as well as from the ārūḍha lagna for social status during the daśā. The pratyantardaśā has particular importance placed on its position from lagna.

10) Graha Dṛṣṭi

The graha dṛṣṭi (aspects) of a planet will be most active during its daśā. Therefore the graha aspects of daśā lord will show what the person will be desiring at this time. Rāśi aspects function regularly throughout the life, while graha aspects function primarily during daśā.

The story the aspects create will come alive during the daśā and antardaśā of the planets by showing what the planet is interested in and what it is trying to achieve. If Jupiter is in the twelfth house, it will have fifth aspect on the fourth house, seventh aspect on the sixth house, and ninth aspect on the eighth house. It will try to improve the fourth house significations of education, home and happiness. Aspecting the sixth house it will desire and work to overcome enemies. Aspecting the eighth house it will desire and work to overcome debts and losses. In this way during Jupiter daśā the main desires of the native will be understood.

11) Argalā

Parāśara has mentioned in his argalā chapter that the fruits of argalā are given in the appropriate daśā. He tells us that argalā will show the definite *(dṛḍha)* results of a house and the fixed *(sthira)* results of the planets. Argalā shows the objectives of the native, as opposed to graha aspects that show the desires of the native, or rāśi aspects that show the physical influences in situations of the native.

यत्र राशौ स्थितः खेटस्तस्य पाकान्तरं यदा ।
तस्मिन् काले फलं ज्ञेयं निर्विशङ्कं द्विजोत्तम ॥ ९॥

yatra rāśau sthitaḥ kheṭastasya pākāntaraṁ yadā |
tasmin kāle phalaṁ jñeyaṁ nirviśaṅkaṁ dvijottama || 9||

In the frutiful season (daśā/antardaśā of the argalā),
know with certainty, best of Brahmins, the rāśi (and its contents),
and the planetary placements will be in their ripe period (will give results).

The results of argalā are seen differently according to the daśā being used. Both Viṁśottari (or special uḍu-daśā) and Nārāyaṇa daśā work very well. The argalā will deepen the reading of these time periods immensely and show when the argalā results will be given to the native.

For rāśi daśās, the argalā is seen from the daśā sign, results are predicted accordingly. For example, an Aries lagna having Jupiter in the fifth house is in Taurus daśā. This means that Jupiter is giving sukhārgalā for that daśā. Because it is placed in the fifth it will be bringing happiness through learning, mantra, children, or some other indication of Jupiter in the fifth.

For graha daśās, like Viṁśottari, one wants to see what argalā the daśānātha gives to the chart. For the same Jupiter in the fifth house of an Aries lagna, it gives argalā to:

2nd house argalā to the 4th house
11th house argalā to the 7th house
4th house argalā to the 2nd house
5th house secondary argalā to lagna
8th house seconday argalā to 10th house

That Jupiter will give gains to the home or education, the person may enter a romance with a spiritual person, they will be happy with earnings, their intelligence will increase, and there will be a promotion in the work place. All these predicitions are according to unobstructed argalā. A planet in virodha will obstruct the indication according to that graha's nature.

For the same case, if the planet was a malefic like Mars one has to consider the significations of Mars and its relationship with the bhāvakāraka. Mars is friendly to the fourth house (bhāvakāraka Moon) signification of land, but not for education. Therefore gains in land or improvement of the lands is possible but there will be fights relative to gains in education. Mars and Venus are neutral to each other and Mars and Jupiter are friendly. For a male chart, Mars would give gains of a love relationship or improvement of passion in the relationship. For a female chart, Mars may bring a relationship but could also bring quarreling and other Mars significations into the relationship. Mars and second house kāraka Jupiter are friends, and therefore the fourth house Argalā on the second will make a person work extra hard to attain happiness in the area of finances. In this way, benefics and malefics need to be seen giving their results in various daśā. Review planetary friendships and enmity.

The kāraka of a house will force a house to perform its duty if it has obstruction to the house. For example, the Moon giving obstruction to the 4th house will force the person to go home during its period. The kāraka will force the person to perform the significations relative to the house. Jupiter having obstruction on the fourth house of education will force the native to go to school. Venus obstructing the seventh house will force a person into a relationship.

There are many derivations of the argalā rules used in interpreting daśā. This is an important one used in timing. The signified bhāva rāśi lord from any kāraka brings the signification in its daśā. For example, for timing love relationship, the seventh lord (kāraka house) from Venus (kāraka) will bring the spouse in its daśā. The ninth lord from Jupiter will bring the Guru. Here one can see the basis of this rule and the various ways that the results can be obstructed.

Practice Exercise:

11. Review the argalā chapter and your understanding, then interpret the argalā of your present daśā (both *from* the daśā lord and on the daśā lord).
12. Calculate which daśā is more likely to bring (1) a lover, (2) a guru, (3) your children?

12) Jīva of the Daśā

Count from the mahādaśā lord to the antardaśā lord and then that many signs from there to see the sign that becomes the Jīva. This will show the main aims and experiences of the daśā. It is where the energy is going, and what we will be "aware" of. The exception to the rules of ārūḍha calculation do not apply. The only exception is if the planets are in the same house, then the 7th house becomes the Jīva.

13) Navatāra Chakra

Navatāra chakra particularly corresponds to Viṁśottarī daśā. The following graph is a good example of how to perceive the Navatāra chakra through the daśās. This is the same chart as the calculation example.

Vimśottarī Daśā			Starting Dates		
Navatāra	Planet	Period	Y	M	D
Janma	Venus	19-3-18	1976	10	09
Sampat	Sun	6	1996	01	27
Vipat	Moon	10	2002	01	27
Kṣema	Mars	7	2012	01	27
Pratyak	Rāhu	18	2019	01	27
Sādhana	Jupiter	16	2037	01	27
Naidhana	Saturn	19	2053	01	27
Mitra	Mercury	17	2072	01	27
P.Mitra	Ketu	7	2089	01	27

Each daśā is given its lord and length according to the Nakṣatra progression. In this way, the first daśā is one's janma daśā. While the second daśā is the sampat daśā. The third daśā is the vipat daśā and is less favorable. As mentioned previously by Parāśara, death can occur in the Vipat, Pratyak, or Naidhana nakṣatras. Which one of these will depend on whether the person has short, middle, or long life (a calculation done to begin longevity timing). As negative health experiences are more prominent in negative tāras, positive experiences are more likely in beneficial daśās. Jātaka Pārijāta (18.25) says to first take into account the house lordship of the planet, then to utilize the navatara chakra. The saṁpat, kṣema, sādhaka, mitra, and paramamitra daśās will bring general prosperity *(samṛddhi)* as long as those planets have beneficial lordship.

There are three cycles of nine. The first is the janma nakṣatra group *(janmarkṣa)*, the second is the karma nakṣatra group *(karmakṣa)*, and the third set is the ādhana nakṣatra group *(ādhanamarkṣa)*. Jātaka Pārijāta (18.23) says the guṇa (sattva, rajas, tamas) of the planet will manifest itself in the beginning of the daśā if it is in the janma nakṣatra group. The guṇa will manifest in the middle of the daśā if it is in the karma nakṣatra group, and will manifest itself towards the end of the daśā if it is in the ādhana nakṣatra group. Therefore, if Jupiter is in the first nine nakṣatras, it will create more sattva in the life from the very beginning of the daśā. If Jupiter is in the second set of nine nakṣatras it will bring its primary sattva in the middle of the daśā, etc.

For specific health purposes the navatāra chakra is calculated from the lagna nakṣatra.

Practice Exercise:

14. Review Navatāra chakra notes and fill out your own daśās accordingly.

	Viṁśottarī Daśā		Starting Dates		
Navatāra	Planet	Period	Y	M	D
Janma					
Sampat					
Vipat					
Kṣema					
Pratyak					
Sādhana					
Naidhana					
Mitra					
P.Mitra					

14) Division of Daśā Results

The results of the daśā have been divided in several ways. The day one enters a daśā, they don't throw away all the qualities of the previous daśā and go buy all new attire. The results will happen slowly. In a daśā of 20 years, the main results may be in the beginning, middle, or the end of the daśā. Different aspects of the results will become prominent at various parts of the daśā.

Parāśara states[135] that the results are based on the strength *(graha-vīrya)* of the planets. If the planet is in the first drekkāṇa (first ten degrees of the rāśi) then the results of this strength will be felt at the beginning of the daśā. If the planet is in the second drekkāṇa it will show the results of its strength in the middle of the daśā, and at the end of the daśā if in the last ten degrees. This strength will relate to the natural significations of the planet. For example, if Venus is in the last drekkāṇa the full artistic nature of it will bloom towards the end of the daśā. If Venus is in the middle drekkāṇa, the full artistic nature will bloom in the middle of the daśā.

Jātaka Pārijāta (18.24) divides the general fulfillment of results to the beginning and end of the daśā. The **front rising** *(śīrṣodaya)* signs give their results in the beginning of the daśā. The **back rising** *(pṛṣṭodaya)* signs give results in the end half of the daśā (chart shown in rāśi chapter with day and night rāśis). The both rising (Pisces) gives results throughout the daśā. Some astrologers say that the front rising give results in the beginning, the both rising in the middle, and the back rising in the end of the daśā. Since this technique is based on sign it will show the results relative to the situation and resources available in the daśā.

[135] Bṛhat Parāśara Horā Śāstra, Daśā-Phala-Adhyāya, v. 3-4

	Division of Results	Factors activated
1	Drekkāṇa	Avasthā/ naisargika
2	Navatāra	Guṇa and Emotions
3	Type of Sign	General indications
4	Benefic/ Malefic	Blessings or suffering

Malefic planets give the results of *strength* (uccha, nīca, etc) in Rāśi and varga in the beginning of the daśā (first three antardaśā). The results of the *ownership* and *house placements* will be felt in the middle third of the daśā (middle three antardaśā). The results of the planet's aspects and aspects on it will be felt primarily at the end of the daśā (last three antardaśā). **Benefics** will give the results of their ownership and house placement in the beginning third of the daśā. The results of the strength through out the various divisions will be felt primarily in the middle of the daśā, and their aspects in the last part of the daśā[136].

These variations to aid timing will help one in predicting the correct fulfillment of the results indicated. They are to be used with care and understanding. So take your time with them, pay attention and watch how different fruits ripen at different times of the year.

15) Carakārakas

The Viṁśottarī daśā of the ātmakāraka planet is said to be painful. It is a time when we suffer the karmas associated with the ātmā on a mental level. The planet that lords the ātmakāraka (AK dispositor) will also show results of the AK. If the AK is under affliction, the suffering of the soul will be felt; if the AK is giving a Rāja Yoga, the effects of this can also be felt.

All the planets except Ketu have some signification related to the carakārakas. The Ātmakāraka shows ones own soul, the bratṛkāraka shows the soul of one's brothers and guru, the darakāraka shows the soul of the lover, partner, etc. These indications will influence the daśā by showing which people (ātmās) have importance at that particular time of the life. Their importance will often be felt most in the particular third of the daśā that the planet gives its results.

16) Divisional Chart Placement

The effects indicated by the various varga charts will show effects in the daśās. This will be discussed more next chapter. The main principle to understand is that every aspect of the chart will factor in to the final result of a daśā. There is nothing that you do not use. The only important thing is to understand how to use the various tools of Jyotiṣa correctly, so they can be applied in the daśā correctly.

The divisional charts have their own daśās for specific events related to their area of life. They will also give general effects relevant to the nakṣatras daśās.

[136] Jātaka Pārijāta 18.58-59

17) Gochara

The present and moving position of the planets is called their gochara (transit). As they move they cause effects similar to a daśā. The most important planets to be aware of are the Sun, Moon, Jupiter and Saturn. These are the luminaries and the large slow moving planets. All planets will give effects but these can modify everything, so pay particular attention to them. Also, the transit of the lord of the daśā becomes very prominent. This means that during the daśā of fast moving planets there will be more ups and downs, while during the daśā of slow moving planets there will be more steadiness.

There is a technique called *Aṣṭakavarga* which shows the strength of transiting planets. This is explained by Parāśara[137] when Maitreya asks,

"You have mentioned the effects of the planets and houses as have other sages, but these results are modified by the transiting effect of the planets. Please teach the science through which a person can get an understanding about their happiness, sorrows, and longevity merely by delineating the positions of planets in transit."

The great sage Parāśara replies, "You have asked a good question, so I will set forth to you the science which will indicate the results relating to the life of the native and their longevity. The results of this technique will not contradict nor repeat those taught earlier, and it will benefit one and all."

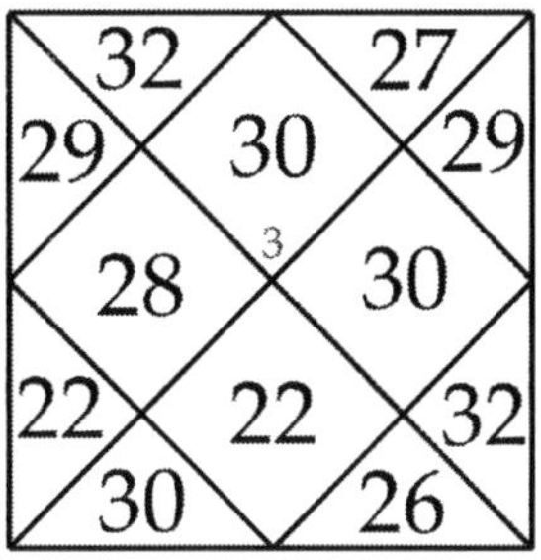

Parāśara then teaches that all the other techniques are applied and that this system of Aṣṭakavarga is used to show the modifications caused by transiting planets. Aṣhtakavarga is a system where the position of planets give points (*bindhu* and *rekha*) to the houses. The total points are called the Sarvāṣṭakavarga and will average between 10-50, with 28-30 being average. Planets transiting through a house with low points will give worse results. Planets transiting through houses with high points will give good results.

A. Calculating Aṣṭakavarga

At *www.learnvedicastrology.org* there is a PDF of a group of 8 circles. Copy them onto card stock and closely cut them out. Put a pin in the middle to allow them to spin. The ascendant is the first house. Line up the moon with the dark lines into their appropriate houses from the lagna in your natal chart. Keeping the moon there, align the planet Mercury (*Budha*) into the correct house in your natal chart using the houses listed on the outside circle. Then continue till all the planets are in their proper placements.

Count how many planets fall into each house and add them up. Create a chart that has each house with the aṣṭakavarga total written into the houses.

[137] Bṛhat Parāśara Horā Śāstra, Aṣṭakavarga-Adhyāya (66/68)

B. Interpretation of Results

When a planet transits a house with low points it will give worse results. If all the houses have an average number of points then the planet gives steady results. If some houses have high numbers and others very low, then there will be lots of ups and downs through various transits. It is important to observe the transits of the slow moving planets (Jupiter, Saturn, Rāhu) as well as the transit of the daśā lord. This is a small introduction to the science of aṣḥtakavarga of which Parāśara spends a huge amount of space.

18) Daśā Sandhi

Just like rāśi have transition points where they are weaker, the daśās also have sandhi times where they change from one planetary period to the next. These daśā sandhi are called *daśā-chhidra,* where chhidra means an opening, hole or weak spot. In these places, the previous daśā is ending which is an increase of tamas, and a new daśā is beginning which is an increase of rajas. This increase of tamas can bring out the worst aspects of the daśā period as well as signaling external changes. Therefore during these periods of time new large ventures are avoided. Sometimes if the daśā-chhidra is giving negative results a pacification ceremony (*śānti pūjā*) is done to calm the energy of the transition.

The intensity of change will relate to how the planets are placed in the chart. If they happen to be in the same house, or in a similar situation the change will not be as profound. While if there is extreme difference by the indications, like one planet causes celibacy and the other indicates sensuality, this will show a harder time of transition. Human nature attaches itself to its situation. A person who does the karma of a doctor believes that they are a doctor. This attachment will cause suffering when they are no longer doing the karma of a doctor. For the ātmā (soul) is beyond all the factors of identity attachment in life. Yet the mind is constantly identifying itself with the material world and the individual's situation. In this way, when things change there may be suffering.

Predictions

Jyotiṣa gives us the tools to make accurate predictions about the past, present and future. It is up to us to learn the techniques and apply them correctly. This requires a serious study, good teachers, and the experience that comes from analyzing many charts. In the *Spaṣṭabala-Adhyāya*, Parāśara says,

गणितेषु प्रवीणो यः शब्दशास्त्रे कृतश्रमः ।
न्यायविद् बुद्धिमान् देशादिक्कालज्ञो जितेन्द्रियः ॥ ३९ ॥

gaṇiteṣu pravīṇo yaḥ śabdaśāstre kṛtaśramaḥ |
nyāyavid buddhimān deśadikkālajño jitendriyaḥ || *39* ||

ऊहापोहपटुर्होरास्कन्धश्रवणसम्मतः ।
मैत्रेय सत्यतां यादि तस्य वाक्यं न संशयः ॥ ४० ॥

ūhāpohapaṭurhorāskandhaśravaṇasammataḥ |
maitreya satyatāṁ yādi tasya vākyaṁ na saṁśayaḥ || *40* ||

Maitreya,
the one skilled in mathematics *(gaṇita),*
who makes great efforts in grammar *(śabda-śāstra),*
has knowledge of the laws of logic *(nyāya),*
is possessed of intelligence *(buddhi),*
who adjusts their thinking according to the
culture, the locality, and the time *(deśa-dik-kāla-jña),*
having controlled senses *(jitendriya),*
good comprehension *(ūha),* clear reasoning *(apoha-paṭu),* and
has learned the branch of Horā from an authoritative source *(sammata),*
the pronouncements *(vākya)* of that one will definitely be true *(satyatā).*

Chapter 13

Varga Chakra:
Divisional Charts

Varga Chakra (Interpretation of Divisional Charts)

Divisional charts are the fine-tuning of the birth chart. They give us deeper insight into what we are seeing within the natal chart. They do not give results on their own but work on refining the indications of the natal chart. Just as the signs of the Rāśi chart are broken smaller and smaller through the divisions, the results given by them are more and more refined. There are whole books on each of these various divisional charts (also called harmonic charts). This is just a small introduction to some general principles of divisional charts that will help you navigate through the information available through the tradition.

Divisional Charts

There are sixteen vargas listed by Parāśara and many more listed by various traditional authors. Parāśara teaches about the navāṁśa deeply but for the other varga charts he only gives a few examples, and references but no direct teaching. These vargas are understood by utilizing principles enunciated by Parāśara *in the specific area of life* the varga indicates which the sage has taught. Finer details are found throughout the astrological literature.

The nomenclature will change for the same divisions for a variety of reasons. Sometimes the name will be based on the number of the divisions of the sign, like navāṁśa is the nine *(nava)* divisions *(aṁśa)*. Sometimes the name refers to the area of life studied in the chart, like dharmāṁśā is a name for the navāṁśa where the individual's dharma is studied. It is also called the bhāgyāṁśa because one can study one's luck *(bhāgya)* in the navāṁśa. In the same text, a varga can be referred to by multiple names. So one must slowly become accustomed to the various names of a varga, like a friend who may be called Matty by his mother, Mateo by you and Dīnanāth in a spiritual gathering.

Multiple Variations

For a particular division there are different ways to break down the same sign. One numerical division may have several different ways to divide itself. For example, the D-3 has four common ways to break down a sign. This could be confusing but each different division has a different purpose and a different way to be read.

Parāśara first says the dreṣkāṇa (also called drekkana or D-3) is for coborn *(bhrātṛ)* and welfare, comfort, health *(saukhya)*. Later he adds that, "The 22nd drekkāṇa counted from the lagna can cause destruction of the individual." This has nothing to do with brothers, and shows that there are multiple ways to use the various divisions.

The first exercise (in the Rāśi chapter) broke down each of the various varga into the traditionally used formats. But when we begin to interpret the meanings of these charts we must get a little more specific. For example, the drekkāṇa (D-3) is an insight into the third house. The third house shows siblings, it also shows our skills, it also shows our parākrama (power, courage, energy), as well as being the house of copulation (*maithuna*). There is a way to calculate the D-3 which will give insight into each of these areas more deeply.

8
4
12
1 5 9
2 6 10
3 7 11
7
3
11
4
8
12
Paraśara"
Drekkana
6
2
10
9
5
1
5 1 9
4 12 8
3 11 7
6
10
2

The **Parāśara D-3** is calculated in the south Indian sign chart format with the numbers in the division relating to the signs. Therefore the first sign Aries is divided into (1) Areis, (5) Leo, and (9) Sagittarius. All three elemental trines exist in one sign. This is the same one utilized in the previous lesson on vargas, which is utilized to see siblings. The third house in this drekkāṇa is for younger siblings, and the eleventh house is used for older siblings. The third from the third (the 5th house) will show the next younger sibling, and the third from that the sibling after that. The circumstances of their birth is related to the house that significates them and the lord of the house used as an ascendant will tell all the qualities of that sibling relative to you.

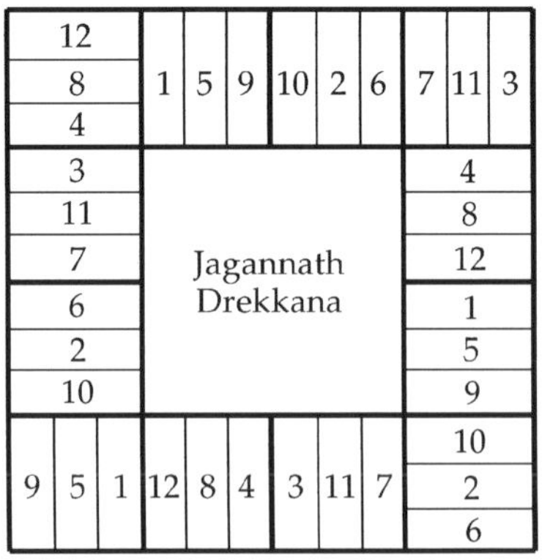

12
8
4
1 5 9
10 2 6
7 11 3
3
11
7
4
8
12
Jagannath
Drekkana
6
2
10
1
5
9
9 5 1
12 8 4
3 11 7
10
2
6

The **Jagannāth Drekkāṇa** is similar to the Parāśara D-3 in calculation of elemental trines yet each signs starts with the primary moveable sign in kendra to it (either 1, 10, 7, or 4 which is Aries-fire, Capricorn-earth, Libra-air or Cancer-water). The Parāśara D-3 starts each sign with the sign itself with out the focus on kendras.

The Jagannāth drekkāṇa shows the karma phala (the results of our actions). It will give an understanding about the ignition and sustenance of yogas. It in general shows the parākrama, courage and energy of an individual. An independent study of the Jagannāth D-3 will show what the life is focused around, or where the person is putting their effort in life.

Parivṛtti-traya D-3 is a regular cyclic division of the three parts of each sign. The first division *(aṁśa)* is Aries and the rest continue forward in normal zodiacal progression. It shows how you manifest your abilities and whether there are any blocks to manifesting these abilities. This is used in conjunction with the abilities indicated in the navāṁśa.

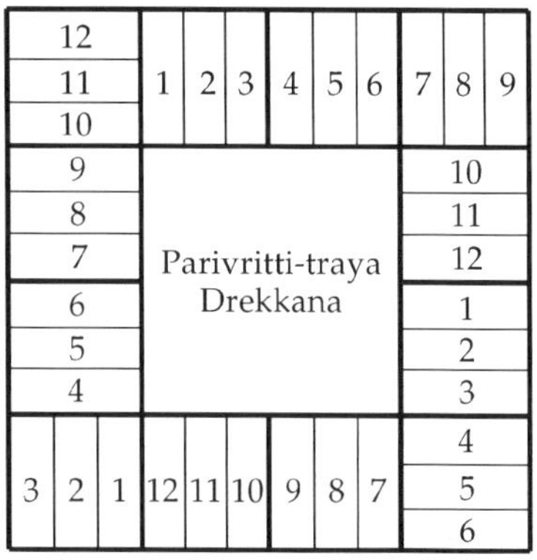

In this D-3, the kendras *(Viṣṇu-sthāna)* show what skills are used the most, and whether you will manifest those abilities in this life, while the trines are the skills you want to master in this life. All other houses are skills less used in daily life. [In the navāṁśa (D-9) the trines *(Lakṣmi-sthāna)* show what abilities you have.] Planets can block the skills of other planets based on the *dig chakra;* Jupiter is obstructed by Rāhu, Venus is obstructed by Sun, Mercury is obstructed by Mars, etc.

The third house also shows the ear, and what you hear. Therefore this division is important for talents learned from a teacher. It also shows the performance of artistic skills like musical performance, performance of plays and concerts, etc.

The **Somanāth Drekkāṇa** goes in a cyclic format through the signs but it is zodiacal in odd signs and anti-zodiacal in even signs. It relates to the maithuna (copulation) aspect of the third house and utilizes the male (odd) and female (even) signs in calculation. The Somanāth D-3 will show one's inner drive, sexual drive, and passion. It shows the sexual ideals, sexuality and celibacy. It directly relates to the level of the Ojas which shows the immunity, health and stamina of the person.

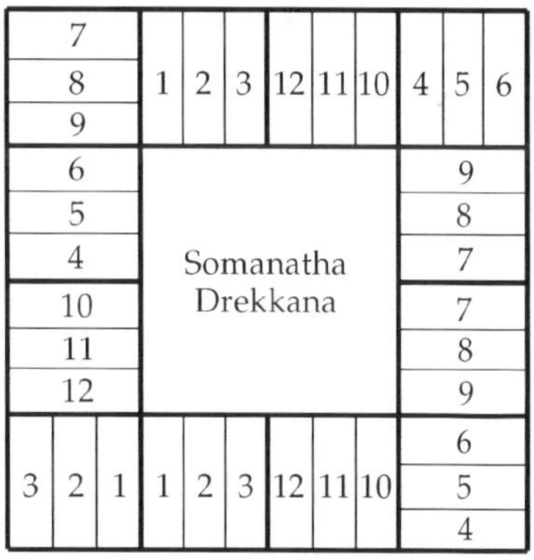

Ojas is the final dhātu in the body. First there is food, then the essence of this becomes rasa, then the essence of this becomes rakta, and then the best part of this becomes maṁsa, to medas, to asthi, to majja, to śukra (the last physical dhātu). The best part (essence) of śukra becomes Ojas. Ojas supports śukra dhātu and śukra dhātu supports Ojas. So if there is no sexual urge, there is a lack of ojas. If there is a lack of ojas (vitality, immunitiy) then there will be a lack of sexual desire because there is not enough energy to support it.

When someone has cancer or AIDS or some disease that destroys the immune system, you will find that they will lose their sex drive at the first level of degeneration. It is the first thing to go in all chronic disease. This is the relationship between Ojas and sexuality. In the same way there is a relationship between the Agni (digestion) and Ojas. If the primary Jaṭharagni (stomach fire) does not digest right, then how will the food ever get refined properly to become Ojas. Each dhātu has a *dhātu-agni*, which also digests each dhātu till it reaches Ojas. Different diseases are based on the level of where the dhātu-agni is not working. On a more subtle level, in the liver are five more bhūta-agnis to digest each of the five elements. Giving us a total of 13 Agnis that can be afflicted and lessen the Ojas in the body.

In this way, there is one division called the drekkāṇa where the sign is divided into three parts. Yet there are four different ways to do this division (in this case). Parāśara drekkāṇa is for siblings. Jagannāth D-3 is for parākrama. Somanāth D-3 is for sexuality, Parivṛtti-traya drekkāṇa is for abilities and skills. Each of these divisions relate to a different aspect of the third house and are interpreted in their own specific way according to the general principles you are about to learn.

Practice Exercise

1. Note the difference in each calculation. Calculate each of the four types of drekkāṇa for your own chart.

General Principles

There are certain general principles that will apply in all divisional charts. When these simple techniques are used correctly there will be a large amount of general information given in the specific area of life (more specific than the Rāśi yet general for the specificity of the varga). These should be learnt and applied always.

I. Kāraka Planet

Each house (bhāva) has a significator (kāraka) planet, and each area of life has a kāraka planet. When we look at the varga charts that kāraka planet becomes very important. The 10th house kāraka Sun in the daśāṁśa (career division) becomes important to show your respect and level of attainment, while the 10th house kāraka Mercury becomes extremely important to show the skills you employ at work. In the Parāśara drekkāṇa the placement of the third house kāraka Mars becomes very important, while in the Somanāth drekkāṇa the placement of Venus, the kāraka of ojas and maithuna, becomes extremely important.

If the kāraka planet is well placed, the significations of that varga fructify. If that kāraka is suffering, then the area of life suffers. In general, the kāraka planet should not be in the twelfth house or the significations will be lost. For example, the navāṁśa will show aspects related to the spouse. If the kāraka of spouse, Venus, is in the twelfth house, the native will not get married. If they do it will not be a normal marriage nor will it last long. In the saptāṁśā, which shows children, Jupiter, the kāraka for children becomes one of the primary planets. If it is in the twelfth house, the chances of having children are very small. In the same chart (D-7) the Moon, kāraka of motherhood, will show if the woman has the ability to sustain a pregnancy. In this way the placement and strength of the kāraka planet become very important to analyze first.

II. Kāraka Bhāva

The kāraka bhāva is the house related to the significations of the area of life being investigated. This kāraka bhāva in the varga chart is the most important to determine results. Analysis is to be done both from the lagna and from the house itself. For example, the kāraka bhāva for the daśāṁśa is the tenth house. From the daśāṁśa lagna the 10th house is the career and all aspects of the career are seen from it, while aspects related to your own nature in work are seen from the lagna. The fifth house from the daśāṁśa lagna shows subordinates, those who are your students or children at the workplace. The fifth house is the eighth house from the kāraka bhāva, which means that it will show transformation/longevity of the career, or when you change jobs. The sixth house from the daśāṁśa lagna shows the general employees and labor that work for you. From the kāraka bhāva it is the 9th house and shows that which supports your career which is the service and labor that you and the other employees perform. The houses from the divisional lagna are seen in relation to you in that area of life.

The houses from the kāraka bhāva are seen according to the principle of bhāvat *bhāvam* (the houses from a specific house having the similar natural house significations relative to that specific house), as well as the principle of *argalā* (the means of a house fulfilling its objectives). These techniques are utilized to understand the indications of the divisional chart houses and thereby the planets placed in them.

III. Lagna lord

The lagna of a divisional chart always represents the native in that specific area of life. The lagna of the D-10 shows the native at work, the lagna of the D-7 shows the person relative to their children and in child-rearing.

The lagna lord will show the person's nature, intelligence, and ideals. If the lagna lord is exalted the person will have high ideals and standards, if the lagna lord is debilitated the ideals will also be less. In a chart like the Somanāth drekkana the lagna lord being exalted will show an high idealism to health and sexuality, the will be concerned about their health and take the best car of their body, as well as be very respectful in areas of sexuality. If the lord is debilitated or weak, the person will have lower ideals and will not consider their long term health when making decisions, nor will they hold a strong sense of purity related to sexuality.

Debilitated planets are good is in the daśāṁśa. In this case, debilitated planets are good for making money. They still will have low ideals, but it is often this lack of ideals that allows the person to make lots of money. If a salesman couldn't bend the truth, he would never be able to get the larger commission of the more expensive product that you didn't really need. Therefore debilitated *(nīca)* planets are good for money.

IV. Rāśi and Varga Integration

The planet ruling the kāraka bhāva in the rāśi chart can be seen in the varga chart to see how the consciousness is being applied in that area of life. For example, the kāraka bhāva for the daśāṁśa is the tenth house. Therefore one can take the tenth lord in the Rāśi chart and see where and how it is placed in daśāṁśa to understand how the individual is applying their consciousness towards work and career. The kāryeśa needs to be well placed in both the Rāśi and the related divisional chart to give the full results.

Varga Nārāyaṇa

Nārāyaṇa daśā shows how we apply our consciousness in the world, it is a *rāśi-dāśa* taught later. It shows what you apply your consciousness to and the results of this application. In the varga charts, it will show what houses are active and thereby give more detailed information about that specific area of life.

Nārāyaṇa daśā and Viṁṣotarri daśā are utilized together. For example, Viṁṣotarri daśā in the daśāṁśa may show you are feeling anxiety at work, while Nārāyaṇa daśā will show what is happening that is causing anxiety. The two daśās do not show different results, they are utilized together to get the depth of good prediction. All the various daśās are used like this.

Varga Arrangements

There are five different varga systems to utilize. These are based on the reason for reading the charts in the first place. For the quick reading of a praśna chart (answering a question) one uses 3 charts for the past, present and future. For general purposes in the lives of average people the ten varga system is used. Traditionally the sixteen varga system is used only for kings and powerful people who influence the karma of many others, though in the modern world these sixteen charts are used more often.

Parāśara teaches the sixteen varga system. These sixteen relate to the maturity of Jupiter at the age of sixteen, or the sixteen years of Jupiter. Sixteen is a sacred number. It relates to the sixteen tantric kalas of the Moon, in which it achieves its fullness. This fullness relates to Lalita, the goddess Tripura Sundari, who is a sixteen year old girl achieving the complete fullness of a woman. Knowledge of the sixteen divisions is the blessing of this goddess.

Arrangement	Containing		Purpose
Trivarga (3)	1, 3, 9	Rāśi (present situation), Drekkāṇa (future after the reading), Navāṁśa (past before the reading)	General Praśna
Ṣaḍvarga (6)	1, 2, 3, 9, 12, 30	Rāśi (father), Horā (mother), Drekkāṇa (brothers), Navāṁśa (relatives), Dvadasāṁśa (children) and Trimsāṁśa (wife)	Traditional Praśna
Saptavarga (7 divisions)	1, 2, 3, 7, 9, 12, 30	Rāśi, Horā, Drekkāṇa, Saptāṁśa, Navāṁśa, Dwadasāṁśa (Sūryāṁśa), and Trimsāṁśa	Muhūrta
Daśavarga (10 divisions)	1, 2, 3, 7, 9, 10, 12, 16, 30, 60	Rāśi, Horā, Drekkāṇa, Saptāṁśa, Navāṁśa, Dasāṁśa, Dvadaśāṁśa, Ṣoḍāśāṁśa, Trimsāṁśa and Ṣaṣṭyāṁśa	Average Person
Ṣoḍaśavarga (16 divisions)	1, 2, 3, 4, 7, 9, 10, 12, 16, 20, 24, 27, 30, 40, 45, 60	Rāśi, Horā, Drekkāṇa, Chaturaṁśa, Saptāṁśa, Navāṁśa, Dasāṁśa, Dvadaśāṁśa, Ṣoḍāśāṁśa, Viṁśāṁśa, Chaturviṁśāṁśa (Siddhāṁśā), Bhāṁśa (Nakṣatrāṁśa), Trimsāṁśa, Khavedāṁśa, Akṣavedāṁśa, and Ṣaṣṭyāṁśa	Powerful individuals, Kings

Specific Charts

The beginner fundamentals have been explained. Now the breakdown of a few specific charts will be examined. The two most important, and most used divisional charts are the navāṁśa (married life) and the daśāṁśa (career). Relationship is ruled by Venus, and career is ruled by Mercury. These are the two rajas planets and therefore the ones causing the most thought, conflict, confusion and thereby questions to be asked of an astrologer. It is therefore important to have a good understanding of these charts. Then we will cover the saptāṁśa for ability to see gender in a varga chart. The others will be brushed over, to get a general understanding and to set the stage for latter study.

Navāṁśa (D-9): Soul, Skills, and Love

The navāṁśa is the deepest and most complex of all the varga charts. There are so many different techniques given in the scriptures and through the tradition. This section will introduce one to the aspects of the soul seen in the navāṁśa, the skills and abilities inherited from past lives and the dharma of relationships.

When a planet is in the same sign in the Rāśi and navāṁśa it is called vargottama which mean it is in the uttama (best) varga (division). The sign placement of planets in the navāṁśa is as important as the placement in Rāśi for the strength of the planet. If a planet is debilitated in the Rāśi and exalted in the navāṁśa it will get nīca-banga, reversal of debilitation: meaning it will act like an exalted planet, the situation may not be the best but there will be luck and resources and support to be successful. In the same way even if a planet is exalted in the Rāśi yet debilitated in the navāṁśa it becomes uccha-banga and gives the results of a debilitated planet; the situation will be good, but there will be a lack of resources, support and luck in that area of life. In this way, the navāṁśa has the power to change all aspects of our life.

The navāṁśa can be read at multiple levels: from the kārakāṁśa showing the nature of the soul, from the lagna as part of the Rāśi chart showing the abilities one has incarnated with and as an independent chart relative to relationship and sexuality.

In a praśna, the navāṁśa is the life of a person up to the present. The drekkāṇa is the future after the praśna while the D-1 is the actual situation and choices at the moment. In this way we must be versatile, and able to change perspectives and views to open up the multi-dimensions of the navāṁśa.

I. Kārakāṁśa

The navāṁśa shows the blessings we receive from our past good action, as well as our blessings from god (which at a higher conscious level cannot be differentiated). It is the ātmā that carries the blessings throughout various incarnations. The soul is signified in a chart by the ātmakāraka planet. The ātmakāraka in the navāṁśa is called the *kārakāṁśā* (the division of significance). It is from here that the astrologer can tell the desires of the soul and the forms of the divine that are supporting the deep goals of the native.

Parāśara has an entire chapter on the kārakāṁśa[138] in BPHS in which he gives many secrets on the navāṁśa. We will start with the spiritual aspects. He teaches that the twelfth house from the kārakāṁśa shows where one spends their energy and will show where they go after death (verses 63-67). If malefics are in the twelfth, the ātmā will give energy to negative actions and will suffer after death, while benefics will show the native spends energy on good things and goes to higher planes after death. Ketu there represents one who is close to attaining liberation *(mokṣa)*. Parāśara then lists the deities the native will worship according to the planets associated with the twelfth house from kārakāṁśa; Śiva for the Sun, Gauri for the Moon, Kartikeya for Mars, etc.

---

[138] Bṛhat Parāśara Horā Śāstra, Kārakāṁśa-Phala-Adhyaya, (33/35)

According to the Chandra-Kāla-Nāḍi, the twelfth from the Kārakāṁśā (KK) is called the *Jīvanmuktāṁśa*, the division which shows the liberation of the jīva (individual soul). The deity indicated by this position is called the *Iṣṭa-devatā*[139]. The twelfth house of the Rāśī shows the loss of your body which happens every night when you sleep, but more so when you die, this is not liberation of the soul, just of the body. The ātmakāraka shows the persons individual existence- your soul. The twelfth house from the ātmakāraka in the D-9 will show what can liberate your soul, how it can lose the individual nature to merge with that which is eternal.

The ninth house from the kārakāṁśa is called the *Vijñānāṁśa* (the division of higher knowing), and from here the *Dharma-devatā* is seen. The Dharma-devatā is the protector of one's dharma in life and will guide the native to their correct path in life, or keep them on their correct path. Both the twelfth and ninth house from the KK relate to the natural signs of Jupiter, who at this level represents the form of god that is all pervasive *(sarva-vyāpakeśa)*, everywhere in everything, known as Viṣṇu in India. Therefore, in the Śrī Achyutānanda Tradition, the forms of these deities are generally given Viṣṇu forms if the native does not have a strong attachment for some other pantheon.

If the 12th house from the KK contains the Moon, the form will be Kṛṣṇa or Gauri.
If there are two planets there, then the one with higher degrees is used.
If no planets are there then the lord of the sign is utilized to indicate the deity.
Aspects will show which deities lead you to your Iṣṭa-devatā.

The Iṣṭa-devatā will guide the native in all situations. If there are curses, the Iṣṭa will help the native overcome them. If there is confusion, the Iṣṭa will guide the native to the right place to get help. Worship of the Iṣṭa-devatā is best done every day, and can be done anywhere. Worship of the Dharma-devatā is best done in a temple (as it relates to the ninth house). Most afflictions to the Rāśi ninth house (and all it significates) can find a remedy with the help of the Dharma-devatā.

The sage Parāśara then mentions that the same can be applied to the sixth house from the amātyakāraka (verse 74). That is all he states and Jaimini in the *Upadeśa Sūtras* says the same thing. The sixth house from the amātyakāraka is called the *Preṣyāmśa* (the division of the servant). According to the Śrī Achyutānanda Tradition this indicates the *Pālana-devatā*, the deity who takes care of your sustenance; nourishes and protects. The same rules apply for the determination of the planet indicating the Pālana-devatā in the sixth from the amātyakāraka (AmK). The AmK is the second highest degree planet. As the ātmakāraka is like the Sun, the AmK is like the Moon. The Palana-devatā is the feminine aspect of the divine who looks after your welfare, and will generally take a sattvic form of the divine mother, to nourish one like a child. When there are problems with sustenance, money, or food this form is used.

---

[139] Iṣṭa can mean *chosen* by choice which relates to deities of the 5th house of the Rāśi, but here it means the deity which has the ability to liberate you.

The third highest degree planet is the brātṛkāraka (BK), which represents brother's in the Rāśi. In the navāṁśa this planet will represent the Guru. The relationship (bhāva sambandha) between the ātmakāraka and the BK in the navāṁśa will indicate the relationship between the native and the guru's souls. If they are in trines, or a yoga then the native has a wonderful relationship with their guru in this life. If they are 6-8 then the chance of meeting the single one guru is very small. If they are in a 2-12 relationship then the guru is very likely not embodied in this life with the native. In this case you will often find people who associate a passed on saint as their guru.

The BK in the navāṁśa is called the *Ajñānāmśa* (division of the third eye) and will indicate the Guru-devatā. It shows the inner personal guru within you. Everything outside is just a reflection of your own self, and the external guru is just a reflection of your own innate guru (and karma with guru). The Guru-devatā is the archetypal energy that teaches you about the universe and when this energy is pleased it manifests one of its worshippers to guide the individual. Therefore when there are problems with learning, with the guru, to find a guru, etc., then the Guru-devatā is worshipped. The archetypal guru is Śiva, and therefore the form of Śiva the native worships as the Guru is indicated by the Brātṛkāraka in the navāṁśa.

Division	Location	Deity
Jīvanmuktāṁśa	12th from KK	Iṣta Devatta
Vijñānāṁśa	9th from KK	Dharma Devatta
Preṣyāmśa	6th from AmK	Pālana Devatta
Ajñānāmśa	Position of BK	Guru Devatta

The Iṣṭa-devatā is like the Sun, the Pālana-devatā is like the Moon and the Guru-devatā is like Jupiter. These are the three sattvic planets that are the tripod of life. By their proper propitiation all things in life will eventually achieve harmony.

These deities will work on the subtle inner level of our being. When there are constant issues in an area of life related to these deities there propitiation becomes important. If a person is having financial problems and they do a Vedic remedy that gives them a job, but then lose that job relatively soon- it shows there is a problem in the area of sustenance and support. One can analyze the condition of the Pālana-devatā and see if this planet is weak or afflicted. If there is a problem with the planet indicating the Pālana-devatā then this must be propitiated in the indicated form (Śakti-rūpa for the Pālana-devatā), before the remedy given for the Rāśi will give full results. If there is a problem in the area of learning, understanding and teacher-student relationship then one should insure the Guru-devatā planet is strong and if not then that form of Śiva should be given to improve the situation, as well as taking care of the indications seen in the Rāśi.

Deities of the Navāṁśā Signs

The Deities of the various navāṁśas was mentioned in the chapter on Rāśi divisions. The navāṁśa is divided into Deva (divine), Manuśya (human), and Rakṣasa (protectors/ demons). This relates to the temperament. The deva signs relate to sattva and the search for knowledge, understanding, and awareness. Manuśya signs relate to the rajas of mankind and the search for wealth, possessions and sustenance. Rakṣasa signs relate to the tamas and the search for power, control and dominion over others.

The placement of the lagna lord shows the focus of the intelligence. The placement of the daśā lord will show what is happening in the life at the moment. If the daśā lord and the lagna are different then there is less success as the person may pursue power when they should be pursuing knowledge, or pursuing knowledge when they should be in politics. When they align then the daśā is set to achieve the blessings of one's intelligence.

The placement of the ninth lord (and planets in the ninth house) will show what the dharma is focused around. The placement of the Moon will show the view and general attitude of the person.

Practice Exercise:

2. Calculate your Iṣṭa-devatā, Dharma-devatā, Pālana-devatā and Guru-devatā.
3. Find the navāṁśa deity of each planet, and compare this with the daśās you have been through and will experience next.

II. Trines: Skills and Abilities

The navāṁśa works in trines. The dharma trines will show your abilities and skills in this life which you have been blessed with due to your works in a previous incarnation. The trines to the tenth will show fortune related to money (artha trines), the trines to the fourth will show fortune related to health (mokṣa trines), and the trines to the seventh will show fortune relative to sexuality (kāma trines).

Parāśara teaches that the dharma trines will show the skills we have in this life. The Moon represents melody and shows singing (that's why people sing in the shower-showers are ruled by the Moon). The Sun rules rhythm and therefore gives the ability to play instruments. If the Moon is in the navāṁśa lagna then the native will have a good voice with melody to sing. If Sun is in the navāṁśa lagna then the native will have good rhythm and the ability to play an instrument. All the planets will give the skills they indicate in the navāṁśa trines.

The difference between the first, fifth and ninth house is the level of depth the ability manifests in. Planets in lagna will show that the skill is a natural inborn ability in the native that just takes application. The fifth house will give the skills related to the planet but the native will need to work at the skill with some effort. Ninth house planets will give their skills with the guidance of a teacher. Planets in the sixth, eighth, and twelfth house will generally not give the ability of their significations easily, or the native will generally not like that area of work or study.

The graph below is what Parāśara teaches in the kārakāṁśa chapter about various planets skills followed by some additional indications.

Graha	Skills and Abilities
Sun	*kārakāṁśe ravau jāto rājakāryaparo dvija |13a|* Oh twice-born, the Sun in kārakāṁśa will show royal (government) service. Leadership, a very direct person, rhythm, stringed instruments and drums, knowledge of music *(gītajña)*, traditional dance, Vedānta philosophy- high spiritual concepts about the nature of the self and Oneness, airplanes and flying if related to Ketu
Moon	पूर्णेन्द्रौ भोगवान् विद्वान् शुक्रदृष्टे विशेषतः ॥ १३ ॥ *pūrṇendrau bhogavān vidvān śukradṛṣṭe viśeṣataḥ | | 13b| |* The Full Moon will show a bhogavān (one who enjoys the pleasures of life), and a vidvān (intelligent, learned, scholar), and the aspect of Venus on that will show the ability to excell in this area. Social work, nursing, food preparation, hotel management, literary knowledge *(sāhityajña)*, knowledge of Purāṇas or folklore, melody, singing *(gāyaka)*, saṁkhya yoga philosophy *(sāṅkhya-yogajña)* or philosophy related to dual creation, the working of the physical world, āyurveda, good at natural medicine and curing disease if conjunct Mercury *(vaidya-sarva-rogahari)*, surgeon if conjunct Mars, pharmaceuticals if conjunct Venus
Mars	स्वांशे बलयुते भौमे जातः कन्तायुधीभवेत् । वह्निजीवी नरो वाऽपि रसवादी च जायते ॥ १४ ॥ *svāṁśe balayute bhaume jātaḥ kantāyudhī bhavet |* *vahnijīvī naro vā'pi rasavādī ca jāyate | | 14| |* Strong Mars in svāṁśa will make the native happy to fight, one who works with fire (transformation of things through heat), and a rasavādī (one who works with alchemical medicine[140]). Fire related work and hobbies like glass blowing, metallurgy *(dhāturvādī)*, or welding. Engineering (of the type related to the conjunct planets or signs), electrical work (especially if associated with Ketu), Tai Chi, martial arts, use of arms, especially the spear *(kauntāyudh)*, knowledgable about warfare, analytical, strong logic (follower of nyāya philosophy), acupuncture, surgery
Mercury	बुधे बलयुते स्वांशे कलाशिल्पविचक्षनः । वाणिज्यकुशलश्चापि बुद्धिविद्यासमन्वितः ॥ १५ ॥ *budhe balayute svāṁśe kalāśilpavicakṣanaḥ |* *vāṇijyakuśalaścāpi buddhividyāsamanvitaḥ | | 15| |* Strong Mercury in svāṁśa will be skilled in the arts, be a sculptor, be clear-sighted, having good discernment *(vicakṣana)*, a merchant or businessman, and associated with science and learning. Product design, giving form to ideas, pottery and handicrafts *(śilpa)*, merchant *(vaṇija)*, business skill, retail work, salesman, if the native is spiritual Mercury can also make one an ascetic of high order *(paramahaṁsa)*, hatha yoga, body-related sciences like massage, writing (generally small articles or technical writing), mīmāṁsaka-investigator/examiner, legal knowledge, lawyers, good at debate, multiple opinions, waivering focus

[140] In that time, Rasa-Śāstra (alchemical medicine) was made through heating various metals and minerals for long periods of time in ovens that were very hot. This could now be someone working in a laboratory/factory with various chemical reactions taking place. All indications must be analyzed within a modern context (deśa, kāla, pātra).

Graha	Skills and Abilities
Jupiter	सुकर्मा ज्ञाननिष्ठश्च वेदवित् स्वांशगे गुरौ । *sukarmā jñānaniṣṭhaśca vedavit svāṁśage gurau* । Jupiter in svāṁśa will show one who does good works (*su-karma*), possessing higher knowledge/understanding (*jñāna*), and one who is knowledgable in Vedas. Steady focus, broad knowledge, well-read, interested in spiritual literature, knowledge of religious rituals, priests, conjunct the Moon the native is an author *(grantha-karta)* and conversant in all areas of knowledge *(sarva-vidyā-viśārada)*, Jupiter gives broad knowledge but not good at speaking in assemblies *(na vāgmī ca sabhādiṣu)*, knowledge of correct expression and grammar *(śabdajñana)* and excelling in Vedas and vedānta *(viśeṣeṇa-vedavedāntavit)*
Venus	शुक्रे शतेन्द्रियः कामी राजकीतो भवेन्नरः ॥ १६ ॥ *śukre śatendriyaḥ kāmī rājakīto bhavennaraḥ* ।। *16*।। Venus will make one śatendriya (having a hundred senses[141]), sensual/passionate, and having royal/political position. Passionate person in all activities, Venus can make one patriotic- passionate about their country, political *(rājakīya)*, beaurocrats, diplomacy, diplomats, art, painting, modern dance, good at finding loopholes in the law, chemistry, eloquent speech *(kavirvāgmin)*, knowledge of poetry *(kāvyajñana)*, author of smaller books if with Moon *(kiñcidūna-grantha-kara)*
Saturn	शनौ स्वांशगते जातः स्वकुलोचितकर्मकृत् । *śanau svāṁśagate jātaḥ svakulocitakarmakṛt* । Saturn going to the svāṁśa makes a person who practices the profession of their family/tribe/community (*kula*). [Jaimini adds that Śani is one who can get success in whatever line of work he performs (*prasiddha-karmajivaḥ*).] Traditional work, work in the profession of one's family, a jack of all trades, Saturn in navāṁśa lagna gives stage fright or individual is seen as a simpleton *(bāla)* in an assembly, Saturn in the navāṁśa fifth house gives one skills in archery *(dhānuṣka)* or the ability to be steady and pierce things
Rāhu	राहौ चौरश्च धनुष्को जातो वा लोहयन्त्रकृत् ॥ १७ ॥ विषवैद्योऽथवा विप्र जायते नाऽत्र संशयः । *rāhau cauraśca dhanuṣko jāto vā lohayantrakṛt* ।। *17*।। *viṣavaidyo'thavā vipra jāyate nā'tra saṁśayaḥ* । Rāhu will make one a thief/dishonest/an unfair dealer, a bowman[142], or a metal worker (as one who works on machines), or a doctor working with poisons. Metal smithing, jewelry making, manufacturing *(loha-yantri)*, factory work, heavy machinery, physics, handles poisons and chemicals, modern medicine, curing poisons if conjunct Gulika with beneficial aspect *(viṣavaidya)*, poisoning others if with Gulika and malefic aspect *(viṣārdita)*, Rāhu with Jupiter will show sound engineering or working with modern sound equipment

[141] Interested in perfumes, essential oils, beautiful clothes, good tasting foods, pleasing all their senses, etc.

[142] One using a bow and arrow to hunt; so this could also be translated as a hunter or one who eats meat or catches their own food, etc., and the various implications and jobs that go along with this. At the level of warfare, Saturn and Rāhu are archers, Mars is a lancer, and Sun is a swords-man- this would translate relative to various modern positions in the armed forces.

Graha	Skills and Abilities
Ketu	व्यवहारी गजादीनां केतौ चौरश्च जायते ॥ १८ ॥ *vyavahārī gajādīnāṁ ketau cauraśca jāyate* ǀǀ 18ǀǀ Ketu makes one vyavahārī (one who does trade, trafficing, mercantile transactions, legal procedures, contracts, litigation, or administration of justice), or one who works with elephants (modes of large/mass transportation), or a theif (one who makes things dissapear). Knowledge of mathamatics *(gaṇitajñāna)*, proficience in astrology *(jyotiḥ-śāstra-viśārada)*, works with small machines, watch maker *(ghaṭikā-yantri-kāraka)*, computers, computer languages, quantum physics, non-linear thought, intuition, if Ketu is conjunct Jupiter it gives the teachings of a tradition/lineage *(sampradāya-saṁsiddhi)*

There are also certain skills that come through the combination of certain planets. If Rāhu and Sun are conjunct in the svāṁśa there is fear of snakes. If a malefic aspects this the native will die of snake bite, if a benefic aspects this they will be a doctor who has the ability to heal people from poisons. If Mars has sambandha with the Rāhu and Sun combination the person may burn their house down, or others houses, or work in a job like a trash incinerator (verses 19-20). Venus (ruler of the water element) aspecting such a combination can make a fireman. In this way, Parāśara has given us some small indications of certain planetary combinations. Other combinations are to be discerned in a similar way.

Parāśara uses the term *svāṁśa* for each of these significations. Sometimes he says kārakāṁśa (KK), referring to the ātmakāraka in the Navāṁśā, but more so he says svāṁśa (even though the present *Sharma* and *Santhanam* translations don't show this). An understanding of the term svāṁśa is very important, *sva* (self) *aṁśa* (division). It is the division representing one's self. The fact is that we are multi-dimensional beings, and there are many facets to what we call ourselves.

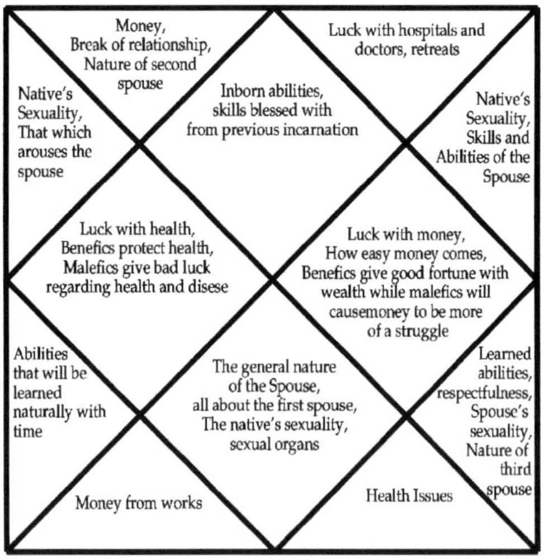

The sage Parāśara in the *Kārakāṁśa-Phala-Adyāya* is utilizing the concept of svāṁśa to mean all the aspects of the self starting with the kārakāṁśā and including the navāṁśa lagna and the ārūḍha lagna. When The Moon is in the fifth house from the kārakāṁśa the native has a soul desire to sing. When Moon is fifth from the navāṁśa lagna the native has the inherent ability to sing. When the Moon is in the fifth house from the ārūḍha lagna the native is seen by others as being good at singing. The combinations from kārakāṁśa will show the soul's desire. The combinations from navāṁśa lagna will show one's abilities, while the combinations from lagna and ārūḍha lagna will show the actual manifestation in the world.

The ability to deepen a reading of the chart by differentiating these factors is very important. For example, there was a chart where the native was confused about their spiritual path and sexuality. From the KK there were combinations to make them a celibate, but from the navāṁśa lagna, lagna, and ārūḍha lagna this combinations were contridicted by some very sexual combinations. The native was confused because they felt celibacy was th path for them and weren't able to came to terms with what their body and mind was desiring. Unless such things line up, they will not be successful. I was able to explain the soul level of celibacy, and the state of mind that can achieve this even will living in the world of enjoyment. He was able to except his sexuality in a new light and not have the confusion he felt before. In this way, these combinations and all others should be seen from the svāṁśa, the various aspects that represent who we are.

Rectification

The navāṁśa changes approximately every fifteen minutes. There is tremendous variability of birth time determination, whether it is based on the head out of the womb, the entire body out of the womb, the first cry, or the time the umbilical cord is cut, etc will create a great variability. Since there is such specific detail given in the varga charts, they can be used to *rectify* the time; to adjust the time the doctor gave in order to find the correct astronomical moment of birth which gives correct results through the birth chart.

For example, if the native is a singer and the Moon is in the twelfth house right next to the first but in a place that indicates bad singing we can tell the time may be slightly off. If by moving the time by a few minutes we can rectify the Moon to be in lagna which correctly fits the natives abilities, then w have rectifies the navāṁśa which would mean the time is correct up to fifteen minutes. As the varga charts increase, the time change goes down, to the point of 30 seconds. In this way the birth time can be rectified down to the exact half minute of birth. Most of the time the rectification process starts in the navāṁśa.

Practice Exercises:

4. Read the *Kārakāṁśa-Phala-Adhyāya* (chapter 33/35) in Bṛhat Parāśara Horā Śāstra. Let the information go into the subconscious mind, at the next course level we will be studying this chapter in great depth. Analyze your own navāṁśa and practice determining the results of the different planets

III. Kalatra: Spouse

The navāṁśa shows all aspects of spouse. The spouse is the one with which we fulfill our dharma-mārga (path of duty) in the world. A monk is fulfilling the mokṣa-marga (path of spirituality) for the world. To sustain dharma in the world, one takes on the householder stage of life, marries and has a family. Whether one gets a good or evil spouse is the blessing or curses of our fortune, seen in the navāṁśa.

The seventh house of the navāṁśa becomes the lagna for the spouse. All their qualities and skill can be seen here in the same way that they are seen from the navāṁśa lagna for the native. The seventh will show the inherent nature of the spouse, the 11th house (5th from the 7th) will show the abilities the spouse gains with some practice, and the third house (9th from the 7th) will show the abilities the spouse learns from a teacher. This will show you what the native is attracted to in general.

When Parāśara speaks of the navāṁśa seventh he talks about the qualities of the spouse. For example, he says that Jupiter and Moon in the navāṁśa seventh make the spouse extremely beautiful, Venus in the seventh will make the spouse sensual, Mercury will make the spouse versed in the fine arts, the Sun will make the spouse focus on domestic activities only, Saturn will make the spouse, older, or traditional, or sickly, and Rāhu will indicate one marries a widow/er. The planets in the 7th house will indicate the characteristics of the natives spouse.

The first spouse is seen from the seventh house, but how can you tell the difference between the qualities of the first spouse and the next one, and if there are three marriages how can one tell about the qualities of that spouse. They will all be different in some ways. The first spouse is seen from the seventh, the second spouse is seen from the eighth house from that which is the second. So the second house shows the second spouse. The third spouse is eighth from that which is the ninth house, and the fourth spouse would again be eight more houses, making the fourth spouse seen from the fourth house and its trines. So if Venus is in the D-9 seventh and Mercury in the second, and Rāhu in the ninth, the first spouse will be sensual, the second will be skilled in fine arts, a writer, or yogi, and the third spouse will be a widow.

Because the second house is the first change of relationship it will show the nature of fidelity of the native in general. Parāśara says that if Venus and Mars associate with the second house here, the native will be unfaithful *(pāradārika)*. And if they both associate this will be a lifelong habit[143]. The second is the eighth from the seventh which makes it how the first relationship ends or suffers. Venus and Mars indicate other relationships. Both of them there/aspecting will insure this. Ketu placed there will cancel this while Rāhu will make it an extreme and with prostitutes and immoral activities. Sambandha is when the sign in the D-9 second house is ruled by Mars and Venus is there, or ruled by Venus and Mars is there. Also, Mars may be placed there and aspected by Venus, or some such combination. Do not confuse the second house rules with the kāma trine rules, as the planets will have different effects on sexuality in these different places.

[143] Bṛhat Parāśara Horā Śāstra, Kārakāṁśa-Phala-Adhyāya, v.30-31

Sexuality

The kāraka for sexuality is Venus, which should be examined in the Rāśi and the navāṁśa first. If Venus is in sattvic signs (ruled by Sun, Moon, or Jupiter) then the sexuality will be pure and with love. If Venus is in a rajasic sign, the sexuality will be a lover for the purpose of sharing activities and pleasure and there may be a neediness in the relationship. Venus in a tamasic sign will show the view of a partner as a sexual object or for sustenance. The guṇa of planets associated with Venus will modify this.

As the navāṁśa works in trines, the kāma trines show sexuality. The third house relates to mithuna (copulation) and therefore we see the 3rd house and its trines (3, 7, 11) for analyzing about sexuality. The kāma trines from the lagna show your sexuality. The partner is represented by the seventh house and the third house from that is the ninth house. The ninth and its trines are the kāma houses for the partner (9, 1, 5). In this way, the partner's sexuality is part of one's dharma.

The seventh house is the fifth from the third and shows the mind regarding sexuality. Planets in the seventh will therefore indicate our sexuality. These types of techniques are good to learn after some discretion is learned about what to say and what not to say when looking at a chart with an individual.

When a slow moving planet such as Saturn is placed in the seventh house then a person takes a long time to be aroused. When a fast moving planet such as the Moon is placed in the navāṁśa seventh house the individual is easily aroused and enjoys daily sexual activity. Other combinations can show a person that is ready to have sex any time with little discrimination.

Jupiter in the trines to the seventh house will create a very dharmic sexuality, which will make the person keep their virginity till later in life, as well as keep them faithful and chaste. At the opposite side of the spectrum, when Rāhu associates with the kāma trines sorrow and shock in the realm of sexuality are created. It is good for sex but not good for the intentions behind it. A benefic Rāhu will be a "player", the native will want just sex but will dress it up nice. While when Rāhu is weak and under malefic association it will significate situations like rape. These types of indications are seen in the kāma trines of the navāṁśa.

The seventh house relates to the sexual organs, size, shape, taste, etc. For example, Jātaka Tattva says that if the seventh lord *(madeśa)* is associated with a malefic *(sapāpa)* then the woman *(strī)* will have a long *(dirgha)* vulva *(bhagā)*. The ślokas for men and women relate as the same tissue differentiates into the male and female sexual organs. The labia majora relate to the scrotum, the labia minora relate to the shaft skin of the penis, the hood of the clitoris relates to the foreskin and the clitoris relates to the glans penis (head). So when a śloka says that when the D-9 seventh house is ruled by Leo there is a large hood on the clitoris, this would also refer to a large foreskin. Taste will also remain the same for male and female. This may seem like a bit too much information for some but having an understanding of this is needed when there are sexual problems and can sometimes be an easy way to rectify a chart. Since this is a physical situation, it can be a clear yes or no when rectifying.

The third house relates to the act of sex, the general virility, and longevity. It is also the house from which we will be able to attract the spouse (on a sexual level). If Jupiter is there, it is the native's courtesy, dharma and wisdom that attracts the spouse. If Mars is there, it is the native's forcefulness, if Mercury is there it is the natives skills or youthfulness that attract the spouse. In this way the third house can be seen for helping the native be more attractive to their spouse.

Homosexuality is seen from the neuter planets Mercury and Saturn and the signs they own (Gemini, Virgo, Capricorn and Aquarius). First there must be indications in the Rāśi chart for homosexuality before D-9 is consulted. In the navāṁṣa, if Mercury is in a Saturn sign or Saturn is in a Mercury sign in one of the kāma trines, this will indicate bi-sexuality, or temporary periods of homosexuality. If there is a strong sambandha like parivartana yoga with Mercury and Saturn in a kāma trines this will show homosexuality. These type of combinations become very helpful in rectification as well as relationship counseling and compatibility.

Once I was traveling with my Jyotiṣa Guru and we were at a Boston Astrology Conference. An older Indian man brought my Guru his daughter's chart to ask about her marriage and complained that she wasn't interested in getting married. In her chart was a parivartana yoga with Saturn and Mercury connected to the seventh house, she was also a student at a university known for its lesbian population. She would never have a straight marriage, a tough one to tell a traditional Indian Brahmin about his daughter.

The primary attributes about an individual's sexuality are seen in the navāṁśa- positive and negative. This type of information needs maturity and discretion to be discussed with a client, but is necessary for a full understanding of the individual and their compatibility in relationships.

Daśāṁśa (D-10): Profession and Career

The daśāṁśa is the magnifying glass to get intricate details on the tenth house and its significations. The tenth house in the Rāśi shows your career karma being positive or negative and general indications, while the daśāṁśa will show the specifics of profession, changing of jobs, interaction with employers and employees, and the times and levels of rise in career.

It is important to integrate this information with the Rāśi chart. As a mechanic takes into account the type of car he is working on before he even looks at the engine of a car. We must take into account the individual's career karma indicated in the Rāśi chart first and then analyze the information gained in the daśāṁśa through the filter of these indications.

See the tenth lord of the Rāśi chart first. If it is placed in the second house there may be work with the family business (if it is Saturn) or the food industry (if it is Moon), or consulting (Venus), etc. The placement will give very general indications of how the person is applying themselves toward career. The tenth lord should also be strong and well placed in the navāṁśa for full achievement potential.

Then analyse the eleventh house from the ārūḍha lagna. This will show what type of people the person will make gains through. If Saturn is positioned there the person will gain through old or sick people. If Moon is there the person will gain through women, especially of the mothering age. Then understand the skills and abilities indicated by the navāṁśa (one can also fine tune that in the dreṣkāṇa). The Amātyakāraka and any planet conjoined it in the Rāśi will also color the direction of career.

The tenth house from the Moon will show social success with career and preferences for work. While the tenth from the navāṁśa lagna will show luck with money or ease of earning potential. The relationship (bhāva sambandha) between the Dārākāraka and the Ātmakāraka in the Rāśi will show the soul's relationship to money, while the relationship of the AL and A7 will show the social relationship with money (these are finer details to just take note of). With these components, a mindset related to work is understood and then the D-10 is analyzed.

1. Tenth house and tenth lord of the Rāśi
2. Eleventh from AL in the Rāśi chart
3. Skills and abilities in the Navāṁśa
4. Daśāṁśa
    A. Kāraka planet: Mercury, Sun, Jupiter, Saturn
    B. Kāraka-bhāva: tenth house and houses from there
    C. Daśāṁśa Lagna and lagna lord
    D. Rāśi tenth house lord in daśāṁśa

A. Kārakas Planets

Kārakas planets for the daśāṁśa are the kāraka planets of the tenth house. Mercury shows the application of skills which is most important in the work place; the signs of Mercury become important for the way a person likes to express their skills. Mercury also represents business, money (cash), banks and trade. Saturn shows the ability to do hard work or labor and put in the extra effort to accomplish the goals. Jupiter shows the resources and blessings of knowledge in work and represents intellectual professions. The Sun shows respect, name, and the ability to rise to power as well as government influence in one's work. The analysis of the placement and strength of these planets in the D-10 will give more detailed indications of their status in career.

B. Kāraka-Bhāva

The tenth (Sun), sixth (Saturn) and seventh (Mercury) houses are the most important houses for understanding a person's career. The **first house** of any divisional chart represents the native themselves in that specific area of life. The daśāṁśa first house shows the native in the work place. The first house has sukhārgalā to the tenth and shows one's happiness in career. Malefics or weak planets in the first house create hard times from one's work while benefics or strong planets give happiness from career. The **fifth house** of the daśāṁśa shows subordinates (one's children at work) and if its lord is well placed then they are beneficial to the native. If the lord of the fifth is not well placed there may be problems with subordinates. If the fifth house is strong then one's knowledge of work is more and there are also lots of subordinates making one have more power and authority. The **ninth house** is your superiors or more specifically the boss. Benefics or strong planets there show learning and good mentoring from the boss while malefics or weak planets will give problems from the boss or superiors. If the ninth lord is in the eighth house there will be problems with the boss, while if the ninth lord is in the ninth one will get good guidance from the boss. If the daśāṁśa lagna is in the ninth house, the native will want to be their own boss.

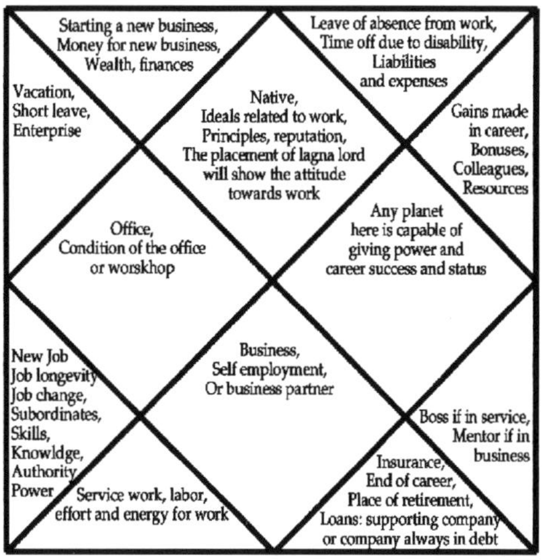

The **sixth house** shows servants or staff, while the fifth house shows people under you who will one day replace your position. The fifth relates to the assistant executive under a senior executive while the sixth is the administrator, janitor, or door security who will not replace a senior executive job from their current position. The sixth lord itself can show business enemies or business competition.

The important daśāṁśa aspect of the sixth house is that it shows service professions while the **seventh house** shows business. Whichever house has more planets or is stronger will determine the way the person works. If there are planets in both houses, then the person may work for others before entering their own business, or it may change depending on the daśā. If there are malefics in the seventh or the lord is weak, it can indicate problems from business partners and even problems in business, indicating that service may be a better choice or a remedy should be done for that planet. Saturn is the kāraka for the sixth house of service and Mercury is the kāraka for the seventh house of business. Their strength should also be understood- one should follow their strengths for success to be achieved. The seventh lord of the daśāṁśa will also relate to business activity as the sixth lord will also relate to service. If one of these house lords is placed in the daśāṁśa tenth house or lagna it will give a leaning to their particular direction.

Mars is maraṇa-kāraka-sthāna in the seventh house and will show problems having partners in business. Venus represents the private sector of business and is maraṇa-kāraka-sthāna in the sixth house of service. The house of maraṇa-kāraka-sthāna planets will show suffering in that area of one's career or company.

The **fourth house** is the office and planets there will show the attributes of the place work is performed. The strength of the house will show the size and status of the office. Remedies to planets in the fourth can be done in the office as part of placement or decor. If the Moon or Venus is in the fourth house then the office will be beneficial if it is near a body of water, or with water visible out the window. If this is not possible then using decoration such as a water fountain for the Moon or other comforts/art for Venus can be installed in the office. The fourth lord in the tenth or tenth lord in the fourth can show working from one's home or living at work. The fourth lord also represents the administrative assistant who makes the office run as they are a part of the office's functioning existence.

The **eighth house** shows loans which can support business (2nd from 7th) and career (11th from 10th) if the planets are beneficial and the lord of the house is strong. If there are afflictions to the house and malefic placements, then there may be debts that continue to grow. The eighth lord shows insurance claims and other troublesome indications. For service work the eighth house shows the ending of a job or unemployment. The fifth house is the transitioning of a job or company as it shows either promotion with benefics/ strong planets or being fired/demoted if malefics or weak planets are placed there. In this way, planets in the fifth house should be strengthened for career progress. The second house shows starting of a new job or resources beginning a new company, the eighth is loss of job or company failure while the fifth is transition within the job or the career. For a company the loan (energy) of the eighth house generally needs to become resources of the second house in order to start.

Planets in the **twelfth house** can show inabilities related to the significations of the planet and thereby things that will cause losses or mistakes related to those significations. The twelfth house shows time off of work- generally negatively caused by things such as injuries or loss of job due to the company cutting expenses. The third house shows short leaves of absence or vacations, or travelling from the office, which is beneficial time off. The karmeśa (tenth lord from the Rāśi) or the daśāṁśa lagneśa in the twelfth house can show better opportunities working abroad. To a business the twelfth house also relates to sales and marketing- the expenses on advertising as well as giving away free samples. Benefics here will show the company will benefit from giving free samples or trials of their products.

Planets placed in odd signs in the daśāṁśa show a strong self focus is needed to succeed in work while planets placed in even signs show a focus on social duty or dharma. Different daśā will show shifts in the individual's focus and purpose of work. In this way the houses and planets placed throughout the D-10 should be considered.

C. Daśāṁśa Lagna and Lagna Lord

The daśāṁśa Lagna itself will show the native and the daśāṁśa lagna lord will show their ideals and attitudes related to career. Planets in lagna will modify attitudes and ideals. The strength of the lagna lord will show how much energy and to what level the individual wants to rise in career and to what level they have standards about what work they will perform and how it is performed. Remember that nīca planets are good for money in the D-10. If a planet is in an enemy's sign, or great enemy's sign it will not do well. But if it is completely debilitated it will make lots of money, though the planet will not show strong abilities related to its significations.

House lord placements in the daśāṁśa lagna will have a large influence on career. The daśāṁśa fourth lord in the lagna will show the native is always at the office or has the office on their mind. The daśāṁśa fifth lord in the lagna will show the individual is always helping subordinates if the planet is benefic or bothered by subordinates if it is malefic or weak. The daśāṁśa ninth lord in lagna shows the native is always interacting or troubled by the boss. In this way the interaction of house lords in the daśāṁśa becomes important to show the work related area of life.

The placement of the lagna lord of the D-10 will reveal the nature of how one works. If it is in the ninth house, the person will be their own boss, if it is in the third house, the person will always be taking vacations or have a job that involves short journeys. The house lords in lagna will 'chase' the native while the placement of the daśāṁśa lagna lord will be what the native is 'chasing'.

D. Rāśi tenth house lord in Daśāṁśa

The Rāśi tenth lord in the daśāṁśa is called the *karmeśa*. It shows how consciousness is applied to work. The house placement of the karmeśa is important. The natural significations of the houses and their daśāṁśa significations will both be applicable to this planet. The significations of the karmeśa and the yogas created by planets it joins will influence the choice of career. The strength of the karmeśa in the daśāṁśa can indicate the ease of rise in career- exaltation and digbala become important to show success over obstacles.

E. Svargāṁśa

The D-10 is also called the Svargāṁśa or the division of the realm of heaven (Svarga). This is the heaven where the various archetypal gods are situated. It is the heaven that is spoken of by religions as the place you go where the streets are paved with gold, and you see all your old friends and you get to enjoy yourself. Svarga is the heavenly realm of enjoyment, where Indra, the king of gods, sits on a throne. It is not the highest heaven sought after by yogis, but an intermediary realm where one enjoys there good karma before being reborn on earth. In this way it shows that which gives us power and rewards that we will be able to enjoy on a material level.

The deities of the daśāṁśa are the lords of the directions who are called the dikpāla-literally the 'direction protecters'. They are the administrators of the directions which relate to a specific type of work. The ten Mahāvidyā also relate to the ten directions and have the ability to bring the knowledge of that direction so that the work *(karma)* can be done in the right way. The Mahāvidyā will give the right knowledge and the dikpāla will give the right utililzation of the knowledge while the śakti of the direction will give the fruits of that direction/type of work.

Dik	Deity	Mantra		Remedy
East	Indra	ॐ लं इन्द्राय नमः	auṁ lam indrāya namaḥ	Worship Iṣṭa-devatā
SE	Agni	ॐ रं अग्नये नमः	auṁ ram agnaye namaḥ	Mṛtyunjaya-Homa
South	Yama	ॐ मं यमाय नमः	auṁ maṁ yamāya namaḥ	Propitiation of ancestors (pitṛ)
SW	Nirriti	ॐ क्षं नैर्त्तये नमः	auṁ kṣaṁ nairttaye namaḥ	Brahma-Rakṣasa Śānti
West	Varuṇa	ॐ वं वरुणाय नमः	auṁ vaṁ varuṇāya namaḥ	Rudra-Abhiṣeka
NW	Vāyu	ॐ यं वायवे नमः	auṁ yaṁ vāyave namaḥ	Orament, decoration, etc
North	Kubera	ॐ शं सोमाय नमः	auṁ śaṁ somāya namaḥ	Worship on birthday auṁ viṣṇave namaḥ
NE	Iśana	ॐ हं ईशानाय नमः	auṁ ham īśānāya namaḥ	Bhajan and scriptures auṁ namaḥ śivāya
Down	Brahma	ॐ अं ब्रह्मने नमः	auṁ aṁ brahmane namaḥ	
Up	Ananta	ॐ ह्रीं अनन्ताय नमः	auṁ hrīm anantāya namaḥ	

Pandit Sanjay Rath teaches that if an individual is suffering career problems caused by a particular antardaśā lord then the deity ruling that planet in the daśāṁśa can be propitiated. For example, if the career is fine and during a Mercury antardaśā there starts to be problems with the boss and it is noticed that Mercury is in an enemy's sign in the ninth house. One can see that the cause of the problem relates to the D-10. In this case, the divisional deity may be used as a remedy.

Saptāṁśa (D-7): Children

The saptāṁśa is the chart used to see the individual nature of one's children. It is said to also reveal other creative endeavors as well as show certain animal instinctual lusts in a person. For this study, we will focus on children specifically in relation to determining the sex of the child. It is easiest to apply these rules of determining male and female in this chart and the rules can be applied in all other areas, like seeing whether the boss is male or female, see whether the D-3 is indicating brothers or sisters, etc.

Before utilizing the D-7 analyze results indicated by the natal chart. See the fifth house for male charts and the ninth house for female charts (according to standard rules of Śrī Jātaka-female horoscopy). Are these houses beneficial in the chart? Is the A5 conjunct benefics, or malefics (Saturn the worst, then Rāhu)? Malefics will cause delay or no children at all. After understanding these indications then proceed to the D-7.

The kāraka planet for the saptāṁśā is Jupiter for children. The Moon also plays a crucial role related to sustenance of a pregnancy to nurturing of the children after birth. Even though the division is into seven related to the seventh house (where children are made), the kāraka-bhāva is the fifth house. The lagneśa will show the ideals related to raising and caring for children.

Rule: If the lagna is odd sign, read the chart zodiacal, if it is an even sign read the chart anti-zodiacal.

Exception: *Taurus and Leo because they variate from the vimsa/sama pada nature related to odd and even signs. So Taurus although even will go zodiacal, and Leo even though odd will go anti-zodiacal.*

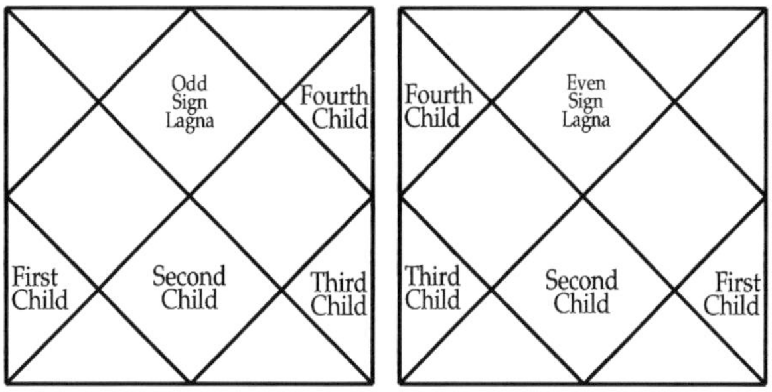

The first child (zodiacally) is seen from the fifth house, then the third from the fifth house (the seventh) will show the sibling to the first child. The third house from the seventh (ninth) will show the next child, and so on. The children will continue coming until a malefic situation or the nodal axis. Jupiter is the main kāraka for the D-7 and Rāhu is its worst enemy. The nodal axis will end more children unless there is a strong enough Jupiter (or beneficial aspect) to jump the nodes.

The strength of each of these houses will show whether they produce a child or will indicate why another child was not born. Abortions/miscarriages are also indicated in the same houses. If there is an indication for an abortion in the fifth house of an odd sign lagna chart, then the first child was aborted. The next child will be seen from the third house from there (the seventh) even if there is no physical child with the parents. In this way, the life of an unborn fetus is seen in the vedic charts, yet its abortion is also seen due to the shared karma of the mother and the child.

Sun	M
Moon	F
Mars	M
Mercury	F/M
Jupiter	M
Venus	F
Saturn	F/M
Rāhu	M
Ketu	F
Exalted	M
Debilitated	F

An animate being is seen by a planet while a sign shows the place and situation. The actual child is shown by a planet, the lord of the 5th, 7th, 9th etc shows the child respective[144]. The lord of the fifth house (for an odd sign lagna) will be the lagna for interpreting the sex, characteristics, personality, career, etc., of the first child. If the fifth lord is in the second house then the chart is read from there. The second becomes the first and whatever signs and planet that lord this will indicate the sex and character of the native. A female planet in a female sign will indicate a female child. A male planet in a male sign will indicate a male child. Neuter planets (Mercury and Saturn) will give results based upon the sign they are placed in. Mixed indications need to be studied more deeply to see what sign/planet is giving the stronger influence. Then there are a few exceptions that need to be remembered.

M	M	F	F
F			M
F			M
M	F	M	F

Exceptions:

1. Parivartana in lagna reverses all sexes in the D-7
2. Parivartana in specific house reverses the sex of the child
3. twins are possible for Gemini, Virgo, and Scorpio
4. Many planets with Moon aspect will show a split personality
5. If the significations are Male, but there is a strong Female influence, then the child may be a feminine male, etc.

Other notes:

The planet indicating the lagna for the child shows can be seen relative to the planet significating the lagna of the other siblings. You can see their relationship to each other with bhāva sambandha principles (if in kendras they work effectively with each other, 6-8 they quarrel, etc).

[144] If lord has already been used, occupation of the house (5/7/9/etc) can be used.

Horā Chart (D-2)

The **Parāśara Horā** is only two signs, Leo and Cancer, ruled by the Sun and the Moon. The Sun horās shows resources, wealth, and *supply*. The Moon horās show the use of resources, *demand*, and sustenance. Jupiter, Sun and Mars do well in Sun horās. Moon, Venus, and Saturn do well in the Moon horās. Mercury is adaptable and can do well in any area of business, thereby good in both horās. The Parāśara D-2 utilizes only the Sun and Moon (showing wealth and prosperity) while the D-30 has no Sun and Moon, only the five tattva (elements) related planets and it shows destruction and suffering.

The **Parivṛtti-traya Horā** is a cyclical division, meaning that the aṁśas are divided into the regular order of the zodiac. This is used to define one's family perception and how you relate to your family or those close to you that are considered family. The second house is called kuṭumba by Parāśara, which means family, or household and can refer to those you are living with in the confines of your home.

The **Kaśināth Horā** is calculated using the day and night strong signs. The first half of the sign will become the sign itself if it is a day strong planet and will be the opposite male/female sign if it is a night strong planet. This chart will show the flow of wealth. The lagna shows the one who is receiving wealth. In this chart the special ascendant called the Horā Lagna is utilized to see from whom and where the native is acquiring the wealth in their life.

Kaśinath Horā	Sun	Moon
Aries	Scorpio	Aries
Taurus	Libra	Taurus
Gemini	Virgo	Gemini
Cancer	Leo	Cancer
Leo	Leo	Cancer
Virgo	Virgo	Gemini
Libra	Libra	Taurus
Scorpio	Scorpio	Aries
Sagittarius	Pisces	Sagittarius
Capricorn	Aquarius	Capricorn
Aquarius	Aquarius	Capricorn
Pisces	Pisces	Sagittarius

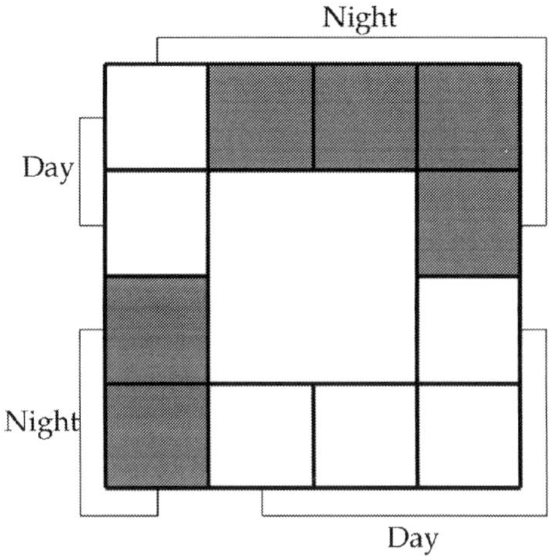

Caturaṁśa (D-4)

The caturaṁśa (also called the Turyāṁśa) shows lands and properties. Vehicles are in the D-16, which is 12 X 1 + 4, meaning it will also show the results of the fourth house. The D-4 comes into use in the 16 varga arrangement (for kings) and thereby indicates the use for those who are actually home owners or for property that is actually owned by the individual. It can be used by those that are renting or leasing but the main aspecting seen in the chart will not be utilized.

Parāśara states that the D-4 shows one's bhāgya, or fortune. There are two main charts used to see bhāgya (or blessings); the D-9 and the D-4. There are two main things that will change your overall karma in life, the two most important things that need a good Muhūrta to begin. The first is the wedding day where you marry your spouse and take on the burdens of their karma for better or worse. The second is the day you purchase a home and you marry your fortune to the Vāstu (Feng Shui) of the property. This property will fully change your fate for better or worse depending on the condition of the energetic arrangement of the land to make you more prosperous and healthy, or cause all sorts of problems. In this way, bhāgya (fortune or luck) is seen from these charts.

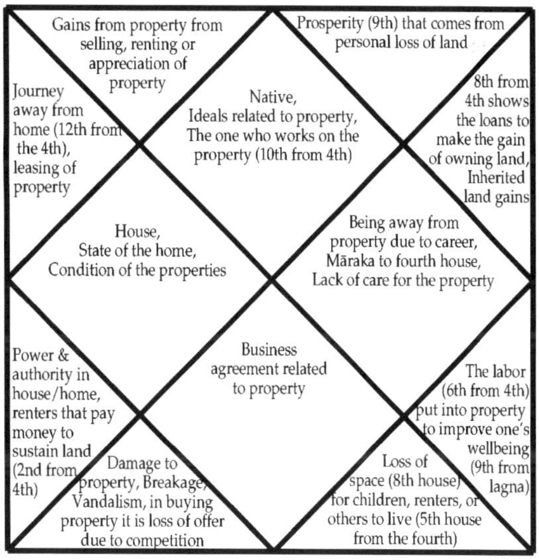

The kāraka planets for the D-4 are Mars for land *(bhūmi)*, Ketu for buildings *(gṛha)* and the Moon for personal home situation. Mars is the natural state of the earth, while Ketu is like Mars but unnatural, as the mud being baked into a brick. Saturn and Rāhu cause problems in most area of this chart. The kāraka-bhāva is the fourth house and all houses are understood from there.

Pañcāṁśa (D-5) and Ṣaṣṭhāṁśa (D-6)

The D-5 and D-6 are not part of the sixteen vargas used by Parāśara, they are given by Jaimini and other authors. The D-5 is used for the political power and fame related to the fifth house. It is connected to the energy of the natural sign of the fifth house, Leo. The natural rules of varga interpretation are applied. It is used only for those in very powerful positions with regards to conditions of the state of their power; acquiring, losing, and the type of power and authority. Those who have an affect on the lives of hundreds of people because of their position need to use the pañcāṁśa. The kāraka planet is the Sun and the kāraka-bhāva is the fifth house.

There are two uses for the ṣaṣṭhāṁśa (D-6), one for litigation and battles with enemies, the other for disease pathology. Large scale war between countries is seen in the rudrāṁśa (D-11). The ṣaṣṭhāṁśa shows smaller situations primarily seen as legal battles in the modern world. For litigation, the lagna and its trines represent the individual and their problems. The sixth house and its trines represent the opposition. In order to be successful in litigation one should take on such battles during times favorable to the ṣaṣṭhāṁśa lagna and while the ṣaṣṭhāṁśa lagna lord is strong. Mars is the kāraka for the opponent/competition/enemy. Jupiter is the kāraka for the individual's lawyer or counsel.

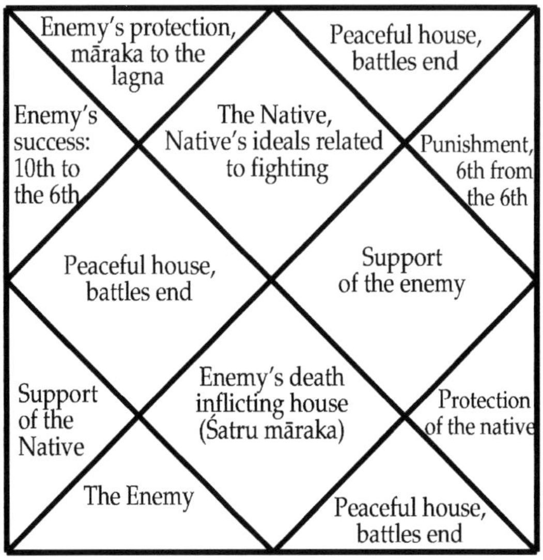

Saturn is the kāraka for the D-6 representing both enemies and disease. In the ṣaṣṭhāṁśa for disease, the chart is actually a division of the drekkāṇa. Each drekkāṇa (of 10°) is split into two parts of 5° each called *kaulakas*.

The rāśī chakra shows a general overall map of the entire body. The drekkāṇa fine tunes the portion or area of the body and the kaulaka determines the internal or external suffering of the problem to the body. If there is a problem indicated by the on the head, the kaulaka will determine whether this will be on the hair (external) or on the brain (internal). In this way, the D-6 becomes very important for medical astrology.

Dvādaṣāṁśa (D-12): Parents

The dvādaṣāṁśa (dva-two, daśā -ten, aṁśa-division) which is the twelfth divisional chart was called the dodecatemoria by the Greeks. It is also called the sūryāṁśa, the division of the Sun (or twelve solar months) and relates to your ancestral karma. Parāśara says the D-12 relates to *Pitṛ* which are means ancestors or parents. The twelfth house relates to the debts we owe our ancestors and the debt we owe our parents for birthing and raising us. The dvādaṣāṁśa will give finer details on the nature and situation of the Mother and the Father.

Each sign is composed of 2.5 degrees which creates 144 dvādaśāṁśas. The kāraka planets are the Sun and the Moon. The kāraka bhāvas are the fourth and the ninth house. The state of these planets will show the situation with the quality of time the native had with their parents. If the Sun is in the twelfth and a malefic is in the ninth the native will not have spent the time needed with the father. As the parents are living beings, the lord (graha) of the kāraka bhāva is utilized to read about the nature, character and situation of the parent. The condition of the kāraka bhāva from the lagna will show the parents relationship with the native, while information on the parent is seen using the kāraka bhāva lord as the ascendant. Timing of all events relative to the parents can be done with this chart including sickness and death of the parents and grandparents.

The varga deities of the planets in the D-12 will also have a strong influence on the beneficial or negative indications of the positions. The deities are Ganeśa (lord of removing obstacles), Aśvinī Kumāras (divine healers), Yama (lord of death) and Sarpa (snakes). Gaṇeśa and the Aśvinī are benefic divisions. If Saturn is in the ninth house, it could show the father was very harsh to the native, or that he was a traditional teacher. If Saturn is in a Sarpa dvadaśāṁśa then it is acting negatively, while if it is in a benefic dwadaśāṁśa then the indications will be more positive. The lords need to be integrated with status of the planets sign placement in the D-12. Gaṇeśa divisions show encouragement, education and protection from the parents and the Aśvinī divisions show nurturing and caring. The Yama division can show early loss of the parent or aspect of childhood, and the Sarpa divisions will show negative karma that needs to be experienced.

Ṣoḍaśāṁśa (D-16): Comforts and Vehicles

The ṣoḍaśāṁśa is (12 X 1) + 4 and therefore relates to the fourth house. It is a higher harmonic than the first twelve divisions and therefore shows a subtler level of reality. Parāśara says it reveals Comfort and prosperity *(sukha)* or lack of it *(asukha)*, and vehicles *(vāhana)*. In some modern places people take owning a vehicle for granted. A vehicle to move swiftly from one place to another is a very high comfort that should not be overlooked. The D-16 will show all attributes of ones vehicle or multiple vehicles. It will also show the ability to appreciate and enjoy material comforts. It is a very important varga for seeing the level of happiness and contentment the person has.

The kāraka planets are Moon and Jupiter for the mental and emotional happiness and comforts or lack thereof. Jupiter will show where happiness *(sukha)* is coming from. Venus is the kāraka for vehicles and signs and planets connected to Venus will modify karma related to vehicles. For those that have a large number of vehicles, like a company, the D-16 chart can be read just like the D-4 but relative to vehicles instead of property. All the general rules can be applied.

Aṁśa Lord	Strong Attachment to:
Brahma	Knowledge and learning
Viṣṇu	Home, vehicles, materialism
Śiva	Relationships
Sūrya	Work and its fruits

There are four deities of the Ṣoḍaśāṁśa and they will give a deeper insight into where the person is seeking to attain happiness from. The Moon and the lagna should be examined for general tendencies.

Viṁśāṁśa (D-20): Spirituality

Parāśara utilizes the D-20 for *upāsana* which is translated to mean worship. It is the combination of two words, upa meaning to be near and āsana meaning seat. It literally means to sit near, and is used in the context of what we practice to get nearer to the divine. Therefore the viṁśāṁśa is used to see a native's spiritual inclinations. The viṁśāṁśa is (12 X 1) + 8 and therefore relates to the eighth house. The eighth house is the house of death, and it is the fact that we die and leave this body which forces us to think about something beyond right here and now. The fourth, eighth and twelfth houses are the mokṣa trines. The eighth is the fifth house from the fourth, showing that it is the knowledge, skills and practices used to attain mokṣa.

The Sun is the significator of spirituality. The bhāva sambandha between the Sun and the lagneśa will indicate the degree of energy a person puts towards spirituality. If any planet is linking (creating sambandha) between the Sun and the lagneśa then that planet will bring spirituality. The relationship between the Sun and the ātmakāraka will indicate the deeper level of spirituality in the person. The state and relationship of Jupiter can also be seen to see ones religiosity. The Sun and Jupiter are then seen in the viṁśāṁśa as the kāraka planets.

The fifth house of the rāśi chart is seen to determine the *preferred* deities of worship. Planet there will indicate the deity according to their state (exalted-Viṣṇu forms, own sign-graha forms, Mars in odd sign-Kartikeya, Mars in even sign-fierce form of the goddess, etc.). The fifth house is the house of mantra, yantra and tantra as well as the house of speculation and planning. Therefore it shows what one desires, which deities those desires manifest as, and the practices one does to fulfill those desires and ambitions (both spiritual and material). The fifth house is the tenth house from the eighth, showing it is the work we do for the occult power of the eighth house. The viṁśāṁśa fifth house is the main kāraka-bhāva relative to what the person worships, but the lagna and trines, as well as the lagna lord need to be studied in depth for the type and depth of the spirituality.

Multiple planets in the lagna and its trines show more spiritual awareness, as well as planets conjunct the lagna lord. The second house shows the spiritual community and the family deity that community is traditionally based around. The deity indicated by the second house in the viṁśāṁśa is called the *Kula-devatā* (family deity) and will bring harmony within the family. Whenever there is suffering from everyone in a family (the father is sick, the mother lost her job, the brother is addicted to drugs, the sister is suffering... etc,) then this is an indication that family deity is not happy and should be worshipped.

The ninth house will show the spiritual views and opinions. Mercury gives a modern or celebratory view, Venus will give a sensualist or artistic approach, Jupiter will give a strict and ritualistic approach, Saturn will give a very traditional or orthodox view. The fifth house shows the nature of ones bhakti (devotion), if it is strong and associated with beneficial lords then the bhakti will be strong. The nature of the planets placed there will reveal the nature of the deities the person worships as well as the practices that will increase bhakti.

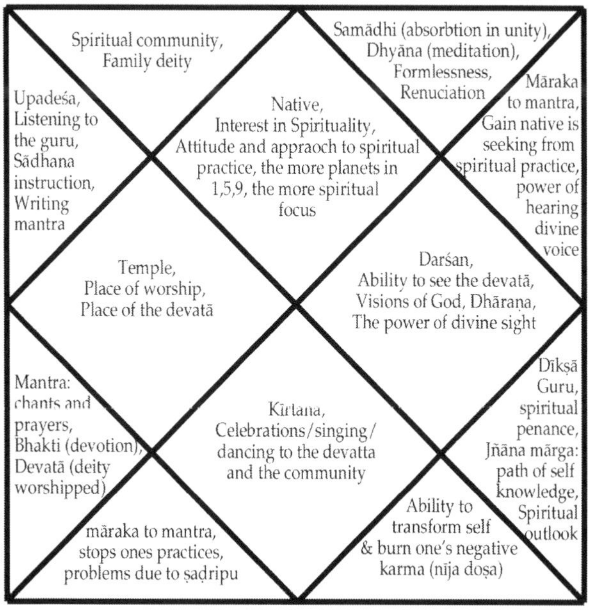

Caturviṁśāṁśa (D-24): Knowledge and Learning

The caturviṁśāṁśa (catur-four, viṁśa-twenty, aṁśa-division) is the division dealing with vidyā. Vidyā means knowledge, learning, science, and the state of understanding. It is the opposite of ignorance. It is also called the siddhāṁśa, from the word siddhis which means perfection. Siddhi has the meaning of supernatural power, but perfection is supernatural power. By the fact that we are humans there is nothing that is completely perfect. Therefore when something is perfected it become super human, beyond natural, supernatural. The D-24 shows our knowledge (vidyā) and our ability to perfect that knowledge of the universe.

The D-24 contains the twelve signs of the zodiac repeated twice. The variation is that the odd signs begin with Leo and ends with Cancer while the even signs begins with Cancer and end with Leo. The importance of Leo and Cancer reveals the importance of the Sun and the Moon in true education. The Moon shows the knowledge that is important to live in the material creation; for career and sustenance, etc. This worldly knowledge is called aparavidyā. The Sun shows the knowledge that helps us to transcend the world, this transcendental knowledge is called aparavidyā. The D-24 calculation shows the esoteric balance of these two forms of vidyā (knowledge). This balance of the lunar (intuitive) energy and the solar (logical) energy is the key to gaining the highest level of knowledge. This is the third eye understanding that comes from balancing the left and right channels of energy in the body and mind.

The kāraka planets for the D-24 are Mercury for mental ability, education, analysis and learning with the Moon for mental focus of the mind. These are the kāraka planets relative to aparavidyā (material knowledge). Jupiter is kāraka of knowledge, wisdom, and understanding while the Sun is the guidance of the atma to higher forms of knowledge. Jupiter and Sun show the aparavidya.

The situation of Mercury and the lagna lord is very important for understanding the enfoldment of the educational process. The situation of the Moon will show the concentration of one's studies. The moon in fixed *(sthira)* signs is very focused, in moveable *(cara)* signs the mind wandering in many areas in studies and outside of studies or through various topics. Dual *(dvisvabhāva)* signs give mixed results. The placement of Jupiter will show the enfoldment of the higher spiritual learning as well as aspects of the higher levels of aparavidyā (Masters degree and PhD). The Sun will show the availability to the teachings of high spiritual knowledge and ones ability to mentally access this knowledge.

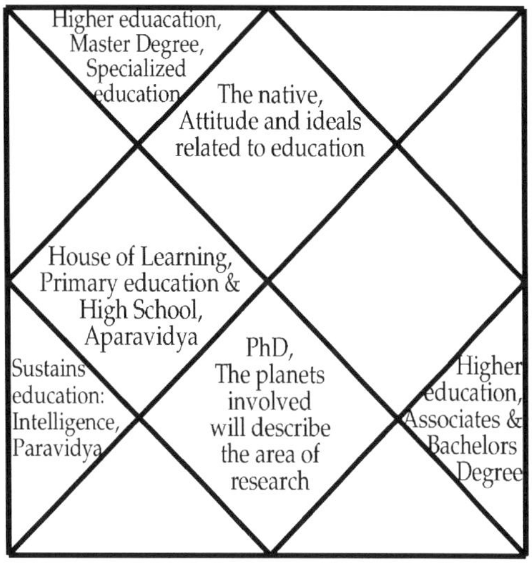

The fourth house (natural sign Cancer) is the environment for learning aparavidyā. The fifth house (natural sign Leo) is the method of learning paravidyā. This is why the D-24 is mapped from the natural fourth and fifth house signs (Cancer and Leo). The Caturviṁśāṁśa lagna lord shows the intelligence, and the fourth lord in the D-24 shows how consciousness is applied to learning.

The kāraka-bhāvas change depending on the level of education. The fourth house is the primary kāraka-bhāva for formal education. It will show the general learning that everyone receives in childhood. The next level of education is seen from the sixth house from the fourth, as it is an addition to the knowledge. In general when something ends and something new begins it is the eighth house from the kāraka, while when something grows it grows to the sixth house. The sixth from the fourth is the ninth house which shows the next level of higher education, like an associates or bachelors degree. The sixth house from this is the second house which shows the more specialized study of knowledge, like a masters degree. The final level of education is the sixth from that which is the seventh house, which shows the PhD level of education, or expertise in a field of study. Planet in the seventh house (or kāraka house) will relate to the subject of the research. The lord of the house will relate to the level of success at that level of education. All houses are read according to standard rules from the kāraka-bhāva. For example, that which sustains the PhD level of study is the eighth house of research and loans; lots of research and lots of loans will allow one to finish their PhD.

If one of the kāraka bhāvas is weak or afflicted this will stop education from continuing according to the reasons indicated by the weaknesses. In general, Saturn and Rāhu are detrimental to education. Saturn will cause monetary lack, or will be too hard, or will make the native start working. It is also the kāraka for forgetfulness. Rāhu will block education by bringing other factors into more focus, making the native travel, or other similar unfocused reasons. Rāhu will also cause confusion related to the path of education.

Triṁśāṁśa (D-30): Misfortunes

The D-30 shows Results of misfortune, bad-luck *(Ariṣṭaphala)*. The Triṁśāṁśa is (12 X 2) + 6 showing its relationship to the sixth house. The sixth house gives diseases which are caused by the bad karma we do against ourselves, while the eighth gives disease based on the bad karma we do against others. The sixth house shows disease which is caused by external factors *(aguṇṭaka)*, while the eighth house shows disease that is caused by internal factors *(nija-doṣa)*.

House	Types of Karma	Two Types of Manifestation
Sixth	Agaṇṭuka	Disease caused by dṛṣṭa (seen) causes
		Disease caused by unseen causes
Eighth	Nija-Doṣa	Disease and suffering of the body
		Disease and suffering of the mind

The external disease caused by the sixth house can be divided into two types; that caused by known (seen) sources, and that caused by unseen sources. Seen (dṛṣṭa) factors are things like car accidents, falls, contagious skin rashes, rape, etc. Unseen factors include past karma, curses, anger of deities or ancestors (badhaka). The D-30 specifically focuses on the seen aguṇṭaka (external) factors of disease, suffering and bad luck.

All malefics (especially Saturn) and debilitated planets become kārakas in the triṁśāṁśa. The lord of the sixth house of the Rāśi becomes very malefic in the D-30 and if it has any association with the eighth house or the lagna it will give misfortunes.

The dusthānas are important kāraka bhāvas, especially the Triṁśāṁśa eighth house. If a planet is placed in the eighth house, then the signs of that planet will also show bad results. These events will happen both according to Naisargika dāśa as well as the Viṁṣottari dāśa of the planets involved. The D-30 lagna lord will show the type weaknesses and problems the person will have. For example, if Venus is the lagneśa the person will have problems with love relationships, marriage, rape, etc. If Saturn is the lagneśa the person will have problems that make them suffer and feel huge amounts of sorrow, grief, or separation. This issues with the lagneśa will be more pronounced if connected to the D-30 eighth lord or the Rāśi sixth lord.

In the D-30 there is no sign of Cancer or Leo, just the signs ruled by the five planets that rule over the elements (tattva). There are also only five deities in the D-30 relating to each of these five tattvas. When utilizing the D-30 for deeper insight into disease pathology the tattva of the sign is very important to take into consideration. The D-30 will show the reasons for disease.

Tattva	Element	Deity
Agni	Fire	Agni
Vāyu	Air	Vāyu
Ākāśa	Space	Indra
Pṛthvi	Earth	Kubera
Jala	Water	Varuṇa

The D-60 shows the karmic reason for all happenings in life as well as disease and suffering, while the D-30 gives deep insight into this suffering and specifically focuses on the subconscious level of the mind and its manifestation into physical reality.

The D-30 chart shows the darker misfortunes of life like operations that leave a person impaired instead of healed, a spouse that goes crazy and harms you, murder, abuse, disfiguration, and addictions. When you analyze these varga chakras you are looking into a field of energy in a person's life, and connecting with that energy. When you look at the D-20 you are connecting to the spiritual realms of the person and the energy generally gets light and fresh. When you utilize the D-30 you are looking at the evils and weaknesses that exist inside of humans, and a heavier, darker energy is felt.

There are two other forms of the D-30, one is Paravṛtti (regular and cyclic), the other is calculated like the D-60 and called the *Ṣaṣṭyāṁśa Triṁśāṁśa*, which is used for a finalization on determining the form of the deity a planet will manifest itself to the individual.

Khavedāṁśa (D-40): Maternal Lineage
Akṣavedāṁśa (D-45): Paternal Lineage

The D-40 is composed of 40 aṁśas of 45 degrees, while the D-45 is composed of 45 aṁśas of 40 degrees. The khavedāṁśa is (12 X 3) + 4 which shows its link to the fourth house of the Mother. The akṣavedāṁśa is (12 X 3) +9 which shows it is connected to the ninth house of the father. The first 12 vargas are the material level, the second harmonic of 12 (13-24) is the mental plane, while the third harmonic of vargas (25-36) relates to a more sub-subconscious plane. The fourth harmonic (37-48) relates to the super-conscious level of reality where consciousness is shared between groups of people.

Parents are seen at the physical level in the D-12 chart. The physical reality of your parents and even grandparents is seen from the D-12, especially when it is physical related like health and death related issues. For example, if you wanted to time the death of the maternal grandmother, the fourth from the fourth in the D-12 will give excellent results. The D-40 and D-45 are at the realm of the super conscious, they represent what you have not really seen, that which has come before you, yet is influencing you. It is the generations of our family that have passed into the super-conscious realm. Our karma will affect our offspring for seven generations, and we are affected by the karma of our ancestors seven generations back.

When a disease is inherited, the D-12 and D-40/45 can be studied to see the genetic karma of this disease, as well as showing a remedy to put an end to the genetic transmission by fulfilling karmic debts. When genetic disease or similar karmic situation affects every other generation, this is seen by comparison of the Rāśi and the D-40/45. When an affliction or curse is seen in the Rāśi and it is possibly genetic, the same signification will show itself in either the D-40 if it is from the maternal lineage or from the D-45 if it is from the paternal lineage. Sometimes there are issues like addictions or abuse in marriage that run through generations and can be seen in these divisions.

When I asked my Jyotiṣa Guru about these vargas some years back, his first reply was, "Why do you want to look at skeletons in the closet?" The suffering caused by our ancestors' misdeeds becomes clear. The D-40/45 are part of the 16 varga system for kings and powerful people, as few rise to king from nothing. Being born in a powerful family sets the foundation for power. The son of a king who persecuted a particular race or religion would still share the karma of that persecution and would suffer that karma unless he balanced this with an equal opposite karma.

Parāśara says that the D-40/45 shows good *(śubha)* and bad *(aśubha)* results. In this way it shows our curses as well as our blessings from the ancestors. If the great grandfather was a great devotee of a particular deity, that deva would bless the person and there entire lineage. Therefore we inherit curses and blessings, which give good and bad results in our life.

The kāraka planets are Venus for the D-40 and Jupiter for the D-45. If Jupiter is in the 12th house of the D-45 there will be little to no connection with the paternal lineage. If Jupiter is in the third house (māraṇa-kāraka-sthāna) then the person will also loose connection to the paternal lineage, except when there is sickness or dying. In this way the kārakas will show the connection to the lineage.

The lagna represents the individual and the lagna lord their ideals. The fourth house is the kāraka-bhāva for the D-40 and the ninth house for the D-45. The matṛkāraka (MK) and the pitṛkāraka (PiK) are to be analyzed in these vargas. In order for a blessing or an affliction in the D-40/45 to be transferred genetically it needs some association to the MK, PiK , otherwise it is an event that is not a shared karma. The lagneśa needs some association in order for the individual to experience the karma, otherwise it could be a brother or sister, or cousin that may experience the karma seen in the D-40/45.

Ṣaṣṭyāṁśa (D-60): Past Life

The D-60 carries the most weight of planetary placement according to Parāśara. The ṣaṣṭyāṁśa is (12 X 4) + 12, it relates to the supra-conscious plane of the ātmā and its past lives. The great sage Parāśara teaches that the D-60 gives the complete view *(akhila- īkṣa)*, or the view of the various lifetimes without the gap of the different bodies we take on. It is therefore the root karma that the soul is carrying with it through various incarnations, and brings an understanding of why certain situations exist in our life (in the Rāśi).

When each of the twelve signs is divided into sixty parts it creates a total of 720 aṁśas of thirty minutes of arc each (30′), which divides each degree in half. The Ṛgveda mentions this division in prayer to the Sun:

द्वादशारं नहि तज्जराय वर्वर्ति चक्रं परिद्यामृतस्य ।
आ पुत्रा अग्ने मिथुनासो अत्र सप्त शतानि विंशतिश्च तस्थुः ॥११ ॥

dvādaśāraṁ nahi tajjarāya varvarti cakraṁ paridyāmṛtasya|
ā putrā agne mithunāso atra sapta śatāni viṁśatiśca tasthuḥ||11||

"The twelve-spoked wheel, of the true (Sun) revolves around the heavens, undecaying, seven hundred and twenty children in pairs, Agni, abide in it.[145]"

The twelve-spoked wheel is the Rāśi chakra of twelve signs through which the Sun revolves around. Each of the 360 degrees are divided in half to create 720 paired divisions. When the triṁśāṁśa is divided similar to the D-60 it is called the *ṣaṣṭyāṁśa triṁśāṁśa*, and relates to the form of the deity a planet is perceived as by the native. When this is divided in half (into D-60) it shows the particular karmic story associated with each of the planets. The importance of the ṣaṣṭyāṁśa cannot be overlooked.

As the navāṁśa has a multitude of techniques, so does the D-60 because of its level of importance. Only a few basic techniques will be introduced here. The D-60 changes every two minutes of time, so unless the time is rectified to this level the accuracy of the past life reading will be questionable. There are many ways to use the D-60 once it is rectified and also a way to use it as it is. Since it is only the D-60 lagna that changes every two minutes, the other planets will stay in their D-60 sign much longer. Therefore we can analyze this position.

[145] Wilson & Sāyaṇācārya, Ṛgveda Saṁhitā, p.422

Ṣaṣṭyāṁśa Deities

Each aṁśa of the D-60 has a deity which will show the nature of the past karmic situation a planet carries[146]. For example, if Venus is in the ninth house and it is placed in Daṇḍā-yuddha-ṣaṣṭyāṁśa, which means a fighting staff, it will show an unfinished fight in past life that came into this life. Since it is Venus in the ninth the person has some fight with tradition (ninth house) in their past life that they are still struggling with in this life. If that same Venus in the ninth house was in Pravīṇa-ṣaṣṭyāṁśa, which means clever and expertise and shows the person perfected a skill from a past life, then Venus will have been some dharmic mastery in the last life that the person is utilizing in this life. If that Venus was in *Kulaghna-ṣaṣṭyāṁśa* which means one who destroys the family, or a home wrecker, or one who stops the lineage, then that Venus would lead to some sexual scandal in the ninth house (temple, or university, etc) that would destroy the family. If that Venus was in *Amṛta-ṣaṣṭyāṁśa*, which means Nectar, nourishing, or rejuvenating then the native will be gaining all sorts of blessings and support from the Guru or the father because of the help they have given in the last life.

If malefics (especially Saturn or Rāhu) are placed in the ninth house, then the native may be disrespectful or disgrace their guru and lineage. The situation with the ṣaṣṭyāṁśa will clarify to what level and why this will happen. If Rāhu was in *Amṛta-ṣaṣṭyāṁśa* then the native would be healing in this life from the negative karma they did to tradition in their last life. While if that Rāhu was in a negative ṣaṣṭyāṁśa there could be severe problems for the individual's guru. In this way, the ṣaṣṭyāṁśa deities are integrated into the entire chart. The planets must be read according to the situation that planet is placed within the chart, while the D-60 is revealing the gentle or harsh karma associated with the situation.

The lords of houses can also be seen. The ṣaṣṭyāṁśa of the ninth lord will show the situation with the native's dharma. If the ninth lord is in *Daṇḍā-yuddha-ṣaṣṭyāṁśa* then the native will be struggling between dharmas. If the ninth lord is *Amṛita-ṣaṣṭyāṁśa* the native will be rejuvenating dharma in this world. Again all these indications need to be seen according to the Rāśi placements.

The ṣaṣṭyāṁśa deity of the Rāśi lagna should tell about the general nature of the individual. If it does not, then one may consider looking at the lords just before and just after their lagna to locate the one most fitting, which is one method of D-60 rectification.

"After death, the soul goes to the next world bearing in mind the subtle impressions of its deeds, and after reaping their harvest returns again to this world of action. Thus, he who has desires continues subject to rebirth."

-Śukla Yajur Veda, Bṛhadāraṇyaka Upaniṣad 4.4.6

[146] List of deities and their meaning are found in the Chapter on Strengths, page 172-174

The Past Life and Present Karma

Reading the chart from the lagna will show what results of past karma that are due in this life. Therefore it can be read just like the Rāśi chart. This is done with a timing tool called *mūla daśā,* which shows the manifestation of our past life karma. When a planet has a blessing or a curse, the reason for this is seen in the D-60 chart. The timing of the curse is done in the rāśi and the understanding is seen in the D-60.

The D-60 shows karmas that were not completed in the past lokas (heavens) or talas (hells) and so the individual has taken birth to complete these karmas. The indications of the properly rectified D-60 are guaranteed to fructify and this is why there is so much importance placed upon this varga chart by seasoned astrologers.

It is read relative to why things happen more than what is happening, though the two things are not able to be separated. For example, if Jupiter is malefic in the D60 chart the person may not meet their guru in this life. If Jupiter is malefic in the second house they may have been supposed to help financially and didn't or might have broken their word. If Jupiter is malefic in the eleventh house they may have been supposed to earn and then give but didn't. If Jupiter is malefic in the sixth house they may have become enemies of the guru and caused the guru such pains. If Saturn is aspecting Jupiter it shows disobedience to the guru, if Rāhu is aspecting Jupiter it shows the native cheated the guru. In this way, the D-60 is read as the reason behind the manifestation of the nature of the life.

The ārūḍha lagna of the D-60 is read as the past embodied life of the individual. It is read just like the Rāśi chart but for the body of the last incarnation. For the ārūḍha lagna to be correct the D-60 lagna must be accurate. There are many advanced methods to rectify this. For example, the third house from the D-60 ārūḍha lagna will show what phobias a person has as it shows how the person died in their last life. If the third from the D-60 AL is Pisces with the Moon in it, the person may have drowned while in a ship at sea, which would give them a fear of the ocean. In this way, there are many techniques to rectify the ṣaṣṭyāṁśa so that the ārūḍha lagna is correct and a good view of the last life is seen. In many cases, past life readings from the D-60 have been verified by the nāḍī readers and psychics. They often bring a wider understanding to an individual as to certain emotions and tendencies in their life.

Practice Exercises:

5. Try to deepen the interpretation of all your planets with their ṣaṣṭyāṁśa lords. With any powerful yogas in the chart see the graha that lords them.
6. See if the D-60 lagna fits you and if not look at the deities just before and just after to try to determine the most fitting, explain why you think this to be the case.

Higher Divisional Charts

The vargas discussed so far are the classic sixteen vargas needed for the complete fullness of understanding a person. These 16 relate to the full Moon, the maturity of Jupiter at age 16, the dawning of the power of wisdom and understanding. The mastery of these 16 varga charts is the considered the blessing of the goddess of the Śrī Chakra.

There are also many higher divisional charts used by traditional astrologers for very intricate results. For example, the Aṣṭottarāṁśa (D-108) is used to see the relationship between the Sun and the Moon as the ātma and the mind. It will show what happens in the dream world when a person is asleep and there is no physical body. In the dream there is just the interaction between the ātma and the mind. Whether the guru comes to you in your dreams or not can be seen in this chart. The nature of the dreams from rehashing of materialistic mental jargon to the visit of great mystics on the astral plane are understood here.

The most important of the higher divisions is the nāḍyāṁśa (D-150). Each sign is divided into 150 aṁśās called nāḍīs. The present day nāḍī astrology relates mostly to pre-written horoscopes that are kept in magical libraries. People arrive and there are ancient palm leafs with their charts and horoscope written long ago. The detail seen in these charts is extremely accurate and detailed. There are many modern nāḍī texts available for study. The one used most by our school is the *Chandra-Kāla-Nāḍī* (also called the *Deva-Keralam*).

This chart changes about every 30 seconds and accuracy is extreme. All charts before this need to be accurate. Once the D-60 has been rectified, then the D-108 is rectified, then the D-150 can be rectified. One of the methods of rectification is utilizing the deities of the nāḍyāṁśa. The deity of the lagna will directly relate to the name of the individual. The level of detail this chart gives is very extreme and will be discussed in later lessons. The highest division is the ardha-nāḍyaṁśā (D-300) which divides each of the D150 division in half. Such vargas are only for experts. I was lucky enough to be in the company of my guru while he taught these higher harmonics to particular advanced students.

Conclusion

The divisions of a sign are a complex system of numerology that give great detail into specific areas of our life. Kalyāṇa Varma in *Sārāvalī* says one cannot take a step forward in Vedic Astrology without divisional charts. This small introduction is enough to understand the general principles and importance of varga charts. There are thousands more techniques that will take time to learn and master.

Chapter 14

Upāya:
Introduction to Remedies

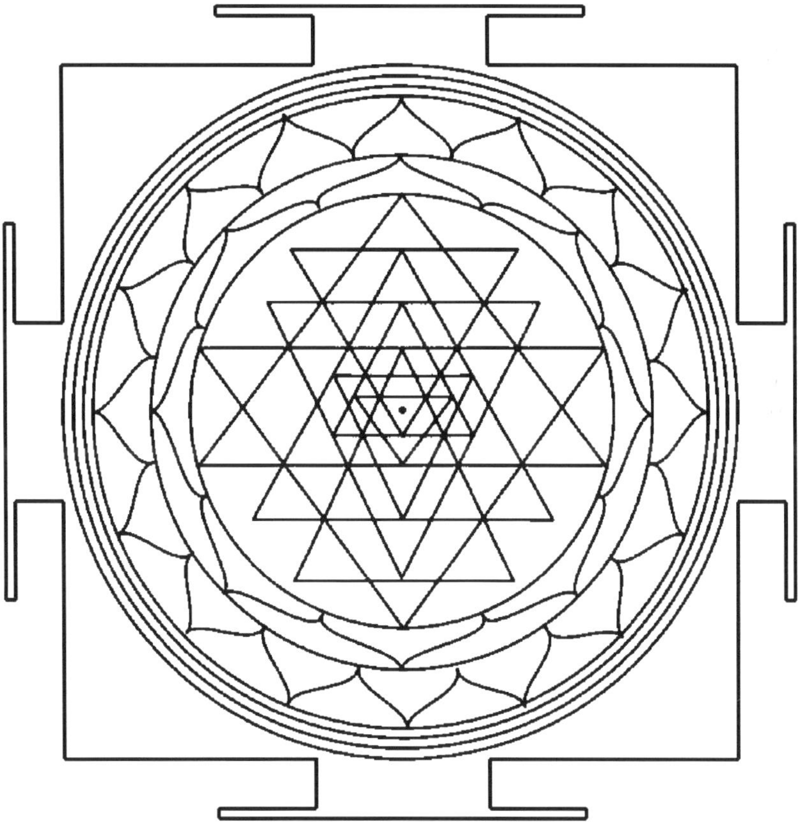

Introduction to Remedies

Planets represent our positive and negative karma and the results we experience in our life. What is the use of knowing our karma if we can't do anything about it? Did you get a mother with a healthy mind who was always there and loving, or a mother who was crazy, or not present? This is all based on our own karma. We may not be able to exchange our mother, but we can improve the situation -calm the craziness, open our hearts and the hearts of others, or find a new and healthy way to nurture ourselves in life.

One of the most beautiful aspects of Vedic astrology are the remedies available to help improve one's present state, brighten one's outlook, balance the neurochemistry of the brain and find fulfillment in life. The gross level remedy is the proper advice guiding an individual to activities, colors, foods, etc. so that they are in alignment with their highest nature. The subtle level remedies include methods to work on the karmic factors creating the individual's reality -similar to fixing the intelligence so that we make good decisions instead of constantly correcting the wrong decisions.

If the decision-making process was to be remedied, one would have to decide how and why it was not working properly. Is the process flawed due to lack of decision-making strength (fifth lord or kāraka weak), in which case you would strengthen it or planets that are supporting it. If bad decisions are made because of malefic influence on the fifth house, fifth lord or kāraka then the planet needs to be purified. Or if decisions are blocked because of argalā, obstacles or a curse, then remedies to remove these need to be performed. These are principles that guide the astrologer to determine specialized remedies that give perceivable results. Parāśara teaches śanti methods for each graha which is a generalized method to improve a planet's results.

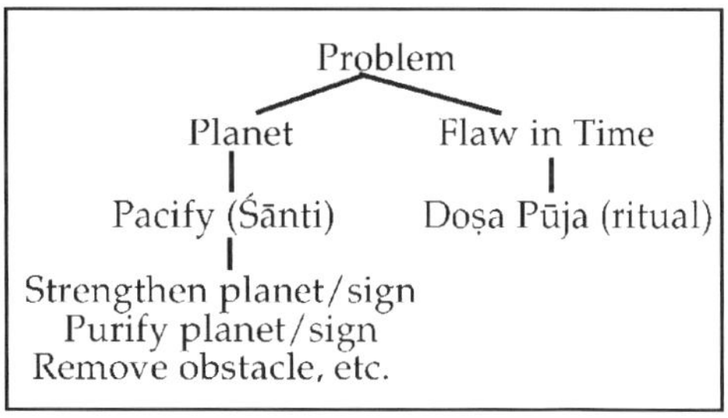

In BPHS, there are two main types of remedies presented -the first is the pacification *(śānti)* of the planets. When a planet is not giving good results due to some affliction or weakness then a remedy is performed to allow that planet to give beneficial results. The second type of remedy is the removal of a problem (*doṣa*) that is indicated by the time of birth. A doṣa requires a remedial procedure be performed to overcome the obstacle indicated by the doṣa. This chapter will introduce methods to *pacify* the planets. Doṣas will be introduced in the following chapter after one understands the *pañchāṇga*. More specialized remedies to strengthen, rejuvenate, purify, etc. a planet will be introduced in the next volume.

The Great Sage Parāśara first introduces remedial measures in the Graha Śānti chapter[147]. Maitreya asks,

ग्रहाणां दोषशान्त्यर्थं तेषां पूजाविधिं वद ।
मानवानां हितार्थाय संक्षेपात् कृपया मुने ॥ १ ॥

grahāṇāṁ doṣaśāntyarthaṁ teṣāṁ pūjāvidhiṁ vada |
mānavānāṁ hitārthāya saṅkṣepāt kṛpayā mune || 1||

Sage, have compassion to benefit the welfare of humankind. Please explain the procedure for worship *(pūjā)* for the purpose of pacifying *(śānti)* the planets.

The Great Sage Parāśara replied,

ग्रहा सूर्यादयः पूर्वं मया प्रोक्ता द्विजोत्तम ।
जगत्यां सर्वजन्तूनां तदधीनं सुखाऽसुखम् ॥ २ ॥

grahā sūryādayaḥ pūrvaṁ mayā proktā dvijottama |
jagatyāṁ sarvajantūnāṁ tadadhīnaṁ sukhā'sukham || 2||

Best of the Intitiated, I have described earlier the planets from the Sun onwards which control *(adhīna)* the happiness and suffering *(sukha-asukha)* of all objects *(jagatyāṁ)* and created beings *(jantūnāṁ)*.

तस्मात् सुशान्तिकामो वा श्रीकामो वा सुचेतसा ।
वृष्टायायुः पुष्टिकामो वा तेषां यज्ञं समाचरेत् ॥ ३ ॥

tasmāt suśāntikāmo vā śrīkāmo vā sucetasā |
vṛṣṭāyāyuḥ puṣṭikāmo vā teṣāṁ yajñaṁ samācaret || 3||

Therefore to fullfill the desire for tranquility *(su-śānti-kāma)*, the desire for prosperity *(śrī-kāma)*, good intelligence *(su-cetas)*, rainfall *(vṛṣṭa)*, longevity *(āyus)*, the desire to be well-nourished and complete *(puṣṭi-kāma)*, rituals *(yajña)* are practiced.

Parāśara teaches that all aspects of life are in their present state based on the situation of the planets, and that appropriate rituals to them will help in the fulfillment of the beneficial desires of life. This is supported by the teachings of the Bhagavad Gītā, where it speaks of success in the material world based on the performance of rituals. As an astrologer, it is important to help people achieve the four goals of life: dharma (right path), kāma (pleasure), artha (prosperity) and mokṣa (spirituality). Therefore, the use of remedies is very important to help the individual overcome any weaknesses in their chart and achieve their full potential. A good astrologer is competent in giving the proper remedial measures.

[147] Bṛhat Parāśara Horā Śāstra, Graha-Śānti-Adhyāya, (84/86)

Doctors spend eight years in university to be competent enough to administer medicine. Though anyone can administer aspirin for a headache, the more severe the affliction, the stronger the medicine needs to be as well as the more important having a good doctor becomes. Do not think it is possible to learn about remedies in a single chapter or even a single book, as it requires a complete understanding of the foundational principles of Jyotiṣa, their implications and everything that branches and fruits from these. Even after a doctor has studied years at university they still need to perform internships before being able to practice on their own. In this same way, let upāyas be a gradual learning that takes time to mature.

We will discuss some basic foundations from which to begin guiding the mind in the right direction of thinking about remedies. How well you have mastered the art of remedy (and the principles behind the remedies) will become clear when you need to give a remedy to a person of foreign religion, like a Catholic, or Muslim, or other non-Hindu practicing individual. All remedies need to be adjusted to fit the religious belief system of the client as well as their level of spiritual advancement and understanding. Here is a list of basic factors to be considered when advising a remedy, followed by a more in depth look at each.

I. What is the cause of the affliction and how is it affecting the individual
II. Which planet or rāśi is indicating the remedy
III. Which form of the remedy planet or rāśi is indicated by its placement
IV. What form of upāya is indicated by that planet or sign placement
V. What form of upāya is indicated by the house, trines and aspects
VI. What length of time is needed to perform the remedy to get results
VII. When or at what time should the remedy be performed

I. Cause of Affliction

The first aspect of prescribing a remedy is to find what needs to be remedied. The cause of the affliction needs to be understood astrologically, and then *how* it is making the individual suffer is to be understood. For example, if there is a relationship problem, determine whether it is the seventh house, the seventh lord, or the upapada lagna that is afflicted. See what is activating the problem - the time of life, the daśā or a bad transit, etc. Or conversely, if while reading a chart you see that the seventh lord is afflicted, determine how this is afflicting the individual. The indication may hurt their business partners, or their love life values, or they may not be able to find a partner, etc. Determine how a negative combination is actually affecting the individual.

If a person receives the best liver medicine in the world and it is actually the kidneys that are causing a problem, their illness will not improve. The correct cause and root of the cause needs to be understood based on general principles, then the remedy can be sought in a way that will guarantee remediation.

II. Planet Giving the Remedy

If a house is weak strengthening the lord of the house or its kāraka is needed and the remedial planet is the planet itself. Other times the planet may be afflicted and need help to be lifted out of its suffering. This will happen if the planet is badly placed, a malefic house lord or if it is cursed. For example, if Mars was badly placed in the eighth house, then by performing remedies that strengthen it one could incur debts or accidents. Also, if Saturn is the lord of the twelfth house, and is placed with the image (AL), then a remedy that strengthens it may actually lower the image and give the person more bad reputation. If a planet is cursed it can recover itself more quickly with the help of another planet, as the cursed planet is in a bad situation itself.

Curses are created by the graha aspect or conjunction of two or more malefic planets (specifically Rāhu, Saturn and Mars). The tamasic malefics are the cause of the suffering due to curses. The association of Mars will show the planet has suffered from violence, the association of Saturn will show suffering and sorrow, the association of Rāhu will show cheating and deceit. If a planet is "hammered" by malefics its natural significations will suffer in this life and it will need to be remedied to get good results.

Bhāva	House	Aspects that uplift the house
Bhāveśa	House Lord	Beneficial planet well placed
Bhāva-kāraka	Significator of House	Beneficial planet well placed

Determine the planet that will help the person out of the cursed situation. There are three factors to analyze; bhāva, bhāveśa, and bhāva-kāraka of the cursed planet. See if there are beneficial aspects to the house of the cursed planet by Rāśi or Graha aspect, helping to lift the planet out of suffering by providing help according to the benefic significations. If there are such indications, then strengthen that planet. For example, if the Moon is afflicted in the sixth house, but has the beneficial aspect of Jupiter from the second house then strengthen his aspect by eating good Jupiter food, using positive speech, etc and the Moon will benefit. If the Moon was afflicted in the seventh and Jupiter was aspecting from the third house, then strengthen Jupiter, perform his māraṇa kāraka remedies, and listen to spiritual music to strengthen his ability to help the Moon. Gemstones of planets should be used after this principle is fully understood. In the case where the Moon was in the seventh it may be good to where its gemstone, but in the case where the Moon was placed in the sixth house it would be better to wear the gemstone of a benefical planet aspecting. Gemstones strengthen a planet they do not give śānti to the planet.

See if the house lord is well placed as a benefic so that by strengthening it the situation in the house will improve by the situation getting better. See if the significator of the house (Moon for fourth, Jupiter for fifth, etc.) is a benefic and well placed so that the lord of the natural significations can be strengthened. Curses in the sixth, eighth, and twelfth have Saturn as bhāva-kāraka and therefore show less chance of removal of the suffering.

If all three remedy factors are afflicted then the karma is fixed and there will be suffering due to the curse. If one of these factors is beneficial, then that planet can be used to lift one out of suffering, or in the daśā of that planet a remedy may naturally come through the means indicated by that planet. The transit of Jupiter over the curse or any other affliction will also prove beneficial for finding a remedy.

It is important to know which planets are helping a person and which planets are hurting them, which planets are in difficult situations and which are ready to uplift the person. Increase the energy of the planets that are in a position to help to provide a remedy, while performiong śānti methods to the suffering planet.

III. Form of the Remedy Planet or Rāśi

The graha will take a personified form, which a human mind can relate to. There are general forms of the planets called *graha-rūpas*. Rūpa means form, and a graha-rūpa is the planet personified as a "planet deity;" i.e. the Sun God, the Moon God, Lord Saturn, etc. Parāśara explains both the visual imagery associated with the planet as a deity, as well as the materials to make the image.

ताभ्राच्च स्फटिकाद्रक्तचन्दनात् स्वर्णकादुभौ ।
रजतादयसः सीसात् कांस्यात् कार्याः क्रामद् ग्रहाः ॥ ४ ॥

tābhrācca sphaṭikādraktacandanāt svarṇakādubhau |
rajatādayasaḥ sīsāt kāṁsyāt kāryāḥ krāmad grahāḥ || 4||

The grahas are made out of copper *(tābracca)* for the Sun, quartz crystal *(sphaṭik)* for the Moon, red sandlwood *(rakta-chandan)* for Mars, gold *(svarṇa)* for Mercury and Jupiter, silver color *(rajata)* for Venus, iron/steel *(ayas)* for Saturn, lead *(sīsa)* for Rāhu, and brass *(kāmsya)* for Ketu.

पूर्वोक्तैः स्वस्ववर्णैर्वा पटे लेख्या द्विजोत्तमैः ।
स्वस्वोक्तदिग्विभागेषु गन्धाद्यैर्मण्डनेषु वा ॥ ५ ॥

pūrvoktaiḥ svasvavarṇairvā paṭe lekhyā dvijottamaiḥ |
svasvoktadigvibhāgeṣu gandyādyairmaṇḍaneṣu vā || 5||

Otherwise, best of the iniiated, draw/paint *(lekhya)* on a canvas *(paṭa)* the color of the planet *(svasva-varṇa)* previously mentioned *(pūrvokta)*, install these in the direction of the planet and adorn it *(maṇḍana)*.

पद्मासनः पद्महस्तः पद्मपत्रसमद्युतिः ।
सप्ताश्वरथसंस्थश्च द्विभुजश्च दिवाकरः ॥ ६ ॥

padmāsanaḥ padmahastaḥ padmapatrasamadyutiḥ |
saptāśvarathasaṁsthaśca dvibhujaśca divākaraḥ || 6||

The two-armed form of the day-maker (Sun) is perceived with the radiance of a lotus and seated on a lotus *(padmāsana)*, holding a lotus flower in one hand, and standing on a chariot *(ratha)* drawn by seven horses *(sapta-aśva)*.

श्वेतः श्वेताम्बरो देवो दशाश्वः श्वेतभूषणः ।
गदाहस्तो द्विबाहुश्च विधातव्यो विधुर्द्विज ॥ ७ ॥

śvetaḥ śvetāmbaro devo daśāśvaḥ śvetabhūṣaṇaḥ |
gadāhasto dvibāhuśca vidhātavyo vidhurdvija || 7||

The two-armed form of the Moon is perceived as pure white *(śveta)* in color, dressed in white, having white ornaments, the lighted one (*deva*) in a chariot pulled by ten horses, holding a mace *(gada)* in hand.

रक्तमाल्याम्बरधरो शक्तिशूलगदाधरः ।
वरदस्तु चतुर्बाहुर्मङ्गलो मेषवाहनः ॥ ८ ॥

raktamālyāmbaradharo śaktiśūlagadādharaḥ |
varadastu caturbāhurmaṅgalo meṣavāhanaḥ || 8||

The four-armed form of Mars *(maṇgala)* is perceived as wearing a red *(rakta)* garland *(māla)* and red clothes, holding a sword *(śakti)*, spear *(śūla)*, mace *(gada)*, and a hand granting wishes, while riding on a ram *(meṣa)*.

पीतमाल्याम्बरधरः कर्णिकारसमद्युतिः ।
खड्गचर्मगदापाणिः सिंहस्थो वरदो बुधः ॥ ९ ॥

pītamālyāmbaradharaḥ karṇikārasamadyutiḥ |
khaḍgacarmagadāpāṇiḥ siṁhastho varado budhaḥ || 9||

Mercury wears a yellow garland *(māla)*, having the radiance of a yellow flower *(Pterospermum acerifolium)*, riding on a lion, holding a small angled sword *(kaḍga)*, a sheild *(carma)*, a mace *(gada)*, and with his fourth hand granting wishes *(varada-mudrā)*.

गुरुशुक्रौ क्रमात् पीतश्वेतवर्णौ चतुर्भुजौ ।
दण्डिनौ वरदौ कार्यौ साक्षसूत्रकमण्डलू ॥ १० ॥

guruśukrau kramāt pītaśvetavarṇau caturbhujau |
daṇḍinau varadau kāryau sākṣasūtrakamaṇḍalū || 10||

Jupiter is yellow *(pīta)* in color and Venus is pure white *(śveta)* both having four arms, offering fulfillment of wishes *(varada-mudrā)*, holding a staff *(daṇḍa)*, a rosary *(sākṣa)*, wearing the sacred thread *(sūtra)* of brahmins, and holding a sacred water pot *(kamaṇḍalu)*.

इन्द्रनीलद्युतिः शूली वरदो गृध्रवाहनः ।
वाणवाणासनधरो विज्ञेयोऽर्कसुतो द्विज ॥ ११ ॥

indranīladyutiḥ śūlī varado gṛdhravāhanaḥ |
vāṇavāṇāsanadharo vijñeyo'rkasuto dvija || 11||

Saturn is perceived as having the brilliance of a blue sapphire, holding a spear *(śūla)*, offering fulfillment of wishes *(varada-mudrā)*, holding a bow and arrow, and riding on a vulture *(gṛdhra)*.

करालवदनः खड्गचर्मशूली वरप्रदः ।
सिंहस्थो नीलवर्णश्च राहुरेवं प्रकल्प्यते ॥ १२ ॥

karālavadanaḥ khaḍgacarmaśūlī varapradaḥ |
siṁhastho nīlavarṇaśca rāhurevaṁ prakalpyate || 12||

Rāhu is fixed by the mind *(prakalpya)* as having a gaping mouth, protruding teeth and terrible face, holding a short sword *(kaḍga)*, a sheild *(carma)*, and a spear *(śūla)*, and hand in varada-mudrā, he is blue *(nīla)* in color, and riding on a lion.

धूम्रा द्विबाहवः सर्वे गदिनो विकृताननाः ।
गृध्रासना नित्यं केतवः स्युर्वरप्रदा ॥ १३ ॥

dhūmrā dvibāhavaḥ sarve gadino vikṛtānanāḥ |
gṛdhrāsanā nityaṁ ketavaḥ syurvarapradā || 13||

Ketu is smoky color *(dhūmra)*, with two arms, armed with a mace *(gadin)*, and bestowing wishes *(varaprada)* living estranged or unnatural *(vikṛta)*, sitting on a vulture *(gṛdhra)*, and eternal *(nityaṁ)*.

सर्वे किरीटिनः कार्या ग्रहा लोकहितप्रदाः ।
स्वांगुलेनोच्छ्रिता विज्ञैः शतमष्टोत्तरं सदा ॥ १४ ॥

sarve kirīṭinaḥ kāryā grahā lokahitapradāḥ |
svāṅgulenocchritā vijñaiḥ śatamaṣṭottaraṁ sadā || 14||

To give benefit (*hita*) to beings on this plane (*loka*) the planets are ornamented with a crown or tiara (*kirīṭin*), and they are 108 of your own fingers in length.

These images wearing their crowns can be made as a statue, a yantra or as a picture of one of these. Parāśara has given the official form of the planet to be worshipped for pacification. In this same way, other texts will give the specific form of other various deities. For example, Parāśara mentions to worship Mṛtyuñjaya during Moon-Saturn viṁśottari daśā, but does not list a form as this is found in the text of the respective deity. In the sixteenth chapter of the tantric text *Mantramahodadhi*, Mṛtyuñjaya-Śiva is described,

We meditate upon the three eyed *(tryakṣa)* Lord Mṛtyuñjaya, who is adored *(bhaj)* by the daughter of the mountain king *(sa-girija)*.
With his first two lotus-like hands he holds a pair of water pots (kumbha). The second pair of hands splashes water onto his head *(ghṛtya-toya-śira)*. His lower hands hold a pot on his lap, while the others hold a mālā and mṛga-mudrā. The crescent Moon on his head *(mūrdha-stha-candra)* drips nectar *(pīyūṣa)* and makes his whole body wet *(ardra-tanu)*. || 19 ||

The various ancient texts that are devoted to a particular deity are to be studied for information related to that deity. Parāśara has only given the planet forms in Bṛhat Parāśara Horā Śāstra as it is an astrological text. The more one learns about the various deities the more one will be able to help people achieve their highest potential.

To get a more specific form of the remedy giving planet or rāśi, determine which form is indicated by the planet's dignity. For example, an exalted planet will manifest itself in the form of Viṣṇu *(Viṣṇu-rūpa)* while a debilitated planet indicates a Kāli-rūpa. If the planet is the guru-devatā it will take a Śiva-rūpa. In this way, one should apply the basics given in the chapter on planets to determine the form the planet will manifest as. Advanced astrologers will also utilize the deities of the varga charts and determination of deity according to varga placements. By using the correct form, the remedy will be the most effective. The form controls the fire aspect of the mind which is what allows an offering to be made (as Agni carries the offerings to the devas).

IV. The Planet and Sign Placement

The form of upāya (remedy) is indicated by the planet and/or its sign placement. One needs to see what elements are imbalanced and therefore what the individual needs to do to achieve pacification of the graha or deity it is representing.

The average westerner is not familiar with Vedic pūjā (worship), which is dualistic and non-dualistic at the same time. God is outside of you and god is inside of you, you are worshipping god, and you are part of god. From the highest view, it is all god, so it is only god that is actually worshipping god. But for the materially manifested mind, the energy of the divine is personified outside of oneself to interact with. The *Bhagavad Gītā* teaches,

देवान् भावयतानेन ते देवा भावयन्तु वः ।
परस्परं भावयन्तः श्रेयः परम् अवाप्स्यथ ॥११ ॥

devān bhāvayatānena te devā bhāvayantu vaḥ|
parasparaṁ bhāvayantaḥ śreyaḥ param avāpsyatha||III.11||

May you cause the gods to exist, and the gods will cause you to exist,
By bringing each other into existence you will attain the highest welfare.

Material offerings representing the elements or other aspects of time and space are offered to the deity who is a personified aspect of the divine energy in the universe as well as an energy inside of you, personified, but still a fully existing aspect of reality. They are not offered as if the person believes the image is a real 108 finger tall god. They are offered to the image which is a portal for the mind to connect to the specific archetypal energy of the universe. Cherish the gods so they cherish you, and by cherishing each other you will attain the highest *(param)* happiness *(śreyasa)*.

Parāśara speaks of pūjā and tells us what to offer to the planets,

यथावर्णं प्रदेयानि सुदुष्पाणि वसनानि च ।
गन्धो दीपो बलिश्चैव धूपो देयश्च गुग्गुलुः ॥ १५ ॥

yathāvarṇaṁ pradeyāni sudṣpāṇi vasanāni ca |
gandho dīpo baliścaiva dhūpo deyaśca gugguluḥ || 15||

Giving flower and clothes in that planet's color, giving *(deya)* fragrant essential oils *(gandha)*, offerings *(bali)*, incense *(dhūpa)*, guggulu[148], and offering lamps/candles *(dīpa)*.

In general, fabric in the planet's or deity's color is wrapped around the image. Then, flowers of a similar color are offered to the planet. Flowers will create harmony and a good relationship between the worshipper and the deity/archetypal energy. The other offerings are part of standard Vedic pūjā (worship). One is advised to learn *pañcha-upachāra pūjā* and do this offering in a traditional way. Then, when recommending remedies one can prescibe them in the proper way, or be able to make adjustments based on the correct method. For example, if dīpa (lamp) is indicated, one can instruct a yoga practitioner in the appropriate method to make a ghee lamp and offer it. Or if a Catholic comes for a reading, they can light candles to the appropriate saints.

Mars/Sun	Lamp, candle, illumiation
Venus/Moon	Milk, rice pudding, ghee
Mercury	Sandal paste or fragrant oil
Jupiter	Garland of flowers
Saturn	Ornaments (jewelry), clothing

All five offerings related to the five elements can be offered in pūjā, or in some cases, just one aspect of the elements is indicated. *Praśna Mārga* (XV.12) teaches that "if the planet occupies a sign of Mars or the Sun (fire element) then light or a candle *(pradīpa)* is prescribed. If it occupies the signs of Venus or Moon (water element) then rice pudding *(pāyasa)*, or ghee *(ghṛta)* or milk *(kṣīra)* are offered repeatively *(punar)*. If in the sign of Mercury (earth element) then sandalwood paste *(chandana)* or other sweet fragrance is offered. If in the sign of Jupiter *(ākāśa element)* then offer a flower garland *(mālā)*. And if in the sign of Saturn (air element) then offer adornments *(bhūṣaṇa)* and clothing *(vāsana)*. This will please the planet." For example, if the remedy was based on Jupiter placed in Aries, then simply a lamp lit to the Guru can be offered. If the remedy involved the Moon placed in Capricorn, then a beautiful dress and precious gemed necklace could be offered to Mother Kāli. Incense also relates to Saturn and the pacification of the vāyu (air element), and planets in Saturn's signs benefit from being offered incense.

[148] Guggulu is an āyurvedic resin, that is burned before worship. It clears the energy of an area and removes energy blockages from the body. It is similar in effect to Native American smudging with sage.

When utilizing a higher form of the planet there can also be some additional offerings to the deity. For example, Gaṇeśa is particularly fond of being offered sweets. When worshipping Ketu in the form of Gaṇeśa to get over the blockages of Rāhu, offering sweets will please this archetypal energy faster and give results sooner. Just as if someone gave you a gift to make up with you, you would be nicer to them, yet if it was exactly what you wanted you would be even more pleased and beneficial to them. Imagine a lover trying to make-up with your least favorite flowers instead of your favorite flowers. These specifics will take time to learn as one studies the devas. There are many texts that talk about worship and the deities. For example, here is a quote from *Mantramahodadhi*, Taraṇga 17:

> Prostrations/modesty/humility (*nati*) are the favorite *(vallabha)* of the Sun god *(mārtaṇḍa)*, Mahāviṣṇu is fond *(priya)* of praises *(stuti)*, Gaṇeśa is fond *(priya)* of being satisfied with food and drink *(tarpaṇa)*. || 116 ||
> Durgā is fond of worship and veneration *(archana)*, Śiva is fond immediately *(nūnam)* by ablution or sacred bathing by anointing with water *(abhiṣeka)*, therefore to give these devas the best pleasure *(pratoṣa)* use this knowledge to worship *(ādṛta)* them. || 117 ||

As well as making offerings to the image of the deity, one is advised to give donations of the objects that the planet or deity is fond of. Parāśara tells us,

यस्य ग्रहस्य यद्द्रव्यमन्नं यस्य च यत् प्रियम् ।
तच्च तस्यै प्रदातव्यं भक्तियुक्तेन चेतसा ॥ १६ ॥

yasya grahasya yaddravyamannaṁ yasya ca yat priyam |
tacca tasyai pradātavyaṁ bhaktiyuktena cetasā || 16||

Objects/substances *(dravya)* and food *(anna)* that the planet enjoys *(priya)* are given away *(pradātavya)* with full devotion *(bhakti)* by the intelligent.

Rāmakṛṣṇa Paramhaṁsa used to say that if you want to find a pearl, then look inside a clam shell. If you want to find god, then look inside of man. The deities are existing in all of the people around us, and will come to us through them. Therefore donation of substances related to them is beneficial to pacify the planet. The most common is the giving away of sesame seeds for Saturn. Some people will even put sesame seeds in bread and offer it to black crows. It is said that the ancestors come through the crows to take the offerings. Pearls can be given to your mother to pacify the Moon, as the substances are given to the people significated by the planet. In this way, there are innumerable remedies when one understands the substances ruled by the planet. One should keep in mind, that the gifting should be pure (sattva) in order to get long term good results. Feeding alchohol to gangsters will pacify Saturn, but only for a short time. Donating root vegetables or sesame oil to people in poverty will pacify Saturn and give long term good effects as it is a higher conscious action with positive energetic ripples.

V. House Placement, Trines and Aspects

The remedy indicated by the house is spoken of by Harihara in *Praśna Mārga* (XV.14). Understanding the remedies associated with the house will help fine tune the type of remedy used to alleviate the suffering of the native. For example, if Rāhu is in the ninth house causing problems, the house indicates worship of the deity in a temple, and Rāhu represents Durgā, so the native can worship Durgā in a temple to get relief from Rāhu. If there is another situation where the ninth lord is involved this will also bring temples in as part of the remedy. Afflictions in the fifth house can be alleviated with mantras, or if there is association with the fifth lord, then also mantra will be most beneficial. Remedies for the sixth house relate to donation of time toward the significations of the planet. If Jupiter is in the sixth or the sixth lord Jupiter is in the third house, then volunteering at a place to help sick children will be a good remedy. In this way, the houses will help fine tune the remedy based upon the planet or sign.

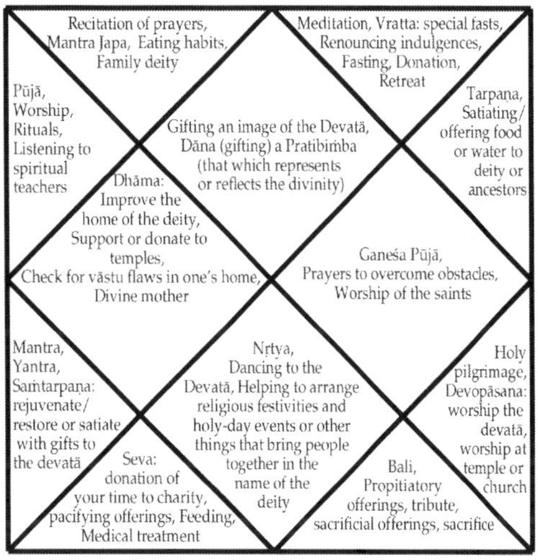

VI. Length or Amount of Remedy

The length to perform the remedy in order to get results will be determined. Some pūjās for doṣas will require a one time ritual. Others will require a certain number of mantras or a certain number of months of fasting. Parāśara advises the number of mantras to be chanted for the pacification of the planets. He reccommends 7,000 mantras for the Sun, 11,000 thousand for the Moon, 11,000 thousand for Mars, 9,000 for Mercury, 19,000 for Jupiter, 16,000 for Venus, 23,000 for Saturn, 18,000 for Rāhu, and 17,000 for Ketu. Many south Indian traditions use the number of mantras as the years of the planet's viṁśottari daśā. For example, Jupiter would be 16,000 mantras, while Venus is 20,000 mantras, etc. Then there are also other variations that will be discussed in later lessons.

Parāśara also gives traditional Vedic mantras in verses 17 and 18 by listing the first words of the Vedic hymn. For example, he lists *"bṛhaspate ati yadaryo"* as the mantra for Jupiter. This comes from book 2, hymn 25 where the full mantra is:

बृहस्पते अति यदर्यो अर्हाद् द्युमद् विभाति क्रतुमज्जनेषु
यद्दीदयच्चवस ऋतप्रजात तदस्मसु द्रविणं धेहिचित्रम्

bṛhaspate ati yadaryo arhād dyumad vibhāti kratumajjaneṣu
yaddīdayaccavasa ṛtaprajāta tadasmasu draviṇaṁ dhehicitram

"Bṛhaspati, born of truth, grant us that wonderful treasure, wherewith the pious man may worship exceedingly; that (wealth) which shines among men; which is endowed with lustre, (is) the means of (performing holy) rites, and invigorates (its possessor) with strength[149]."

These mantras require the guidance of a teacher to learn proper pronunciation and intonation. It is recommended that a beginner start with simple *nāma-mantras*. A *'nāma'* mantra is a *'name'* mantra. You put Auṁ in front of the planet or diety's name and namaḥ afterward, with *'āya'* added to the name as an english preposition. Namaḥ is a praise, so it is *Auṁ praise to the planet*. For example, Auṁ Chandrāya namaḥ means "Auṁ praises *(namaḥ)* to *(āya)* the Moon *(Chandra)*." Or use the appropriate deity mantra for the planet. When the Sun is worshipped as Śiva one says *"Auṁ namaḥ Śivāya"* or for Viṣṇu one can do *"Auṁ Viṣṇave namaḥ"*. In later work, we will study the science of mantra more in depth.

Planet	Namaḥ Mantras[150]	Sādhu Sandkuli Tantra Mantras
Sun	auṁ namaḥ sūryāya	klīm aiṁ śrīṁ hrīṁ sūryāya namaḥ
Moon	auṁ namaḥ chandrāya	hrīṁ hrīṁ huṁ somāya svāhā
Mars	auṁ namaḥ maṅgalāya	hrīṁ auṁ aiṁ kujāya svāhā
Mercury	auṁ namaḥ budhāya	auṁ klīṁ auṁ budhāya svāhā
Jupiter	auṁ namaḥ gurave	raṁ yaṁ hrīm aiṁ gurave namaḥ
Venus	auṁ namaḥ śukrāya	huṁ huṁ śrīṁ śrīṁ naṁ raṁ śukrāya svāhā
Saturn	auṁ namaḥ śanaiścarāya	hrīṁ klīm śanaiścarāya namaḥ
Rāhu	auṁ namaḥ rahave	bam aiṁ baṁ baṁ klīṁ baṁ tamase svāhā
Ketu	auṁ namaḥ ketave	śrīṁ śrīm āṁ baṁ raṁ laṁ ketave svāhā

[149] *Ṛgveda Saṁhitā*, Parimal Publications translation
[150] Namaḥ goes in the front of the planet name making it a safe mantra, unless the specific planet name has been given according to the mantra chakras and the first letter is beneficial to the individual.

Note on Fire Ceremony:

Parāśara then teaches about the *havana* (verse 21-22), which is the fire ceremony used to worship the planets. He mentions the *bhojana* (verse 23-24) and donation (verse 25) done afterward. Whenever a fire ceremony is done, these two things are performed for completion. The fire offers the prayers to the form of the deity that lives outside of us. The feeding (bhojana) is done with foods specific to the planets to make offerings for the aspect of the deva that exist inside of the human being. We still find this in our culture where after a marriage, graduation, or funeral there is food for everyone who attended the ceremony. Some say that the planet or deity will eat the food through these people to become pacified. For the Sun, Parāśara recommends rice with raw sugar (jaggary), and rice with milk (rice pudding) for the Moon, Rice with curd (sour cream) for Venus, rice with ghee for Jupiter, etc. The food will relate to the planet being propitiated. Then after the fire ceremony, donation is made.

Donation of objects that will benefit people ruled by the planet or deity are given away. A milk giving cow (dhenu) is donated for the Sun, conch shell (śaṇkha) for the Moon, etc according to Parāśara. These objects need to be updated for the modern day relative to what the planet rules. Gifting a vehicle to a woman's shelter for Venus, books to a school for Mercury, or computers to an impoverished school district for Ketu. In this way, the beneficial effects of the pūjā are continuing to create good karmas long after the ritual has finished. It is a **standard** practice, that after a fire ceremony, feeding and donation is performed.

The Bhagavad Gītā says,

काङ्क्षन्तः कर्मणां सिद्धिं यजन्त इह देवताः ।
क्षिप्रं हि मानुषे लोके सिद्धिर् भवति कर्मजा ॥१२ ॥

kāṅkṣantaḥ karmaṇāṁ siddhiṁ yajanta iha devatāḥ|
kṣipraṁ hi mānuṣe loke siddhir bhavati karmajā||IV.12||

In the world of men desiring success in actions, they worship the devas,
and quickly success born from ritual actions is accomplished.

VII. Time to Perform the Remedy

It is important that a remedy be performed at a beneficial time. If you go to the movies and get there two hours late you won't be able to catch the movie. In the same way, time has a certain frequency and specific use that will allow the remedy to give the best results. When the transit of Jupiter is either over or trine to the affliction, then the suffering is possible to overcome. It is beneficial to perform the remedy on a good day of the week and a beneficial tithi. The proper mūhurta (starting time) is also needed. Parāśara mentions,

यस्य यश्च यदा दुःस्थः स तं यत्नेन पूजयेत्।
एषां धात्रा वरो दत्तः पूजिताः पूजयिष्यथ ॥ २६ ॥

yasya yaśca yadā duḥsthaḥ sa taṁ yatnena pūjayet ǀ
eṣāṁ dhātrā varo dattaḥ pūjitāḥ pūjayiṣyatha ǀǀ 26ǀǀ

When the planet will be of ill condition (*duḥstha*) ritual (*pūjā*) is performed
The creator *(dhatṛ)* has granted *(datta)* the blessing *(vara)*
that the worshipper's request *(eṣā)* will be honored *(pūjita)*.

Remedies are an important aspect of Vedic astrology, which will take time and further study to master. The more one learns about the deities, what they represent, how they are worshipped and the secret archetypal meaning behind them, the better one will be able to prescribe the best remedy. For example, the root ginger is a good aid for digestion. If you give a person ginger their digestion will improve. Cinnamon is a carminative (removes flatulence) and when added to ginger improves digestion and assimilation. Though cinnamon is heating and if used alone with ginger it will increase the heat too much. If added with cumin, a cooling digestant, it will promote better digestion and remove flatulence in a balanced way. Or a beginner could just prescribe ginger and it would take a little longer, but would eventually work. In this way, the basic remedies will be beneficial, and the more fine-tuning applied, the more efficient the remedy will be for the individual.

मानवानां ग्रहाधीना उच्छ्रायाः पतनानि च ।
भावाऽभावौ च जगतां तस्मात् पूज्यतमा ग्रहाः ॥ २७ ॥

mānavānāṁ grahādhīnā uñchrāyāḥ patanāni ca ǀ
bhāvā'bhāvau ca jagatāṁ tasmāt pūjyatamā grahāḥ ǀǀ 27ǀǀ

Humans are subject *(adhīna)* to accumulation of prosperity or
falling into ruin according to the planets *(bhāvā'bhāvau)*,
because of that beings therefore honour the grahas with rituals *(pūjā)*.

Chapter 15

Pañchāṅga:
The Five Limbs of Time

Pañchāṅga: Five Limbs of Time

Maharṣi Parāśara declares the relationship of the five elements to the grahas in the third Chapter where he describes the planets.

अग्निभूमिनभस्तोयवायवः क्रमतो द्विज ।
भौमादीनां ग्रहाणां च तत्त्वानीति यथाक्रमम् ॥ २० ॥

agnibhūminabhastoyavāyavaḥ kramato dvija ।
bhaumādīnāṁ grahāṇāṁ ca tattvānīti yathākramam ।। 3.20।।

Fire, Earth, Ether/Sky, Water and Air, are respectively governed by Mars, Mercury, Jupiter, Venus, and Saturn.

The five planets removing Sun and Moon, and Rāhu and Ketu are the primary rulers over the five elements. This is seen in the Pañcha-mahāpuruṣa yogas where each of the five elements takes predominance in a chart and is also represented by the 33 devas where the Sun and Moon are their own manifest devas while the other grahas manifest among the five elements of the aṣṭa vasava. In certain techniques Sun and Moon will show fire and water, but their primary significations are transcendent of the five elements.

Mercury	Venus	Mars	Satun	Jupiter
Earth	Water	Fire	Air	Ether
pṛthvi	jala	agni	vāyu	ākāśa

The five elements make up the manifest world both relative to space and time. In space (the material world) everything is composed of the combination of the five elements, and everything exists in the five states of matter (solid, liquid, combustion, gaseous and ether). This is the foundation of the material world and therefore fundamental to āyurveda. Time, in the same way, is composed of the five elements. These five elements give Time its qualitative nature. The Astrologer must be able to read the condition of these five elements of Time as the *Vaidya* (Āyurvedic doctor) reads the conditions of space. Therefore, both beneficial times (festivals) and negative times *(doṣas)* need to be seen and understood.

The Vaidya learns to watch the five elements in nature (space) to understand how they work in the body. This is based on the concept that we are a microcosm which is reflective of the macrocosm. That which makes the universe work makes the human work. In the same way, what the grahas significate on the material plane will be reflected in the quality of the element connected to the Time.

When the five elements display themselves as the five aspects of time they are called the **Pañcha** (five) **aṅga** (limbs) of time. These form the Vedic analysis of Time and its effect on ALL created things. The pañchāṅga is something that astrologers read every morning to be in tune with the stars and planets. As a tree has roots, bark, leaves, flower and fruit, so does time take on its own dimensional form which is perceived by the trained astrologer.

Element	Planet	Anga	Qualities
Fire	Mars	Vāra	Health, vitality, strength, protection
Air	Saturn	Nakṣatra	Prana, disease, bodily ailments, suffering
Water	Venus	Tithi	Love, passion, desires, relationships
Earth	Mercury	Karaṇa	Work, career, achievements, skill
Ether	Jupiter	Yoga	Harmony, general relations, friends

I. Vāra (Solar Day)

There are seven solar days that together make the period of time called the week. In the pañchāṅga, the solar day is ruled by Fire element *(agni tattva)*. Mars (fire) rules over energy, vitality, and strength, therefore the vāra lord will show the general strength and vitality of a person.

#	Day *(English)*	Vāra *(Sanskrit)*	Graha
1	Sunday	Ravivāra	Sun
2	Monday	Somavāra	Moon
3	Tuesday	Maṅgalavāra	Mars
4	Wednesday	Buddhavāra	Mercury
5	Thursday	Guruvāra	Jupiter
6	Friday	Śukravāra	Venus
7	Saturday	Śanivāra	Saturn

According to Āyurveda, the strength of the agni in the body is important for the digestive/transformative processes. There are 13 types of agni in the body; the digestive fire in the stomach, the agni that digests each element, and the agni of each tissue (*dhātu*). When the digestive fire is strong it removes all toxins (*ama*) from the body. When the agni is low there are toxins present causing low ojas. Whereas when ama is removed ojas increases and the person has a strong immune system. When each of the seven dhātu agnis are healthy it allows each tissue to be formed properly, thereby allowing the next tissue in the process to be formed healthy and strong. This leads Ojas (the final result of dhātu digestion) to be formed properly and in a larger amount. Thereby the body is healthier, stronger, has more energy and vitality. If the vāra lord is poorly placed in a natal chart, the agni will tend to be weak and there will be problems related to ama and improper formation of dhātus. If the vāra lord is well placed the body complex will tend to be strong and have more vitality.

The days of the week are based on the seven physical grahas. The chāya-grahas (nodes of the Moon) do not have physical bodies and therefore do not relate to the vāra. The order of the days is systematically calculated based on the horās (hours) of the day, therefore one must understand the horās.

A rāśi takes about 2 hours to rise while half a rāśi, called a horā-aṁśa, takes one hour to rise. This is the root of the time period called the hour *(horā)* which comes from the movement of the 12 signs of the zodiac. Twelve signs divided in half portions of lunar and solar parts create twenty-four horās in a day. Each hour of the day is ruled by a physical planet.

The order of the lordship of the hours is based on slowest to fastest motion. Saturn is the farthest from the Sun and therefore the slowest, then Jupiter, then Mars. Earth is the next closest planet to the Sun but in Jyotiṣa we are using the geocentric view for Horā calculations (helio-centric for gaṇita) - and therefore the Sun moves the speed of the Earth making the Sun the next fastest planet. Next in speed are Venus, then Mercury and the fastest moving body in the sky is the Moon. This is the order of the horās and logic behind it.

According to *Sūrya Siddhānta* (I.51-52), the lordships of the days of the week are calculated from the day of entering Kali Yuga. This is also the day of the flood according to Christian/Muslim astrologers.

The Vedic day starts at sunrise and the day is owned/named by the horā at sunrise. Every seven days the cycle of horās repeat creating the week.

LMT	Hora	Sun	Mon	Tues	Wed	Thurs	Fri	Sat
6AM	1	Sun	Mon	Mar	Mer	Jup	Ven	Sat
7AM	2	Ven	Sat	Sun	Mon	Mar	Mer	Jup
8AM	3	Mer	Jup	Ven	Sat	Sun	Mon	Mar
9AM	4	Mon	Mar	Mer	Jup	Ven	Sat	Sun
10AM	5	Sat	Sun	Mon	Mar	Mer	Jup	Ven
11AM	6	Jup	Ven	Sat	Sun	Mon	Mar	Mer
12AM	7	Mar	Mer	Jup	Ven	Sat	Sun	Mon
1PM	8	Sun	Mon	Mar	Mer	Jup	Ven	Sat
2PM	9	Ven	Sat	Sun	Mon	Mar	Mer	Jup
3PM	10	Mer	Jup	Ven	Sat	Sun	Mon	Mar
4PM	11	Mon	Mar	Mer	Jup	Ven	Sat	Sun
5PM	12	Sat	Sun	Mon	Mar	Mer	Jup	Ven
6PM	13	Jup	Ven	Sat	Sun	Mon	Mar	Mer
7PM	14	Mar	Mer	Jup	Ven	Sat	Sun	Mon
8PM	15	Sun	Mon	Mar	Mer	Jup	Ven	Sat
9PM	16	Ven	Sat	Sun	Mon	Mar	Mer	Jup
10PM	17	Mer	Jup	Ven	Sat	Sun	Mon	Mar
11PM	18	Mon	Mar	Mer	Jup	Ven	Sat	Sun
12PM	19	Sat	Sun	Mon	Mar	Mer	Jup	Ven
1AM	20	Jup	Ven	Sat	Sun	Mon	Mar	Mer
2AM	21	Mar	Mer	Jup	Ven	Sat	Sun	Mon
3AM	22	Sun	Mon	Mar	Mer	Jup	Ven	Sat
4AM	23	Ven	Sat	Sun	Mon	Mar	Mer	Jup
5AM	24	Mer	Jup	Ven	Sat	Sun	Mon	Mar

The first horā on Monday is ruled by the Moon and the first horā on Tuesday is ruled by Mars. This is a standard rule that applies to months, years, etc- the lord of a month is the day the first day of the month starts. In Jyotiṣa, the beginning is what counts- in your chart it is the moment of birth/start that tells about your whole life, the chart at the beginning of a journey tells about the whole journey. So the lord of the first hour of the day gives the day its energy, the horā lord flavors the day.

Therefore, the vāra lord is calculated based on the lord of the first horā of the day. This makes the entire day beneficial for the particular activities of the bhāvas ruled by the lord of that particular day. Vāras and horās have an impact relative to the bhāvas they rule. For example, the best day to go for a job is the day of the tenth lord (career). The best day to go to the doctor is the day of the fourth lord (cure). The vāra will show what activities have strength (agni) behind them for the day. If you can't go for a job interview on the day of the tenth lord, then second best choice is the horā of the tenth lord.

"All activities that are started during the horā which is ruled by the lord of the related bhāva in the birth chart shall surely fructify. Similarly, activities started during the horā of the badhakeśa [obstacle planet] from the concerned bhāva shall suffer obstruction and activities started during the horā of the rogeśa (8th house lord) from the concerned bhāva shall suffer annihilation[151]."

For a Gemini ascendant trying to get a job, the tenth house is Pisces and ruled by Jupiter, which makes Thursday the best day to apply. If the individual cannot apply on Thursday then they should insure that the time is Jupiter horā for their interview. Eighth from the concerned bhāva is Libra ruled by Venus, the individual should avoid Venus horā for trying to get a job.

Practice Exercises:

1. What is the lord of the day you were born? How is that planet placed in your chart? Look at the charts of a few people you know who are prone to being sick, and see the situation of their vāra lord.
2. What is the best day for you to apply for a new job, or ask for a raise? What is the best day to buy a new car or house? If you can't do this activity on this particular day, then what time on a Monday would be beneficial for these activities?
3. Review in the chapter on strengths the varṣādi-bala and see the level of importance given to the horā-lord.
4. Study the chart on the horās and days closely and make sure you understand the pattern. You should be able to take any hour of any day and be able to mentally calculate the lord of the hour (*horā lord*) from your head without using the chart.

[151] Rath, Sanjay, Kala Hora

II. Nakṣatra (Lunar Constellation):

In a sidereal month it takes the Moon 27.3217 days to complete one revolution of the zodiac. This motion is the basis of the nakṣatra. For material plane calculations the time is rounded down to 27 lunar signs. For spiritual purposes the time is converted to 28 lunar signs. The nakṣatra relate to the Air Element *(vāyu-tattva)* and thus relate to the planet Saturn.

The nakṣatras show the direction and state of the vāyu (which becomes prāṇa in the human body). The mind (concentration) goes where the prāṇa is directed, and the prāṇa goes where the mind is directed. By thinking of devotion and love the prāṇa will go to the heart area and make it warm where by thinking about sex, the prāṇa will go to the sexual organs and arouse them. In the same way, by meditating (focusing the mind) on the third eye center in the forehead, then the mind will think about spiritual understanding. By meditating on the root chakra the mind will dwell on security, home and health issues. The state of the prāṇa will show the direction and state of the mind. The state of the mind when beginning an event will show the intentions and ideas in the mind of the people starting the event. This state of mind will fructify within the existence of that created object or event. If the mind is focused on destruction or infidelity at the time of marriage, the union will not last long; while if the mind is focused on love and sharing (by the Moon being in the appropriate nakṣatra at the time of the event) then that energy will merge the two people into each other in a happy marriage.

The nakṣatras will show how the overall success of an event will fructify. If the prāṇas are good the event will be healthy (well enjoyed). If the prāṇas are weak or in the wrong direction, there will not be health to the event. The strength and placement of the viṁśottari graha lord of the nakṣatra will indicate the strength of the mind/prāṇa within the event or created object or person. In the natal chart, if the *viṁśottari graha lord* of the *natal nakṣatra* is ill placed then the prāṇas of the individual are weakened. This will lead to ill health and lack of focus in the mind which leads to suffering.

In āyurveda there are two main aspects to health, agni-ojas and the balance of the five vāyus (prāṇas in the body). The vāra relates to agni and the strength of the body complex. The nakṣatra relates to the state of the proper or improper flow of prāṇa in the body. When the prāṇa becomes blocked or does not flow correctly disease begins in the body. Vāra relates to disease that is based on the physical level so physical medicine is best to cure it. The disease may disrupt the mind, but the primary treatment is of the physical body, the root of the disease. Nakṣatra shows disease that starts in the *prāṇa-maya-koṣa* (energy body) and the *mano-maya-koṣa* (mind). This disease should be treated primarily through energetic medicine and treatment of the mind through yoga, psychological therapy, meditation, etc. When the disease manifests in the physical body, physical treatment can work but only temporarily. Both physical treatment to alleviate the symptoms and subtle therapy should be used. In summary, vāra shows the strength of the body while nakṣatra shows the functioning (flow of energy).

#	Nakṣatra	Graha	#	Nakṣatras	Graha
1	Aśvinī	Ketu	15	Svātī	Rāhu
2	Bharaṇī	Venus	16	Viśākhā	Jupiter
3	Kṛttikā	Sun	17	Anurādhā	Saturn
4	Rohiṇī	Moon	18	Jyeṣṭhā	Mercury
5	Mṛgaśira	Mars	19	Mūla	Ketu
6	Ārdrā	Rāhu	20	Pūrvāṣāḍhā	Venus
7	Punarvasu	Jupiter	21	Uttarāṣāḍhā	Sun
8	Puṣya	Saturn	(28)	Abhijit	- - -
9	Āśleṣā	Mercury	22	Śravaṇa	Moon
10	Maghā	Ketu	23	Dhaniṣṭhā	Mars
11	Pūrvaphalgunī	Venus	24	Śatabhiṣa	Rāhu
12	Uttaraphalgunī	Sun	25	Pūrvābhādra	Jupiter
13	Hasta	Moon	26	Uttarabhādra	Saturn
14	Citrā	Mars	27	Revatī	Mercury

Practice Exercises:

3. What is the state of your nakśatra lord in the rāśi chart?
4. Is your ill health more likely to the malfunction of the agni or to the vāyu element? What can you do to protect your health with this information?

III. Tithi (Lunar day):

The Moon has 15 tithis in the waxing half called the *Śukla-pakṣa* (white/bright half). The 15 tithis of the waning Moon are called *Kṛṣṇa-pakṣa* (black/dark half). The new Moon is called *Amāvāsya*; amā means together, and vāsya means to dwell. Amāvāsya is when the Sun and the Moon dwell together; this is seen as a conjunction of the luminaries. When they begin to move apart, with the Moon surpassing the Sun, the waxing Moon begins. The eighth tithi is the half Moon. The fifteenth śukla tithi is called *Pūrṇimā* which comes from the word pūrṇa meaning full, complete, abundant, filled, satisfied. It is the Full Moon when the Sun and the Moon are 180 degrees apart.

Śukla-Pakṣa (Bright Half)

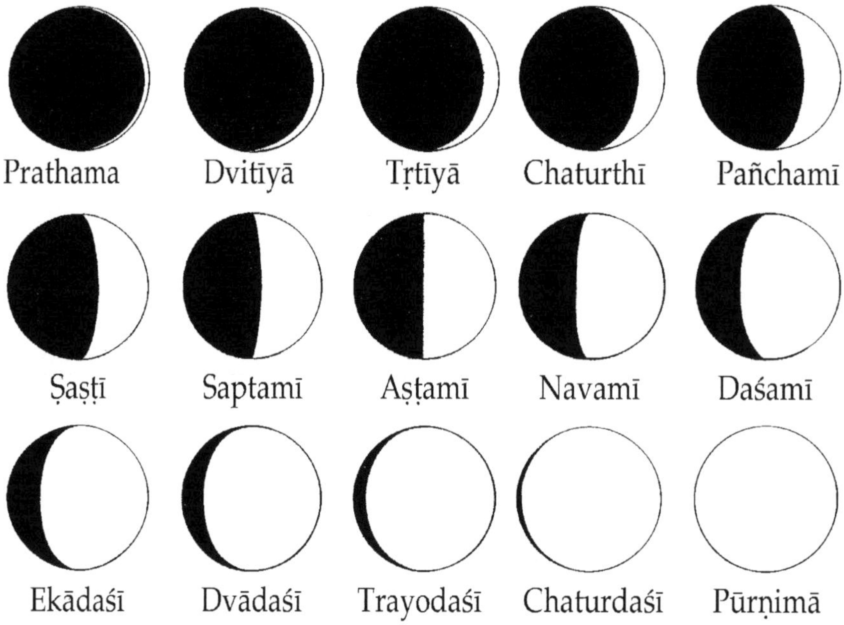

Kṛṣṇa-Pakṣa (Dark Half)

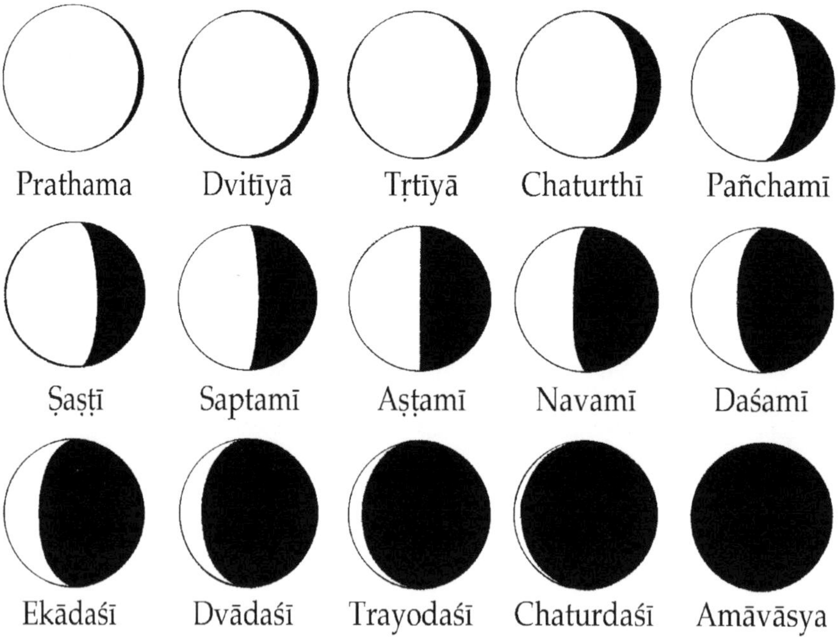

There are 30 Tithi related to the 29.5306 days it takes the Moon to go through one synodic cycle. The Lunar day is approximately .9483 that of a solar day. It is calculated according to every 12 degree motion of the Moon. The Tithi is calculated by subtracting the Sun's longitude from the Moon and dividing by 12 degrees. This is to calculate how many 12 degree portions (Tithis) the Moon has moved forward.

The differentiation of the Sun and the Moon gives the Tithi, while the addition of the Sun and Moon's longitude gives the *pañcāṅga Yoga*. The subtraction of the Sun and Moon relates to the asura-guru[152] Venus, while the addition of the Sun and Moon relate to the deva-guru Jupiter. Venus relates to the water element *(jala-tattva)* and shows desires and passions of the mind. Venus also relates to Lakṣmi and thereby shows prosperity.

Using a tithi in muhūrta, one will see the desires of the mind at that time of the event or creation, what people will want and what will make them happy, how easily they will be gratified or not satisfied. This relates to the quality of the desire that is experienced, while the nakṣatra will show how the emotion arising with it is integrated into the person and utilized by the mind.

In the natal chart, the placement of the lord of the tithi will show how love relationship is experienced. If it is weakly placed, there will be problems indicated in the relationship aspect of life.

Tithi	Tithi Name	Graha lord
1 & 9	Pratipad, Navamī	Sun
2 & 10	Dvītiyā, Daśamī	Moon
3 & 11	Tṛtīyā, Ekādaśī	Mars
4 & 12	Caturthī, Dvādaśī	Mercury
5 & 13	Pañcamī, Trayodaśī	Jupiter
6 & 14	Ṣaṣṭhī, Caturdaśī	Venus
7 & Full Moon	Saptamī, Pūrṇimā	Saturn
8 & New Moon	Aṣṭamī, Amāvāsya	Rāhu

[152] Venus is the teacher *(guru)* of the demons *(asuras)*. Asura is those who are lacking light *(sura)* or understanding, and focused on the material plane of enjoyment. Jupiter is the teacher *(guru)* of the devas *(light beings)* who follow the path of higher works and good character.

The fifteen tithis are ruled by the planets in the order of the days of the week plus Rāhu. Sun (Sunday), Moon (Monday), Mars (Tuesday), etc and this repeats twice through each pakṣa (half lunar month). The lord of the tithi should be well placed for starting any events that involve love, passion or the longevity of relationship. When the lord of the tithi is weak, the factors that show problems in relationship will make themselves dominant in a person's chart/life.

These fifteen tithis are also broken down into five groups given below according to the five elements within the tithi. These are the five elemental aspects of desire (tithi-water-Venus).

Name	Tithi			Tattva[153]
Nanda	Pratipad (1)	Ṣaṣṭhī (6)	Ekādaśī (11)	Agni
Bhadra	Dvītiyā (2)	Saptamī (7)	Dvādaśī (12)	Pṛthvī
Jāya	Tṛtīyā (3)	Aṣṭamī (8)	Trayodaśī (13)	Ākāśa
Ṛkta	Caturthī (4)	Navamī (9)	Caturdaśī (14)	Jala
Pūrṇa	Pañcamī (5)	Daśamī (10)	Pūrṇimā/Amāvāsya	Vāyu

These elements are seen in the center of the Sarvatobhadra-cakra (seen in the nakṣatra chapter). The *nanda* tithi is associated with Tuesday and Sunday, the *bhadra* tithis are connected to Wednesday, *jāya* is connected to Thursday, etc. The planet which lords the tithi is used to determine the strength of desire on that particular lunar day. The element is used to see the qualitative nature of the desire. The elements are seen to create cycles of a six pointed star when mapped into the degrees of the zodiac, the example star at the left is of nanda tithis.

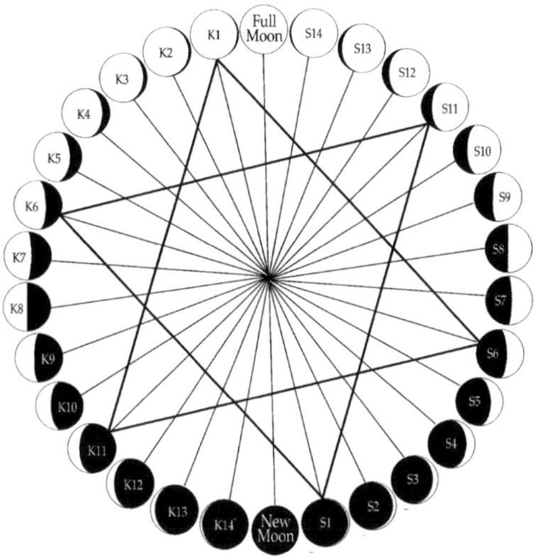

Tṛtīyā tithi (3rd) is ruled by Mars but as it is Jāya (ruled by ākaśa/ Jupiter) so it can bring two people together, as ākāśa is the binding force that holds things together. Ekādaśī tithi (11th) is ruled by Mars and it is nanda (ruled by fire-Mars) so the fighting desire is very strong. Mars is passionate, energetic, and creates conflict, it is not good for marriage, though good for war and leadership. Fasting on ekādaśī will get one over anger, because Mars is the lord and it is a nanda (fire) tithi. Vaiśṇavas fast on the 11th Tithi to be perfect peaceful devotees. No one will fight with the one who has done this fast for some time. Fasting on aṣṭamī will make it so you never cheat anyone,

[153] Rath, Sanjay, *Triṁśāṁśa D-30*

so will not get cheated. Fasting on the full Moon will give you truth as it removes the negative effects of Saturn.

To get a better understanding of the tithi one can relate them to their respective deity. Varāhamihira says in the *Bṛhat Saṁhitā* (chapter XCIX) that "Since Rohiṇī star and pratipada are presided over by Brahmā, all works that are allowed under the star can be performed under the tithi too. Similarly in regard to the star Abhijit and dvītiyā; Śravaṇa and the 3rd lunar day, Bharaṇī and the 4th lunar day, Mṛgaśira and the 5th lunar day", etc. When one understands the deities one can use the nakṣatra and tithi more readily and deeply.

Varāhamihira, Bṛhat Saṁhitā, chapter XCIX, verses 1-3			
Tithi	**Tithi Name**	**Graha lord**	**Deity**
1	Pratipad	Sun	Brahmā
2	Dvitīyā	Moon	Vidhāṭṛ *(Hari)*
3	Tṛtīyā	Mars	Viṣṇu
4	Caturthī	Mercury	Yama
5	Pañcamī	Jupiter	Chandra
6	Ṣaṣṭhī	Venus	Agni *(Subrahmaṇya)*
7	Saptamī	Saturn	Indra
8	Aṣṭamī	Rāhu	Vasus
9	Navamī	Sun	Nāga
10	Daśamī	Moon	Dharma *(Aryamā)*
11	Ekādaśī	Mars	Rudra
12	Dvādaśī	Mercury	Āditya *(Savitṛ)*
13	Trayodaśī	Jupiter	Manmatha *(Bhaga)*
14	Caturdaśī	Venus	Kāli
Full	Pūrṇimā	Saturn	Viśvadevas
New	Amāvāsya	Rāhu	Pitṛs

Practice Exercises:

5. What is the tithi lord for the day you were born and how is it placed in the natal chart? What is this indicating about your relationship karma?

Interaction between the Vāra and Tithi

When specific tithis line up with certain vāras they are considered auspicious or treacherous combinations. One such group called *siddhi-yogas* show that the work on those days is accomplished successfully. If pratipada (1st), ṣaṣṭhī (6th), or dvādaśī (12th) fall on a Friday, it is considered auspicious. [These are based on ghātaka-cakra correlations to the days.]

Nanda	Bhadra	Jāya	Ṛkta	Pūrṇa
1, 6, 11	2, 7, 12	3, 8, 13	4, 9, 14	5, 10, 15/30
Friday	Wednesday	Tuesday	Saturday	Thursday

In the same way there are certain combinations that are inauspicious, where there will be hurdles in accomplishing works. These inauspicious days have been called Dagdha, Viṣa, and Hutāśana. *Dagdha* means burnt, scorched, inauspicious, consumed by fire, pained, or tormented. Viṣa means poison or venom. *Hutāśana* means fire, the oblation-eater, purified by fire, fear, and alarm.

	Sun	Mon	Tues	Wed	Thurs	Fri	Sat
Dagdha	12th	11th	5th	3rd	6th	8th	9th
Viṣa	4th	6th	7th	2nd	8th	9th	7th
Hutaśan	12th	6th	7th	8th	9th	10th	11th

Kālacakra Remedies

Pūjās done to propitiate planets can be done at specific times that give them the power to overcome the problems of negative combinations, aspects and placements. Using the Kālacakra one can calculate which day and tithi would be best to fast, do pūjās and other upāyas (remedies). Some remedies only require a one time pūjā for results. These pūjās can be expensive and time consuming and the results should be successful the first time. For example, if a person has had several failed operations, and then they learn of a karmic problem causing the malfunction in their chart, they can do the pūjā remedy before the next operation. In this case, we need to perform the puja at the most powerful time to ensure positive results for the individual.

The most powerful time to do a pūjā is when the vāra of a planet aligns with the tithi opposite it on the Kālacakra. These certain days are very powerful for planetary propitiations. For example, worshipping the Sun on ṣaṣṭī or caturdaśī is auspicious because they are tithis ruled by its Kālacakra opposite. Worshipping the Moon on pañchamī and trayodaśī is auspicious because these tithis are ruled by the Moon's opposite, Jupiter. Jupiter upāya (remedy) is most powerful on a Thursday that falls on a dvitīyā or daśamī. When Thursday falls on a daśamī it is called *Sudaśā-vrata,* which means the su (good) daśā (time period) begins and the dur (bad) daśā ends. There are various rituals performed on that day to empower Jupiter.

Worshipping a Mercury rūpa (form) is auspicious on aṣṭamī and Amāvāsya to destroy/remove the evil effects of Rāhu. When Wednesday falls on an aṣṭamī it is called *Buddhāṣṭamī*, where the Rāhu deluding the memory of Mercury can be removed with appropriate rituals. So propitiations for these planets should be done on the most powerful days. These days are used when a certain upāya such as a single pūjā is advised to remove the ill effects of a planet.

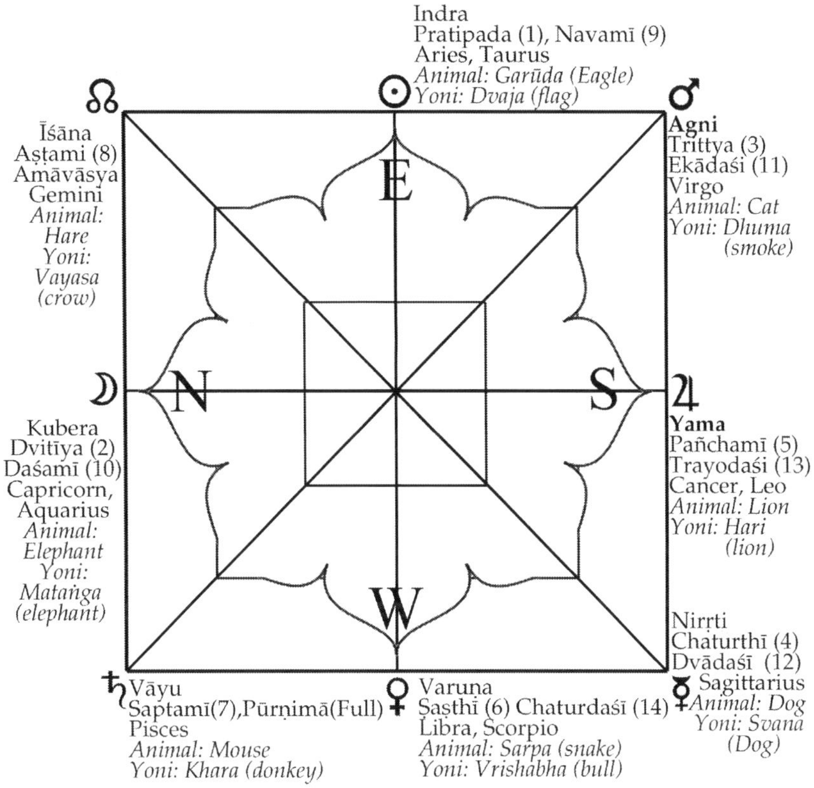

Worship	On this Tithi for Suppression of:	Kālacakra Opposite
Sun	Ṣaṣṭhī, Caturdaśī	Venus
Moon	Pañcamī, Trayodaśī	Jupiter
Mars	Saptamī, Pūrṇimā	Saturn
Mercury	Aṣṭamī, Amāvāsya	Rāhu
Jupiter	Dvitīyā, Daśamī,	Moon
Venus	Pratipad, Navamī	Sun
Saturn	Tṛtīyā, Ekādaśī	Mars
Rāhu	Caturthī, Dvādaśī	Mercury

IV. Karaṇa (Half Lunar Day)

The tithi of twelve degrees is divided into two halves of six degrees each making up a karaṇa. These two halves show how the desire (of the tithi) is achieved. The karaṇas relate to earth element *(pṛthvi-tattva)* and are associated with Mercury. The earth element is the physical action taken to achieve the water element, just as earth (a container) is what gives water form.

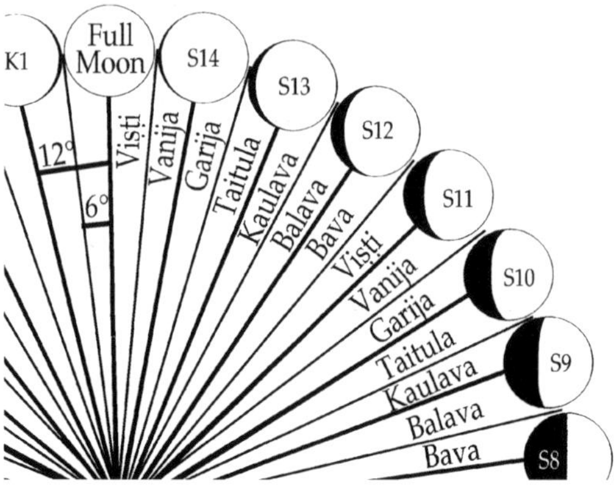

Mercury relates to the tenth house of profession and therefore shows career, applied skills, and achievements. In muhūrta, the karaṇa will become important when work is needed to achieve the desired result. A beneficial karaṇa will ensure the work is done correctly and on time. The division of the tithi into karaṇas is slightly different for each phase of the Moon.

Tithi	Śukla-Pakṣa Karaṇas		Kṛṣṇa-Pakṣa Karaṇas	
Pratipad (1)	Kinstughna	Bava	Balava	Kaulava
Dvitīyā (2)	Balava	Kaulava	Taitula	Garija
Tṛtīyā (3)	Taitula	Garija	Vanija	Viṣṭi
Caturthī (4)	Vanija	Viṣṭi	Bava	Balava
Pañcamī (5)	Bava	Balava	Kaulava	Taitula
Ṣaṣṭhī (6)	Kaulava	Taitula	Garija	Vanija
Saptamī (7)	Garija	Vanija	Viṣṭi	Bava
Aśtamī (8)	Viṣṭi	Bava	Balava	Kaulava
Navamī (9)	Balava	Kaulava	Taitulaa	Garija
Daśamī (10)	Taitula	Garija	Vanija	Viṣṭi
Ekadaśī (11)	Vanija	Viṣṭi	Bava	Balava
Dvādaśī (12)	Bava	Balava	Kaulava	Taitula
Trayodaśī (13)	Kaulava	Taitula	Garija	Vanija
Caturdaśī (14)	Garija	Vanija	Viṣṭi	Śakuni
Pūrṇimā/Amāvāsya	Viṣṭi	Bava	Chatuspad	Nāga

In the natal chart the lord of the karaṇa is seen for issues related to the tenth house and Mercury. If the karaṇa lord is poorly placed or afflicted in the natal chart it will show problems relative to profession. Their lordships are given in the table below:

#	Karaṇa	Graha	Deity
1	Bava	Sun	Jyeṣṭhā/Indra
2	Balava	Moon	Rohiṇī/Brahmā
3	Kaulava	Mars	Anurādhā /Mitra
4	Taitula	Mercury	Uttaraphalgunī/Aryamā
5	Garija	Jupiter	Jyeṣṭhā/Indra (Bhū- Earth)
6	Vanija	Venus	Śravaṇa/Viṣṇu (Śrī)
7	Viṣṭi	Saturn	Bharaṇī /Yama
8	Śakuni-Brahma	Lagna Lord	Āśleṣā/Nāga
9	Catuspada-Viṣṇu	Fourth lord	Rohiṇī/Brahmā
10	Nāga-Maheśa	Seventh lord	Āśleṣā/Nāga
11	Kiṁtughna-Sūrya	Tenth lord	Svātī/Vāyu

The strength and placement of the karaṇa lord will show the overall strength of the career related area of life. This can be seen before even looking at the tenth house and D-10 chart. The lord of the karaṇa or any planet conjunct this lord will influence the type of career a person will follow. The pañcāṅga takes precedence over almost all other indications, and is looked at in the beginning of a chart reading. This is why traditional astrology charts will always have the pañcāṅga placed right next to the birth chart.

V. Yoga (Union of Sun and Moon)

The sum of the longitudes of the Sun and the Moon give the factor of time called the yoga (or pañcāṅga-yoga). In viṁśottari daśā, the years of Jupiter (16) relate to the addition of the Sun (6) and the Moon (10). The pañcāṅga-yogas relate to Jupiter and the space element *(ākāśa tattva)*. Space holds the entire universe together pervading everything. In an interpersonal interaction, if the space element is strong the two people get along; if it is weak then the two people will fight. This is why Harihara says in *Praśna Mārga* that if Jupiter is strong all deities will favor you and if it is weak all deities will show you their wrath. This is because the ākāśa element/space is how one relates to the world.

Yoga #	Pañchāṅga-Yoga Name	Graha
1,10,19	Viṣkumbha, Gaṇḍa, Parighā	Saturn
2,11,20	Prīti, Vṛddhi, Śiva	Mercury
3,12,21	Ayuṣmān, Dhruva, Siddha	Ketu
4,13,22	Saubhāgya, Vyāghāta, Sādhya	Venus
5,14,23	Śobhana, Harṣana, Śubha	Sun
6,15,24	Atigaṇḍa, Vajra, Śukla	Moon
7,16,25	Sukarma, Siddhi, Brahmā	Mars
8,17,26	Dhṛti, Vyātipata, Indra	Rāhu
9,18,27	Śula, Variyān, Vaidhṛti	Jupiter

If the lord of the Yoga is strong in a chart there will be harmony in inter-personal relationships, if the lord is afflicted or weak then there will be fighting, enmity, lack of understanding and an inability to connect deeply.

The pañcāṅga-yoga is used in muhūrta during big events where many people will be gathering. A strong pañcāṅga-yoga lord ensures that the crowd will get along. It is important in events like peace rallies and projects geared to bring a closer relationship between two people or multiple organizations.

Practice Exercises:

7. Who is the lord of your karaṇa, how is it placed and how does this influence your career? Look at the karaṇa lord in the chart of friends or family members who have a hard time with that area of life.
8. What is the situation of your pañcāṅga-yoga lord in the Rāśi chart and how does this affect your ability to get along with others? Look at the chart of someone who gets along with every one and analyze their pañcāṅga-yoga lord. Look at the chart of some people who have a hard time getting along with others and analyze their pañcāṅga-yoga lord. Note the differences in the state of these planets.

Pañcāṅga Doṣas: Flaws in Time

Now you have a general understanding of each limb of the Pañcāṅga and ways to use each of them both in the natal chart as well as in muhūrta (choosing a good time for an event). Parāśara teaches that there are certain times (according to the pañcāṅga) that are indicative of problems or suffering. The entire last portion of Bṛhat Parāśara Horā Śāstra is decicated to analysis of combinations that indicate suffering from the last birth and the remedies to overcome these combinations.

Amāvāsya Doṣa

Birth on Amāvāsya (new Moon) causes poverty or hardship for the parents. This is the first individual pañcāṅga doṣa that Parāśara teaches[154]. Its remedy lies in worship of the Sun and Moon by the parents of the child. Then complete pūjā and homa are done. Alternative remedies for the doṣa are based upon the form of Kālī indicated by the New Moon placement.

Specifics of the Śānti pūjā are given by Parāśara in BPHS. Images of the Sun and Moon are to be made in gold (or silver and copper according to one's budget). Parāśara gives the mantras used to worship the Sun and Moon for this pacificication ritual. In them you can see the intent behind the ritual.

Mantra for the Moon:

आ प्यायस्व समेतु ते विश्वतः सोम वृष्ण्यम् भवा वाजस्य संगथे ॥

ā pyāyasva sametu te viśvataḥ soma vṛṣṇyam bhavā vājasya saṅgathe||1.91.16||

Grow to fullness, Soma, may you gather strength from everywhere,
focusing on success and prosperity. (Ṛgveda 10.36.14)

Mantra for the Sun:

सविता पश्चातात् सविता पुरस्तात् सवितोत्तरात्तात्सविताधरात्तात्
सविता नः सुवतु सर्वतातिं सविता नोरासतां दीर्घमयुः ॥१४ ॥

savitā paścātāt savitā purastāt savitottarāttātsavitādharāttāt
savitā naḥ suvatu sarvatātiṁ savitā norāsatāṁ dīrghamayuḥ||10.36.14||

May Savitṛ on the West, Savitṛ on the east, Savitṛ on the north,
Savitṛ on the South, may Savitṛ send us all desired wealth,
may Savitṛ bestow upon us long life. (Ṛgveda 1.91.16)

[154] Bṛhat Parāśara Horā Śāstra, Darśajanmaśāntyādhyāya (86/88)

Kṛṣṇa-Chaturthī Doṣa

Birth in the 14th waning tithi is a doṣa (problem causing lunar day). The tithi is divided into 6 parts.

1	0-16.6666%	Auspicious, no doṣa
2	16.6666-33.3333%	Early death of Father
3	33.3333-50%	Early death of Mother
4	50-66.6666%	Ruin of Maternal Uncle
5	66.6666-83.3333%	Destruction of Family
6	83.3333-100%	Downfall of self and loss of wealth

The remedy is found in Bṛhat Parāśara Horā Śāstra[155] and consists of worshiping Śiva with the crescent Moon on his head, in white clothes, white mālā, and riding his bull Nandi. Varuṇa mantra, Śiva pūjā, worship of the nine planets, and recitation of the Mṛtyuñjaya mantra are performed.

Eka Nakṣatra Doṣa

When two people in close family are born on the same nakṣatra the younger one will suffer loss of wealth and happiness, this often relates to some similar project the elder has started. If they share the same pada (navāṁśa), then the health will also suffer and even death can occur. The doṣa will activate when the two people separate from each other. The remedy[156] lies with proper worship of the deity ruling the nakṣatra. It must be performed on an auspicious vāra and nakṣatra while the Moon is strong. According to Parāśara the remedy cannot be performed on a Ṛkta-tithi nor a Viṣṭi-karaṇa.

A doṣa like this will not be seen by looking at the native's chart only. If you are looking at the entire family's chart it will be possible to notice; otherwise, it is determined through logical analysis. For example, if a person says they are having health or money problems and you notice it started just after the older brother moved out of the house, or just after they moved out from their own parents home, then you would look to see if there may be some nakṣatra similarity. In the same way, in Vāstu (Vedic Feng Shui) if health or marriage problems start just after a person moves into a new home, then one can look towards getting a Vāstu consultation to help overcome these problems. An astrologer should integrate all aspects of reality through logical analysis to determine the root problem. Only when the root problem is discovered can a proper remedy address the situation.

[155] Bṛhat Parāśara Horā Śāstra, Chapter 87/89
[156] Bṛhat Parāśara Horā Śāstra, Chapter 89/91

Saṅkrānti Doṣa

Saṅkrānti is when the Sun changes sign and has not yet reached greater than one degree, therefore making the Sun's position between zero and one degree. The day the Sun enters another sign there will be Saṅkrānti-doṣa for the entire day. In a natal chart, the vāra lord's houses will be destroyed by the Saṅkrānti-doṣa (the houses lorded by the lord of the day are destroyed). Those areas of life, planets and ārūḍhas placed there will not fructify until remedial measures are performed. Parāśara says it will bring poverty *(daridra)* and suffering *(duḥkha)* to the individual. This is because the Sun being in Saṅkrānti is said to show the wrath of Śiva.

There are 7 types of Saṅkrānti-doṣa depending on the day it occurs, each having its own name. These variations of the Saṅkranti are explained in depth in *Murhūrta-Cintāmaṇi*. Some will be worse or better for an individual depending on their position in life[157].

Saṅkrānti-doṣa pūjā consists of the ceremonial worship of the Sun, Moon and Śiva in kalaśa and bathing with the blessed water afterward. The Sun and Moon represent the left and right eyes while Śiva represents the third eye. The specific form is Mṛtyuñjaya Śiva who has the power to rejuvenate. Then the stated repetition of Mṛtyuñjaya japa is performed regularly.

Sunday	Ghora	Horrible
Monday	Dhvāṅkṣi	Beggar, Caw of crows
Tuesday	Mahodari	Big bellied- edema, swollen
Wednesday	Manda	Drunk, intoxicated
Thursday	Mandākini	Simple, foolish
Friday	Miśra	Mixed, diverse
Saturday	Rākṣasi	Demoness

Grahaṇa Doṣa

Birth on either a solar or lunar eclipse can cause sickness, suffering and poverty. The deity of the nakṣatra in which the eclipse took place is worshiped with the appropriate rituals. If it is a solar eclipse a gold image of the Sun is also made. If it is a lunar eclipse a silver image of the Moon is made. For both, an image of Rāhu is made in lead. According to Parāśara, each image is worshipped with the appropriate rituals for the particular deity by the parents of the child and then the sacred water of the kalaśa is used to bath the child to remove the afflictions.

[157] Muhūrta Cintāmaṇi, 3.1

Gaṇḍānta Doṣa

There are three types of gaṇḍānta and divisions among that given by Parāśara[158]. They indicate death (health problems) during birth, traveling, and auspicious ceremonies like marriage, etc.

Tithi	First two ghatis of Pūrṇa-tithis (5, 10, 15) and last two of Nanda-tithis (1, 6, 11) totaling four ghatis (ghati is 24 minutes)
Nakṣatra	Revatī - Aśvinī, Āśleṣā –Maghā, Jyeṣṭhā- Mūla (two ghatis of each)
Lagna	Pisces-Aries (Sva-gaṇḍānta), Cancer-Leo (Mātṛ-gaṇḍānta) , Scorpio-Sagittarius (Pitṛ-gaṇḍānta), half ghati of each

For nakṣatra gaṇḍānta, when a planet is in between nakṣatras, the remedy should be done in the first 10 days of birth before the father sees the child. The remedy (Abhiṣeka) should be done with the Father if it is in the first half of the gaṇḍānta and with the Mother if it is in the second half of the gaṇḍānta.

Tithi	Donation of a bull	Gold image of lord of tithi
Nakṣatra	Donation of cow with a calf	Gold image of lord of nakṣatra
Lagna	Donation of Gold	Gold image of lord of lagna

Parāśara says in the next chapter that birth in the gaṇḍānta between Jyeṣṭhā and Mūla is highly inauspicious because the deities Indra and Rakṣasi are highly inimical to each other. Birth in Mūla is called **Abhukta-Mūla**. The affliction will result in the child losing their father after the 8th year. The remedial ritual is much longer and more complex than the other remedies.

In the chapter following that, Parāśara talks of Jyeṣṭhā-gaṇḍānta which gives problems to the son and the father, or the daughter and the brother of her husband. A child born in the last 3 padas of Āśleṣā-gaṇḍānta will cause death of the mother-in-law while birth in first 3 padas of Mūla will cause death of father-in-law. In these cases, remedial measures should be done before marriage.

[158] Bṛhat Parāśara Horā Śāstra, (92/94)

Tattva Doṣas (Element Problems)

Water and fire are inimical to each other, as are earth and air. Space (ākāśa) removes conflict and has no enmity towards the other elements. Jala (tithi) and Agni (vāra) conflict while Pṛthvī (karaṇa) and Vāyu (nakṣatra) conflict. When a graha links the two limbs the planet becomes weakened and its natural significations and the houses it lords are hurt. This will occur when the tithi lord and vāra lord is the same planet, or the karaṇa and nakṣatra lord is the same planet.

For example, if a native was born on a Monday (vāra ruled by Moon), on a Kṛṣṇa-dvitīyā (tithi ruled by Moon), on Śravaṇa (nakṣatra ruled by Moon), and Taitula-karaṇa (ruled by Mercury), then the fire (vāra) and water (tithi) are being linked by the Moon. This will hurt the Moon and its houses. The remedy is the worship of the element connected to the planet that links them. Moon relates to water, so the worship of water is to be performed.

Offering (Dravya)	Face	Bīja	Mantra
Milk *(Pāyas)*	Ākāśa	hauṁ	auṁ īśānāya namaḥ
Curd *(Dadhi)*	Vāyu	hyaiṁ	auṁ tatpuruṣāya namaḥ
Ghee *(Ghṛta)*	Agni	hruṁ	auṁ aghorāya namaḥ
Kṣaudra *(Honey)*	Jala	hvīṁ	auṁ vāmadevāya namaḥ
Śarkarā *(Sugar)*	Pṛthvī	hlaṁ	auṁ sadyojātāya namaḥ

The five elements are worshipped on the Śiva-liṅga with five mantras to the five faces of Śiva. When a tattva-doṣa occurs the particular element becomes imbalanced. For the above example of water tattva imbalance, the mantra "auṁ vamadevāya namaḥ" is said pouring honey over the Śiva-liṅga.

Conlcusion

Time is more real than can be seen with the naked eye. The Astrologer looks at the pañcāṅga and sees more deeply into the entire chart of an individual or at any moment in time. These aspects of time are also responsible for making people rise up in life or can be blocking them from reaching their full potential. When the Time is wrong success is denied. The Vedic Astrologer sees the flaws in time, and remedies these prior to the smaller details within the chart. When the Time is right, all possibilities will be open.

कारणेन विना कार्यं जायते जगतीतले ।
यदि तर्हि सदा सर्वं जायेतैवानिरोधतः ॥

kāraṇena vinā kāryaṁ jāyate jagatītale |
yadi tarhi sadā sarvaṁ jāyetaivānirodhataḥ ||

In this universe nothing happens without a cause.
Once this concept is clear, a person can achieve anything.

Chapter 16

Interpretation

Interpretation

The calculations and strength analysis of Vedic Astrology are a science, while the interpretation of what it means and how to benefit human life with the information is an art.

There are various ways to read a chart depending on the situation and intention of the reading. People constantly ask my Jyotiṣa guru for a lesson or teaching on how to read a chart, and every time he has agreed, I have heard him teach totally different systems. I have tried to organize the various methods and this is a presentation of the techniques I consider foundational, which a beginner astrologer should be acquainted with for general birth chart analysis.

Sometimes an astrologer looks at a chart with no prior information, other times one already knows the individual well. Some readings are general and the individual expects you to know the important areas and other times there is no waste of time on other areas of life, the person wants to know about a specific area of life and nothing else. Therefore the order of the analysis needs to be modified for the situation which comes with experience. Interpretation is an art.

Beginners always ask what to look at when dumbfounded by the plethora of techniques of Vedic Astrology. The seasoned astrologer is looking at multiple aspects of the chart simultaneously. It is not a linear process when looking at a chart; it is a multi-dimensional, multi-tasking analyzing process. This is a very generalized list of the approach I take when first looking at a chart.

I. Start with a Gaṇeśa mantra, then a Sūrya mantra, and your Paramparā mantra.

II. Analyze the Lagna and Lagneśa (placement and situation).

III. Planets in houses (quickly see placements; don't interpret-just feed the information into the mind so you know the basic positions).

IV. Planets conjunct (yogas, see degrees for how tight the conjunction).

V. Look at Moon's nakṣatra (from here you put on colored shades to view the rest of the chart. Other events will be interpreted through the shade of this color.)

VI. Look at AK (charakārakas/charakāraka replacements), ārūḍha lagna and other ārūḍha placements.

VII. Look for curses and blessings/uplifting yogas (curse of graha, kalasarpa, mahāpuruṣa yoga, parivartana- to get a general state of the planets and their involvements).

VIII. Pañcāṇga Lords to determine focus of problem areas in the life.

IX. Check which daśās apply in the chart and then check daśās that are running presently.

X. Look at navāṁśa trines (and other houses) to see bhāgya (the fortunes of life).

XI. Make a few statements to confirm the chart, rectify if it's not correct, don't move forward until you are sure the chart is correct or you may make inaccurate predictions. Predict the past before the future.

XII. Assess the issues of the native from the information just scanned (and consulting if in-person, with Praśna if not in-person) and then begin to apply techniques relative to the individual's issues.

XIII. Begin telling the native the meaning of all this information you have just taken in. Begin speaking after you have seen how all the planets are interacting and their strength and condition.

XIV. Give Remedies, and end on a positive note.

The Art of Interpretation

Every reading will be different from different astrologers as they are human and will flavor the reading according to their own perception of the world and spiritual maturity. Even a reading from the same astrologer at different periods of the astrologer's life will yield different interpretations. There is a karmic bond between the astrologer and the client. Some people have the karma to receive bad advice and will go to an inexperienced or unlearned astrologer who misinterprets their chart. Or if they have the money to go to a good astrologer they may even give the wrong information so their reading is incorrect. If a person has the karma to get good advice, they will arrive at the correct place for knowledge. In this way, the universe guides everyone to the perfect astrologer at the correct time. The situation of the A7 will indicate the type of clients a person has. The ninth house, A9, and the amātyakāraka planet will indicate the type of advice the individual receives and the type of people they receive it from.

In the beginning, the new astrologer starts with a list as presented above. Slowly, the factors in this list will be analyzed simultaneously. For example, in the beginning one reads a chart from the lagna (physical situation), then reads it from the ārūḍha lagna (social situation), then reads it from the kārakāṁśa (soul's intention) all separately and then slowly integrates the three stories presented, but after time the seasoned astrologer will be able to see all these sides of the human being simultaneously at a glance. The analysis of the pañcāṅga and the nakṣatras, and the degrees and charakārakas is all seen in one glance. The curses, yogas, lagna, strengths and rectification are all done simultaneously. After this becomes simple, then higher techniques are added to give more details because there is more time for this.

I. Proper Mantra

Start with a Gaṇeśa mantra and then a Sūrya mantra, and Parampara mantra (mantra of your Jyotiṣa tradition) if applicable and/or your dīkṣā mantra (if initiated by a spiritual teacher).

Gaṇeśa is worshipped for mathematical skill (represented by Ketu). He ensures the calculations are correct and if they aren't that a correct reading is still given. Mistakes are ruled by Ketu and mantra to Gaṇeśa helps us avoid making mistakes or any other obstacles to the correct data for reading the chart. Here are two mantras to Gaṇeśa, a small one for beginners and a larger one for advanced students.

ॐ ह्रीं ज्योतिर्गणेशाय नमः

auṁ hrīṁ jyotirgaṇeśāya namaḥ

Auṁ, universal power, I praise the Light giving Gaṇeśa

गणानां त्वा गणपतिं हवामहे कविं कवीनामुपमश्रवस्तमम्
ज्येष्ठराजं ब्रह्मणां ब्रह्मणस्पत आ नः शृण्वन्नूतिभिः सीदसादनम्

Gaṇānāṁ tvā gaṇapatiṁ havāmahe kaviṁ kavīnāmupamaśravastamam
Jyeṣṭharājaṁ brahmaṇāṁ brahmaṇaspata ā naḥ śṛṇvannūtibhiḥ sīda sādanam

Oblations to the Lord of all calculations, the highest wisdom of the wise, "Thou art the precursor (auṁ) of all prayer and the lord of all souls; we pray for thy guidance for success in all good actions[159]." (Ṛgveda 2.23.1)

The Sun is worshipped for the ability to "see" into the chart. The Sun gives the logical reasoning and inference needed to understand the intricacies of a chart. With the blessings of the Sun the aspects of the person hidden within the chart can be seen. When looking for something misplaced (Ketu) take a moment to worship the Sun and then look for the item. The Sun helps us find what we are looking for. In a chart, the Sun will help us do a proper analysis and find the correct issue that needs to be remedied. This is a simple mantra for the Sun, or one could do the Gāyatrī mantra.

ॐ नमः सूर्याय

auṁ namaḥ sūryāya

Auṁ, praises to the Sun

[159] Translation by Sanjay Rath

The Parampara mantra is for the guidance of the Guru. The Guru is your own awakened third eye, or the teacher outside until that time has come. The Guru mantra helps to open the third eye or invoke the blessings of your teacher and lineage to guide you through the reading, to see the correct factors, and to ensure you guide the person to achieve their highest potential. When the ego stands in the way and thinks it can accomplish anything alone, it is bound to achieve less than planned. When one surrenders body, mind and soul to the Supreme Guru, then the higher consciousness has the space (ākāśa) to come in and guide. This mantra is the most important and should always be on the mind and consciously invoked before a reading. The Acyutānanda-Paramparā mantra is the Janaka-Ṣaḍakṣari Mantra "Hare Rāma Kṛṣṇa". One can also do the Śiva pañcākṣari mantra "Namaḥ Śivāya", if not initiated into any other mantras.

The mantra given by a spiritual teacher is important to have on your lips before you begin a reading, as what you say will come from your mouth, pass over your tongue and lips, so they should be having a high vibration. This higher vibration will allow you to go deeper and farther in the reading. If at any time you become confused in a reading, remember these mantras (of Gaṇeśa, Sūrya, and Guru) and say them in your mind to guide you.

II. Lagna and Lagneśa (placement and situation)

The Lagna will show the personality, guṇa and general make-up of the individual. Planets placed there will have a heavy influence as well as planets having an aspect. The sign ruling the lagna will determine the lordship of all the planets. Jupiter is the first and tenth lord for Pisces, while the third and sixth lord for Libra. Therefore the quality of planets is also determined relative to lagna.

The placement of the lagneśa will show the direction the person applies their intelligence in the world as well as their overall physical make-up and strength. A strong lagneśa involved in powerful yogas gives overall success and vice versa.

III. Planets in Houses

Notice the placement of planets in houses, notice their signs, and how strongly placed they are. Don't interpret at first; just feed the information into the mind to know positions. Visualize the chart so it is a yantra entering the mind (both conscious and subconscious). If you begin interpreting before having taken a full look at the chart you will start going into one area without taking a holistic look at the whole chart. Note the strengths of the planets, so that this is in your awareness as you take account of everything in the chart.

IV. Planets Conjunct

Notice the conjunction of planets (yogas) and see the degrees between them to see how tight the conjunctions are; what combinations are standing out the most, are they beneficial or harmful to the life. Take the time to research the combinations so as not to miss out on important combinations that change everything. Look for parivartana yogas that will switch results around.

Notice specifically which planets are affecting which other planets. For example, is Jupiter aspecting all the malefics, or are all the planets either in Saturn's signs or aspected by Saturn. Are all the planets in one quarter of the zodiac creating a nābhasa yoga; in this way, look at the combinations present in the chart. If there are multiple important combinations see which are stronger to influence the individual according to the lagna and the Moon.

V. Moon's Nakṣatra

Look at Moon's nakṣatra and determine the flavor of the individuals mind. This is the color the mind will filter through, like shaded glasses to view their life. Look at aspects to the Moon which will also color the thinking process. The Moon is like white paint, the smallest amount of color will stain it another color. If Mars aspects, it is like red paint dropped into white, the red color will dominate, only slightly diluting the red color. The house will influence the mind, fifth house Moon is always speculating, sixth house Moon is always arguing or debating, seventh house Moon is always thinking about relationship and extroverted, eighth house Moon is vulnerable and uncomfortable always trying to protect itself, ninth house Moon is focused on philosophy, etc.

Use this information to adjust how you will talk to the person. If the Moon is in the ninth house you can talk about the higher philosophical aspects of astrology as you read the chart (according to the level of intelligence and interest). If the Moon is in the sixth or eighth house, you must be careful and gentle with how you say the things you see. You don't want to hurt or argue about anything, so phrase yourself correctly to be extra supportive.

Utilize this with the constitution of the native. Vāta people like to hear things quickly and move on to the next thing, but easily forget. So speak faster and just repeat yourself more than once. Pitta constitution likes to go deep into one area of the chart and focus. They also want to feel in control, so you have to let them lead you to the areas they wish to discuss. Kapha constitution is slow to get things but remembers well, so speak slowly and clearly and ensure you get the concept across but once you have there is no need to repeat it. Vāta people will easily make changes in their life but have a hard time keeping a steady routine, so you can focus more on the importance of the continuation of remedies and how much needs to be done for results. They are better with a lot at once but not over a long period of time. The Pitta people need to understand things logically and so you must give them intellectual reasoning for the remedies given in order for them to follow through. Kapha people are slow to make change but very steady. You can focus on inspiring them to begin a remedy and telling them the importance of it. They need motivation and you can be harsher with them to get them motivated, while you must be gentler with the vāta constitution.

Get a sense of the person whose chart you are reading. Don't speak to them as you would anyone else, or they might not be able to hear all the advice you have for them, and your advice will not really be best suited for them either. Understand the way they think, and interact with them through the method that allows them to be most receptive to the information you are sharing.

Note on Sensitivity:

The astrologer must take into account the situation of the client they are reading for. The strength of the Moon (how well they can handle sensitive information) and the nature of their personality (how you need to present the information) need to be analyzed. I will give two examples for the reader to think about, in the hope that you won't make similar mistakes.

When I first started reading charts, I saw the 8th house lord, Sun, strongly placed in the eleventh house. The lord of inheritance in the house of gains as the Sun (father) showing that gains would come through the father in the form of inheritance. The woman was about to enter Sun Mahādaśā and in my first phone reading I predicted that she would soon be gaining a large in heritance from her father. She was quiet for a moment, more than usual, and I went on with the reading telling her other things. The reading ended with no excitement. The friend who recommended her to me consulted me later saying that I devastated her. Her father was fighting cancer and she was doing everything in her ability to save him. I ruined all her hope. One could argue that we should always speak the truth and others should accept it, but things need to be shared in a gentle way after assessing the situation. Saying she was about to get an inheritance from the father is predicting his death, but I did not take into account that future consideration. I should have assessed his health in the chart and discussed this with her first and then gently indicated the results of the inheritance.

Another situation was when I was with two other astrologers and the one was applying for a job doing readings in a store. He was giving the employees readings to prove his accuracy to the store manager to get the position. He looked at the chart of a woman of 18 years of age, and said that she would marry a man she didn't love and have a child outside of the marriage. This was truly indicated by the navāṁśa but as an 18 year old woman it was not the most appropriate thing to say. Instead he could have said that she should marry based about true love and not just material situation, as a material based relationship would prove to be filled with problems. In this way, we can advise without making the person feel like they are doomed by some type of karma. Speaking in a way that allows a person to feel their freewill is important for their digestion of the information. It is a science to see karma, it is an art to talk with a person about this in an appropriate way.

VI. Ātmakāraka and Ārūḍha Lagna

Look at individual's AK as this will influence their inner being and soul's desires. A Venus AK will enjoy art, beauty and sensuality in their life. A Saturn AK will focus on the suffering of life and its alleviation or increase. In this way look at the individual's ātmā and then note the other carakārakas. Check if there are any carakāraka replacements happening by the planets being in the same degree.

Look at the ārūḍha lagna, to see how other people perceive the person. Look at positions from the ārūḍha lagna to see how they are interacting with society. See the placement of other bhāvapadas. If the bhāvapadas are conjunct important yogas, then the people indicated by these bhāvapadas will help achieve these good results or harmful events.

With these two areas you are looking at the inner soul nature of the person and outer social nature to get a well-rounded view of how they operate in life. The other carakārakas will indicate the soul nature of other people in their life, and the other bhāvapadas will indicate their interaction with these people on the social level.

VII. Curses and Blessings

Look for curses and blessings. Blessings are caused by the aspect or conjunction of two or more benefics. Curses are created by the aspect or conjunction of two or more malefic planets (specifically Rāhu, Saturn and Mars). If a planet is afflicted by malefics its natural significations will suffer in this life and it will need to be remedied.

Parāśara talks about curses in the *Pūrva-Janma-Śāpadyotana-Adhyāya* or the chapter on Curses of Previous Birth. He focuses totally on the fifth house as an example. Parāśara can be studied for a deeper understanding.

For a curse to give its full results it must be associated with the ātmakāraka, the eighth lord or the lagneśa. If the lagneśa is involved then the person has a direct physical experience of the curse's suffering. If the eighth lord is involved then the person feels punished by the affliction. If the ātmakāraka is involved then the suffering is felt deep in the person's soul and is carried for a long time.

When the curse is in a good house, the person has the ability to gain from the situation after experiencing the suffering of the curse. This happens when a person created some negative situations in a past life without intending to do so. When a negative situation happens with malefic intention the curse will be placed in a dusthāna and then the suffering will continue to be an issue even after the curse has given its results. Also take into account the situation of benefics and malefics: Benefics are better when weak if in a dusthāna or strong in a kendra. When they are in a kendra they can do good and should be strong, when they are in a dusthāna they will cause suffering and the weaker they are the less suffering they will cause. While the opposite is the situation with malefics, malefics can do much harm in kendras, so if they are placed there they are better weak, but when they are in dusthānas they are better strong. Integrate this concept into the level of suffering a curse causes.

VIII. Pañcāṅga Lords

First, check the pañcāṇga for any doṣas in the quality of time that require remedial measures. Then look at the quality of time. You have already taken in a general understanding of the planets and their situation in the chart. Now look at the quality of time to see where in the chart you will begin your reading and deeper focus. There are so many directions you can begin to look to uncover deeper understanding, and many techniques to utilize. The time to share your understanding of the chart is limited to a small period of a reading; therefore you must be able to see where you should begin.

Take lord of the Moon's viṁśottari nakṣatra and look at it in the Rāśi. Its placement will show health, the vāra lord will show energy, see the tithi for relationship, the pañcāṅga-yoga for social connections, and the karaṇa for career. If one of these planets is weak or afflicted then the area of life significated by its pañcāṅga lordship will suffer. Therefore look at that area of life more in depth. For example, if the nakṣatra lord was Venus and Venus was debilitated in the sixth house, then we would look at health issues first in the chart. In this way use the natal pañcāṅga to guide you in a reading.

IX. Daśā Applicability

Check which daśās apply in the chart and then check daśās that are running presently. There are multiple special daśās that may work better than normal Viṁśottari. Check to the best of your present knowledge which are applicable to the chart and best for the purposes of your present reading. There are various layers of time that can be seen with different daśās. When you are lost on a journey you will look at a road map which contains the main highways or streets you are driving on. When you are looking at buying land for commercial mining you will look at a map that locates various minerals and relevant geological formations. When you are looking at buying land for agriculture you will be looking at maps of ground water and percentage of rainfall per year. In this way, you can look at different maps of the same area for different purposes. You can also look at various daśās of time depending on your intention when you look at a chart. Daśās are maps of time as time can be mapped just like space.

After deciding the daśās to be used, see what time periods the person is running. Look at what they have come from, what are they in presently and where will they be going. First look over this at the level of the Mahādaśās and get the big picture of their life. Then take into account the antar-daśās to get the more immediate focus of their present time period.

You have already understood the beneficial or malefic nature of the planets and their position; therefore the initial analysis of the daśā should be easy. The general understanding is what is important when you first analyze the chart. You can research deeper into the effects of the daśā with argalā and other techniques or wait until the reading to begin applying more intricate analysis. Take account of transits at this time and see what houses these transits are benefiting or hurting, as well as the aṣṭakavarga of the houses being transited by key planets.

X. Navāṁśa Trines

Look at navāṁśa trines (and other D-9 houses) to see the *bhāgya* (fortune) of the individual. The navāṁśa chart is always placed beside the Rāśi chart for the purpose of deeper insight and ensuring the correctness of the birth time. See the skills and abilities of the individual, their karma with money and health as well as the guiding deities shown in the navāṁśa. When you analyzed curses and their remedies, if any remedy planet is also the Iṣṭa-devatā then it is best to use this form as a remedy.

XI. Confirm the Chart

Make a few statements to confirm the chart based upon the navāṁśa, the Rāśi and the daśā. Rectify the chart if it's not correct, by trying to make the navāṁśa match the nature of the individual. Don't move forward until you are sure the chart is correct or you may make inaccurate predictions. You must be able to correctly predict the past and have the client confirm this before you try to predict the future or give any important advice.

There are very famous astrologers, who charge very high fees for their readings, who do not rectify first (as they see so many people a day) and they can give completely incorrect readings because of the lack of time. It is important to take your time in ensuring you have the correct data or else you will not be helping anybody, not your reputation or the welfare of the client.

For example, once I saw a woman who was born in Illinois at a time before they had accepted the daylight savings time throughout the entire state; only in Chicago did they actually change the time on the clocks, other more rural areas kept the same time year round. The computer program was inaccurate about this. I always check calculations in two different computer Jyotiṣa programs and compare. When the results don't match it indicates that I need to do further research. I found out that some counties used DST and others didn't and those that did sometimes would not record birth data according to DST even if the county was using it for the work day. This left a very large variability that no average program or data search was able to answer. The client assured me that she had a terrible reading when she utilized DST and that she had confirmed that there was no DST in her time. As I am the one giving the reading, I cannot trust another astrologer's analysis, even if they are considered 'famous'. I looked at the woman's charts with two different possible times. I told her about her marriage if she had the first chart, then told her about her marriage if she had the second chart. She quickly confirmed the chart she had insisted was correct (without knowledge of which was which). I then proceeded to give her a reading from this chart. In this way ensure that you have the correct chart to be reading from.

XII. Assess the Issues of the Native

You have come to a general understanding about what is going on and what you need to talk about. Don't try to be a big shot, talk to the person and make sure you are on the same page as they are. There are famous doctors in India, who will just take your pulse and give you medicine without asking any other questions. Some see hundreds of people a day in this fashion. Sometimes they are very accurate, and other times I have seen their medicine not work, as it did not fully fit the client's situation. Talk to the client.

You should have already gained some trust while rectifying the chart. They will want to see you prove you can actually see them, so make a few predictions about the past and what they are seeking, but be open and receptive to what they have to share. Active speakers will find it easy to tell you that you are completely wrong when you are not seeing them as they are. Passive speakers will let you give a whole reading on the wrong chart and just say O.K. at the end. In that case, they loose from useless information and the astrologer looses from the ability to learn about human life seen through the stars and human interaction.

If you are not doing an in-person consultation then consult a praśna chart to check accuracy of the natal chart as well as determine pertinent issues of life to discuss. For praśna accuracy, the person's natal lagna will match the trines (or seventh) from the praśna-navāṁśa. The placement of the praśna lagneśa and Moon will give some indication about their situation and where their mind is focused. Praśna is a huge science in and of itself and should be learned in detail.

XIII. Talk about the Chart

Begin the real reading of the chart. Put the information together to get a life sketch of the person, and interpret the story of their life. Parāśara says,

संयोज्य स्थानसंख्याया दलमेतत्समं फलम्।
एवं सखेटभावानां फलं ज्ञेयं शुभाऽशुभम्॥२०॥

saṁyojya sthānasaṅkhyāyā dalametatsamaṁ phalam|
evaṁ sakheṭabhāvānāṁ phalaṁ jñeyaṁ śubhā'śubham||[160]

The results of all factors of placement should be counted and brought together, then the good and bad results of planets in houses is known.

Parāśara talks about adding up all the various factors and coming to a conclusion about the situation. Add positivity for a strong planet and negativity for a weak planet, subtracting results for malefic aspects and adding better results for a benefic aspect, etc. He also mentions that when there are two sign lords (for Aquarius and Scorpio) to also factor the results according to the average of both planets' situation[161]. Parāśara teaches to calculate all factors for understanding the results. We must take all factors into account and then percieve the sitatuation of the individual. The chart is the yantra of a person's life, we must understand the life of the person through the chart.

[160] Bṛhat Parāśara Horā Śāstra, Atheṣṭa-Adhyāya, v. 20
[161] Bṛhat Parāśara Horā Śāstra, Atheṣṭa-Adhyāya, v. 18

XIV. Remedies

The entire last section of Bṛhat Parāśara Horā Śāstra is filled with curses and doṣas and their various remedies. Some of these have been briefly mentioned under the pañchaṇga-doṣas and others in the section on curses. The science of remedies (called upayas) is an entire book in itself. The better one understands upayas the better one is able to alleviate the general suffering of others.

- What is the cause of the affliction & how is it making the individual suffer
- Which planet or rāśi is indicating the remedy (or is it a doṣa with a specific remedy mentioned by the sages, ie Saṁkranti doṣa)
- Which form of the remedy planet or rāśi is indicated by its placement.
- What form of upaya is indicated by that planet or sign placement
- What form of upaya is indicated by the house it is placed in
- What form of propitiation is indicated by planets in trines and aspecting
- What is the length to perform the remedy to get results
- When or at what time should the remedy be performed

The intention to help others is the most important principle. It is our duty to use this knowledge to benefit mankind and make the world a better place.

Appendix

Appendix I: Sanskrit Lessons

This is a very basic lesson to begin to familiarize the Jyotiṣa student with Sanskrit. As the student is learning a large amount of new Sanskrit terminology it is best to learn it the first time with correct pronunciation, or you will have to learn it twice. For proper pronounciation of mantras for yourself and as remedies, the understanding of the Sanskrit alphabet is imperative.

Part A is the pragmatic aspect of learning the letters. Part B is learning a little in depth about each letter to understand it and be better able to pronouce it. It is impossible to learn correct pronuciation without a teacher, and verbal help of a teacher is advised. Students are advised to download Itranslator from

http://www.omkarananda-ashram.org/Sanskrit/Itranslt.html. This free program will install all Sanskrit and transliteration fonts one needs to learn basic Sanskrit.

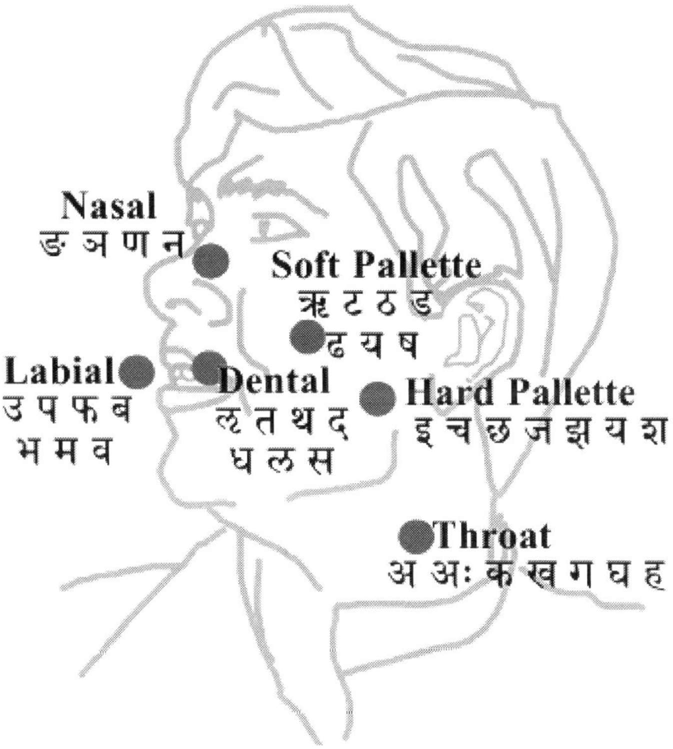

Part A

This is the written Sanskrit alphabet and a pronunciation guide. Students are to learn the sound of the letters and practice writing the letters.

Sanskrit Vowels:		
अ	a	as in but, indra, aditi, [one beat *(mātrā)*: the sound lasts for one second, short]
आ	ā	as in father, āśrama, grāha, [two beats *(mātrās)*: the sound lasts for two seconds, long a]
इ	i	as in bit, fit, iṣṭa-devatā, citrā *(short: one mātrā)*
ई	ī	as in meet, police, lakṣmī, jīva, klīṁ, *(long: two mātrās)*
उ	u	as in full, put, uttaraphalgunī, rudra
ऊ	ū	as in boot, bhūmi, sūrya, pūṣān, pūrvaphalgunī
ऋ	ṛ	as in bṛhaspati, ṛṣi, mṛgaśiras, kṛttikā, ṛgveda; the tongue rolls on the on the top of the mouth to make a continuous sustained rrrrrr sound *(one matra)*
ॠ	ṝ	same as short but two matras, is created when two words with ṛ combine
ऌ	lṛ/ḷ	as in kḷpta *(engaged, connected)*, the tongue rolls on the top of the mouth to make a continous sustained llllll sound *(one mātrā)*, [lṛ Itrans99/ḷ Itrans2003]
ॡ	lṝ/ḹ	same as short but two mātrās
ए	e	as in fate, pray, whey, āśleṣā
ऐ	ai	as in fight, aisle, pie
ओ	o	as in go, ojas,
औ	au	as in down, hound, cow
अं	aṁ	nasal sound that falls between ang and am, a nasal 'M' without closing the lips
अः	aḥ	As in namaḥ, slightly pronouced ah, a vowel *(not consonant like h ha)*

Sanskrit Consonants:		
क	ka	as in kill, Kevin, Kāli, prakāśa *(to illuminate)*, pakṣa *(half lunar month)*
ख	kha	as in bunkhouse, khaga *(moving in the air/planet)*; the same ka is said with an added expiration coming from the navel
ग	ga	as in goat, give, bug, gātha, gītā, Gaṇeśa
घ	gha	as in loghouse, ghaṇṭā *(bell)*; the same ga as before but with an added apiration at the end coming from the navel center
ङ	ṅa	as in xing, aṣṭāṅga-yoga; created in the throat not the mouth
च	ca	as in church, cello, chair, candra, Cāmuṇḍā
छ	cha	as in coach-horse, chandas (meter)
ज	ja	as in john, Jagannātha, Jyeṣṭhā
झ	jha	As in jhillīka *(a cricket)*, khujjhaṭi *(fog)*; apirated ja
ञ	ña	as in single, pañchamī, cañcala *(unsteady)*
ट	ṭa	as in aśṭamī, ṣaśṭyāṁśa; this group of sounds starts with the tongue on the top of the mouth and then the sound is made, this makes the sound cerebral instead of dental
ठ	ṭha	as in dhaniṣṭhā, jyeṣṭhā; the same 'ṭa' is aspirated
ड	ḍa	paṇḍita *(scholar)*; this is a cerebral 'ḍa' that starts with the tongue on the top of the mouth
ढ	ḍha	as in Uttarāṣāḍhā, dṛḍha-karma
ण	ṇa	as in guṇa, gaṇapati, pūrṇimā, purāṇa; very similar to a normal na except that the sound starts with the tongue at the roof of the mouth
त	ta	dental 'ta' as in table, want, Revatī, pratipada
थ	tha	dental 'ta' with an aspiration as in tithi, chaturthī
द	da	dental 'da' as in day, dog, dusthāna, deva, Candra
ध	dha	dental 'da' but with an aspiration from the navel; dhī *(intelligence)*, sambandha, dharma, dhāna-yoga, Dhaniśtha
न	na	dental "na" as in never, nut, neat, Candra, Punarvasu, Anurādhā
प	pa	as in Pat, Pete, Pūrvābādra, Paraśurāma
फ	pha	aspirated "pa" as in the name Pam, Pūrvaphalgunī,
ब	ba	as in be, cab, imbibe, buddha
भ	bha	aspirated 'ba' as in clubhouse, bhadra-mahāpuruṣa-yoga
म	ma	as in machine, matter, mokṣa
य	ya	as in yellow, yantra
र	ra	as in red, read, rāśi

Sanskrit Consonants:		
ल	la	as in late, learn, lagna
व	va	as in very, variable, varga, vāstu, viṁśāṁśa
श	śa	deep 'śa' coming from the same place in the throat as the sound 'cha'; as the word sure, śukra, Viśākhā, Aśvinī, navāmśa
ष	ṣa	cerebral 'ṣa' as in share, shave, bush, Dhaniṣṭhā, Puṣya, Kṛṣṇa
स	sa	dental 'sa' as in send, saint, sever, sandhi, saptamī
ह	ha	as in hurry, help, hat, horā, Hasta
This next group are some common conjunct letters (which are combinations of the previous letters).		
क्ष	kṣa	the letter क and cerebral ष् put together to make *kṣa* as in kṣetra
त्र	tra	dental त् and the semi-vowel र combine to make *tra* as in trikoṇa
ज्ञ	jña	the letter ज् combines with palletal ञ to make *jña* which is pronounced together as in jñāna *(knowledge)*. Hindi *jña* and Sanskrit *jña* are not pronounced the same.
द्ध	ddha	dental द् combines with its aspirate ध to makes a two mātrā aspirate *ddha* sound as in siddha *(perfected one)*, vṛddhi *(to grow/prosper)*
द्य	dya	dental द् combines with semi-vowel य to make *dya* as in vidyā
श्र	śra	palatel श् combines with to semi-vowel र to make *śra* as in śrīṁ, Śravaṇa

[Assignment 1]

These letters are to be printed for the practice of writing the letters:

अ आ इ ई उ ऊ ऋ ॠ ऌ ॡ

ए ऐ ओ औ अं अः

क ख ग घ ङ

च छ ज झ ञ

ट ठ ड ढ ण

त थ द ध न

प फ ब भ म

य र ल व

श ष स ह

क्ष त्र ज्ञ द्ध द्य श्र

Combining Consonants and Vowels

Consonants are considered lame without a stick, they cannot walk without a vowel. K (क्) becomes ka (क) when an a (अ) is added to it, so that it can be pronounced. Consonants cannot be pronounced without a vowel. G (ग्) becomes gā (गा) when ā (आ) is added. C (च्) becomes ci (चि) when i (इ) is added. So all letters are considered to have a silent a (अ) as part of them so they can stand (be pronounced).

a	ā	i	ī	u	ū	ṛ	ṝ
ा	ाा	ि	ी	ु	ू	ृ	ॄ
	e	ai	o	au	am	aḥ	
	े	ै	ो	ौ	ं	ः	

K (क्) becomes

ka	kā	ki	kī	ku	kū	kṛ	kṝ
क	का	कि	की	कु	कू	कृ	कॄ
	e	ai	o	au	am	aḥ	
	के	कै	को	कौ	कं	कः	

[Assignment 2]

On a separate sheet of paper practice writing each of the primary 33 consonants with each of the 16 vowels, like the example of ka (क).

Part B

This section contains more in depth knowledge about the letters of the Sanskrit language. It is to be studied after one has general familiarity with the letters so that you can get to know them better. I thank my Sanskrit teacher, Vāgīśa Śāstrī of Vārāṇasī, for my deeper understanding of the Sanskrit language, and from where a large part of this information comes from.

The Sanskrit Alphabet

The word alphabet comes from the word alpha (a) and bet (b), in the same way the tantrics call the group of letters *akṣara-mālā* which means the necklace (mālā) from a (अ) to kṣa (क्ष). The letters themselve can be called *akṣaras* as well as *varṇas* (colors), and sometimes the alphabet is called the varṇa-mala. In the Purāṇic period the alphabet was called the *ahaṁ*, again representing a (अ) to ha (ह), as the conjunct letter was not accepted as part of the alphabet at that time. In the time of the Sanskrit scholar Paṇini (500 BC), the alphabet was called the *Varṇa-Samāmnāya*. In Vedic times the alphabet was called *matṛkā*, which means mothers. The letters are considered not just the mother of all literature (composed of words, composed of letters), but the mother of the whole universe which is composed of sound. In this way it is said that tantriks don't worship statues as gods but instead worship letters as gods.

The four primary vowels (svāra)

अ and आ (a ā) is called acyuta (a= not, cyuta= changeable). It can be chanted continously without change as it needs no help of the tongue. It is connected to Viṣṇu.

इ and ई (i ī) is called śakti (energy/goddess) as it will change.

उ and ऊ (u ū) is called śambu and is connected to śiva.

ऋ and ॠ (ṛ ṝ) and ऌ and ॡ (lṛ lṝ) are connected to the ṛṣi (sages) and agni (fire). The Ṛ is pronounced as 'ri' in north India and 'ru' in south India, but it is actually a vowel not found in English that is created by rolling the tongue. The ṛ becomes lṛ and has many of the same connotations.

4 Dipthongs
(vowels created from the primary vowels but differing)

ए (e) is a combination of अ (a) and इ (i), which is called the guṇa vikāsa of इ (i). If you were to pronounce अ (a) and then open the mouth as if saying इ (i) then you get the sound of ए (e) as in the word rate.

ऐ (ai) is a combination of अ (a) and ए (e). If you were to pronounce अ (a) and then open the mouth saying इ (i), then you get the sound of ऐ (ai).

ओ (o) is made when अ (a) is pronounced and the mouth is opened as if saying उ (u) then you get the sound of ओ (o) as in boat.

औ (au) is a combination of अ (a) and ओ (o). If you were to pronounce अ (a) and then open the mouth saying ओ (o), then you get the sound of औ (au) as in out.

2 Ayogavāhas (Anusvāra and Visarga):
The Ornaments of Sanskrit

अं (aṁ) is called anusvāra which means that which is spoken after *(anu)* a vowel *(svāra)*. It is nasal resonance that is made without closing the lips. If you close the lips it will resonate on the lips instead of at the sahasrāra chakra.

अः (aḥ) is called visarga and relates to creation a destruction, it has fire and can make things sprout or burn things to make them end. Anusvāra is one point *(bindu)* and is connected to śiva. While visarga has has 2 points and is connected to śakti.

The vowels *(svāra)* are ruled by the Sun. They are *'svā'*- self *'ra'*-effulgent/ shining. They can stand alone without support. They are Puruṣa, and represent consciousness.

The consonants cannot stand alone, they need the support of a vowel. The Prakṛti (creation) cannot stand (exist) without Puruṣa (consciousness). Every consonant is lame without a stick, so *'a'* (अ) is already part of the each letter. In this way *k* (क्) becomes *ka* (k) when an a (अ) is added to it. In Sanskrit a consonant is not written without a vowel. The svāra are self shining in that they are consciousness, they do not need anything added to them to be pronounced, to shine.

Consonants-Vyañjana

There are five vargas (divisions) of letters relating to the five major planets of the Mahāpuruṣa yogas and the five elements; Mars, Venus, Mercury, Jupiter, and Saturn. Each of these divisions contains 5 letters, making 25 group letters. Then there are 8 additional out of group letters connected to the Moon. Added up 25 and 8 equals 33, which relates to the 33 major deities of the Vedic pantheon who are the foundation of Jyotiṣa. The 2 ayogavāhas (anusvāra and visarga) represent the Aśvini-kumāras residing as the prāna in the nostrils and the other 14 vowels represent the 14 lokas.

क ख ग घ ङ
ka kha ga gha ṅa

Hard क (ka) is the grandfather of the ka-varga (also called Ku (कु)- as 'u' is the 5th letter it means the 5 letters of ka). This varga are gutteral (kaṇṭhavya) and come from deep in the throat. Kha (ख) is the aspirate of ka. It is said as *'a'* is superior of the svāras that *ha* (ह) is superior of the vyañjana. *'A'* comes from the throat while *'ha'* it comes from the navel. Aspirate kha has *'ha'* merged in the letter, so the mouth is open saying *'ka'* and with it *'ha'* comes from the navel. Soft *ga* (ग) is the same as its grandfather *'ka'* except softer. Take a moment to say *'ka'* and *'ga'* and to feel the hard and soft sound coming from the same place in the throat. Then *gha* (घ) is the aspirate of its father letter. The first to letters are hard, the 3rd generation becomes soft, and the 5th generation becomes even softer. The nasal *ṅa* (ङ) is said to be like 3rd consonant but even softer with *anunāsika* (गँ). So it starts in the same place in the throat and resonates in the nose like a nasal sound. The ka-varga is connected to the planet Mars.

च छ ज झ ञ
ca cha ja jha ña

Ca (च) is the great grandfather from which the other letters descend. The ca-varga comes from the hard pallete *(tālu)* and are called palletal *(tālavya)*. *Cha* (छ) is the aspirate *(mahāprāṇa)* of its father non-aspirate *(alpaprāna)* ca, both are hard. The third letter, *ja* (ज), originates from the same place as *ca* (च) but it is soft. The J on j can be seen to similar looking to the english letter *'j'*, this will help keep *ca* and *ja* separate in your mind. Take a moment to practice saying both seeing how they are coming from the same place in the mouth yet the first is hard and the second is soft. *Jha* (झ) is the mahāprāṇa of *ja* (ज). The present letter used in modern Sanskrit is from Maharastra script, the traditional way to write *jha* is झ. The 5th letter is similar to the 3rd letter but softer and nasal (जँ), it is written as *ña* (ञ). Like all other vowels *ñ* (ञ्) cannot stand alone and takes *'a'* (अ) to become *ña* (ञ). The nasal ña comes from the same place in the mouth as the rest of its varga and then resonates in the nose. The *cu* (चु) are ruled by the planet Venus. And one can see the bījas like *caṁ* (चं) for the Moon, *jaṁ* (जं) for water, and *juṁ* (जुं) for rejuvination *(mṛtyuñjaya bīja)* come from these letters.

Hard		Soft		Soft/Nasal
Alpaprāṇa	Mahāprāṇa	Alpaprāṇa	Mahāprāṇa	Alpaprāṇa
क	ख	ग	घ	ङ
च	छ	ज	झ (भ्र)	ञ
ट	ठ	ड	ढ	ण
त	थ	द	ध	न
प	फ	ब	भ	म

ट ठ ड ढ ण

ṭa ṭha ḍa ḍha ṇa

The ṭa-varga comes from the soft pallete *(murdhana)* and are called cerebral *(murdhanya)*. The letters of the division are created by strinking the tongue on the roof of the mouth while starting the sound. The rest remains in the same pattern as the previous vargas. *Ṭa* (ट) is the hard grandfather which has *ṭha* (ठ) as the mahāprāṇa. Becoming soft it makes *ḍa* (ड) and *ḍha* (ढ). Then the nasal is almost like the normal na in english except its cerebral sound with the tongue at the roof of the mouth creating *ṇa* (ण). The loop on the line (ण) is said to represent the tongue on the top of the mouth. The *ṭu* (*qu*) are ruled by the planet Mercury.

त थ द ध न

ta tha da dha na

The ta-varga comes from the teeth (*danta*) and are called dental (*dantya*). Ta (त) is the normal ta we see in Tom and tap, while its aspirate is said with more force from the navel. When you say aspirate tha (थ) you can feel the breath coming out of the mouth with force while non-aspirates do not have the same ability to feel the breath. Da (द) and dha (ध) come from the tongue touching the teeth but are softer. And na (न) is the normal English sound westerners are familiar with. The tu (तु) is ruled by Jupiter.

प फ ब भ म

pa pha ba bha ma

The pa-varga comes from the lips *(oṣṭha)* and they are called labials *(oṣṭhya)*. *Pa* (प) is the grandfather from which the others arise from according to the rules of the group letters. The nasal *ma* (म) comes right from the lips. The *Pu* (पु) are ruled by Saturn.

4 semi-vowels
(out of group consonants)

य र ल व

ya ra la va

The semi-vowels are called such because they are consonants that are developed from vowels. They are actually two vowels that when said together create a consonant sound.

i (इ) + a (अ) = ya (य)

u (उ) + a (अ) = va (व)

ṛ (ऋ) + a (अ) = ra (र)

ḷ (ऌ) + a (अ) = la (ल)

If you chant 'iiii' and then open your mouth and say 'aaa' you will see the creation of *ya* sound. In the same way, chant the vowel and then open your mouth with 'a' and hear the consonant be created. With the group letters, these all fall into the non-aspirate and soft 3rd group (ga, ja, ḍa, da, ba).

The semi vowels *(ardha-svāra)* are combinations of vowels with अ (a) and are known as the *antastha*. They are vowels (Puruṣa/consciousness) that when pronouced with अ (a) take on the shape of Prakṛti as consonants. As the Moon is just a reflection of the Sun's light, these semi-vowels are ruled by the Moon, they are half Sun, a reflection.

The vowels are Puruṣa relative to the soul, while the consonants are Prakṛti relative to the body, the Moon is that which links the body and soul, it is the inbetween. The 1st set of the Moon's letters are connected to Ketu (the semi-vowels) and the 2nd set of the Moon's letters are connected to Rāhu (the syllabants and ha).

3 syllabants (they sound like shhhhh)

श ष स

śa ṣa sa

There are three syllabants in Sanskrit versus the two common in English. First is pallatel *(tālavya) śa* (श), that comes from the same place as the cha-varga. It sounds much like the English word sure. Next is the cerebral *(murdhana) ṣa* (ष), that starts deep in the throat and comes out like the ṭa varga it is associated with. It is the same sha as in show, shower, and shadow. Last is dental *(dantya) sa* (स) that is a hard s coming on the teeth as in saint or sinner. The syllabants are apirate and hard like the 2nd group (kha, cha, ṭha, tha, pha).

Last (and Superior)
ह
ha

The letter *ha* (ह) is the last official letter of the Sanskrit alphabet. *Ha* is aspirate and soft so it falls into the 4th group (gha, jha, ḍha, dha, bha).

Saṁyukta (3 Famous Combinations)
क्ष त्र ज्ञ
kṣa tra jña

These are common combinations often shown that are not officially different letters, they are wriiten along with the modern script but not written as the ancient Sanskrit alphabet, as they are combinations of previous letters in themselves.

k (क्) + ṣa (ष) = kṣa (क्ष)

t (त्) + ra (र) = tra (त्र)

j (ज्) + ña (ञ) = jña (ज्ञ)

[Assignment 3]

Chant (say aloud) the *varṇa-mala* every morning. First do the vowels, then do the group letters 3 ways: 1. practice them downwards (ka, ca, ṭa, ta, pa, kha, cha, etc), 2. practice them right to left (ṅa, gha, ga, kha, ka, ña, jha, ja, etc.) and 3. practice them left to right ka, kha, ga, gha, ṅa, ca, cha, ja, etc.). Then continue with the rest of the letters. As you say the letter feel where they are coming from in your mouth, throat, nose, body. Become aware of the anatomical order of the letters in the Sanskrit language.

Study Question: Complete sentences are not required, charts are good for # 3 & 7.

1. What are the names of the letters?
2. What are the 5 original vowels?
3. What are the four dipthongs and what are they composed of?
4. What are the two ayogavāhas and what deities are they connected to?
5. What are the six places of pronunciation?
6. Explain the five groups withing the labial division.
7. What are the four semi-vowels and what composes each?
8. What are the 3 types of "s" and where are they pronounced (what varga do they correlate to)?

Appendix II: Bhāveśa-Phala-Adhyāya

This Appendix is a translation of the chapter on the results of house lords (*Bhāveśa-Phala-Adhyāya*) in Bṛhat Parāśara Horā Śāstra. It has been put into a graph format for ease of reference and study. Some of the significations given by Parāśara in this chapter follow simple logic. For example, when the seventh lord is in the second house the native acquires wealth through the spouse (second house is wealth and the seventh lord represents relationship). When the seventh lord goes to the eighth (house of troubles) the individual gets little happiness from relationship and the spouse may have health concerns.

The beneficence or treacherousness of house lords and the concept of Bhāvet Bhāvam has been explained in the Bhāva chapter. These concepts will help explain many of the results listed but not all of them. Some principles have not been taught directly in Bṛhat Parāśara Horā Śāstra. For example, Parāśara says that the seventh lord in the first or seventh house causes vāta vitiation, the eighth lord in the lagna causes boils (pitta aggravation), while the twelfth lord in lagna causes kapha problems. This follows a rule that the kendra houses relate to vāta, the paṇaphara houses to pitta, and the āpoklima houses to kapha. This has not been given in a dictum but is considered an implied rule.

If one seriously studies the bhāveśa and bhāva chapters they will see the usage of very advanced principles only explained in the nāḍī saṁhitās. In this way, in these seemingly simple chapters, Paraśara shows full knowledge of various advanced principles and support of their usage. When a person can explain the logic for the results of all the placements mentioned in this chapter as well as the results listed in the chapters on each individual bhāva in BPHS then they actually understand Parāśara. All the significations given have a logic that can be learned. Some of the logic is beyond a beginner book's grasp, but will be learned on the path of Jyotiṣa. One should read through this appendix and apply one's own logic with one's present knowledge where possible.

Parāśara mentions strength and the difference between benefic and malefic placements altering results. When the eighth lord is in the eighth house it can give long life unless it is weak- which it then gives medium life. The eighth lord in the eleventh gives long life (especially if it is combined with a benefic). The eighth lord in the twelfth gives short life and even more so if with a malefic. All the house lord placements are also modified by various other influences like the position of planets and other house lords as well as aspects, special ascendants, ārūḍhas, etc. For example, the eighth lord in the fifth house can make one dull-witted, have few children and be long lived. If Jupiter (the planet of intelligence) is placed with strength in the ascendant then the native is intelligent. Jupiter aspects the fifth house and so will give some children, Jupiter protects health and will support the indications of being long lived. In this way, all factors are to be integrated.

The various, sometime contradicting, indications will be activated according to the daśā of the individual. In the above example, there will be some issues with intelligence or speculation (fifth house indications) in the daśā of the eighth lord. Children may come only in the daśā of Jupiter or Jupiter may need to be strengthened as a remedy to bring children. In this way daśā will show the various results of the planetary placements and their lordship.

Appendix II: House Lords *(Charts continue from left to right)*

	1 Lagna	2 Dhanabhāva	3 Sahajabhāva	4 Sukhabhāva	5 Sutabhāva	6 Ripubhāva
1 lagneśa	Lagneśa in lagna gives bodily happiness *(dehasukhabhāg)*, good strength *(bhujavikramī)*, intelligent/ clever *(manasvī)*, fickleminded *(cañcalaścaiva)*, has two spouses *(dvibhāryaḥ)* || 1||	Strength *(bālaḥ)*, endowed with gains *(lābhavān)*, scholar *(paṇḍitaḥ)*, happy *(sukhī)*, well mannered *(suśīlo)*, law abiding *(dharmavin)*, respectable *(mānī)*, many spouses *(bahudāra)*, good qualities *(guṇairyutaḥ)* || 2||	Lagneśa in the 3rd house makes one brave as a lion *(siṁha-tulya-parākramī)*, able to accomplish *(sarva-sampadyuto)*, respectable *(mānī)*, two spouses *(dvi-bhāryaḥ)*, intelligent *(matimān)*, happy *(sukhī)* || 3||	Lagneśa in the 4th house gives one Strength *(bālaḥ)*, makes parents happy *(pitṛmātṛsukhānvitaḥ)*, many siblings *(bahubhrātṛyutaḥ)*, passionate *(kāmī)*, good qualities and form *(guṇa-rūpa-samanvitaḥ)* || 4||	Happines from children *(suta-saukhyaṁ)*, reasonable *(madhyamam)*, loss of first child *(prathamāp atyanāśaḥ)*, respectable *(mānī)*, easily angered *(krodhī)*, liked by authorities *(nṛpapriyaḥ)* || 5||	Lacks bodily happiness *(deha-saukhya-vivarjitaḥ)*, enemy problems if aspected by malefics *(pāpāḍhye śatrutaḥ)*, pain if not aspected by benefics *(pīḍā saumya-dṛṣṭi-vivarjite)* || 6||
2 dhaneśa	Has many children *(putravān)*, connected to wealth *(dhanasaṁyutaḥ)*, causes problems for the family *(kuṭumbakaṇṭakaḥ)*, desirous *(kāmī)*, harsh speaking *(niṣṭhura)*, performs others duty *(parakāryakṛt)* || 13||	Wealthy *(dhanavān)*, arrogant *(garvasaṁyuta)*, has two spouses *(dvibhāryaḥ)*, or many spouses *(bahubhāryaḥ)*, devoid or abondaned by children *(sutahīna)* || 14||	Courageous and strong *(vikramī)*, wise *(matimān)*, has good qualities *(guṇī)*, desirous *(kāmī)*, covetous *(lobhī)*, wealth by both good and bad means[162] *(śubhāḍhye ca pāpāḍhye)* and an atheist *(devanindaka)* || 15||	Second Lord in the 4th house can make one endowed with all types of achievments *(sarva-sampata-samanvita)*, if conjunct Jupiter, in own sign or exalted then the person will be comparable to a king *(guruṇā saṁyute svocce rājatulyo naro bhavet)* || 16||	Second Lord in the 5th house can make one endowed with wealth *(dhanasamanvita)*, and get a son *(dhano-pārjanaśīlāśca jāyante tatsutā)* || 17||	With benefics one will make money from enemies and litagation *(saśubhe śatruto dhanam)*, with malefics one will loose through enemies and have deficient shins- or be unable to stand their ground *(sapāpe śatruto hānir-jaṅghā-vaikalyavān)* || 18||
3 Sahajadīśa	Wealth earned by ones own hands *(vabhuja-arjita-vittavān)*, knowledge of selfless service *(sevājñaḥ)*, impulsive *(sāhasī)*, lacking formal education but intelligent, *(vidyāhīno'pi buddhimān)* || 25||	Thick body *(sthūlo)*, lacking courage *(vikrama-varjita)*, Small initiative *(svalpa-arambhī)*, lacking happiness *(sukhī na)* may covet another's wealth and wives *(syāt rastrī-dhanaka-amukaḥ)* || 26||	Happiness from siblings *(sahodara-sukha-anvitaḥ)*, having wealth and children *(dhana-putra-yutaḥ)*, merry *(hṛṣaḥ)*, eats well, consumes *(bhunakti)*, making noises while drunk with happiness *(sukha-madbhutam)* || 27||	Happy *(sukhī)*, associated with wealth *(dhana-saṁyutaḥ)*, intelligent *(matimān)*, childish *(bālo)*, suffering in marriage *(duṣta-bhāryāpatiśca saḥ)* || 28||	Having children *(putravān)*, having good qualities *(guṇasaṁyuta)*, if house lord or conjunct planet is malefic will have a cruel wife *(bhāryā tasya bhavet krūrā krūragrahayutekṣite)* || 29||	Inimical to sibling *(bhrātṛ-śatru)* great wealth *(mahā-dhanī)*, enmity between maternal uncle and native *(mātulaiśca samaṁ vairaṁ)* but love of maternal aunt *(mātulānīpriyaḥ)* || 30||
4 Sukheśa	Endowed with education *(vidyā)*, good qualities*(guṇa)*, ornaments *(vibhūṣita)*, land *(bhūmī)*, vehicles *(vāhana saṁyukto)*, maternal happiness *(mātuḥ sukha-samanvita)* || 37||	One who enjoys the pleasures of life *(bhogī)*, possesses all types of wealth *(sarvadhanānvitaḥ)*, close to the family *(kuṭumbasahito)*, honourable *(mānī)*, impulsive *(sāhasī)*, good at deception *(kuhakānvitaḥ)* || 38||	Courageous *(vikramī)*, have servants *(bhṛtya-saṁyutaḥ)*, digestive diseases *(udāro'rug)*, good qualities *(guṇī)*, generous *(dātā)*, earns wealth by own hands *(svabhuja-arjita-vittavān)* || 39||	Counsellor/ minister *(mantrī)*, all types of wealth *(sarvadhanānvitaḥ)*, skillful, dexterous *(caturaḥ)*, good conduct *(śīlavān)*, honourable *(mānī)*, knowledgable *(jñānavān)*, loves spouse *(strīpriyaḥ)*, happy *(sukhī)* || 40||	Happy *(sukhī)*, loved by all the people *(sarva janapriyaḥ)*, devotion to the sattva form of god, *(viṣṇu bhakto)*, good qualities *(guṇī)*, honourable *(mānī)*, earns by own hands *(svabhuja-arjita-vittavān)* || 41||	Lacking maternal happiness *(mātṛ-sukhavivarjitaḥ)*, easily angered *(krodhī)*, theiving with charms and spells *(cora-abhicārī)*, acting as one pleases *(svecchācāraśca)*, troubled,sad *(durmanāḥ)* || 42||

[162] See argalā chapter relative to the third house

Appendix II: House Lords *(Cont'd from Page 432)*

	7 Dārabhāva	8 Randhrabhāva	9 Bhāgyabhāva	10 Karmabhāva	11 Lābhabhāva	12 Vyayabhāva
1 lagneśa	If the 7th lord is a malefic then relationship longevity is shortened *(pāpe bhāryā tasya na jīvati)*, if it is a benefic lord it will show traveling *(śubhe'ṭano)*, poverty *(daridro)*, or indifference *(vā virakto)*, or associated with authoriy *(vā nṛpo'pi vā)* || 7||	Lagneśa in the 8th house can make one skilled in occult knowledge *(siddha-vidyāviśāradaḥ)*, diseased *(rogī)*, a theif *(cauraḥ)*, get very angry *(mahākrodhī)*, a gambler *(dyūtī)*, and adulterous *(paradāragaḥ)* || 8||	Fortunate *(bhāgya)*, well like by people *(vāñjanavallabhaḥ)*, worshipper of sattva devatās *(viṣṇubhaktaḥ)*, clever and eloquent in speech *(paṭurvāgmī)*, has wife, children and wealth *(dāra-putra-dhanairyutaḥ)* || 9||	Happiness and comforts from father *(pitṛ-saukhya-samanvitaḥ)*, royal honor *(nṛpamānyaḥ)*, popular among people *(jane khyātaḥ)*, self-made *(svārjita)* || 10||	Always gaining/ aquiring *(sadā lābha-samanvitaḥ)*, well-mannered *(suśīlaḥ)*, popularity *(khyāta)*, fame *(kīrti)*, many wives *(bahu-dāra)*, good qulaities *(guṇairyutaḥ)* || 11||	Lacking bodily comfort *(dehasaukhyavivarjitaḥ)*, wastes money on useless items and is eaily angered if not aspected by benefics *(vyarthavyayī mahā-krodhī śubha-dṛg-yoga-varjite)* || 12||
2 dhaneśa	Will have sexual desires for other's spouse *(paradāra-rataḥ)*, a healer *(bhiṣek)*, if lorded by or conjunct a malefic *(pāpekṣitayute)* the spouse will be improper or an adulteress *(tasya bhāryā ca vyabhicāriṇī)* || 19||	Endowed with abundant land and wealth *(bhūribhūmi-dhanairyuta)*, little happiness from spouse *(patnī-sukhaṁ bhavet svalpaṁ)*, no happiness from elder brother *(jyeṣṭha-bhrātṛ-sukhaṁ na hi)* || 20||	Will rise to prosperity *(dhanavān-udyamī)*, clever *(paṭuḥ)*, sickly when young but happiness later in life *(bālye rogī sukhī paścāt)*, observes pilgramages, religious rites, dharma, etc *(tīrtha-dharma-vratādikṛt)* || 21||	Desirous *(kāmī)*, honourable *(mānī)*, learned, scholar *(paṇḍita)*, lots of wealth and wives *(bahu-dārya-dhanairyuktaḥ)*, loss of hapiness through children *(kiñca putra-sukhojjhitaḥ)* || 22||	All types of gains *(sarva-lābha-samanvitaḥ)*, always exerting oneself, diligent *(sada-udyoga-yutaḥ)*, honourable *(mānī)* well known, famous *(kīrtimān)*, || 23||	Proud, inconsiderate *(sāhamī)*, lacking wealth *(dhanavarjita)*, desire and depend on other people's wealth *(parabhāgyaratastasya)*, no happiness from eldest child *(jyeṣṭha-apatya-sukhaṁ nahi)* || 24||
3 Sahajadīśa	service to another king, *(rājasevāparaḥ)*, suffer in childhood *(bālye duḥkhī)*, will no doubt get happiness *(sukhī cānte)* || 31||	Will be a thief *(jātaścairo)*, makes a living by serving others *(āsavṛttyopajīvī)*, will die at the gate of the king *(rājadvāre mṛtirbhavet)* || 32||	Devoid of the paternal *(pituḥ sukha-vivarjitaḥ)*, make fortune through wife *(strībhir-bhāgya-udayastasya)*, happiness through sons, etc. *(putrādi sukha-saṁyutaḥ)* || 33||	Possesses all types of happiness *(sarva-sukhānvitaḥ)*, wealth earned by owns own hands *(svabhujārjivitta)*, procures corrupt women for sexual pleasures *(duṣṭa-strībharaṇe rataḥ)* || 34||	Always gains from one's work *(vyāpāre lābhavān sadā)*, Lacking formal education but strong mental capacity *(vidyāhīno'pi medhāvī)*, impulsive *(sāhasī)*, helps others *(parasevakaḥ)* || 35||	Expenses on negative things *(kutārye vyayakṛjjanaḥ)*, father will be cruel *(pitā tasya bhavet krūraḥ)*, wealth through the wife *(strībhir-bhāgya-udayastathā)* || 36||
4 Sukheśa	Highly educated *(bahu-vidyā-samanvitaḥ)*, not taking the wealth earned through father *(pitrārjita-dhanatyāgī)*, will be quite in assmebly/ stage fright *(sabhāyāṁ mūkavad)* || 43||	Lacking domestic happiness *(gṛhādisukhavarjitaḥ)*, little paternal happiness *(pitroḥ sukhaṁ bhavedalpaṁ)*, will be equal to a unich/neuters sex *(klībasamo)* || 44||	Loved by all the people *(sarvajanapriyaḥ)*, love of god *(devubhuktu)*, good qualities *(guṇī)*, honourable *(mānī)*, will have all types of hapiness *(sarvasukhānvitaḥ)* || 45||	Will have royal honours *(rājamānyo)*, alchemist *(rasāyanī)*, great partier *(mahāhṛṣṭo)*, happy with the pleasures of life *(sukhabhogī)*, overcoming the senses *(jitendriyaḥ)* || 46||	Fear of genital disease *(gupta-roga-bhayānvitaḥ)*, liberal *(udārī)*, having good qualities *(guṇavān)*, charitable *(dātā)*, gratified by helping others *(paropakaraṇerataḥ)* || 47||	Lacking domestic happiness *(gṛha-ādisukha-varjitaḥ)*, negative propensity *(durvyasanī)*, foolish, confused *(mūḍhaḥ)*, always slothfull or lazy *(sada-alasya-samanvitaḥ)* || 48||

Appendix II: House Lords

	1 Lagna	2 Dhanabhāva	3 Sahajabhāva	4 Sukhabhāva	5 Sutabhāva	6 Ripubhāva
5 Suteśa	Learned *(vidyān)*, has happiness from children *(putrasukhānvitaḥ)*, stingy *(kadaryo)*, crooked/ dishonest *(vakracittaśca)*, seizes other peoples property *(para-dravya-apahāraka)* ॥ 49॥	Many children *(bahuputro)*, wealthy *(dhanānvitaḥ)*, maintainer of the family *(kuṭumbapoṣako)*, honourable *(mānī)*, loves spouse *(strīpriyaḥ)*, famous throughout the earth *(suyaśā bhuvi)* ॥ 50॥	Love of siblings *(sodarapriyaḥ)*, speaks slander *(piśunaśca)*, stingy *(kadaryaśca)*, always occupied with one's own work *(svakāryaniratah sadā)* ॥ 51॥	Happy *(sukhī)*, maternal happiness *(mātṛsukha-anvitaḥ)*, wealthy/Lakṣmi is with them *(lakṣmīyuktaḥ)*, intelligent, good discrimination *(subuddhiśca)*, a king or minister or perhaps a teacher *(rājño'mātyo'thavā guruḥ)* ॥ 52॥	Has children *(putravān)* if earning wealth through good means *(śubhāḍhye)*, is without children if earning through sinful means *(pāpāḍhye-patyahīno-sau)*, good qualities *(guṇavān)*, fond of their friends *(mitra-vatsalaḥ)* ॥ 53॥	Children will be like enemies *(putraḥ śatrusamo)*, or perhaps a child may die *(mṛtāpatyo'thavā)*, or perhaps native will adopt a child *(dattakrītasuto'thavā)* ॥ 54॥
6 Ṣaṣṭheśa	Sickly *(rogavān)*, famous *(kīrti-saṁyutaḥ)*, one's own enemy, wealthy *(ātmaśatrurdhanī)*, honourable *(mānī)*, impulsive *(sāhasī)*, good qualities *(guṇavān)* ॥ 61॥	Impulsive *(sāhasī)*, notorious one of the family *(kulaviśrutaḥ)*, foreign country *(paradeśī)*, happy *(sukhī)*, good speaker *(vaktā)*, always occupied with one's own work *(svakarmanīrataḥ sadā)* ॥ 62॥	Easily angered *(krodhī)*, lacking courage *(vikrama-varjitaḥ)*, like an enemy to the brother *(bhrātā śatru-samastasya)*, a servant who talks back *(bhṛtya-uttara-dāyakaḥ)* ॥ 63॥	Lacking maternal happiness *(mātṛ-sukha-vivarjitaḥ)*, intelligent *(manasvī)*, speaks slander/ betrayer *(piśunā)*, disliked *(dveṣī)*, rich and fickle-minded *(calacitto'tivittavān)* ॥ 64॥	Wealth and other things fluctuate *(yasya calaṁ tasya dhanādikam)*, hostility with son and friends *(śatrutā putra-mitraiśca)*, happy *(sukhī)*, selfish *(svārthī)*, compassionate *(dayānvitaḥ)* ॥ 65॥	Quarrelsome/ revengeful within one's own cirlce of kin *(vairaṁ svajñāti-maṇḍalāt)*, friendliness with others *(anyaiḥ saha bhaven maitrī)*, medium happiness though wealth etc *(sukhaṁ madhyaṁ dhanādijam)* ॥ 66॥
7 Dareśa	Desirous of anothers wife *(paradāreṣu lampaṭaḥ)*, corrupted *(duṣṭo)*, clear-sighted and constant *(vicakṣaṇo'dhīro)*, pained by vata disorders *(vātarujānvitaḥ)* ॥ 73॥	Has many wives *(bahustrībhiḥ samanvitaḥ)*, aquires wealth through spouse *(dāra-yogā-ddhanāptiśca)*, pracrastinates *(dīrghasūtrī)*, enjoys honour *(mānavaḥ)* ॥ 74॥	Death of an offspring *(mṛtāpatyo hi)*, enjoys honour *(mānavaḥ)*, sometimes daughter is born and son stays alive *(kadācijjāyate putrī yatnāt putro'pi jīvati)* ॥ 75॥	The spouse is never obediant *(jāyā nāsya vaśe sadā)*, the native loves truth *(svayaṁ satyapriyo)*, is intelligent *(dhīmān)*, religious minded *(dharmātmā)*, dental disorders *(dantarogayuk)* ॥ 76॥	Honourable *(māni)*, has all good qulaities *(sarvaguṇānvitaḥ)*, always joyful *(sarvadā harṣa-yuktaśca)*, therefore working with all types of wealth *(tathā sarva-dhanādhipaḥ)* ॥ 77॥	Spouse is in pain/ sick *(bhāryā tasya rujānvitā)*, spouse is defiant or hostile *(striyā sahā'tha vā vairaṁ)*, native is easily angered *(svayaṁ krodhī)*, and lacks happiness *(sukhojjhitaḥ)* ॥ 78॥
8 Randreśa	Deprived of bodily happiness *(jātas-tanu-saukhya-vivarjita)*, abusive of god and holy people *(devānāṁ brāhmaṇānāṁ ca nindako)*, has sores/ boils/ ulcers/ tumours *(vraṇasaṁyuta)* ॥ 85॥	Will ruin the strength/vitality very much *(bāhubalahīnaḥ)*, will give little wealth *(dhanaṁ tasya bhavet svalpaṁ)*, will not recover lost wealth *(naṣṭa vittaṁ na labhyate)* ॥ 86॥	No happainess from brothers *(bhrātṛsaukhyaṁ na)*, lazy *(sālasyo)*, none or defective servants *(bhṛtyahīnaśca)*, without strength *(balavarjitaḥ)* ॥ 87॥	Neglected by mother *(mātṛhīno bhavecchiśuḥ)*, devoid of happiness from house and property *(gṛha bhūmi sukhairhīno)*, malicious/ treachery towards friends *(mitradrohī)* ॥ 88॥	Senseless/ stupid *(jaḍabuddhiḥ)*, little understanding *(svalpaprajño)*, long life *(dīrghāyuśca)*, endowed with wealth *(dhanānvitaḥ)* ॥ 89॥	Will overcome the enemy/ competition *(śatrujetā)*, body is with disease in childhood *(roga-yukta-śarīraśca bālye)*, fear of snakes and water *(sarpajalād bhayam)* ॥ 90॥

Appendix II: House Lords *(Cont'd from Page 434)*

	7 Dārabhāva	8 Randhrabhāva	9 Bhāgyabhāva	10 Karmabhāva	11 Lābhabhāva	12 Vyayabhāva
5 Suteśa	Honourable *(mānī)*, tolerant of all dharma *(sarva-dharma-samanvitaḥ)*, happiness from children etc *(putrādi-sukha-yuktaśca)*, gratified by helping others *(paropakaraṇe rataḥ)* ।। 55।।	Little happiness from chilren *(svalpa-putra-sukha-anvitaḥ)*, having cough and/ or asthma *(kāsa-śvāsa-samāyuktaḥ)*, easily angered *(krodhī)*, devoid of happiness *(sukha-varjitaḥ)* ।। 56।।	Child will be a prince or equal to *(putro bhapo vā tatsamo)*, or native be a prince themselves *(svayaṁ vā)*, author *(grantha-kartā)*, famous/renown *(vikhyātaḥ)*, the light of the family *(kuladīpakaḥ)* ।। 57।।	Powerfull position *(rājayogo)*, much happiness from worldly life *(anekasukhabhogī)*, will be well known and famous *(khyātakīrtirnaro)* ।। 58।।	Educated *(vidyāvān)*, desired by the people *(jana-vallabhaḥ)*, author *(grantha-kartā)*, great skills *(mahādakṣo)*, many children and wealth *(bahu-putra-dhana-anvitaḥ)* ।। 59।।	Without happiness from own children *(putra-sukhojjñitaḥ)*, adopted child *(dattaputra-yuto)*, or perhaps aquire a purchased child *(vā'sau krīta-putra-anvito'thavā)* ।। 60।।
6 Ṣaṣṭheśa	Devoid of happiness in relationship *(dārasukhojjhitaḥ)*, famous *(kīrtimān)*, good qualities *(guṇavān)*, honourable *(mānī)*, impulsive *(sāhasī)*, wealthy *(dhanasaṁyutaḥ)* ।। 67।।	Diseasesd *(rogī)*, inimical to the wise *(śatrurmanīṣiṇām)*, covet other people's property *(paradravyābhilāṣī)*, makes other people's wives unchaste *(paradārarato'śuciḥ)* ।। 68।।	Seller of timber and stone/ building materials *(kāṣṭhapāṣāṇa-vikrayī)*, experiences ups and downs in trade/ commerce *(vyavahāre kvacid-dhāniḥ kvacid-vṛddhiśca)* ।। 69।।	Enjoys honor *(mānavaḥ)*, notorious one of the family *(kulaviśrutaḥ)*, speaks to father without devotion *(abhaktaśca piturvaktā)*, foreign country *(videśe)*, will be happy *(ca sukhī bhavet)* ।। 70।।	Gain of wealth through enemies *(śatruto dhanamāpnuyāt)*, good qualities *(guṇavān)*, impulsive *(sāhasī)*, honourable *(mānī)*, devoid of happiness through children *(kintu putra-sukhojjhitaḥ)* ।। 71।।	Always spending on one's desires/ attachments/ addictions *(vyasane vyayakṛt sadā)*, disliked by the learned *(vidvaddveṣī)*, addicted to violence toward living beings *(jīvahiṁsāsu tatparaḥ)* ।। 72।।
7 Dareśa	Happiness in relationship *(dārasukhānvitaḥ)*, intelligent *(dhīro)*, clear-sighted *(vicakṣaṇo)*, wise *(dhīmān)*, self-focused *(kevalaṁ)*, vata disorders *(vātarogavān)* ।। 79।।	No happiness from relationship *(dārasukhojjhitaḥ)*, spouse is afflicted by disease *(bhāryā'pi rogayuktā'sya)*, and ill-behaved *(duḥśīlā'pi)*, as well as disobedient *(na cānugā)* ।। 80।।	Union with many women *(nānāstrībhiḥ samāgamaḥ)*, no devotion to wife *(jāyāhṛtamanā)*, starts many tasks/projects *(bahvārambhakaro)* ।। 81।।	Spouse does not act as desired *(nāsya jāyā vaśānugā)*, native enjoys righteous action *(svayaṁ dharmarato)*, has wealth, children, etc *(dhana-putrādi-saṁyutaḥ)* ।। 82।।	Earning through the relationship *(dāra-artha-samāgamaḥ)*, little happiness from sons, etc *(putrādi-sukham-alpaṁ)*, will have many daughters *(kanyaprajo bhavet)* ।। 83।।	Poor *(daridraḥ)*, or miserable *(kṛpaṇo'pi vā)*, spouse is always spending *(bhāryāpi vyayaśīlā'sya)*, will have a livelihood through clothing/textiles *(vastrājīvī)* ।। 84।।
8 Randreśa	Will have two spouses *(bhāryādvayaṁ bhavet)*, certain loss in business if conjunct a malefic *(vyāpāre ca bhavedhānistasmin pāpayute dhruvam)* ।। 91।।	Long life *(dīrghāyuṣā)*, though middle life if 8th lord is weak *(nirbale madhyama-ayuḥ)*, may be dishonest or a thief *(syāccauro)*, abusive to self and others *(nindyo'nyanindakaḥ)* ।। 92।।	Betrayer of righteousness *(dharmadrohī)*, atheist/ non-believer *(nāstikaḥ)*, bad marriage *(duṣṭa-bhāryā-patiścaiva)*, takes away/ steals other people's property *(para-dravya-apahārakaḥ)* ।। 93।।	Deprived of paternal happiness *(pitṛ-saukhya-vivarjitaḥ)*, slanderer/ informer *(piśunaḥ)*, jobless *(karmahīnaśca)*, these results won't happen if the house lord is benefic *(yadi naiva śubhekṣite)* ।। 94।।	Devoid of wealth if with a malefic *(sapāpe dhanavarjitaḥ)*, suffers in childhood *(bālye duḥkhī)* but happy later in life *(sukhī paścāt)*, long life if joined a benefic *(dīrghāyuśca śubhānvite)* ।। 95।।	Always spending on bad actions *(kukārye vyayakṛt sadā)*, short life *(alpa-āyuśca)*, especially if with a malefic *(sapāpe ca viśeṣataḥ)* ।। 96।।

Appendix II: House Lords

	1 Lagna	2 Dhanabhāva	3 Sahajabhāva	4 Sukhabhāva	5 Sutabhāva	6 Ripubhāva
9 Bhāgyeśa	Fortunate *(bhāgyavān)*, respected as a prince *(bhūpavanditaḥ)*, amiable disposition *(suśīlaśca)*, well formed/ handsome *(surūpaśca)*, well educated *(vidyāvān)*, aknowledged by the people *(janapūjitaḥ)* || 97 ||	Scholar *(paṇḍito)*, loved by the people *(janavallabhaḥ)*, wealthy *(dhanavān)*, desirous *(kāmī)*, endowed with happiness from wife, children, etc *(strī-putrādi-sukha-anvitaḥ)* || 98 ||	Happiness from siblings *(bhrātṛ-sukha-anvitaḥ)*, wealthy *(dhanavān)*, virtous *(guṇa-vāṁścāpi)*, possesses good body and habits *(rūpa-śīla-samanvitaḥ)* || 99 ||	Endowed with happiness through house and vehicles *(gṛhayāna-sukha-anvitaḥ)*, all types of good fortune *(sarva-sampatti-yuktaśca)*, devoted to mother *(mātṛbhakto)* || 100 ||	Possesses children and good fortune *(suta-bhāgya-samanvitaḥ)*, enjoys devotion to teachers and guides *(guru-bhakti-rato dhīro)*, religious *(dharmātmā)*, scholar *(paṇḍito)* || 101 ||	Little fortune *(svalpabhāgyo)*, devoid of happiness with maternal uncle *(mātulādi-sukha-hīnaḥ)*, always troubled by enemies *(śatrubhiḥ pīḍitaḥ sadā)* || 102 ||
10 Karmeśa	Learned *(vidvān)*, famous *(khyāto)*, wealthy *(dhanī)*, a poet *(kavīḥ)*, sickly in youth *(bālye rogī)*, happy in later age *(sukhī paścād)*, wealth increases day by day *(dhana vṛddhir dine dine)* || 109 ||	Wealthy *(dhanavān)*, has good qualities *(guṇasaṁyutaḥ)*, honoured by the authority *(rājamānyo)*, friendly/ liberal *(vadānyaśca)*, happiness through father, etc *(pitrādi sukha-saṁyutaḥ)* || 110 ||	Happiness from brothers and servants *(bhrātṛ-bhṛtya-sukha-anvitaḥ)*, courageous *(vikramī)*, endowed with good qualities *(guṇa-sampannaḥ)*, eloquent speech *(vāgmī)*, devoted to truth *(satyarato)* || 111 ||	Happy *(sukhī)*, devoted to mother *(mātṛhite rataḥ)*, vehicles, land, houses, etc *(yāna-bhūmi-gṛhādhīśo)*, good qualities *(guṇavān)*, wealthy *(dhanavānapi)* || 112 ||	Endowed with all types of education *(sarva-vidyā-samanvitaḥ)*, always cheerful *(sarvadā hṛrṣasaṁyukto)*, wealthy *(dhanavān)*, has children *(putravānapi)* || 113 ||	Devoid of paternal happiness *(pitṛ-saukhya-vivarjitaḥ)*, skillful *(caturo'pi)*, lacking wealth *(dhanairhīnaḥ)*, tormented by enemies *(satrubhiḥ paripīḍitaḥ)* || 114 ||
11 Lābheśa	Sattva nature *(sāttviko)*, wealthy *(dhanavān)*, happy *(sukhī)*, looks on all equally *(samadṛṣṭiḥ)*, poet with eloquent speech *(kavirvāgmī)*, always gaining *(sadā lābhasamanvitaḥ)* || 121 ||	Endowed with all kinds of wealth *(sarvadhanānvitaḥ)*, all sorts of acchievements, *(sarvasiddhiyuto)*, charitable *(dātā)*, religious *(dhārmikaśca)*, always happy *(sukhī sadā)* || 122 ||	Competant in any types of work *(kuśalaḥ sarvakarmasu)*, wealthy *(dhanī)*, happiness through siblings *(bhrātṛsukhopetaḥ)*, may suffer disorder with sharp pains *(śūlarogabhayaṁ kvacit)* || 123 ||	Will have gains through mother's family *(lābho mātṛkulād)*, make pilgrimages to sacred places *(tīrthayātrākaro)*, endowed with happiness from house and land *(gṛha-bhūmi-sukha-anvitaḥ)* || 124 ||	Children will be happy *(sukhinaḥ sutāḥ)*, educated *(vidyavanto'pi)*, of good character *(sacchīlāḥ)*, the native will be religious and happy *(svayaṁ dharma-rataḥ sukhī)* || 125 ||	Endowed with disease *(roga-samanvitaḥ)*, cruel-minded *(krūra-buddhiḥ)*, dwelling abroad *(pravāsī)*, tormented by enemies *(śatrubhi paripīḍitaḥ)* || 126 ||
12 Vyayeśa	Will always be spending *(vyayaśīlo)*, weak *(durbalaḥ)*, kapha disorders *(kapharogī)*, lacking wealth and education *(dhana-vidyā-vivarjitaḥ)* || 133 ||	Always expenditure on good actions (*śubhakārye vyayaḥ sadā*), religious (*dhārmikaḥ*), kind in speech (*priya-vādī*), endowed with good qualities and happiness (*guṇa-saukhya-samanvitaḥ*) || 134 ||	Lacking happiness from siblings (*bhrātṛ-saukya-vivarjitaḥ*), hostility towards other people (*bhavedanya-jana-dveṣī*), supports oneself by one's own body (*svaśarīrasya poṣakaḥ*) || 135 ||	Lacking maternal happiness *(mātuḥ sukha-vivarjitaḥ)*, regular losses in property, vehicles, home, etc *(bhūmi-yāna-gṛhādīnāṁ hānistasya dinedine)* || 136 ||	Lacking children and education *(suta-vidyā-vivarjitaḥ)*, will visit many places and spend lots of money to gain a child *(putrārthe ca vyayastasya tīrthāṭanaparo)* || 137 ||	Will make enmity with own people *(svajanavairakṛt)*, easily angered *(krodhī)*, sinful *(pāpī)*, suffers *(duḥkhī)*, enjoys other people's spouses *(parajāyārato)* || 138 ||

Appendix II: House Lords *(Cont'd from Page 436)*

	7 Dārabhāva	8 Randhrabhāva	9 Bhāgyabhāva	10 Karmabhāva	11 Lābhabhāva	12 Vyayabhāva
9 Bhāgyeśa	Happiness in relationship *(dārayogāt sukhodayaḥ)*, good qualities *(guṇavān)*, famous *(kīrtimāṁścāpi)*, a spiritual person *(dvijasattamaḥ)* || 103||	Ninth lord in the eighth house can make one devoid of fortune *(bhāgyahīno)*, and have no happiness from the elder brother *(jyeṣṭha-bhrātṛ-sukhaṁ naiva)* || 104||	Endowed with much fortune/ good luck *(bahu-bhāgya-samanvitaḥ)*, possessed of good qualities and looks *(guṇa-saundarya-sampanno)*, much happiness from siblings *(sahajebhyaḥ sukhaṁ bahu)* || 105||	A king or equal to a king/ powerful position *(rājā'tha tatsamaḥ)*, minister/counselor *(mantrī)*, army general *(senāpatirvā'pi)*, good qualities *(guṇavān)*, praised by the people *(janapujitaḥ)* || 106||	Constantly gaining wealth *(dhanalābho dine dine)*, devotion to elders *(bhakto guru-janānāṁ)*, good qualities *(guṇavān)*, one who does good karma *(puṇyavānapi)* || 107||	Causes loss of one's fortune *(bhāgya-hānikaro)*, constantly spending on good deeds *(śubhakārye vyayo nityaṁ)*, becomes poor through excess hospitality *(nirdhana-atithisaṅgamāt)* || 108||
10 Karmeśa	Has happiness in relationship *(dāra-sukha-anvitaḥ)*, intelligent *(manasvī)*, good qualities *(guṇavān)*, eloquent speech *(vāgmī)*, always devoted to truth and righteousness *(satya-dharma-rataḥ sadā)* || 115||	Without work *(karmahīno)*, associated with lonevity *(dīrgha-āyur-apyasau)*, resorts to abuse of others *(paranindā-parāyaṇaḥ)* || 116||	A king *(rājā)*, or from a royal/ powerful family *(rāja-kula-udbhavaḥ)*, or equal to a royal family *(tatsama-anyakula-utpanno)*, has wealth, sons, etc *(dhana-putrādi-saṁyutaḥ)* || 117||	Capable of all types of work *(sarvakarmapaṭuḥ)*, happy *(sukhī)*, courageous *(vikramī)*, speaks the truth *(satyavaktā)*, devoted to teachers and guides *(gurubhaktirato)* || 118||	Edowed with wealth and children *(dhanasutānvitaḥ)*, cheerful *(harṣavān)*, has good qualities *(guṇavāṁścāpi)*, always speaks the truth *(satyavaktā sadā)*, happy *(sukhī)* || 119||	Expenditure on royal favors *(tasya rājagṛhe vyayaḥ)*, constanly in fear of enemies *(śatruto'pi bhayaṁ nityaṁ)*, skilled *(caturaścāpi)*, worried *(cintitaḥ)* || 120||
11 Lābheśa	Always gaining through the spouse's family *(lābho dāra-kulāt sadā)*, noble *(udāraśca)*, good qualities *(guṇī)*, desirous *(kāmī)*, native obediant to spouse *(jano bhāryā-vaśānugaḥ)* || 127||	Failure and losses in endeavors *(hāniḥ kāryeṣu)*, long lived *(tasyāyuśca bhaveddīrghaṁ)*, spouse will die first *(prathamaṁ maraṇaṁ striyaḥ)* || 128||	Fortunate *(bhāgyavān)*, skilled *(caturaḥ)*, keeps promises *(satyavādī)*, praised by authority *(rājapujyo)*, wealthy *(dhanādhipaḥ)* || 129||	Venerated by government *(bhūpavandyo)*, good qualities *(guṇānvitaḥ)*, enjoys owns own path/religion *(nijadharmarato)*, intelligent *(dhīmān)*, speaks the truth *(satyavādī)*, overcomes the senses *(jitendriyaḥ)* || 130||	Gains from all works *(lābhaḥ sarveṣu karmasu)*, will have knowldge *(pāṇḍityaṁ)*, and happiness *(sukhaṁ)*, increase day by day *(tasya varddhate ca dine dine)*	Will always spend on honourable works *(satkāryeṣu vyayaḥ sadā)*, desirous *(kāmuko)*, many spouses *(bahupatnīko)*, mixes with low caste people *(mleccha-saṁsarga-kārakaḥ)* || 132||
12 Vyayeśa	Always spending on the spouse's activities *(vyayo dārakṛtaḥ sadā)*, lack happiness in relationship *(tasya bhāryā-sukhaṁ naiva)*, lacking strength and education *(bala-vidyā-vivarjitaḥ)* || 139||	Always endowed with gains *(lābhānvitaḥ sadā)*, many friends *(priyavāñ)*, medium life span *(madhyama-āyuśca)*, full of good qualities *(sampūrṇa-guṇa-saṁyutaḥ)* || 140||	Will disrespect the teachers and guides *(gurudveṣī)*, hostile towards friends *(mitrairapi bhavedvairaṁ)*, gain of one's own goal is foremost *(svārtha-sādhana-tatparaḥ)* || 141||	Expenditure on royal family/ government officials *(vyayo rāja-kulādbhavet)*, little happiness from father *(pitṛto'pi sukhaṁ tasya svalpameva)* || 142||	Income problems *(lābhe hāniḥ)*, will gain through others's savings *(pareṇa rakṣitaṁ dravyaṁ kadācillabhate)* || 143||	Will have abundant expenses *(vyayādhikyaṁ)*, no bodily happiness *(na śarīrasukhaṁ)*, easily angered *(tasya krodhī)*, filled with hatred/ spiteful *(dveṣaparo)* || 144||

Bibliography

Bibliography

Bloomfield, Maurice, trans. *Hymns of the Atharvaveda*. Sacred Books of the East, volume 42. 1897.

Burde, Jayant. *Rituals, Mantras, and Science,* An Integral Approach. Motilal Banarsidass Publishers, Delhi, 2004.

Bhat, M. Ramakrisna. *Varāhamihira's Bṛhat Saṁhitā,* Part One & Two. Motilal Banarsidass Publishers, Private Limited, Delhi, 2003.

Chand, Devi. *The Atharvaveda Veda*. Munishiram Manoharlal Publishers Pvt. Ltd. New Delhi, India, 2002.

Chand, Devi. *The Sāma Veda*. Munishiram Manoharlal Publishers Pvt. Ltd. New Delhi, India, 2004.

Chand, Devi. *The Yajur Veda*. Munishiram Manoharlal Publishers Pvt. Ltd. New Delhi, India, 2004.

Danielou, Alain. *The Myths and Gods of India*. Inner Traditions International, Rochester, Vermont, 1991.

Das, Gauranga. "Suryamsa (D-12 Chart)", *Varga Chakra*, SJC 2002 Hyderabad conference compilation, Sagar Publications, New Delhi, 2002.

D.H. McNamara, J.B. Madsen, J. Barnes, and F.B. Ericksen. *The Distance to the Galactic Center*. Publications of the Astronomical Society of the Pacific, Vol. 112, pp. 202-216, Febuary 2000.

Frawely, David. "The Shaktis of the Nakshatras". *Vedic Astrologer*, vol. II, Issue 2, New Delhi, March-April 1998.

Goel, G.K. "Kaulaka (Shastamsa)", *Varga Chakra*, SJC 2002 Hyderabad conference compilation, Sagar Publications, New Delhi, 2002.

Harrison, Peter, and Hill, Stephen. *Dhātu-Pāṭha, The Roots of Language*, Munshiram Manoharlal Publishers Pvt. Ltd., New Delhi, 1997.

Joshi, K.L. trans., *Viṣṇu Purāṇa*. Parimal Publications, Delhi, 2002.

Kaufmann III, William, and Freedma, Roger. *Universe, Fifth Edition*. W.H.Freeman and Company, New York, 1999.

Keel, Bill. *Milky Way Central Region Map*. University of Alabama, http://www.seds.org/messier/more/mw_map.html

Larsen, Visti. Lessons: *Argalā or Intervention*, unpublished.

Larsen, Visti. *Kalamsa-The Fortune of Luxuries*, http://Śrīguruda.com/articles.htm , updated article originally published as "Shodasamsa- The Fortune of Luxuries", *Varga Chakra*, SJC 2002 Hyderabad conference compilation, Sagar Publications, New Delhi, 2002.

Larsen, Visti. Rath's Lectures: *Upāsanāṁśa*, http://Śrīguruda.com/articles.htm , released 2006.

Macdonell, Arthur Anthony. *A Vedic Reader, For Students*. Scanned at www.sacred-texts.com August 31, 2000, Original publication 1917.

Mani, Vettam, *Purāṇic Encyclopedia*. Motilal Banarsidass, Delhi, 1979.

Muller, Max, and Eggeling, Julius, *The Satapatha- Brahmana*, Part-V, Sacred Books of the East Vol. XLIV, Low Price Publications, Delhi, 1996.

Moore, Patrick. *Venus*, Cassell Illustrated, a division of Octopus Publishing Group Limited, London, 2002.

Pingree, David. *The Yavanajātaka of Spujidhvaja*, Volume II. Harvard University Press, Cambridge, Masschusetts, 1978.

Podder, Sarajit. RE: [Om Krishna Guru] #3 *"Count from Lagna to it's lord..."*, Śrījagannath@yahoogroups.com, Sunday, March 13, 2005.

Podder, Sarajit. *The Karakas I*, translation of Kalidasa's Uttara Kalamrita, www.varahamira.blogspot.com, February 2005.

Pujan, Shiv. "Trimsamsa", *Varga Chakra*, SJC 2002 Hyderabad conference compilation, Sagar Publications, New Delhi, 2002.

Rai, Ram Kumar. *Mahidhara's Mantra Mahodadhiḥ*. Prachya Prakashan, Varanasi, 1992.

Raja, Dr. C. Kunhan. *Asya Vāmasya Hymn*. Ganesh and Co. Pvt. Ltd., Madras, 1956

Raman, B. V. *Praśna Mārga*. Motilal Banarsidass Publishers Pvt. Lmt., Delhi, 2003.

Rao, Bangalore Suryanaryan. *Varahamihira's Brihat Jataka*. Motilal Banarsidass Publishers, Delhi, 2001.

Rao, S.K. Ramachandra. *Ṛgveda Darśana*. Kalpatharu Research Academy, Bangalore, 1998.

Rao, S.K. Ramachandra. *The Āgama Encyclopedia*. Sri Satguru Publications, Delhi, 2005.

Rath, Sanjay. *Argalā*, Lecture at Śrī Jagannath Center Conference, Edison, New Jersey, 2003.

Rath, Sanjay. *Bṛhat Parāśara Horā Śāstra*, Graha Guṇasvarūpa Adhyāya, Śrī Jagannāth Center, Singapore, 2004.

Rath, Sanjay. *Career and the Daśāṁśā*, BAVA lecture at the Theosophical Society, London, July 30, 2005.

Rath, Sanjay. *Crux of Vedic Astrology*. Sagar Publication, New Delhi, 1998.

Rath, Sanjay. *Jaimini Maharishi's Upadesa Sutras*. Sagar Publications, New Delhi, 1997.

Rath, Sanjay, Kala Hora, http://srath.com/lectures/kalahora.htm

Rath, Sanjay. *Opening Lecture*, 0017 The Guṇas of Grahas and Rāśis, Vyāsa SJC, 2005.

Rath, Sanjay. *Pañcha Mahāpuruśa Yoga*, Jyotish Digest, Vol. 3 Issue 3, July –September 2004.

Rath, Sanjay. *Rashi and Drishti*. sohamsa@yahoogroups.com, Monday, May 08, 2006.

Rath, Sanjay. *Steps to Horoscope Interpretation*. Śrī Jagannath Center East Coast workshops 2003

Rath, Sanjay, *Triṁśāṁśa* D-30, Articles, www.Srath.com

Rath, Sanjay. *Vedic Remedies in Astrology*. Sagar Publications, New Delhi, 1998.

Sadagopan, V. trans., *Sudarshana Ashtakam*, copmased originally by Swami Desikan, http://www.ramanuja.org/sv/acharyas/desika/stotras/sudarsana.html
or http://sanskrit.gde.to/doc_deities_misc/sudarshan8.html , 1995.

Sastri, Dr. P.S. *Uttara Kalamrita [of] Kalidasa*. Ranjan Publications, New Delhi, 2001.
Sastri, V. Subramanya. *Vaidyanatha Dixita's Jātaka Pārijāta*, Ranjan Publications, New Delhi, 2004.

Sharma, Girish Chand, *Maharshi Parasara's Brihat Parasara Hora Satra*, Volume 1 & 2, Sagar Publications, New Delhi, 1995.

Sharma, Girish Chand, *Daivagya Acharya Shri Ram's Muhurta Chintamani*, Sagar Publications, 2003.

Sharma, T.R.S. (chief editor). *Ancient Indian Literature: An Anthology*, Volume I. ISBN 81-260-0794-X, Sahitya Akademi, New Delhi, India.

Smith, Gene. *The Structure of the Milky Way*, Gene Smith's Astronomy Tutorial, http://cassfos02.ucsd.edu/public/tutorial/MW.html

Strobel, Nick. *Nick Strobel's Astronomy Notes*, Primis/McGraw-Hill, Inc., Columbus, Ohio, 2004.

Swami Shivananda. *Hindu Scriptures Part 1*, The Divine Life Society, Rishikesh.

Yano, Michio, (digitalizer), Sugita, Mizue (proof reader). *Varāhamihira's Bṛhatsaṁhitā*, based on the edition of A.V.Tripāṭhī, (SarasvatI Bhavan GranthamAlA Edition), Version 3, June 5, 1992.

Wandahl, Finn. *Jyotish in the Rgveda*, http://www.wandahl.com /Pages/Articles/RigVeda.htm, 25.10.2002.

Wilson, H.H. and Bhāṣya of Sāyaṇācārya. *Ṛg Veda Saṁhitā*, Parimal Publications, Delhi, 2001.

Williams, Monnier. *Sanskrit-English Dictionary*. Munshiram Manoharlal Publishers Pvt. Ltd., New Delhi, 2002.

Wise, Micheal, & Abegg, Martin, & Cook, Edward. *The Dead Sea Scrolls: A New Translation*. Harper Collins Publisher, San Francisco, 2005.

Zharotia, Ajay (trans). *What Gurudev Said...*, Translation of Sanjay Rath lecture, SJC Atri Class 4, New Delhi, November 2005.

Chandrasekharendra Saraswathi MahaSwamiji. *Hindu Dharma: The Vedas* is a book which contains English translation of certain invaluable and engrossing speeches of Śrī Śrī Śrī Chandrasekharendra Saraswathi MahaSwamiji (at various times during the years 1884 to 1994). http://www.kamakoti.org/hindudharma/part5/cha 3.htm

About The Author

Freedom is an internationally known and respected Vedic astrologer, Yoga teacher and Yoga therapist. From an early age, he has practiced Haṭha Yoga and successfully incorporates the wisdom of yoga and Āyurveda into his classes and readings.

Freedom graduated with honors from the University of Massachusetts with a BA in Psychology and concentration in Religious Studies. At age 19, he met his first yoga Guru who introduced him to the science of Āyurveda. It was at this point that he met Vedic astrologers and began the study of Jyotiṣa. From here, he attended the New England Institute of Āyurvedic Medicine and went to India for a clinical internship with the International Academy of Āyurveda. His skill in astrology was recognized here after he gave his first lecture among esteemed astrologers from Pune and Bombay.

Freedom learned to integrate his āyurvedic practice into the western framework at the California College of Āyurveda. At this time he studied Jyotiṣa through the American College of Vedic Astrology.

Freedom deepened his study of yoga with a variety of respected teachers in America and India, while continuously looking for a traditional Jyotiṣa Guru. He eventually met Pandit Sanjay Rath and began to study Jyotiṣa in the Orissa Paramparā of Śrī Achyutānanda Daśa. He traveled to many areas of India with his Guru, and met a number of astrologers who would have otherwise been inaccessible.

Freedom spent years living closely with his guru, learning how astrology is practiced in both the modernized areas of Delhi and Bhubaneshwar, as well as in rural areas still maintaining very traditional practices. He has also lived in Vārāṇasī studying Sanskrit with Vāgīśa Śāstrī, which has helped him give many of his own translations to various sections of this book.

Freedom has met with Indian, Nepali, and Tibetan astrologers, sharing in a variety of both ancient and modern astrology techniques. He has visited nāḍi readers, palmists, and forehead readers whose accuracy was astounding. He has studied with sadhus, nāth yogis, pujaris and tantrics. He carries the teachings of the Vedic astrology lineage of Śri Achyuta Daśa and his understanding is apparent as you read his writings or hear him lecture. Freedom is presently settled in the Nevada City, California and teaches regular classes in astrology and yoga. Learn more at www.shrifreedom.org.

35097143R00263

Made in the USA
Lexington, KY
31 August 2014